Polarized Politics

Polarized Politics

The Impact of Divisiveness in the US Political System

edited by
William Crotty

LYNNE
RIENNER
PUBLISHERS

BOULDER
LONDON

Published in the United States of America in 2015 by
Lynne Rienner Publishers, Inc.
1800 30th Street, Boulder, Colorado 80301
www.rienner.com

and in the United Kingdom by
Lynne Rienner Publishers, Inc.
3 Henrietta Street, Covent Garden, London WC2E 8LU

Library of Congress Cataloging-in-Publication Data
A Cataloging-in-Publication record for this book
is available from the Library of Congress.

ISBN 978-1-62637-167-5 (hc : alk. paper)

British Cataloguing in Publication Data
A Cataloguing in Publication record for this book
is available from the British Library.

Printed and bound in the United States of America

The paper used in this publication meets the requirements
of the American National Standard for Permanence of
Paper for Printed Library Materials Z39.48-1992.

5 4 3 2 1

Contents

List of Tables and Figures   vii

Preface   xi

1   Polarization in US Politics and Policy
William Crotty   1

2   Ideology as a Polarizing Force
William Crotty   7

3   Voter Turnout and the Path to Plutocracy
Walter Dean Burnham   27

4   From Umbrella Parties to Polarized Parties
Arthur C. Paulson   71

5   Big Money, Mass Media, and the Polarization of Congress
Thomas Ferguson   95

6   Structural Sources of Political Polarization
Gerald M. Pomper and Marc D. Weiner   129

7   Religious Groups as a Polarizing Force
Lyman A. Kellstedt and James L. Guth   157

8   Women's Political Leadership Roles
Barbara C. Burrell   187

9   African Americans and Party Politics
William Crotty   209

10   Latinos, Partisanship, and Electoral Engagement
     John A. Garcia   241

11   Gay Rights and the Party Divide
     Paul R. Brewer and Shawn C. Fettig   257

12   Aging Policy: A Partisan Paradox
     Christine L. Day   285

13   The Debate over Health Care
     Thomas R. Marshall   309

14   Representation in a Dysfunctional Democracy
     William Crotty   327

References   355
The Contributors   389
Index   391
About the Book   409

Tables and Figures

Tables

3.1a	Recent Comparative Voter Turnouts Around the World	29
3.1b	Selected Examples of High and Low Voter Turnouts in the United States, 1866–1958	30
3.2	The Long View: Voter Turnout Among the Potential US Electorate, 1788–2008	35
3.3	Demobilization Strategies, 1890–1920	40
3.4	Election Turnout in New Jersey, 1900–1919	41
3.5	Estimated Turnout vs. Composition of US Voting Electorate, by Socioeconomic Status, at Posited Global Turnout Rates	46
3.6	Realignment, Mobilization, Demobilization: A Tale of Two Cities	48
3.7	Big Bangs in US House Elections: Greatest Two-Party Vote Swings, 1892–2012	60
5.1	Industries Within Big Business Above-Average in Fundraising Support for Newt Gingrich, 1995–1996	98
5.2	Campaign Spending Growth Through Time, 1970–2008	117
5.3	How Polarization Paid in the House GOP: Gingrich, DeLay, and Armey vs. Michel	120
7.1	Religious Traditions and Party Identification, 1940–2012	163
7.2	Religious Belonging, Beliefs, and Behavior and Partisanship, 1964–2012	167
7.3a	Religious Affiliation and the Republican Party Coalition, 1940–2012	170

vii

7.3b   Religious Affiliation and the Democratic Party
        Coalition, 1940–2012   171
7.4a   Religious Restructuring and the Republican
        Party Coalition, 1964–2012   173
7.4b   Religious Restructuring and the Democratic
        Party Coalition, 1964–2012   174
7.5   Predicting Republican Party Identification: Religious
        and Social Demographic Variables, 1964–2012   176
7.6   Predicting Republican Identification: Issues, Religious
        Groups, and Demographic Influences, 2008–2012   182
10.1   Voting-Eligible Population, Actual and Projected,
        2012 and 2030   243
10.2   Latino Naturalizations by Nation of Birth, 2007–2008   246
11.1   Congressional Votes on Gay Rights Issues,
        by Chamber and Party, 1993–2010   265
11.2   Presidential Nominees' Positions on Gay Rights
        Issues, 1992–2008   268
11.3   US Supreme Court Votes in Gay Rights Decisions,
        with Ideology Scores for Justices   270
11.4   Determinants of Public Support for Allowing Gays
        to Serve in the Military, 1996–2008   277
11.5   Determinants of Public Support for
        Gay Marriage, 2004–2008   279
14.1   Real Income Growth, 1993–2011   337

Figures

3.1a   Voter Registration in San Francisco as Percentage
        of Potential Electorate, 1922–1960   50
3.1b   Voter Realignment in San Francisco: Percentage
        Democratic of Two-Party Registration, 1922–1948   51
4.1   States in Presidential Elections: Realignment, 1896–2012   82
4.2   Coalitions of States in Presidential and Congressional
        Elections, 1896–2012   84
5.1   Party Unity Votes in the House, 1953–2008   97
5.2   Party Unity Votes in the Senate, 1953–2008   100
5.3   The Opportunity Cost of Doing Good: Maximum Salaries
        of Regulators Compared with Incomes of the Regulated,
        1949–2007   114
8.1   Women as a Percentage of Congressional Democrats
        and Republicans, 1975–2011   195

8.2	Number of Republican and Democratic Women in Congress, 1975–2011	196
8.3	Number of Democratic and Republican Women in State Legislatures, 1983–2011	197
8.4	Number of Female Primary Entrants by Party, 1994–2010	198
8.5	Democratic and Republican Women as a Percentage of Party Candidates, 1994–2010	198
10.1	The Latino Presidential Vote, 1980–2012	244
10.2	Party Affiliation Among Latino Registered Voters, 1999–2011	248
10.3	Latino Participation in Presidential Elections, 1988–2012	252
10.4	Election Capsule, 2012	253
11.1	Public Support for Gay Rights, 1992–2011	272
11.2a	Public Support for Allowing Gays to Serve in the Military, by Party, 1992–2008	273
11.2b	Public Support for Allowing Gays to Serve in the Military, by Ideology, 1992–2008	273
11.3a	Public Support for Gay Marriage, by Party, 1996–2011	274
11.3b	Public Support for Gay Marriage, by Ideology, 1996–2011	274
12.1	Average ARA/NCSC Ratings of Representatives, US Congress, 1996–2011	304
12.2	Average ARA/NCSC Ratings of Senators, US Congress, 1996–2011	305
14.1	Income Share of the Top 10 Percent of Earners, 1917–2011	334
14.2	Income Share of the Top 1 Percent of Earners and Top Marginal Tax Rate, 1913–2011	338
14.3	Unions and Shared Prosperity, 1918–2008	340
14.4	Wealth Inequality: Europe vs. the United States, 1810–2010	341
14.5a	Moderates in the House, 1916–2012	349
14.5b	Extremists in the House, 1916–2012	349
14.6a	Liberal and Conservative Party Differences in the House, 1879–2011	350
14.6b	Liberal and Conservative Party Differences in the Senate, 1879–2011	350

Preface

This book concerns what may be the biggest threat facing the United States and electoral democracy, a threat that is currently endangering our concept of a fair and just society. The emergence of an ever widening gulf between those with money, power, and influence and those at the lower end of the socioeconomic spectrum has the potential to undermine US future stability and security as a country. In the pages that follow, we examine the evidence of these disparities across groups and the underlying structural roots and political considerations that provide insight into the nature and extent of the problem.

* * *

A number of people have contributed to this project. Most notably among these is our publisher, Lynne Rienner, whose compelling insights and sound judgment were crucial for the book. I would like to thank Jessica Gribble, former political science editor at Lynne Rienner Publishers, who participated in the development of the book from its inception. Shena Redmond, senior project editor, applied her professional expertise to the manuscript to great advantage. Jason Cook was a thorough and conscientious copyeditor. The research skills of Roxanne Palmatier of the Northeastern University Library were most welcome. James Dunne, my research associate, added his political insights, perceptive analyses, and highly professional approach to all aspects of the project, which were appreciated. Finally, I am grateful to my wife, Mary, for her consistently invaluable contributions and to my brother, Walter, for his assistance at critical points in the process.

To all, thank you.

—*William Crotty*

1

Polarization in
US Politics and Policy

William Crotty

Polarization is a term meant to describe the condition of hyper-partisan/ideological extremism, policy representational imbalance, and institutional paralysis that combine to make contemporary governing so problematic. It connotes a divisiveness that moves well beyond normal politics and political parties to the end points of the US ideological spectrum. The result is a dysfunctional politics, identified primarily by its rejection of reasoned compromise, the lifeblood of a democratic system. Relied on as the basis for electoral and issue decisionmaking, it can come to challenge the ability of a nation and its political institutions to effectively represent the interests of its citizenry. It responds most directly to the demands of the narrow, economically well-off strata of the population who benefit from a rejection of a mainstream political culture. The proportion of the electorate who profit from an asymmetric political discourse may be small, but the results of such actions have extraordinarily important consequences.

Polarization results in a continual loop in which the system overrepresents and responds most directly to the resources of those who have established themselves as the most economically powerful in the political culture. Those who suffer the most by the inability to address in a meaningful manner the social needs of a society tend in turn to be the mass citizenry. The dominant subgroup in the context of contemporary politics is those with the economic resources to move the nation's politics, decisively in recent decades, in the direction most beneficial to their interests.

In the United States, conditions of polarization in its politics have been present for over a generation, increasing in emotion and intensity and in effectiveness in shaping issue outcomes as the years pass. This is frequently seen as a political condition that contrasts markedly with earlier times when

1

partisan differences without question existed and, however firmly held, seldom came to paralyze decisionmaking. The political parties, while moving in clear left-right directions in an earlier time, had multiple factions, regional interests, social group demands, and issue factions within the coalitions. Interparty compromises became a necessity for electoral success. In a hyper-partisan/ideological age, such an ability to reach mutually satisfactory agreements, while recognizing that each side will have to give up something in the interests of a broader governance, is rare. It is, and unlike several generations earlier, not an outcome or process of decisionmaking that is prized.

There is a level of "truth" and rigidity certainly in service to an ideological master that comes to see compromise as a surrender of principle, an unacceptable voiding of the electoral bond with constituents of similar views, to an opposing belief system. As indicated, governing under such conditions makes effective representation of multiple social interests especially difficult. Such a system prizes principle above political bargaining and denigrates pragmatism as little beyond a sellout, as evidence of a moral corruption in the body politic. Pushed to the extremes, such a culture can bring into question the essence of what a democratic system is meant to stand for and how and for whom it is intended to operate.

It is necessary to understand such issues when discussing polarization. A hyper-partisan, value-driven policy calculus does benefit some, and it does so handsomely. At the same time, it is necessary to realize that polarization is not the product of some mysterious or mystical "silent hand" to be found in a society or an act of whatever god has relevance in this context. It is a planned outcome, a dynamic achieved with great effort and seemingly unlimited funding. It is one that benefits its sponsors to levels unimaginable in previous times. It is then a product of a certain type of politics, justified by a convenient and useful philosophic reasoning as to what best rewards a society and fed into the political system by the political parties. In short, polarization, however it would be explained, approached, or rationalized, is a product of self-interest, namely, economic self-interest in the US system, taken to extremes. It is best approached as a political problem, one that maximizes the resources of wealth in shaping policy outcomes and most dominantly the society's economic reward structure. It takes advantage of a policymaking structure that is porous, open to influence at innumerable stages, and makes actions in the interests of a mass public extraordinarily difficult.

Defining Polarization

Polarization can be defined as an emphasis on extremes in the politics, partisanship, and policymaking of a society. The emphasis is on divisiveness as seen at present, resulting in the hyper-partisanship and ideologically based conflicts that have come to dominate the nation's politics. The principle underlying the concept is easy enough to grasp. It is roughly adapted from physics and from explanation of momentum as in magnetic or electric polarity with opposing force fields moving in precisely opposing directions. The intent in politics is not to carry over the theoretical or measurement specificity to be found in science, but to supply a broad and easily understood if imprecise level of understanding to a phenomenon that has come to transcend all levels of present-day politics.

While the essential idea is clear and not a subject for debate, more open to argument is the manner in which a severely polarized politics impacts party developments and group representation in crucial areas of the society. Sorting through and assessing developments in these more critical areas of importance provides the basis for the analysis to come.

A Partisan Bent

Before addressing the topics of individual concern, there is a dynamic that needs to be mentioned in order to put in context what is to follow. It is less discussed than other aspects of polarization, but important—critical even— for appreciating exactly what has been, and continues to be, developing. There is a partisan imbalance to the polarization controversy. This is not to say that both political parties are not products of a hyper-partisan/ideological approach to political issues. They are. Each sees governing and decisions as to the distribution of the nation's resources, who benefits, who pays, and how and what is to be valued and promoted and what is not, through intense and contrasting ideological lenses. They represent different groups and interests in the society, competing for attention and dependent, whatever their claims to independence may be, on the outcomes. In these regards, both parties have moved their center of gravity over recent generations. They have undergone a process of unification of their coalitional factions around accepted value premises, in the process becoming increasingly partisan in elections and in institutional decisionmaking. Fundamental changes that have occurred in party ideological and issue cohesion have come to restructure the party system. Still, one party, the Republicans, has moved further and more emphatically to the right than the Democrats have to the left. This has had major consequences for policymaking. Polarization is substantially more of a Republican/conservative phenomenon than it is a Democratic/liberal emphasis. This becomes clear with a more intensive identification of its roots and the dynamic of the forces most active in funding the movement and gaining the most in the process from such conditions, and should be kept in mind when evaluating policy outcomes in the areas to be critiqued.

Structure of the Book

In Chapter 2, I explore the belief systems that underlie the hyper-partisan, intensely ideological politics of the current era. In Chapter 3, Walter Dean Burnham, building on his pathbreaking contributions to the understanding of political representation and its consequences, addresses issues of competitive disequilibrium, party representation, and the policy implications of both for a class-sensitive electoral order. Burnham also places the US experience in an international comparative context, making clear the distinctive upper-level tilt of election turnout and electoral decisionmaking in the United States as compared to that in other advanced democratic nations.

In Chapter 4, Arthur C. Paulson traces the evolution of the US ideological party system from the 1960s to the present—a process that he describes as the most fundamental electoral realignment in US history. His incisive analysis raises basic issues for a political system undergoing the uncertainty of a transformative era.

The ultimate focus of polarization is policymaking, and the epicenter of policymaking at the national level is to be found in Congress. Thus in Chapter 5, Thomas Ferguson offers a sharp, comprehensive analysis of the factors—primary among them "big money"—that most influence congressional decisionmaking.

In principle and seen comparatively, US governing institutions were established more to force lengthy deliberation than to effect efficient, rapid decisionmaking processes. By any standard, the US approach to policymaking is demanding and complicated. Much has changed, however, since the Constitution was written, diluting and reprogramming the original intentions of the Founders and serving to reframe the operations of the state. The result is a current institutional framework that raises the question of how far a governing system can evolve and continue to remain true to its founding values. This issue is met head-on by Gerald M. Pomper and Marc D. Weiner in Chapter 6. Their bold, thought-provoking analysis of the impact of polarized politics on a society is one of major importance for our understanding of where the nation and its representative institutions are and where they are heading.

Religion has always played an important role in the political life of the United States, typically serving as a dividing line between Republicans and Democrats. In Chapter 7, Lyman A. Kellstedt and James L. Guth provide a major reinterpretation of the reengineering of the parties along a secular/religious divide. With an emphasis on the electoral alignment over the past seventy years, they make an important contribution to our understanding of both the changes that have taken place and the severity of their impact.

The struggle for the equal recognition and political empowerment of women in the United States has been long and contentious. In a number of respects, it has broadly paralleled African Americans' post–Civil War battle for voting rights. In Chapter 8, Barbara C. Burrell explores the ways in which gender politics is related to and has an impact on contemporary partisan polarization. Her focus is on political leadership and the recruitment and election of women to political office.

Racial polarization in politics is the subject of Chapter 9, in which I trace the evolution of controversies surrounding the social and political rights of African Americans from the Reconstruction period to the present.

In recent elections, Latino political mobilization has drawn significant attention from the political parties, and Latinos have been making use of their increasing political capital. John A. Garcia, in Chapter 10, explores two dimensions of the political world of Latinos: the extent of their electoral engagement, and their partisan affiliations, preferences, and interactions.

The subject of Chapter 11 is gay rights in the context of polarized party politics. Paul R. Brewer and Shawn C. Fettig explore how gay rights issues, such as the lifting of the ban on military service and the legal recognition of gay marriage, have emerged and evolved over time as partisan and ideological battlegrounds.

A more recent issue to enter the political arena as an area of major concern is aging. As the baby boomers reach their mid-sixties, the call for government programs to meet increasingly complex needs has become an important part of each party's electoral agenda—and brought into high relief opposing conceptions of the nature of the state. In Chapter 12, Christine L. Day develops the dimensions of that controversy and explores the often corrosive ideological orientation of the debate.

One of the intractable fault lines in US politics in recent decades has been over the adoption of a national health care plan. In Chapter 13, covering the mid-1930s to the present, Thomas R. Marshall explores when, why, and how health care became a partisan issue.

In Chapter 14, the concluding chapter of the book and admittedly a sobering one, I trace the upward redeployment of wealth in the United States and its concentration in a tiny fraction of the population. I argue that the explanations for this polarization of wealth are political and not economic, the results of a conservative, neoliberal program meant to reward the richest of Americans. The vehicle for redefining the country's economic structure has been the political parties, recipients of the substantial corporate and individual donations needed to compete effectively for public office (an "investment theory of politics"). The parties are themselves increasingly polarized, from their base in the electorate to their policy votes in Congress. The relationship creates a cycle that continues to add to the imbalance. The transference of wealth to the richest on such a massive scale raises questions as to the representative nature of the parties and the quality of representation in a mass democratic society.

2

Ideology as a Polarizing Force

William Crotty

In this chapter, I seek to answer simple (or seemingly simple) questions in relation to political ideology. My intention is to look at political ideology in relation to its substantive roots as encountered in the two major political parties and, also, to identify the extent to which differences in party ideology have contributed to the polarization of the parties on policy issues. The questions to be addressed are basic to an understanding of US politics in general, as well as to an understanding of political polarization in the current age. As is usually the case, what appears to be reasonably straightforward conceptually can be anything but in practice.

The guiding assumptions underlying the analysis are that there are identifiable ideological distinctions between the parties, and that these fundamental differences in worldviews contribute to the polarization of the political parties and US politics in the contemporary age. The development of such a thesis calls on the substantive context of the political thinkers and events presumed to establish the marking points for each party's views. Thus, I begin by reviewing the characteristics of ideology and the classical conceptions of conservatism and liberalism, before exploring these two philosophies in practice. I conclude the chapter by raising issues and questions of concern relevant to an understanding of ideology as a polarizing force underlying the policy and political differences that establish the parties' identities.

The Characteristics of Ideology

The first question to be answered is what we are referring to when we discuss "ideology." Robert Lane can be helpful in the effort to provide a degree

7

of clarity to the subject and a set of criteria relevant to the discussion. In *Political Ideology,* Lane set out, among other things, to develop some ideas about the origins and maintenance of ideologies generally. And to deal "with the way in which the American common man's ideology—or any ideology, supports or weakens the institutions of democracy" (1962: 30).

In his review of the various definitional approaches to identifying politically relevant ideologies in the literature, Lane acknowledged that "the range and variety are formidable" before settling on the criteria he chose for these ideologies:

1. They focus on those who rule, how they are selected, and the values they embrace.
2. They are meant to persuade.
3. They deal with the most significant of values for the individual and the society.
4. They call for change.
5. They are rationalizations of individual and group interests.
6. They are normative and moral in substance and assumptions.
7. They are (inevitably) removed from their context and placed in a more politically marketable belief system with appeal to a broader audience.

And all ideologies, like all other beliefs, imply an empirical theory of cause and effect in the world, and a theory of the nature of man (Lane 1962: 14–15). This discussion of ideology is not meant to provide a precise, empirical, and measurably strict application to the term as in the case of research on voting behavior. The explorations and definitional approaches put forward long ago by Philip Converse (1964) and more recently by William Jacoby (2002, 2010), among others, have focused on developing a school of thought that presents such a base for the attitudinal dimensions of ideology to be found in the electorate. The approach here is looser, broader, and of more substantive emphasis, and based on a review of the roots of each party's ideological themes and their expression in policy terms.

This is not to say that elite and mass ideological perspectives are not important to an appreciation of voter decisionmaking. Clearly they are. There are different ways to make the argument. Ideology can be seen as a psychological device for reducing to manageable proportions and adding coherence to the welter of disparate information sources available to the citizen. The ability to think in terms of and to use ideological mappings to evaluate candidates and party programs can be taken as an indication of intellectual sophistication, political knowledge, and attention to the political process. This can also be taken one step further to argue the necessity of such informed and relevant citizen decisionmaking to the vitality, durability, and representativeness of the democratic system. A liberal-conservative continuum has in addition proven valuable in cross-national party analyses in understanding the political dimensions shared in common and the placement of parties and voters in relation to programmatic offerings. As Jacoby states, the "national operation of the political system and effective democratic representation are impossible unless people have some understanding about the policy stands of relevant actors within the political world. . . . Ideology provides a tool that people could use to get a sense of those policy positions without expending an undue amount of effort" (2010: 2).

With this as an introduction to the complexities of the subject matter, we enter into a discussion, clearly selective in nature, of the intellectual roots that modern conservatism and liberalism call on in framing their conceptions as to governance.

Classical Conception of Conservatism and Liberalism

Liberalism as initially conceived called on the writings of philosophers such as John Stuart Mill, John Locke, Jeremy Bentham, Adam Smith, and Jean-Jacques Rousseau. "The core liberal value is individualism. A liberal political order attempts to create and maintain an environment [and governing structure] that will facilitate individual self-development and fulfillment" (Conradt 1983: 317). The principles underlying the realization of these objectives would include efforts to maximize human freedom, constitutionalism, individual rights, and popular sovereignty.

Ironically perhaps, modern conservatism in its free-market emphasis is closer to a redesigned version of this early view of liberalism. The liberal movement that has come down to the present would not disavow such principles, but given the harshness and human costs encountered in capitalist societies and industrial economies, it turned to the state as the vehicle to help reduce social and economic inequities. The New Deal's social welfare state and Sweden's and other European governments' socialist societies would be examples of both the movement that took place and the framing of liberal objectives in the contemporary era. Modern liberalism, as can be seen, is a far cry from its historic beginnings.

Conservatism presents a starkly different conception of both human nature and society. Calling on the views of Edmund Burke, its defining assumptions (see Conradt 1983: 16) have little in common with those of liberalism:

1. "Conservatives view society as a natural, organic product . . . [that] embod[ies] the wisdom of the ages." Change therefore must be slow, well considered, and incremental.

2. The nonrational is more important than the rational. The whole is of more importance than its individual units. Inequality is acceptable and unavoidable.
3. Leadership ability is found in only "natural leaders." Elitism is an important element of a society.

In its original form, more evident in Europe and in the United States (in the Eisenhower years), conservative governments did not reject the welfare state. "The national leaders have a responsibility to protect and care for the weaker members of the community" (Conradt 1983: 316). This is not an aspect of conservative thinking of prominence in the polarized politics of the United States. Also it could be argued that when the conservative tradition moved into the 1930s and beyond, as found in the writings of Frederick Hayek, Milton Friedman, and others, the movement was redefined and reduced basically to an economic program with attendant government responsibilities designed to protect the dominance and subsidize the activities of the groups represented.

The Conservative Tradition

The conservative philosophies in US politics are more coherently developed and argued than are liberal ones. We turn to the intellectual roots of such thinking as found in the writings of Edmund Burke. We then move to Frederick Hayek, an exemplar of the Austrian school of economics (along with Ludwig von Mises and Joseph Schumpeter, among others), which was profoundly influential in setting the terms of the current debate.

In a more explicitly American view, several individuals provide the basis for a selective look at contemporary conservative thinking: William F. Buckley, a popularizer of conservative principles and a propagandist for the cause second to none; Milton Friedman, an economist of major policy and political importance; Irving Kristol and the neoconservative movement; and Ayn Rand and her more extreme laissez-faireism. Rand is included primarily for her impact in contemporary politics.

The starting point then for a discussion of the conservative tradition would be Edmund Burke. His was a now classical conception of a conservative philosophy of government sensitive to real-world interests. In his *Reflections on the Revolution in France* (1790), Burke rejected revolution and mass-based, anti-establishment movements in favor of a gradual and measured process of accommodation and social change. He celebrated tradition, individual rights (recognizing they had yet to spread to the mass public), and the stability and investiture in an orderly society provided by the protection of private property. Wisdom was embedded in the evolution of institutional forms, and he celebrated the critical value of a constitution in establishing both the limits of public conduct and the rights of the citizenry.

The Eisenhower presidency in particular and to an extent its extension by the Nixon presidency could serve as examples of an adaptation of Burkean views to US politics. The Reagan and George W. Bush presidencies decidedly did not. Politically, the rise of Goldwaterism, with its turn to a hard-right, more doctrinal US brand of conservatism, brought to an end the more centrist and accommodationist thinking of a less rigid, more accepting pre-polarized political era.

Frederick Hayek (1889–1992), a celebrated Viennese economist and considered one of the most thoughtful and penetrating of conservative thinkers, is central to the dominant modes of contemporary right-wing thinking on the primacy of the economy and the role of government in facilitating its ends. Hayek is representative of the Austrian school of economics of the pre-Nazi European period of the 1930s. It would later move its base to the United States, with great effect on anti-statist, free-market thinking. From the late 1930s to the 1950s, Hayek especially and his colleagues more broadly left a permanent mark in defining and providing an intellectual rationale for the conservative model of government.

In a series of publications, notably *The Road to Serfdom* (1944) and *The Constitution of Liberty* (1960), Hayek argued for the primacy of freedom and liberty as the organizing principles of a society. He was against concentration of power, the theme underlying all of his arguments. In the wake of the seeming collapse of capitalism in the 1930s, many European countries took to experimenting with various forms of planned economies or what Hayek considered to be socialism, an arrangement of the economic and political order that he strongly opposed. Hayek rejected socialism in all its forms, from Britain's relatively mild flirtation, through Sweden's socialist state, to Hitler's National Socialism (although and despite the labeling, Nazi Germany was closer to a corporatist state). It included even Franklin D. Roosevelt's social welfare state. In short, the road to totalitarianism (or "serfdom") was to be fought and rejected at every turn. In turn, Hayek advocated competition, a laissez-faire, unregulated economic order, constitutionalism and the rule of law, minimal government, a classic liberal sense of political rights, and localism and federalism in the administration of services. A free-market economic order and a state built to facilitate such an end, he argued, would best free the capacity of the individual to achieve.

Possibly the most politically influential if not one of the strongest proponents of a Hayekian perspective in recent times has been Milton Friedman of the Chicago school of economics, adviser to presidents and foreign heads of state and a serious and effective spokesperson for a purist free-market economics together with all that this implies for governance. Among his many publications, one of the clearest in setting forth his views on the relationship between a capitalistic free-market economic system and political freedom is *Capitalism and Freedom* (1962). Friedman's themes are similar to Hayek's, a debt he acknowledges. He has been the economist–political exponent of choice for many conservatives, and an influence on domestic policymaking, especially during the presidencies of Reagan and George W. Bush.

The question Friedman asks of each of us (playing off John F. Kennedy's 1961 inaugural address) is what we can do to protect our political freedom. The answer is to support and believe in a capitalist free-market economic structure that in turn will lead to greater political freedom. This is identified as minimal government interference in the economic, political, and social life of the individual. While some government regulation is called for to enforce the established rules of the society and to preserve social order, the least amount of regulation tolerable is the standard to be observed. "Economic arrangements play a dual role in the promotion of a free society. On the one hand, freedom in economic arrangements is itself a component of freedom broadly understood, so economic freedom is an end in itself—economic freedom is also an indispensable means toward the achievement of political freedom" (Friedman 1962: 8).

It is conceivable that the associations made could be open to debate. Nonetheless and taken in its entirety, Friedman presents a plausible, succinct, and easily understood defense of a free-market-based politics. It takes little imagination to understand why such writings have served as a bible of sorts for modern proponents of conservatism or why Friedman's views have had such an impact on policymaking. There is an intuitive appeal to the points made that, when combined with the critique of the welfare state, serve to draw the battle lines clearly and forcibly.

William F. Buckley Jr. (1925–2008) may have seen himself, and could be considered, as the inspiration for and conservator of present-day conservatism. He was unquestionably its most prominent spokesperson and its best-known celebrity. Beginning with his *God and Man at Yale* in 1951, he positioned himself as the advocate for and arbiter of all things conservative. He could be seen as the prosecutor, judge, and jury for a form of political conservatism, and a pillar of orthodoxy for the tradition. His brand of conservatism demanded a strict adherence to the established code as pronounced by him. It had within it a reliance on moral values, a rigidity in application, and even an element of authoritarianism. Consequently it was not always acceptable to those who shared the movement's broader principles.

Buckley in addition had a controversial background as an employee of what is now the Central Intelligence Agency; was a supporter of Franco's Spain, a defender of the Vatican, a sympathizer with apartheid in South Africa; and, less known, supported racial theories of politics in the United

States. He was also a fervent anticommunist and a defender of McCarthyism. In his more publicly recognized persona, Buckley was an author, editor of the *National Review,* spy novelist, mentor, publicist, television celebrity and host of a PBS talk show, newspaper columnist, debater, and fierce Republican. It is in these public roles, more than in anything of greater depth in his writings, that he had his greatest impact. All in all, it amounted to a long and impressive career in shaping the practice of conservatism and in framing the debate over, and the alternatives to, the New Deal welfare state. Overall, his influence was widespread. Conservative columnist George Will celebrated his contributions: "Without Buckley, no *National Review* [the magazine Buckley edited for twenty-five years], without *National Review,* no conservative takeover of the Republican party; without that, no Reagan, without Reagan no victory in the Cold War" (quoted in Brookhiser 2009: 1).

For some, it would appear that Buckley was the dominant force in the US conservative movement and, through him, in its political success. The underlying foundation of Buckley's thought was a form of religious morality (if differentially applied) based on Catholic teachings (Buckley was an ardent practitioner of the religion) and as incorporated into arguments in favor of a free-market state.

In line with his other views, Buckley held an intense dislike for those he considered liberal or for those he believed did not do enough to advance the conservative cause. President Dwight Eisenhower fell into the latter category. A centrist and moderate, Eisenhower accepted the New Deal welfare state and chose to attempt to coexist rather than challenge Soviet communism aggressively, and implicitly, militarily.

Buckley's dislike of liberals was visceral; he thought that "social and individual differences, if they are not rational, are objectionable and should be scientifically eliminated; and that all peoples and societies should strive to organize themselves upon a rationalist and scientific paradigm" (quoted in Allitt 2009: 76; see also Buckley 2012: 7). Liberals, in contrast, according to Buckley, rely on reason; they seek equality; and they rely on the state to achieve their objectives.

It would be difficult to determine who would agree to such a description of liberalism. What it does show, and vividly, is all that Buckley found intensely objectionable and was committed (to the extent it existed) to reversing. His conception of liberalism appears closer to what was believed at that point in the Cold War to be the essence of a repressive Soviet communism. The belief that it also applied in US politics to a social state liberalism begins, along with the causes and figures of prominence he chose to support, to indicate the intensity and ideological rigidity inherent in his approach to his political world. Buckley would make his mark as the most active and one of the most effective and influential conservatives of his generation.

A bridge between principle and practice was provided by the neoconservative movement of the late 1960s, 1970s, and 1980s. The development was distinctive in a number of respects. It introduced an intellectual perspective into conservative politics that had been missing, and it was a major factor in rejuvenating the Republican Party and reviving its electoral prospects. It was also distinctive in its views and in the composition of its membership. It had begun among Jewish Democratic intellectuals in New York City reacting to the excesses and social chaos that had marked the 1960s. Among its principal outlets were the magazines *Public Interest* and *Commonweal*. The latter was edited by Irving Kristol, considered the "godfather of neoconservatism," along with, at various points, Daniel Bell and Nathan Glazer, respected figures in the academic world. It eventually came to provide an alternative home for disgruntled Democrats alarmed by both the challenges to authority in the movement in the 1960s and early 1970s, along with what they saw as the less than forceful efforts by their party to challenge the Soviets in the Cold War.

The neoconservative movement, unlike the more theoretical defenses of conservatism to be found in Hayek, Friedman, and the like-minded thinkers who codified conservative principles, had a decidedly practical bent. It was motivated by a desire to directly influence the course of US government, especially as it related to foreign policy. The movement itself was relatively small in numbers, although its impact on politics was to be great. It could claim support from a number of prominent authors, journalists, politicians, and intellectuals. Among these, in addition to Kristol, his wife, Gertrude Himmelfarb, and his son William, were Michael Novak, Ben Wattenberg, Charles Krauthammer, James Q. Wilson, Jeane Kirkpatrick, Robert Kagan, Norman Podhoretz, David Brooks, Seymour Martin Lipset, and Joshua Muravchik. All were politically involved in one way or another. William Baroody Sr., founder of the American Enterprise Institute (AEI), Elliott Abrams, John R. Bolton, Richard Perle, Dick Cheney, Donald Rumsfeld, Kenneth Adelman, and Douglas Feith provide a sampling of those who served in government or otherwise did the most to give the neoconservatives a political voice. Think tanks developing and promoting the movement's principles included, in addition to the AEI, the Manhattan Institute, the Hudson Institute, the Cato Institute, and also, although most often identified as libertarian, the Heritage Foundation. The chief beneficiaries of the neoconservative wave as well as the most effective implementers of Kristol's policy programs were to be found in the more unrelenting politics of the Reagan and George W. Bush presidencies.

Jeane Kirkpatrick described its origins and relationship to other conservative strains: "The neocon had embraced liberal values. . . . The neoconservative was born from a reaction to the counter-culture that dominated American politics through the sixties and seventies. . . . The counter-culture . . .

constituted a sweeping rejection of traditional American attitudes, values, and goals" (2004: 235).

Irving Kristol put it this way: "The student rebellion and the rise of the counterculture, with its messianic expectations and its apocalyptic fears . . . certainly took us by surprise, as it did just about everyone else. Suddenly we discovered that we had been cultural conservatives all along" (2004: 341; see also Wolfson 2004).

There was another motivating dimension to the emergence of the neo-conservatives. That was the endorsement of what came to be called a "muscular" foreign policy designed to aggressively confront the Soviets and all forms of communism. Their belief was that this did not represent the position of the liberals and the Democratic Party, and that their views on the conflict were more compatible with the traditional stands on defense taken by conservatives and by the Republican Party. At the same time, and distinguishing the neoconservatives from the more traditional conservatives, they were considerably more liberal on domestic issues and did not necessarily reject the New Deal welfare state. As Kristol explained, his discontent with social democracy and liberalism "had absolutely nothing to do with economics" (2011: 336). These sentiments, however, were subordinated to what the neoconservatives saw as the gravity of the communist threat.

The neoconservative movement added a vital life force and a distinctive intellectual reasoning to practical conservatism, which helped advance the fortunes, and contributed to setting the direction, of the Republican Party. It helped to reframe the national debate in terms of a modern US conception of conservative principles and priorities, a reorientation whose political appeal has continued to this day.

An idiosyncratic offshoot of the Austrian school, but one that proved politically attractive, was found in the views of Ayn Rand. Her commitment to individualism, limitations on government, and the deification of a free-market capitalism, combined with an ardent anticommunism, attracted supporters. In orientation, Rand's views were similar to those of mainstream conservatism, but more extreme and abstract in practice. Rand's arguments against altruism and on behalf of the unrestrained advancement of individual self-interest moved well beyond the arguments of others.

Rand (1905–1982), a novelist, screenwriter, philosopher, celebrity, proponent of atheism, and devotee of a fierce and unrestricted laissez-faire capitalism, developed a cultlike following through her writings, personality, and formidable intellect. Rand was a Russian émigré from a background of wealth and privilege who relocated to the United States when the Soviet communists appropriated her family's holdings. She was intensely anticommunist and opposed any form of collectivism, including the New Deal social welfare state, which she saw as the road to totalitarianism. She spoke primarily through her novels, *Atlas Shrugged* (1957) and *The Fountainhead* (1943), and a philosophy she created called objectivism. Her message was complicated and not easily deciphered, and its "true" meaning is still under discussion. It centered on the benefits of capitalism, entrepreneurship, personal ambition, and motivation. It was built on an argument for a self-interest that rejected any form of what it called collectivism. It was her belief that such an approach would provide the potential for historic individual achievements if left unrestricted by social conventions and government restrictions. Rand established the boundary for US ideology, one that rejects any conception of broad social or public action or social responsibility that would place any limit on the individual.

Her teachings held a fascination for ambitious young males in particular and influenced Alan Greenspan, former chairman of the Federal Reserve and a member of her inner circle; Representative Paul Ryan (WI), Republican vice presidential nominee in 2012; and Representative Ron Paul (TX) and his son Senator Rand Paul (TN). The elder Paul, while a Republican, ran two presidential campaigns based on arguing her principles in what within the political world came to be called libertarianism. Ayn Rand's priorities were not all that different from those of the conservative Republicans more generally, but were considerably more radical. The impact of her philosophy on politics in the United States continues, as the ongoing fascination with and influence of her writings attest.

The Practice of Political Conservatism

Politically, the most pronounced examples and the most successful applications of the "new conservatism" (i.e., post-Goldwater) can be found in the presidencies of Ronald Reagan and George W. Bush. The two clearest expositions of conservative principles and policy options can be found in Barry Goldwater's *Conscience of a Conservative* (1964) and the Republican National Committee's Newt Gingrich–inspired *Contract with America* (1994). Both, of course, are explicitly political tracts. Still, to the extent anything does, they lay out the assumptions behind the politics of the right and the issue positions to be taken to realize the society conservatives envision. These continue to set the agenda for conservative candidates and administrations and, to varying extents, the issue agendas that Democratic presidents (Jimmy Carter, Bill Clinton, and Barack Obama) have had to deal with and, to an extent, embrace.

The ideas are familiar: an unyielding opposition to the New Deal system and the social welfare state it created, and a commitment to roll back and eventually eliminate it and the social net it built; a capitalist economic system with free-market guarantees; a minimal government presence (outside of defense) in the economy; an elimination of regulations pertaining to the economy, environment, financial industry, trade, and the like; a strong defense and an aggressive international promotion of the national interest; and the now familiar association between a social-service state and encroaching totalitarianism. The thinking can prove to be a rigid and inflexible doctrinaire base for politics, differentiating the hard-right conservative views of the present era with the more inclusive, coalitional approach of earlier times. Also, conservatism as practiced contributes directly to and defends the continually increased disparities in individual wealth, a class-structured society (although this is denied), and the social inequities to be found in everyday life.

Goldwater's *Conscience* and its prescriptive remedies for the country were not well received at the time of their publication, judging by the voters' reception of Goldwater's candidacy. In the light of hindsight, there is little that is surprising (with one possible exception) in the reasoning presented or the policy directions proposed. They are common currency in today's politics.

Should anyone miss or misconstrue the message, in *Conscience* Goldwater claims that the Democrats of his day and even some Republicans "propound the first principle of totalitarianism: that the State is competent to do all things and is limited in what it actually does only by the will of those who control the State" (2009: 9).

It is an extreme charge by any measure. It rejects the institutional arrangements in the United States designed to ensure no such outcome, the country's history and democratic value structure, and its operations to date. It did serve to energize a nascent conservative movement and give it a cause beyond simply preserving or altering the status quo or rationalizing excessive accumulations of corporate and personal wealth.

In addition, there is the attention given to military power and the forceful promotion of a bellicose, anticommunist foreign policy: "Our national posture must reflect strength and confidence and purpose." To do this, Goldwater proposes a foreign policy built on military power; encourages "captive peoples to revolt against their Communist rulers"; confronts the Soviet Union and its allies directly; and seeks to force "the Communist leaders to choose between total destruction of the Soviet Union" or to accept regionally localized defeats. "Such a policy involves the risk of war. . . . Of course; but any policy, short of surrender, does that." He considers the risks of nuclear war worthwhile in order "to save our country" (Goldwater 2009: 70–74). For nonbelievers, this is a frightening argument. It was, however, an argument that proved attractive to the neoconservatives.

The *Contract with America* reflects Goldwater-type principles but is more of a campaign manifesto, emphasizing a long list of policy positions (as did Goldwater's *Conscience*) that meant to appeal to voters and to achieve the type of society conservatives embraced. As a consequence, it has a different tone and focus than the broader call to arms found in *Conscience of a Conservative*.

The *Contract with America* (Republican National Committee 1994: 4) lists five principles of the values underlying the society it hoped to achieve: individual liberty, economic opportunity, limited government, personal responsibility, security at home and abroad. The "vision" put forward "seeks to renew the American dream by promoting individual liberty, economic opportunity, and personal responsibility, through limited and effective government, high standards of performance and an America strong enough to defend all her citizens against violence at home or abroad" (1994: 5). While few of its recommendations were to become law, it is a fair statement of the political objectives of contemporary conservatism.

Several themes in conservative thought tend to converge. This is especially evident in the practice of contemporary conservative politics. The emphasis is placed on the importance of a weakly regulated (or largely unregulated), capitalist, free-enterprise economics and the political institutions and politics designed to support it. One difference, as viewed in a broader historical perspective, from a once dominant, more flexible, and inclusive mainstream conservatism, is the rigidity, certitude, and reductionism found in the present conservative message and as practiced in politics. The tradition of gradualism in an effort to adjust to the social needs of a public as well as the veneration of wisdom in the form of customs and governing institutions as found in the writings of Edmund Burke are not part of the present conservative school of thought. In terms of political consequences, it represents more of a dogma, intolerant of modifications or concessions and not open to other viewpoints.

The Liberal Tradition

Liberalism is distinctly different from mainline conservatism in substance, as would be expected, but also in its sporadic development. Conservatism, as contrasted with liberalism, has a broad coherence in themes, a historical depth, and a consistency of views, qualities often found lacking in the liberal tradition. In contrast, liberalism, in its search for an authentication and legitimization of its beliefs, calls on a variety of authors and their writings on a wide range of often political topics of more immediate concern. Liberals do have their own priority of values, equality and social justice, but the body of advocacy work in presenting and defending these is distinctly less uniform and more diverse in sources and development than that of its conservative counterparts. To an impressive degree, it does end up at much the same place in an emphasis on defending its principles and in protecting from dismemberment, and as the occasion permits allowing for an expansion of, the social welfare state. It is argued more as an empirical position, a reaction to historical experience and the abuses of an unrestrained capitalism, than it is beholden to any one theorist or group of theorists and their resultant schools of thought.

One way of explaining the modern conception of liberalism as contrasted with classical liberalism is the emphasis on "positive" protections in society as against a "negative" conception of solely individual rights. It does not reject the latter and in fact incorporates it into its belief system, but moves well beyond it.

Charles Forcey explains: "Equality has been expanded to mean not merely formal equality before the law but also social, religious, and racial equality insured by considerable legal coercion. . . . The new liberalism . . . has turned away from a dream of automatic progress by the free-wheeling exercise of individual rights to a conviction that only the conscious, co-operative use of governmental power can bring reform" (1961: xiv).

There is a search in liberal thought for a historical identity, one identified with the quality and quantity of views sufficient to match the conservative experience. It does not exist. In an earlier age, John Dewey, Walter Lippman, Herbert Croly, Charles A. Beard, and other pre–New Deal observers, and even earlier aspects of the populist and progressive movements, could be called on to present various criticisms of economic and state-based actions. Each was in one way or another a reaction to the brand of capitalism as practiced at the time. All made a cumulative, if varied, contribution to contemporary liberal thinking.

The defining moment for liberals, however, came with the birth of the New Deal and its introduction of a safety net (left unfinished as it was) to cushion the worst of free-market exploitation for the mass of the citizenry. In addition, the New Deal devised a regulatory framework intended to set the boundaries of accepted economic entrepreneurism, provide a level of accountability to the public at large, and avoid the periodic recessions that marked an unrestricted capitalistic order. Roosevelt, as well as the balance of the liberal movement, was not against capitalism per se, and, as some historians claim, the New Deal could be seen as a conservative movement intended to protect a free-market economy from itself. It would provide a level of stability in operation and a public responsiveness to social conditions not otherwise a part of the economic application of neoliberal free-market principles. The New Deal in its response to the economic collapse of the Great Depression employed an activist, redistributive model new to American society. It was intended to achieve a number of ends, including providing for the longevity and continued relevance of a private enterprise economy, rather than create a revolutionary new state. The New Deal galvanized the liberal political world and gave it a focus and systematic, politically relevant plan of action suited to achieving the ends it thought important.

Be that as it may, the belief in a state embracing progressive social legislation and a regulatory role in the economy has been under sustained attack. In the decades following Lyndon Johnson's Great Society and its enactment of such programs as Medicare and Medicaid, the War on Poverty, and civil rights legislation (in particular the Voting Rights Act of 1965, which transformed the political landscape), the effort has been to limit, repeal, or starve funding programs of essence to the social welfare state (Mackenzie and Weisbrot, 2008).

Beginning with the presidency of Ronald Reagan and proceeding through that of George W. Bush, the campaign to dismantle the New Deal legacy has enjoyed significant successes. In its place has been the move to adopt a conservative framework for governance, with an emphasis on deregulation, a balanced budget, restriction of social services, minimal state interference in the economy, a revised tax structure sympathetic to monied interests and corporate America, an acceptance of the profound inequalities of wealth, and a stronger military and a reliance on its power in international affairs. In the post–September 11 years, restrictions on civil liberties could be added to the list. As one measure of its success, the Democratic presidents during the period—Jimmy Carter, Bill Clinton, and Barack Obama—seen to be representing the party believed to be the conservator of Roosevelt's reforms, have operated to varying degrees within a conservative neoliberal framework for governing. All in all, a far cry from any conception of a vibrant social welfare state.

Liberal author and critic Chris Hedges claims that liberals "lack the vision and fortitude to challenge dominant free-market ideologies. They have no ideological alternatives, even as the Democratic Party openly betrays every principle the liberal class claims to espouse" (2010: 14). Nonetheless, given what has been said and the dissatisfaction with politics as currently practiced, an effort will be made here to indicate the current state of liberal thinking. There have of course been challenges to the conceptions of a capitalist state as practiced in recent decades. To illustrate the major themes of the liberal movement, three who have contributed to it will be visited: John Kenneth Galbraith, economist and disciple of Keynesian thought (although his arguments as to the responsibilities of the state go well beyond it); Paul Krugman, Nobel Prize–winning Princeton economist and op-ed columnist for the *New York Times*; and, from a different and broader perspective, democratic theorist Alan Wolfe.

First Galbraith: an author with more than twenty-five books to his credit, provider of an antidote to Milton Friedman and his thinking, political activist, counselor to presidents, ambassador to India in the Kennedy administration, and a highly visible advocate for an expanded social welfare state as best suited to meeting the needs of the society. Among Galbraith's better-known works are *The Affluent Society* (1958) and *The New Industrial State* (1967) (although other of his writings can be called on as needed to clarify his views).

Galbraith's writings are a wide source of systematic arguments in favor of an economic redistribution of economic resources within the society in particular and the corresponding role of the state he believed important to achieve such an end. It is arguable certainly that the quality and significance of his views may have been undervalued given his highly visible public role as counselor to Democratic leaders from Harry Truman and Adlai Stevenson onward during the period when much of his work appeared. He could be seen as trumpeting an economic philosophy already broadly accepted by Democrats and Republicans (with limits) in the pre-Goldwater period, one that was familiar and that had traction and one that resembled much of the liberal thinking at the time. In reality, the arguments as to the intersection of the economy, the state, and society were both clearly developed and could be seen as providing the in-depth gravitas that much of liberal thinking lacked.

Galbraith's argument is unadorned, a straightforward defense of the reigning liberal creed. It is meant to address the imbalance in economic terms between private goods and the private opulence it can confer, and public goods and the poverty and social neglect it creates. The lesson if needed: "It is scarcely sensible that we should satisfy our wants in private goods with reckless abandon, while in the case of public goods . . . we practice extreme self-denial." (1958: 193). He went on to predict what was to become a reality of the late twentieth and early twenty-first centuries: "With affluence [will come] a comfortable disregard for those excluded from its benefits and its culture. . . . As so often in the past, we will develop a doctrine to justify the neglect. . . . Influential is the argument that stresses the inefficiency of government and sees its costs and taxes (those for defense apart) as a threat to liberty" (1958: 262). The end result, as Galbraith wrote: in addition to the celebration of unrestrained individual affluence came a rationalization for limiting government programs intended to help the poor.

There is in Galbraith's opinion a problem with a society that measures itself and its success in terms of goods produced, profits, and gross domestic product at the expense of a broad public good. For economists, the basis for judging the utility of an economic system rests on two criteria: "whether it serves man's physical needs and whether it is consistent with his liberty. . . . It has always been imagined especially by conservatives, that to associate all or a large part of economic activity with the state is to endanger freedom" (1967: 483–484). Conservatives may fear the state, but they have failed to notice, or chose not to notice, that a corporately organized, planned economy has ever more closely aligned itself with the state, resulting in an abridgment of freedoms, economic and otherwise. Put more bluntly, corporatism not free enterprise best describes the country's economic arrangements (less union representation). The state is intimately involved in the economy, with its principal role defined as promoting the interests of a corporate free-enterprise system. The neoliberal free market is a myth, a convenient illusion to be used in redirecting public attention from what in actuality is the economic reality.

The only means available to transform such economic-state interdependence or alleviate its worst excesses is through a politics committed to the creation of a greater balance between state and economy, private and public goods. The one initiative that could begin to achieve such an objective would be an activist, redistributive state.

Nobel Prize–winning economist and *New York Times* op-ed columnist Paul Krugman, reputedly the most read economist worldwide, in his book *Conscience of a Liberal* (2007), builds on Galbraith's position by adding a more contemporary touch. Krugman is a fierce critic of the inequalities of social life and the neoliberal economic dogma that gave birth to them. It is an economic strain of thinking as practiced in contemporary politics that Krugman finds self-serving, sloppy, and naive or even intentionally ignorant of social consequences, yet it drives real-world conditions. As he sees it, it is a tired and unworkable formula robotically and endlessly repeated by conservative commentators and politicians.

As Krugman explains it, the evolution of the conservative ascendancy was built on a rejection of the moderation of the post–World War II years; an obsessive and consuming reaction to Soviet communism; and an intense reaction to government aid for the unworthy poor. "Reagan taught the movement how to clothe elitist economic ideas in populist rhetoric. Nixon . . . showed how the dark side of America—cultural and social resentments, anxieties over security at home and abroad, and above all, race—could be exploited to win elections" (2007: 171). It attracted large-scale funding, as Krugman saw it, creating the conservatism we find in contemporary times.

For Krugman, economic inequality is at the heart of party polarization and in turn of the embrace of a conservative to hard-right political philosophy. He finds Democrats as well as Republicans making a contribution: "On economic issues from welfare to taxes, Bill Clinton arguably governed not just to the right of Jimmy Carter, but to the right of Richard Nixon." The Republicans in turn "don't just take America back to the way it was before the New Deal. They take us back to the way we were before the Progressive Era" (2007: 5). Some liberals would add the Obama administration to the indictment.

On race, Krugman believes that the white backlash against blacks began with Richard Nixon and his 1968 and 1972 campaigns. Nixon borrowed the slogans and appeals from George Wallace presidential campaigns. The approach gained respectability and enjoyed great political success with Reagan's candidacy. Speaking of Reagan, Krugman adds, "His early political successes were based on appeals to cultural and sexual anxieties, playing on the fear of communism, and, above all, tacit exploitation of white backlash against the civil rights movement and its consequences" (2007: 11).

It is a subject Krugman acknowledges that most Americans are uncomfortable talking about. He credits such appeals as the reason efforts to roll back welfare, dissolve the safety net, and oppose a national health care plan encountered such success. In addition, a race-based politics provided for the Southern support for Republicans that allowed the party to win a congressional majority for the first time in forty years in 1994, and for Newt Gingrich to become Speaker of the House.

Galbraith and Krugman speak in a language most liberals would be familiar with in both identifying the basic problems in American society and arguing for a social welfare state along the lines of an expanded and more inclusive New Deal. These can be considered the principal theme of contemporary liberalism.

There are, however, broader conceptions of what liberalism is or what it should be. One vision is offered by Alan Wolfe, a democratic theorist, who sees in liberalism both a temperamental state of mind combined with a more benign concern for the welfare of the average person. Wolfe finds procedural liberalism based on an appreciation of the core importance of political rights in both liberalism and conservatism. Substantive liberalism, seen as support for or opposition to the welfare state, is another matter.

Wolfe adds another dimension to liberalism relevant to the national security state. It is one that should be a shared conviction of liberals and conservatives, Democrats and Republicans, but is not. That is, the homage paid to classical liberalism (i.e., procedural rights) has become less honored (to a large extent ignored) in practice in the post–September 11 national security state.

Liberalism, Wolfe concludes, not only has a place in the contemporary period but also contains within itself qualities unique to meeting the demands of the modern world. "Liberalism . . . stand[s] on the side of democracy. . . . It has backed movements to extend the suffrage and to increase racial and gender equality. . . . It views war as a failure in the quest for peace. . . . It defends the concept of an open society because it truly detests those that are closed" (2010: 286–287). Perhaps optimistically, Wolfe argues that liberalism accepts the terms of a modern society and contains within itself confidence about the future.

His arguments stand in marked contrast to those, for example, of a Buckley or a Rand or the political world of Ronald Reagan and George W. Bush. For those who choose to share such beliefs as Wolfe's, his is a strong argument on behalf of a liberal politics and a liberal democratic state.

Conclusion

Thus the ideological and policy lines are clearly drawn, as seen in the two parties' appeals, their definitions of the role of government, and their prescriptions for achieving social progress. However, in this contemporary period the political battle is far from even. Whatever virtues liberalism may hold for its adherents, liberals have been in the minority for decades. Whatever it might have been or might become, liberalism is not in a good place in the early twenty-first century. Most Americans see it as an outworn testament to a time long past, of limited relevance to the immediate concerns of the contemporary period.

Approached from a reductionist perspective, the dominant political ideologies of the present era can be traced back to two economists, John Maynard Keynes and Frederick Hayek. Keynes's assumptions as to the value of an activist intervention in the economy as contrasted with the argument of Hayek that the social good is best achieved when the market is left to its own dynamics represent the essence of the competing ideologies. The Hayek approach rejects any extension of state power, however justified, as the pathway to authoritarianism, similar to what fascism brought to Europe. The Keynesian argument does not have such an emotionally charged core and makes its case more in terms of economic balance and accelerated recoveries from depression and recession (a dominant world problem at the time he wrote) and, as practiced in liberal democracies, social equity and individual justice and well-being.

The movement politics of the 1960s, as discussed in this volume, added a policy dimension to the Democratic Party coalition and, to an extent, refined its voice and message. It also fit the party's historical mission and its receptivity to newly emerging social groups and their concerns. The values of the movement politics as to the nature and role of the state were fully in accord with Keynesian assumptions and, of more relevance at this point in time, with the principles and practices of the Democratic Party.

The same can be said for the movement of the neoconservatives toward the Republican Party in the late 1960s and the 1970s, a union solidified during the Reagan years and an intrinsic part of the Republican governing, issue, and value framework since. It was in fact the substance of Republican politics as endorsed by Reagan and subsequent national candidates specifically in relation to the uses made of government power in international affairs and especially in relation to communism. The chaos, assault on authority, anti-Vietnam stance of the 1960s, and rediscovered love of tradition (1950s Cold War–style) were motivating factors in the embrace of a conservative Republican program. Neoconservatives were destined to play a major policy role as well as evolve an intellectual foundation for conservatives of consequence and as practiced during the years of Reagan, George W. Bush, and the Tea Party.

The fundamentalist Christian moral crusade put forth restrictive views on social morality and what it depicted as an increasingly amoral, decadent, God-distancing, and overly secularized society. They added, or more accurately fully drew out and developed, an explicitly political language. Such beliefs are inherent in present-day conservatism and are articulated in Republican Party campaigns. These hardly constituted a rejection of old-school economic conservatism. Again as with liberalism and the Democratic Party on the other side of the movement politics of the 1960s, they fit comfortably within conservative Republican principles as to a limitation on the state intervention in economic affairs and the voiding of social welfare policy programs.

The approach can be selective in practice. An extension of the Republican/conservative conception of the state was added in the advocacy of the government, politics, the courts, and the law as championed through party actions to implement moral and religious objectives (the "intrusion of politics into the bedroom" decried by civil rights advocates). However the merits of such a movement might be debated, it proved to be a powerful electoral dynamic for Republicans.

However, the question as to the role of ideology in party politics and policymaking remains. Unquestionably it is there, embedded in each party's DNA, paraded before voters in campaigns and legislature debates, and put forth to rationalize and to place in a broader perspective an assumingly democracy-reinforcing theory of the state.

With this in mind, a persuasive argument can be made that conservatism and liberalism in the contemporary period can be seen in, and reduced to, attitudes on issues of economic and social policy—that is, issues of who gets what. These views in turn predict attitudes on government and its responsibilities, what is best for the society, and the means for stabilizing and maintaining the democratic state. The ideological foundations for such an overarching worldview, based on the foregoing arguments, begin with support for the socioeconomic issues that reflect each party's core beliefs and establish the divide that at present results in the polarization between the parties and the stalemate in policymaking.

It is unlikely at this stage that much thought is given to the roots, validity, or assumptions of the ideologies being put forward. It has essentially become a repetitive, time-worn, and largely automatic response by conservatives and liberals meant to advance the self-interest of coalitional supporters. William Safire got it right when he defined political ideology: "Originally, a system of ideas for political or social action; in current political attacks, a mental straight-jacket, or rigid rules for the philosophically narrow-minded" (2008: 336).

Nonetheless, and even though this viewpoint may be on target, the contemporary political parties and the policymaking process exist in an intensely ideological, distinctly partisan political climate. The respective intellectual frameworks explored both define the differences in belief systems, policy objectives, and governing principles that separate the parties and also fuel, in a fundamental and nonnegotiable way, the society's increased levels of polarization.

Should anyone question the relationship or relevance of ideology to political action, a look at the two-party platforms of any presidential year in the twenty-first century should make the case. These platforms are clear and unadorned by moderated appeals in presenting the worldviews and programmatic thinking of the parties, their core supporters, and those who hold elective office in their name in a bimodal political era.

3

Voter Turnout and the Path to Plutocracy

Walter Dean Burnham

Men make their own history, but they do not make it just as they please;
they do not make it under circumstances chosen by themselves, but under
circumstances directly encountered, given and transmitted from the past.
The tradition of all the dead generations weighs like a nightmare on the
brain of the living.
　　—Karl Marx, "The Eighteenth Brumaire of Louis Bonaparte" (1852)

I attempt no compliment to my own sagacity. I claim not to have controlled
events, but confess plainly that events have controlled me.
　　—Abraham Lincoln, Letter to A. G. Hodges, April 4, 1864

The subject of participation by American citizens in the elections that determine their rulers is a very well plowed research field. Many have helped to elucidate the facts of the matter over the past half century. I, too, have my own contributions, the most recent of which—*Voting in American Elections: The Shaping of the American Political Universe Since 1788* (Burnham 2010b)—contains much data and some reflections. Does more need to be said at this late date? I think the answer is yes, and that it would be advantageous to review the subject in broad comparative contexts and over the long term.

This requires rather extensive treatment of that great historic anomaly, the South (i.e., the eleven former Confederate states), and also of the dynamics associated with one particular party system or historical era of US electoral politics, what I have called the "system of 1896" (which survived until 1932). Levels of turnout reflect, of course, electoral mobilization—and demobilization—of the potential electorate.[1]

For the relatively recent period, including the New Deal, I look here in some detail to three urban case studies of the ebb and flow (and ebb) of voter participation: Boston, Pittsburgh, and San Francisco. I then briefly review issues and problems affecting the conduct of elections today. Finally, there will be an effort to integrate this material into a broader vision of the whole subject.

This is an area in which facts very often speak through numbers. Controversies in this domain, particularly involving the turnout "optimum" of 1840–1900, have been remarkably persistent, suggesting the possibility that some unvoiced agendas within Americanized political science have been involved. But by now there is some general agreement on the bare facts of the case. Beyond numbers, however, lies something that is perhaps less frequently discussed: the *quality* of the vote.

I begin by placing contemporary voter turnout rates in the United States into a comparative perspective, and then add a few sample instances—highs and lows—from the nineteenth and twentieth centuries (see Tables 3.1a and 3.1b). Electoral regimes, of course, differ considerably among the twenty-one nations whose recent (valid-vote) turnout rates are presented in Table 3.1a. One would expect that states imposing compulsory voting would be in a class by themselves—as indeed they are, with an overall participation-rate mean of 88.1 percent. Some are federal systems, in which constituent states retain considerable powers; in other cases (e.g., Spain and the United Kingdom), considerable devolution to subordinate governmental units has recently occurred. Still others are unitary—a class that is more numerous than any other.

By what means are votes at the ballot box translated into bits of political power? Since the advent of democratic laws in the late nineteenth and early twentieth centuries eliminated explicitly discriminatory franchises (*régimes censitaires*, etc.), several major methods have been employed. The oldest and simplest, which has been consistently in use in US general elections since the Constitution went into effect in 1788–1789, is the first-past-the-post system (one ballot, simple plurality). This has often been associated with the centripetal (center-seeking) force of two-party systems (though by no means always), but has important liabilities in the accurate translation of votes into seats—a matter constantly discussed among British politicians and electoral experts. In countries with multiple cleavage structures in the population, considerations of representative equity and the maintenance of system legitimacy resulted in the emergence of proportional-representation schemes. Questions posed here are likely to include issues of representational thresholds: What proportion of the total vote suffices to give a particular party seats in the legislature? Post–World War II Germany, with a disastrous experience with "pure" proportional representation during the Weimar period (1919–1933),

**Table 3.1a Recent Comparative Voter Turnouts Around the World
(valid vote as percentage of potential electorate)**

	Period	Maximum Poll
Compulsory voting (legislative elections)		
Australia	1975–1996	91.6
Belgium	1977–1995	86.4
Luxembourg	1979–1994	86.2
Mean		88.1
Partial or full proportional representation (legislative elections)		
Austria	1974–1995	88.3
Denmark	1977–1997	84.1
Finland	1975–1995	74.2
Germany[a]	1976–1994	84.5
Iceland	1975–1996	87.9
Israel	1977–1996	77.9
Italy	1976–1991	85.8
	1992–1996	78.6
Netherlands	1977–1994	83.1
Norway	1977–1993	81.4
Portugal	1979–1995	74.5
Spain	1977–1996	73.1
Sweden	1976–1994	88.0
Switzerland	1975–1993	46.7
Mean[b]		81.6
Scrutin à deux tours (two ballots, two rounds)		
France (presidential elections)	1978–1995	79.7
Greece (legislative elections)	1978–1993	81.8
Mean		80.8
One ballot, district plurality (legislative elections)		
Canada	1979–1993	72.5
Japan	1976–1994	69.9
New Zealand	1975–1993	85.3
United Kingdom	1979–2005	70.6
Mean		74.6

United States	Period	Mean
Presidential elections (one ballot)	1976–2008	55.9
Legislative elections (US House, off-year)	1974–2006	38.0[c]

Source: Burnham 2010b.
Notes: a. For 1990–1994, West Germany only.
b. Excepting Switzerland (due to a historical accident).
c. Voter turnout ranged from 36.0 to 40.4.

Table 3.1b Selected Examples of High and Low Voter Turnouts in the United States, 1866–1958

High Turnouts: States of the North and West, Pre-1900 (percentages)

	Presidential Elections			Legislative Elections (US House, off-year)	
	Year	Turnout		Year	Turnout
Indiana	1896	97.6	Indiana	1866	96.0
Illinois	1896	96.9	Ohio	1866	85.9
Iowa	1896	96.9	Pennsylvania	1866	84.9
Ohio	1880	96.7	Delaware	1866	84.7
Indiana	1880	96.3	West Virginia	1894	83.1
New York	1868	96.0	South Dakota	1894	82.7
Ohio	1896	95.5	New Hampshire	1866	81.8
Wisconsin	1896	95.4	New York	1866	81.8
Michigan	1896	95.2	Illinois	1894	80.4

Low Turnouts: States of the South (Ex-Confederacy), Post-1900 (percentages)

	Turnout in Presidential Election	Turnout in Legislative Elections (US House, off-year)		
	1924	1926	1942	1958
Alabama	13.7	8.5	4.3	13.1
Arkansas	15.3	8.5	8.9	27.3
Florida	15.1	9.2	8.3	17.6
Georgia	9.5	3.2	3.4	6.7
Louisiana	9.7	5.3	6.4	10.3
Mississippi	9.5	2.8	4.3	5.2
North Carolina	36.0	25.5	15.7	24.2
South Carolina	6.4	1.8[a]	2.3	6.2
Tennessee	23.3	7.7	8.9	18.0
Texas	21.8	9.8	7.2	14.6
Virginia	18.1	8.6	5.4	19.1
South	19.0	8.5	7.2	15.1

Source: Burnham 2010b.

Note: a. The turnout in South Carolina in 1926 represents the lowest voter participation ever recorded in the United States since at least 1798 (though this turnout is somewhat higher than the mean 1.1 percent turnout in France under the extreme *régime censitaire* conditions imposed under the Restoration regime of 1815–1846; see Sternberger and Vogel 1969: 514. The year 1926 was, of course, fifty-six years after the adoption of the Fifteenth Amendment, but very much had happened in the meanwhile.

settled for a mixed system: some seats are apportioned by party lists at the level of the *Länder* (Germany's sixteen states), while the others are allocated by plurality vote by individual districts. Most proportional-representation systems are centered on calculations linked to party lists of candidates— where indeed the entire country (e.g., Israel or the Netherlands) forms a single constituency. Some have advocated a single transferable vote (the so-called Hare system), in which voters list the preferences in some form of rank ordering (Australia and Ireland are instances).

And then there is France—a country with five historical republics, two empires, and also (since 1789 as well as before) some monarchical traditions. Electoral regimes here have followed a kind of zig-zag pattern: some proportional-representation elections in the Third Republic (1870–1940), proportional representation as the standard in the Fourth Republic (1946–1958), and the current system, which divides the country into district constituencies and provides a one ballot win for any candidate polling an absolute majority, but otherwise requires a second ballot where a simple plurality suffices to elect. This system—*scrutin à deux tours*—was also employed in Imperial German Reichstag elections from 1871 to 1912. It is similar to the runoff primary elections in the United States, mostly in the South; but there, only two candidates are permitted in the second election.[2]

With the exception of Switzerland, a confederation with the bulk of politics taking place at the cantonal level, rather than nationally, the comparative profile in Table 3.1a underscores US turnout—even for president—as a negative outlier. The achievement of democratic norms and rules affecting the franchise was a long and often conflicted process in most of these countries from the early nineteenth century until the early to middle twentieth. But at the end of the day, these norms and rules were based on a now uncontested set of assertions: "one person, one vote, one value."[3]

As a comparative proposition, the state as such has always been problematic, and its manifestations very often bitterly contested in the United States. (This was, after all, a large part of what the Civil War was all about, a huge event whose legacy is not yet exhausted.) The United States still—in an opaque way—has not entirely transcended the Putney debates of 1647 and the colloquy there between General Ireton and Colonel Rainborough.[4] No such debates have had any contemporary relevance in any other country for many decades now. In practice (and normatively), each adult citizen's right to participate in elections is viewed as fundamental, which it is the duty of government to protect and promote. This means in practice that no burdens on the individual's access to the ballot box such as personal-registration requirements exist in such countries. Adequate funding is provided to maintain enrollment of adult citizens by public authority. Techniques vary. Thus, in Germany one finds in the official returns the following (Der Landeswahlleiter 1995):

- Total eligibles (*Wahlberechtigte*)—that is, the potential electorate not by estimate but by enumeration.
- Total vote cast by party, including scattering and, separately, invalid votes, for each of two ballots that each voter casts (*Erst- und Zweit-stimme*).
- In the detailed reports—here, Berlin in the 1994 general election—total votes for each party are given for 1990 and 1994 (*Zweitstimme*, or the proportional-representation fraction of the election) for each of the city's twenty-three districts (*Bezirke*), and by precinct in each district (e.g., seven precincts in proletarian Marzahn and five in middle-class Wilmersdorf).

And there is much, much more. Germany is a federal state, and in each of its sixteen *Länder,* an official called "der landeswahlleiter" is responsible for the conduct of *Länder* and federal elections, and for maintaining and updating electoral registers of eligibles. In Canada and Great Britain, "chief electoral officers perform the same functions for elections at the federal level and, in Canada, for elections in each of the country's ten provinces. Naturally, since there is no second ballot in Canada and Great Britain as in Germany, and since both Canada and Great Britain determine district elections by first-past-the-post, reporting is less voluminous (though at the precinct level and upward in Canada), but certainly adequate. A chief duty of these officers is to compile and update registers of eligible voters, and post the same so that people inadvertently missed can appeal and be added to the register. A situation such as Jimmy Beare encountered in Corpus Christi, Texas—denied the right to vote because of a particularly abusive personal-registration requirement—would be literally inconceivable in any of these other countries. For them, at least, the date is not 1647 anymore.

If there is any one arena where the rights of US states have survived the twentieth century, the New Deal, and all other expansions of the scope of the federal government, it is the conduct of elections. The limitations are relatively few and specific: constitutional amendments (the Fourteenth, where equal protection claims by citizens are litigated; the Fifteenth, as and when not nullified by state action; the Nineteenth, enfranchising women; the Twenty-Third, giving the citizens of the District of Columbia a vote for president; the Twenty-Fourth, banning the poll tax in federal elections; and the Twenty-Sixth, lowering the minimum voting age to eighteen years). Of course, none of these limitations existed before 1868; and in ways and with effects to be discussed later, the Fourteenth and Fifteenth Amendments were progressively nullified in the former Confederate states between 1875–1877 and 1904.

Despite the demonstrated fact that the imposition of personal-registration requirements reduces the turnout rate by about 10 percent, all other things being equal, these requirements have never been subject to effective challenge in the courts. Additionally, states are free to determine the dates of nonfederal elections and specify the form of ballots to be used at polling places. Very recent efforts—by conservative legislatures, of course— to require picture identification of would-be voters are still pending litigation in the courts.

As often happens in very close elections, the imbroglio in the presidential election of 2000 in Florida disclosed a parade of horrors usually concealed from the public eye. The bulk of election administration was devolved by the state to officials in its sixty-seven counties. Great diversity prevailed in the form of ballots used. Additionally, as might be expected, expenditures at this local level had to compete with more immediate and continuous local-government obligations. Thus, in the case of the notorious butterfly ballot (punch-card type) in Palm Beach County, Florida, some 4,000 votes reportedly cast for Pat Buchanan were in the main intended for Democratic candidate Vice President Al Gore. While the notional Republican plurality was 537 votes, it seems very probable that Gore won the state by between 10,000 and 20,000 votes. But Republicans controlled all relevant instances at the state level except the Florida Supreme Court. Eventually, in mid-December 2000 in *Bush v. Gore,* the US Supreme Court disgraced itself by ending the recount. It needn't have bothered: the Florida legislature, controlled by Republicans, gave every sign that, if necessary, it would seize control of the state's twenty-five electoral votes and award them to George W. Bush. There would have been nothing in precedent to overturn such a choice: the last such occasion was in 1876, when the Colorado legislature chose (Republican) electors.

The federal-bargain deviation from democratic norms has elicited a huge critical literature going back more than a century, so far as the Electoral College is concerned. Three times since the Civil War, the loser of the national popular vote has won the day via the Electoral College (1876, 1888, 2000), and almost did so in 1916 and 1976 as well. Many diverse proposals have been advanced to replace the Twelfth Amendment (1804) with something else, but so far, to no avail.

And then there is the US Senate, the quintessence of the federal bargain of 1787. This body was never intended by the Framers of 1787 to be directly elected by the people. This was an important federal function of state legislatures until 1913, when they were replaced by direct popular vote. But this is an unapportioned and unapportionable body: one potential voter in Wyoming was equivalent to 53.8 in California in 2008. A radical Democrat might propose any one of three solutions to this problem: abolish the Senate, strip it of its powers as "the world's most powerful second chamber," or proportionalize it. Such reform notions would, however, collide head on with Article I, Section 3, and the unamendable Article V. So this part of the federal bargain will, no doubt, live on indefinitely, but at a cost that seems to be rising every year. Extreme partisan polarization intersects with the arcane rules of the Senate: filibusters by minorities, now endemic, require sixty votes to end. As well, there is what is now a promiscuous use by individual senators of "holds" to block nominations at their will or whim. This body today makes its own unique contribution to an ever more obviously dysfunctional US government. Those of a historical-comparative frame of mind might recall the pre-1791 Polish Diet and its *liberum veto* ("free veto"), which paralyzed all action: by 1795 the Polish state was extinct; and, of course, it made no pretense of democracy during its lifetime.

Viewed over the past century and a half, the countries in Table 3.1a, except for the United States, show a common pattern: so far as mass mobilization is concerned, of a shift from less to more. Very often, this process was associated with progressive expansions of the electorate, until the gap between what the French call *le pays reél* ("the real country") and *le pays légal* ("the legal country") was eliminated, first for males and then for women, with their enfranchisement in the early twentieth century. To be sure, this was not always the case. Imperial Germany (1871–1912), with its multiple cleavages, provided universal male suffrage in its Reichstag elections from the beginning. What Bismarck and other elites called *Reichsfeinde*—Catholics and the working class—won larger and larger shares of the potential electorate as turnout swelled above 80 percent in 1912.[5] After the lapse of Bismarck's antisocialist legislation in 1890, this huge input from the party of nonvoters was very largely associated with the growth of the Social Democratic Party, which became the largest party in the 1912 election. After 1890, forces supporting the Reich's power structure moved from a hegemonic position in Bismarck's time until reaching a minority status in the last elections held under this regime. Not surprisingly, the political right and many in the circle of the imperial court gave more and more attention to the possibilities of a military coup to redress this balance (Berghahn 1993: chap. 8).

The long-term picture in the United States could not be more different than the non-American pattern of less-to-more mobilization of the citizenry (i.e., the integration, at this primordial level of voting, into the political system). Summary turnout data are presented in Table 3.2, covering the whole history of the United States since the adoption of the Constitution in 1788.

During the first century of the country's existence, the comparative pattern of less-to-more prevailed, too. For the Northern and Western states, in the aggregate of the 1876–1896 period, the 84.9 percent presidential turnout rate was virtually identical, say, with Germany's performance in 1912. Participation rates in excess of 90 percent can be found at the state level at various times from 1840 to 1900. Indeed, in the pivotal region of the Midwest (and outside that area, too, in West Virginia), in the pivotal election of 1896, turnouts in excess of 95 percent were registered in six states. Kansas and Texas fell just short of the 90 percent threshold.

Table 3.2 The Long View: Voter Turnout Among the Potential US Electorate, 1788–2008 (percentages)

	Presidential-Year Elections		Off-Year Elections, US House	
	President	US House		
National				
1788–1796/1797	12.5	22.4	1790–1794/1795	23.2
1800–1824/1825	26.5	48.7	1798–1826/1827	45.4
1828–1836/1837	56.9	58.7	1830–1834/1835	59.3
1840–1852/1853	75.5	69.6	1838–1854/1855	63.9
1856–1872	78.1	75.6	1858–1874	67.5
1876–1896	79.5	78.6	1878–1894	65.4
1900–1916	65.1	62.9	1898–1914	52.3
1920–1928	51.7	48.2	1918–1930	36.3
1932–1948	57.9	54.3	1934–1950	41.3
1952–1968	63.3	59.1	1954–1970	45.6
1972–1988	51.7	50.9	1974–1990	37.4
1992–2008	57.2	53.3	1994–2006	37.5
North and West				
1788–1796	12.4	21.2	1790–1794/1795	23.3
1800–1824/1825	30.9	47.7	1798–1826/1827	42.6
1828–1836/1837	61.3	59.5	1830–1834/1835	59.4
1840–1852/1853	77.6	72.4	1838–1854/1855	63.9
1856–1872	82.2	80.8	1858–1874	70.9
1876–1896	84.9	84.4	1878–1894	72.1
1900–1916	73.9	71.8	1898–1914	63.0
1920–1928	59.9	56.0	1918–1930	43.0
1932–1948	68.1	64.6	1934–1950	51.8
1952–1968	70.4	67.2	1954–1970	53.7
1972–1988	58.0	55.2	1974–1990	41.4
1992–2008	59.1	55.3	1994–2006	39.7
South				
1788–1796	18.0	30.4	1790–1794/1795	22.5
1800–1824/1825	17.9	50.2	1798–1826/1827	54.8
1828–1836/1837	40.6	55.3	1830–1834/1835	62.1
1840–1852/1853	69.8	62.0	1838–1850/1851	58.7
1856–1860	74.0	62.1	1854–1858/1859	65.5
1861–1867	Civil War	Civil War	1861–1867	Civil War
1868–1876	71.2	67.5	1869–1874	64.9
1880–1896	61.7	60.1	1878–1894	46.9
1900	43.5	41.6	1898	35.8
1904–1916	29.8	27.8	1902–1914	20.3
1920–1928	21.4	19.6	1918–1930	11.7
1932–1948	24.9	22.0	1934–1950	10.6
1952–1960	38.8	31.8	1954–1962	18.5
1964–1968	49.1	41.0	1966–1970	31.3
1972–1988	47.4	41.1	1974–1990	29.0
1992–2008	53.1	48.6	1994–2006	32.2

Source: Burnham 2010b.
Notes: "North and West" comprises the following census divisions: New England, Mid-Atlantic, Delaware, East North Central, West North Central except Missouri, and Mountain and Pacific. "South" comprises Alabama, Arkansas, Florida, Georgia, Louisiana, Mississippi, North Carolina, South Carolina, Texas, and Virginia (ex-Confederacy).

Thereafter, a huge demobilization of the electorate continues through 1930, with very little interruption outside the South, and with a colossal interruption in that region that was not seriously reversed until the 1960s. This transformation is well known and has received considerable attention in the literature, ranging from studies in the 1920s by Charles Merriam and other University of Chicago political scientists, to those of more modern times (e.g., for the South: Kousser 1974; for the North: McGerr 1986).

The Last Century: Down, Up, and Down Again

Michael Lind (1996) has proposed the existence of three US republics. For so complex a subject as the government of the United States, more than one periodization scheme can claim some legitimacy, depending on the specific part of the story one is analyzing. Lind's version deals with the early republic, from 1789 to 1861, which perished in the flames of civil war and from 1828 was dominated by the Democratic Party; the second republic, from 1861 to 1932, which was dominated by the takeoff to full capitalist development and its political carrier, the Republican Party; and the third, which rose from the ashes of the Great Depression and the New Deal response (beginning in 1932), with the Democratic Party in usual ascendancy. Within the context of such a republics framework, I think it would by now be necessary to add a fourth republic, starting around 1980, and with some remarkable similarities to the second—including the ascendancy of the Republican Party, big business, and the financial sector of the economy—dedicated to repealing as much of the third as possible.

This all makes sense at the most macro level, but the evolution of electoral politics has its own periodicities. These have historically been punctuated by nationwide sequences of critical realignment. The peaks of the realignment process are conventionally centered on such dates as 1800, 1828, 1860, 1896, 1932, and, in many ways, 1968. It is scarcely possible to do more here than to suggest such a grid and then center attention on the fourth party system: the period 1896–1932.[6]

What could be described as the turnout optimum occurred in the wake of the Civil War and extended to the end of the nineteenth century (the third or Civil War party system). (The South, with its unique electoral history from the end of Reconstruction [1875–1877], will be discussed later.) This was also the Gilded Age, dominated by the rapid takeoff of the political economy toward its early twentieth-century domination by industrial and finance capital. This huge transition produced enormous stresses in the traditional agrarian United States, as well as the initial upsurge of class-struggle politics.

Two singularities marked this epochal transition period.[7] First, unlike developments elsewhere in the Western world, the United States was unique in that it had achieved (for its time) the full panoply of democracy as early as the 1820s. Elsewhere, elites and ruling classes were usually insulated from pressures arising from the mass of the ruled classes—at least short of revolution—by various institutional limitations on the extent of suffrage, party formation, and other devices. In the United States, on the other hand, elites were always potentially threatened by overthrow through constitutionally legitimate means, including mass use of the ballot box. The first intimations of this problem occurred during the explosion of strikes in 1877, and the temporary peak of the Greenback Party in 1878. It became acute during the general crisis of the 1890s, culminating in the rise of the Populist Party and its absorption by the Democrats in the pivotal election of 1896.

The second singularity was the fact that the very high turnouts, particularly in the emerging metropole (or core) of the greater Northeastern quadrant, were associated with extraordinary immobility of the partisan vote from election to election. A key to understanding this apparent anomaly can perhaps be found in the very name given to the third party system, the Civil War system. This enormous event essentially annealed the partisan preferences of the vast majority who were old enough to fight in 1861. The vast dynamism of economic development, coexisting with political immobilism, produced a continuously widening gap between base and superstructure until, by the 1890s, crisis generated the trigger that produced a critical realignment that brought the third system to an end. But in the meantime, professional politicians constructed machines with the capacity to drill their followers and dependents. Even as early as the 1880s, the post-Jackson spoils system, following the assassination of President James Garfield, was partially supplanted at the national level by the Pendleton Civil Service Act of 1883. But no such thing was usually done at the local or state level. By the mid-1880s, a presidential candidate was widely attacked: "He wallows in spoils like a rhinoceros in an African pool." The goo-goos of 1884 came on the scene too soon, but in a real sense paved the way for the antipartisan, demobilizing developments that swept through the political system shortly after 1900.

But what of the capitalist elite in the crisis of the 1890s? This crisis truly terrified them: it was possible that William Jennings Bryan might win the 1896 election. Quite a few of them panicked. Mark Hanna, the impresario of the 1896 Republican presidential campaign, had to calm down his timorous fellow industrialists: "You're just a bunch of damned fools. There ain't going to be no revolution. Bryan's talking silver all the time, and that's where we've got him." Justice Oliver Wendell Holmes Jr., in 1913, gave an address, "Law and the Court." Among the other riches in his presentation, he observed,

> It is a misfortune if a judge reads his conscious or unconscious sympathy with one side or the other prematurely into the law, and forgets that what seems to him first principles are believed by half his fellow men to be wrong. I think that we have suffered from this misfortune, in State courts at least, and

that this is another and very important truth to be extracted from the popular discontent. When twenty years ago a vague terror went over the earth and the word socialism began to be heard, I thought and still think that fear was translated into doctrines that had no proper place in the Constitution or the common law. (quoted in Lerner 1943: 390)

"Twenty years ago" brings us back, or near enough, to the Supreme Court's invalidation of the income-tax provision in the Wilson Tariff of 1894: *Pollock v. Farmers' Loan and Trust Co.* (1895). This was part of a network of decisions tilting the balance between private enterprise and government authority strongly to the right, and setting up a long generation of judicial supremacy that lasted until 1937–1941 (Wiecek 1998). Until recently, we had thought that such matters were permanently settled, but there has been more than one counter-revolution in US history. Attorney Joseph Choate led the charge against the tax: "The Act . . . is communistic in its purposes and tendencies, and is defended here upon principles as communistic, socialistic— what shall I call them—populistic as ever have been addressed to any political assembly in the world" (quoted in Paul 1960: 192–193). Addressing the Court directly, Choate said, "There is protection now or never." Where there's a will there's a way. To invalidate this communistic income tax, it was necessary to disregard the fact that, between 1862 and 1872, the income tax was used to help defray the gigantic costs of the Civil War. Moreover, it was necessary to overrule a century of error, enshrined in *Hylton v. United States* (1796), in which the Court had ruled that a federal tax did not require apportionment among the states. It was during the "system of 1896" that began what Robert Jackson (1941) was to term the "struggle for judicial supremacy." For those critics who have claimed that there was little policy change immediately after 1896, I would reply that the chief policy organ during the period of 1895 to 1933–1936—certainly wherever the always-contested boundary between the private and the publics was concerned—was the Supreme Court rather than Congress or the presidency. Since the whole thrust of the fourth (1896–1932) system was the dismantling of democracy— partially in the North, near totally in the South—this adaptation of the Court's policy role fit other developments like a hand fits a glove (see Burnham 1991).

But not everything that changed after 1900 could be processed through the judiciary. In what follows, it should not be supposed that any nefarious conspiracy was involved. Mentalities changed remarkably rapidly in and after 1896. That climacteric really decided something. Put in comparative terms, the city beat the country, and the victory (or defeat) was final. Meanwhile, however, stormy economic development continued. As good a date as any for the rise of the corporation question was the creation of United States Steel in 1901 from a number of smaller producers. At the same time, there was a profound shift more broadly in the political culture, with a now-delegitimized nineteenth-century party system, toward a political order in which the most valued institution was the business corporation. How to cope with the corporation question and the machine-led corruption and inefficiency of state and local governments? Reform was the mantra of that protean movement called progressivism: the cure of the ills of democracy was, of course, more democracy. Sometimes very consciously, sometimes not, elite searches for order included multiple changes whose effect was to demobilize the electorate and overcome corruption at the ballot box. Table 3.3 provides a general profile of these demobilization strategies between 1890 and 1920.

Thus, turnout cascaded downward in both presidential and off-year elections from 1898 through 1926–1930. At the same time, there was a spectacular shift toward democratic one-partyism throughout the South, of course; but there was also another shift (favoring the Republicans) throughout the Pacific Coast states and in such core areas of the industrial metropole as Michigan and Pennsylvania. By the 1920s, the Democratic Party was unassailable in the South (and hence could not be replaced nationally), while reduced to an incoherent jumble of fragments clinging to ethnocultural and regional traditions (see, e.g., Burner 1968).[8]

In Pennsylvania, the twin paths of turnout and partisanship displayed the existence of the usual systems or eras, though (prior to 1932) a shift toward plummeting turnout and one-party balance that was considerably more extreme than in most states outside the South. Pennsylvania emerged as a Republican state in 1858, but with very high levels both in turnout and partisan competitiveness. The realignment displacement between 1892 and 1896 inaugurated the next cycle, particularly noteworthy for the near collapse of both turnout and the Democratic Party. This was followed by a shift into a new era that began in 1932 and was rapidly consolidated between 1934 and 1940: significant improvement in turnout, though nowhere near to the pre-1900 levels, and intense competitiveness. It is noteworthy, by the way, that personal-registration requirements were not enacted until 1906—and then only to Pennsylvania's large cities—and not imposed on the rest of the electorate until 1937.

Quite a few state studies describe the dynamics of this vast post-1900 depression in electoral participation. One of the very best and most penetrating of such studies is *Testing Democracy* by John F. Reynolds (1988), which deals with New Jersey. The whole work is a gold mine of information as to the processes through which electoral politics in the Garden State was transformed (perhaps a better word would be "revolutionized") between 1880 and 1920. It is particularly good in discussing the very rapid change in mentalities that made it possible for the progressives' New Idea to sweep aside all before it. Here I will focus on twin purification laws adopted in 1911, a

Table 3.3 Demobilization Strategies, 1890–1920

Target Groups	Opponents	Rationales	Sanctions
Urban	Middle class; technocratic programs; upstate and small-town agrarians	Anticorruption; white Anglo-Saxon Protestant values; inefficiency; Sodom and Gomorrah	Ballot reform; nonpartisanship; corporate ideal; city manager; malapportionment; discriminatory voter registration laws
Political parties General	Progressives and many others; see *Urban*	Lack of representation; "old politics" (cf. 1968!) corruption	Detailed legislative regulation of party organization and activity; direct primaries
Minor	Both major parties;	See *Populists*	Some corruption and pressure on dependent voting population; later, raising party ballot-access thresholds to impossible heights; "Red scares" key moments; see also *Immigrants*
Socialists	Both major parties	See *Immigrants*	
Immigrants	Small-town and metropole white Anglo-Saxon Protestants; agrarians	Low cultural development; Romanism; anarcho-communists (drunk, lazy, etc.)	Elimination of alien voting; personal periodic registration for cities only; literacy tests (e.g., Massachusetts)
Populists (North and West)	Corporate elite; urban and town middle class, especially metropole Republican Party	Danger of revolution by the "backward" (Alexander Hamilton's old nightmare of the 1790s)	Electoral activity; some corruption and pressure on dependent voting population; antifusion laws
Populists (South)	Regional and local elite; Democratic Party	Same as against populists of the North and West, plus fear of black balance of power in intrawhite conflicts	Fraud and violence, often very widespread (e.g., race riot in Wilmington, North Carolina, in 1898
Blacks (South 85%)	Southern white conservatives; Southern white progressives	Racism; "traditionalist Southernism"; anticorruption	Violence and terror, endemic 1871–1900 (with pulses up and down); later, "institutionalization": poll taxes, literacy tests, white primaries, etc.
Lower classes in general	Middle-to-upper classes; many major-party leaders (state and local) (down to present; see Piven and Cloward 1988)	Anticorruption; "voting is not a right but a privilege"; individualist/voluntarist liberalism; "states' rights"	

personal-registration statute and a corrupt-practices act. The registration
statute applied only to the state's cities and was of the periodic type (i.e., if a
voter missed an election, he or she had to reregister), and the registrations
were available on only four days.

The impact of these purifying changes was very substantial. As shown
in Table 3.4, a striking before-and-after profile emerges for turnouts among
native-born, foreign-born, and black voters in New Jersey. A few excerpts
from Reynolds's trenchant conclusion (1988: 168–171) seem to be called for,
as it summarizes very many of the forces for comprehensive change that
emerged across the country:[9]

> The main components of the System of 1896 were in place in New Jersey
> after 1911: a fragmented electoral system, weakened partisanship, waning
> participation, and an entrenched political elite.

> Throughout much of the nineteenth century, elections were communal affairs
> that brought adult men together in a variety of highly ritualized social activ-
> ities on or before election day. The voting process was uncomplicated and
> only loosely administered. In a nation of "island communities," the conduct
> of elections was necessarily placed in the hands of local partisans. The par-
> ties enlisted a small army of ticket peddlers, poll watchers, ward heelers and
> others to ensure that a full vote was realized in every ward and township. A
> very sizable sum of money was required to compensate the workers and even
> the voters for their efforts. . . . At the turn of the century, a vociferous dissent
> was lodged by the self-described better element who came to be known first
> as mugwumps, then as New Idea men, and still later as Progressives.
> . . . They brought a different set of values and perspectives to the electoral
> process shaped by a more centralized, hierarchical and formal social struc-
> ture characteristic of corporations, professional associations, and labor
> unions.

Table 3.4 Election Turnout in New Jersey, 1900–1919 (percentages)

	Native-Born Voters	Foreign-Born Voters	Black Voters
Presidential elections			
1900–1908	86.5	76.9	61.9
1912–1916	79.7	55.2	40.2
Delta (absolute)	–6.8	–21.9	–21.7
Delta (relative)	–7.9	–28.2	–35.1
Off-year elections			
1901–1910	71.1	74.3	63.4
1913–1919	64.7	44.7	40.4
Delta (absolute)	–6.4	–29.6	–23.0
Delta (relative)	–9.0	–39.8	–36.3

Source: Reynolds 1988: 150, tab. 6.2.

Reform swept through New Jersey's electoral system in three waves. The first culminated with the adoption of the secret and official ballot in 1890; the second materialized in 1903 with the direct primary and the voting machine; and the last introduced rigid voter registration and the blanket ballot in 1911.

The greater regulation imposed over the electoral process was to have three main effects. First, it officially recognized the major role played by the Democratic and Republican party organizations in the electoral process. In this way, it allowed these bodies to impose more discipline in their ranks and better defend themselves against raids on their voting bases by third parties and independent candidates. Second, by eliminating the necessity of local machines, the new electoral system eventually cut the candidates loose from the electorate and encouraged a spirit of independence and nonpartisanship that would later permeate the entire political process. Lastly, the new sets of laws made heavier demands of the public *by converting the voting process into a more complicated, onerous, and even intimidating experience.* (emphasis added)

The South's Apartheid Regime

As historian Eric McKitrick (1960) has noted, following the collapse of the Confederacy and the outbreak of an epic struggle between President Andrew Johnson and the Republican Congress, the former Confederate states (except Tennessee) were placed under military Reconstruction in 1867. The final settlement of the war depended on a peace treaty in two major parts: the Fourteenth and Fifteenth Amendments to the Constitution (1868, 1870), with readmission to the Union depending on ratification of the former by state legislatures elected by universal male suffrage. As was the case with the Versailles Treaty of 1919, this was viewed by most of the defeated population as a diktat, to be subverted and nullified at the earliest opportunity. At the same time, however, even after so-called Redemption and the removal of the last federal troops from the South in 1877, the amendments had apparently given Congress power to resume intervention to protect the rights of blacks to vote. In that context, a number of Southern states did not move toward an outright purge of this huge minority from the voting population until they were sure that they could get away with doing so. The date of the failure of the Lodge Force Bill in the Senate (February 1891) may be regarded as the moment of departure; by the time Republicans regained full control of the federal government, they were no longer interested.

The Supreme Court also took a hand. On all sorts of fronts, starting with the *Slaughterhouse Cases* (1873), which essentially gutted the Fourteenth Amendment's "privileges and immunities" clause, the Court developed a network of rationales aimed at reducing the enormous nationalizing thrust of the Civil War amendments and civil rights legislation enacted pursuant to them. The net cumulative effect of these decisions was to restore full pre-1861 control of elections to the states. The first case involving voting rights (racial exclusion from the polls) was *U.S. v. Reese* (1876). In this case (an 8-to-1 ruling), Chief Justice Waite observed that "the Fifteenth Amendment did not positively confer the right of suffrage on anyone." The Court then struck down Section 3 of the Enforcement Act of 1870 on the grounds that it did not explicitly include the words of the amendment. In *Plessy v. Ferguson* (1896), the Court endorsed the constitutionality of racial segregation in transportation; thus *Plessy* was, in the narrow sense, not a case about voting rights, but it did enshrine, until 1954, a central aspect of the region's emerging "apartheid" regime.

The circle was closed just a few years after the *Plessy* case. In *Williams v. Mississippi* (1898), a black man indicted by an all-white grand jury and convicted of murder by an all-white petit jury appealed on the grounds that since only voters could serve as jurors, and since the state had adopted a network of election-law changes to exclude blacks from the suffrage, he had been deprived of equal protection of the laws under the Fourteenth Amendment. It seems that Williams had not shown that the actual administration of the Mississippi suffrage provisions was discriminatory. As well, in *Giles v. Harris* (1903), the Court affirmed the constitutionality of Alabama's disfranchising constitution of 1901. By 1908 at the latest, all the former Confederate states had joined the parade. And that was that for more than sixty years.

The subject then turned to Southern (white) primary elections. When the white primary was established by state legislation that was explicitly race-exclusionary, this was a bridge too far: in *Nixon v. Condon* (1932), the Supreme Court ruled that such action was an unconstitutional deprivation of equal protection of the laws under the Fourteenth Amendment. The state (Texas) promptly repealed its primary laws, converting the hegemonic Democratic Party into a private organization that—like the Elks or the Kiwanis Club—was free to determine the qualifications of its members. This dodge was affirmed by the Supreme Court in *Grovey v. Townsend* (1935). After all, if the Democratic Party's processes were those of a private organization, its activities and processes did not constitute state action. As well, in *Smith v. Allwright* (1944), the Court concluded that the primary election system was an integral part of Texas's election procedures, and *Grovey v. Townsend* was explicitly overruled. By now, seventy-four years had passed since the Fifteenth Amendment was ratified. But the end was not yet.

The poll tax as a requisite for voting was an integral part of the purge machinery in many of the Southern states in the 1890–1908 period, and by the 1930s was duly challenged in the Supreme Court. In 1937 in *Breedlove v. Suttles,* the Court ruled (unanimously) that such taxes were valid state controls over elections. With extremely few exceptions, the legal norm favored state controls over elections, until the voting-rights revolution of the mid-1960s culminated in the Twenty-Fourth Amendment (1964), barring the poll tax as a prerequisite for voting in federal elections, and the Voting Rights Act of 1965. But what about state elections? As of 1966, three states, of which Texas was one, retained the poll tax at that level. In that year, the Supreme Court invalidated this requirement in *Harper v. Virginia State Board of Elections*. Justice Douglas's opinion for the six-man majority asserted that political franchise is "so fundamental a right that it cannot be denied because of wealth, property or economic status," that such efforts to do so violated the equal protection clause of the Fourteenth Amendment. This was rather sweeping: the real issue here was racial rather than economic, and it is noteworthy that the decision drew three dissents, from Justices Black, Harlan, and Stewart. Their view continued this age-old, singularly American debate: the dissenters claimed that there was a rational basis for the Virginia poll tax, and that states should have broad constitutional leeway under the equal protection clause to establish voter qualifications. From this perspective, both property qualifications and poll taxes are legitimate parts of the constitutional framework. As I have emphasized, the states have been and still are quasi-sovereign concerning the conduct of their elections, chiefly subject since the 1960s to federal constraints on "suspect classifications"—that is, race-based classifications.[10]

There is a reason for my brief discussion here of what V. O. Key Jr. (1949) and others, especially J. Morgan Kousser (1974), have so thoroughly documented over the past six decades. The one-party South, buttressed by small-to-tiny turnouts, ensured that, whatever happened elsewhere in the country, the Democratic Party could not be dislodged during the lifetime of the system of 1896–1932. More than this, the regional variants of the politics of domination and control that were at the core of that system persisted all the way through the New Deal, surviving a full generation after the accession of Franklin D. Roosevelt to the presidency. It is well known that FDR's second term was a much less happy experience than his first. His Court-packing initiative of 1937 foundered, in part because he was outmaneuvered by Chief Justice Hughes; then came his effort to purge the Democratic Party of conservative undesirables in the party's 1938 primaries; and also the return of economic slump from October 1937 through 1938–1939, and the spectacular Republican gains in the 1938 elections, followed by the clear emergence of a "conservative coalition" in Congress that was to survive into the 1960s.[11]

In discussing the New Deal and its aftermath, I probably break no new ground, except perhaps in some details. Some remobilization occurred with the Al Smith-Hoover election, in 1928, in which the Democratic candidate's Catholic religion and other ethnocultural factors played the crucial role. The first clear account of this was presented not by a professional political scientist, but by a particularly astute journalist, Samuel Lubell, in 1952.[12] Lubell coined the term "the Al Smith revolution" as a stage-setter for the massive national swing in metropolitan areas that was central to the New Deal realignment that began in 1932. This was true for the Upper West Side of New York City and other places with substantial numbers of Catholics, but there was also a marked Hoover surge that year in metropolitan areas such as Detroit, Denver, Seattle, and Los Angeles. It is also noteworthy that political scientists did not predict or expect that Harry Truman would be the victor in 1948. Only then, it seems, did light dawn that 1948 was a maintaining election, a systemic property not dependent on the existence of a candidate named Roosevelt.[13]

For a very long time it has commonly been understood that the New Deal realignment—the first time in US political history—entailed a new system in which the electorate was very significantly polarized along the lines of social classes. Sociologist Robert Alford (1962), reviewing evidence from Gallup public opinion polling, found that 1940 and 1948 represented the high points of salience in this explanatory variable. Perhaps a personal word may be offered here. In 1940, I, as a ten-year-old with an already developed interest in politics, lived in a "real" (i.e., bourgeois) Pittsburgh suburb, Mt. Lebanon Township. Political socialization worked very well in my case for quite a considerable time. The partisan balance in this township in 1940 was 18.1 percent for Roosevelt, 81.9 for Republican candidate Wendell Willkie. In the town of Homestead, overwhelmingly inhabited by steelworkers and their families, the tally was 84.3 percent for Roosevelt, and 15.7 percent for Willkie. Turnout was close to identical: 10,388 of a total 1940 population of 19,571 in Mt. Lebanon (53.1 percent), and 9,307 of 19,041 in Homestead (48.9 percent), with quite a few more resident aliens in the latter population compared to Mt. Lebanon.[14] Anyway, shortly before election day, I took the bus from the suburb to downtown Pittsburgh with a Willkie button on my jacket. Very shortly after I got off the bus, I was surrounded by not very well dressed men in cloth caps, who made it very clear that they objected to that button. I took it off, they dispersed. Later, I encountered Alford in graduate school and came to his discussion of class polarization in 1940. I could very easily relate to that.

Beginning in 1964, and with a much more useful series from 1968 onward, the Bureau of the Census has produced Series P-20, on registration and voting participation. Table 3.5 presents, on a 1968–1988 base, estimates of turnout by occupation at various posited global turnout rates, from 30 to 90 percent. The occupational stratification is taken from the male labor force in 1980 as a benchmark. Since the female segment of the labor force was (and probably still is) disproportionately concentrated in lower-to-middle status white-collar jobs, lumping this segment together with the other tends to blur the class-stratification pattern.

Naturally, the data in Table 3.5 constitute just a snapshot from a particular slice of historical time. But it seems to be a reasonable approximation of the real relationship between social class and voting participation. The table

Table 3.5 Estimated Turnout vs. Composition of US Voting Electorate, by Socioeconomic Status, at Posited Global Turnout Rates (percentages)

Socioeconomic Status	Percentage of 1980 Male Labor Force Electorate	Posited Global Turnout Rate			
		30		40	
		Est. Turn.	PV	Est. Turn.	PV
"Owning" middle class	30.6	60.0	57.0	65.4	48.2
Subaltern middle class	11.4	42.7	15.1	51.6	14.2
Subtotal: Middle class/ white collar	42.0	55.2	72.1	61.5	62.4
Upper working class	28.1	20.4	17.8	32.2	21.8
Lower working class + unemployed	29.9	10.9	10.1	22.1	15.9
Subtotal: Working class + unemployed	58.0	15.5	27.9	27.0	37.6

(continues)

compares the estimated turnout rate at each level of socioeconomic status, with composition of the voting electorate.[15] At the posited 90 percent turnout (about that in contemporary Sweden), the turnout at each level of socioeconomic status, except for the bottom two levels (lower working class + unemployed, and working class + unemployed), is very close to the global total. Conversely, at the posited 30 percent turnout, the turnout for what I call the "owning" middle-class male labor force, at 60.0 percent, is 30 percent higher than its share of the 1980 male labor force, at 30.6 percent, though this class constitutes 57 percent of the voting electorate (i.e., the party of voters who actually voted). And a turnout of somewhere between 35 and 40 percent corresponds to virtually all off-year elections to the US House of Representatives since 1974. As the structure of these summary turnouts shows, at the bottom of the participation rollercoaster, the mean socioeconomic status level of the voting electorate is distinctly higher than when the rollercoaster reaches some sort of peak. If, as is common abroad, participation levels are very high and invariant, then there is little or no gap between the political *pays légal* and the *pays réel*. In the United States, this has not always been true, and it is not true now. For a time, the New Deal realignment did (outside the South, of course) considerably reduce that gap.

I take two faces from the crowd here, as shown in Table 3.6. Not individuals as with Democratic senator Cotton Ed Smith of South Carolina, but

Table 3.5 Continued

				Posited Global Turnout Rate					
50		60		70		80		90	
Est. Turn.	PV	Est. Turn.	PV	Est. Turn.	PV	Est. Turn.	PV	Est. Turn.	PV
70.7	42.6	75.9	38.7	81.3	35.9	86.7	33.7	91.0	32.0
60.5	13.6	69.4	13.2	78.2	12.9	87.0	12.6	95.8	12.4
67.8	56.1	74.1	51.9	80.4	48.7	86.7	46.4	93.0	44.4
44.0	24.3	55.6	26.0	67.3	27.3	79.0	28.2	90.6	29.0
33.2	19.5	44.3	22.1	55.5	23.9	66.8	25.4	78.1	26.6
38.4	43.9	49.8	48.1	61.2	51.3	72.7	53.6	84.2	55.6

Source: US Bureau of the Census, Series P-20.
Notes: Est. Turn.: estimated turnout. PV: party of voters (voting electorate). Base for the turnout estimates is 1968–1988. Nonvoters = 1 – PV in each turnout category. The "owning" middle class comprises professional-technical workers, managers except farm owners and managers; the subaltern middle class comprises sales and clerical workers; the upper working class comprises servicemen, craftsmen, and foremen; and the lower working class comprises operatives and laborers (including farm laborers).

two urban areas at the heart of the regional metropole that dominated the national political economy for much of the twentieth century. The time frame is 1912 through 1980/1988. The urban areas are metropolitan Pittsburgh (some 150 units of Allegheny County, including the thirty-two wards of the city) and the forty-six cities and towns in greater metropolitan Boston that were part of that area in 1940. Ecological regression was performed on the relationship between socioeconomic status categories of the male labor force—in the case of Pittsburgh, including both ethnicity and social class, and in the Boston area just social class alone.[16]

There are quite a few stories that can be told from these arrays. But first, one aspect of background. At the time, the steel capital Pittsburgh was controlled by a Republican machine, as was the state, before the New Deal realignment (see Stave 1970).[17] The region's working class was a medley of ethnic groups, chiefly from Eastern Europe. The middle class was, of course, not exclusively Anglo-Saxon, but had few in its composition of what Boston mayor James Michael Curley called "the newer races." The Boston area had

Table 3.6 Realignment, Mobilization, Demobilization: A Tale of Two Cities (composition of potential electorate in percentages)

Pittsburgh Metro Area, 1912–1980

	Solid Anglo-Saxon Bourgeoisie					Solid Ethnic Working Class			
	Nonvoting	Democrat	Republican	Other		Nonvoting	Democrat	Republican	Other
1912	28.8	20.9	55.3[a]	-5.0		54.8	8.1	24.5[a]	12.6
1916	25.3	16.1	57.2	1.4		57.4	19.1	20.1	3.4
1920	30.0	10.7	57.7	1.6		77.8	5.0	10.5	6.7
1924	37.6	7.2	53.0	2.2		68.1	1.7	9.7	20.5
1928	19.9	11.4	68.8	0		59.1	36.7	3.5	0.7
1932	30.5	13.9	55.3	0.3		58.6	35.9	2.8	2.7
1936	23.0	12.1	63.2	1.7		33.0	4.2	0.8	2.0
1940	14.5	0.4	84.7	0.4		28.3	70.0	1.5	0.2
1944	21.4	3.8	74.5	0.3		39.6	58.4	1.8	0.2
1948	24.4	-2.6	77.8	0.4		35.3	63.4	0.8	0.5
1960	18.5	12.4	69.1	—		37.4	71.9	-9.3	—
1980	17.5	12.3	59.6	9.6		63.1	44.9	-7.0	-1.0

Boston Metro Area, 1912–1988

	Solid Anglo-Saxon Bourgeoisie				Solid Ethnic Working Class			
	Nonvoting	Democrat	Republican	Other	Nonvoting	Democrat	Republican	Other
1912	22.7	16.4	61.3[b]	-0.04	36.2	27.2	32.8[b]	3.8
1916	16.6	14.5	68.6	0.3	37.0	42.0	17.9	3.1
1920	19.3	8.6	72.6	-0.5	57.1	19.2	19.6	4.1
1924	28.8	5.0	67.6	-1.4	49.7	18.51	18.5	13.2
1928	11.0	8.6	81.0	1.4	31.7	54.2	3.0	1.1
1932	14.1	4.8	81.0	0.1	36.6	53.7	6.8	2.9
1936	13.0	2.2	84.7	0.1	27.8	59.3	3.7	9.2
1940	8.4	0.3	91.1	0.2	26.2	65.5	7.6	0.7
1944	6.9	9.0	84.0	0.1	40.7	52.7	6.5	0.1
1948	16.6	-1.1	83.1	1.4	33.8	63.6	0.8	1.8
1960	4.4	20.2	75.3	0.1	27.1	74.9	-2.1	0.1
1980	9.8	28.0	43.5	21.0	59.5	28.8	9.6	0.1
1988	-1.6	53.7	47.9	—	74.0	18.0	8.0	—

Source: Burnham 2010b.

Notes: Negative numbers are ecological regression estimates based on aggregate data, and such negative numbers can be expected whenever there is deviation from the underlying assumptions of the model; for an accessible and brilliant discussion of ecological regression, see Gienapp 1986: 475–481.

a. The 1912 Republican vote in Pittsburgh: among the solid Anglo-Saxon bourgeoisie, 15.5% Republican, 39.8% Progressive (55.3% total); among the solid ethnic working class, 9.9% Republican, 14.6% Progressive (24.5% total).

b. The 1912 Republican vote in Boston: among the solid bourgeoisie (middle class), 29.8% Republican, 31.5% Progressive (61.3% total); among the solid working class, 17.1% Republican, 15.7% Progressive (32.8% total).

multiple manufacturing industries, but was sharply socially segregated: the working class was heavily Irish Catholic (although with some Yankee, French, and other minorities); the middle classes were predominantly Yankee Protestants. "The war between the top and the bottom of Beacon Hill" was legendary and persisted for many decades. Even before Al Smith came on the scene in 1928, the Democratic party was much more robust than in the Pittsburgh area, hence the differences in mobilization rates.

At all times before 1936 (Pittsburgh) or 1928 (Boston), middle-class turnout was very much higher than in this modeled working-class segment of the potential electorate. Afterward, this declined, but persisted. In the Pittsburgh area, the dynamics of realignment, from 1928 to 1940, were those of bilateral mobilization, toward the Republicans among the middle-class segment (note the Hoover surge in 1928) and with a huge evacuation of the party of nonvoters into the Democratic Party. By 1940, we have a political profile that closely mirrors the differences between Mt. Lebanon and Homestead discussed earlier. Noteworthy in both settings is the significant conversion effects as well—the post-1924/1928 decline in the Republican share of the potential electorate. This same profile is evident in the 1922–1960 voter registration data for San Francisco, as indicated in Figure 3.1a. The fre-

Figure 3.1a Voter Registration in San Francisco as Percentage of Potential Electorate, 1922–1960

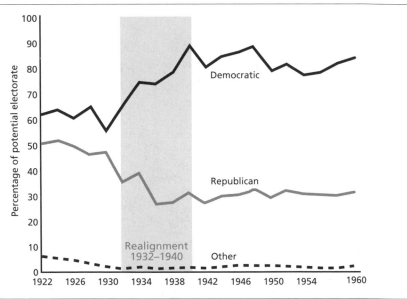

Source: Burnham 2010b.

quently discussed question of whether mobilization or conversion was chiefly responsible for the expanded Democratic share of the voting universe indicates that in San Francisco, at least, the contribution of each was about the same (see Figure 3.1b).

The profiles in Table 3.5, once established, persisted with respect to both partisanship and turnout through 1960, though it is perhaps worthy of note that in that year John F. Kennedy won a notably larger share of the middle-class portion of the potential electorate in the Boston area than any previous Democrat had achieved, though Wilson came close to that level in 1912 and 1916. What happened across the quarter century and later had two counter-vailing themes: a shift toward the Democrats among the middle-class vote (particularly, by 1988, in the Boston area), and an enormous collapse toward demobilization, not conversion, in the working-class segments in both cities, as seen in Table 3.6.

In the Pittsburgh region, the share of nonvoters among the solid ethnic working class rises from 37.4 percent to 63.1 percent between 1960 and 1980. The situation in the Boston area, by 1988, is even worse among the solid ethnic working class, with the share of nonvoters up from 27.1 percent in 1960, to 59.5 percent in 1980, to 74.0 in 1988—the latter, one may infer,

Figure 3.1b   Voter Realignment in San Francisco: Percentage Democratic of Two-Party Registration, 1922–1948

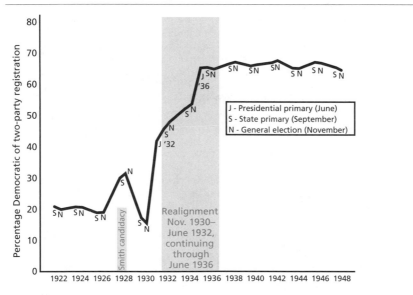

Source: Burnham 2010b.

higher than at any time since well before 1840. By contrast, the nonvoting segment of the potential electorate among the solid bourgeoisie (middle class) in both the Pittsburgh region and the Boston area is tiny and essentially invariant from 1940 onward. Nor is this merely an artifact of a possibly defective methodology: there is a 1992 Harvard University bachelor dissertation by Marshall Louis Ganz, "Where Have All the Voters Gone? The Decline of Voting and the Disintegration of the New Deal Alignment," with subtitle, "A Case Study of Five Boston Wards, 1960–1988." The title more or less says it all.

Ganz spelled out the post-Watergate partisan profiles so astutely that an extensive quotation seems appropriate. Written in the early 1990s, it seems a remarkably accurate picture of the situation in the contemporary period:

> [In 1988] Republicans based their success on a combination of the three elements referred to throughout this inquiry—ideology, social groups, and institutions. They developed a conservative laissez-faire ideology which emerged from the Goldwater campaign of 1964 and reached fruition in the two terms of the Reagan presidency. The ideology successfully defines the middle class as needing protection from government, rather than protection by it. Within this context, conservative Republicans identified a coalition of social groups both North and South, a substantial number of whom used to be Democrats, who provided their base. They also created a set of party institutions well-tuned to modern fundraising and media campaigns in combination with a capacity for grass-roots mobilization based on conservative activists and evangelical churches.
>
> Democrats did not have a clear ideological message and seemed to vacillate between Carter's "outsiderism," Mondale's traditional liberalism and Dukakis' technocratic Progressivism. While their new social base of ethnic [i.e., racial] minorities, feminists and environmentalists remains reasonably loyal when they participate, many do not participate. Their relationship to the white working and middle class voters—many of whom, outside the South, have remained loyal—remains tenuous and tense. They have turned to modern electronic campaigning, but their traditional institutions have decayed and their grassroots activists do not seem driven by the same ideological commitment that provides the conservative populists and religious right with so much of their energies.
>
> Meanwhile, about 50 percent of the electorate remains entirely outside the process, aligned only in their dealignment. Of some 85 million citizens who failed to vote in the 1988 presidential election, at least 55 million had become eligible since and they may never have cast a ballot. (Ganz 1992: 45–46)

I find myself trying to place President Barack Obama among the three Democrats Ganz mentioned. "Outsider," yes; "technocratic progressive," definitely; "traditional liberal," not really—hence the manifestly apathetic-to-disaffected base (and his disaffection with the base is also only too apparent). A Democrat might well say, in the words of the first stanza of William

Butler Yeats's prophetic poem "The Second Coming" (1920): "The best lack all conviction, while the worst are full of passionate intensity."

I would, however, part with Ganz on one point: the vast turnout decline among working-class voters has counted for considerably more than any voting apathy on the part of those fragments of new middle classes that form so important a part of the modern Democratic Party. Most of it comes from far lower down the social structure, among people whom Democrats condescendingly characterize as being wedded to their "religion and guns."

One may add a final note from the two places in Allegheny County, Pennsylvania, discussed earlier: the township of Mt. Lebanon and the borough of Homestead. In 2008, Mt. Lebanon looked as prosperous and "desirable" a suburb as it was in 1940. With the complete disappearance of the steel industry, Homestead is now depopulated and desolate. It remains heavily Democratic: Obama won 88.5 percent of the vote in 2008, but that vote represented only 28 percent of the 1940 Democratic total. Mt. Lebanon, on the other hand, managed to gain 3.4 percent in 2008, even while the county as a whole had been losing population for several decades. The most striking feature of Mt. Lebanon's behavior is that in 2004, it went Democratic for president for the first time since it was founded in 1911. And, in 2008, Obama won 54.9 percent of the vote to John McCain's 45.1 percent. It's still very much of a middle-class place, but the composition of the middle class has undergone enormous change, just as the steel-oil empires of Pittsburgh's past are now replaced as major industrial sectors by health care, higher education, and electronics. (In 2008, within the city limits, Pittsburgh's total population was less than half of what it was in 1940.)

Margaret Thatcher of the United Kingdom believed and said that there was no such thing as society, just individuals. Her policies were aimed at dissolving traditional social solidarities among the ruled classes, from breaking the grip of the unions (e.g., in the declining coal industry), to selling off council housing to former tenants, and more. The advent of Ronald Reagan launched a new era, whose objectives were similar to those of his British soul mate. Laissez-faire ideology prevailed: in the words of its prophet in the heyday of the system of 1896, William Graham Sumner (1919), this proposed way for people to relate to their world was, simply, root, hog, or die.

The post-1960 decline in voter participation has presented certain problems or puzzles for political scientists operating within the survey research tradition. For a powerful predictor of an individual's propensity to vote is her or his education level: the higher the latter, the more likely one is to vote rather than abstain. Of course, for many purposes education level can be read as a surrogate or proxy for position in the class structure, though it is not always clearly understood that way. Access to higher education in particular has always been an economically rationed fact of life. Based on data from the *Historical Statistics of the United States, Colonial Times to 1970* (US Bureau of the Census 1975) the following are the number of bachelor degrees or equivalent per thousand population at various times: 1920, 26; 1940, 81; 1960, 160; 1970, 223; and much higher still in 2010. So the puzzle: the electorate is much better educated now than it was in 1960, and vastly more so than in 1940 (as a careful listening to the actors' accents in the 1930s movies will convey). But despite this, turnout—which could be expected to rise alongside rising levels of formal education—instead falls, in some cases (outside the South, of course) to levels not seen since the 1820s or earlier.

Nor can this be attributed to the addition of the eighteen-to-twenty age cohort to the electorate in 1971. At an increment of about 1.06 × the 21-and-over base, it is too small to do the job. Tightening of personal-registration requirements, for example, has also not occurred, but rather the converse.[18]

One possible answer to the puzzle is that, given all that has been said so far about an electoral system whose leaders have never fully committed themselves to the basic canonical rule of democracy—one person, one vote, one value—and its implications for organizing the political system, the post-1960s shift toward massive abstention levels is essentially to be found in the behavior (or nonbehavior) of the electorate. In other words, transformations in the contexts of the electoral process since the 1960s have progressively hollowed out the active electorate. (A full enumeration of these changes would require a far, far longer chapter.) A catalogue of such changes virtually compiles itself when one thinks about them, many of which were prophetically evaluated by V. O. Key Jr. (1956) more than fifty years ago, and of which the insulation of major state elections from national political tides is one of the more important.

Conclusion

Interested elites and their allies have frequently gamed the machinery of elections for more than a century now, and they continue to do so. For example, the computer-led, frequently bipartisan, drawing of congressional-district boundaries has—except in upheaval or wave crises such as those of 1994, 2000, 2008, and 2010—significantly contributed to the number of one-party seats in the House of Representatives and in situations in which, as in 1988 and other years, well over 95 percent of incumbents running are duly reelected.[19]

A major contributor to this hollowing out of the electorate has almost certainly been the huge, and greatly increasing, input of interested money into campaigns in recent decades, and the continuing constitutional problems presented by the courts in creating and sustaining anything looking like coherent controls by government over the money flow. In a complex but collectively unanimous decision in 1976, in *Buckley v. Valeo,* the Supreme Court ruled that the Federal Election Campaign Act, as amended in 1974, was constitutionally void so far as candidate expenditures were concerned; in other words, in this interpretation of the First Amendment, money is speech and thus its expenditure by candidates, or independent groups, was shielded from regulation. In 1996 came *Colorado Republican Federal Campaign Committee v. Federal Election Commission,* which virtually completed the task of demolishing expenditure constraints. As the editors of a leading textbook put the matter, "the Court seems to have placed the First Amendment squarely across the path of those wanting to curtail independent spending by either parties or groups" (Mason and Stephenson 1999: 454). It goes without saying that any such license by private groups to buy the government would be unthinkable in any other Western democracy. But there is more.

In January 2010, the Supreme Court handed down a case that President Obama criticized to the justices' faces in his 2010 State of the Union message: *Citizens United v. Federal Election Commission.* Back in 1907, at the behest of a Republican president (Theodore Roosevelt), an overwhelmingly Republican Congress enacted an anticorruption statute, forbidding corporations to make direct contributions to political campaigns. This was done out of revulsion for the heavy and obvious corporate giving in the elections of 1896 through 1904. Back in 1886, the Court decided a case, *Santa Clara County v. Southern Pacific Railroad,* that, though otherwise obscure, retains one vitally distinctive element. In the words of one commenter on the case, "In an unusual preface, entered before argument, Chief Justice Morrison R. Waite observed that the Court would not consider the question 'whether the provision in the Fourteenth Amendment to the Constitution which forbade a state to deny to any person within its jurisdiction the equal protection of the Constitution, applied to those corporations. We are all of the opinion that it does'" (Hall 2005: 881).

And there matters rested. Obviously no one in 1907 imagined that these creatures of the state, as constitutional persons like you and me, could not find their political money cut off by government action. But an ideological right-wing majority in 2010 linked this juridical person to the money-is-speech rationale of *Buckley* and its successor cases to strike down this precedent of 103 years and turn the money taps back on. The circle launched by Roscoe Conkling's argument in the Gilded Age, and embraced without dissent in the *Santa Clara* case and now fused with *Buckley* and its successor cases, fully closed the circle.

It may be true, in the contemplation of Pius X and other Catholic popes, that error has no rights, no matter how long persisted in. While this may be satisfactory for defenders of religious doctrine, it is harder to defend if people are supposed to accept respect for precedent as a normal canon of judicial action. There is, however, another precedent for the century of error, bringing us back to the 1895 income-tax case, *Pollock v. Farmers' Loan and*

Trust Co. There were, as we have seen, emotional issues involved in the dis-ordered, crisis-ridden atmosphere of 1895. The specific legal-constitutional issue was whether certain kinds of federal taxes had to be apportioned among the states. (If so, they essentially could not be created in practice.) The issue was raised and decided by Court in 1796, so far as a federal tax on carriages was concerned (*Hylton v. United States*): such a tax did not have to apportion among the states. There matters rested for ninety-nine years. Meanwhile, dur-ing the Civil War, the Internal Revenue Service was created in 1862, and an income tax was imposed, lasting from 1862 to 1872, when it expired. In the 1894–1895 arguments in the *Pollock* case, Joseph Choate and others argued explicitly that it was time to "reverse a century of error," which (by a vote of 5 to 4, as in *Citizens United* in 2010) the Court's majority duly did. Restora-tion of this segment of federal taxing power had to wait until 1913, with rati-fication of the Sixteenth Amendment.[20]

In an outraged dissent, Justice Henry Brown got right to the point:

> The outcome of this case involves nothing less than a surrender, of the tax-ing power to the moneyed class. . . . Even the spectre of socialism is conjured up to frighten Congress from laying taxes upon the people in proportion to their ability to pay them. It certainly is a strange commentary . . . that Con-gress has no power to lay a tax which is one of the main sources of revenue of nearly every civilized State. . . . I hope it may not prove the first step to-ward the submergence of the liberties of the people in a sordid despotism of wealth. (Paul 1960: 212)

I hope that readers will agree that the Supreme Court's activities in 1895 and 2010 have a remarkable parallelism. The system of 1896 was one in which the Supreme Court was the most important of the three branches of govern-ment, not in what it positively did but in what it forbade Congress and state legislatures from doing, in areas of direct concern to the monied class. It may be asserted that *Citizens United* was not, after all, such a big deal, since the curtailment of federal efforts to find a way to control the huge flood of interested money was already very far advanced. But, as they say, it's the principle of the thing. I certainly share Justice Brown's hope that this "may not prove the first step toward the submergence of the liberties of the people in a sordid despotism of wealth," but think that this hope is pretty forlorn: in the domain of money in elections, of buying America, *Citizens United* is not the first step, but the last. Welcome to 1895, every-body! Indeed, one wonders whether we might change the country's name to "United States of Plutocracy."[21]

The hollowing out of the electorate, reflected in substantial part by the declines in turnout, has, I think, had much to do with the emergence of money-driven, media-saturated "permanent campaigns" as traditional parti-san and other solidarities have disintegrated. If so, the connection between nonvoters whose chief explanation is in the "not interested" category and voters who are disaffected with "Washington" and available (as with the Perot candidacy in 1992) for third-candidate insurgencies against "the system" would seem clear enough. As I remarked at the time, the fact that Ross Perot won 18.9 percent of the total vote in 1992 (with a significantly rising turnout, by the way) was a warning. Not that Perot was in any sense a dangerous character; but the fact that this was the largest third-candidate vote in our post–Civil War history[22] was telling us something. Given a large enough crisis—especially economic—active and passive disaffection can make all sorts of pathologies envelop the electoral system and the country as a whole. In previous critical-realignment crises, the transition at the level of the electorate very much involved large-scale entries by previous nonvoters, the large majority of whom lined up with the winners. The same interplay between former nonvoters and winners of realignment also happened in the history of Weimar Germany, with the Nazis filling the lion's share of the previous vacuum (Burnham 1972).[23]

Predictions are not offered here. A general review of the multiple crisis points afflicting the United States today is far beyond the scope of this chapter. It is perhaps enough to say here that the contradictions have reached the point where they are standing on their hind legs and screaming at the tops of their voices. A key element reflecting them is what journalist Ronald Brownstein (2007) has termed "the second civil war."[24] There is a general legitimization crisis at work, and it has grown a lot more intense since the bank-driven near-collapse of the economy into the Great Recession of 2008–2010. This should not be surprising. It is well understood that capitalism had a near-death experience in the Great Depression, as originating in a stock market crash in 1929. President Herbert Hoover, who is often miscast as an unthinking apostle of laissez-faire, put his hand on a major part of the problem. "The trouble with capitalism," he commented, "is capitalists. They're too damned greedy." Much debate followed during the 1930s, raising such questions as, Can capitalism be saved? Should it be saved? What can government do to save it? The ultimate answer that was found, then as later, was the liberal (or social-democratic) welfare state. In 1929 as in 2008, foundational relations of power in political economy and society were stripped bare, and stood forth in their true nakedness. A chief virtue of the so-called interest-group liberal state was its ability—among other things—to re-clothe the Emperor. The twin fulcrums were government regulation of potentially runaway enterprise on one hand, and the pursuit of social harmony through welfare-state payments for the bulk of the ruled classes. This meant that the Lords of Creation had to accept that the costs of doing business had increased, but many surely realized that the price of social peace was worth paying, in particular because the adoption of Keynesian demand-side economic policies contributed to flattening the business cycle.

Of course, in the postwar period a lot more than economic policy was changing. The United States became an empire after 1945, and eventually a very costly and deeply unpopular war in Vietnam shattered much of the consensus of the Eisenhower years. (The response was characteristic. As the Vietcong and the North Vietnamese won the war while the United States looked the other way, policymakers abolished the draft and thus neutralized dissent on college campuses. But the empire was kept anyway.)[25] To this was added the large upheavals, North and South, involved with the second Reconstruction and the civil rights revolution. But we need not attempt any further recitation here of the historically obvious. From the advent of Ronald Reagan in 1980, New Deal liberalism and its supporting coalition became increasingly passé. The so-called Great Moderation of 1984–2007—led especially by then-venerated Federal Reserve Board chair Alan Greenspan (1987–2006)—appeared to justify conservative rule and the liberation of the (of course, always efficient) free marketplace. Undercurrents of popular discontent did not cease, of course; witness Ross Perot's exceptional showing in 1992. These undercurrents were muted, as in reality the banks essentially seized control of the government. After mergers and liquidations, the six largest banks[26]—obviously too big to fail—by 2009 were "worth" some 64 percent of gross domestic product, up from 19 percent in 1995 (Johnson and Kwak 2010: 203). They had now become a near-hegemonic force in US politics, perhaps equaled only by the military/imperial sector.

Vast rage permeates the American population. With the nakedness of oligarchy fully exposed, the collision between republican ideals and a certain populism on the one hand, and the realities of power on the other, is jarringly obvious to almost anyone without a job, to those who fear losing their jobs, to the millions whose houses are "underwater" (that is, their mortgages are larger than their sale value), to those whose incomes have been stationary (or declining) in constant-dollar terms since 1973, to those who worry about the future of their children in an ever more globalized and fragmented labor market—and the list goes on and on.

Disappointed expectations are endemic, and no wonder. The question arises: Who or what will be able to formulate a narrative that will explain what has been happening to people like you and me? The comparison is worth making in detail, even granted that the Great Depression was much worse by any measure than today's Great Recession: What does the political *raise en scène* of the 1930s look like when compared and contrasted with that of the twenty-first century? Who or what will seize control of the narrative? The omens are not bright. For as political theorist Louis Hartz once observed, "where there is no socialism (i.e., organized social democracy), even liberals look demonic" (1955). The final word might, however, rest with Supreme Court justice Oliver Wendell Holmes Jr., who, speaking in 1913, during some then-present discontents, observed, "When the ignorant are taught to doubt, they do not know what safely they may believe" (quoted in Lerner 1943: 388).

Putting the 2012 Election into Context

As space is not unlimited, I must be concise. What follows is a series of propositions about the 2012 election and its aftermath.

Proposition 1

The widespread view of the 2012 race is that it was a status quo contest. This view is correct. But just what *status* is *quo*? President Obama was one of thirteen incumbents in the period 1900–2012 who ran for a full second term. Of these, nine were reelected and four were defeated (Taft in 1912, Hoover in 1932, Carter in 1980, and George H. W. Bush in 1992). But of the nine who were reelected, Obama stands out as the only one who won a smaller share of the two-party vote the second time around (53.7 percent in 2008 compared to 52.0 percent in 2012, or a negative swing of 1.7 percent). This had consequences, as we shall see.

Proposition 2

At the congressional level, the true benchmark—when things really changed—was the 2010 election. A full account of 2012 cannot be made without placing 2010 at the center of analysis. This was an earthquake of remarkable proportions by any standard. For at least half a century, US House elections had displayed the huge power of incumbency in determining the vast majority of their outcomes. In 2010, the Democrats suffered a real debacle at all levels of election, as compared with "big bang" elections dating back to 1892, as shown in Table 3.7.

In 2010, at the state-legislature level, Democrats lost 727 of the 4,075 seats they had secured in 2008, or 17.8 percent of them, reducing that party's share of the total to levels not seen since 1928. In the wake of this rout, Republicans secured thirty governorships, and in twenty-four states their party won control of both houses of the state legislature. Nor was 2010 an ordinary year, since decennial reapportionment of legislative seats was at hand.

At the level of congressional elections, the 2008–2010 vote swing was 9.2 percent. Table 3.7 places that in a seventy-transition sequence that began in 1872–1874. This result virtually completed the reduction of the South's Democratic Party cohort, and more generally, across the country, virtually wiped out the "blue-dog" contingent within the party. The influx of Tea Party–backed candidates radically propelled the House GOP toward the very far right.

Table 3.7 Big Bangs in US House Elections:
Greatest Two-Party Vote Swings, 1892–2012

Transition	Swing (%)	Comment
1930/1932	+10.3	New Deal critical realignment
2008/2010	–9.2	2012 swing: +3.8
1892/1894	–9.0	Critical realignment (1896 system)
1946/1948	+8.0	Counter-deviating election (reinstating)
1920/1922	+7.8	Counter-deviating election (reinstating)
1918/1920	–7.0	Deviating election

Source: Burnham 2010b.
Notes: Vote swings of plus or minus 7.0% or greater. Number of transitions = 70, with transitions 7–70 following 91.4% of cases.

The policy impact of these changes and their occasional follow-through in 2012 (as in North Carolina) has been a notorious matter of record, leading squarely to the checkmate scenario now playing out in Washington, D.C. Most notably, while the Senate remained Democratic after 2012, that party gained only ten seats net from the post-2010 Republican House majority. On the Democratic side, it is often noted that the party's House candidates received over 1.7 million more votes than did their GOP counterparts (59.7 million compared to 58.0 million). But the result—201 Democrats compared to 234 Republicans in the House—was not just the result of extremely skillful Republican gerrymandering; geography was involved.

Proposition 3
The negative swing against Obama was unevenly distributed. With the extremely important exception of Ohio, the centerpiece of the struggle with Mitt Romney, Pennsylvania and most of the Midwest showed considerably larger swings than the national swing of 1.7 percent. Well over a hundred counties that Obama carried in 2008 swung to Romney in 2012, and many of them were concentrated in the Midwest. Nationally, Obama won 669 counties compared to 2,946 carried by Romney, or just under one-fifth of the total (18.5 percent). Overall, the number of votes per Obama county in 2012 was 98,516, contrasted with 24,910 per Romney county. When, after election night, vice presidential nominee Paul Ryan said that his ticket had been defeated by the "metropolitan vote," he was correct, at least correct enough.

There is a little more to this story. The GOP reapportionment of Pennsylvania seems a noteworthy example of how it was that Republicans in the House elections won a majority of thirty-three seats, despite losing the popular vote by 1.6 million votes nationwide. For while Democratic House candidates won a 50.8 percent majority of the two-party popular vote, they won just five of the state's eighteen seats. But we also have presidential data for both 2008 and 2012 by congressional district (see Barone and McCutcheon 2013). In 2008 in Pennsylvania, with a state vote share of 55.2 percent, Obama actually carried ten of these eighteen seats. In 2012, by contrast, with 52.7 percent of the vote, he carried just the same five districts that House Democrats won. The additional five, carried by Obama in 2008 but not in 2012, all went Republican, but very narrowly at the presidential level.

Finally, one can do a little thought experiment—applying an often touted remedy, the district system, for apportioning the electoral vote (the formula for either party would be congressional district + 2 [if it wins the statewide vote] = electoral vote). Applying this in 2008—since Obama won a majority of thirty-six congressional districts—produces an electoral-vote tally of 299 Democrats and 239 Republicans. But in 2012 Obama won only 208 districts (plus the District of Columbia, or 209), while Romney won 227. Now the total tally becomes 263 for Obama, and 275 for Romney—and presto, the latter is "elected"! What is involved, of course, is a huge geographical "lumpiness." Note as well, of course, that since Obama won only 208 congressional districts, his "coattails" were largely nonexistent. Naturally, Republicans in charge of reapportionment know all about this, and have a word for it: as in the new third congressional district of Ohio (Columbus), put all the Democrats you can find into a "vote sink" and then try to carry everything else (Barone and McCutcheon 2013: 1306). In 2012, in sharp contrast to 2010, 95 percent of all incumbents in both parties running for reelection achieved their goal. This suggests a kind of "new normal," such that the US House of Representatives seems likely to remain usually, if not always, in Republican hands until at least the 2020 reapportionment cycle.

Proposition 4

The creation of what appears to be a hegemonic Tea Party bloc of seventy or more congressional Republicans is a specific legacy of 2010. So was its counterpart, the near-annihilation of "blue-dog" Democrats. As events in 2011 in Wisconsin and in 2013 in North Carolina have vividly demonstrated, the big story of both elections is the emergence of near-monolithic Republican solidarity on the extreme right. In the presence of a strikingly passive president, this "new" GOP has, to a remarkable extent, framed the national policy agenda. There is, of course, a large and rapidly growing literature on this fundamental change in US politics (e.g., Brownstein 2007; Balz 2013; Mann and Ornstein 2012).[27] Since political checkmate appears to be the destiny of the United States for at least the next several years, there is almost certainly to be considerably more in the offing.

Proposition 5

There are a few features of the 2012 election that merit a little more attention.

The white vote. This component of the electorate shrank from 83 percent in 1992 to 72 percent in 2012. At the same time, Romney scored a real landslide among white voters: 59 percent compared with 39 percent for Obama, representing an anti-Obama swing of 4 percent. Historically, when minorities once cast tiny shares of the vote, this would equal, say, the 1904 Republican landslide favoring incumbent Theodore Roosevelt, or the 1928 election, in which Republican Herbert Hoover defeated Democrat Al Smith by an equivalent margin. The Romney campaign operation, and it also seems the Gallup poll, which seriously projected a misestimate, had models that assumed (1) a white component of 74 percent, like that in 2008, and (2) much greater intensity among Republican than Democratic voters. But reality falsified these assumptions: (1) The growing Latino share of the vote showed a positive (pro-Obama) swing of 4 points (67 percent to 71 percent); (2) for the first time probably in history, the black turnout rate actually exceeded the white; (3) the enthusiasm differential supposedly favoring the GOP ticket did not materialize. Nevertheless, one could imagine circumstances in which the declining white vote could be even more lopsidedly Republican, say in 2016, when it will constitute something like 70 percent of the electorate. Thoughtful Republicans like Senator Lindsey Graham of South Carolina are very aware that changing demography is not on the party's side and that constructive steps on the immigration front should be taken. But the preferred solution, so far, has been to enact voter identification and other vote-suppression legislation at the state level—which of course does not endear the GOP to minority voters.

Gaming the system: back to 2010 again. First, gerrymandering has played a real role in entrenching Republican control of both the US House of Representatives and the numerous state legislatures that swung into the party's control in the 2010 electoral earthquake. But creative redistricting is virtually as old as the republic—first gaining wide notice with Elbridge Gerry's 1812 masterpiece in Essex County, Massachusetts. We can note it and set it aside.

Second, the combination of Barack Obama's election in 2008, the catastrophic impact among Main Streets from coast to coast of the economic collapse that unfolded in 2008–2009, and a widespread sense that "they" were "taking it away" ("it" being the American dream) from "us" produced a real radicalization within large sectors of the white population, and especially that part of it that makes up the Republican base. These developments happened to have coincided with an off-year election.

Back in 1956, V. O. Key Jr. noted a disturbing trend: more and more states were moving their major state elections from presidential years to off years. This involved insulating state politics from national political tides. When he wrote in 1956, about half of the states had made the move toward off-year elections for major state offices (Key 1956: 41–51). Since then, this shift has been nearly consummated. In 2012, only eleven of the fifty states, representing 53 of the US House's 435 representatives (12.2 percent), still held elections for major state offices during presidential election years.

What was not perhaps fully appreciated in Key's day is that presidential-year and off-year elections involve two quite different electorates. Over the period from 1972 through 2012, the mean presidential-year turnout nationally was 56.7 percent for president and 49.1 percent for the US House. In the off-year period 1974–2010, the mean US House turnout was 37.4 percent (at 41 percent, 2010 saw the highest turnout in the series). The 2010 turnout was 65.1 percent of the 2008 presidential figure, and 70.9 percent of the 2008 US House participation rate. Voters who turn out in off years are notably whiter, more affluent, and older than their presidential-year counterparts. Usually this doesn't seem to matter structurally. But 2010 was clearly different. So, of course, were 1854, 1858, 1874, 1894, 1910, and 1930.

And third, there are primaries to consider. V. O. Key (1956: 85–132) was also suspicious of these, viewing them as destructive of grassroots organizations of the parties. In very recent years, extreme forces in and around the Republican base have discovered and used the threat (and actuality) of "primarying" less ideologically pure incumbents of their own party. A crazed base, very often constituting less than one-fifth of the larger electorate, has responded. This has notably resulted in forfeited near-certain party wins in November, as for instance in the 2010 Delaware Senate election, in which Christine ("I'm not a witch") O'Donnell lost a Senate seat that Republican representative Michael Castle could easily have won; or as in Indiana in 2012, when long-standing and statesmanlike Republican incumbent Richard Lugar was defeated by Tea Party favorite Richard Mourdock—who then promptly lost the seat to Democrat Joe Donnelly, while the latter's presidential running mate, Obama, was losing the state to Romney by 267,656 votes.

Such cases have a huge radiance among the rest of the congressional rank and file. The threat of being "primaried" if one doesn't toe the ultra-right line is very real, and may account in part for the remarkable specter of some forty-three (or more?) virtually unanimous House GOP votes to repeal Obamacare. The frame of reference is a very familiar one: "We'd like to win elections, but our first objective is to win and maintain control of the party." In various ways, in the 1920s and 1930s, this was the recipe for Stalinist politics.

Proposition 6

The upshot of the 2012 election, refracted as it importantly was by what happened in 2010, amounts to a virtual checkmate. Even in Bill Clinton's time, Republicans in Congress and elsewhere refused to accept his legitimacy as president despite the election returns. This has been raised to the nth power so far as the present situation is concerned. The governing system of the United States is perceived as scarcely legitimate to many in the electorate, and not a few in Congress.

One could imagine a "way out" of sorts: a true-red conservative Republican wins the presidency in 2016, alongside a Republican majority in the Senate (produced in 2014 or 2016) and continued Republican control of the House. In that case, the poet laureate of such a regime would be the late Ayn Rand, who is after all the favorite author of Wisconsin's Republican representative Paul Ryan.[28] Alternatively, we could have more of the same indefinitely, except that we really can't, since in the traditional British view of the matter, "The King's government must be carried on."

So how does 2012 look? One could end on the kind of cheerful note that British poet Robert Southey struck in reviewing the once famous victory of John Churchill, Duke of Marlborough, over Louis XIV's forces in 1704 (a victory that led nowhere, since the war was settled nine years later on the basis of the status quo). As Southey wrote in his 1798 poem "The Battle of Blenheim,"

> "And everybody praised the duke,
> who this great fight did win."
> "But what good came of it at last?"
> Quoth little Peterkin.
> "Why, that I cannot tell," said he;
> "But 'twas a famous victory."

But affairs seem rather more somber than that. Of course, the logjams over the budget, the deficit, and the raising of the debt ceiling may find some sort of resolution short of government shutdown or government default. But if so, something else will come along. We are deeply into an era that I call the Gilded Age II. But it is also one that has been labeled "the second civil war." I have not the faintest idea when, how, if, by whom, or by what means this impasse in our collective affairs will be overcome. But there may be something to be said to the point that economist Paul Krugman has raised: "Of course, the coming confrontations are likely to damage America as a whole, not just the Republican brand. But . . . this political moment of truth was going to happen sooner or later. We might as well have it now" (2013a: A27). Or as president-elect Lincoln put the matter in a letter to a senator, "Let there be no compromise on the question [of extending slavery]. The instant you do, they have us under again; all our labor is lost, and sooner or later must be done over. . . . The tug has to come, and better now than at any time hereafter" (December 10, 1860). And the tug came. Ten days after this letter was written, South Carolina seceded from the Union. And the rest, as they say, is history.[29]

Notes

1. Compare to the discussion in Burnham 1986, but especially Burnham 1970. Persistent conflicts seem endemic in this whole field of action. See, for example, Burnham 1971 and the statistical assessment of the controversies that Burnham 1970 generated in Ferguson and Chen 2005.

2. An excellent summary of all this history, and more, is Rokkan 1970.

3. Compare Rokkan 1970, especially chap. 1 ("The Comparative Study of Political Participation") and chap. 3 ("Nation-Building, Cleavage Formation, and the Structuring of Mass Politics"). For an earlier but still valuable analysis, see Tingsten 1937. And for a typically thorough and detailed German survey of historical developments in European democracies, see Sternberger and Vogel 1969.

4. This is not entirely a matter of inference. As late as 1970, the attorney general of Texas defended the January 30 registration cutoff date in the 1966 Texas statute on grounds of "maintaining the purity of elections." See Burnham 1971: 341–342.

5. *Reichsfeinde* means "enemies of the Reich." About one-third of the German population was Roman Catholic. In the 1870s, Otto von Bismarck launched a *Kulturkampf* against them, which in the end led only to a consolidation of Catholic support for their confessional party, the Zentrum; and he also secured enactment of anti-socialist legislation to stunt the growth of the other "enemy." For a graphic presentation of this mobilization pattern, see Burnham 1972.

6. For various reasons, my work in this genre has recommended itself more to historians than political scientists. See Kleppner 1987 (note especially his appendix, "Realignment Theory After Key"). See also Burnham 1981.

7. For a starkly unfriendly account of politics (and constitutional law) in this period, see Beatty 2007. See also the analysis of the "distended society" in Wiebe 1967.

8. One of the distinguishing characteristics of the 1896–1932 system was that it was the most sectionally polarized in US history. The GOP usually dominated the metropole (or core) and the Pacific Coast, except when it committed binary fission in 1912–1914. It had become virtually invisible in the Southern "colony" or periphery, while it had to contend with progressive and even socialist movements in the other periphery (far Midwest and Mountain states). By 1920, the "search for order" had largely been consummated. But, as Robert H. Wiebe (1967) and others have pointed out, the Great American Middle underwent two huge scares: the first, the Great Hun Scare (by 1917–1920), against the numerous German American minorities, especially in the Midwest; and the second, the Great Red Scare (1918–1920), which destroyed what was left of the socialist movement in the United States, by no means always peacefully. Finally (1921–1925), the Ku Klux Klan became something of a national force for the first time. It is a pity that the Great American Middle is often prone to panic attacks and scapegoat-hunting. Just the out-group targets change with time, it seems.

9. Of course, by no means everything serving to depress turnout in New Jersey—especially recently—can be traced to the Geren Registration Act of 1911. A summary provides a useful overview:

Election Turnout in New Jersey, 1876–2008 (percentage of potential electorate)

	Presidential Years	Off Years	
	President	Governor	US House
1876–1892	91.9	74.6	75.3
1894–1910	84.9	74.1	78.1
Geren Registration Act, 1911			
1912–1919	69.9	57.8	52.8
Suffrage of women, 1920			
1920–1931	65.3	51.2	44.9
1932–1949	71.0	52.6	52.2
1950–1970	71.3	55.5	50.6
Suffrage of 18- to 20-year-olds, 1971			
1972–1984	60.8	43.7	40.9
1985–1998	57.4	41.6	32.6
2000–2008	62.3	39.1	36.3

Indeed, in 1986, just 28.3 percent of the potential electorate voted in US House elections, the lowest turnout since the 1822 election. As elsewhere in the non-Southern states, a remarkable and abrupt downshift in turnout for US House elections occurred in the off year 1974, without significant recovery thereafter, from 1978 through 2006.

10. The classic study of the South's apartheid regime not long before its termination is Key 1949; see especially pt. 5, "Restrictions on Voting." Key's (typically understated) judgment was that, overall, in a disorganized politics, the have-mores profit more than the have-lesses.

11. We can take a face from the crowd: Ellison Durant Smith, Democratic senator from South Carolina from 1909 until his death in 1944. Born in 1866, Smith was a colorful character who became universally known as "Cotton Ed." He was very conservative as well as an outspoken racist. (When he attended the 1936 Democratic convention, a black minister delivered the invocation. Smith exclaimed, "That man is as black as the ace of spades!" and walked out of the convention hall.) A brief summary of his electoral career provides a useful overview (see table on top of p. 67). Senator Smith was one of the targets of President Roosevelt's attempted purge in the 1938 primaries. As was usually the case, Roosevelt lost; only death removed Smith from the scene.

12. Nevertheless, Lubell was the first to identify the "revolt of the city" as crucial to the formation of the New Deal majority coalition.

13. This is discussed by Theodore Rosenof in *Realignment: The Theory That Changed the Way We Think About American Politics*. Rosenof quotes a letter from Austin Ranney to fellow political scientist E. E. Schattschneider that is worth including here: "However pleased they were about the electoral result as Democrats, 'as political scientists we should be downright depressed.' The outcome indicated 'that we just don't know as much about the nature of American politics and public opinion as we may have thought we did on November 1st.' Not that we are any worse than any other kinds of 'experts' but it's humiliating all the same" (2003: 13). Shades of the anything-but-stellar performance of the vast majority in the economics profession in their failure to predict the great meltdown of September 2008 (and after).

Ellison Smith's Performance in Senatorial Elections, 1920–1938

	Potential Electorate	Smith	Republican	Total	Percentage of Potential Electorate Total	Percentage of Potential Electorate Smith
General elections						
1920	777,000	64,388	—	64,388	8.3	8.3
1926	801,000	14,560	—	14,540	1.8	1.8
1932	852,000	104,472	1,976	106,448	12.5	12.3
1938	955,000	45,751	508	46,259	4.8	4.8
Primary elections						
1920	777,000	65,861	42,735	198,596	14.0	8.5
1926	801,000	82,753	77,559	160,312	20.0	10.3
1932	852,000	150,468	114,840	265,308	31.1	17.7
1938	955,000	186,519	150,437	336,958	35.3	19.5

14. Today, Mt. Lebanon remains a quite popular and prosperous place. Homestead, with the steel mills gone, is a desolate wasteland where few people still live.

15. The only US case that Herbert Tingsten was able to find in his early but still valuable study *Political Behavior* (1937: 158) was that of Delaware, Ohio, in the 1924 election. While categories differ, the pattern is obviously similar. The days when Ohio could and did produce turnouts in excess of 90 percent were long gone by 1924.

16. In the case of Pittsburgh, two other categories, while available, are omitted here (solid ethnic bourgeoisie, and solid Anglo-Saxon working class).

17. Pittsburgh is a very well documented city. In 1912, for example, the Russell Sage Foundation produced a mammoth, six-volume survey of Pittsburgh and its environs that was an extraordinary "tour de force" of early social science.

18. A positive point for Texas: after the end of the 1966 registration statute, it moved toward an extremely user-friendly system: (1) registration by mail, with postcards in English and Spanish available at grocery stores and the like; (2) no-fault absentee voting before election day. Despite which the turnout in 2006 was less than one-third of the potential electorate.

19. Richard Scher's *The Politics of Disenfranchisement: Why Is It So Hard to Vote in America?* (2010) covers all the bases. There have been some very recent parades of horrors—notable in the infamous 2000 election in Florida. But other such cases occur. Once upon a time, I taught at Kenyon College in Gambier, Ohio (1961–1963). Gambier is a very small, intimate town. I voted there in the 1962 election, before personal registration had been extended in that part of the state. One went in to the polling place, received four ballots for deposit in four milk cans on a dais, said "howdy" to everybody, and departed. In the 2004 election, Gambier gained national exposure when students who persevered had to stand in line—in some cases, I gather, for more than eight hours—to cast their vote. Whether there was a deliberate

effort to suppress the vote, or sheer administrative incompetence, I do not know. Either way, the notable Gambier incident of 2004 starkly revealed one of the themes that Scher discusses. See also the discussion in Overton 2006.

20. A historical note: the Sixteenth Amendment achieved the necessary two-thirds majority support in both houses of a solidly Republican Congress, in 1909, and was ratified by the necessary three-quarters of the state legislatures, a substantial majority of which were controlled by the GOP.

21. Compare the discussion in Ferguson 1995b, but also the story in *USA Today,* October 15, 2010, titled, "Campaign Spending by Groups Gone Wild: Amount Double That of the 2006 Midterm Elections." Some excerpts from this story (Schouten 2010: 4A):

> Spending by outside groups to influence congressional races surged past the $220 million mark this week, as party committees and conservative groups pump last-minute cash into ads in advance of the Nov. 2 elections. . . .
>
> The total is roughly twice the $111 million similar groups spent at this point in the last midterm elections in 2006, an analysis by the non-partisan Sunlight Foundation shows. . . .
>
> Many of the most active players, including the U.S. Chamber of Commerce, operate under tax code provisions that do not require them to publicly disclose their donors, even as they spend at an unprecedented rate. A Supreme Court ruling in January [i.e., *Citizens United*] freed groups to spend unlimited corporate and union money on independent ads that call for the election or defeat of candidates. . . .
>
> "We are standing at the precipice of unlimited political spending," said Ellen Miller, the Sunlight Foundation's executive director. . . .
>
> Richard Hasen, a campaign-finance expert at Loyola Law School in Los Angeles, said the "staggering" spending also demonstrates that special-interest groups are prepared to spend heavily in the 2012 fight for the White House. "We may look back at the 2008 election and its $4.2 billion price tag as a quaint time when money in politics didn't matter so much."

End of story. And of democracy? Only in the United States—literally.

22. Excluding Theodore Roosevelt's Progressive Party of 1912, product of a Republican rupture.

23. My 1972 article, titled "Political Immunization and Political Confessionalism: The United States and Weimar Germany," has acquired a certain intellectual history. The confessionalism model it develops is considered, along with radicalized lower-middle-class and mass-society explanations, in what is probably the definitive work on the origins of the Nazi vote, Falter 1991. It has also been reprinted in Rotberg 2001.

24. Its subtitle: *How Extreme Partisanship Has Paralyzed Washington and Polarized America.* Books with a "decline and fall" tendency have recently become legion. See, for example, Jacobs and King 2009.

25. The literature on the empire and its malign influence on democracy at home is now enormously large.

26. Bank of America, JP Morgan Chase, Citigroup, Wells Fargo, Goldman Sachs, and Morgan Stanley.

27. For a state-of-the-art political science analysis, see Jacobson 2013. A particularly penetrating account, which includes discussion of politics in the states, is Davis 2013.

28. Ayn Rand's masterpiece is *Atlas Shrugged,* first published in 1957. The pure doctrine is found in Part Three, Chapter VII: "This Is John Galt Speaking." For a useful discussion of this libertarian/anarchist intellectual, see Burns 2009.

29. A broader view of the *mise en scene* is Perry Anderson's essay on modern US politics, "Homeland," in which he concludes, "In the U.S., the regalian rights of the dollar have mitigated the effects of the crash. But the system-wide deadlock in the regime of accumulation persists, politically over-determined by the local *Kulturkampf* of colours and mores. The upshot is the unbalanced balance of partisan forces of which commentators wring their hands today. The neo-liberal order has become a political no-man's land, in which no organic formula of rule is now in sight" (2013: 32). Or as Antonio Gramsci once commented, "The old is dying and the new cannot be born. In the interval, a large number of morbid symptoms appears" (1971: 2).

4

From Umbrella Parties
to Polarized Parties

Arthur C. Paulson

In November 2012, President Barack Obama, the incumbent Democrat, was reelected, narrowly defeating Republican Mitt Romney. The Democrats retained their majority in the US Senate, while the Republicans retained their majority in the House of Representatives. The election of 2012 resulted in little change in the balance of divided government in the United States.

Even before our elected leaders began their new terms, they faced the challenge of negotiations over finding a plan to move the federal budget toward balance. Throughout the campaign, Obama had advocated a balanced approach involving spending cuts and revenue increases, the latter specifically including increased income taxes for Americans with the highest incomes. Republicans generally stood in favor of more in the way of spending cuts and less reliance on tax increases, and they entered negotiations in opposition to an increase in income tax rates. If in the future the president and the Republican leadership in Congress cannot do a better job of arriving at agreements that can be passed by the House and Senate than they did in dealing with the debt ceiling, the country will continue to face deep budget cuts and tax increases, what we have come to call the "fiscal cliff."

This debate, with the related public posturing, is about more than the federal budget and national debt. It is an ideological confrontation about the fundamental role of government in American society. The issues and positions in the current debate are not new. What is relatively new in the American experience, tracing back over about a half century, is the development of a party system that is polarized along ideological lines.

I have previously argued that electoral realignment remains a periodic reality in US politics (Paulson 2000, 2007, 2009, 2012). Political scientists

71

generally missed what was the most profound electoral realignment in US history, between 1964 and 1972, because that realignment was fundamentally ideological and insufficiently partisan to be recognized widely. Nevertheless, it resulted in the end of the New Deal era and was followed by three decades in which the rule was divided government, most often featuring a Republican president and a Democratic Congress. Divided government, however, did not represent electoral chaos. The swing vote during this period was composed mostly of conservative Democrats, disproportionately Southern, who voted Republican for president and Democratic for Congress. The three decades after 1964 also involved a long secular realignment, in which those conservative Democrats shifted to the Republicans in congressional elections as well.

The result is a new ideologically polarized party system in which there will be more party-line voting in the early twenty-first century than there was in the middle and late twentieth. For the past decade, presidential and congressional elections have presented an evenly divided, ideologically and culturally polarized electorate, with the Democrats strongest in the Northeast and on the West Coast, and the Republicans strongest in the South and the Interior West. The 1964–1972 realignment in presidential elections has been married to the more recent secular realignment in congressional elections, defining the current electoral era. How did such ideologically polarized parties, so contrary to the historic American experience, develop? What are the implications of the new party system for US democracy in the twenty-first century?

Two Vignettes

In the spring and summer of 1944, as President Franklin D. Roosevelt, the incumbent Democrat, was preparing to run for a fourth term, and after Wendell L. Willkie had been defeated for renomination for president in the Republican primaries, the two planned to meet to discuss what they might do to produce a deliberate realignment of the party system along ideological lines. FDR, according to the account of his aide, Samuel Rosenman, was enthusiastic. The president instructed Rosenman to set up a meeting with Willkie, commenting, "I think the time has come for the Democratic Party to get rid of its reactionary elements in the South and to attract the liberals in the Republican Party. Willkie is the leader of those liberals. He talked . . . about a coalition of the liberals in both parties, leaving the conservatives in both parties to join together as they see fit. I agree with him one hundred percent and the time is now—right after the election."

Willkie indicated his interest in a meeting. "Both parties are hybrids," he told Rosenman. According to Rosenman, Willkie was interested in a realignment of the parties, "between all the liberal forces on the one hand and all the conservative forces on the other" (Barnard 1966: 480–481).

Because both FDR and Willkie preferred to wait until after the election to meet, the meeting never took place. Willkie died before the election, at the age of fifty-two, after a series of heart attacks, and Roosevelt died in office the following year, no action having been taken. Nevertheless, much of their vision has been realized in today's party system.

Twenty years later, Senator Barry Goldwater of Arizona, a conservative Republican who would have agreed on little else with Roosevelt or Willkie, agreed with their view of what parties and party systems should be. When his name was first placed before a Republican convention in 1960, he withdrew and beseeched conservatives to support the party ticket: "Let's grow up conservatives! If we want to take this party back, and I think we can, some day, let's get to work!" Goldwater and his supporters believed that the party should stand on conservative principles, offer "a choice, not an echo" and belittled liberal Republicans as "me, too Republicans" (White 1965: 89). "Some day" turned out to be 1964, when Goldwater's nomination proved to be the crucial turning point toward an ideological polarization between the major parties that Roosevelt and Willkie could only dream of.

The Party System in the United States: Two Parties, Many Factions

The United States has had a two-party system throughout the life of the republic, but there have generally been more than two sides to every issue. US political parties are best understood when examined as factional systems, rather than as rational-acting organizations. Across all alignments until the 1960s, both major parties were umbrella parties, loose coalitions among interests and factions, each spanning the ideological spectrum of American life (Aldrich 1995; Paulson 2000, 2007, 2009, 2012). The Republicans, generally more conservative on economic issues, were also the party of "modern" values and were more liberal on racial issues. The Democrats, more progressive on economic issues, were also the party of "traditional" values, and on balance were more conservative on racial issues, if only because of the Southern white supremacist faction (Jensen 1978; Paulson 2000, 2007, 2009, 2012; Rae 1989, 1994, 1998).

The Democratic umbrella has covered a multifactional system: the party regulars, including labor, the big-city organizations, and a working-class electoral base; the more middle-class reformers; and the more rural, Southern, and generally conservative faction (Mayer 1996; Paulson 2000, 2007, 2009, 2012; Rae 1994). The first two factions are relatively liberal, and there was little difference between them until they held the presidency and emerged as a majority within the Democratic Party during the New Deal. Since then, party regulars usually have prioritized economic issues, while the reformers have focused more on the causes of emerging social movements.

The South was once, of course, the factional home of white supremacy in US politics. Southern conservatives held their power within the Democratic Party through seniority in Congress that landed them committee chairs when the Democrats were in the majority, and through the two-thirds rule that gave the South an effective veto power over nominations at Democratic National Conventions. The two-thirds rule was finally replaced by majority rule at the 1936 convention, as FDR's renomination was uncontested.

The multifactional divisions of the Democrats are illustrated by the closest convention roll call on record, when the Democrats declined to condemn the Ku Klux Klan in 1924, and by the 1948 roll call that endorsed a platform plank for civil rights reform, causing the Dixiecrats to bolt and form a third party. The latter roll call signified a decisive shift of national power within the Democratic Party away from its Southern and rural conservatives toward its liberal factions.

The Republican umbrella has historically appeared to cover a more bifactional system: the relatively moderate-to-liberal Wall Street faction, with its more cosmopolitan, internationalist, big business interests, and the Main Street faction, with its more conservative, small business, nationalist, or isolationist interests. A somewhat more complex understanding is offered by Nicol Rae (1989, 1998), who has analyzed the Republicans as a multifactional system, Wall Street as composed of the progressives and the moderates, and Main Street as composed of the stalwarts and the fundamentalists.

While conservative Republicans have composed the majority of their party in Congress for well over a century, between the New Deal and the 1960s they were unable to deliver presidential nominations. Their candidate, Senator Robert Taft of Ohio, was "Mr. Republican," but he was denied the nomination three times, as moderate-to-liberal Republicans secured majorities of delegates at national conventions that nominated Wendell Willkie, Thomas Dewey, and Dwight Eisenhower for the presidency between 1940 and 1952. The Republicans remained the party of Lincoln until 1964, when Senator Goldwater won the Republican presidential nomination. The nomination of Goldwater signified not only the shift of power within the Republican Party toward its conservatives, but also the shift of power among conservative Republicans toward the fundamentalists.

Party Realignment and Electoral Realignment

The two-party system has been a dynamic one, going through periods of fundamental change periodically. Party and electoral change has been widely illustrated using the concept of realignment, introduced by V. O. Key Jr.

(1955, 1959), and developed most notably by Walter Dean Burnham (1970). Realignment involves significant and persistent shifts in the electoral coalitions of our major parties, which tend to occur periodically, often resulting in new majority parties, governing coalitions, and policy agendas (Andersen 1976, 1979; Bartels 1998, 2000; Burnham 1970, 1991, 1996; Clubb, Flanigan, and Zingale 1990; Ladd 1978; Ladd with Hadley 1978; Lawrence 1997; Paulson 2000, 2007; Pomper 1972, 1996; Pomper and Lederman 1980; Stonecash 2006; Sundquist 1983). Critical realignments have been placed in the 1830s, 1860s, 1890s, and 1930s, and more controversially in the 1960s. Whether electoral change since the 1960s is called "realignment" or not, the "sixth party system" emerged between 1964 and 1972 (Aldrich and Niemi 1996).

Electoral realignment has always been associated with the birth of a new political party (the Democrats in the 1830s and the Republicans in the 1850s) or a decisive shift in factional power within a major party (the nominations by the Democrats of William Jennings Bryan in 1896 and Alfred E. Smith in 1928). What makes the 1964–1972 period unique is that for the first time in US history, there were decisive factional shifts within both major parties almost simultaneously, with an enduring impact on the party system.

The sixth party system emerged in three stages. First, liberal Democrats and conservative Republicans became the dominant factions in their parties. Second, party change between 1964 and 1972 was accompanied by electoral realignment in presidential elections. Third, the 1964–1972 realignment in presidential elections was followed by a period of frequently divided government, until realignment in congressional elections reached critical proportions in the 1990s.

In an ideologically polarized party system, the parties have become ideologically homogenized internally (Mayer 1996; Paulson 2000, 2007, 2009, 2012). The shift of factional power was more gradual in the Democratic Party, more sudden for the Republicans.

Democrats

As late as 1924, at the national convention that featured the 103-ballot battle for the Democratic presidential nomination, conservative Democrats, with their base in the South, had the votes to narrowly defeat the motion to condemn the Ku Klux Klan. The factional strength of liberal Democrats grew during the New Deal period, and FDR made an effort to take advantage of it. In 1936, with the president unopposed for renomination, the Democratic National Convention replaced the two-thirds rule with majority rule over nominations. In 1938, FDR led a mostly unsuccessful campaign in the congressional primaries to "purge" conservative Democrats. By 1944, liberal Democrats still did not have the votes at the national convention to deliver renomination to Vice President Henry Wallace, who lost to Senator Harry Truman of Missouri and a coalition of moderates and conservatives.

The 1948 convention was the first at which liberal Democrats commanded a majority, when they overcame the opposition of moderates and conservatives to pass the ambitious endorsement of civil rights. But they encountered two problems. First, they needed the South to win national elections. And second, liberals faced a collective action problem about power within the party. By 1968, when liberal Democrats were deeply split among themselves over the Vietnam War, party regulars generally supported the Johnson administration, and reform liberals generally opposed the war. The commitment of that year's national convention to party reform reflected an effort to heal the divide.

In 1972, Senator George McGovern of South Dakota, an antiwar liberal, defeated Senator Hubert Humphrey of Minnesota, a more moderate liberal, and Governor George Wallace of Alabama, a segregationist, for the Democratic presidential nomination. Since 1972, liberal Democrats have generally retained their advantage in national nominating contests. Contested presidential nominations have been won by moderate Democrats under two conditions: when the liberal Democrats failed to unite on a candidate (1976 and 1992), or when a moderate Democrat was an incumbent president (Jimmy Carter in 1980) or an heir apparent (Al Gore in 2000).

The infusion of African Americans into the Southern Democratic electorate, facilitated by the Twenty-Fourth Amendment to the Constitution and the Voting Rights Act, has changed the national Democratic Party. While Southern moderate Democrats like Carter, Clinton, and Gore have been instrumental in moving the Democratic Party back toward the ideological center in recent years, their emergence has nonetheless played a major role in the ideological polarization between and ideological homogenization within the parties. Their victories in primaries have eliminated the old "white supremacy" faction of the Democratic Party. Today, voters who once would have supported George Wallace are practicing Republicans, no longer a factor in Democratic primaries. The Democratic Party is now the more liberal of the major parties across the country, even in the South.

Ironically, party unity on ideological issues probably increased the image of divisiveness in the unexpectedly long contest for the Democratic presidential nomination in 2008. Senator Barack Obama of Illinois and Senator Hillary Rodham Clinton of New York agreed on most issues, differing only on matters of salience and degree about the Iraq War, the economy, and health care. Without ideological cues, the campaign was waged on demographic and personal issues, which heated up the discourse. Certainly, there was lingering racial tension at points in the primary campaign. But even the spirited contest in the primaries could not cover the fact that the Democrats are America's liberal party.

Republicans

Nicol Rae's multifactional analysis of Republican politics illustrates the decline in the national power of moderate-to-liberal Republicans, the emergence of conservatives as the majority within the party, and the movements of both the party and its conservatives to the ideological right.

The two nominations of Governor Thomas Dewey of New York, a moderate Republican, in 1944 and 1948, were explained by different factional dynamics. In 1944, Wendell Willkie was seeking renomination for president, campaigning as an internationalist with the support of party "progressives." As a result, Dewey had the support of conservatives in the primaries and won the nomination without organized opposition at the convention. In 1948, Dewey faced opposition from both his ideological left and right. He outlasted Harold Stassen of Minnesota, then still the serious candidate of progressives, in the primaries; he then led Senator Taft, the conservative, on the first two convention ballots. The opposition then collapsed and the convention cast a unanimous vote for Dewey on the third ballot.

Four years later, Dewey was among the leaders of a coalition of moderates and progressives that delivered the Republican presidential nomination to General Dwight Eisenhower, frustrating Senator Taft and his conservative supporters for the third time. Taft actually went to the convention as the frontrunner, but Eisenhower's forces won important procedural roll calls on rules and credentials with the support of delegates pledged to progressive favorite sons Stassen of Minnesota and Governor Earl Warren of California. When Eisenhower led on the first ballot, the shift of Stassen's Minnesota delegation delivered the nomination to Ike.

The bitter 1952 convention, featuring the showdown between Eisenhower and Taft, turned out to be a warm-up for 1964, when conservative Republicans secured the GOP presidential nomination for Senator Barry Goldwater of Arizona, defeating Governor Nelson Rockefeller of New York in the primaries and Governor William Scranton of Pennsylvania at the convention. The salience of civil rights presented conservative Republicans with a viable Southern electoral strategy, and they organized to take over the party at the grassroots. The conservatives who supported Goldwater were not only more numerous than the supporters of Robert Taft, but also more ideological. While Taft supporters were "stalwarts" in Rae's conceptualization, Goldwater supporters were movement conservatives, ideological "fundamentalists," for whom the Republican Party was a means to an ideological end (Rae 1989). Yet in 1964, the party remained seriously divided. Before the convention, liberal Republicans mounted a serious, if doomed, campaign to stop Goldwater, and many of them never did endorse the nominee, even after the convention.

The last major ideological showdown in the Republican presidential primaries came in 1976, when President Gerald Ford, a moderate, won the nomination. But the president won only because he was the incumbent, however accidentally installed by Watergate and the resignations of President Nixon and Vice President Spiro Agnew. Ford had the support of moderates and progressives, but it was not enough. Ronald Reagan had the backing of the fundamentalists. Stalwarts were torn between their president and their ideology, and gave Ford enough support to deliver the nomination. Reagan came so close precisely because conservatives already had the upper hand in GOP nominations.

In 1980, Reagan paid no penalty for his challenge to an incumbent Republican president. He had the support of conservative Republicans, stalwarts and fundamentalists alike, who amounted to a clear majority of the primary electorate. His opposition was split between George H. W. Bush, the candidate of the moderates, and Representative John Anderson of Illinois, the candidate of the progressives. Reagan clinched the nomination well in advance of the convention, and Bush withdrew. Unlike 1964, the Republican National Convention in 1980 was a celebration of party unity. Anderson ran for president as an independent, practically acknowledging that there was no longer room for progressives in the Republican Party.

Since 1980, Republican presidential primaries have become contests among conservatives and moderate conservatives, also known as fundamentalists and stalwarts. By 1988 there was little evidence of ideological factionalism in the distribution of the vote in Republican presidential primaries. Ideology revived as a factor in the 2000 primaries, with Governor George W. Bush of Texas inheriting the coalition that had supported Goldwater and Reagan in 1964 and 1980, respectively. Indeed, three states where his father had won primaries against Reagan in 1980 held primaries before George W. Bush clinched the nomination in 2000: Michigan, Connecticut, and Massachusetts. He lost all three to Senator John McCain of Arizona, who enjoyed the support of moderate Republicans. Nevertheless, although the contest between Bush and McCain featured intense rhetoric, it did not feature a return to the degree of ideological factionalism that once had marked the showdowns between Eisenhower and Taft or Goldwater and Rockefeller.

Just as Reagan paid no price for his 1976 insurgency in 1980, McCain was able to overcome his 2000 defeat to win the Republican presidential nomination in 2008. Certainly, McCain is the most moderate conservative to have won any of the 2008 primaries, but he is no Nelson Rockefeller. Indeed, McCain won the nomination after a campaign in which he and all of his Republican opponents tried to promote themselves as the new coming of Ronald Reagan. Moreover, McCain won the nomination only because conservative Republicans were unable to unite in the primaries on either Mitt Romney, who appealed to stalwarts, or Mike Huckabee, who appealed to fundamentalists. But if John McCain is not a conservative Republican, he is a conservative and a Republican.

Since 2008, we have seen the emergence of the Tea Party within Republican ranks. Tea Party candidates won several primaries in advance of the 2010 midterm elections. But there is less new about the Tea Party than its media coverage would indicate. The Tea Party greatly resembles the Goldwater movement before 1964, with its grassroots rebellion against the party establishment, and represents today's "fundamentalist" faction in Republican politics. Its emergence certainly has shaken factional politics within the Republican Party, but it only enhances the trend toward ideological polarization between the parties. Indeed, the Tea Party presents us with the question of just how conservative America's conservative party is going to become.

The 2012 Republican Presidential Nomination

Rae's multifactional analysis informs us about the contest for the Republican presidential nomination won by Mitt Romney in 2012. Throughout the contest, Romney found his strongest support among moderate Republicans. His persistent opposition came from much more conservative fundamentalists. During the "invisible primary" a number of candidates supported by fundamentalists rose to challenge Romney. Representative Michelle Bachmann of Minnesota, Governor Rick Perry of Texas, and Herman Cain each had their moment, only to fade from the scene.

The two candidates who survived to face Romney in the primaries and caucuses both found the base of their support among fundamentalists: former senator Rick Santorum of Pennsylvania, and former House Speaker Newt Gingrich. They won contests where there was fertile ground for fundamentalists. Santorum won Iowa and several other caucus states, plus primaries in border states and the South: Missouri, Oklahoma, Tennessee, Alabama, Mississippi, and Louisiana. Gingrich won primaries only in South Carolina and Georgia.

Romney's task, which he accomplished, was to hold his moderate base and persuade stalwarts that he was conservative enough. His most important victories came in primaries in blue states, later won by Obama in the general election: New Hampshire, Florida, Michigan, Ohio, Illinois, Maryland, and Wisconsin. By the time Santorum and Gingrich had withdrawn, Romney had outpolled their combined vote among moderate-to-liberal Republicans, and secured a plurality among conservatives. Santorum and Gingrich had cut each other off from making a more serious challenge by splitting the fundamentalist vote. Romney had won by uniting moderates and stalwarts. Like John McCain, who had defeated him four years before, Romney may not be a conservative Republican, but he is a conservative and a Republican, and he was the presidential nominee of America's conservative party in 2012.

In the second stage of the development of the sixth party system, party change between 1964 and 1972 was accompanied by electoral realignment in presidential elections. This realignment did not look like the previous ones, and David Mayhew (2002) has artfully stated his doubt that periodic realignment is a reality in US politics. While I vigorously defend realignment to be a historical reality and a useful concept for electoral analysis (Paulson 2007), we can concede the point for the sake of argument. If we were to stipulate that periodic electoral realignment is a figment of our imagination, we still find one compelling realignment in the 1964–1972 period. Rather than the "surge" realignment, in which a general shift creates a new majority party, the 1964–1972 sea change was an "interactive" realignment, in which decisive minorities within each party coalition engage in a crosscutting shift toward the opposing party (Clubb, Flanigan, and Zingale 1990). The decisive shift was among white Southerners, who moved from their historical home in the Democratic coalition toward the Republicans.

In 1944, the old umbrella party system and the New Deal alignment still seemed stable. But that was the last time the Democrats won a majority in a presidential election based on the New Deal coalition. Over two decades, a new party system and electoral alignment emerged. Four Deep South states broke from the national Democratic ticket in the Dixiecrat revolt of 1948. Republicans cracked the South in the next three elections. Then, in 1964, Senator Goldwater, the Republican nominee for president, ran even with President Johnson across the South and swept the Deep South while losing the national election by a landslide of near record proportions.

Since then, the Republicans have carried most or all of the South in every presidential election except 1976, when Democrat Jimmy Carter of Georgia was elected president. For four decades, the South has been the central building block for the GOP in winning seven out of thirteen presidential elections, placing Republicans Richard Nixon, Ronald Reagan, George H. W. Bush, and George W. Bush in the White House. The last four Republican victories in presidential elections all included a solid South in their coalition.

Even Southern Democrats no longer carry the South in presidential elections (Paulson 2007). When Carter carried ten of the eleven states of the old Confederacy in 1976, it was only because of an African American vote that did not exist for the most part in the South until the Voting Rights Act. Even against Carter, President Ford won the Southern white vote. Ronald Reagan carried most of the South in 1980, when he defeated Carter. When Bill Clinton of Arkansas was elected president twice, he carried only four states across the South each time. Finally, when Vice President Albert Gore narrowly lost the 2000 presidential election, he carried no states in the South, not even his own Tennessee, the Florida controversy notwithstanding.

Meanwhile, the Northeast has gone in the opposite direction, even if the electoral change was not as extreme and is often overlooked (Speel 1998; Reiter and Stonecash 2010). For a century after the founding of the Republican Party, the base of its coalitions was found in the Northeast. Republicans carried all or most of this quadrant of the country in eighteen of the twenty-six presidential elections between 1856 and 1956, including all sixteen of its victories. Then, in 1960, Senator John F. Kennedy, Democrat of Massachusetts, carried most of the Northeast in his narrow election victory. Since then, the Northeast has been the base of the Democratic coalition, always voting generally more Democratic than has the country as a whole, and for all of the Democrats who won.

Thus, while there has been a partisan realignment of the states, the coalitions of states found historically in presidential elections are not broken (Archer et al. 1988; Archer et al. 1996; Burnham 1970; Jensen 1978; Kleppner 1987; Ladd with Hadley 1978; Paulson 2000, 2007; Rabinowitz and MacDonald 1986; Schantz 1996; Schneider 1978; Sundquist 1983; Wright, Erickson, and McIver 1985). Instead, the partisan coalition of states is reversed almost intact. The once solidly Democratic South remains almost as solid, but Republican in most elections since 1964. The Northeast, once the base for the Republican Party of Lincoln, has become the most Democratic region of the country. Figure 4.1 compares an electoral map for presidential elections between the critical election of 1896 and 1944, with an electoral map for presidential elections since 1964. The maps present a valid comparison almost identical to the aggregate election results. Republicans won seven of thirteen presidential elections between 1896 and 1944, and seven of thirteen presidential elections between 1964 and 2012. The maps show that what is now the Republican "L" of the South and Interior West (Cook 1996) was once the Democratic "L," and that what is now the Democratic base in the Northeast was once the Republican base.

Finally, as the sixth party system developed, the 1964–1972 realignment in presidential elections was followed by a period of frequently divided government, until realignment in congressional elections reached critical proportions in the 1990s. While the Republicans won five out of six presidential elections between 1968 and 1988, the Democrats retained their majorities in both houses of Congress most of the time, and in the House of Representatives all of the time, until 1994. This led political scientists to argue that we were in a period of dealignment and party decay (Broder 1978; DeVries and Terrance 1972; Jacobson 1990; Ladd 1981, 1991; Silbey 1991; Wattenberg 1990). Somewhat more perceptively, James Wilson (1985) called it "realignment at the top, dealignment at the bottom."

Divided government was not so much "party decay" as the result of split tickets, cast disproportionately in the South, in states and congressional districts carried by Republicans in presidential elections, while incumbent conservative Democrats were being reelected to the House and Senate. Over time, as conservative Democrats retired, or lost primaries to more liberal Democrats, or switched parties, their states and districts became as Republican at the "bottom" as they had been at the "top."

Figure 4.1 States in Presidential Elections: Realignment, 1896–2012

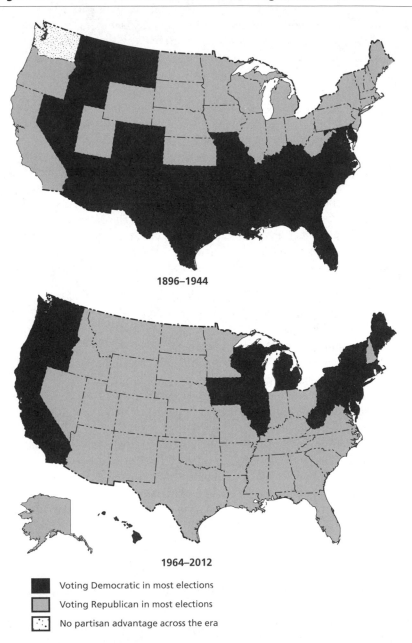

1896–1944

1964–2012

■ Voting Democratic in most elections
▨ Voting Republican in most elections
⬚ No partisan advantage across the era

Source: Derived from David Leip, *Dave Leip's Atlas of U.S. Presidential Elections,* http://www.uselectionsatlas.org.

Then came the midterm elections of 1994, when the Republicans, led by Newt Gingrich in proposing their *Contract with America* (Republican National Committee 1994), won both houses of Congress, the House of Representatives for the first time in forty years. For the first time since Reconstruction, Republicans won majorities of House and Senate seats across the South. Coalitions of states and voters now looked very similar to the coalitions that had emerged in presidential elections since the 1960s, providing renewed evidence of realignment (Burnham 1996; Paulson 2000, 2007; Wilcox 1995). In a play on Wilson's words, I called it "critical realignment at the top, secular realignment at the bottom." More efficiently and originally, James Campbell (2006) has called it "staggered realignment."

The new coalitions have remained stable. The electoral maps in Figure 4.2 illustrate that increased split-ticket voting in the late twentieth century was more a realigning transition than a linear trend toward dealignment or party decay. From 1896 to 1944, the Republicans carried the Northern tier, and the Democrats carried the Southern tier, particularly the solid South, in both presidential and congressional elections. From the presidential realignment in the 1960s until the congressional realignment three decades later, the Democrats gained in the Northeast, and the Republicans gained in the West, in both presidential and congressional elections. But while Republicans usually won the South in presidential elections, Democrats retained their hold on the region in congressional elections. Since the congressional election of 1994, coalitions in presidential and congressional elections have come to resemble each other, with Republicans winning most of the South and Interior West, and Democrats winning most of the Northeast.

Ideological polarization between the parties in Congress increased slowly after 1980, and became pronounced after the 1994 election. Between the New Deal and the 1990s, the voting records of Southern conservative Democrats had been clearly distinguishable from those of Northern Democrats, particularly when the issue of civil rights was at the top of the congressional and public agenda. Scattered Republicans in Congress tended to vote on the liberal side of issues. But after 1994, party-line voting became the rule. In 1999, Congressional Quarterly stopped publishing its scoring of "conservative coalition" voting in Congress, roll calls on which a majority of Republicans and Southern Democrats were on one side of an issue, and a majority of Northern Democrats were on the other. That sort of roll call no longer occurred often enough to be statistically useful (Congressional Quarterly 1999).

Since the 1990s, the ideologically polarized party system has been in place. The Republicans are now the conservative party, and the Democrats are the liberal party, in both presidential and congressional elections, in every region of the country.

Figure 4.2 Coalitions of States in Presidential and Congressional Elections, 1896–2012

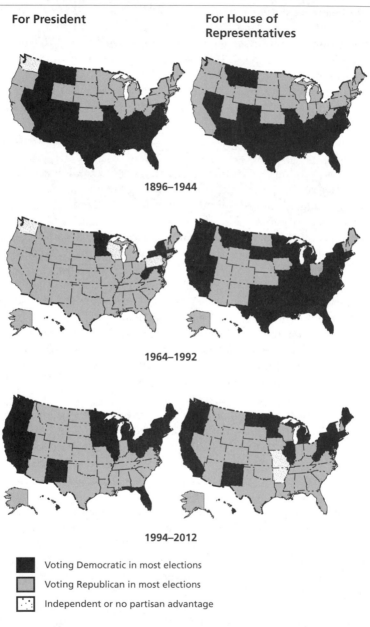

For President

For House of Representatives

1896–1944

1964–1992

1994–2012

███ Voting Democratic in most elections

▓▓▓ Voting Republican in most elections

▒▒▒ Independent or no partisan advantage

Source: Derived from David Leip, *Dave Leip's Atlas of U.S. Presidential Elections,* http://www.uselectionsatlas.org.

Voter Realignment and Elite Realignment
in the Sixth Party System

The distribution of opinion among American voters is probably no more or less polarized today than it has been historically (Fiorina, Abrams, and Pope 2011), but party change has polarized the distribution of their votes. After the realignment in presidential elections in the 1960s, the swing voters were typically conservative Democrats (often called "Reagan Democrats") and disproportionately Southern whites, the types of voters who supported George Wallace in 1968, and for nearly thirty years thereafter split their tickets, voting Republican for president and Democratic for Congress. Since 1968, the historically Wallace voter appears to have been voting the Republican ticket. Meanwhile, historically liberal Republican voters have shifted the other way, toward the Democrats. The moderates left behind by this electoral change seem to be today's swing voters, while electorates in both party's primaries are more ideologically homogenized.

Electoral realignment has been accompanied by the sort of elite realignment between the parties that Roosevelt and Willkie once planned to do together. The party-switching parade at the leadership level started mostly with liberal Republicans becoming Democrats: Senator Wayne Morse of Oregon, Mayor John Lindsay of New York, Representative Ogden Reid of New York, and Representative Donald Riegle of Michigan, for example. Then there were the conservative Democrats becoming Republicans: Senator J. Strom Thurmond of South Carolina, Representative John Bell Williams of Mississippi, and former Governor John Connally of Texas led the early waves; Representative Phil Gramm of Texas followed in the 1980s; while Senator Richard Shelby of Alabama led another wave of conservative Democrats into the Republican Party after the 1994 congressional election. Finally, there are the moderates in both parties who became independents: former senators Lowell Weicker of Connecticut and Lincoln Chafee of Rhode Island, who were elected governor; both Senator James Jeffords, Republican of Vermont, and Senator Joseph Lieberman of Connecticut, the latter of whom had been the Democratic nominee for vice president in 2000, left their parties to serve as independents. Prior to the 2010 campaign cycle, Senator Arlen Specter of Pennsylvania, the veteran liberal Republican, switched parties, hoping to avoid a difficult Republican primary and win reelection as a Democrat. His plan was frustrated when he was defeated in the Democratic primary.

The net result of this party switching is ideological polarization between the parties in Congress that reflects the outcome of electoral realignment— not the decline of political parties per se, but the decline of the umbrella parties born in the nineteenth century. They have been replaced by new, more nationalized, more ideologically cohesive parties in an ideologically polarized party system.

Toward a "Responsible" Party System?

As E. E. Schattschneider (1942) put it, "democracy is unthinkable save in terms of parties." As long ago as 1950, the American Political Science Association's Committee on Political Parties advocated reform in the direction of a "responsible" party system in the United States, on the theory that elections serving democratic norms should present clear issue alternatives and more predictably link public opinion to public policy. In the decades since, the idea of such a responsible party system and party government in the United States has found support among political scientists (Manuel and Cammisa 1999; Paulson 2000, 2007; Sundquist 1988, 1992).

There were more critics than supporters, however. V. O. Key (1966) supported the democratic values advanced in the American Political Science Association's committee report, but argued that the US electorate was already "responsible," even without party reform. Evron Kirkpatrick (1971), in his classic critique, found the report to be a polemic, without empirical foundation.

But the most common argument against a responsible party system in the United States was that it was practically impossible. According to this line of argument, based on the realities of the old umbrella parties, there have been a number of almost insurmountable constraints operating against responsible parties. First, the United States has a separation-of-powers system, not the sort of fusion of powers found in Britain that promotes collective responsibility in a parliamentary system (Dahl 1967; Epstein 1967). Second, the United States has a two-party system, supported by state laws, single-member districts, and winner-take-all electoral systems (Duverger 1954). To win in a two-party system, parties must avoid ideological extremes to appeal to the center of the electorate (Downs 1957; Scammon and Wattenberg 1970).

Third, the US two-party system functions within a Lockean classic liberal culture (Hartz 1955; Tocqueville 2000). Both parties support individual liberty and limited government, private property and capitalism. Moreover, US political culture is known for its very limited degree of class consciousness (Aronowitz 1973; Bell 1960; Centers 1949; Hartz 1955; Lane 1962; Schlozman and Verba 1979; Tocqueville 2000; Turner 1947). Neither major party can assemble stable majorities by making narrow, doctrinaire appeals to a limited class base. This social consensus historically promotes retrospective voting (Fiorina 1981) tied closely to incumbent performance and economic growth. Thus, historically, our parties have performed the function of interest aggregation more than interest articulation, as their umbrellas covered diverse factions that spanned the US ideological spectrum.

Without distinct national ideological programs, the umbrella parties were patronage-oriented more than issue-oriented, and decentralized, focused on winning office at the local, state, and national levels. Issues were fundamentally a tool for building coalitions to win elections, assembling legislative majorities, and governing (Aldrich 1995).

These observations of constraints on the operation of responsible parties in the United States, however, were reasonably accurate reflections of the umbrella parties that came unraveled in the electoral realignments of the late twentieth century, but they no longer reflect the realities of the US party system. We still live with a constitutional separation of powers and a two-party system. The American people have not necessarily polarized as citizens and voters (Fiorina, Abrams, and Pope 2011). But our major political parties have, by the standards of the American experience, become more ideologically polarized and nationalized. As Gerald Pomper has argued, while the parties still market themselves to the center of the electorate, they are doing so from more distinct ideological positions (Pomper 1996), and "parliamentary government" is developing in the United States (Pomper 1999).

The Party System and the Constitutional System

The irony of US electoral politics in the early twenty-first century is that political parties appropriate to parliamentary government and a responsible party system have developed, but the constitutional form of a parliamentary party government has not (Mann and Ornstein 2012). The behavior of political elites in the following cases illustrates the disjunction.

Divided Government

Under the umbrella party system, vigorous national policy was often the result of unified government operating through partisan majorities across the elected branches of government, and it sometimes resulted from bipartisan coalition building in a divided government. On the other hand, even partisan majorities sometimes failed to overcome factionalism, and divided government sometimes resulted in "gridlock." In the polarized party system, partisan majorities seem necessary, although not sufficient, to policy change. President Barack Obama was successful in passing seriously watered-down health care reform legislation, but the effort was almost frustrated by filibuster in the Senate. It would appear that a partisan majority needs to control the presidency and both houses of Congress, with a filibuster-proof majority in the Senate, in order to build and pass a policy agenda.

What happens with divided government today is illustrated by executive-legislative relations after the midterm elections of 1994 and 2010, two cases where the Republicans won majorities in both houses of Congress with a Democratic president in the White House. After the 1994 election, the Republicans were operating as if they were a parliamentary majority, with a national party program based on the *Contract with America*. When President Bill Clinton and the Republicans could not agree on a budget in 1995, the administrative functions of government shut down for a period of time. This almost happened again after the 2010 election, and Democrats and Republicans became anchored in the debate and negotiation over the increase in the national debt limit, with the prospect of default looming. After the presidential election of 2012, we again faced the debate about the federal budget and the looming "fiscal cliff" in an environment of divided government.

Impeachment

In 1974, President Richard Nixon was facing the prospect of impeachment as the Watergate episode neared its conclusion. He was counting on Southern Democrats to join his fellow Republicans on the House Judiciary Committee and on the floor of the House to head it off. That is, as the Democrats controlled both houses of Congress, Nixon was counting on factionalism to overcome partisanship to save him, hoping for the support of Southern conservative Democrats (White 1975). As it happened, factionalism worked against him, as moderate-to-liberal Republicans on the committee joined all of the Democrats to send bills of impeachment to the House floor.

Twenty-five years later, President Bill Clinton could not count on factionalism to prevent impeachment. The Republicans had a majority in the House, and they acted like a parliamentary majority. The vote to impeach the president, in the House Judiciary Committee and on the House floor, was a virtual party-line vote, with Republicans voting for impeachment, Democrats against. What saved Clinton from removal from office was constitutional form. He was not a prime minister in a fusion-of-powers system, faced with a vote of no confidence by simple majority. He was the president of the United States in a separation-of-powers system, and conviction required a two-thirds vote of the Senate. Nevertheless, in the Clinton episode, the congressional parties acted like parliamentary parties.

Disputed Elections

In 1960, when Republican Richard Nixon lost the presidency to Democrat John Kennedy by only 49.7 percent to 49.6 percent of the popular vote, Nixon decided to forego recount efforts in Illinois and Texas, despite very close results and suspicions of vote fraud. From what we know of Nixon, his decision was not explained by timidity. Rather, the party system of his day was much more oriented to elite consensus than is today's party system. If Nixon wanted to run for president again, and we know he did, he could not afford to place his personal political interests ahead of the country's stability.

Forty years later, the Florida election controversy of 2000 could not be kept behind closed doors. Neither side fundamentally trusted the other, and it proved impossible even to agree on standards for counting ballots. A thirty-six-day standoff was resolved only when the US Supreme Court in

Bush v. Gore voted 5 to 4 to halt the recounts, effectively handing the presidency to George W. Bush (Ceaser and Busch 2001; Pomper 2001). The questioned legitimacy of his election hounded Bush politically throughout his presidency.

Evaluating the New Party System

American voters may not be as ideologically polarized as the electoral map makes them appear, but their votes are cast for ideologically polarized parties in a two-party system. This reality once again presents the normative question posed in the American Political Science Association's 1950 committee report: Is an ideologically polarized party system good for US democracy?

We can infer from public opinion polls that most Americans think not. Before his reelection, President Obama was having problems securing the support of a majority of Americans in job approval. According to public opinion polls, support for Congress has been well below a majority throughout the Obama presidency. By Obama's secnd term, it fell to less than a 20 percent approval rate for the way Congress did its job. Except for the period around the first-term inauguration of Obama, throughout his presidency a majority of Americans have considered the United States to be on the "wrong track." While these polls do not address the idea of a responsible party system directly, the answers can be tied to an apparent general feeling that elected officials are far too engaged in partisan bickering, and not enough in serious policymaking. The problem with parliamentary-style political parties in the US separation-of-powers system is that divided government is likely to result in policy gridlock.

But the US system of umbrella parties has not been consistently effective in policymaking, just as an ideologically polarized party system need not be consistently ineffective. The umbrella party system has certainly been periodically effective at making policy, particularly around the turning points of electoral realignment. The Jeffersonian Republicans expanded national authority beyond the level they initially supported in order to buy the Louisiana territory and promote the building of wilderness roads and canals to the interior, important developments in the economic modernization of the United States. The Jacksonian Democrats reversed the National Bank and annexed Texas. The Republicans and Democrats alike contributed to the policies of the "progressive era," which promoted the political development necessary to US industrialization. The Democrats in the 1930s passed the New Deal, and both parties cooperated in integrating new government functions into American life. Both parties contributed to the postwar Bretton Woods system, postwar macroeconomic policy, and the bipartisan foreign policy. And Reaganomics was a creative moment, passed with bipartisan support from Republicans and conservative Democrats.

But the umbrella party system also contributed to the biggest policy failure in American history. Neither the Democrats nor the Whigs could effectively handle the issue of slavery. While the Whigs passed from the scene, the Democrats were split between two national conventions in 1860, could not decide on a single presidential candidate, and ended up as divided as the country was with the Civil War approaching. The birth of the Republican Party and its nomination of Abraham Lincoln for president turned out to be essential steps in the salvation of the republic. But the Civil War is certainly not an example of the legitimate democratic or constitutional institutions working effectively—by definition, quite to the contrary.

The issue of race and civil rights in our own time also illustrates the limits of the umbrella party system. Southern conservative Democrats used seniority and the committee system in Congress for decades to block civil rights legislation. The Civil Rights Act of 1964 became law only because it had bipartisan support, and then only because President Lyndon Johnson and other Democratic leaders were willing to make an appeal that would put the national Democratic coalition in jeopardy (Paulson 2000).

While the maintenance of electoral and legislative coalitions is often a worthy goal for political elites, periodically those coalitions have become part of the problem. Periodically, we see the majority develop a serious collective-action dilemma in trying to set the policy agenda, while the opposition offers no viable alternative. The pre–Civil War party system failed to produce governance necessary for its time. The parties of the progressive era and the New Deal succeeded. The Democrats in the 1960s failed to keep the New Deal coalition together, and no stable partisan majority took its place. Today, once again, we seem to be encountering one of these moments in US political life, in which we find ourselves facing urgent issues and looking for a governing coalition capable of providing the leadership necessary to the resolution of those issues.

Polarized Parties and Polarizing Issues

When the issues on the public agenda lend themselves to a high level of consensus, the umbrella party system has worked well. But the issues of the past four decades have not been consensus issues, and the issues of the early twenty-first century appear likely to be just as polarizing. The ideologically polarized parties that have developed in recent years seem likely to remain in place for the foreseeable future. Thus, the question becomes not whether we prefer the umbrella party system or a responsible party system, but whether a polarized party system can work in the United States.

If Americans are dissatisfied with how our leadership and political institutions are operating, the problem at the moment would appear to be that liberals and conservatives alike are still fighting the battles of the 1960s, in what we now refer to as "culture wars."

The issues we face in the early twenty-first century are polarizing issues that are compelling in their own right (Paulson 1998, 2007). They all involve fundamental change in the structure of the economy and our relationship with the world. They are big issues we have yet to address meaningfully, and they are so interrelated that a macropolicy approach involving very basic questions of political philosophy and economic theory will be unavoidable. To simplify, I will organize these issues into three categories: first, war and peace, the threat of anti-American Islamist terrorism, and our broader changing relationship with the world; and second, fundamental structural change in the economy, both the national economy in the postindustrial age and the international economy. Neither of these two issues can be addressed separate from the other as a matter of analysis or effective policy. Taken together, these two issues present us with the third, which is fundamentally a political issue: Will we be able to manage change effectively with democratic political institutions?

War and Peace

The tragic events of September 11, 2001, certainly reset the public agenda in the United States, and landed us in what we have since called the "war on terror." As Americans have become exhausted with war in Afghanistan, Iraq, and more recently Libya, we have encountered the temptation to conduct the debate as if it were Vietnam all over again. But "war" is an incomplete title for this episode in our history, and this war will not be won by military means alone, or even primarily. Indeed, no one even has the authority to surrender on behalf of the terrorists. This involves a long-term global commitment, and it will involve nothing less than a fundamental reordering of our relationship with the world. What regimes will be allies? What social movements around the world will we support, and for what purposes? A war is successfully conducted only if it obtains worthy political objectives, and neither the George W. Bush administration, nor the Obama administration, nor their critics, have clearly stated what our objectives are, or ought to be. Even if we are engaged in a fight for our way of life, keeping our way of life as we know it will prove an inadequate policy goal. Global change is presenting political and economic realities we hardly understand, and a fundamental reordering of our relations with the world seems inevitable.

Postindustrial Modernization and the International Economy

Twice in the latter half of the twentieth century, the US economy was proclaimed an ultimate success, once on behalf of government intervention policies promoted by liberals, once on behalf of free-market policies promoted by conservatives. Keynesian economists confidently claimed victory over the business cycle, with the "full employment" balanced budget in the 1960s, and social analysts declared an "end of ideology," a final decline of class conflict born of affluence (Bell 1960). The "social bargain" (Cornwall 1994) of that time was one in which the government invested in national defense and social programs, the private sector made profits in a growing economy, and people benefited. But the bargain, together with the Bretton Woods system, was dismantled when President Nixon floated the dollar in 1971. Two decades later, after Reaganomics, victory over economic cycles was again being declared with an "end of history" (Fukuyama 1992), an ultimate triumph of capitalism, free markets, and new technologies.

But Nixon's 1971 decision fundamentally altered the structure of the international economy, ending an era of cheap access to foreign oil and opening an era of floating exchange rates. Budget deficits after the oil shocks of the 1970s, stagflation, and Reaganomics effectively reduced the policy flexibility of the federal government in domestic macroeconomics. Even when the business cycle turned up in the 1980s, and again in the 1990s, economic growth was only about half as high as it had been in the 1960s. Moreover, growth since the 1980s has been based much more on both private and public debt than were the previous waves of economic growth.

We live in a structurally low-growth economy. The recession makes us feel it more, but recovery, when it comes, will not change the reality of structural low growth. Economics, the political environment, and the policy agenda all indicate a period of austerity. Whether the issue is a structural deficit in the federal budget, or health care and health insurance reform, or the decline of manufacturing as an employer and the increase in structural unemployment, or energy policy, or climate change and the environment, the debate is increasingly politicized and ideological. These issues all deal with questions of fundamental disagreement about the role of government in society. However, both major parties remain classic Lockean liberal parties, defending different vested interests in American life, different corners of the status quo. Within that context, the parties represent ideologically distinct alternatives, with Democrats usually defending vested interests in the public sector, while Republicans usually defend vested interests in the private sector, each against change proposed by the other. On each issue, the constitutional separation of powers operates against the proponents of change.

* * *

But the actual choices are not really between the status quo and change. They are about facing alternative futures involving differing visions of rapid structural change. The status quo as we know it is really not one of the alternatives, and the policy choices of the early twenty-first century are likely to become more polarizing.

In his original classic on realignment, Walter Dean Burnham (1970) pointed out the difference between ideological polarization on cultural issues, such as civil rights or the Vietnam War, and the relative ease with which economic issues could then be finessed. He argued that these are fundamental issues that involve a worldview and cannot be treated the same as, for example, taxes, the budget, and so on. But Burnham wrote this before the "social bargain" was dismantled, at a time when robust economic growth was still considered the rule. In today's low-growth economy, we have developed a zero-sum politics, in which any new public investment in any interest is connected to disinvestment from some other interest. Economic issues today have become "either-or" issues.

This reality threatens the "American dream" and makes US political institutions at least appear to be dysfunctional. What Alexis de Tocqueville called the "equality of conditions," a belief in equal opportunity and upward social mobility tied to a reality of economic growth in American life, has always had much to do with the very limited presence of class consciousness in American political culture. Democracy and capitalism have coexisted in advanced liberal societies precisely because the pie has been growing, most of the time. So long as economic growth is the default situation, pluralist democracy works, because bargaining can be based on how the increments of growth are divided; no one has to live with less. But advanced democratic capitalist societies are in an age of austerity, and Americans no longer live in a setting where the odds are necessarily good that each generation will be better off than the previous one. With a relatively static economic pie, anybody's gain is somebody's loss, presenting the zero-sum political challenge.

Ideological polarization in American political life reflects the issues we face as much as it does the party system that has developed since the 1960s. Whether we prefer umbrella parties or not, they will not be reincarnated anytime soon. The polarized party system is here to stay for the foreseeable future. The essential question is whether democratic institutions can facilitate debate about the very difficult policy agenda of the next few decades. Can our ideologically polarized party system become, in both the empirical and normative sense of the word, a "responsible" party system?

5

Big Money, Mass Media, and the Polarization of Congress

Thomas Ferguson

*Should any political party attempt to abolish Social Security, unemploy-
ment insurance, and eliminate labor laws and farm programs, you would
not hear of that party again in our political history. There is a tiny splinter
group, of course, that believes you can do these things. Among them are
H. L. Hunt (you possibly know his background), a few other Texas oil mil-
lionaires, and an occasional politician or business man from other areas.
Their number is negligible and they are stupid.*
　　　　　　　　　　　　　—President Dwight Eisenhower, 1954[1]

*There are two things that are important in politics. The first is money and I
can't remember what the other one is.*
　　　　　　　　　　　　　—Mark Hanna, 1895[2]

This is a small chapter on a big subject: the polarization of US politics since
the mid-1970s. In its early stages this process of polarization bore more than
a passing resemblance to the opening scenes of a Grade B disaster movie:
with almost everyone's attention focused elsewhere, a series of tiny, seemingly insignificant departures from long-standing routines took place. Just
about all of these stayed well beneath the radar. Then, in the mid-1980s,
came the shock of recognition: everyone suddenly woke up and realized that
the US political system had altered dramatically.

Polarizing Parties: The Problem Defined
Some episode in the Nixon administration usually prefigures just about
everything that happens later in US politics. So it is with polarization. Today
we know that the burglar-in-chief and his principal advisers loathed Demo-

crats, foreign policy "weakness," and anyone who strayed too far from a *Reader's Digest* view of American culture as much as any of their less reserved successors on the Republican right. But at the time, the bitter passions that animated Watergate's fatal illegality were only occasionally glimpsed for what they were. Most records were restricted and only snippets of the tapes were available. Thus the break-in, the cover-up, the "enemies list," and the rest could be easily written off as isolated pathologies by those who were determined to do so.[3]

The Ford administration's brief, fitful half-life and the economic crises of the 1970s further distracted anyone from focusing on what was happening at deeper levels of the political system. The distaste for Democrats and what might euphemistically be termed the unwavering commitment to "peace through strength" that consumed the former Nixon aides in the White House, such as Dick Cheney and Donald Rumsfeld, showed through only occasionally before they departed the scene—for a while (Mann 2004).

By contrast, the stormy early days of the "Reagan Revolution" created a bigger public stir. But the folksy image of a "Great Communicator" chatting one-on-one with Democratic House Speaker Tip O'Neill, together with all the propaganda about Reagan being the most popular president of all time, though totally untrue, once again distracted many. Although the Republicans were well into their giant naval buildup, had put through the "supply side" tax cuts, and were intent on "starving the beast," studies of press content show that party polarization remained a distinctly subordinate theme almost into Reagan's second term (Levendusky 2009).

The first signs of the coming storm that attracted wide notice came in the mid-1980s. A group of insurgent Republicans, tired of being perpetually in the minority and emboldened by the Reagan Revolution in presidential politics, broke with the long-established norms governing how the US House of Representatives transacted business. Led by Newt Gingrich, they derided older Republican House leaders as timid, unimaginative, and too inclined to compromise with Democrats.[4] The self-styled "revolutionaries" launched vigorous public attacks on Democrats as they trumpeted their own agenda of deregulation, budget cuts, lower taxes, and a baker's dozen of social issues, from abortion to opposition to all forms of gun control. Their noise and energy reverberated in the mass media, triggering a cascade of institutional and cultural changes that sent the political system veering off in a startling new direction.

House debates swiftly turned increasingly bitter and highly personal. Gingrich and his colleagues began a frontal attack on Democratic Speaker Jim Wright of Texas for alleged corruption. Eventually, after a formal inquiry, Wright was forced to resign. Bringing down the Speaker created a sensation. It elevated Gingrich to the status of a demigod on the right and catapulted him into a leadership position among House Republicans.

As he and his group redoubled their energies, the House boiled over. Party-line voting jumped sharply (see Figure 5.1).[5] Gingrich and his allies emphasized fundraising, not just through the usual publicly reported vehicles (election committees of individual senators and representatives; the new "leadership" political action committees [PACs] that many of these individuals were opening; the National Republican Congressional Committee and, more equivocally, the Republican National Committee), but also GOPAC, a political action committee that Gingrich had controlled since 1986, but that operated mostly in secret (Sabato and Simpson 1996).[6] In public, Gingrich and other Republican leaders talked incessantly about "small business." But as Table 5.1 shows, large firms in many industries where regulation was a front-burner political issue, including oil and gas, tobacco, trucking, pharmaceuticals, accounting, and insurance, were overrepresented in Gingrich's own fundraising.

In 1990, congressional polarization drew worldwide attention. Backed by major GOP financiers, Gingrich and other GOP conservatives revolted when George H. W. Bush reneged on his "read my lips: no new taxes" prom-

Figure 5.1 Party Unity Votes in the House, 1953–2008

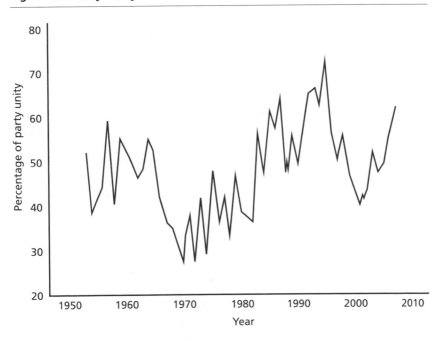

Source: Ornstein, Mann, and Malbin 2008.

Table 5.1   Industries Within Big Business Above-Average in Fundraising Support for Newt Gingrich, 1995–1996

	Percentage of Firms	Significance Level	
Glass	60	(.07)*	$N = 5$
Accounting	50	(.11)*	$N = 6$
Tobacco	50	(.20)*	$N = 4$
Pharmaceuticals	47	(.02)*	$N = 17$
Trucking and			
ground transport	41	(.07)*	$N = 17$
Insurance	37	(.01)	$N = 43$
Oil and gas	28	(.21)	$N = 53$
Aircraft	36	(.19)*	$N = 14$
Chemicals	32	(.17)	$N = 28$

Source: Ferguson 2001, based on Federal Election Commission data as described there.

Notes: The comparison is to large firms and major investors as a whole, not firms of any size. Period covered is "early money" for 1995–1996. (Mean = 21 percent, $N = 875$)

* Significance levels are the result of the Fisher's exact test; expected value in a chi-squared test is less than 5 (warning of low power).

ise and signed a bill that raised revenues to close a budget deficit. Throughout the rest of Bush's term, Gingrich and his supporters waged a running battle with the White House over whether to press for further cuts in the capital gains tax (Ferguson 1995b).

In 1992, in the midst of a recession, the Republicans lost the White House. But their dreams of a sweeping political realignment did not die. In fact, by clearing centrist Republicans out of their perches in the White House, the loss probably helped Gingrich and his allies. Completely undaunted, Gingrich, Republican National Committee chair Haley Barbour, and National Republican Senatorial Committee chair Phil Gramm orchestrated a vast national campaign to recapture Congress for the Republicans in the 1994 elections. With the economy stuck in a "jobless recovery" and Democratic fundraising sputtering after the White House passed a modest tax increase on the highest brackets and cratered in its attempt to pass sweeping national health care legislation, the Republicans won control of both houses of Congress. The House result was a true shocker: it marked the first time Republicans controlled that body since 1954 (Stiglitz 2004; Ferguson 1995b, 2001).

The improbable victory stamped Gingrich as the man of the hour, and he triumphantly ascended to the Speakership. Almost like Shakespeare's Julius Caesar, for a brief period he bestrode the political world like a colossus, often conducting himself as though he considered himself to be co-president.

The New Polarized Congress Emerges

Before a series of political reverses and another corruption investigation forced him from the scene, Gingrich and his leadership team, which included Dick Armey and Tom ("the Hammer") DeLay, institutionalized rule changes in the House and the Republican caucus that vastly increased the leadership's influence over House legislation. They also implemented a formal "pay to play" system that had both inside and outside components. On the outside, DeLay and other GOP leaders, including Grover Norquist, who headed Americans for Tax Reform, mounted a vast campaign (the so-called K Street Project) to defund the Democrats directly by pressuring businesses to cut off donations and avoid retaining Democrats as lobbyists. Inside the House, Gingrich made fundraising for the party a requirement for choice committee assignments (see Currinder 2009; Heberlig, Hetherington, and Larson 2006). The implications of auctioning off key positions within Congress mostly escaped attention, as did the subsequent evolution of the system into one of what amounted to posted prices (Currinder 2009).[7]

The GOP's external effort to defund the Democrats drew wide criticism. Eventually it crashed. Senator John McCain and other GOP leaders supported an investigation into the business dealings and campaign finance activities of several aides of DeLay, who had become majority leader after Gingrich and Armey departed. The aides were eventually convicted. DeLay himself was forced to resign from the House after being indicted in another money-laundering case (see, among many sources, Continetti 2006).

By contrast, the changes in House procedures and rules that the Republicans instituted proved durable. Democrats rapidly emulated the formal "pay to play" system for House committee assignments, leading to a sharp rise in campaign contributions from members of Congress of both parties to their colleagues and the national fundraising committees. Soon leaders of the Democrats, too, were posting prices for plum committee assignments and chairmanships. They also centralized power in the leadership, which had wide discretion in how it treated bills and more leverage over individual members:

> Under the new rules for the 2008 election cycle, the DCCC [Democratic Congressional Campaign Committee] asked rank and file members to contribute $125,000 in dues and to raise an additional $75,000 for the party. Subcommittee chairpersons must contribute $150,000 in dues and raise an additional $100,000. Members who sit on the most powerful committees . . . must contribute $200,000 and raise an additional $250,000. Subcommittee chairs on power committees and committee chairs of non-power committees must contribute $250,000 and raise $250,000. The five chairs of the power committees must contribute $500,000 and raise an additional $1 million. House Majority Leader Steny Hoyer, Majority Whip James Clyburn, and Democratic Caucus Chair Rahm Emmanuel must contribute $800,000 and raise $2.5 million. The four Democrats who serve as part of

the extended leadership must contribute $450,000 and raise $500,000, and the nine Chief Deputy Whips must contribute $300,000 and raise $500,000. House Speaker Nancy Pelosi must contribute a staggering $800,000 and raise an additional $25 million. (Currinder 2009: 38)[8]

From 1991 to 1995, Texas senator Phil Gramm headed the National Republican Senatorial Campaign Committee. The 1994 Republican triumph made him chair of the Senate Banking Committee, where gale-force political winds in favor of financial deregulation were already blowing. Under Gramm and like-minded Senate Republicans, partisanship in the upper chamber grew at close to the same rate as in the House, if less flamboyantly (see Figure 5.2). A radically different tone began to envelop a body long celebrated for comity: constant threats of filibusters by defiant minorities meant that working control came to require not fifty-one votes, but a sixty-vote "super-majority," while confirmations of presidential nominees slowed to a snail's pace when different parties controlled the White House and the Senate ("divided government"). The spirit was catching—not only new members, but older senators

Figure 5.2 Party Unity Votes in the Senate, 1953–2008

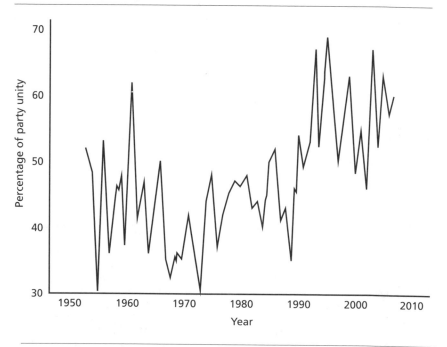

Source: Ornstein, Mann, and Malbin 2008.

and members of the House with previously moderate records, joined the headlong rush to extremes (see Theriault 2006, 2008). In both the Senate and the House, leaders increasingly resorted to complex parliamentary procedures to make life difficult for the other party and sometimes for minority factions within their own (see, for example, Theriault 2008).

Though existing data are fragmentary, the mass media appear to have polarized right along with Congress. Pushed by private broadcasters, the Reagan administration extensively deregulated broadcasting (Mazzocco 1994). (The broadcasters included William J. Casey, a former top official of Capital Cities Communications, which eventually purchased ABC, who continued to hold his stock in the concern outside a blind trust while serving as head of the Central Intelligence Agency.) The president also eliminated the so-called Fairness Doctrine by executive order. Fairly soon, a dense network of ties emerged between conservative Republicans and parts of the media (Brock 2004). In particular, talk radio became a conservative bastion (Barker 2002).

Over time, television networks, led by Rupert Murdoch's Fox News (headed by Roger Ailes, a former Nixon campaign consultant), increasingly abandoned even the appearance of objective reporting, in favor of evident partiality toward one or the other major party, but especially toward conservatives and the center-right members of both parties.[9] Subsequent statistical studies of media content reveal an important link between media deregulation and the evolution of polarization in Congress: the proportions of "buzzwords" used in news stories—that is, the "slant" of the news—closely tracks the mix used in congressional debates and speeches; for reasons explained later, it is likely that this "echo effect" was already operating in the mid-1980s (Gentzkow and Shapiro 2010).

The feedback loop running from Congress to the mass media and back again amplified the process of polarization, though the exact degree is difficult to determine. How the system worked in outline is clear enough: congressional leaders of both parties now focused intently on creating sharper party profiles ("brands") that would mobilize potential outside supporters and contributors. So they spent enormous amounts of time and money honing messages that were clear and simple enough to attract attention as they ricocheted out through the media to the public.

As means to this end, leaders staged more and more votes not to move legislation, but to score points with some segment of the public or signal important outside constituencies. For the same reason, they sometimes made exemplary efforts to hold up bills by prolonging debate or, in the Senate, putting presidential nominations on hold. Meanwhile, they set formal or informal quotas for senators and representatives—here even conservative Republicans stoutly defended equal rights—for member contributions to the national congressional committees. The national fundraising committees, in turn, poured resources into elections to secure and hold majority control.[10] Contests for relatively rare "open seats" that had no incumbent running, or races in which incumbents looked unsafe, received particularly heavy attention, since those were most likely to sway the balance of forces inside each chamber.

Allusions to congressional "Leviathans" had been flying around for some years; here, at last, the real thing was taking shape: centralized parties, presided over by leaders with far more power than in recent decades, running the equivalent of hog calls for resources, trying to secure the widest possible audiences for their slogans, and projecting their claims through a mass media that was more than happy to play along with right-thinking spokespersons of both parties.[11] The members, in turn, scrambled to raise enough money to meet the quotas the leaders set as the price of securing influence in the House or the Senate.

A Familiar Story: See No Evil

Not surprisingly, some observers worried about the long-term effects of these practices on public life. In particular, a few drew attention to a tidal wave of political money flooding into both major parties (Ferguson 1995b).

But such misgivings gained little traction during the decade-long Rose Bowl parade of weird and weirder that followed Gingrich's resignation as Speaker—the circus over impeachment and Monica Lewinsky; the GOP strong-arm tactics and sudden, sharply partisan Supreme Court decision not to respect state courts after the 2000 election; the Swift Boats and "girlie men" rhetoric of 2004; the Schiavo case; the rush to war with Iraq; and the rest. Political commentators mostly affected not to take the high jinks at face value. More than few made light of them, asking what else was new. Reaching back to another age, they invoked H. L. Mencken's famous characterization of US politics as a "carnival of buncombe."

Much work by social scientists reinforced these dismissals. Most studies of campaign finance by political scientists come out of a formal-legal tradition. There is no question that the work is valuable—this chapter draws upon it, for example—but inquiry tends to rest with the production of tables detailing total campaign spending across the maze of legally allowable categories. Or researchers simply track total spending (often just total spending by political action committees). Neither gambit sheds much light on what should be the decisive research question, which is what the patterns of political contributions reveal about bloc and coalition formation among major investors as they sort through candidates and policy alternatives. The handful of scholars on Congress who recognize that money influences leadership selection do not pursue their sometimes very interesting research results to their logical conclusion.

Some economists and political scientists who embraced the fashion for applying neoclassical economics to politics provided uniquely disarming reassurance. In a move strikingly reminiscent of the appeals to free-market "reputational" economics that Alan Greenspan and others regularly deployed against critics who worried that financial markets were running amok, these scholars tried to stand reality on its head by highlighting a few highly stylized facts interpreted through the lens of a starkly simple version of neoclassical economic theory.[12]

They argued that most people who were donating those millions of dollars to politicians did not do this because they wanted or expected something in return. They were doing it because in some way it made them feel good—perhaps because they thought it was the right thing to do, or for the thrill of it all, or simply because it was fashionable—at any rate for some expressive, not instrumental reason. "Campaign contributions," they asserted, "should be viewed primarily as a type of consumption good, rather than as a market for buying political benefits" (Ansolabehere, de Figueiredo, and Snyder 2003: 105).[13]

Somewhat inconsistently (since, after all, rates of return should be irrelevant to contributors animated by expressive values), these scholars also suggested that the real mystery of US campaign finance was why there was "so little money" in US politics, since by their calculations, rates of return were impossibly high—a few million dollars, they argued for example, sufficed to deliver billions in defense or transportation spending (Ansolabehere, de Figueiredo, and Snyder 2003). As recorded campaign spending soared into the billions and deregulation of financial and other markets became manic, other analysts delivered still more good news. With straight faces, they reported a decline of "material motivation" among politically active citizens.[14]

No Longer So Funny

As long as the economy boomed and deregulation and market fundamentalism remained the conventional wisdom of policymakers, minds in the Open Society mostly stayed closed, and reassuring story lines about polarization ruled the roost. The year 2008, however, brought a stunning end to the party. World financial markets melted down and the bottom fell out of the world economy. Henceforth the polarization of the US political system has increasingly come in for anguished reappraisal.

The first occasion for reconsideration came fast—during the fatal days of September 2008. After allowing Lehman Brothers to go bankrupt, Federal Reserve chair Ben Bernanke, New York Fed president Timothy Geithner, and Treasury secretary Hank Paulson made their famous decision to rescue the American International Group (AIG) (and through AIG, many large private banks). But with world markets freezing up (Ferguson and Johnson 2010a) and giant runs threatening even the mightiest US financial institutions, Paulson and Bernanke approached Congress for a bailout. The stunning rejection by the House of their proposal for what became the Troubled Asset Relief Program (TARP), followed by that body's breathtaking reversal days later amid a saturnalia of pork and campaign subventions, was widely viewed by world markets as the political equivalent of the Arizona Meteor Crater (Ferguson and Johnson 2009b). It pried open many previously closed minds in a hurry, despite a wide diversity of views about the merits of the bailout itself.

The political system's response to a host of challenges since has only deepened concerns. Whatever responsibility one assigns to the administration's timid initial proposals, the congressional compromises that resulted in the Dodd-Frank financial "reform" legislation plainly failed to fix the problems that caused the financial crash. "Too Big to Fail" has been institutionalized. Bank concentration is rapidly increasing. Many derivatives are clearly going to escape regulation. Consumer banking has not been fixed. Mortgage markets now depend entirely on the state, while both the administration and Republicans in Congress are seizing on the budget crisis as an excuse to defund the regulators who are supposed to implement the new rules (see especially Johnson and Kwak 2010; see also Admati and Hellwig 2013).

As one energy-related environmental disaster after another hits and the world price of oil bounces up and down, Congress has done little besides talk about climate change or energy policy. Both friends and foes of the health care legislation that finally passed in 2010 express disgust at the process that produced it. Many acknowledge that the failure to permit the government to bargain with pharmaceutical firms will cost the public trillions of dollars in the next few years (Stiglitz 2010b), while event analysis of Senate committee voting confirms widespread suspicions that major features of the final health care bill mainly aided the bottom lines of insurers, not the populace as a whole (see in particular Dube 2009).

For many, though, the last straw is the way Congress has dealt with economic policy since the financial crisis. Since 2008, US elections have parodied so-called retrospective-voting theories of voter choice. In a pattern reminiscent of many countries at the start of the Great Depression, the US electorate appears to be applying a simple rule: in, out; out, in. But with unemployment remaining high and millions of discouraged workers dropping out of the labor force, the number of citizens expressing pessimism about "our system of government and how well it works" has risen to record levels (see ABC News and *Washington Post* 2011).

Yet nothing seems to deflect the parties from their now customary posture, especially the Republicans. The sudden, shocking bipartisan agreement after the November 2010 congressional elections to extend the George W. Bush tax cuts for two more years showed up all the talk about the urgency of cutting budget deficits as so much cant. In the meantime, many plans to cut the budget are being excitedly talked up in the press, but all of those garnering plaudits mostly decline to challenge politically entrenched interests in health care, defense, or the financial sector in favor of simply cutting benefits for ordinary Americans (Ferguson and Johnson 2010c). Most recently, the spectacle of a superpower brought again and again to the brink of shutting down its government has unsettled many.

The contrast with China and other countries that are managing recovery from the Great Recession far better is glaring and is rapidly emerging as a concern in its own right. In the 1990s, Thomas Friedman and other American analysts talked excitedly about how television and the Internet stimulated citizens of many third world countries to invidiously compare their circumstances to life in the United States (Friedman 2000). Now Friedman wistfully compares the gleaming new skyscrapers and long-distance rail systems of China and other Asian countries with the dilapidated, ramshackle infrastructure of the United States, where even crossing bridges can be hazardous. As China forges ahead with its vast programs of state-led economic reconstruction while the United States stagnates, the specter of the United States becoming, in Richard Nixon's memorable phrase, a "pitiful, helpless giant," is concentrating minds even on the right.[15] Bismarck famously compared the process of legislation to making sausage. Many Americans are now alive to the fact that in Washington, D.C., the process of sausage making has virtually ground to a halt. They want to know why this happened and what can be done about it.

Alternative Explanations

Alas, neither the mass media nor existing scholarship has much to offer. The most popular theory about the origins of polarization is the "cultural wars" approach. In this view, American society has fractured into warring segments over a set of "hot button" issues. America's highly polarized politics, runs the argument, just reflects the deep differences that now divide Americans—differences that some television commentators profess to believe run deeper than at any time since the Civil War (see Fiorina and Abrams 2009).

But while the theme is a staple of popular political discussions, there is virtually no truth to it. Quite like claims in the 1980s that American public opinion had shifted markedly to the right and that Ronald Reagan's magic powers as a "Great Communicator" had established his position as the most popular US president of all time (Ferguson and Rogers 1986; Page and Shapiro 1992), it is easily refuted by simply aligning data on public opinion over time. As Morris Fiorina (Fiorina and Abrams 2009) shows, whether we rely on Gallup, General Social Survey, or National Election Survey data, sharp ideological shifts in American opinion are not to be found. Between 1972 and 2004, for example, even the much-touted shift in the percentage of the population styling themselves "liberal," "conservative," and "moderate" bounced very little. Between the 1970s and the 2000s, the "liberal" label declined slightly in popularity, but only by about 5 percentage points. All through the period, the largest category of people who expressed a preference self-identified as "moderates," while the percentage of people thinking of themselves as extreme conservatives actually fell. As Morris Fiorina and Samuel Abrams commen, "The percentage of exact middle-of-the-scale placements was 27 percent in 1972 and 26 percent in 2004" (2008: 570).[16]

Time graphs of levels of these and related measurements typically look like near-straight lines (Fiorina and Abrams 2009). To the extent that any ideological change at all shows, it is as often as not slightly leftward. On some issues, such as same-sex marriage, public opinion has moved sharply in that direction.

Given the mass of contrary data, analysts intent on finding electoral explanations for polarization appeal to a variety of epicycles. Most of these involve some version of political "sorting." The idea is that even if there is no basic change in the trend of opinion, perhaps the population is somehow shoehorning itself into more homogeneous political units that then battle out their differences. The most obvious suggestion, again much touted in the media, involves the gerrymandering of legislative districts. This is a testable hypothesis, and many have tested it. The upshot is that while some stunning examples of gerrymandering for partisan advantage certainly exist, such as the lurid Texas case that led to DeLay's conviction, many countercases can also be found. In general, redistricting cannot possibly account for the observed degree of polarization (Theriault 2008). This actually should have been obvious all along: US Senate districts have not changed at all, but the Senate exhibits about as much polarization as does the House over the same period.

Many other "sort" theories have been advanced. Everyone knows that Republican strength in the South has surged. But a substantial part of the population was more conservative there to begin with; they didn't change much. It also turns out that some of the sharpest increases in polarization occurred in the North and East (Fiorina and Abrams 2009). Most studies of geographic polarization thus end up concluding that geography has been at best a marginal factor (see the review in Fiorina and Abrams 2009).

Complicating the story by adding references to migration—of African Americans from South to North and whites to the South—does not help much. The changes in each party's regional strongholds undoubtedly strengthen dominant viewpoints in each party by increasing the ranks of relative liberals in, for example, the Northeast, and conservatives in the South and West. Thus differences between the parties should grow more distinct. But Fiorina's points about the lack of change in Southern opinion on policy and polarization above the Mason-Dixon line remain stumbling blocks.

Pointing to all the intensely partisan Republicans who come from the Sunbelt is not an answer, but just reframes the question.[17]

The one form of "sort" theory with traction undermines the logic of explaining political change over time through it. Morris Fiorina (Fiorina and Abrams 2009) and Matthew Levendusky (2009) are persuasive in their argument that individuals who hold specific "hot button" attitudes that political parties choose to highlight, on such issues as abortion, gay rights, or stem cell research, tend to migrate toward the party championing those issues. But this research also shows that the phenomenon is distinctly modest—usually resulting in a migration of only a few percentage points. Huge numbers of people holding hot button attitudes continue to affiliate with the "wrong" political party. Most also do not change their broader ideological label when they drift, so that the overall ability of labels like "liberal" or "moderate" or "conservative" to predict positions even in sensitive issue areas is still usually limited. The conclusion has to be that "sorting" was a minor part of all the sound and the fury that came with polarization; it cannot be the Archimedean lever that moved the American political world.

Persuaded by the lack of empirical evidence for mass polarization, many, perhaps most, political scientists now point to party "elites." These are said to entertain sharply different opinions from the rest of Americans on a variety of issues, including their customary answers to survey questions about what America's number one problem is. The result is a theory that looks persuasive at first glance. Unrepresentative party "elites" now control both parties; these party elites do not attempt to maximize votes. Instead they make appeals to their bases by cobbling together different sets of "special interest" voters. Refinements of the approach sometimes add claims about the organizational isolation of increasing numbers of Americans, who are described as "bowling alone" (for a general sketch of various views, see Fiorina and Abrams 2009).

Acknowledging the "base" strategy in contemporary elections has to be a major step forward for empirical social science. It is high time political science and history abandon simple median-voter accounts in which parties try to maximize votes. But this step should be complemented by a frank avowal that throughout much of US history, including the last three decades of increasing polarization, both major parties have often declined to chase new voters and often made strenuous efforts to hold down voter turnout (Burnham 1970, 1984, 2010a, 2010b; Overton 2006; Ferguson and Chen 2005).

In most discussions, however, the identity of these "elites" is strangely elusive.[18] Almost no names are ever used, save for those of pop celebrities or a handful of high-profile political spokespersons. Many analysts point to data concerning "convention delegates." Others invoke "activists" and, occasionally, "contributors." The latter are nowhere investigated empirically. Instead, most analysts gesture toward groups prominently discussed in the mass media. More than a few such lists, including some of Fiorina's, read like faint caricatures from Karl Rove or the *Wall Street Journal*: "Although both parties continue to have support in broad social groupings like blue-collar workers and white-collar professionals, their bases now consist of much more specifically defined groups. Democrats rely on public sector unions, environmentalists, and pro-choice and other liberal cause groups. Republicans rely on evangelicals, small business organizations, and pro-life and other conservative cause groups" (Fiorina and Abrams 2009: 157).[19]

Polarization and Parties: An Empirical Account

It has long been clear to a few close observers that accounts along these lines leave out something important. But the financial crisis reveals their hollowness for everyone to see. Current theorizing about party "elites" in political science and journalism is really a twenty-first-century reincarnation of the old "political amateurs" thesis that Edward Banfield, James Q. Wilson, and the first generation of neoconservatives used to hammer McGovern Democrats. It has been updated and stretched to cover the Republicans, but it does not begin to do justice to the facts of how political parties actually function.

Its basic defect is easily stated: anonymous convention attendees or nameless group leaders did not organize the mighty effort by the GOP to capture control of Congress that eventually triumphed in 1994. That was put together by particular political leaders at a definite, historically specific point in time. The three politicians who led it—Newt Gingrich, Phil Gramm, and Haley Barbour—were not bowling alone.

Clearly forces of the religious right played a role in their calculations. But almost two decades later, no one should still be fooled. Evangelicals and conservative Catholics did not determine Republican grand strategy. It was mostly as elections approached that the GOP leaders pushed social issues to the fore. Christian Coalition leader Ralph Reed's stunning e-mail unearthed during the congressional investigation into DeLay's aides memorably records that the most prominent of the religious leaders working closely with Gingrich, DeLay, and company were not planning to lay up their treasure in heaven.[20] If only because all the major political preachers—Jerry Falwell, James Robison, Pat Robertson, and the rest—had close relations with conservative Republican donors themselves, pressure from the Amen Corner was never going to be intense enough to break the Republican leaders' concentration on their real priorities.[21] Candidates who took the religious right's claims at face value or swallowed the GOP's own propaganda on this point, such as Pat Buchanan in 1992 or Mike Huckabee in 2008, could stir up the flock, but then always got sheared.

Once again, against the backdrop of the world-shattering events of September 2008, the values that Gingrich, Gramm, Barbour, and company held sacred stand out in bold relief. It is probably unfair to characterize Phil Gramm in the 1990s simply as the strongest champion of financial market deregulation in the United States. There might be some question whether that accolade belongs to his wife, Wendy Gramm, who helped block derivatives regulation as chair of the Commodity Futures Trading Commission before heading off to the board of directors of Enron. But Gingrich and Barbour appear to have been every bit as committed to that cause as was Gramm, not to mention the phalanx of Wall Street financiers who poured millions of dollars into the fundraising vehicles of all three for years (Ferguson and Johnson 2009a; Ferguson 2001).

But financial deregulation scarcely amounted to half of what the three who made the 1994 revolution were aiming at, though in no small part thanks to their success, profits in the financial sector reached 47 percent of all domestic corporate profits just before the crash (Kirshner 2011). Gingrich, Gramm, Barbour, and their allies were free-market fundamentalists. They were intent on targeting the entire legacy of the New Deal, not just financial deregulation. They wanted to deregulate not one market, but virtually every market, and cut back government's role across the board. They favored eliminating or cutting back the Environmental Protection Agency, spoke up for the tobacco industry (Barbour was a lobbyist for it), and tried to hamstring the Environmental Protection Agency, the Federal Communications Commission, the Federal Trade Commission, the Consumer Product Safety Commission, and the Federal Drug Administration. They all championed "American" energy (i.e., oil, nuclear power, and coal), and pushed unceasingly for still more tax cuts weighted toward the super-rich, sweeping cutbacks in social spending, Social Security privatization, and, of course, higher spending in the one area of big government they approved of, defense spending (Gingrich organized a special defense caucus early in his career and was famously close to Lockheed).[22] Generally, climate change was something they were trying to accomplish in the United States, not arrest.

Speculations about whether their personal commitments to these views ran much deeper than Gingrich's to evangelical family values is unlikely to be fruitful in the present state of our knowledge. Certainly, on many occasions, Gramm and Gingrich talked like true believers in the religion of the free market.

What matters for this chapter is what mattered in reality: that the leaders of the Republican surge lucidly understood that, in sharp contrast to the world of classical democratic theory, where the cost of political action barely registers, real-life politics is now very expensive. Despite occasional appearances to the contrary, political money is not available in perfectly elastic supply just for the asking. Money, in other words, does not grow on trees. Whatever else they are—"networks" of campaign consultants and specialists, party leaders, allied interest groups—political parties are first of all bank accounts that have to be filled (Ferguson 1995b).

Gingrich and his allies were painfully aware that transforming the GOP's gains at the presidential level into a true "critical realignment" of the political system as a whole required breaking the Democratic lock on Congress. So they shattered all records for congressional fundraising in their drive to get control of the House. Their success in this is what polarized the system. The tidal wave of political money they conjured allowed Gingrich, Gramm, Barbour, and their allies to brush aside the older, less combative center-right Republican leadership and then persist in their efforts to roll back the New Deal and remake American society in the image of free-market fundamentalism.

In power, the Republicans restructured their national political committees and the Congress into giant ATMs capable of financing broad national campaigns to protect and extend their newly won position in Congress. The Republican success left the Democrats facing the same dilemma they had in the late 1970s, as the Golden Horde first formed up behind Ronald Reagan: they could respond by mobilizing their older mass constituencies or emulate the Republicans. That battle had been settled in favor of so-called New Democrats (Ferguson and Rogers 1986). Dependent for many years on campaign money from leading sectors of big business where regulation kept recreating divisions—notably finance and telecommunications (Ferguson 1995b)—the Democrats reconfirmed their earlier decision to go for the gold. They followed the Republicans and transformed both the national party committees and their congressional delegations into cash machines, with the leaders in each chamber, but especially the House, wielding substantially more power than at any time since the famous revolt that overthrew Speaker Joseph Cannon in 1910–1911. As the Republicans moved further and further to the right, the Democrats did too, constrained only by the need to preserve something of their mass base.[23]

The Spectrum of Political Money

The mighty wave of political money that carried Gingrich, Gramm, and company to the heights of power is plain in the broad statistics on campaign finance collected by the Federal Election Commission and the Treasury (where so-called 527s and some other special vehicles report). But assessing it properly requires waving a series of yellow flags first.

Political money is complex; it strikingly resembles the electromagnetic spectrum. Vast stretches of it are normally invisible to humans, including newspaper reporters and scholars, because campaign spending as tabulated and released to the public by government agencies in many countries amounts to but a fraction of it. Thus, although the size of some parts of the political money spectrum can be approximated (see box), it makes little sense to try to estimate the size of other parts. For example, George Stigler (1975) was surely right in arguing that the reason so many lawyers flock to politics is not extraordinary zeal for the public welfare, but because they so easily receive legitimate business thrown their way as a legal form of payoff. But while Internal Revenue Service investigations confirm his point, they have been too few and far between for anyone to say with confidence what percentage of all legal receipts really represents payments for political ser-vices. The heavy representation of lobbyists—who are often lawyers—and attorneys on most lists of campaign contributions is clear, however, and is surely no accident.

The Spectrum of Political Money

1. *Payments to political figures.* Comprise many hundreds of millions of dollars, including certain director fees and speaking fees, and some "research" and philanthropic "advice" from consultants.
2. *Lobbying.* The legal definition of lobbying is very narrow. For 2010 for Washington, D.C., on-the-record lobbying money totaled approximately $3.5 billion (Center for Responsive Politics, http://www.opensecrets.org). Lobbying at the state and city level is also large.
3. *Think tanks.* These institutions have experienced rapid growth especially since the 1970s, both within and outside Washington, D.C. In 2005, major D.C.-based think tanks spent approximately $411 million (Weidenbaum 2009).
4. *Foundations and charitable grants.* Most foundations and charitable grants are not political (perhaps just 3–5 percent are). Of those that are, some go through think tanks. In 2006, total giving amounted to $296 billion.
5. *Payments to lawyers for services.* Substantial, but unknown.
6. *Value of stock tips and initial public offerings to political figures.* "Event analysis" studies suggest that this value is very large in certain periods.
7. *Formal campaign spending.* In 2008, total expenditures on federal campaigns alone amounted to $5.2 billion. Formal campaign spending at the state and local levels is also heavy.
8. *Public relations spending.* Some of this spending certainly affects politics.

Another big slice of the spectrum reflects consulting fees and payments flowing to essentially political figures by investment houses and other outside groups with clear interests in public policy. In recent years, studies using "event analysis" methods to analyze political influence on firm profitability have proliferated. These indicate that some firm directors carry significant political weight; at least part of the fees received by such directors should count as payments for political services (Ferguson and Voth 2008). Many such payments, however, go to complete outsiders. Payments to academics or think tank–based researchers who derive substantial parts of their living from giving overpriced speeches, academic studies, and "advice" to business groups and individual firms also belong here.[24]

This is an old practice that appears to have risen in importance in the years in which polarization has been increasing. Though detailed quantitative assessments are lacking, it seems clear that the party "networks" that are now the focus of so much work in political science are heavily salted with such "designated hitters." They are far overrepresented among the talking heads that dominate television talk shows and network news "analysis," and their ties are virtually never disclosed, unless they face Senate confirmation. Not long ago, for example, it came out that a top White House adviser had been paid almost a million dollars for advising a major investment house on "philanthropy." Those are not market rates; and like financial tips, they nowhere appear in records of campaign contributions. But they should be reckoned as political money, though they appear as ordinary business expenses. The meager disclosures that are currently on the record suggest that the totals must be fairly large, running at least into hundreds of millions, with some filtered through organizations, but many others coming directly from individual large firms.

Two similar forms of political money that never show in anyone's official campaign finance statistics also elude precise specification. One reflects the value of tips and inside financial advice on legislators (and perhaps other officials, including staff; existing statistical studies cover only legislators). Some excellent work on the investment portfolios of US senators and members of the House of Representatives has been published. Both indicate that in the latest stages of party polarization, such assistance reached disturbing levels, until perhaps the press began to pay attention. The knowledge that someone was watching may have encouraged better behavior—an illustration, perhaps, that real reform is not impossible at all if the press pays more than fleeting attention.[25]

Imprecision also attends estimates of the degree to which charitable contributions by businesses involve political considerations. Here caution must be the watchword. Many donations are doubtless pure philanthropy—this always needs to be frankly acknowledged. But industries vary substantially in the rate at which they contribute to charity. In some cases, as in the pharmaceutical industry, for example, some large gifts probably represent a form of investment in scientific research that can reasonably be expected to produce results of interest to the firm or donors. That may be self-interested, but it is not politics.

But where image is a concern, politics cannot be far away. So-called deep public relations that aims at preparing the public's mind and defusing criticism over the long run is a fact of life, as a spokesperson for one of the world's largest chemical companies forcibly explained to me some years before he made a splash as an adviser to George W. Bush's White House. I would not take seriously denials by oil companies and other large firms that contributions to PBS, public radio, and some Internet sites (such as Politico.com) are not fraught with political implications. A good part of what appears as "public relations" in the national income accounts is really politics, even if no lobbying is involved—enough, I think, that jibes about how advertising expenses tower over actual campaign expenditures are really jokes on the skeptics who find the comparison so amusing. The legal meaning of "lobbying" is also quite narrow, so that the commonsense application of the term applies to far more than the admittedly gigantic sums nowadays on record.

On the other hand, a quarter century after John Saloma (1984) and I and Joel Rogers (Ferguson and Rogers 1986) analyzed the role right-wing foundations and think tanks played in the Reagan Revolution, these and related topics now attract notice (Rich 2004; Weidenbaum 2009; McGann 1995). So the numbers, at least in regard to think tanks, if not foundations, are tolerably good: they are very large indeed. How to set a value on media coverage, though, is a problem. Conceptually, the question is relatively clear: How much would it cost to gain exposure of the same quality through paid time? This answer, though, is unhelpful. It is obvious that attention and exposure on Fox News and the programming of other networks are priceless, which just repeats the problem. Setting a figure on its value in the economy as a whole is a mug's game. The best one can do is to remind analysts who keep reporting impossibly high rates of return on firm political investments that such rates of return are indeed impossibly high.

A final aspect of political money that no campaign finance statistics ever catch, but that has clearly played a key role all through the process of polarization, is shown in Figure 5.3. It plots incomes on Wall Street versus the salaries of financial regulators over nearly six decades. The implication for naive views about campaign finance as the root cause of the breakdown of electoral accountability is extremely important. Put simply, there is a point beyond which economic inequality in its own right complicates electoral control. The appropriate comparison is perhaps with a powerful magnetic field. When The Force is with them—when, that is, senators and representatives, their staffs, presidential aides, and federal regulators can be sure of walking out of their offices to become multimillionaires when they retire or

Figure 5.3 The Opportunity Cost of Doing Good: Maximum Salaries of Regulators Compared with Incomes of the Regulated, 1949–2007

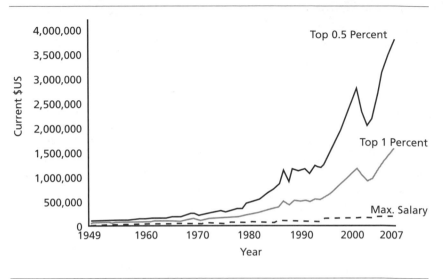

Source: Ferguson and Johnson 2010b.
Note: Top 0.5 percent and 1 percent incomes proxy financial sector.

step down—expecting them to act consistently in the public interest is naive, even if all were elected on 100 percent public funding.[26]

Campaign Finance and Polarization

The invisible stretches of the spectrum of political money include myriad smaller players, whose spending aggregates to nonnegligible sums. But a plenary share of funds with national political objective surely comes from big players—major firms, investors, foundations, and the like. In the mid-1970s, as the process of polarization got under way, the evidence is overwhelming that many of these, especially foundations, think tanks, and lobbyists representing major businesses and investor groups, streamed more and more of their resources toward right and right-center groups and politicians (Ferguson and Rogers 1986; Saloma 1984).[27] None of this shows in official campaign statistics.

But formal campaign finance also played a vital part in shaping polarization, and its role since the mid-1970s is now much easier to document, thanks to the official statistics. Several twists to the story, however, are all but unknown. They require a word if we are properly to understand how the surge in big money interacted with internal changes in Congress to produce the fiery, fabulously expensive stalemate machine we have now.

Ironically, Democratic liberals were the ones who opened Pandora's Box. In the early 1970s, House Democrats, who had controlled the institution for decades, implemented sweeping rule changes. The reforms were multifaceted and accomplished in several stages. Their thrust was to decentralize the House and put more power in the hands of the caucus to determine committee decisions and allocate resources.[28] Though the norm of seniority remained a factor for a considerable time, the changes made it less important as a guide to selecting committee chairs and assignments; indeed, the rule changes marked the beginning of the end for that hoary system, which expired in the subsequent decade as the Republicans also jettisoned it.

Up to that point, congressional changes in rules had been mostly glacial, though the 1960s had witnessed significant developments. As a result, the rule changes in the 1970s have attracted extensive discussion. The usual story portrays the switch as a kind of Indian Summer of the expiring New Deal party system, in which Democratic liberals, chafing under the hegemony of Southern Democratic barons with ultra-safe seats (and thus immense seniority), succeeded after years of agitation in taking back a measure of control.

But John Wright (2000), in a uniquely penetrating analysis, shows that the fundamental problem was a growing squeeze on Democratic campaign finance. Though by later standards, congressional campaign costs in the 1960s look almost risible, that decade nonetheless saw sharp rises in the costs of congressional campaigning—more than 50 percent between 1964 and 1968, for example. Not only were expenditures for broadcasting rising, but the boom of the 1960s led to a surge of new money. For a while organized labor, the traditional mainstay of House Democrats, tried to keep up. Presidential politics was somewhat different (Ferguson and Rogers 1986; Alexander 1976), but the handwriting was on the wall.

Aware that substantial numbers of businesses were willing to contribute to Democrats who sat on congressional committees with authority over them and perhaps sensing that business-based political action committees could provide a convenient vehicle for such contributions, anxious Democrats decided to follow the money. They inserted provisions into legislation on campaign finance reform that facilitated business spending via PACs around the publicly stated intent of the law.[29]

In the early 1970s, this did not strike many liberals as particularly dangerous, as they successfully pushed through bills (or pressured the president into issuing executive orders) establishing the now celebrated "third wave" of regulatory institutions, including the Environmental Protection Agency, the Occupational Health and Safety Administration, and the Consumer Product Safety Commission. The same liberal Democrats, with some important liberal Republican support, also passed landmark legislation authorizing tighter regulation of tobacco, water purity, nuclear power, and many other potentially hazardous activities, while the Labor Department and Health, Education, and Welfare established offices to enforce compliance with legal standards.

By the end of the decade, liberals felt rather different. Campaign costs— or at least spending totals, which jumped 120 percent between 1976 and 1980 while the price level rose only 35 percent—continued to skyrocket. Organized labor's position in American life started to slide, at first slowly, and then with a rush. At the end of the decade, as income inequality started taking off while wages of ordinary Americans stagnated, campaign contributions flowed readily and steadily into Republican coffers via both direct mail and more conventional small, face-to-face group solicitations of major investors and businesses.

The Democrats, by contrast, struggled. They played catch-up. In contrast to the GOP, for the Democrats direct mail was not an attractive option, both because of its high unit cost and because of the simple facts that Democratic mass constituencies were hard hit by the economic downturn and less affluent in the first place. But the party did have success with PACs, as did some interest groups friendly to Democrats. It was in this period, for example, that trial lawyers emerged as major Democratic funders, though in the aggregate, members of the corporate bar command far larger purses. Like the Republicans, Democrats also learned to work around post-Watergate restrictions on individual contributions. Donors allied to the party did also; some organized their own issue PACs, and pressed suppliers, key employees, and family members to contribute. But the restrictions were annoying and probably did constrain both major parties—for a while.

Political scandals in the United States customarily exhibit half-lives rivaling those of subatomic particles. As Watergate faded from public memory and campaign costs continued spiraling upward, both parties found it in their interest to quietly let big money back into the system via the rear door. Most Republicans were hostile to campaign finance restrictions on principle. In addition, they could readily calculate that they were likely to gain the lion's share of new money. But many Democratic leaders were intent on reorienting the party away from labor and its dwindling legions, to business (Ferguson and Rogers 1986; Wright 2000). As usual, the parties and the increasingly conservative courts, which were also players, were backstopped by political scientists, lawyers, and journalists who, without pausing to ask why anyone might want to pour millions of new dollars into the political system, celebrated the democratic potential of more "competition" through more lavishly financed parties and candidates.

So the dikes were breached. The post-Watergate reforms putting relatively strict limits on campaign spending did not last through even two presidential elections. A 1979 legal change and rulings by the compliant Federal Election Commission (which is uniquely and totally subservient to Congress in a way unlike any other government agency; see Urofsky 2005) opened up the wonderful world of "soft money." This could be raised in any amount by the national parties and spent for so-called party-building purposes.[30]

Table 5.2 represents a rough effort to track the flood over time. It subtracts out narrowly defined presidential and congressional expenditures (which include a plenary share of large—that is, over $250—contributors, but which came also with nettlesome ceilings on their size) from total contributions to all federal candidates.[31] What's left over (the "other" category in Table 5.2) is mostly, but not entirely, big money, including individual contributions to parties, which have a higher ceiling. Because of the way the rules channel "soft money" and its later avatars (various forms of "independent" expenditures, so-called 527 spending, etc.), these expenditures show up in a

Table 5.2 Campaign Spending Growth Through Time, 1970–2008 (millions of current dollars)

	Total Federal	Total Presidential	Total Congressional	Other	Union PAC Spending
1970					
1972	236	138	77		
1974					
1976	300	160	88		
1978					19
1980	698	275	239	184	25
1982					35
1984	1,245	325	374	546	48
1986					58
1988	1,598	500	458	640	74
1990					85
1992	2,188	550	678	960	95
1994					88
1996	2,877	700	765	1,339	100
1998	1,619		646	970	98
2000	3,849	645	900	2,304	129
2002	2,182		807	1,375	158
2004	4,575	958	949	2,668	183
2006	2,853		1,265	1,588	197
2008	5,980	1,829	1,197	2,954	265

Sources: Compiled by the author; see text and especially note 31.

bewildering variety of guises. Sometimes they appear as party-related funding; other times as "independent" expenditures. The method of subtracting out from total federal contributions is an approximation, but it is not a bad one.[32]

Because the Watergate-era reform legislation set higher contribution and spending limits for parties than for individual candidates, it secured a significant place for parties in federal elections. Soft money, however, carried this process to a whole new level, at the same time that it cemented the parties' dependence on large contributors, while further regulatory changes weakened remaining legal restrictions on party expenditures. Eventually, the law (and Federal Election Commission enforcement practices) distinguished between direct transfers from parties to candidates, which had legal limits; coordinated expenditures, which had limits, albeit high ones; and "independent" expenditures by parties, which had no limits at all.

The same pressures that made soft money attractive to parties also made PACs appealing. Greater public scrutiny made many presidential candidates, especially Democrats, reluctant to take PAC money, which was easy for journalists and political scientists to analyze, since the Federal Election Commission made lists of PAC contributors readily available. But press coverage of Congress is more sporadic and careful statistical studies suggest that it is also often biased. Senators and representatives, especially the latter, were less reserved than presidential candidates; they craved the money and were happy to open for business in many senses.

More and more individual senators and representatives began setting up new PACs of their own, so-called leadership PACs. At first these were mostly limited to real leaders, senators and representatives who held formal leadership positions. Tracking them is harder than one might suppose, since official statistics collect them in other, larger categories of PACs. By a very conservative reckoning, as late as 1994, there may have been as few as 38. But then they multiplied like a deadly virus. By 1998 there were 120, then 176 by 2000, 291 by 2002, and at least 298 by 2008.[33]

Leadership PACs operated alongside the senator or representative's own election committees. In effect, they were a completely legal second pocket that friendly interest groups and supporters could stuff with cash if they wanted to. Funds from them could not be directly used for reelection purposes, but they could be used for all kinds of other useful purposes—staff, infrastructure, even, it appears, what unsympathetic observers might characterize as slush funds. Most important of all, however, they could be used to make campaign contributions to other senators and representatives.[34] Contributions from them to other congressional candidates rose sharply through time: from $11 million in 1998 to $21 million in 2008.[35] But total contributions from members of Congress for election campaigns increased much more, because their donations to national congressional campaign committees from both their leadership PACs and their election committees increased (see Bedlington and Malbin 2003). By 2006, direct and indirect donations (through the national campaign committees) topped $60 million (Currinder 2009).

Leadership PACs accelerated the emergence of the new, comprehensively money-driven Congress. As seniority withered in the 1970s, several California Democrats shocked many of their colleagues by openly using campaign contributions to enlist support from their colleagues for committee chairmanships they desired. Here was pay-to-play with a vengeance. The practice became widespread in both parties. In the 1990s, the movement to place term limits on the number of years senators and representatives could chair committees took hold, first among Republicans, but later among the Democrats too. The effect was to throw open more positions, at least potentially, and get aspirants thinking ahead about how to amass the requisite resources. The decline of seniority, term limits, the surge in campaign cash, and leadership PACs were transforming Congress into a Hobbesian jungle, with money as the weapon of choice in the war of all against all.

As their desires for resources surged, however, senators and representatives quickly found themselves in a position uncomfortably reminiscent of the hunting bands that killed off the mammoths. In the early 1980s, donations from individuals to congressional campaigns hit a ceiling. Small donations, in particular, stagnated (Conlon 1986). The gap was filled by more and more money from PACs, mostly from business; more aid from large contributors; and help from the national parties and affluent groups and businesses that spent "independently."

Not surprisingly, Gingrich pioneered other ways of garnering political money as he stepped forward to challenge the older Republican leadership in the mid-1980s. In 1986, he took over GOPAC, a political action committee founded to promote Republicans by Pete DuPont, whose family had been mostly Republican stalwarts for generations. Claiming to have spotted a loophole in the law, Gingrich began cultivating rich businesspeople and major concerns. Incomplete press accounts mention a circle of 172 donors who committed to providing him with at least $10,000 a year for "party building." Over the next eight years, he appears to have raised perhaps $13 million dollars, at a time when the average cost of winning a House seat was about half a million dollars. He also established a foundation that paid him for teaching a history course; the foundation, in turn, had links to a center that promoted telecommunications deregulation.[36]

One thing became clear very fast: as the "Right Turn" of so many businesses and investor groups picked up speed in the late 1970s, polarization paid (see Ferguson and Rogers 1986). Virtually from the start, on-the-record contributions to Gingrich and his "revolutionaries" leaped past those to the older Republican leaders whom they eventually brushed aside, such as

Robert Michel. The attacks on Jim Wright and the Democrats, the epic clashes with the White House over taxes, and the other battles sent Gingrich's fundraising soaring, along with the fundraising of his allies, such as Armey and DeLay (see Table 5.3).[37] They far outpaced Michel's war chest, even though he served as the Republican leader in the House for years.

After the Republican revolutionaries took power, polarization and the search for funds spiraled upward. When a very special party-line vote from the Supreme Court awarded the White House to George W. Bush after the 2000 election, the process took another mighty qualitative leap upward. As this chapter's tables and figures show, fundraising kept climbing, as did party unity votes in Congress. Though not shown here, so did member contribu-

Table 5.3 How Polarization Paid in the House GOP: Gingrich, DeLay, and Armey vs. Michel

	Receipts ($)	Expenditures ($)
Gingrich Career Totals		
1997–1998	6,831,829	7,578,716
1995–1996	6,252,069	5,577,715
1993–1994	2,012,572	1,817,792
1991–1992	1,963,435	1,962,810
1989–1990	1,558,934	1,559,052
1987–1988	851,786	838,708
1985–1986	738,258	736,607
1983–1984	356,626	336,065
1981–1982	367,636	365,750
1979–1980	278,317	277,585
(Note text caution about GOPAC secret funding.)		
DeLay Career Totals		
2005–2006	3,780,923	3,836,376
2003–2004	2,909,844	3,143,559
2001–2002	1,350,115	1,274,921
1999–2000	1,342,920	1,298,995
1997–1998	1,340,997	1,170,867
1995–1996	1,620,227	1,621,708
1993–1994	669,010	701,245
1991–1992	341,516	371,362
1989–1990	324,134	297,153
1987–1988	364,837	361,255
1985–1986	316,191	294,850
1983–1984	555,459	530,147

(continues)

tions to their colleagues, demonstration votes, holds on presidential nominations, and the rest.

By then, the role that large contributors were playing was almost mind-numbing. In the mid-1990s, Bill Clinton and the Democrats found another loophole that the Federal Election Commission quickly blessed, allowing parties to spend unlimited sums on expenditures made supposedly independently of the campaigns they were in fact intended to benefit. In 2002, Senators John McCain and Russ Feingold promoted what became the Bipartisan Campaign Finance Reform. This abolished "soft money," but gave a pass to so-called 527 spending that could be raised and spent in any amount by organizations allegedly independent of the national parties. The measure also raised the limits on individual contributions to levels high enough to make chasing them eminently rewarding in its own right.[38]

Not surprisingly, the legislation changed the ways parties and candidates chased funds, but did not alter big money's evolving role in the sys-

Table 5.3 Continued

	Receipts ($)	Expenditures ($)
Armey Career Totals		
2001–2002	588,818	476,913
1999–2000	1,373,930	1,323,416
1997–1998	2,061,340	2,125,437
1995–1996	1,248,706	1,673,388
1993–1994	1,177,630	900,871
1991–1992	483,928	495,128
1989–1990	440,375	198,555
1987–1988	419,632	314,903
1985–1986	557,096	567,923
1983–1984	392,963	368,869
Michel Career Totals		
1993–1994	64,121	313,513
1991–1992	646,637	636,430
1989–1990	705,878	579,258
1987–1988	877,026	861,969
1985–1986	689,849	639,765
1983–1984	681,434	707,734
1981–1982	697,084	687,875
1979–1980	168,667	134,540

Source: Federal Election Commission data, organized by *Congressional Quarterly* money line.

tem. Various entities close to the parties reorganized as 527s and opened for business. New 527s with obvious partisan tilts also emerged. Meanwhile, encouraged by the Bipartisan Campaign Finance Reform Act and various court rulings, outside interest groups and affluent investors began setting up 501(c) groups that claimed the right to spend unlimited amounts of money on their own.

Researchers analyzing press coverage discovered a striking pattern: that the language newspapers used to describe politics varied systematically depending on whether Republicans or Democrats predominated in the regional media market. The economists who wrote the paper celebrated the apparent triumph of the market; they claimed that their research showed that "bias" in newspapers represented an accommodation to market demands (Gentzkow and Shapiro 2010). But their write-up was less precise than their econometric specification. Though they talked about voters, in fact the scholars had no measure of voter behavior in their equation. What they did have was a term that reflected the local mix of campaign contributions in national politics. Their work was consistent with—and their specific measure actually supported—the proposition that contributors rather than the general population drive local media markets.[39] This was top-down polarization with a vengeance.

In 2010, a Supreme Court whose apparent partiality to the political right had drawn wide comment finally threw open just about all remaining doors to political money. In *Citizens United v. Federal Election Commission,* it ruled that corporations (and any labor unions that still had money) were free to spend funds directly from their corporate treasuries in any amount, as long as they did so independently of campaigns mounted by federal candidates or parties.

As a flood of new, anonymous money begins washing over the landscape of American politics and observers get set for yet another record in presidential campaign fundraising, it is hard to think of many reasons why polarization should abate. As Eisenhower suggested in 1954, the conservative and center-right investor blocs that are the final cause of the polarization of US politics have come a long way. They are closer than ever before to rolling back the legacy of the New Deal. Accordingly, they have little incentive to compromise. We are not watching a rerun of *Cabaret,* but plenty of people out in the heartland who know little of the subtleties of political money appear to believe that bringing back laissez-faire will somehow snatch back the broad-based prosperity that the regulated, interventionist New Deal state once secured them. Big money playing on aroused minorities, amid low voter turnout (with often strenuous efforts to keep it that way), has been a potent political formula for a generation. A few faint signs suggest that this formula is wearing through (see Parramore 2010). But that is a topic for another day.

Notes

I am grateful to Walter Dean Burnham, Jerome Grossman, Robert Johnson, and Peter Temin for many discussions of points at issue in this chapter. I am particularly grateful to Paul Jorgensen, Ben Page, and Lynn Parramore for reading drafts under considerable time pressure and to Robert Wade for some comments on part of the argument. Obviously, neither any of them nor any institution I am associated with bears responsibility for the final product.

To keep documentation to manageable length, notes are often collected and placed at the ends of paragraphs. Unless otherwise indicated, newspaper and magazine citations are normally to the Internet versions. Note that many papers publish stories on the Internet late in the day before they appear in hard copy.

The preliminary version of this chapter was initially presented at the second annual conference of the Institute for New Economic Thinking at Bretton Woods in April 2011 and published on the institute's website. Discussion was widespread, eventually reaching even the *Financial Times*. The chapter has been redeveloped, and points raised have been analyzed in significantly greater depth, with new points added regarding the relevance of the role of money as it impacts the political process. For more detailed discussions, especially of campaign finance data and congressional bloc formation, see Ferguson, Jorgensen, and Chen 2013.

1. Presidential Papers of Dwight David Eisenhower, Document no. 1147, Letter to Edgar Newton Eisenhower, November 8, 1954, http://www.eisenhowermemorial .org/presidentialpapers/first-term/documents /1147.cfm.

2. Hanna was the political boss who organized William McKinley's campaign for the presidency. The quotation is from Urofsky 2005: 4.

3. The discussions have never stopped, but see, for example, Hersh 1983.

4. The literature is vast. On Gingrich, a study with much useful detail is Sabato and Simpson 1996.

5. Figure 5.1 shows the percentage of roll call votes in which a majority of voting Democrats opposed a majority of voting Republicans. Many indices of polarization have been computed. A lot are good; for the period in the figure, they all give more or less the same results. Compare, for example, the well-known Poole-Rosenthal scores, which do suggest that the connection with Reagan is important.

6. Note that the Republican National Committee was not clearly controllable by Gingrich at that time.

7. See also Powell 2010, especially fig. 3, which I did not see until several years after its date of presentation.

8. Marian Currinder adds that the Republicans do not have a formal dues requirement; instead, the inventors of the *Contract with America* (Republican National Committee 1994) have tended to rely on separate sets of contracts between members and the leadership. The target numbers on the GOP side, of course, are also huge. The means vary, but not the end. Both procedures are tantamount to posting prices, though technically the GOP procedure is closer to a silent auction. Incidentally, on the Democratic side, the House Financial Services Committee counts as one of the power committees, with the colossal requirements for contributions. Probably those are waived for some very junior members, but it is easy to understand why in 2010, as the Dodd-Frank "reform" legislation went through, more than seventy members of the House served on the committee. Banks, as everyone who has passed Economics 101 knows, can create money. And now, so too can members of Congress. On the Democrats and Pelosi, see Chaddock 2010.

9. As many as five individuals mentioned as potential GOP presidential candidates in 2012 were on the payroll of the Fox network during parts of 2010; two who

formed formal exploratory committees then withdrew their candidacy. For the media concentration on the right and center right, see, for example, the surveys of network appearances over the years by FAIR, available at its website, http://fair.org.

10. Alan Abramowitz, Brad Alexander, and Matthew Gunning (2006) suggest that in recent House elections, money rather than incumbency per se has played an increasingly important role in making most House seats relatively safe. I disagree with these authors on a number of key points, but the incumbency finding is interesting.

11. Much of the literature on party finance sees contemporary national parties as "service" organizations. There is a clear point to this characterization, but it shorts the ways those who control the party can grant or withhold these "services" to coerce would-be candidates for open seats. I am confident that this happens in both parties, but cannot consider the point in more detail here. To the extent that distinct blocs, such as Tea Party Republicans, form in Congress, quite distinct patterns of financial support exist for them. See the discussion in Ferguson, Jorgensen, and Chen 2013.

12. On Greenspan and especially the still little-discussed decision to close down the New York Fed's primary dealer regulatory unit, see Ferguson and Johnson 2009a. For the neoclassical arguments on campaign finance, see especially Ansolabehere, de Figueiredo, and Snyder 2003.

13. The essay by Stephen Ansolabehere and colleagues has the merit of posing several important questions very clearly. But its discussion of contributions over time in American political life and other key factual questions is seriously flawed. Judgments about some of the theoretical issues depend on the exact nature of the purported facts. But parts of the essay's reasoning are inconsistent with clear realities. If, for example, playing the game or aiding someone with certain values is really the thing, then the probability of winning should not influence the players. That is, if "participation" truly were the motivation for most contributions, then money should not abruptly stop flowing to losers after reverses; nor should lucre rain on winners. But both often happen. See the discussion in the extended version of Ferguson 2005. I hope to revisit this discussion in the near future.

14. See the references to other works discussed in Fiorina and Abrams 2009. It does not seem to have occurred to anyone that such claims were inconsistent with the massive pressures for market deregulation in the political system. By contrast, some excellent work showed up earlier claims that most blue-collar workers were not still concerned principally with bread-and-butter issues. See especially Bartels 2008; Gelman et al. 2010.

15. The Nixon quotation comes from his "Address to the Nation on Southeast Asia," April 30, 1970, http://www.mekong.net/cambodia/nixon430.htm.

16. The long discussion of multidimensionality in these studies is not, alas, something I can take up in this chapter.

17. One can respond that voter turnout is heavily skewed in many of these districts. This is an argument to which I am very sympathetic. But it begs the question of who or what is responsible for the low turnouts. That question, of course, is easily answered from the perspective of the investment approach to congressional evolution that I adopt in this chapter. But without such a framework, the response is arch in the extreme, verging on incoherence. There is a simpler way to make the point: there are Republicans and Republicans. As the Eisenhower quote that opens this chapter suggests, what the label stands for has evolved through time. Whether this shows according to one or another standard of measurement adopted in the congressional literature is a secondary question; it is a fact. The current argument over Social Security would have been unthinkable in, say, the 1950s.

18. The relatively few papers on leadership selection and fundraising in Congress constitute an exception.

19. Compare to the discussion of the facts about Democratic campaign contributions and industry sectors in Ferguson, Jorgensen, and Chen 2013.

20. "I need to start humping in corporate accounts!" wrote Ralph Reed (*Time* 2006). This from someone who had loudly denounced the "insiders" game in Washington and had been hailed in public as the "right hand of God." Later, it also came out that this public opponent of gambling was lobbying on gambling-related issues.

21. On Falwell and Bunker Hunt, see the discussion in Ferguson and Rogers 1981. On the others, see Ferguson and Rogers 1986.

22. Table 5.1's list of industries that were heavy contributors to Gingrich's fundraising is instructive in pointing to regulation, but see also the discussion in Sabato and Simpson 1996 on Gingrich's many efforts to intervene for GOPAC and other contributors.

The long list of very concrete aims should be a warning to the carefree way much of the literature on Congress and campaign finance throws around the term "ideological." It is fine to say that the backers of the Republican surge had ideological goals. So they did. But wrecking the government agencies, for example, implied very concrete increases in profits for many firms and investors. If one loses sight of the vast sums of money involved, the point of the whole business rapidly disappears.

23. In the final analysis, it was the "Right Turn" of so much political money that pulled and pushed the Republicans to the right. The Democrats, also intent on following the money, trailed along at a pace constrained by what remained of their mass constituency (which does still retain some resources that the party needs; witness the battle over the status of organized labor and community groups). The gap between the parties at any point in time will, accordingly, vary with both the financial incentives and pressures from the mass base. The policy preferences of the median voter do not drive the system's dynamics; the investor blocs do. See Ferguson 1995a.

24. Obviously, appointees with business backgrounds have been serving in federal posts since the beginning of the republic, and many politicians have always had external ties. What is distinctive about recent developments is the extent to which such ties appear to be extending down even to midlevel party operatives. This really illustrates the problems attendant to sharply rising inequality.

25. On investment portfolios of senators, see Ziobrowski et al. 2004; on investment portfolios of representatives, see Ziobrowski et al. 2011. Mostly negative results for later periods have been reported in Eggers and Hainmueller 2011; the differences may relate to the period covered. Procedures for accessing data on congressional portfolios, while intensely supervised, did become simplified around the time the essay by Ziobrowski and colleagues (2004) appeared. That, in turn, received substantial press coverage, though only modest attention within political science. But the press coverage raises the possibility that the dynamics discussed in Dyck, Moss, and Zingales 2008, a recent paper on publicity and congressional behavior, took hold.

26. Effective civil service bureaucracies with real career ladders and appropriately high salaries are as important as campaign finance reform itself in preserving popular control of the state.

27. The phenomenon cut across state lines, of course. This point is obvious, but bears some reflection. Some political scientists have recently begun backhandedly acknowledging the breakdown of median-voter models by running regressions on state data to see which income groups get the most out of state policy. This procedure is well intentioned, but not wise. Money crosses state lines. There is no reason to

assume that representatives who take it are acting only for their legal constituents, however wealthy.

28. As Wright summarizes, "By the mid-1970s, the selection of committee chairs was made subject to caucus approval; subcommittees were established for most committees and then provided with staff, funding, fixed jurisdictions, and referral of appropriate legislation; the Ways and Means Committee was expanded and Democratic members stripped of their authority to make committee assignments; bills could be referred to multiple committees; committee hearings and markups were opened to the public; teller votes were introduced; and the Speaker was allowed to nominate Democratic members of the Rules Committee. Generally, then, power over legislation was dispersed more widely within the House, the powers of the Speaker were enhanced, and the entire legislative process became more accessible to the public" (2000: 219).

29. Wright asserts that the Democrats had their eyes explicitly on PACs at the time. There is no question that many Democrats wanted to chase money from business; see, for example, Ferguson and Rogers 1986. But there were comparatively few PACs aside from those run by labor then. Various accounts of the legislation are not easily reconciled; compare, for example, Urofsky 2005; La Raja 2008; and Epstein 1979. The whole episode could benefit from a close, archival-based study.

30. With conditions, some of the money could be shared with state parties. But this level of detail is unnecessary in this chapter.

31. Reliable information on total campaign spending is harder to come by than one might imagine. Alas, the redesign of the usually very useful Center for Responsive Politics makes it far less helpful for serious research purposes. Many of its data series have been shortened to the point that they impair inquiries. Its series on total costs of federal elections, for example, goes back only to 1998, even though it plainly has the data. I began with those numbers (at http://www.opensecrets.org/bigpicture /index.php). I then combed back through the series of volumes started by Herbert Alexander and continued by John Green and David Magleby and his colleagues on the financing of individual elections, to produce similar numbers for past elections. (The major pitfall here is the effort involved in separating out money spent on state and local elections; for reasons only those who work with these numbers are likely to appreciate, that is complex. There are also problems with internal inconsistencies among sources. I sorted these out as carefully as possible. There is no question that all the estimates here are rough.) The rationale for subtracting the narrow presidential totals (which do contain modest amounts of public funds; these are too small, especially in recent years, to make it worthwhile to refine them further) and the narrow congressional contributions is that both of these are fairly easy to partition between large and small individual contributions on the basis of available statistics. The "Other" category does contain some small contributions, but soft money, 527 spending, and the several varieties of independent expenditures included in "Other" come mostly from large contributors and major corporate interests.

In recent presidential elections, the role of small contributors has been less than the noise in the press about them would suggest. Some tendency to overstate their significance stems from data-processing problems. The name-matching programs in common use do not pick up all the contributions from apparently different individuals that are in fact coming from the same person. This happens for many reasons—different addresses, initials, occupations, zip codes, and so forth. In 2008, the Obama campaign also famously encouraged donors to write several smaller checks, instead of one large one, making special problems in that election. There is a strong tendency, therefore, to underestimate the weight large donors actually play in elections. See Ferguson, Jorgensen, and Chen 2013 for a detailed discussion of 2008 and, especially,

2012. This demonstrates that politics in the United States is substantially a game reserved for the 1 percent. The contrast with earlier estimates by, for example, the Campaign Finance Institute is substantial.

By contrast, congressional campaigns rely less on individual donations and more on PACs to begin with. Campaign Finance Institute tabulations for recent elections (which are not consolidated as in Ferguson, Jorgensen, and Chen 2013, and thus are likely to underestimate big-donor concentration) suggest that individual contributions of less than $200 usually provide less than 10 percent of House candidate receipts and 14–17 percent of all Senate candidate receipts. Contributions over $1,000 make up about a third of House candidate receipts and somewhat over 40 percent of Senate campaign contributions. PACs provide about a third of receipts in the House and a sixth or so in the Senate. Both Senate and House campaigns get help from the parties and are affected by independent expenditures. As members of Congress don't bowl alone, neither do they campaign alone.

The union numbers reported by the Center for Responsive Politics are fraught with errors; I found a substantial mistake there, which the Center for Responsive Politics corrected. But I believe the center's totals are still too low; they do not in fact catch all the 527 funds. The labor numbers in Table 5.2 come from Stanley and Niemi (2010: 92); they are for all PACs. For better estimates, see again Ferguson, Jorgensen, and Chen 2013.

32. Scale economies in campaigns are fairly large; there is also a good deal of joint production, as state and even local campaigns piggyback on federal race expenditures and vice versa. There are some rules regulating these practices, but they are of doubtful effectiveness and enforcement is normally exiguous. See Ferguson, Jorgensen, and Chen 2013.

33. Many tabulations of leadership PACs exist. A close look suggests that many often include other PACs besides those of members of Congress. Some leadership PACs also try to hide their sponsors. I rely on the conservative reckoning by Kathy Gill at http://uspolitics.about.com/od/finance/tp/leadership_pac_data.htm. Hers is lower than many others, but I prefer to err on the side of caution. As discussed earlier, subsequent work with Paul Jorgensen and Jie Chen (Ferguson, Jorgensen, and Chen 2013) suggests that the true figures run appreciably higher.

34. This was also possible from the electoral committees, but that represented a dollar-for-dollar loss to the representative donating the funds. Leadership PACs reduced the element of competition; indeed, to the extent that investors maxed out in both (by no means always the case), it meant there was no competition at all.

35. Total contributions from leadership PACs come again from Gill at http://us politics.about.com/od/finance/tp/leadership_pac_data.htm.

36. For the foundation, see Sabato and Simpson 1996. For the 172 donors, see Kranish 1994. For the link between the foundation and the telecommunications center, see Ward 1997.

37. Gingrich's effort to win control of the House was widely viewed as a long shot during most of the period he waged it. This rules out various "reverse causality" hypotheses such as that attributed to Robert van Houweling in Heberlig, Hetherington, and Larson 2006. In this view, money flowed to the right-wing Republicans because donors expected them to win. The whole discussion of money and votes in House elections needs reexamination in light of the "linear model" discussed in Ferguson, Jorgensen, and Chen 2013; see especially fig. 1 there.

38. Especially when the presidential contribution could be combined with another, larger contribution to a political party. Such "joint" fundraising events have become very popular; they amount to a one-stop shop for big money.

39. Matthew Gentzkow and Jesse Shapiro's (2010) finding, I think, is historically conditioned; it reflects the spiraling polarization of Congress and the political culture. For that reason, studies of media coverage for slightly earlier periods probably would find similar results. Note, however, that presidential endorsements by the media may well not follow the proposed pattern; unpublished research indicates that they do not. To the extent that media manipulation is subtle, it also may escape detection by such methods. Even studies of Fox News that report finding effects on voters do not suggest that those effects are very large.

6

Structural Sources
of Political Polarization

Gerald M. Pomper and Marc D. Weiner

The partisan polarization currently dominating American public
life is a serious threat to the long-term political health of the United States.
We argue that there is a deep and troubling cause of our present discontents:
a fundamental change in the nation's political institutions.

We contend—and fear—that these long-term institutional changes dis-
tort the electorate's capacity to assess political accountability as well as chill-
ingly inhibit the Madisonian system's capacity to check both individual and
institutional political ambition. While taking note of the 2012 presidential
election results and subsequent events, we expect these perils to continue
during and after Barack Obama's second term.

These changes in US political institutions are of major and enduring significance. Political realities have in effect rewritten the Constitution. In practice, it now reads (with virtual amendments in italics),

The Legislative Process
Every Bill which shall have passed the House of Representatives *by vote of*
the majority political party and the Senate *by a three-fifths majority* shall,
before it become a Law, be presented to the President of the United States.
[Article I, Section 7]

Powers of Congress
The Congress shall have Power . . . to regulate Commerce with foreign
Nations, and among the several States, and with the Indian Tribes, *when*
approved by the Supreme Court. [Article I, Section 8]

The validity of the public debt of the United States, authorized by law . . .
shall not be questioned, *but the Congress may default on payment of such*
debt. [Fourteenth Amendment, Section 4]

129

Election of Congress

The House of Representatives shall be composed of Members chosen every second Year by the People of the several States, *after nomination in direct primaries.* [Article I, Section 2]

The Senate of the United States shall be composed of two Senators from each State, elected by the people thereof, for six years, *after nomination in direct primaries.* [Article I, Section 3; Seventeenth Amendment, Section 1]

Election of the President

Each State shall appoint, in such Manner as the Legislature thereof may direct, *upon the approval of the Supreme Court,* a Number of Electors, equal to the whole Number of Senators and Representatives to which the State may be entitled in the Congress. [Article II, Section 1]

Presidential Powers

The President shall be Commander in Chief of the Army and Navy of the United States, *and may conduct War in the absence of a Declaration of War by the Congress.* [Article II, Section 2]

He shall take Care that the Laws be faithfully executed, *according to his privileged definition of the Laws.* [Article II, Section 3]

Presidential Appointments

He shall . . . nominate, and by and with the Advice and Consent of *three-fifths of* the Senate, shall appoint Ambassadors, other public Ministers and Consuls, Judges of the Supreme Court, and all other Officers of the United States. [Article II, Section 2]

The President shall have Power to fill up all Vacancies that may happen during the Recess of the Senate, *the times of such Recess to be established by the President,* by granting Commissions which shall expire at the End of their next Session. [Article II, Section 2]

Judicial Power

The judicial Power shall extend to all Cases, in Law and Equity, arising under this Constitution, the Laws of the United States; . . . *and to all Cases involving elections, notwithstanding other powers granted by this Constitution to the Congress and state legislatures.* [Article III, Section 2]

While these new words will not be found in the literal text of the Constitution, they define the actual workings of our government today. Although we do not expect perfection in either people or politics, and do not think that the Constitution has ever been a perfect instrument of government, we despair at these changes. We share the doleful realism of the authors of *The Federalist Papers,* James Madison in particular, who were of the mind that human ambition, often tawdry, was the root motivation of politics. But ambition, they hoped, could be turned to better purposes.

Now, however, poisoned by the toxicity of these extraconstitutional structures, the new system sabotages Madison's hope that social diversity, the virtue of officials, and the necessity of compromise would overcome the ills of individual ambition and the clash of institutions. Today, unchecked, political ambition weakens democratic accountability and effective government while promoting unfettered ideological conflict and personal aggrandizement.

The Federalist Papers: Madison Agonistes

We begin with a core premise of our foundational theory, that personal ambition is the driving force of politics. "To [the Founders] a human being was an atom of self-interest. They did not believe in man, but they did believe in the power of a good political constitution to control him" (Hofstadter 1948: 3).

Two key *Federalist* papers present distinct guides to future political practice under the Constitution. *Federalist* no. 10 (Pole 2005: 48–54) presents a slow yet efficacious collaborative model that promotes the common welfare, while *Federalist* no. 51 (Pole 2005: 280–284) provides the template for resolving the inevitable political deadlock that results from the narrow ambitions of politicians seeking to maximize personal power. These two papers—both authored by Madison—as well as the Constitution itself, simultaneously acknowledge and seek to constrain ambition. As Madison wrote in *Federalist* no. 10, "The latent sources of faction are thus sown in the nature of man. . . . We know that neither moral nor religious motives can be relied on as an adequate control." Later, in *Federalist* no. 51, he more directly warned against political naiveté: "If men were angels, no government would be necessary. If angels were to govern men, neither external nor internal controls on government would be necessary."

However, the thrusts of these two papers are quite different. In *Federalist* no. 10, Madison finds "a republican remedy for the diseases most incident to republican government." Representation will "refine and enlarge the public views," so that virtuous leaders are more likely to be recruited to office, while it will be "difficult for unworthy candidates to practise with success the vicious arts." By establishing a large republic, factions inimical to the public good will either be outvoted if a minority, or fragmented if a majority. In either case, mischievous factions will be "unable to concert and carry into effect schemes of oppression." In essence, Madison relies on a sociological solution: the plurality of groups will prevent domination by any one group advancing any one interest. In *Federalist* no. 10, he leaves institutional regulations aside, optimistically relying on a virtuous elite and the diversity of a large nation to provide protection for liberty.

When, a few months later, Madison considers the detailed structure of the Constitution in *Federalist* no. 51, his tone and prescriptions are darker; here he focuses increasingly on the power urges of officeholders. While a constitution "must first enable the government to control the governed," he stresses the need to "oblige it to control itself." Now he enlists, even elevates, the self-interest of politicians into a prime merit through a "policy of supplying by opposite and rival interests, the defect of better motives . . . [so] that each may be a check on the other; that the private interest of every individual may be a centinel over the public rights."

To prevent the "tyranny" they so feared, the Founders erected institutional barriers against anything other than slow, incremental policy development and change. They also, though, expected the federal government to be strong and active, guided by "representatives, whose enlightened views and virtuous sentiments render them superior to local prejudices, and to schemes of injustice." In *Federalist* no. 51, however, Madison expressed pessimism about this prospect, as he urged "giving to those who administer each department the necessary constitutional means, and personal motives, to resist encroachments of the others."

Just as Madison apparently came to doubt the virtue of representatives, we no longer rely on any such virtue in today's political culture. Instead, we *expect* representatives to be self-interested; we *expect* them to be enthusiastically self-promoting. At the same time, however, we must observe that modern political ambition, catalyzed by the extraconstitutional structural changes we describe, has a stranglehold on political decisionmaking and policy development. Indeed, we see interest groups that are no longer prevented from promoting their self-interest by majoritarian doctrine; we see the rages of local politics violently elevated to national prominence; we see politicians deploying modern technology in the service of those "vicious arts by which elections are too often carried"; and we see the Supreme Court extensively involved in the thickets of politics, serving as an active political contender for conservative causes. And, as a result, we see institutional clogs throughout the arteries of US government.

We write after the election of 2012, the bitter conclusion to Barack Obama's first presidential term. That tenure began with the Senate minority leader's declaration that his party's first priority was factional victory: "The single most important thing we want to achieve is for President Obama to be a one-term president" (Seib 2010). He and the Republican party were good to their word, as that goal defined their strategy for the next four years, effectively thwarting any possible political consensus on such vital policy issues as health care, national debt management, climate change, and foreign relations.

In this chapter, we ask three questions. What is the state of our present institutions? How did US politics change so radically? And what are the prospects for improvement after the elections of 2012?

The Present Institutional Decay

The Constitution established majority rule as the basic operating procedure for the federal government. The use of simple-majority rule was a major change from the Articles of Confederation, which had required a super-majority of nine of thirteen states to pass any legislation. Even with all of the checks and balances, and even with some unusual counting rules, majorities were to inevitably prevail under the new Constitution. Majorities would elect the members of Congress, pass legislation in both chambers (although the Senate might not reflect a majority of the nation's voters), elect the president (although mediated through a unique and occasionally out-of-step Electoral College), and, in the Senate, a majority would confirm presidential appointments. The only instances where support beyond a simple majority was required were the approval of treaties, impeachments, and constitutional amendments.

Article I in the New Constitution

Today, however, silently and without the required formal action by Congress or the states, the Constitution has been amended to drastically alter the original majoritarian principle. In Congress, the two chambers have made this change in very different ways. Now, the Senate operates under minority rule and the House observes unrestricted rule by the majority party.

Senate rules now require a three-fifths super-majority vote to make law. In practice, the upper chamber will neither pass nor necessarily consider bills unless sixty senators support cloture on debate. This stricture comes not from the Constitution, but from the filibuster, established by the Senate's rules governing debate. Despite its extraconstitutional origin, it has become as binding as any of the explicit provisions of the Constitution itself, effectively operating as a mute addition to Article I. As a leading analyst declares, "Over the last fifty years, there has been a quiet revolution in American politics. A major hurdle has been added to the legislative process. . . . It just happened, and it happened so quietly we barely notice" (Koger 2010: 3).

Unlimited debate existed in practice in the Senate in the early twentieth century, even after it expired in the House in the late nineteenth century. The first formal restriction on filibusters came in 1917 at the urging of President Woodrow Wilson, and the new strictures required a two-thirds vote to end debate. The new cloture rule was first invoked in 1919, to force a vote on the Treaty of Versailles. Setting aside Jimmy Stewart's speech in the 1939 film *Mr. Smith Goes to Washington,* the most famous use of the filibuster was by Southern segregationist Democrats opposing civil rights legislation. Proving, however, that at least at that time majority rule still prevailed in the Senate, those passionate opponents were still outvoted and desegregation bills were passed, most notably the Civil Rights Acts of 1964 and 1965.

In 1975, the second formal restriction further lowered the required vote to three-fifths of the Senate, the now famous sixty votes. Although it could still prevent a majority from acting, the cloture rule was used sparingly, reserved for matters that aroused passionate opposition from minority factions. Through this time, then, as Madison had hoped, the republican principle of majority rule still prevailed.

Since 1993, however, the filibuster—or even the mere threat of a filibuster—has become standard practice. In the fifty-four years (1917–1971) since the first cloture rule was enacted, there typically was only a single cloture motion filed each year. By the time of the 111th Congress, of 2009–2010, there were two such efforts a week—usually futile—to achieve action in the Senate (Ornstein 2010). This sharp increase in filibusters has remade the Senate into a legislative roadblock. In failing to meet the two major criteria for legislative effectiveness, "deliberation and decisiveness," the Senate usually only accomplishes delay (Matthews 2010).

Several political developments led to the vastly increased use of the filibuster. First, filibusters are no longer true contests. Traditionally, a filibuster required one or more senators to hold the Senate floor in order to stall a roll call vote. Because physical presence was required, dissenting senators could eventually be worn down. Now, perhaps due to empathy for aging senators, the mere threat of a filibuster can throw a bill off the legislative calendar with no political cost to the minority opposition. This outcome results not from the minority's will to obstruct, but from the "unwillingness of majorities of less than sixty senators to engage in wars of attrition and incur the attendant costs" (Wawro and Schickler 2006: 262). What had once been a calculated and costly tool of government with potentially grave political consequences is now deployed with ordinary casualness. This change undermines the fundamental seriousness of the filibuster, rendering it, in essence, a nuclear weapon routinely used for muggings.

Second, the filibuster is no longer limited to legislation that inspires fierce debate on the very nature of government and the American way of life, as was the case with Southern Democratic segregationists; rather, today the filibuster is used to threaten most legislation that contains significant party-aligned policy differences. For example, as Norman Ornstein (2010) noted, the filibuster was employed in 2009 to delay unemployment benefits in the midst of the nation's economic collapse, even though the bill eventually passed on a vote of 98 to 0.

Third, filibusters have become ordinary tools of chamber partisanship. Previously, a cloture requirement of sixty votes might be met by policy-preference alliances across party lines. Now, to enact its legislation, a party usually must look for all of the required sixty votes within its own ranks. However, save for a brief and tenuous eighteen-month interregnum of 2009–2010, no party has held sixty seats in the Senate since 1978. Thus, it is essentially impossible to achieve a three-fifths vote from only one side of the aisle. Over a longer span, since 1940, except for two periods, from 1962 to 1966 and from 1974 to 1978, neither party has held a filibuster-proof minimum.

We now have more filibusters, easier filibusters, more extensive filibusters, and more partisan filibusters. The result of the silent amendment is inaction, or action that is dependent on unsavory deals such as the "Cornhusker Kickback" or the "Louisiana Purchase," employed to pass the Patient Protection and Affordable Care Act. The Senate's inactivity on the debt limit and long-term deficits led conservative Republican senator Tom Coburn to declare the virtual disappearance of the Senate: "Our epitaph will read: Never before in the field of legislating was so much ignored by so many for so long" (Coburn 2011). Writing in *The Federalist Papers,* Alexander Hamilton foresaw the consequences of a super-majority requirement: "But its real operation is to embarrass the administration, to destroy the energy of government, and to substitute the pleasure, caprice or artifices of an insignificant, turbulent or corrupt junto, to the regular deliberations and decisions of a respectable majority" (Pole 2005: 119).

Beyond the filibuster, another development in the Senate hinders the proper functioning of US government: blockages to the confirmation of presidential appointees. The number of positions subject to Senate confirmation has increased vastly from the Constitution's specifications; these positions now include not merely justices, ambassadors, and military officers, but also at least 1,200 civilian nominees. Put another way, one of every six presidential appointments, including heads of independent agencies and subcabinet officials, requires Senate confirmation.[1] Not only does the Senate vet more appointees, but it also is more demanding in its procedures and less supportive of the president. Fewer circuit court judges, for example, are approved: less than 50 percent now pass muster in the 2010s, compared to 90 percent in the 1970s. The combined effect of these practices is seen in a brief comparison of Presidents Ronald Reagan and Barack Obama, both of whom came to power during episodes of marked party turnover: Reagan needed confirmation of 295 key appointees, Obama 422. Reagan had to wait an average of 114 days for confirmation of his subcabinet appointees, while Obama has had to wait an average of 195 days.[2]

Equally as pernicious as the casual use of the filibuster is the Senate practice of allowing individual legislators to decree a "hold" on a nomination until they win a particular goal. Such "holds" are not restricted to (and are, indeed, often entirely unrelated to) the nominee's fitness for office. They include demands for other patronage, for favored local projects, or for other unrelated concessions. Furthermore, the holds may not even be publicly announced, as a secret hold has been as valid as an open fight. In a notorious instance, Alabama senator Richard Shelby put a hold on *every* Obama nominee in an effort to acquire new Air Force and Federal Bureau of Investigation facilities for his state. Madison's worst expectations of the effects of personal ambition have been more than fulfilled.

In the opening days of the 112th and 113th Congresses, the leadership of the slight Democratic Senate majorities (fifty-three in 2011, fifty-five in 2013) vocally supported change. Ultimately, though, fear of the possible loss of control after 2014, and fear of the unknown, overwhelmed those reformist urges, and only minor changes were made. Anonymous holds on nominees were ended, the number of presidential appointees needing confirmation was reduced by about 200 positions (none of them a major office), and debate was limited on nominations, but only for subcabinet positions and district judges.

At the same time, procedural rule changes were also made. Now, if the minority is permitted to offer amendments, proposed legislation will move directly from committees to the floor, ending individual vetoes on legislation. Long-winded debates will face time restrictions before and after cloture is considered, and it will be easier to enter conference negotiations with the House (Bolton 2013). While these changes may increase the efficiency of the Senate, they do not speak to flaws in its fundamental character.

The major blockages—the sixty-vote cloture requirement and allowance of "silent" filibusters—remain, with no further change possible until 2015. Stasis continues, perpetuating, as Ezra Klein has characterized it, "a world in which you can't enact your ideas or govern effectively and so the voters end up thinking you as feckless as the folks across the aisle. . . . That's a world in which the rules of the Senate, and not the policies of the parties, drive outcomes, and thus drive elections. That's a world where voters never know whose ideas are best because neither side can ever enact their agendas. But that's the world the Senate apparently prefers to inhabit" (2011).

The changes in the House of Representatives have been entirely opposite. The Republicans, winning a strong majority in the 2010 elections, and continuing in control in 2012, have remade the chamber into a parliamentary body, rigidly divided along party lines, where almost all floor roll calls are now party-line votes. Only Republican measures are considered, with the Republicans gaining virtually unanimous support from their own ranks and virtually unanimous opposition from the Democrats. In 2011, 76 percent of House roll calls divided the two parties, the highest frequency ever; the average Republican voted with their party on 91 percent of these tallies, also at the top of the charts; and Republicans won 89 percent of these divisions, another near record. In contrast, in the nonmajoritarian Senate, party-line votes occurred on barely more than half of roll call votes, and Democrats won on only 72 percent.[3]

The party division is also strikingly ideological. The degree of party polarization is at a historical high.[4] A single liberal-conservative ideological dimension accounts for almost all variation between the parties. The Republican Party, compared to its stance going back to 1879, has become a severely conservative party, in contrast to a steady moderate liberalism among Democrats and the virtual disappearance of past regional differences among Democrats. Unified in their ideology, the Republicans can pass whatever they want in the House. And they do—as witnessed by fifty separate roll calls to repeal the Obama health care law as of March 2014.

The US House of Representatives, however, is not the British House of Commons. Winning every roll call does not enact legislation, at the very least due to the independent veto power of the presidency. It seems, then, that the Republicans have been attempting to operate the political equivalent of hammering square pegs into round holes. This style of governing is more than futile; indeed, "parliamentary-style parties in a separation-of-powers government are a formula for willful obstruction and policy irresolution" (Mann and Ornstein 2012: xiii).

This irreconcilable conflict among US institutions was repeatedly demonstrated in impotent attempts to resolve the long-term imbalance between the nation's federal budget and its rising national debt. These attempts became a virtual farce of failure with many acts but no resolution. The scenes included congressional failure to establish a national commission with strong powers to recommend a long-term budget solution; a presidential appointment of a similar commission, followed by failure to win support for bipartisan recommendations from House Republican members; failure of extensive negotiations between President Obama and House Speaker John Boehner for a "grand bargain" (Bai 2012); congressional failure to raise the national debt limit, leading to the first downgrade ever in the nation's bond rating; failure of a "super-committee" in Congress to develop a consensual budget solution; and finally, a post-election lame duck session of Congress to avoid falling off a "fiscal cliff" that would raise taxes, cut spending, possibly lead to a default on the national debt, and probably bring on a new economic recession.

To avoid both the "fiscal cliff" and the debt default, while upholding its fiscal principles, the newly reelected Republican House majority had to resort to semicomic verbal gymnastics and abject fiction. To avoid raising income taxes on the wealthiest 2 percent of the nation, it waited until January 1, 2013, when all taxes were formally increased, and then passed a bill to lower them on all but persons with annual incomes above $400,000–$450,000. Refusing to "raise" the national debt limit, it instead decided to "suspend" it until May (and then still later), while pretending to enforce its decision by holding back congressional paychecks, a measure of doubtful constitutionality or persuasive impact.

As this volume neared publication, some changes were made in the legislative process. The most important was a daring reinterpretation of the filibuster rule in the Senate. The Democratic majority, with little warrant in precedent, and only for confirmation of presidential nominations other than justices of the Supreme Court, audaciously eliminated filibusters and imposed a simple-majority requirement. As an immediate result, the Obama administration could finally fill many stalled significant positions. But the filibuster itself remains unchanged and is used still more often on legislation. And so despite this small sign of reform, we hold to our dire views.

Some observers were also cheered when Congress actually passed a budget, quietly raised the federal debt limit, and ended irrational "sequesters" of appropriations already legislated. But these actions did little to resolve the long-term financial straits of the federal government. From late 2013, the House of Representatives continued to be more focused on partisan conflict than lawmaking, so that the 113th Congress has passed less legislation than any in the modern period. Even before the 2014 elections sealed the present deadlock, there was little prospect of action, even at a slow Madisonian pace, on issues where both parties acknowledge the need for change, such as immigration reform, climate change, tax relief, nuclear proliferation, the repair of America's alliances, or even providing fixes for the technical problems of Obamacare (Montgomery and Helderman 2013; Montgomery 2013).

Article II in the New Constitution

The budget battles illustrate another aspect of the changes in US institutions we lament: increased power of and decreased restraints on the president. The Obama administration clearly shows that Congress is less responsive to presidential legislative initiatives, but its tenure continues a trend toward new executive authority beyond the Constitution's provisions. With the growth of a large administrative state since the New Deal, the presidency has become increasingly autonomous of political parties, Congress, and similar traditional checks (Milkis 1993).

This new power of the president is most evident in the most important decision any nation can make, to engage in war. While the Constitution deliberately left that decision to the legislative branch, the last formal declaration of war by Congress was entry to World War II in 1941. Since then, however, much American blood has been spilled in combat. There were nearly as many American military deaths in Vietnam and Korea combined as in World War I; more American soldiers died in Iraq and Afghanistan than in the Revolution.

As the experience of seven decades demonstrates, the president has assumed the effective power to declare war. Congress did attempt to retrieve some of its constitutional power by passing the War Powers Act of 1973, but it has not imposed binding restraints. Sometimes presidents have asked for congressional approval before committing troops; sometimes they have not. President Harry Truman took the nation to war in Korea without congressional action; President Lyndon Johnson used a questionable, if not exaggerated, naval incident to gain approval for an undeclared war in Vietnam; and President George W. Bush obtained unknowing approval for a conflict of unknown proportions in Iraq. Most recently, because US intervention in the desert nation of Libya was confined to airplanes, President Obama saw no reason to involve Congress at all in decisions that led to the conflict there.

Domestically, too, presidents have used or constructed means to strengthen their powers. "Executive privilege" is one technique, whereby presidents refuse to provide documents or notes on discussions they regard as confidential (Miller Center 2012). Although first used by George Washington in regard to treaty negotiations, the scope of the claim has widened considerably in recent years. Bill Clinton attempted to use the doctrine to shield his sexual behavior, and George W. Bush to hinder investigation of political appointments.

A more worrisome tactic is found in presidential assertions of the power to interpret the law, even to nullify congressional acts without using the constitutional veto power. Such claims were rare and largely rhetorical until Samuel Alito, the future Supreme Court justice, suggested the tactic to President Ronald Reagan. Since then, he and later presidents, particularly George W. Bush, have issued "signing statements," announcing their intention to disregard provisions of the laws they have just signed. Although the practice was condemned by the American Bar Association, Bush went on to set the record, issuing 157 signing statements in which he challenged 1,200 provisions of the laws sent to his desk, including limits on torture of alleged terrorists (Savage 2009).

Another expansion of presidential power has come in the use of recess appointments. The Constitution permits the president to make temporary appointments when the Senate is unavailable to confirm the selections. More recently, presidents have stretched this power to put in place persons who are unlikely to win confirmation, giving them full authority for a year or more to implement policies that have incurred Senate opposition and long delays. President George W. Bush did so, appointing ultra-conservative John Bolton as ambassador to the United Nations, and President Obama filled many positions in this manner, including heads of the new Consumer Financial Protection Agency. Even though the Senate was technically in session, it accepted the president's workaround to its own inaction. The D.C. Court of Appeals, however, ultimately declared this action unconstitutional, an indicator also of an extension of judicial power (Barnes and Mufson 2013).

Claims of new presidential power may even extend to illegal acts. After failing in his constitutional subversion in the Watergate scandal, Richard Nixon still believed in total presidential immunity, later explaining, "if the president does it, it can't be illegal." George W. Bush went substantially further than Nixon, with an extensive attempt to expand the president's political authority. His "war on terror" involved a war on the Constitution, with unprecedented claims of presidential power, an attack on the principle of separation of powers, suspension of the right of habeas corpus for terrorist detainees, repudiation of the Geneva Conventions, and illegal spying on Americans (Walker 2012: 281, 457). Using memorandums from a legal subordinate, the president authorized torture, including waterboarding of suspected terrorists, and confined hundreds of them without trial. Although most of these practices—but not recording of domestic phone calls—have been repudiated by the Obama administration, the Bush precedents and memorandums remain ready for revival by a future, less scrupulous chief executive.

Article III in the New Constitution

The Constitution, we have argued thus far, has been de facto amended in Articles I and II, which specify the character of the legislative and executive branches. Effective amendment has also occurred in Article III, leading to an aggrandized judicial branch.

We are concerned with the impact of Supreme Court decisions on the rules of the game of politics. In particular, while *Bush v. Gore* (2000) legitimized ad hoc incursion by the Court beyond its constitutional domain, we are most concerned with the impact of *Citizens United v. Federal Election Commission* (2010). That decision was "transformative" in the sense that it "struck down decades-old limits on corporate and union spending in elections (including judicial elections) and opened up our political system to a money free-for-all" (Hasen 2010).

Electoral democracy requires fairness in the political process. While fairness surely includes integrity in the rudimentary aspects of election process, such as counting votes—the empirical issue at the heart of *Bush v. Gore*—it also includes higher-order normative considerations, such as the role of money in politics. In terms of the case outcome of *Citizens United,* the issue of how to regulate money in politics in a way consistent with the public interest is reduced to a balancing of First Amendment rights (of the political contributor, whether individual or corporate, and of the political recipient) with the democratic obligation to ensure an accessible political conversation and a fair political process.

Structurally, however, the issue of *Who answers the question of how to regulate money in politics?* is the much more important long-term implication of *Citizens United.* Having the authority to decide this issue is a question of political jurisdiction, the balancing of institutional power between Congress and the Court. At one level, it is a relatively simple equation: *Citizens United* invalidated a portion of a federal statute, the Bipartisan Campaign Reform Act. Invalidating duly enacted acts of legislatures is the very hallmark of judicial activism; here, the Court did so under the claim that the ban on activities by corporate entities (including unions and special organized groups) violated the free speech provisions of the First Amendment to the federal Constitution. This is naked judicial activism with a conservative bent.

This particular judicial activism, however, is an extension of the Court's jurisdictional self-promotion in *Bush v. Gore*. It offends the basic premises of participatory democracy not only through the case outcome, but through the jurisdictional implication as well. In terms of outcome, *Citizens United* corrupted decisionmaking about the balance and nature of access to the national political conversation; similarly, *Bush v. Gore* corrupted the constitutional delegation to states of jurisdiction over election proceedings. In terms of jurisdiction, both cases further positioned the federal judiciary as the ultimate arbiter of political elections.

Because election law regulates the process of democratic accountability, it is the law from which all other law comes. It is the first law corrupted when politics goes dark; efforts to appear legitimate by totalitarian regimes almost always involve manipulation of election law. *Bush v. Gore* and *Citizens United* left the door open to unbounded extraconstitutional judicial authority over election law. Judicial review of the administration of politics—because it goes directly to democratic accountability, directly to the legitimacy of our elected officeholders, and because it is so rife with the potential for election outcome mischief—should be the source of great democratic concern.

In the roughly ten years between *Bush v. Gore* and *Citizens United,* the Court expanded its jurisdiction in election law in unprecedented ways. Writing just after *Bush v. Gore* and almost a decade before *Citizens United,* David Ryden predicted the future:

> Although *Bush v. Gore* dominated the headlines . . . it was only one piece of the story surrounding the Court and the electoral area. In other less-heralded cases—involving campaign finance regulations, primary election voting requirements, and racial redistricting—the Court was compiling a record of unprecedented involvement in the electoral process. [This] flurry of cases . . . made it clearer than ever that the electoral process was now fully constitutionalized. The Court had proven willing to weigh in on virtually any aspect of election law, often with dramatic consequences. (2002: xv)[5]

Bush v. Gore watered down the idea that the Court should be more jurisdictionally circumspect in election law cases; rather, and quite to the contrary, it signaled that under the right circumstances, anything goes—the Court is completely without jurisdictional self-limit. We learn from *Bush v. Gore* that if one petitions the Court at just the right time with just the right outcome in mind, the Court can substitute its will for the will of the legislatures involved, and then simply brand the case "limited to the present circumstances" (as it did in *Bush v. Gore*). Knowing that the Court can do this has created a new normal in electoral jurisprudence, perfectly setting the stage for *Citizens United,* "a major upheaval in First Amendment law" (Tribe 2010) that "profoundly affected the nation's political landscape" (MacColl 2011).

We now have a Supreme Court that twice, within a decade, entered into and corrupted electoral politics, signaling no self-limit respecting its jurisdiction. We find ourselves in a political culture in which the Supreme Court will, as needed, readily ignore the constitutional separation of powers, its own long-standing doctrine of avoidance of constitutional issues, and the reputational impact of judicial interference with election law. In *Citizens United* we see the Court substituting its judgment for the will of the legislature in election law, just as it did in *Bush v. Gore.* The difference, however, is that *Citizens United* is not "limited to the present circumstances." Rather—short of a constitutional amendment[6]—*Citizens United* sets the limits on the regulation of money in politics for generations to come.

Bush v. Gore and *Citizens United* are jurisdictional land grabs. If power is to remain adequately balanced so that separating the political and nonpolitical branches matters for the purposes the Founders intended, then we should have seen a coherent congressional response to protecting the integrity of election law and the democratic accountability it is designed to facilitate. None has been evident, and none is likely.

While the new power of the Supreme Court is most apparent in these electoral law decisions, they are not the only instances. In 2012, the nation breathlessly awaited the Court's verdict on the Obama health care reform. A major shift in US public policy, whatever its merits, had been passed through the normal political process of elections, with concessions to particular interests, and near-classical bargain-and-compromise. A presidential election was pending, with candidates offering a clear choice on the statute. The customary political means of democratic resolution were available and operating. But the unelected Supreme Court would make the decision. A near majority, four justices, was ready to overturn the entire law, confident that congressional deadlock would make it the final arbiter (Liptak 2012).[7]

In the end, through some judicial legerdemain by Chief Justice John Roberts, the law was upheld. His innovative reading allowed the democratic process to go forward; President Obama, by winning reelection, ensured the permanent implementation of the law. But the Court still intruded far into the political process. Even in upholding this extension of the social welfare state, Roberts expanded the Court's jurisdiction and power. He redefined the meaning of "interstate commerce" as used in the Constitution itself; he created a new individual right to abstain from a legal federal obligation; and he constructed new barriers to federal action in response to a major public problem (*National Federation of Independent Business v. Sebelius* 2012). In saving the law, and perhaps the reputation of the Court, Roberts also changed the Constitution. Rather than let the fate of the law depend on the voters and their representatives, the Supreme Court, democratically unaccountable and without a single member who ever served in elected office, wrested new, expanded powers to decide the nation's most vital issues.

How Did This Happen?

Although power can never be eliminated from politics, it can be redistributed. When senators are unable to act, House members' influence will swell. When Congress cannot act, the presidency will be aggrandized. When the elective branches are deadlocked, the judiciary will be less restrained. In this simple observation lies the root of the problem.

The Mixed Heritage of Progressivism

The extraconstitutional changes we lament are the ironic heritage of progressivism. Beginning as pushback to blatant political corruption, early twentieth-century progressivism took many forms. Moral outrage led to local reforms such as the ouster of some urban party machines, changes to election procedures to incorporate use of voter registration and the secret "Australian ballot," and efforts to promote disinterested "good government" through expert, nonpartisan city managers, in lieu of cronyism. At the federal level, new institutional rules included partial replacement of the spoils system by the federal civil service, restrictions on the power of congressional leaders, and the direct election of US senators by the public, in lieu of election by state legislators.

Substantively, the movement was a response to major changes in the American society and economy. By 1920, the population topped 100 million with, for the first time in US history, a majority living in urban areas. Moreover, a fifth—20 million—were foreign-born or children of immigrants. The United States became the world's leading economy and a major military and diplomatic power. Disparities in wealth and income grew, spurring protest and political action among farmers and industrial workers and leading to the organization of farm cooperatives and labor unions.

Equality constituted an underlying theme of these changes as evidenced during the presidencies of Theodore Roosevelt and Woodrow Wilson. Trends toward political equality included female suffrage, ballot reform, and direct senatorial election. In economic policy, the egalitarian thrust was evident in antitrust legislation, regulation of basic industries such as railroads and banks, adoption of the income tax, presidential intervention in strikes to the benefit of wage earners, and a ban on corporate contributions to political campaigns.

Equality may be democracy's core principle, but the "real issue" at the founding was the "declared capacity to rule ourselves." Self-government, wrote the late Wilson Carey McWilliams, "is in some ways the American story" (quoted in Pomper and Weiner 2003: 228). And so progressivism came logically to a further emphasis: "The cure for the ills of democracy is more democracy." If the people collectively were given more power, they would promote a better society. Instead of government by representatives, who might be corrupted, the electorate would, as far as possible, make its own decisions. States adopted methods of direct legislation through initiatives and referendums, and means to chasten wayward public officials through recalls. These measures echoed the Anti-Federalists' preference for direct democracy and their contempt for representation. As Patrick Henry acidly put it, "Are we to go so far as to concede everything to the virtue of Congress? . . . I disdain to hold anything of any man. We ought to cherish that disdain."[8]

The Direct Primary

The most significant long-term progressive reform has been the direct primary, by which voters choose not only their representatives, but also the party nominees for those offices. This reform has had its intended effect: party leaders no longer select the candidates who will face the electors; aspirants must first win the approval of those who vote in state-regulated party primaries. First adopted for state elections in the progressive period, direct primary elections are now also the principal means of choosing presidential candidates.

Yet, like all of life's plans, democracy does not always work as intended. The direct primary system of nominations is a basic source of our present problems. Primaries are not exercises in mass participation or representative of the breadth of popular opinion. They instead facilitate extremism in candidates and polarization in government.

Party polarization is particularly evident among elite voters—those who pay the most attention to politics, vote in primaries, contribute to campaigns, write letters, and shape the legislative environment (Abramowitz 2009; Fiorina and Abrams 2009). As David Mayhew suggests, "ideological activist groups and campaign funding networks have nested within each of the two parties in an unprecedented way recently, infusing special oomph and loyalty into the core of each of the congressional parties. Now, a minority party senator may face trouble back home by not joining a party filibuster on a divisive issue (2010: 1149).

The process of securing primary nominations has increased the intensity of partisan divisions. Primary elections favor more-ideological candidates who are concerned less with success of legislative agendas than with the message itself; they are, then, less likely to seek the compromises that inevitably must accompany effective action. The penalty for moderation was evident in the 2010 and 2012 Senate primaries, particularly among Republicans. Incumbent senators Robert Bennett and Lisa Murkowski, despite their actual conservative positions, were defeated in their party nomination contests, and likely but more moderate winners were rejected in Delaware, Nevada, and Colorado, resulting in the loss of the Senate for the Republicans. In 2012, moderates withdrew or were rejected in Republican primaries in Maine, Indiana, Nebraska, and Missouri. The party reaped the whirlwind: instead of the expected Republican takeover of the Senate, Democrats increased their majority by two seats, despite an unfavorable political lineup. The same effect looms for Republicans in the 2014 primaries, when ideological extremists will likely challenge three Southern but not rabid conservatives. "The war has changed. Republican voters want every fight to be hand-to-hand combat. They don't want to give any ground" (Stuart Rothenberg, quoted in Kane 2013).

In nominations, self-interested ambition will swing Republican aspirants to the right and Democratic contenders to the left. To get nominated, candidates must follow their party bases even if this results in taking more extreme positions than the median voter and perhaps losing support in the general election. The Republican presidential nominating contest in 2012 showed the effect, as Mitt Romney abandoned his previous moderate philosophy to appeal to the conservatives dominant among primary voters. In the early states critical to his party victory, self-identified conservatives composed from 61 percent to 84 percent (in the first critical test, the Iowa caucuses) of the turnout; half of them identified as "very conservative."[9] But Romney was then handicapped in the general election, when he attempted to resume his previous moderate posture.[10]

The ideological devotion required in the direct primary has altered two other important aspects of electoral politics. The first is candidate recruitment. There has been a significant shift in the incentives that motivate political ambition. When parties were stronger, ambition could be furthered by material incentives, including party patronage and the financial rewards of office. But the material rewards have declined considerably; patronage is extremely limited and officeholders are legally held to very rigid standards, not only on the obvious bans on bribery but even on accepting minor gifts or meals. Virtually the only reason to seek a political office now is ideological, because a potential candidate is devoted to a particular policy position.

The second and related aspect is the decline of interparty competition. "As a result of population movement, immigration and party realignment within the electorate, Republicans increasingly are surrounded by other Republicans and Democrats by other Democrats" (Abramowitz 2010: 101). In the House, by 2004, nearly half of all districts were safe seats, and barely more than a fourth were marginal. Candidates therefore must worry more about their primary contests and less about the general election contest, which creates another incentive to cater to the ideological preferences of the small number of primary voters and to give less attention to general interest.

Once elected, ideological representatives have few incentives to moderate their positions, as seen particularly among House Republicans. They are less likely to respond to the blandishments of party leaders because, adopting the pose of the ordinary citizen as legislator, they often pledge to self-imposed term limits. Leaders have fewer rewards to offer, because "earmarks" to benefit local constituencies have been eliminated. Legislators can even reject their own leadership, as House Republicans did regularly in turning down the budget deals worked out by their own Speaker of the House, John Boehner—and were joined in this rigidity by some House Democrats who rejected the initiatives of President Obama.

In an early analysis of primary nominations, V. O. Key observed, "So few votes determine the primary nomination that aspirants for office need only command the loyalties of a relatively small following to win a place on the party ticket" and "primary participants are often by no means representative of the party." The consequences, Key speculated, might be that "the miniscule and unrepresentative primary constituency may . . . handicap the party in polling the maximum party strength in the general election . . . [or] may lead to general election victories embarrassing to the responsible elements of the party as well as impairing the usefulness of the party in the larger cause of the government of the state" (1956: 140–141, 145, 153–154).

Madison obviously knew nothing about primary nominations, but he did have a remedy for extremism. He confidently expected that local fires would be cooled in a temperate continental pool: "The influence of factious leaders may kindle a flame within their particular states, but will be unable to spread a general conflagration through the other states. . . . A rage . . . for any other improper or wicked project will be less apt to pervade the whole body of the union, than a particular member of it" (Pole 2005: 54). But Madison wrote before the modern age of national politics, during which rapid travel and instantaneous communication have destroyed the Founders' firewalls. Rages are easy to ignite while cooling ponds leak.

Political Polarization

Extreme candidates become extremist legislators. With legislators pushed to extreme positions by the primary voters, Congress loses both its moderates and its policy moderation. Indeed, a study of the Congresses elected in 2006 and 2008 shows that almost all House members are more extreme in their policy views than both the median voter and the median member of the same party in their state, a phenomenon of the Senate as well. The result is a distortion of representation: public opinion tends to cluster toward the middle of a bell-shaped curve, while representatives—and voters in primaries—form a contentious bimodal distribution. As a consequence, the electorate gets an odd "leapfrog representation," as extreme Republicans (or Democrats) are eventually defeated by extreme Democrats (or Republicans). In the process, moderate voters are neglected and public policy veers from one pole to the other (Bafumi and Herron 2010).

Polarization also manifests among campaign contributors, large and small, who fuel the extremism of candidates. Extremism and polarization are parts of a self-sustaining vicious cycle that includes not only substantive policy positions, but also the processes of politics. As James Morone writes, "Moral politics transform the political process itself. They draw fierce partisans into the fray and blow right past the usual checks-and-balances, deals and compromises. Who logrolls with evil-doers? . . . [Ideological extremists] scoff at politics as usual, they will not compromise. After all, they see a nation teetering between right and wrong, salvation and perdition" (2003: 10).

The flight from moderation can be measured by party-line voting in Congress, now at record levels. Instead of forging cross-party alliances, Republican and Democratic legislators have become entrenched in deeply opposed camps. An indicator of this intense and increased partisan attitude can be measured in terms of the crossing of party lines on policy votes. In 2010, by one ranking, there were *no* moderates in the Senate. None. Every Republican stood on the conservative side of the aisle, and every Democrat on the liberal side. By contrast, compare that mapping to the 1982 Senate, in which fifty-eight senators could be located between the most liberal Republican and the most conservative Democrat. Incredibly, the House is even more polarized. As recently as 1999, a majority of the House could be located among the party dissidents; by 2010, there were only nine mavericks—a decline to less than 1 percent of members in a decade. The infrequent dissenters "now face pressures from their colleagues; a cold shoulder from the leadership; blistering criticism from the overtly partisan media aligned with each side; and, with growing frequency, primary challenges bankrolled by powerful party interest groups" (Brownstein 2011: 25).[11]

Aside from the accomplishment of their policy goals, legislators have two pathways to success: by achieving prominence in their chamber and by reelection (Mayhew 1974). To navigate either path successfully now requires ideological purity. Within the halls of Congress, party loyalty is rewarded; moderation and compromise are disdained. As Richard Mourdock, the Tea Party winner of the Indiana Republican senatorial primary, scoffed, "I think bipartisanship ought to consist of Democrats coming to the Republican point of view" (Mourdock 2012). Those who defect from the party are likely to be punished by unfavorable committee assignments, denial of election funds, and social ostracism. Bipartisanship is not practiced or even tolerated; it is actively disdained.[12]

The foundation for these results is a marked ideological shift in the mass bases of the parties. Through most of US history, the parties could be described as "umbrellas" or "big tents," general interest groups with a wide ideological range. As recently as 1992, Republican liberals and moderates were as numerous as Republican conservatives, while Democratic liberals were outnumbered two to one by their party's conservatives and moderates (Pomper 1993: 138, tab. 5.2). By 2010, the character of the parties' mass bases had changed considerably. If moderates are excluded, Republican conservatives outnumbered Republican liberals eleven to one (65 percent to 6 percent), while Democratic liberals predominated over conservative Democrats by seven to four (42 percent to 24 percent) (Pew Research Center 2010). These end points are part of a more general trend toward ideological cohesion and separation in the electorate (Weiner 2005). Ideology is now the defining predictor of partisanship, "much more central to voters' partisan identities than social characteristics such as class, gender, and race" (Abramowitz 2010: 59).[13]

Ideological differentiation and party differentiation have become virtually synonymous. "An array of economic, racial and new social and religious values issues have become aligned more visibly to partisanship and to liberal-conservative labels and cues, producing an increasingly issue-based and ideologically based partisan alignment" (Bafumi and Shapiro 2009: 19). As the parties have become more ideologically coherent, their rank-and-file identifiers have also become increasingly antagonistic.[14] This "new partisan voter" both encourages political leaders to appeal to issue extremists within their parties and limits their ability to move toward moderate positions between the parties.

Political polarization reflects other important divisions in American life, particularly in the economy, in location of residence, and in the information environment. Economic differences among Americans are now the most extreme in a century. Those in the top 1 percent of income recipients now garner 18 percent of the nation's total income, a marked gain from relative economic equality from 1960 to 1980 (when the share of the top 1 percent was less than half as large, 8 percent). More broadly, the top tenth of income earners now garner as much of the national income as all other Americans—a disparity not evident since the Great Depression.[15] Significantly, party polarization and income inequality are closely associated, a correlation of .90 since the end of World War II.[16]

Widening economic differences are also reflected in increased residential separation of income groups, which is likely to be reflected in the social separation of Republicans and Democrats. "Mixed income neighborhoods have grown rarer, while affluent and poor neighborhoods have grown more common." From 1970 to 2009, "the share of families living in middle-income neighborhoods dropped from 65 percent to 44 percent" (Reardon and Bischoff 2011). Living apart, and, in turn, not interacting in community or social engagements, partisans in different economic classes are also likely to become more polarized politically.

The Belittling Effect of Bigger Media

The polarization of the United States is furthered by major changes in the information environment of Americans. In times past, the United States had common sources of information. Newspapers generally held to standards of objective journalism, and relied on similar sources such as the Associated Press and the *New York Times*. Three networks dominated television, with large audiences for nightly news programs, and audiences had no choice but to watch such events as the party conventions or major presidential speeches.

That commonality no longer exists. With the advent of electronic media, the print press has declined, new television networks have emerged, and both newspapers and television have become politically aligned. While there is much reporting about politics, there is less useful information. News about politics is now constant, repetitive, virtually inescapable, and, more often than not, trivial. While cable television's nonstop news reporting has surely led to more news, it has not led to better news reporting or increased public understanding. The new media generally neglect interpretative journalism, providing instead short pieces, repeated often but not elaborated. Competition by the media for the public's attention privileges attention-grabbing "breaking news"—sex scandals and other personal transgressions—over the intricacies of policy deliberation. Politicians understand the power of immediacy, and exploit it through a provocative assertion or personal attack. But politicians have been slow to learn the danger of immediacy. Because all statements are now permanently recorded, whether by the media directly, or by a surreptitious cell phone camera, politicians cannot show irresolution or change their position; they must always be wary of questioners and they must expect constant investigation and intrusions on personal privacy. Every candidate must live in fear—sometimes justifiably so—of a "Macaca moment" that will permanently damage their career (Karpf 2010).

A still greater change in the media environment arrived via the Internet—the birthing of blogs, social networks, individual commentary, and wide, often anonymous, discourse. The Internet is often commended for its asserted egalitarian effects. Every computer user now can access unlimited data sources and can participate in political discussion with a single click. Isolated individuals can form communities of interest (Kennedy 2008). Political interests can be rapidly mobilized, and may even achieve revolutionary change, as in the epochal transformations of 2011 in the Middle East.

These opportunities are epitomized by the spreading "blogosphere." Blogs, short for "web logs," are now innumerable, perhaps approaching a billion. An early study found astonishing activity: 100,000 new sources each day and 1.3 million postings daily (Sifry 2006). The Pew Institute testifies to their popularity: one in ten Internet users contributes to a blog, one in three reads blogs,[17] and bloggers are now officially recognized at sites such as the party nominating conventions. These communications include many thousands of explicitly political blogs and millions of political commentaries: in 2010, two out of nine persons online used Facebook, MySpace, or Twitter for politics (Smith 2011). Moreover, there is no evident party bias in blog authorship or readership; Republicans and Democrats use political blogs in similar proportions (Karpf 2008).[18]

Politics as a process, however, is not necessarily the same as democratic politics as a goal. The generally accepted standards of democratic discourse include accurate information, elaboration of arguments, two-sided discussion, identifiable sources, and sufficient time for community discussion (Kelley 1960: chap. 2). Much Internet traffic falls far short of these standards; indeed, the lightning speed of electronic communication favors immediate responses, not considered judgment. Editing, much less considered argument, is largely absent even in the Internet's "political" content. Sources are commonly anonymous, making open exchange impossible while fomenting personal nastiness. Quantitatively, "only a small proportion [of bloggers] focus their coverage on politics, media, government, or technology" (Lenhart and Fox 2006); qualitatively, bloggers and readers largely confine themselves to producing and reading political content consistent with their ideology.

A comprehensive study of 5,000 political blogs found almost no ideological crossovers among these blogs; liberals linked to and read from liberal news sources, while conservatives confined themselves to conservative sources (Adamic and Glance 2005). Similar conclusions came after an extensive study of blog readers in the 2006 congressional elections. These ideologically sealed readers do participate actively in politics, but they do so from "largely cloistered cocoons of cognitive consonance, thereby creating little opportunity for a substantive exchange across partisan or ideological lines" (Lawrence, Sides, and Farrell 2010: 157). Rather than a marketplace of ideas, the blogosphere more closely resembles a vast unordered bazaar where scattered pushcart peddlers hawk jumbled wares to unseen buyers during a thunderstorm. As another observer aptly put it, "Like the Tower of Babel, there is noise, but little communication."[19]

The Power of Money

Money provides the final element in this "tragedy of the commons," where personal ambitions dominate shared interests. Campaigns now redefine the meaning of the word *expensive*. Political aspirants must find huge buckets of dollars—millions in House races, tens of millions in Senate contests, even billions in a presidential race. By portraying politics as a choice of good and evil, interest groups gain more media attention and financial contributions; candidates solicit funds on a similar logic in making their appeals to the most committed groups and individuals.

The *Citizens United* decision did not create these dynamics, but it has deepened their impact. Its most essential effect is to allow anonymous voices other than the candidates to speak very, very loudly throughout a political campaign. These noncandidate voices, devoid of accountability to voters, make political campaigns severely unequal, not only between the parties but also on lines of social class. While political parties, which still have some accountability for their actions, are limited in their contributions, wealthy patrons, corporations, and extravagant groups known as Super PACs (political action committees), are now unlimited in the timing, sources, amounts, or content of their presumed "independent expenditures." These entities can lawfully disguise their funding, and face no electoral consequences for their actions.

With previous restrictions essentially eliminated, campaign spending in the election of 2012 set extravagant records. Even under earlier legal interpretations, spending had been compared to a tube of toothpaste. If one point of access were curbed, the goo would force a different opening. In 2012, the Supreme Court threw away the tube's cap, and the toothpaste of money flowed freely—on the order of $2.3 billion in the presidential race alone.

Free spending, however, does not promote democratic debate. Total spending was almost equal between Obama and Romney in 2012, but the sources of contributions were quite different. While 20 percent of Obama's cash came from small individual contributions, the figure was but a slight 6 percent for Romney; reversing that sourcing, Romney's campaign drew 37 percent of its funding support from outside groups such as Super PACs, which accounted for only 17 percent of Obama's funding support.[20]

The new campaign structure imposed by the Supreme Court furthers the long-term trend toward class inequality. By dint of incumbency and exceptional campaign organization, Obama was able to equalize the 2012 money race. In future races, however, persons of wealth will probably regain their inherent advantages. The record of Super PACs and other "independent" groups in 2012 foretells that future. Conservative groups outspent liberal groups by a ratio of 2.4 to 1; Republicans benefited from this spending, overwhelmingly used for negative campaigning by both camps, by a similar ratio, 2 to 1. These funds came from a tiny and politically unrepresentative group; of over half a billion dollars given by individuals, only 200 donors gave half of all contributions, dividing 71 percent to 29 percent along conservative-liberal lines.[21]

The Future of the New Constitution

America's current political polarization comes at the end of a long causal chain. Progressivism opened the parties to mass participation in the nomination of candidates through the direct primary. Economic and social developments shifted the stakes in politics to national contestation. Ideological realignment made party elites and identifiers more philosophically coherent and elections more consequential. Candidates realized that their ambitions could be best satisfied by raising funds from committed interest groups, gaining media attention by outlandish arguments, and appealing to their ideological brethren in primaries, while gaining more influence once elected by taking more extreme positions.

This environment recalls Madison's prescient concern that a faction will be ready "to sacrifice to its ruling passion or interest, both the public good and the rights of other citizens." What is far less evident is his hope that the world of politics will attract a virtuous elite, "citizens whose wisdom may best discern the true interest of their country, and whose patriotism and love of justice, will be least likely to sacrifice it to temporary or partial considerations" (Pole 2005: 52).

Ambition has changed the pathways of US politics. Ambitious senators now do better as obstructionist filibusterers, blocking legislation and presidential appointments. Ambitious representatives do better by adhering to an uncompromising party program. Presidents do better by expanding their executive authority. The Supreme Court does better by grabbing control of the electoral process. Candidates do better by appealing to ideological voters and to wealthy ideological contributors in primaries. The media and bloggers do better by giving attention to controversy, exaggerating events, and segmenting audiences.

The authors of *The Federalist Papers* acknowledged ambition as the motor of politics, yet feared its potential harm. Ambition would lead inevitably to factions "sown in the nature of man." To preserve liberty and diversity, Madison established the fundamental premise of the Constitution, "that the *causes* of factions cannot be removed; and that relief is only to be sought in the means of controlling its *effects*." The government the Founders constructed abounded in checks and balances, separation of institutions, elections to determine the popular will, and means of change in the Constitution itself.

Modern developments, however, have not only eroded the original controls but also added new blockages to governmental action. The two houses of Congress not only are different in the bases of representation but also operate through diametrically opposite rules. The president, under cover of democratic legitimacy, has assumed far greater powers than foreseen by even rabid Anti-Federalists. The Supreme Court, once characterized by Hamilton as the "least dangerous" branch, has become a dominant supervisor of virtually all policy, most notably electoral rules, processes, and, if conditions are right, outcomes. Economic disparities have created overweening dominance for the faction of "those with property." Technology has dissolved the barriers of space and time that once made a "co-existent passion or interest . . . unable to concert and carry into effect schemes of oppression." Modern media campaigning and unlimited spending allow "unworthy candidates to practice with success the vicious arts, by which elections are too often carried" (Pole 2005: 49–53).

Through a combination of accident, historical evolution, and some deliberate choices, we have gone beyond checks and balances to near deadlock. But, while institutions may become inert, the real world will still present challenges, and government must act. As Hamilton warned, "The vigour of government is essential to the security of liberty; that, in the contemplation of a sound and well-informed judgment, their interests can never be separated; and that a dangerous ambition more often lurks behind the special mask of zeal for the rights of the people, than under the forbidding appearance of zeal for the firmness and efficiency of government" (Pole 2005: 3).

The revival of US political institutions may come through different paths. Perhaps we can revive the Madisonian system, by small tinkering at the perimeter or even large reconstruction of the whole. Perhaps we can imitate other democracies and adopt an American form of parliamentary government, built upon an updated "more responsible two-party system" (American Political Science Association 1950). Or perhaps the future holds a darker transformation.

These speculations await another occasion and fuller thought. We continue to hope, and believe, that US institutions can show their historical resilience in pursuit of effective democratic government. But as we close, we also are haunted by W. B. Yeats's (1920: 19) dark vision of "a second coming," easily applicable to our politics:

> Things fall apart; the centre cannot hold;
> Mere anarchy is loosed upon the world,
> The blood-dimmed tide is loosed, and everywhere
> The ceremony of innocence is drowned;
> The best lack all conviction, while the worst
> Are full of passionate intensity.
> Surely some revelation is at hand.

Notes

1. "Senate May Vet Fewer Nominees," February 1, 2011, http://congress.org /news/2011/02/01/senate_may_vet_fewer_nominees.

2. http://www.hsgac.senate.gov/public/index.cfm?FuseAction=Press.Majority News&ContentRecord_id=78b6fa7d-5056-8059-7609-0e1add6f1f3e (June 23, 2010).

3. *Congressional Quarterly,* http://media.cq.com/media/2011/votestudy_2011.

4. See Nolan McCarty, Keith T. Poole, and Howard Rosenthal, "House 1879–2010: Party Means on Liberal-Conservative Dimension," http://polarizedamerica .com/polarizedamerica.asp. See also Figure 14.6 in this volume.

5. The "flurry of cases" to which Ryden refers (his through 2002, supplemented with all those from then to 2011) covers seven areas on the subject of elections: (1) the interaction between money and free/political speech; (2) redistricting and appor-

tionment; (3) the processes of initiative and referendum; (4) poll photo-identification and proof-of-citizenship requirements; (5) extensions of the preclearance provisions of the Voting Rights Act of 1965; (6) the voter registration process; and (7) unbiased election administration.

6. This has happened only four times: the Eleventh Amendment overturned *Chisholm v. Georgia* (1793) (federal court jurisdiction); the Fourteenth Amendment overturned *Scott v. Sandford* (1857) (equal protection); the Sixteenth Amendment overturned *Pollock v. Farmers' Loan and Trust Co.* (1895) (income tax); and the Twenty-Sixth Amendment overturned *Oregon v. Mitchell* (1970) (eighteen-year-old vote).

7. Congress reversed Supreme Court rulings, on average, in only 2.7 cases between 2000 and 2012, compared to a historical average of 12 reversals during the period 1975–1990.

8. In the Virginia convention to ratify the Constitution, in Elliot 1888, vol. 3: 167.

9. Results of 2012 exit polls in individual states are available at http://elections .nytimes.com/2012/primaries/states. In New Hampshire, conservatives composed only 53 percent of the primary electorate, but a substantial proportion were independents and Democrats permitted to vote in the state's open primary.

10. Romney campaign spokesman Eric Fehrnstrom showed the difficulties in ideological shape-shifting. Asked how his candidate would make the transition from the primaries to the general election, he overcandidly replied, "Well, I think you hit a reset button for the fall campaign. Everything changes. It's almost like an Etch A Sketch. You can kind of shake it up and restart all of [it] over again." See Bingham 2012.

11. The statistics in this paragraph are from the "vote ratings" in Brownstein 2011. In an update for 2012, the pattern was unchanged. Every Republican senator was more conservative than every Democrat. In the House, ten Democrats were more conservative than the most liberal Republican, and five Republicans were more liberal than the most conservative Democrat. See *National Journal* 2012.

12. A reader now interested in the informal institutional rules of the Senate would likely be shocked by the deterioration of the chamber's classic "folkways": apprenticeship, an emphasis on legislative work, specialization, courtesy, reciprocity, and institutional patriotism. See Matthews 1959.

13. See the convincing argument in Abramowitz 2010: chap. 3.

14. Using a 7-point liberal-conservative ideology scale from American National Election Studies (ANES) data, Abramowitz (2009) shows the close relationships: "On average, Democratic identifiers and Democratic-leaning independents placed themselves at 3.3, the Democratic Party at 3.4 and the Republican Party at 5.1 on the scale, while Republican identifiers and Republican-leaning independents placed themselves at 5.3, the Republican Party at 5.2 and the Democratic Party at 2.4 on the scale." Compare to the classic but very different findings in McClosky, Hoffmann, and O'Hara 1960.

15. "(Not) Spreading the Wealth," http://www.washingtonpost.com/wp-srv /special/business/income-inequality, accessed June 18, 2011.

16. McCarty, Poole, and Rosenthal, "House 1879–2010: Party Means on Liberal-Conservative Dimension."

17. For example, see the blogs at http://www.pewinternet.org/topics/blogs.

18. For David Karpf's useful categorization of the electronic universe, see http://blogosphereauthorityindex.com.

19. Marc S. Pomper, personal communication, June 4, 2011.

20. According to the Center for Responsive Politics, at http://www.opensecrets .org/pres12/index.php#out, reporting finance data available through November 26, 2012.

21. "2012 Outside Spending, by Group," http://www.opensecrets.org/outside spending/summ.php?cycle=2012&disp=O&type=P&chrt=V and http://www.open secrets.org/outsidespending/summ.php?cycle=2012&disp=O&type=P&chrt=P; "2012 Super PACs: How Many Donors Give?" http://www.opensecrets.org/outsidespending /donor_stats.php?cycle=2012&type=I.

7

Religious Groups
as a Polarizing Force

Lyman A. Kellstedt and James L. Guth

Throughout US history, political parties have depended on religious groups to help build winning electoral coalitions. Parties and candidates can mobilize the citizenry in their churches, while pastors and denominational leaders can relay partisan cues to their flocks and voice the concerns of their congregants to party elites. Despite the ubiquity of these efforts, changes in the lineup of religious groups with political parties can and do occur. For example, party coalitions have changed dramatically since the end of World War II, and religious groups have played a significant role in those changes. It is no exaggeration to say that religion has been an engine of partisan realignment in the past generation.

The specifics of this realignment are complex. Religious groups have not only shifted their partisan attachments, but also altered these identifications at different times and for different reasons. In addition, cleavages have emerged within some religious denominations and traditions that mirror the partisan polarization so apparent in contemporary US politics. In this chapter we explore these changes and demonstrate that the underlying basis linking religious groups to political parties has changed in a way that has contributed to partisan polarization in the twenty-first century.

Models of the Ties Between
Religious Groups and Political Parties

Although the earliest social scientific studies of the US electorate focused on the socioeconomic differences between the two major parties, they also confirmed the continuing power of religious divisions (Lazarsfeld, Berelson, and Gaudet 1944; Berelson, Lazarsfeld, and McPhee 1954). Catholics were more

157

likely to identify as Democrats than were their Protestant counterparts in every social class. Conversely, Protestants outside the South were more likely to choose the Republican label than were Catholics during the postwar period. Early research in the American National Election Studies (ANES) (Campbell, Gurin, and Miller 1954; Campbell et al. 1960) reached similar conclusions. Even today, political scientists, pollsters, and pundits talk about candidates' pursuit of religious groups, using the common parlances of the "Catholic vote," the "Jewish vote," or the "white Protestant vote." In recent years, as religious groups have multiplied, the "vote" lexicon has extended to Muslims, Mormons, and even Hindus. In other words, the focus has been on religious affiliation.

Recently the analysis of religious voting has become even more complicated. With the rise of the Christian right in the late 1970s and its increasing influence within the Republican Party, observers have implicitly focused on religion as defined by types of belief, often using terms such as "Evangelical," "fundamentalist," "conservative Christian," or "traditionalist Catholic." On the other end of this implicit "belief" dimension are the rising numbers of nonreligious or secular voters. This dimension of religion is often captured rather crudely in the shorthand of the "God gap," measured empirically by the frequency of church attendance (Sullivan 2008: 4–7). Indeed, anyone perusing the burgeoning popular and scholarly literature on religion in US politics is likely to be confused by the vast array of religious classifications and measures used by analysts. Our basic assumption here is that the scheme that best taps all the important facets of religion in the United States will provide the most insight into political behavior.

To construct such a classification requires consideration of two competing views about the critical components of religion in the United States. The first of these—the ethno-religious perspective—stresses categories based on religious belonging, especially membership in religious traditions, and the long-term political conflicts and alliances among those traditions. The second—the restructuring perspective—emphasizes emerging divisions within religious traditions, based on changes in religious belief and behavior, and the consequent formation of new political coalitions across the boundaries of old traditions. Each perspective stresses different facets of religious faith and, thus, different operational measures, and each has virtues for political analysis. We shall outline the basic contentions of each and then proceed to an empirical examination of the evidence on party identification from 1940 to the present.

The Ethno-Religious Model

The earliest social scientific studies of religion and voting behavior relied implicitly on an ethno-religious interpretation of the links between religion and politics in the United States. As developed in more systematic fashion by historians in the 1960s and after, this theory identifies the key religious groups as the historical denominations and religious families born in Europe and later multiplying on the shores of the United States. Presbyterians, Lutherans, Baptists, Episcopalians, Methodists, and myriad other Protestant denominations combined distinct religious worldviews with cultural attributes such as ethnicity, race, or regional location. They were soon joined by other ethno-religious traditions, including Catholics, Jews, and the Eastern Orthodox. All these groups developed distinct political cultures, fostered by religious leaders, houses of worship, and tight-knit ethno-religious neighborhoods. Although the assumptions underlying this analytic framework are often not articulated, historians in the ethnocultural school usually argued that ethno-religious groups held differing worldviews, cultural preferences, and negative reference groups that shaped their distinct views on public policy (McCormick 1974).

Thus, for these historians, religion influenced US politics primarily through affiliation or belonging, with partisan attachments and voting behavior reflecting "political expressions of shared values derived from the voter's membership in, and commitment to, ethnic and religious groups" (Kleppner 1970: 35). Given a two-party system in the context of great diversity, religious groups naturally sought alliances with compatible groups, as each, no matter how large, needed allies to influence electoral politics. And inasmuch as these groups were often in conflict with others, party politics naturally involved competing alliances of ethno-religious groups (Kleppner 1970, 1979; Jensen 1971; Formisano 1983; Swierenga 1990, 2009). In the nineteenth century, a Whig and later Republican coalition of "pietists" faced a Democratic alliance of "liturgicals," joined by Southern white Protestants as a result of the Civil War and Reconstruction (Kleppner 1970, 1979; Jensen 1971).

By the early New Deal years, these coalitions had reorganized; important changes in the religious world had split white Protestant churches into Evangelical and Mainline traditions, but ethno-religious loyalties remained at their base. Mainline Protestants provided much of the Republican Party's leadership, as well as its most faithful voters, whereas Catholics, Jews, black Protestants, and other religious minorities, such as Southern Evangelicals, constituted the bedrock of the Democracy. As a result, early social science research in the 1940s found religious divisions still vital, even in the context of the supposed dominance of class-based New Deal politics (Lazarsfeld, Berelson, and Gaudet 1944; Berelson, Lazarsfeld, and McPhee 1954).

The Restructuring Model

Despite the virtues of the ethno-religious model for historical analysis, many scholars now argue that it has lost much of its explanatory power in contemporary politics. The underlying bases for ethno-religious politics—the powerful social integration within religious traditions, the social isolation of those traditions, and the strong tensions among traditions—have largely vanished (Kleppner 1979). Nevertheless, the political behavior of certain close-knit ethno-religious groups such as black Protestants, Latino Catholics, Jews, and Latter-day Saints suggests that the model may still have relevance. Indeed, even affiliation with churches in the historical Evangelical, Mainline Protestant, or Catholic traditions may still matter politically, in part because such membership is elective today, allowing believers to choose a congenial religious—or even political—environment (Green and Guth 1993; Hout and Fischer 2002; Putnam and Campbell 2010).

Although many analysts still focus on ethno-religious tradition, variously defined (Manza and Brooks 1999; Steensland et al. 2000; Layman 2001; Leege et al. 2002), some sociologists argue that the ethno-religious description of religious life and its political implications have less and less utility. As ascriptive affiliations break down, ethnic and religious neighborhoods disappear, geographic mobility rises, and intermarriage abounds, Americans move freely among religious settings, ignoring historical ties of denomination, ethnicity, region, and even family (Ammerman 1997; Pew Research Religion and Public Life Project 2008; Putnam and Campbell 2010).

For such theorists, it is now belief, not belonging, that serves as the fundamental basis for religious alignments in politics. As people re-sort themselves into congenial theological environments, religion has been restructured into two camps with opposing worldviews, fostered by competing religious institutions and leaders. As Robert Wuthnow (1988) and James Hunter (1991) have argued, old religious traditions have been polarized by theological, social, and cultural conflicts into a conservative, orthodox, or traditionalist faction on one side, and a liberal, progressive, or modernist bloc on the other. And the growing number of secular Americans would seem to represent a natural extension of the liberal or progressive side—perhaps even the product of struggles over restructuring (Hout and Fischer 2002). Wuthnow saw such developments splitting religious institutions, but Hunter, in line with the apocalyptic title of his book *Culture Wars,* projected the divisions into the polity as a threat to social stability. Hunter's assumption was that religious polarization had clearly led to political polarization.

Although scholarly reaction to the "culture wars" thesis has tended to focus on these purported political manifestations (Williams 1997; Fiorina, Abrams, and Pope 2011; Nivoli and Brady 2006), Wuthnow's and Hunter's original formulations were rooted in theological developments, especially the emergence of opposing worldviews. Their competing camps were characterized by alternative belief systems, different religious practices, and adherence to rival religious movements. Indeed, identification of these polarizing forces probably constitutes the most valuable insight of the restructuring perspective.

Although critics are rightly skeptical about extreme statements of the restructuring theory, anecdotal evidence for a milder version is convincing, especially in "old-line" religious institutions in the United States. The religious press reports continual battles between traditionalists and modernists in almost every major Protestant body, as well as in the Catholic Church, in the United States. Conflicts over how best to interpret the Bible in the Southern Baptist Convention, the controversy over the installation of gay bishops in the Episcopal Church, and the continuing factionalism within the United Methodist Church, are just three examples of the many divisions that have arisen within Protestant churches in recent decades.

Although rooted in theology and practice, these struggles also produce opposing moral, social, economic, and political perspectives. Most of the scholarly literature focuses on the political controversies over social issues, such as abortion and gay rights, but there is growing evidence that these theological divisions have come to influence public attitudes on foreign policy issues and economic policy attitudes as well (Guth et al. 2006; Guth 2009). It is true that some culture war theorists overstate the consequent polarization, both within religious institutions and among the mass public: there are centrists in the religious wars, and moderates in the political wars. However, the religious divisions they identify may well influence the structure of electoral politics, if only because both religious and political elites are polarized, thus shaping the cues presented to the public (Guth et al. 1997; Fiorina, Abrams, and Pope 2011).

A third "hybrid" formulation builds on the insights of the ethno-religious and restructuring perspectives, arguing that both religious affiliation and religious beliefs help to explain how religion shapes US politics (Layman 1997, 2001; Guth et al. 1999; Kohut et al. 2000; Guth et al. 2006; Green 2007; Green et al. 2007; Smidt, Kellstedt, and Guth 2009). According to this perspective, some groups behave as the ethno-religious model would suggest, such as Jews, black Protestants, Latino Catholics, and others. Others respond on the basis of contemporary divisions over beliefs, perhaps with religious behavior added to the mix. For the three largest white religious traditions— Evangelical and Mainline Protestantism and European-origin Catholicism— we expect that the interaction of ethno-religious affiliation and restructuring variables provides the best explanation for political choices and behavior. Not only have these traditions had the longest experience in US politics, but they also are the primary battlegrounds for the theological quarrels identified by restructuring theorists. Each includes many traditionalists, those believers who seek to preserve their tradition against the intellectual encroachments of the modern world. On the other side are modernists, who want to adapt beliefs and behaviors to modernity. Still other members (centrists) retain the beliefs and practices characteristic of their tradition, but with less consistency and commitment than do traditionalists. Centrists are often puzzled by the conflicts between traditionalists and modernists and tend to sit on the sidelines in these controversies.

Thus, given the varied impact of ethno-religious forces and restructuring influences among religious groups in the United States, we think a hybrid model is appropriate, emphasizing the study of belonging, believing, and behaving, as well as the interactions of these factors, as the best means to understand the relationship between religion and politics in the United States. We expect that both ethno-religious affiliation and traditionalism in belief and practice are factors that connect people to contemporary party politics, if in varying degrees (Smidt, Kellstedt, and Guth 2009; Layman and Green 2005).

Religious Groups and Party Identification

Delineating the contours of partisan identification by religious groups since 1940 is by no means an easy task. The available data on religious affiliation have various limitations, especially during the early years of the analysis, and finding evidence on religious belief and behavior is even more arduous. Nevertheless, we have produced a time-series for religious affiliation and partisanship that allows us to trace the transformations in partisan religious alignments with some degree of confidence.[1] And although we cannot test the restructuring thesis for the entire period, given the absence of data on religious belief in the earliest years, we have adequate measures for selected years in the 1960s and beyond.

First, we consider the contours of partisan identification by ethno-religious groups since 1940. Table 7.1 reports the net partisan advantage among major ethno-religious traditions from 1940 to 2012. This figure is calculated simply by subtracting the percentage of Democratic identifiers from that of GOP identifiers, with a negative score representing a Democratic advantage and a positive score a Republican one. Independents are excluded from the analysis. As the last row in the table shows (the "national" figures), there has been a small change in the ratio of Republicans to Democrats from 1940–1944 to 2012, with the GOP making slight gains, despite considerable Democratic margins at times during the 1950s, 1960s, and 1970s. The Democratic electoral victories in 2006 and 2008 brought a small spike in Democratic numbers during the 2008 election year, which dwindled to a two-point difference by 2012.

Despite the small national change over this extended period, the partisan transformations of ethno-religious groups were often dramatic. At the beginning of the era, we see a New Deal religious coalition that fits the picture drawn by the early voting studies. In 1940–1944, both white Evangelical and black Protestants identified as Democrats, as did white Catholics, in the latter case by an enormous margin.[2] Jews were also solidly in the Democratic

Table 7.1 Religious Traditions and Party Identification, 1940–2012

	1940–1944	1956–1960	1964–1968	1970–1978	1980–1988	1992	1996	2000	2004	2008	2012	+/-
Evangelical Protestant	-18	-25	-27	-15	0	16	24	26	32	28	36	54
Mainline Protestant	12	9	3	10	15	14	11	11	4	-1	15	3
Black Protestant	-7	-34	-81	-74	-74	-69	-69	-66	-60	-71	-66	-59
Latino Protestant	—	—	—	-35	-30	-27	-15	-15	-4	-5	9	44
White Catholic	-43	-45	-47	-38	-17	-8	-5	-4	-3	-6	1	44
Latino Catholic	—	—	—	-50	-44	-31	-20	-32	-47	-36	-33	17
Latter-day Saints	—	7[a]	-13	14	22	26	47	38	50	55	32	25
Jewish	-27	-63	-67	-58	-48	-46	-44	-39	-47	-50	-62	-35
All other faiths	-5	1	-17	-42	-43	-28	-19	-14	-33	-40	-35	-30
Unaffiliated	-11	-20	-29	-33	-20	-16	-5	-8	-17	-27	-24	-13
National	-8	-17	-26	-20	-13	-8	-2	-3	-4	-9	-2	6

Sources: Gallup, 1940–1944; American National Election Studies (ANES) Panel Study, 1956–1960; ANES Cumulative File, 1964–1988; National Surveys of Religion and Politics, 1992–2012.

Notes: Cell scores represent the percentage Republican minus the percentage Democratic in each religious group.

a. Number less than 20.

camp, as were the small number of religiously unaffiliated citizens, albeit by a smaller margin, but one that increased over the next three decades. On the other side, the large national body of Mainline Protestants was the sole group with a significant Republican advantage. Ethno-religious groups that play a much larger role in contemporary politics (Latino Catholics and Latino Protestants, Latter-day Saints) were too small even to allow estimates, although the "all other faiths" category in Table 7.1 does show a modest Democratic bias. In sum, a modified version of nineteenth-century ethno-religious politics was alive and well in the 1940s.

As we move across time (and across Table 7.1), we see several clear developments in ethno-religious alignments. First, Evangelical affiliation with the Democrats peaks in the early 1960s, thereafter declining to an even split during the Reagan era in the 1980s. In 1992 a GOP advantage appears that continues to grow until 2004, receding only slightly in 2008, before reaching an all-time high in 2012. Thus, by the 1990s, white Evangelicals, composing one-fourth of the public, had come to exhibit a strong Republican preference. At the same time, the rapidly diminishing cohort of their Main-line brethren retained a clear preference for the Republicans up until the election of 2004, but then abandoned that historical position for a true "swing" status, dividing almost evenly in partisan attachments in 2008. They did revert to a solid GOP preference in 2012, however. During the second half of the twentieth century, black Protestants moved from a modest to an over-whelming identification with the Democrats, reaching a peak in the pivotal 1960s and remaining at a very high level thereafter. On the Democratic side, the New Deal alignment of white Catholics was reduced to a very modest edge for the Democrats by 1992. By 2012, white Catholics had become a pivotal swing group in both partisan alignments and elections. The Jewish preference for the Democrats has fluctuated somewhat, but stayed at a high level throughout the period, while the growing ranks of the religiously unaf-filiated have demonstrated a steady Democratic advantage, one that dimin-ished only briefly in the late 1990s before recovering in more recent election years.

By the 1970s, the smaller ethno-religious groups that previously were hard to identify in ANES (and other) surveys had become both more numer-ous and politically consequential. For example, Latino Protestants and Latino Catholics appeared in considerable numbers in the 1970s, identifying gener-ally as Democrats, although the smaller but rapidly growing Protestant con-tingent moved toward the Republicans in the 1990s and later, becoming modestly more Republican in 2012. The same can be said of Latter-day Saints, whose numbers now surpass those of American Jews and generally give the GOP a strong edge in partisan affiliation. At the same time, the catch-all category of "all other faiths" is not only becoming larger, but also solidly Democratic in preference. All in all, by 2012 religious groups had changed their partisan identities substantially; indeed, all the large groups can be said to have "realigned," by any definition of the much-disputed term.

A focus on changes since 1940 is instructive, but it also neglects the timing, and potentially the causes, of the alterations for particular groups. For example, Evangelical Protestants retained a clear identification with the Democratic Party through the 1960s, but began to move away from the Democrats in the 1970s, voting strongly against McGovern in 1972 (Kellstedt et al. 2007: 273). They became evenly divided between the parties in the 1980s, and joined the Republican ranks after 1990 in massive numbers. Meanwhile, partisan change among the Mainline Protestants was slow; not until the 1990s was their love affair with the Republican Party usurped by that of the Evangelicals. For black Protestants, stronger Democratic attachments came swiftly with the civil rights movement in the 1950s and the Civil Rights and Voting Rights Acts of the 1960s. White Catholic migration from Democratic identification began with voting for Nixon in 1972 (Kellstedt et al. 2007), warmed with affection for Reagan in the 1980s (as so-called Reagan Democrats), and has continued gradually ever since. Ironically, Mainline Protestants and white Catholics, historically the bulwarks of the GOP and the Democrats, respectively, have moved from opposite positions to occupy the middle of the partisan spectrum, although the 2012 data suggest that Mainliners may sometimes feel more of a tug from their old allegiance.

In theoretical terms, Table 7.1 suggests that there is still some support for an ethno-religious model linking religion to political behavior. Jews and Latino Catholics join black Protestants as strong supporters of the Democratic Party, suggesting that religion and ethnicity are critical in partisan attachments, as the ethno-religious model would indicate—a conclusion buttressed by the Democratic tendency of other faiths and, perhaps, the religiously unaffiliated. And the Evangelical religious tradition is now clearly tied to the GOP, more strongly than had ever been the case for the Mainline Protestants (the former "Republican Party at prayer"), and at much the same magnitude as Catholicism was tied to the New Deal Democracy.

In sum, religious traditions still differ in their partisan attachments, as the ethno-religious model suggests, but we also need to examine a religious restructuring model to see if it is a better fit in the twenty-first century. Theorists such as Robert Wuthnow and James Hunter have argued that differences in theological worldview are a better explanation for political divisions among religious people than are the old ethno-religious factors. Although they are not always explicit on this point, the restructuring theorists tend to see such divisions as most potent within the large, "older" religious traditions of the United States, such as Evangelical and Mainline Protestants as well as European-origin Catholics. These groups are increasingly acculturated or assimilated, and well-educated, and engage in high rates of intermarriage, thus reducing ethno-religious sources of conflict (Putnam and Campbell 2010). On the other hand, the influences of higher education, critical approaches to religion, modern communication, and globalization have all served to create the very theological divisions described by the restructuring theorists. If restructuring is occurring and has political implications, it should be most evident in the three largest religious traditions in the United States.

Testing the claims of restructuring theory before the 1960s is quite difficult, given the limitations of available data.[3] Table 7.2 examines more recent periods for which ANES and other survey data are available in the form of questions on biblical interpretation and church attendance. Although these items provide only a minimal measure of what we call religious traditionalism, we use them to classify respondents as traditionalists (literalist view of the Bible and regular attendance), modernists (figurative or "mythic" view of the Bible and infrequent attendance), and centrists (intermediate scores on both). Although the measures are quite crude, they are also quite powerful. As Table 7.2 shows, partisan differences between traditionalists and modernists are nonexistent among Evangelicals in the 1960s, but in the next decade there is a clear monotonic tendency for theological traditionalism to reduce Democratic affiliation.[4] In subsequent decades, the partisan split between traditionalist and modernist Evangelicals grows, reaching truly massive proportions in 2004, 2008, and 2012. The large traditionalist contingent favors the GOP over the Democrats by a huge margin, while the much smaller modernist segment is evenly divided. The impetus for these changes is not entirely clear; the traditionalist/modernist divide coincides with the rise of the religious right and its focus on "social" issues, but by 2004 the division is solidified on foreign policy and economic issues as well (Guth et al. 2006).

The historical patterns for Mainline Protestants and white Catholics differ from the pattern for Evangelicals, but in instructive ways. For Mainline Protestants, through the 1980s, traditionalists are the most Republican, while modernists are the least so. (It is church attendance that accounts for this; Mainline regular attenders appear to have picked up partisan cues more readily than their less observant co-religionists.) This Mainline pattern reversed briefly in 1992 before reemerging in 1996 and reaching its highest point in 2012; even so, the differences between Mainline traditionalists and modernists are smaller than those present among Evangelicals. In some ways the most dramatic changes occurred among white Catholics: in the 1960s it was the traditionalist segment that was the most Democratic; by 2004 this group had become much more Republican, but then reverted to an even partisan division in 2008 and 2012. Centrist Catholics moved from a strongly Democratic bias in the 1960s to a virtual tie by the 2000s, while modernist Catholics started the period as strong Democrats, flirted with the GOP in the 1990s, but reverted to their Democratic loyalties after 1996. Thus, if we con-

Table 7.2 Religious Belonging, Beliefs, and Behavior and Partisanship, 1964–2012

	1964–1968	1970–1978	1980–1988	1992	1996	2000	2004	2008	2012	+/–
Evangelical Protestant										
Traditionalist	–21	–8	17	28	44	47	56	56	61	82
Centrist	–36	–12	–7	4	14	13	18	9	28	64
Modernist	–23	–20	–13	–1	–3	2	0	2	2	25
Mainline Protestant										
Traditionalist	9	24	23	15	22	23	25	14	34	25
Centrist	–1	6	15	13	11	5	–3	5	24	25
Modernist	–10	–5	4	23	–3	8	–1	–17	–6	4
White Catholic										
Traditionalist	–48	–37	–18	–9	–6	9	31	–2	1	49
Centrist	–33	–38	–16	–18	–6	–6	–9	0	10	43
Modernist	–33	–47	–18	3	–4	–10	–20	–27	–11	22
National	–16	–20	–13	–8	–2	–3	–4	9	–2	14

Sources: American National Election Studies (ANES) Cumulative File, 1964–1988; National Surveys of Religion and Politics, 1992–2012.
Notes: Cell scores represent the percentage Republican minus the percentage Democratic in each religious group.

fine our attention to the 1990s and after, we see culture war divisions most strongly among Evangelicals, less strikingly among Mainliners, and opening up even among Catholics.

Our findings suggest that the ethno-religious model was a good fit in the 1960s for all three large white religious traditions. There were relatively few partisan divisions by theological orientation, and the ones that appeared among Mainliners and Catholics show that those believers most attached to their religious tradition tended to adhere most strongly to that tradition's historic "party," whether the GOP for the Mainliners or the Democrats for Catholics. This began to change for Evangelicals in the 1970s. Although all three Evangelical subgroups still identified as Democrats, traditionalists were less likely to do so. By the 1980s traditionalists had moved to the Republican side of the partisan ledger and continued this migration after 1990. Evangelical centrists and modernists moved toward the GOP as well, but not as far as did their traditionalist counterparts. Thus, a restructuring model seems to describe contemporary partisan divisions among Evangelicals exceedingly well.

For the Mainline, traditionalist/modernist differences were substantial in the 1970s and 1980s, driven by the relatively high church attendance of the former. This pattern reversed in 1992 before reasserting itself in 1996 and continuing ever since. The largest traditionalist/modernist differences in partisanship in the Mainline occurred in 2012, although the gaps do not approach the size of those among Evangelicals. Still, this seems to be evidence for a restructuring interpretation. For white Catholics, an ethno-religious explanation is a good fit for partisan attachments until 2000, as traditionalist/modernist differences remained minimal and all three white Catholic subgroups moved toward the Republicans at about the same rate. However, in the four presidential elections since 2000, the partisan gap among Catholic theological factions has varied considerably, depending on the candidates and political circumstances. George W. Bush apparently gained ground for the GOP with his persistent direct appeals to Catholic traditionalists, whereas Catholic traditionalists and modernists both seemed to lack enthusiasm for the candidates and policies offered by the Republican and Democratic parties in 2008 and 2012.

In sum, Tables 7.1 and 7.2 show a linkage between religion and party attachments that suggests that an ethno-religious interpretation is appropriate for black and Latino Protestants, Latino Catholics, Jews, smaller religions, and Latter-day Saints throughout the time period. However, for the three largest white religious traditions, a restructuring model works best in recent decades for Evangelicals, since 1996 for Mainline Protestants, and at times since 2000 for white Catholics. Not only have religious groups and subgroups realigned, but the model that best explains religion and partisan ties has changed as well. Finally, the realignment has probably contributed in a variety of ways to greater partisan polarization in the society. Much of this is related to the shifting religious domination of our two major parties, to which we now turn.

Religion and Partisan Coalitions: The Ethno-Religious Perspective

What is the contribution of ethno-religious groups to the coalitions of the two major parties? How has the importance of each group changed over time? Tables 7.3a and 7.3b look at the ethno-religious composition of the Republican and Democratic coalitions, respectively, from 1940 to 2012. As Table 7.3a demonstrates, the Republican coalition was dominated by Mainline Protestants in the 1940s through the 1970s, as this group provided fully one-half of all party identifiers during those decades, a proportion that slipped slightly over the period, first with the relative and then absolute decline in the number of Mainliners. This decline accelerated during the 1980s, when Mainliners still constituted three-eighths of the GOP, through the 2000s, when the tradition contributed about one-fifth of the GOP religious coalition. At the same time, the Evangelical contribution grew from one-sixth of Republican identifiers in 1940–1944 to almost two-fifths in 2008, before dropping slightly in 2012, making Evangelicals by far the largest single religious component of the GOP. These changes in the contributions of the two white Protestant traditions are due to several factors: the massive decline in Mainline affiliation since 1940, the relative stability in Evangelical membership, and of course the Evangelical movement toward the GOP and the decline in Mainline identification with the Republicans noted in previous tables.

As Evangelicals surpassed Mainliners as the dominant religious force in the Republican Party, the contributions of other religious groups also changed. By the 1980s, white Catholics regularly constituted about one-fifth of the Republican coalition (about the same proportion as in the Democratic coalition). Latter-day Saints and Latino Protestants also contributed a small, if growing, number of identifiers, but the GOP attracted few black Protestants, Latino Catholics, Jews, or members of other smaller religions. The religiously unaffiliated make up an increasing percentage of Republican Party adherents over time, reflecting their increases in the population, although their proportions slipped in 2008 back into the single digits and remained there in 2012. In many ways then, the GOP coalition is ethno-religiously homogeneous: Evangelicals, Mainliners, and white Catholics have accounted for at least 75 percent of Republican identifiers.

The Democratic Party ethno-religious coalition looks very different. No single religious group has ever dominated Democrats as Mainline Protestants once did for the GOP, but the larger components of the Democratic alliance

Table 7.3a Religious Affiliation and the Republican Party Coalition, 1940–2012 (percentages)

	1940–1944	1956–1960	1964–1968	1970–1978	1980–1988	1992	1996	2000	2004	2008	2012	+/−
Evangelical Protestant	16	21	23	26	28	34	32	35	38	39	36	20
Mainline Protestant	56	52	53	46	38	22	21	21	19	18	21	−35
Black Protestant	6	4	1	2	2	2	3	2	3	2	3	−3
Latino Protestant	—	—	—	—	1	1	3	2	3	3	4	4
White Catholic	14	13	15	16	19	21	18	19	19	18	18	4
Latino Catholic	—	—	—	1	2	3	3	3	2	4	4	4
Latter-day Saints	—	1	1	3	2	2	2	2	3	5	2	1
Jewish	2	1	1	1	1	1	2	1	1	1	0.4	−1
Unaffiliated	4	6	3	4	7	12	14	13	12	9	9	5
All other faiths	2	2	2	2	2	1	3	3	1	2	2	0
Total	100	100	99	101	102	99	101	101	101	101	99.4	

Sources: Gallup, 1940–1944; American National Election Studies (ANES) Panel Study, 1956–1960; ANES Cumulative File, 1964–1988; National Surveys of Religion and Politics, 1992–2012.

Note: Totals do not always sum to 100 percent due to rounding.

Table 7.3b Religious Affiliation and the Democratic Party Coalition, 1940–2012 (percentages)

	1940–1944	1956–1960	1964–1968	1970–1978	1980–1988	1992	1996	2000	2004	2008	2012	+/-
Evangelical Protestant	22	25	25	23	21	19	17	17	16	16	13	–9
Mainline Protestant	35	28	28	22	20	13	15	15	16	14	13	–22
Black Protestant	4	7	14	13	18	17	16	17	16	16	19	15
Latino Protestant	—	—	—	—	1	3	4	3	3	3	3	3
White Catholic	25	28	24	25	21	21	19	19	18	18	16	–9
Latino Catholic	—	—	—	2	4	5	4	6	7	9	9	7
Latter-day Saints	—	0.3	1	1	1	1	1	1	1	1	1	1
Jewish	6	4	4	4	3	3	4	3	3	2	2	–4
Unaffiliated	5	6	3	6	8	16	16	15	18	16	18	13
All other faiths	3	2	3	3	3	3	5	4	4	5	5	2
Total	100	100.3	102	99	100	101	101	100	102	100	99	

Sources: Gallup, 1940–1944; American National Election Studies (ANES) Panel Study, 1956–1960; ANES Cumulative File, 1964–1988; National Surveys of Religion and Politics, 1992–2012.

Note: Totals do not always sum to 100 percent due to rounding.

have shifted over time. Although we often think of the Democratic Party as an alliance of ethno-religious minorities, it once attracted substantial numbers of the dominant Mainline community. In 1940–1944, for example, Mainline Protestants actually formed a plurality of Democratic identifiers, reflecting their large share of the national population. White Catholics came in next with about a quarter of the Democratic total, followed closely by Evangelicals. These three groups together made up over 80 percent of Democratic identifiers in the 1940s, with other religious groups contributing only small proportions.

Over time the contribution of the three large groups to the Democratic coalition has declined by 40 percentage points; this was especially true for Mainline Protestants, reflecting their declining numbers—even as the remaining Mainliners moved toward Democratic preferences. Meanwhile, black Protestants, Latinos, adherents of other religions, and the unaffiliated became much more important to the Democrats. The Democratic coalition is clearly not dominated by any single religious group and is much more heterogeneous than the Republican alliance. This explains why religious mobilization efforts in campaigns are difficult for Democrats: religious diversity creates problems in identifying common religious appeals, locating Democratic identifiers, and finding successful themes that attract religious voters without alienating others. Finally, the coalition data highlight something that is often missed by pundits: white Catholics, Evangelicals, and Mainliners, despite their declining importance to the Democratic coalition, are still too numerous to ignore.

Religion and Partisan Coalitions:
The Restructuring Perspective

The substantial contributions that the large white religious traditions make to both parties prompt us to look at the contribution that theological factionalism within those traditions makes to each coalition. The evidence is found in Tables 7.4a and 7.4b. On the Republican side, Evangelical traditionalists have significantly increased their "market share" since the 1960s, accounting for about one-fifth of all GOP identifiers since 2004 and bolstered by a substantial number of Evangelical centrists. At the same time, the proportion of Mainline traditionalists and centrists has dropped precipitously: each group by itself constituted almost one-quarter of the national GOP in the 1960s, but by 2012 they accounted for only one-seventh even when combined. Although the white Catholic contribution to the Republican coalition has increased slightly over time, traditionalists have actually lost ground while centrists and modernists have gained a little. Nevertheless, combining all religious traditionalists in Table 7.4a produces almost one-third of GOP identifiers, a proportion buttressed by theological conservatives in other

Table 7.4a Religious Restructuring and the Republican Party Coalition, 1964–2012 (percentage affiliation)

	1964–1968	1970–1978	1980–1988	1992	1996	2000	2004	2008	2012	+/–
Evangelical										
Traditionalist	12	13	11	13	15	18	21	22	20	8
Centrist	9	10	13	15	12	10	12	13	11	2
Modernist	2	3	4	6	6	6	5	5	6	4
Mainline										
Traditionalist	23	17	8	5	5	6	7	5	7	–16
Centrist	24	21	21	8	9	8	6	7	7	–17
Modernist	6	7	9	9	6	7	6	5	6	0
White Catholic										
Traditionalist	9	9	6	5	4	6	7	6	4	–5
Centrist	5	6	10	7	7	7	7	7	10	5
Modernist	1	1	3	9	7	6	6	5	4	3
Total national share	91	87	85	73	71	74	77	75	75	–16
All other	9	13	15	27	29	26	23	25	25	16

Sources: American National Election Studies (ANES) Cumulative File, 1964–1988; National Surveys of Religion and Politics, 1992–2012.

Table 7.4b Religious Restructuring and the Democratic Party Coalition, 1964–2012 (percentage affiliation)

	1964–1968	1970–1978	1980–1988	1992	1996	2000	2004	2008	2012	+/–
Evangelical										
Traditionalist	11	9	6	5	5	5	4	4	3	–8
Centrist	12	11	11	8	8	7	7	8	5	–7
Modernist	2	4	4	5	5	5	5	4	5	3
Mainline										
Traditionalist	10	6	3	3	3	3	3	3	3	–7
Centrist	14	11	11	5	7	6	6	5	4	–10
Modernist	4	5	6	5	6	6	7	6	7	3
White Catholic										
Traditionalist	16	13	6	6	5	4	3	5	4	–12
Centrist	7	10	11	8	8	7	8	6	7	0
Modernist	1	3	4	7	7	8	8	8	5	4
Total national share	77	72	62	52	54	51	51	47	43	–34
All other	23	28	38	48	46	49	49	53	57	34

Sources: American National Election Studies (ANES) Cumulative File, 1964–1988; National Surveys of Religion and Politics, 1992–2012.

groups, such as Latter-day Saints and Latino Protestants. This supplies a very large number of religious traditionalists who are easy to reach: they are in the pews on Sunday and are active members of a variety of religious organizations and groups. Thus, in both numbers and accessibility, traditionalists have a dominant position within the GOP.

Turning to the Democratic coalition, we recall from Table 7.3b that the three major white traditions accounted for 77 percent of Democratic identifiers in the 1960s—about the same as their contribution to the GOP in 2008—but that this proportion declined to only 43 percent in 2012. That "loss" was not shared equally among all theological factions, however. As Table 7.4b demonstrates, the decline in Democratic coalition contributions among Evangelicals, Mainliners, and white Catholics was most significant among theological traditionalists and, to a lesser extent, centrists. This loss was especially notable among traditionalist Catholics, a very significant cohort of the party in the 1960s, but almost minuscule in 2008. Modernists in all three traditions, on the other hand, actually increased slightly their market shares of the Democratic Party. In sum, the data demonstrate the power of Evangelical traditionalists and centrists in the Republican Party and the massive decline in the importance of Mainline Protestants to the GOP. On the Democratic side, the key findings are the heterogeneity of the coalition and the decline in the importance of traditionalist white Catholics to the coalition. The differing religious compositions of the parties explain not only variations in mobilization strategies but also, more fundamentally, different party priorities and policies.

Party Identification over Time:
The Impact of Religious and Demographic Variables

Ethno-religious tradition and religious traditionalism clearly have an impact on partisan attachments. But are they as important as social demographic variables such as education, income, employment status, age, gender, marital status, and region? Contemporary political scientists and sociologists have often been reluctant to consider religion and related cultural factors as primary sources of party identification, preferring to emphasize social class and related economic issue attitudes (e.g., Stonecash 2000). We cannot begin to provide a full assessment of the relative power of religious and demographic factors in structuring party identification, but we can shed some light on the changing influence of cultural and social-class factors. In Table 7.5, we compare the influence of both kinds of variables in explaining party identification in four periods: the late 1960s, the 1980s, 2008, and 2012. These periods were chosen because we have comparable measures of religion and other

Table 7.5 Predicting Republican Party Identification: Religious and Social Demographic Variables, 1964–2012 (ordinary least squares analysis)

	1964–1968	1980–1988	2008	2012
Religious tradition				
Evangelical	.05	.00	.00	.08*
Mainline	.10***	.10***	−.01	.09**
Latino Protestant	—	−.01	−.03*	.02
Black Protestant	−.16***	−.08*	−.11***	−.24***
White Catholic	−.02	.03	−.13***	.02
Latino Catholic	—	−.05***	−.11***	−.09***
Jewish	−.10***	−.06***	−.08***	−.06**
Latter-day Saints	.04**	.05***	.08***	.02
All other faiths	.06***	−.09***	−.08***	−.06**
Unaffiliated/nonreligious	—	—	−.09***	.00
Restructuring measure				
Traditionalism	−.05	.01	.14***	.20***
Interaction terms				
Evangelical Protestant × Traditionalism	.07	.11***	.11***	.07*
Mainline Protestant × Traditionalism	.10**	.07**	−.02	.04
Black Protestant × Traditionalism	.00	−.01	−.11***	−.07*
White Catholic × Traditionalism	−.04	−.06*	.08**	−.01
Socioeconomic status				
Income	.06***	.09***	.07***	.06*
Education	.19***	.05***	−.03*	−.04*
Employed	−.10*	.01	.04**	.02
Unemployed	−.08	.00	−.01	.02
Other demographics				
Age	.07***	−.05***	.01	.08**
Male	.01	.05***	.12***	.16***
Married once	−.03*	−.02	.01	.03
Single never married	−.02	.01	−.04***	−.03
Female homemaker	.01	.04***	.08***	−.01
Region				
Northeast	.11***	.02	−.01	.00
South	−.09***	−.06***	.01	.04
R-squared	.16	.12	.18	.22

Sources: American National Election Studies (ANES) Cumulative File, 1964–1988; National Surveys of Religion and Politics, 2008–2012.
Note: *p* < .05; **p* < .01; ***p* < .001.

variables needed for the analysis. Although the measures in the four regressions in Table 7.5 are not always exactly the same, we have made them as comparable as possible, even where this results in some loss of information.

First, our analysis includes the religious variables used in previous tables: dummy variables for ethno-religious traditions, a traditionalism measure derived from items tapping biblical authority and attendance at religious services, and interaction terms for traditionalism within the four largest traditions in the United States: Evangelical Protestantism, Mainline Protestantism, and black Protestantism, and white Catholicism. The "religiously unaffiliated" are the suppressed reference category for the first two periods, as they were the religious group closest to the mean, but in 2008 and 2012 that role fell to the subgroup of "unaffiliated but religious" respondents.[5] Age, income, and education are measured in linear fashion, while the remaining variables in the table (male, married once, single never married, female homemaker, employed, unemployed, Northeast and South [regional residence]) are included as dummy variables.

Despite the limitations of our religious traditionalism measure, the results are quite instructive. In the 1960s, some of the ethno-religious tradition variables are significant predictors of party identification. Black Protestants and Jews are significantly more Democratic, while the Mainline Protestant coefficient is solidly Republican. Evangelical Protestants also lean Republican, once the social-class and region variables are in the table, although previous bivariate results showed Evangelicals (predominantly Southern and working-class) still in the Democratic camp at that time. Note that religious traditionalism has no significant effect by itself, although it tends to work in a Democratic direction. The interaction terms do show results: Mainline Protestants who had a literal view of the Bible and who attended church regularly were more Republican in partisanship, even when other variables are controlled for. On the other hand, biblical literalists and regularly church-attending white Catholics leaned in a Democratic direction, although the coefficient does not reach statistical significance. Clearly, theological restructuring was not a major force in the 1960s in explaining partisan alignments, as its clear influence is in the tendency for the most observant to support more strongly their tradition's "normative" party, the GOP for Mainliners and the Democrats for Catholics.

The contours of the New Deal party system are clearly seen in the impact of the socioeconomic and demographic variables. Higher education and income are significant contributors to Republican identification, while older citizens also tended to be more Republican. The historic regional bases for the party system were also still in evidence in the 1960s, as residents of the Northeast were somewhat more Republican, and Southerners still adhered to the old "solid Democratic South." Married respondents were slightly more Democratic, but no gender gap was in evidence. All in all, the results show that both ethno-religious factors and socioeconomic variables made substantial contributions to party identification.

The 1980s are critical both for the rise of Reagan Republicanism and the Christian right, and for the beginning of religious restructuring and the displacing, in part, of the old ethno-religious alignments. Do we see new sources of party cleavages in the data? In the 1980s, the coefficients for the ethno-religious traditions change only modestly, with the addition of Democratic Latino Catholics in larger numbers. Religious traditionalism does not have any pro-Republican effect across the sample, but shows up as a significant interaction among Evangelicals as the most orthodox and observant become substantially more Republican. At the same time, the size of the interaction effect among Mainliners drops somewhat, but is still significant. Among white Catholics, on the other hand, traditionalists are still significantly more Democratic when the remaining variables are taken into account. Thus, in the 1980s the GOP retains its ethno-religious core of Mainliners, also picking up traditionalist Evangelicals and Latter-day Saints, while the Democrats attract an expanding coalition of religious minorities, as the "all other faiths" category leans toward the party of Roosevelt.

As religious influences shifted during the 1980s, the old socioeconomic and demographic markers lost some of their power. Higher education drops significantly as a predictor of GOP identification, while income becomes slightly stronger. Although Southern residence still mildly predicts more Democratic tendencies, Northeasterners no longer lean toward the GOP. Interestingly, however, there is now a gender gap, with males more Republican, and a "homemaker" gap, with stay-at-home moms more Republican as well. Older citizens are now more Democratic when everything else is in the equation. Note that the variance explained by the model decreases from the 1960s, indicating that party identification was not as well explained by the model variables as it was earlier. Still, religious tradition and socioeconomic status remain significant predictors, with some new help from gender and family status.

When we turn to 2008 the results are quite different. First, the coefficients for the Evangelical and Mainline Protestant religious traditions are both virtually zero, indicating that these religious affiliations have no added explanatory power once the other variables are in the equation. On the other hand, significant coefficients appear for all the ethno-religious "minorities": black Protestants, Latino Catholics and Protestants, Jews, all other faiths, and the unaffiliated/nonreligious (secular) citizens are all more Democratic, while Latter-day Saints are more Republican. The coefficient for white Catholics returns to a significant Democratic predictor, although this results from the effects of other variables in the equation. A second significant development is the clear intrusion of religious traditionalism into the explanation, working in favor of the GOP in the sample as a whole and having an added effect among Evangelicals and white Catholics, but not among Mainliners. Only among black Protestants does religious traditionalism reinforce the impact of ethnocultural identity. Thus, religious "restructuring" does seem to have had a considerable impact on party divisions for some groups, but, for others, ethno-religious identity remains more important.

What about the competing socioeconomic and demographic influences? While higher income still predicts somewhat stronger GOP identification, in 2008 higher levels of education actually become a slightly pro-Democratic influence, perhaps confirming the expectations of some party theorists that the future of the party lies with the highly educated, technocratic, and professional classes (Judis and Teixeira 2002). The gender gap continues to rise in importance, as men are much more Republican, joined by female homemakers, while single Americans are more prone to identify as Democrats. At the same time that family status indicators are rising in importance (and deserve much more attention), region has now been reduced to insignificance, with the coefficients for Northeastern and Southern residence virtually zero, as is the coefficient for age. On balance, then, the evidence suggests that ethno-religious status, religious traditionalism, and family status have become more powerful predictors of party identification, while socioeconomic status and region have declined in importance. Note that the variance explained in 2008 is larger than in the 1960s or 1980s.

The 2012 results largely confirm those of 2008, but with some variation. Despite the growing influence of religious traditionalism on GOP identification, Evangelical and Mainline affiliation also predict stronger Republican ties. In contrast, Jews, members of other faiths, Latino Catholics, and in particular black Protestants maintain their links to the Democrats, even after everything else is taken into account. Perhaps surprisingly, in a year that a Latter-day Saint headed the GOP ticket, Mormon affiliation did not add any predictive power to GOP identification—for the only time in the periods covered by the table.

The Ideological Source of Religious Differences and Partisan Polarization

We have demonstrated that ethno-religious tradition and religious restructuring are reflected in the composition of "parties in the electorate" in the United States, but what are the fundamental sources of these differences? Much of the literature on polarization focuses on ideological divisions, with scholars variously emphasizing differences on social, economic, or even foreign policy attitudes. Those who see emerging religious divisions tend to focus on social issues, such as abortion, gay rights, or stem cell research, but there is evidence that religious groups have distinctive positions on other issues that may also contribute to the characteristic party alignments we have shown (Guth et al. 2006).

As a first cut at such ideological differences among religious groups, we draw on the 2008 and 2012 iterations of the National Survey of Religion and Politics, with large batteries of religious and issue items. We calculated three issue scales, covering respondents' positions on social, foreign policy, and economic welfare issues. *Social conservatism* includes culture war issues such as abortion, gay rights, and same-sex marriage. *Foreign policy militancy* includes items such as support for the Iraq War (in 2008), priority of maintaining a strong military, and preference for Israel over the Arabs in the Middle East (for more documentation and discussion, see Guth 2010). Finally, *welfare conservatism* includes several items on desire for more government services, higher taxes, expanded health care, and greater aid for the poor.[6]

The overall patterns can be summarized quite easily. Evangelical Protestants anchored the conservative end of all three scales, buttressed by their Latter-day Saint allies. The liberal pole of each scale was held by the unaffiliated or secular population joined by black Protestants and Latino Catholics (except for the social traditionalism measure), Jews (except on foreign policy), and all other faiths. Mainline Protestants, white Catholics, and Latino Protestants fell in the middle of the scales in both years. And within the three large white religious traditions, theological understandings produced the expected differences: traditionalists were the most conservative on all three scales and modernists the most liberal. Combining ethno-religious and restructuring categories, Evangelical traditionalists were the most conservative across the board; agnostics and atheists were the most liberal.

As a way of summarizing ideological divisions, we used two procedures. First, we ran a secondary factor analysis of the three issue scales, producing a single measure of *issue ideology*. As a second check, we used the z-scores for *self-identified ideology*. Reassuringly, both produce very similar patterns among the religious groups, with Evangelicals and Latter-day Saints being the most conservative across the ethno-religious spectrum, Mainline Protestants and Catholics situated in the center, and most other faiths and the unaffiliated situated well to the left. In restructuring terms, Evangelical traditionalists almost define the conservative pole, on both the issue measure and self-identification, while Jews, other faiths, seculars, and agnostics/atheists are far to the left. On both summary measures, black Protestants look more conservative than one might expect, reflecting their conservatism on social issues (for a detailed presentation of the 2008 results, see Kellstedt and Guth 2011).

To recapitulate: the evidence suggests that the religious divisions we have discovered in party identification are at least partially the result of the distinctive issue positions taken by religious groups. Evangelicals, and especially their large traditionalist contingent, have strongly conservative positions across the board on social, foreign, and welfare policies, while many religious minorities, as well as the increasing cohort of secular citizens, hold distinctly liberal positions on these same dimensions. Mainline and Catholic identifiers tend toward more centrist positions, but traditionalists among them move toward the right, and modernists toward the left. And although we cannot demonstrate conclusively that such differences explain the growing political polarization in US politics, there is certainly a lot of circumstantial evidence pointing in that direction, as Evangelical traditionalists have become a growing presence in the GOP, and religious minorities and seculars have enhanced their position among Democrats.

Are religious influences fully mediated by the issue preferences and ideological identities of religious groups? Or are there still purely ethno-religious factors that account for some degree of party attachment? Or, perhaps, does religious traditionalism exercise some additional direct influence over party identification? In Table 7.6, we address these questions with an ordinary least squares regression, including religious and other variables, using the expanded measures available in both the 2008 and 2012 iterations of the National Survey of Religion and Politics.

The influence of ideological factors in explaining party identification in both 2008 and 2012 is very impressive. Welfare conservatism, foreign policy militancy, and social traditionalism all have very solid impacts on party identification, as does a residual score for the part of self-identified ideology not accounted for by issue attitudes.[7] On the other hand, many of the ethno-religious tradition dummies drop out of the analysis, although in 2008 Latter-day Saints are more Republican than their other attitudes and traits would predict and white Catholics, along with most religious minorities, are more Democratic, indicating an additional influence of ethno-religious status. This tendency is especially strong for black Protestants. In 2012, however, only Jewish, Latino Catholic, and, once again, black Protestant affiliation adds predictive power—all of the other religious traditions drop out. In a similar way, secular and agnostic/atheist respondents do not show any greater Democratic propensities, once other factors are in the equation. And although the religious traditionalism measure has a sign in the right direction, the coefficient is not statistically significant in predicting greater Republican identification in either year, suggesting that the impact of traditionalism seen at the bivariate level is mediated by ideological conservatism.[8] Note once again the extremely modest and almost haphazard impact of demographic factors. When issues and ideology are in the equation, higher education has a mildly pro-GOP effect in 2008, the South is slightly more Republican in 2012, women are more Democratic in 2012, and the employment status variables have a small effect in 2008. Each of the equations explains well over two-fifths of the variance, an impressive performance.

Table 7.6 Predicting Republican Identification: Issues, Religious Groups, and Demographic Influences, 2008–2012 (betas, ordinary least squares analysis)

	2008	2012
Ideological factors		
Welfare conservatism	.271***	.315***
Foreign policy militancy	.237***	.090***
Social traditionalism	.209***	.215***
Self-identification (residual)	.200***	.268***
Ethno-religious tradition		
Evangelical	−.004	−.080
Mainline	−.014	−.030
White Catholic	−.065**	−.085
Latter-day Saints	.033*	−.030
Latino Protestant	−.015	.030
Black Protestant	−.208***	−.241***
Latino Catholic	−.045*	−.086*
Jews	−.043**	−.056**
Other non-Christian	−.033*	−.135
Secular	.018	.027
Agnostic/atheist	.009	.020
Restructuring measure		
Religious traditionalism	.028	.026
Socioeconomic and other demographics		
Education	.035*	.013
Income	.020	.039
Female	−.012	−.090***
Unemployed/student	−.029*	.024
Homemaker (female)	.042**	−.021
Northeast	−.004	.026
South	−.015	.046*
Adjusted R-squared	.403	.421

Sources: National Survey of Religion and Politics, 2008 ($N = 4,000$); National Survey of Religion and Politics, 2012 ($N = 2,002$).
Note: $*p < .05$; $**p < .01$; $***p < .001$.

Conclusion

Religion has served as one of the key social bases of partisan attachments throughout US history. Yet the nature of the ties between religious groups and the major parties has changed over time. For example, it is a commonplace that white Southern Protestants have abandoned their historical linkages to the Democratic Party and joined the ranks of the Republicans, and that white Catholics have lessened their ties to the Democrats in recent decades. This chapter has documented the partisan "journeys" of the major religious groups in this country. The partisan transformations have often been dramatic. Evangelical Protestants have left their previous home in the Democratic Party and become the keystone in the GOP coalition, led by their traditionalist core. Mainline Protestants have lost their preeminence in the Republican Party, partly due to shrinking numbers and partly to decreasing party loyalty. Together with white Catholics, their old opponents and the historical centerpiece of the New Deal coalition, Mainliners have at times become a swing group in national elections, closely divided between Republican and Democratic identifiers. Meanwhile, black Protestants have moved from modest to strong identification with the party of Roosevelt, Kennedy, and Obama. Latinos, Catholic and Protestant alike, were of little political consequence two generations ago, but their growing numbers make them a force in the Democratic Party today. Although their theological traditionalism and social conservatism have often drawn Latino Protestants toward the GOP, especially under George W. Bush, that propensity may be encouraged or thwarted by current Republican strategies on immigration legislation now before Congress. Throughout the time period that we have examined, smaller religious groups have favored the Democrats (with the exception of Latter-day Saints). Jews have been strong supporters of the Democrats, as have members of other small religious faiths and, increasingly, the growing numbers of the unaffiliated.

Party coalitions look much different today than they did in the 1940s. The numerically dominant Mainline Protestants overwhelmed all other groups on the Republican side until the 1990s, and were the largest single group within the Democratic coalition as well until the 1970s. Their demise in the coalitions of both parties has been dramatic. For the Republicans, Evangelicals are now the senior partner in their religious coalition. The Democrats' coalition is marked by extreme heterogeneity, with several religious and nonreligious groups contributing significant numbers to the party ranks, and expecting a significant internal role as well. Indeed, the heated controversy at the 2012 Democratic National Convention over inserting both a mention of God and recognition of Jerusalem as Israel's capital in the party platform highlighted the competing forces at work.

What is less obvious is the exact role that religious affiliation and religious beliefs and behaviors have played in these processes of transformation. We have argued that religious belonging has been the driving force in partisan attachments for most religious groups throughout US history. For black Protestants, Latino Protestants and Catholics, Jews, Mormons, and other smaller religious groups (Muslims, Buddhists, and Unitarians, to name only a few), affiliation with the group is associated with partisan ties. This model of party attachments—the ethno-religious model—was the basis of partisanship in the nineteenth century (Kleppner 1979) and remains so today for these groups. However, for the three largest white religious traditions—Evangelical and Mainline Protestantism and white Catholicism—the basis for party ties has changed in the past generation.

Differences of religious belief and behavior within these traditions, produced by religious restructuring, have become central to partisan attachments. Traditionalists have moved most dramatically in a Republican direction, while their modernist counterparts have resisted this trend. These developments have been most evident among Evangelicals, somewhat weaker among Mainliners, and still developing among white Catholics. All in all, the best explanatory fit for current trends is a hybrid model, given the importance of both ethno-religious tradition, especially for smaller "outgroups," and theological traditionalism, which has increasingly come to shape the partisan choices of the major white traditions.

Most, but not all, of these religious influences on partisanship appear to be mediated by issue attitudes and ideology. Many observers have focused on how social issues, such as abortion, gay rights, and similar questions, have moved religious traditionalists toward the GOP, and religious liberals and secular citizens toward the Democrats, contributing to partisan polarization. But we have demonstrated a broader influence for religious traditionalism, arguing that it also produces attitudes favoring a militant foreign policy and conservative economic welfare policies, benefiting the GOP and furthering partisan polarization by creating a vast constituency of thoroughgoing conservatives, dominated numerically by Evangelicals, Latter-day Saints, and traditionalists from other groups. On the other side, Democrats draw on the support of thoroughgoing liberals, who are numerous in the party's ethno-religious minorities and among the growing ranks of the secular population. This contingent is buttressed to some degree by religious modernists from the Mainline Protestant and white Catholic traditions, who nevertheless are often more left-center than left on these policy dimensions. However these divisions develop in the future, no scholar can afford to tackle the analysis of partisanship in the contemporary United States without accounting for religious factors.

Appendix on Data Sources

Data sources for this chapter include (1) Gallup surveys from 1940 to 1944 (available at http://brain.gallup.com/documents/decadebreakout1940.aspx); (2) the American National Election Studies (ANES) Panel Study covering 1956 to 1960; (3) the ANES Cumulative File covering 1964 to 1988; and (4) the National Surveys of Religion and Politics conducted at the University of Akron, covering 1992 to 2012.

Most Gallup surveys, beginning in 1936, do not include in-depth measures of religious affiliation. Only rarely are belief measures included, although church attendance is regularly measured. When affiliation questions are included, they take the form of "religious family" categories, such as Baptist, Methodist, Presbyterian, or

Lutheran. Assigning these families to the modern Protestant Evangelical or Mainline traditions is somewhat problematic. Although most Methodists, Presbyterians, and Lutherans are affiliated with Mainline churches, some are affiliated with smaller Evangelical denominations. In the early surveys, however, all have to be assigned to the Mainline. White Baptists, on the other hand, must be assigned as Evangelical, despite the existence of Mainline Baptist denominations. A somewhat similar problem exists in working with the ANES data, whether the 1956–1960 Panel Study or the 1964–1988 Cumulative File. The ANES religious affiliation codes for these periods are also not very specific, although they are more detailed than those of Gallup. A church attendance item is included in each survey, but only one religious belief measure is available—a Bible item—and then only in 1964 and 1968 and again in 1980 and subsequent years.

The National Surveys on Religion and Politics, beginning in 1992, have detailed religious affiliation codes and many belief and behavior items (see Smidt, Kellstedt, and Guth 2009: chap. 1). As a result, we have much greater confidence in our findings since 1992. Yet, despite the caveats about earlier surveys, it is worth the effort to go back as far as possible in time to examine the links between religion and partisan attachments.

Notes

1. On our data sources, see the appendix to this chapter. For more discussion of the problems involved in this exercise, see Kellstedt et al. 2007.

2. By contemporary standards, black Protestants in this period seem almost evenly divided between the parties, not yet having completely abandoned the party of Lincoln.

3. We have demonstrated earlier that in 1944 there was little evidence of any politically relevant religious divisions within the major traditions in presidential vote (Kellstedt et al. 2007: 288–289).

4. No Bible item was available in the ANES in the 1970s, so traditionalists are simply frequent church attenders.

5. These are the substantial number of citizens who claim no religious affiliation but attend church frequently and have an orthodox view of the Bible.

6. The three scales differ slightly in 2008 and 2012 because of the availability of items. All the alpha reliability coefficients for the social, foreign policy militancy, and welfare policy scales in both 2008 and 2012 exceed .70.

7. It is interesting to note that within the three large white ethno-religious traditions the issue scores have varying degrees of influence over party identification. In a series of analyses not reported in this chapter we found that in 2008 the foreign policy score had the strongest impact for Evangelicals, followed by social issues, and then welfare conservatism. Among Mainliners, the order was reversed, with economic policy most important, followed by foreign policy, and then social issues. For white Catholics, foreign policy was most important, followed closely by welfare issues, and at a considerable distance by social issues. In 2012, perhaps reflecting the end of the Iraq War and the winding down of the US effort in Afghanistan, foreign policy was not as potent a predictor.

8. Nor does traditionalism interact with ethno-religious tradition to produce higher levels of Republican or Democratic affiliation. In preliminary analyses, we included interaction terms, but none approached statistical significance and thus they were omitted from the analysis reported in Table 7.6.

8

Women's Political Leadership Roles

Barbara C. Burrell

In this chapter, I explore the ways in which "gender politics" is related to and impacts contemporary partisan polarization. Gender politics refers to differences between men and women in their engagement in political activities and how the public perceives those activities depending on whether men or women are performing them. Gender politics is a multidimensional aspect of partisan politics. After a broader introduction, I focus on one particular aspect of that politics—political leadership. Differing cultures in the Democratic and Republican parties have affected their approaches to achieving equity between men and women in public office and leadership within their organizations. There is a growing partisan gap in the presence of women within the elected legislative caucuses of the Democratic Party and the Republican Party. Further, in the aftermath of the 2010 congressional elections, the highlighting of party policy differences—by showcasing female members as ideological partisans advancing their own party's policies through a women's frame of reference and engaging in strong criticism of the opposition party's policies—became a common practice. I describe this practice and consider whether it is a harbinger of change. I conclude with some reflection on the possible effect of polarization on women's ambitions as political leaders.

Historical Evolution of Partisan Gender Gaps

In a 1991 *New Republic* article titled "Parenthood," Christopher Matthews dubbed the Democratic Party the "mommy party" and the Republican Party the "daddy party," appellations that have become common descriptions of these organizations, at least in popular commentary. Matthews's emphasis was on their respective policy interests and rhetoric around those concerns. From a more academic perspective, Christina Wolbrecht has argued that "the two American parties have become polarized over the issue of women's rights, when once there was at the least consensus and, prior to that, perhaps even the opposite alignment." The Democratic Party, Wolbrecht tells us, "stands as the party of women's rights, aligned with feminist organizations and most likely to support feminist policy initiatives. The Republican Party, on the other hand, has generally staked out an opposing position, distancing itself from feminism and siding with those who prefer more traditional women's roles and responsibilities" (2000: 3, 6). Scholar Jo Freeman (1996) has also noted that "feminism has become highly identified with the Democratic Party and anti-feminism with the Republican Party" (see also Freeman 1987). Writing in 1996, she noted,

> In the last 25 years, the two major parties have undergone a realignment, on at least one cluster of issues. They are now polarized around feminism and the reaction to it, with different programs and different visions of how to deal with sex and the role of women. The Republicans are now the party of traditional family values, while Democrats are following the feminist agenda of making the personal, political. Republican feminists are left with an onerous choice: they can stay in the party and suppress their feminist concerns, or they can leave.

More recent research by Brian Frederick on the voting behavior of Democratic and Republican senators provides further evidence of the polarized nature of the two parties on women's issues. As Frederick notes, "Electing Democrats to the Senate regardless of their gender will produce a massive swing in support for women's issues" (2011: 205) (at least as measured from a liberal women's rights perspective).

As these observations illustrate, partisan polarization encompasses gender politics in contemporary times. A number of complex factors are involved in the gender distinctions between Democrats and Republicans. Three lenses regarding the political parties and gender politics have received particular attention: (1) differences within the general public between men's and women's opinions on public policy issues, party identification, and voting behavior; (2) the parties' positions on issues of particular concern to women, often referred to as women's issues; and (3) the recruitment of women to elective office and political leadership positions within both major parties. All three of these aspects of gender politics have relevance in considerations of polarization between the parties, especially in the decades since the commencement of the second women's rights movement in the late 1960s and particularly in recent election cycles.

A substantial amount of literature has explored the nature of the "gender gap" within the general public regarding issue attitudes and voting behavior and how this gap became a political phenomenon (see especially Whitaker 2008) affecting party politics. The idea of a gender gap became part of the US political landscape during the 1980 presidential election. The gender gap was not a feature of political commentary prior to Ronald Reagan's election that year, nor were women viewed as a political force. It was not that men and women had never diverged in their perspectives on public policy issues or voting behavior prior to this election; rather, a group seeking change noted a difference in the votes of men and women after the 1980 election and made the gender gap a political story that has affected political history.

Though Reagan handily won the 1980 election, that election experienced an 8 percent gender gap in votes for the winning candidate, with 46 percent of women voting for Reagan compared with 54 percent of men. The votes of women had been noted during the campaign, but the idea of a women's bloc had primarily been ignored or dismissed. Adam Clymer was the first journalist to address the difference in Reagan's support between men and women, in a post-election analysis piece in the *New York Times*. Clymer reported that "Mr. Reagan's long-standing difficulties in persuading women to vote for him . . . held down his percentages again Tuesday. . . . The [*New York Times* and CBS News] poll suggested that both fear about war and opposition to the Equal Rights Amendment handicapped Mr. Reagan's bid for their support" (1980: 18).

As Kathy Bonk (1988: 85) recounts the story, Eleanor Smeal, president of the National Organization for Women (NOW), recognized the political significance of Clymer's story. At that time, NOW and other women's rights organizations were discouraged over the failure of campaigns to get the Equal Rights Amendment passed. The gender gap in the 1980 election gave these groups a "hook" for media attention and ammunition to press politicians to vote for the amendment. Building on Clymer's story, NOW headlined the December–January (1980–1981) issue of its newspaper with an article titled "Women Vote Differently Than Men, Feminist Bloc Emerges in 1980 Elections." The article went on to state that "the NYT/CBS poll reported that 8 percent fewer women (46 percent) voted for Reagan than did men (54 percent). ABC's poll was similar. This difference calculated in actual votes, amounts to a net loss of 3.3 million female votes for Reagan." NOW edited the article into op-ed pieces that Smeal wrote and that were reprinted in both the *Chicago Sun Times* and the *Chicago Tribune*. The target audience: Illinois legislators who would be voting on the Equal Rights Amendment during the next fifteen months (86). The term "gender gap" first appeared in the media in a Judy Mann piece in the *Washington Post* in

1981. Since that time it has been a major feature of electoral politics in the United States.

Academic audiences were introduced to the gender gap when Kathleen Frankovic published "Sex and Politics: New Alignments, Old Issues" in *Political Science and Politics* in 1982. Noting the lack of earlier scholarly interest in sex differences in public opinion, Frankovic focused her attention on the appearance and persistence of sex differences in basic political evaluation of Reagan's performance. Not only had women been much less in favor of Reagan over Carter in the 1980 election compared to men (women had evenly divided their vote between the two candidates), but they also continued to express greater disapproval of Reagan's policies and performance as president than did men. Frankovic's analysis of public opinion polls led her to conclude that it was not feminist issues but rather issues of war, peace, and the environment, and Reagan's stands on these issues, that accounted for his lower levels of support among women compared to men.

Systemic research on the origins and nature of the gender gap in party identification and voting behavior since Frankovic's publication provides a number of prominent findings. First, trends in the gender gap in party identification have been the result of the movement of men to the Republican Party. Karen Kaufmann, John Petrocik, and Daron Shaw, in their review of myths about the gender gap, note that "the proportion of women shifting to the Democrats has been comparatively modest; by and large women have retained the party identification and voting profile of women from fifty years ago" (2008: 98). Further, as Virginia Sapiro and Shauna Shamas have emphasized, differences in men's and women's opinions on public policy issues have for the most part been minimal, not substantial (2010: 24). Barbara Norrander, in her review of the history of gender gaps, concludes that "a number of gender gaps appear when examining American public opinion and voting patterns. Most of these gender gaps are relatively small, with women differing from men by five to ten percentage points. Additionally, on most issues where a gender gap appears, a majority of both women and men fall on the same side of the issue" (2008: 9). Differences in the opinions of men and women have been greatest on issues that involve the use of force both in the international realm and domestically. Compassion issues are a second area in which gender differences have been found. "Women are more likely than men to favor government actions to assist individuals suffering economic difficulties or inequalities" (Norrander 2008: 11). Few gender differences have been found on "women's issues" such as abortion and support for the Equal Rights Amendment.

Too, several scholars have explored from diverse angles the extent to which the parties have diverged on women's issues and have attempted to appeal to women as a political group (see, for example, Wolbrecht 2000; Sanbonmatsu 2002; Freeman 1987; Dodson 2006). The parties have become most polarized and most vocal in their positions on reproductive rights. They also started in 1980 to espouse very divergent views on the adoption of an equal rights amendment to the Constitution. Both parties seem to have endorsed changing gender roles and women's expanding participation in the economy and political life of the nation. But conservatives and liberals differ greatly on the role of government in supporting this equality. Laws focusing on violence against women and promoting equality for women in the military have been approached from quite different ideological perspectives.

Studies that have focused on the third lens of partisanship and its relationship to women in public office have been less extensive than these other research streams. But it is perhaps here—the presence of women in the parties' elective office caucuses, leadership positions, and efforts to achieve gender equity among their elected officeholders (see Burrell 2010)—that the most substantial gap has emerged between the parties especially since the 1992 election. This gap is not necessarily the result of polarization, but the parties' responses to issues of identity and descriptive representation (that is, the presence of women as lawmakers) and the policy implications of these issues are polarized in nature.

The Democratic Party has become not only the "mommy" party in terms of its issue orientation, and the "feminist" party in terms of its policy orientation, but also a "woman's" party in terms of its elected office caucuses, while the Republican Party remains a "man's" party in its officeholding representation at both the national and state legislative levels and within its elected leadership. Before analyzing this partisan gap and the growing polarization among female representatives in their congressional voting, I first turn to placing this aspect of polarization within the larger normative context of women's representation, that is, why it is important to have more women as elected leaders.

Normative Perspectives on Women's Representation

Normative perspectives have stimulated much research on women and politics. Women and politics scholars have long argued that greater gender equity in political leadership matters from both theoretical and empirical perspectives. The normative stimulus for studying women's quests for political leadership emerges from ideas about justice and fairness, about women's symbolic importance as political leaders, and women's substantive impact on policymaking. Justice and fairness arguments demand a concern with the unequal distribution of men and women in leadership positions. In addition, women's presence among political leaders may have a symbolic importance for women and girls. The invisibility of women as role models among our leaders may discourage girls and young women from envisioning themselves in such positions. Women may ask why they should pay attention to politics, state their opinions, and join in political campaigns if women are not visible among policymakers and leaders. Third, the substantive importance of having a critical mass of women present as public policies are being made is an important representational issue. Female lawmakers may bring distinctive policy preferences and ideas to the legislative agenda, policy debates, and problem solving, and may have a particular effect and influence on policy outcomes.

A number of normative theorists have proposed—and hoped—that greater numbers of women in political office would have a variety of positive effects, such as compensating for past and present injustice, providing a voice for overlooked interests, and contributing to the overall legitimacy of a democratic system (see, for example, Mansbridge 1999; Wolbrecht and Campbell 2006). Justice requires that one-half of the population not be excluded from political leadership; symbolic importance be attached to women's presence among political leaders; and a difference perspective be acknowledged holding that women can bring new issues to the legislative agenda and unique orientations to public policy debates based on their distinctive life experiences.

Fairness demands that men and women be present in roughly equal numbers among political elites, the justice argument contends. The gender, ethnicity, and race of elected representatives serve as evaluations of democratic political institutions. Implicit in these evaluations is the assumption that democratic political institutions that lack any representatives from historically disadvantaged groups are unjust and perceived as illegitimate. It is "grotesquely unfair for men to monopolize representation," Anne Phillips has argued in laying out the justice argument for gender parity in representation. She asks "by what 'natural' superiority of talent or experience could men claim a right to dominate assemblies" (1998: 232). Phillips maintains that descriptive representatives are needed to compensate for past and continued injustices toward certain groups. According to this argument, past and present betrayals by privileged groups create a belief that trust can be given only to descriptive representatives. The presence of descriptive representatives partially compensates for those betrayals.

Jennifer Lawless, too, has recently summarized this normative perspective, stating that "many scholars conclude that there appears to be something wrong with a political system that produces governing bodies dominated by men, when in fact, women comprise the majority of the population" (2004: 81). Structural discrimination has kept women from pursuing political leadership positions on an equal basis with men. Many historical examples exist of the prejudices women faced when they left their traditional roles in the home and sought a place in the public sector. Indeed, it took over seventy years of campaigning for women to attain the right to vote alone.

It might not matter whether public policies incorporated women's perspectives and interests if these perspectives and interests were the same as men's. But we know that this was not the case in the past. Otherwise, why would women have organized, marched, and lobbied for an equal rights amendment? Why would they have sued in court for equal rights over the need for special laws regarding violence, job security, and the like? The distinctive experiences of women's lives have also not been incorporated into the policymaking agenda, or heard in legislative debates without the presence of women to express them (see, for example, Hawkesworth 2003; Dodson 2006).

A further argument advanced in support of the idea of descriptive representation is that female politicians serve as role models inspiring other women to political activism and greater political competence. They perform a symbolic representation function. According to this perspective, women running and serving in high public office have an impact on their female constituents, stimulating greater interest and involvement in the electoral process. Female leaders may impact people's attitudes toward government and their ability to influence it, enabling them to see government as more accessible and open as it becomes more diverse. The presence of female leaders may especially affect women in helping to close their deficit compared to men on political factors such as efficacy, interest, knowledge, and general political participation. These possible effects on women's engagement in the political process bring together descriptive and symbolic representation concerns in advocating for more women in political leadership positions. A number of empirical studies have attempted to measure the symbolic connection between female political leaders and candidates, and female constituents and voters (see, for example, Atkeson 2003; Lawless 2004; Wolbrecht and Campbell 2006, 2007; Atkeson and Carrillo 2007).

Jane Mansbridge has written that the descriptive representation of having women as candidates and elected officials (along with members of minority groups), contributes to a "construction of social meaning that members of these groups are capable of governing. Their very presence as candidates and office holders signals to the public that politics is no longer exclusively a male domain" (1999: 648). Mansbridge also suggests that this altered social meaning of the nexus of "political" and "woman" lends increased "de facto legitimacy" to the polity itself. According to researchers Lonna Atkeson and Nancy Carrillo, "A representative body that shares physical characteristics with its constituency symbolically appears more open to input from more citizens and appears better able to understand citizen interests. Female citizens, therefore, may perceive that their own opinions will have greater value when larger proportions of female representatives are present" (2007: 81). Thus, the enormous philosophical importance of gender equity in the political life of democracies makes an empirical exploration of partisan politics regarding women's quests for political leadership and their performance once in office a necessary inclusion in any assessment of partisan polarization.

The Partisan Gap in Elective Officeholding

In the early years of the second half of the twentieth century, the few women who served in public office were about equally likely to be Republicans as Democrats. Once the second women's movement took off in the late 1960s, female Democrats began to outnumber female Republicans among both state and national representatives, and the notion of a "party gap" was born. Examining the proportion of each party's female representation in the US House from 1956 through 2006, Barbara Palmer and Dennis Simon (2008: 165–166) show that in the election cycles from 1956 to 1990, the proportions of Democratic and Republican women successfully running for the House were relatively equal. In twelve of the eighteen election cycles, the difference in the proportions of women that the two parties sent to the House was less than 1 percent. Then in 1992, the so-called Year of the Woman in American Politics, but perhaps more accurately described as the Year of the Democratic Woman, the proportion of women in the Democratic House caucus nearly doubled, from 7.1 percent to 13.7 percent, while the proportion of Republican women in the House caucus increased from 5.4 percent to only 7.3 percent, as shown in Figure 8.1.

The proportion of Democratic women in the House continued to climb, while the gains of Republican women were much more modest. Democrat Nancy Pelosi made political history by becoming the first woman to be selected by her caucus to be Speaker of the House, at the beginning of the 110th Congress in 2007. The gap grew in 2008, and in the 111th Congress (2009–2010) women made up 22 percent of the Democratic delegation but only 10 percent of the Republican delegation, the largest gap ever.

The gap did close slightly as a result of the 2010 election, in which the Republicans gained sixty-three seats in the House to once again become the majority party. Republican women increased their numbers in the House by eight members. As a result of this increase, and the record-breaking number of Republican women who had mounted campaigns for the House, ten Republican female members of the House issued a press release touting 2010 as the Year of the Republican Woman, highlighting the varied backgrounds of these women. As the press release noted, "these are the stories that made 2010 the year of the Republican woman. They're about farmers, attorneys, teachers, nurses, doctors, small-business owners, law enforcement officials, entrepreneurs, wives and mothers. They're the stories of the dynamic and driven women who will be sworn in as members of the 112th Congress"

Figure 8.1 Women as a Percentage of Congressional Democrats and Republicans, 1975–2011

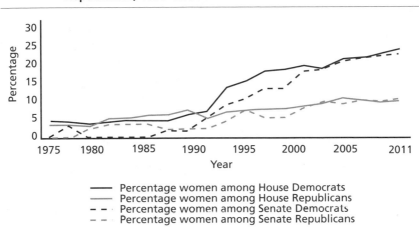

Source: Data compiled from the Center for American Women and Politics databases.

(Politico.com 2010). But even given their enhanced numbers in Congress, women still make up only 10 percent of the Republicans in the House and Senate (see Figure 8.1). While Democratic women saw their numbers in Congress decline in 2010 (see Figure 8.2), they continued to make up nearly one-quarter of the Democratic House caucus (24 percent), and Nancy Pelosi continued as their caucus leader.

A similar partisan gap trend has occurred at the state legislative level. Figure 8.3 shows the trend from 1983 through 2011 in the numbers of Democratic and Republican women in state legislatures. By 2010, 70 percent of the women in state legislatures were Democrats. The expanding partisan gap in favor of Democrats, especially from 1996 through 2009, reversed in 2011, when the Republicans closed the gap somewhat at the state level as they did at the congressional level, as a result of their success in the 2010 elections. The proportion of Democratic women in state legislatures declined to 61 percent in 2011. But the success of Republican women did not translate into a larger share of women in the Republican caucuses overall, as they only increased their representation from 16 percent to 17 percent. Democratic women represented 31 percent of that party's membership in 2011, the same as in 2010 before that year's elections.

A similar partisan gap has also existed in state legislative leadership positions. For example, in 2010, Democratic female state legislators held 21 percent of state legislative leadership positions as opposed to 9 percent for

Figure 8.2 Number of Republican and Democratic Women in Congress, 1975–2011

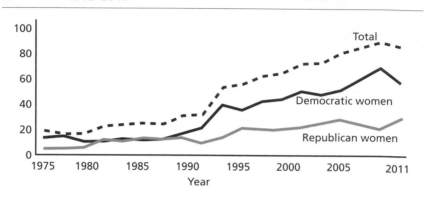

Source: Data compiled from the Center for American Women and Politics databases.

Republican female state legislators. That same year, all of the female presidents of the state senates (five) and all of the female speakers of the state houses (five) were Democrats. Preliminary data from the Center for American Women and Politics (CAWP) for 2011 presenting the numbers of women in these top two leadership positions show that three women, two Democrats and one Republican, were serving as senate presidents, and that two women, one Republican and one Democrat, were serving as house speakers. An expansion of the category of leadership positions to include other offices, to determine the effect that the Republican victories more broadly have had on reversing the leadership trends among women, remains to be undertaken. At the national level, the 2004 election of Nancy Pelosi as the leader of the Democratic caucus in the US House of Representatives, together with her subsequent ascension to the Speakership of the House after the Democrats won control as a result of the 2006 election, was a major and symbolically important achievement in women's quest for political leadership. Beyond Speaker Pelosi, female Democrats have obtained a greater role in party and committee leadership positions in Congress than have their Republican counterparts, as the research of Jocelyn Evans has shown (2005).

Partisan Gap in Running for Office

As with the trend for elected officials, there is a similar gap between the parties for candidacies for public office. Palmer and Simon (2008) report that, from 1956 to 1988, women on average composed 5.1 percent of all Republican primary congressional candidates, and 5.9 percent of all Democratic pri-

Figure 8.3 Number of Democratic and Republican Women in State Legislatures, 1983–2011

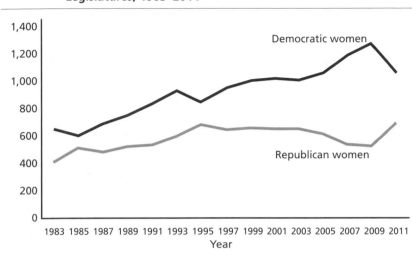

Source: Data compiled from the Center for American Women and Politics databases.

mary candidates in a given election cycle. In seven of the seventeen election cycles in this thirty-year period, the difference between the proportions of female primary candidates in both parties was less than 1 percent. In the 1990s, however, the parties began to drift apart. Figures 8.4 and 8.5 show the number of female Democratic and Republican candidates and their percentage representation among party candidates from 1994 through 2010. Democratic women substantially outnumbered Republican women as congressional primary candidates in all of the elections except the 2010 contests. At the same time, after 1996, Democratic women have been consistently a larger proportion of their party's candidates, even in the 2010 election. Women's increasing incumbency status within the Democratic Party, the political environment of the election cycles, the opportunity structure that open seats present, and the partisan nature of those open-seat opportunities have affected the numbers of women running over the course of these elections and their presence within their party.

A party gap also emerges when women's representation is examined from the recruitment lens. Richard Fox and Jennifer Lawless (2010), in their Citizen Ambition Panel Study, show that Republican women are the least likely to report having received the suggestion to run for office from a gatekeeper. While Democratic and Republican women are equally unlikely to have received encouragement to run for office from elected and party officials, Republican political activists lag in recruiting women. Lawless and Fox

Figure 8.4 Number of Female Primary Entrants by Party, 1994–2010

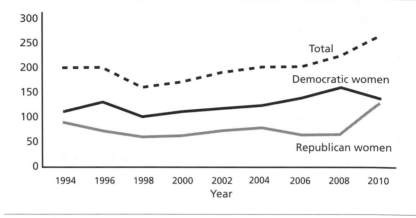

Source: Data compiled by the author.

Figure 8.5 Democratic and Republican Women as a Percentage of Party Candidates, 1994–2010

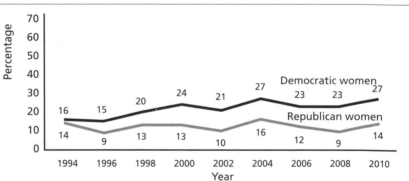

Source: Data compiled by the author.

attribute this difference to the work of women's organizations in encouraging women to run for office and helping them navigate the political process. These groups tend to have a progressive bent and therefore are likely to travel in the same circles as Democratic women.

Voter stereotypes about women's electability and what they would do once in office may also have discouraged potential female Republican candidates from seeking election. Experimental data David King and Richard Matland report (2003) suggest that the biggest hurdle female Republican candidates face is the perception that they are more liberal than their male counterparts, and thus that conservative Republican voters see them as unacceptable candidates in primary elections.

A survey by Kira Sanbonmatsu and Kathleen Dolan conducted in 2006 reveals further difficulties for would-be Republican female candidates, based on gender stereotypes. Respondents were asked a series of questions measuring their perceptions of women's and men's issue competency in the areas of crime and education. They were asked about Democratic and Republican members of Congress separately. Findings revealed potential problems for Republican female candidates. Among their own partisan identifiers, Republican women gain less benefit than do Democratic women based on the stereotype that women are more competent on education and less competent on crime. As Sanbonmatsu and Dolan (2009: 488) report, it seems clear that

> among Republican identifiers, gender stereotypes that benefit women are less important than those that work against women's perceived competence. On an issue that is typically perceived as a traditional woman strength—education—Republican women are less likely than Democratic women to be perceived favorably by their party members. Meanwhile, Republican women are more disadvantaged on a traditional male strength issue—crime—than are their Democratic women counterparts. In general, Democrats are more likely to hold gender stereotypes that benefit women in politics. Democrats are more likely than Republicans to see an advantage for women on the issue of education and are less likely than Republicans to see a male advantage on the issue of crime.

The rise in the number of candidacies of conservative women in 2010 and their distinctive framing of policy perspectives and identity as women may be lessening these stereotypical disadvantages and ushering in a new era of potential for Republican female candidates. Sanbonmatsu (2002) has also hypothesized that the incentive structures of the Republican and Democratic parties have differentially affected the recruitment and election of women to state legislatures. Thus the paths to office for Democratic and Republican women have varied.

The social eligibility pool of women in a state as measured by female labor force participation has had a greater effect on Democratic women's representation in that party's caucus in state legislatures, but has been less important for Republican women. Measures of the professionalism of the state legislature show that it has had little impact on women's numerical representation within either party. Being in the majority party has had a negative effect for Democratic women but not for Republican women. Sanbonmatsu (2002: 804) suggests that there is greater competition for seats within the Democratic Party in Democratic-majority legislatures compared to competition within the Republican Party in Republican-majority legislatures. Therefore, Democratic women may have trouble winning the backing of their party if the primary is competitive. Sanbonmatsu also finds that the extent to which state party organizations have control over nominations has had a negative impact on women's representation in state legislatures, but that the relationship has been stronger within the Democratic Party.

Party Organizations and Women's Political Leadership

The Democratic and Republican parties have developed distinct cultures regarding their internal politics that have differentially framed the opportunities of women's rights activists within them. Jo Freeman has argued that in the Democratic Party, power flows upward, but that in the Republican Party, power flows downward (1987: 235). The Democratic Party is pluralistic; it consists of constituencies who are seen as representing the interests of important blocs of voters whom the Democrats must respond to as a party. The Republican Party has separate units composed of distinct demographic groups, "but they are auxiliaries, not constituencies. The purpose of these groups is to elect Republicans, not to communicate group concerns to the party. . . . The Republicans have a unitary party in which great deference is paid to the leadership; activists are expected to be 'good soldiers,' and competing loyalists are frowned upon" (236).

This structural difference creates different conceptions of legitimacy. In the Democratic Party, whom one represents determines legitimacy. In the Republican Party, whom one knows and who one is as a party activist determine legitimacy. This difference "makes the Democratic Party so much more responsive to demands for reform within it, and the Republican Party so much more responsive to changes in leadership" (Freeman 1987: 236).[1] Thus, women's rights activists have had wider opportunities to promote their caucuses within the Democratic Party.

Building on Freeman's cultural analysis, Jocelyn Evans has more recently summarized the distinctive cultures of the two parties in similar terms, characterizing the Republican Party as being ideologically homogeneous, with a stress on party loyalty, internal competition, hierarchical organization, and elite participation. In contrast, ideological and descriptive diversity, constituent responsiveness, seniority rule, and egalitarian organization and participation have characterized the Democratic Party (2005: 7). Framing an analysis of the behavior of Republican and Democratic female members of the US Congress in terms of party structures, Evans has concluded that, "whether a female Member is a Democrat or a Republican, partisanship is an important factor of the political context serving to shape women's political experience. Female Republican Members do not behave the same way as female Democratic Members. They do not vote the same way on the floor. They do not have the same priorities. And, in the end, while it appears they have some level of success within the Congress, the factors predicting this success are unique to the parties to which they belong" (123).

A comparison of the National Federation of Republican Women (NFRW), the main group within the Republican Party advancing women's involvement in politics, and EMILY's List, the preeminent organization within the Democratic Party promoting the candidacies of women, illustrates the distinct cultures of the parties in recent years. Both groups are independent organizations working somewhat outside formal party structures. The NFRW's range of programs encourages the political involvement of women in the party. Among its activities, it provides training workshops for would-be female Republican candidates, but does not endorse or provide financial aid to female candidates. Its main goal is to foster the principles of the Republican Party. It works for candidates as part of the Republican team. EMILY's List, on the other hand, trains and recruits specific candidates and provides financial support, technical expertise, and on-the-ground help for women candidates whom it specifically endorses. Endorsed candidates must pass a litmus test of being pro-choice regarding abortion rights. EMILY's List will go "head-to-head" with party establishment candidates in primary elections, and thus has become a formidable force within the Democratic Party. Its presence illustrates the distinct culture of the Democratic Party that Jo Freeman has characterized, while the approach and perspective of the NFRW illustrate the distinct culture of the Republican Party.

A group of women within the Republican Party did form the WISH List in the 1990s to promote pro-choice female candidates following the model of EMILY's List, but it had limited success in finding pro-choice women within the party who were willing to mount campaigns that often would challenge the dominant pro-life stance of the party. With declining resources and essentially no nonincumbents to promote, the WISH List in 2010 merged with the Republican Majority for Choice and effectively went out of business. In 2010 it contributed only a total of $1,500 to five female congressional candidates, reflecting the fact that pro-choice Republican women are not viable candidates.

To further explore the theme of advocacy of women candidates, I surveyed the listing of political action committees (PACs) at the OpenSecrets .org website. For 2010, sixteen PACs in the "women's issues" sector contributed a total of $726,512 to candidates in federal elections. This amount is for direct contributions only, and does not include bundled money that might have been funneled to candidates. OpenSecrets.org reports that 81 percent of this money went to Democratic candidates; nine of the PACs gave only to Democrats, three gave only to Republicans, and three donated to candidates of both parties (the final PAC was listed as having contributed a negative amount). Of note, former Republican representative Deborah Pryce's Value in Electing Women PAC, which became the leading Republican PAC, is among this group. In 2010 it gave $112,500 in direct contributions to twenty-two congressional candidates, seventeen for the US House and five for the US Senate. It is unclear whether this PAC donates to female candidates in contested primaries and how involved it is in primary elections, although the total dollar amount in direct contributions to candidates in 2010 suggests some primary donations in contested races. The PAC's website says nothing about recruitment or training of female candidates. These findings regarding women's issue PACs are not distinctive to 2010 alone; I found the same imbalance in 2008 (Burrell 2010).

Polarized Women in Political Leadership

In much of this chapter so far, I have stressed differences between the two parties in their orientation toward the promotion of women as candidates and as party leaders based more on their cultures than on an antiwomen perspective on the part of the Republican Party. Its antifeminist, masculine perspective may have discouraged women from seeking nomination for public office as its standard-bearer, resulting in an indirect relationship between polarization and women's political leadership. In this last section I turn to more direct evidence of the relationship between women's political leadership in the two parties and contemporary polarization.

Interest in the nature of the policy impact of having female representatives in Congress led in the past to a number of studies examining the differences in voting behavior between female and male members. Most of these past studies showed that female members tended to be more liberal than their male colleagues within both parties, and more likely to support issues of importance to women, as Brian Frederick (2009) has noted. However, in extending this line of research through to the 109th Congress (2005–2006), Frederick has demonstrated that "women in the House are more divided along partisan and ideological lines than at any point over the past two decades, [and] even more ideologically distant than their male colleagues" (2009: 181). His conclusion is based on an analysis of Keith Poole and Howard Rosenthal's (2007) ideological scoring of members of the 97th through the 109th Congresses, which shows that Democratic female members have grown more liberal in their voting behavior on the floor of the House, while Republican female members have become more ideologically conservative.

Frederick concludes that the "present ideological position of women is related to the exodus of moderate women from the House and the entrance of more extreme members in both parties" (2009: 186). As he explains, Republican female representatives are being elected from more heavily Republican districts, and "in an era where seniority is no longer the automatic rule for moving up the committee ladder it behooves women in the Republican Party to compile a voting record that demonstrates loyalty to the GOP leadership" (197). On the other side of the aisle, he notes, "Democratic activists are becoming more liberal and women who want to win contested primaries will respond to this development. Women who win these primaries often have the support of EMILY's List. . . . As far as institutional advancement is concerned, compiling a record consistent with party loyalty is crucial. Since most Democratic women are elected from very liberal districts, their policy records will position them nicely to acquire power in the House" (197).

The ideological distance between female Republican and Democratic members of the US House could not be more strongly illustrated than by the House vote on the Lilly Ledbetter Fair Pay Act on January 29, 2009. This act amended the 1964 Civil Rights Act to extend the period in which employees could file equal-pay lawsuits. President Obama signed it into law that day, since the Senate had already passed it. The act was a response to a 2007 Supreme Court decision holding that the statute of limitations for presenting an equal-pay lawsuit begins on the date that the employer makes the initial discriminatory wage decision, not on the date of the most recent paycheck, as a lower court had ruled. The US House passed the bill by a vote of 250 to 177. It was a piece of legislation that liberal women's rights activists had championed. All of the Democratic female members who voted, voted for the act; all of the Republican female members who voted, voted against it. The partisan difference between the female members could not have been greater.[2]

The campaigns of the 2010 elections and the resulting partisan bickering and gridlock further highlight the growing polarized nature of partisan female leaders' positions, their approaches to politics, and their forcefulness in promoting these orientations. While gender was not the main theme of these elections, which were dominated by the rise of the Tea Party movement, there were certainly "gendered moments" in the campaign; some of the more infamous of these were even being initiated by female candidates. For example, Nevada Republican Senate candidate Sharron Angle told her Democratic opponent, Senate majority leader Harry Reid, to "man up." Colorado Republican Senate candidate Jane Norton attacked her opponent, Ken Buck, in the Republican gubernatorial primary by saying he wasn't "man enough." He responded at a public event by saying that Coloradans should vote for him "because I do *not* wear high heels." Norton, having successfully baited Buck, went on to fundraise with the tagline, "Ken Buck may think a woman's place is in the house. We know a woman's place is in the Senate." Karen Handel, running in the Republican primary for governor of Georgia, told her male opponent Nathan Deal that "it's frankly time to put the big boy pants on" (S. Miller 2010). From the male candidate side, US representative

Betty Sutton's (D-OH) Republican opponent, Tom Ganley, sent mailers to voters telling them to "take Betty Sutton out of the House and put her back in the kitchen" (M. Miller 2010).

In some instances, the "gender" moments among the candidates were actually female-on-female barbs. Perhaps most noteworthy was Carly Fiorina's "'God, what is that hair?' Soooo yesterday" comment regarding the hair of her opponent, US senator Barbara Boxer. Mary Fallin, Republican nominee for governor in Oklahoma, played what commentators have called the "mommy card" when she was asked what set her apart from her opponent. "Being a mother, having children, raising a family," she replied. Lieutenant-Governor Jari Askins, the Democratic nominee, had never been married and had no children (Marcus 2010).

The most notorious gender aspect to the election was undoubtedly Sarah Palin's clarion call to "mama grizzlies" to rise up, and the warning she issued that a herd of "pink elephants" were stampeding to Washington, D.C., with an "e.t.a. of November 2. You don't want to mess with moms who are rising up," she intoned at a Susan B. Anthony List fundraiser in May 2010. "If you thought pit bulls were tough, you don't want to mess with mama grizzlies." This language became part of the Republican campaign landscape in that election, with Palin endorsing and characterizing a number of the female candidates as "mama grizzlies"—tough conservative women. "She brought to the Republican Party what some members had once complained did not exist: a concerted effort to tap female candidates for promotion and lift them out of obscurity," Anne Kornblut (2010) noted in the *Washington Post*.

Illustrative is Palin's endorsement of CeCe Heil, one of eleven Republican primary contenders, and the only woman in the contest, competing to oppose Democratic representative Jim Cooper in the general election. In a Facebook posting, Palin described Heil (who had previously run for a seat in the House) as "another tough 'mama grizzly' with the experience, passion, and integrity to restore some common sense to Washington. As a small business owner, attorney, constitutional scholar, and proud mother of two, she will fight tirelessly to protect our freedoms and rein in the excesses of an out-of-control federal government that seems set on spending away our children's future."[3]

Ambition problems and voter stereotyping, features of the political environment that seemingly hinder Republican women's candidacies, may rapidly become outdated with this rise in the promotion of conservative women's candidacies both inside and outside the Republican Party's organizational structure. Marin Cogan (2011), in a Politico.com piece titled "GOP Freshmen Women Go On the Offense," called attention to this new politics. She described a new weapon in the Republican messaging arsenal, "a growing, influential caucus of younger GOP women intent on fighting back against Democratic claims that the party is anti-woman. This new group does not fit the traditional model of women who run for office. Rather they are rock ribbed, younger, conservative working mothers, a new breed of GOP representative the Republican male leaders are more than happy to have deployed on the front lines, to act as the public face for a party that still suffers from a gender gap in their rank-and-file."

Once the 112th Congress commenced, the female members used their distinctive "gendered" position to highlight the ideological distance between the parties. Two events showcase this new gendered aspect of partisanship. On April 8, 2011, in the midst of one of the budget showdowns between the parties, with a government shutdown imminent, the female Democratic senators and the female Republican representatives held competing press briefings to emphasize how their own party's position would help women and how the other party's approach would hurt women. The Democratic senators' theme was that the Republicans would "throw women and children under the bus," a phrase repeatedly used in their briefing.

A key sticking point in solving the immediate budget impasse from the perspective of the female Democratic senators was the Republican insistence that no federal money go to Planned Parenthood. As the federal government was about to be shut down, the Republicans wanted any legislation keeping the government operating to bar federal dollars for Planned Parenthood, the country's largest abortion provider. The overarching issue, Senator Barbara Mikulski declared, was that the Republicans "want to cut funding for prenatal care by $50 million dollars. . . . They want to take our mammograms away from us; they want to take prenatal care away from us, take counseling and family planning away from us and we just say 'no.'" Senator Dianne Feinstein stated that the Republican cuts would "hurt women and we women in the Senate will not let it happen. What is at stake is about the ability of poor American women to get health services."

In response, fourteen Republican female representatives held a briefing that same day, April 8, with the dominant theme being that sound fiscal policy and spending cuts would help their children and their grandchildren. As Representative Shelley Moore Capito of West Virginia put it, "the argument is about spending and there is nothing more important to the health of my granddaughter . . . , my daughter and every woman in America [than] good sound fiscal policy and that the women of America are not swallowed up by a huge debt and deficit." Each of the speakers reiterated this theme, relating spending cuts to the creation of a healthy future for children and grandchildren.

Then on June 21, 2011, Representative Cathy McMorris Rodgers (R-WA), vice chair of the House Republican Conference, led fourteen Republican female members on the House floor for a GOP Women's Special Order. Titled "I Am a Republican Woman," this order highlighted members' backgrounds, their personal stories and policy objectives, and the Republican agenda to create jobs, and each woman spoke briefly on these

topics. Although conservative political thinkers have decried identity politics, these female Republican representatives stressed identity in their
remarks, emphasizing why they were Republican women. They emphasized
their motherhood while also underscoring their professional status and
careers before coming to Congress. Of the fourteen women who participated in this special order, ten highlighted motherhood and grandmother-
hood and talked of their children. Cathy McMorris Rodgers talked of coming home "every night to two beautiful children." Representative Martha
Roby asked rhetorically, "Why in the world would a 34 year old woman
with a six year old and a two year old run for Congress?" Representative
Ann Buerkle shared that she was the mother of six children and grandmother of eleven. Representative Ileana Ros-Lehtinen stated, "I'm a daughter. I'm a mother. I'm a grandmother." These women also spoke of their
experience as nurses, small-business owners, physicians, farmers, educators, and attorneys. They did not talk about social issues. Rather, they
spoke of creating jobs, and limiting government spending and regulations.
They put a distinctive gendered spin on their policy advocacy, stressing the
unique experiences of their roles as women that made them strong, credi-
ble advocates for the economic policies of the Republican Party rather than
emphasizing their similarities with men. Representative McMorris
Rodgers's opening remarks illustrate this theme:

> While our backgrounds and professions may be different, one thing is not:
> We are all conservative reformers committed to leaving America better for
> our children and grandchildren. After all, women in this country know better
> than anyone the effects of harmful economic politics. Why? Because two out
> of three businesses are started by women. Women-owned businesses are the
> fastest growing segment in the United States economy and they generate over
> $3.5 trillion in revenue a year. Women manage 83 percent of household in-
> come, spend two out of three health care dollars, and make up the majority
> of health care providers in America.

This event, according to media accounts, came in response to an earlier
comment made by US representative Debbie Wasserman Schultz, chair of
the Democratic National Committee, that the Republican Party was anti-
women and was engaging in a "war on women." She focused her remarks on
votes to defund Planned Parenthood and Title 10 funding for clinics that perform abortions (Bedard 2011). Contemporary female Democratic and Republican national officials have sharply different worldviews on "women's
issues" and what constitutes equal rights for women, as these events strongly
suggest. Female leaders in the two parties have staked out clear, highly divergent, and substantive policy perspectives centering on women. Both groups
see themselves as representing women, but from quite divergent lenses.
Descriptive representation and substantive representation have taken on a

heightened complexity in this domain. These officials have taken substantive differences to the public forum, contributing distinctively to the polarized nature of national policymaking.

Conclusion

The preceding anecdotes stress dominant, strong, and tough women on both sides of the congressional aisle in prominent positions and the emergence of more conservative women entering elections with forceful articulation of a distinctive gendered message. But a significant alternative lens also must be contemplated regarding the connection between a polarized and uncivil national politics and the creation of a more critical mass of women seeking political leadership. This lens focuses on what effect the polarized nature of our national politics and the incivility within our governing institutions that has accompanied it is having on efforts to create a more gender-equitable political leadership. Is polarization having a negative effect on women's decisions to run for public office, even given the emergence of Sarah Palin's "mama grizzlies"? Little empirical evidence directly addressing this question has been conducted, although some indirect evidence does shed a modicum of light on the situation.

We need to ponder the negative effects of the ugliness and polarization that permeate the political system on the desire of qualified, ambitious individuals to run for and hold public office. This reflection pertains to both men and women and it is not meant to cast women and their ambitions in a Pollyannaish perspective. We have certainly seen that female candidates can be just as negative and just as brash as male candidates. (Besides the anecdotes noted in this chapter, see also Bystrom et al. 2004.) But the nature of contemporary politics has particular relevance to ideas about women and political leadership given normative concern with creating more numerically gender-representative political institutions. Women who have the resources, the credentials, and the ambition to be political leaders, along with many of their male counterparts, may be deciding that they can have greater influence on concerns of importance to them in other venues than political leadership. Is there anything in the election process that would be attractive to them? For example, who wants to "dial for dollars" every day of the campaign process? Or once in office, who wants to be screamed at by one's constituents when trying to effect and explain public policy, or engage in unseemly policy debates in committees and on the floors of the House and Senate?

We need to ask why women would want to run for public office in the first place, given the contemporary atmosphere of scandal, incivility, and polarization. Potential candidates, both men and women, may ask for what purpose they should run for a position in these institutions if their concern is to make a positive contribution to public policy. In an exploratory survey of the extent to which male and female potential candidates were taking advantage of windows of opportunity in open-seat primaries for the US House in 2006, Brian Frederick and I found that 49 percent of the women who were queried about their decisionmaking process regarding entering such a primary who decided not to run checked that "the ineffectiveness of the U.S. House as policy-making institution" was a "very important" or an "important" factor in their decision not to become a candidate, and 56 percent checked that "the inability of members of the U.S. House to work together" was a "very important" or an "important" factor (Burrell and Frederick 2007; see also Fulton et al. 2006). Institutional problems such as these provide a counterbalancing and sobering perspective on incentive structures and on questions about party recruitment and the role of ambition in women's quests for equality in political leadership positions at the same time that those women who have sought such positions have increasingly succeeded in attaining them.

These problems suggest that it may be not just lower levels of ambition that account for the scarcity of female candidates for national office, but also the negativity surrounding the institutions and the political process one must engage in to get there. Fewer male and female community and policy leaders are turning their efforts to influence public policy. Here is a significant political science question ripe for systematic empirical research. The number of candidates running for local office has dropped and elections have been canceled because of a lack of candidates (Macedo et al. 2005: 66), suggesting a larger societal problem than simply lack of ambition among women or lack of recruitment. The role that the contemporary nature of our politics plays in women's career ambitions and candidacies for elective office is an area calling for more research from an ambition perspective, an institutional perspective, and a polarization lens. Such an investigation would complement further research on the ideological distance between Democratic and Republican female public officials and its connection to the representation of women.

Notes

1. Whether the emergence of the Tea Party movement and other conservative groups such as religious-right organizations and the Club for Growth has modified this 1980s conception of Republican Party culture is an open research question.

2. It should be noted, however, that all of the female members of the US Senate, Democrats and Republicans, voted for passage of the Lilly Ledbetter Fair Pay Act.

3. Facebook post, https://www.facebook.com/notes/sarah-palin/cece-heil-for -tennessees-5th-district/406187423434.

9

African Americans and Party Politics

William Crotty

Race is, and has been, the most polarizing force in US politics. Its roots go back to before the United States became a nation. The issue failed to be resolved at the nation's founding, and in fact threatened to derail the entire enterprise; provoked a civil war; led to a de facto reimposition of slavery's conditions, with some modification in a largely token recognition of the Civil War's outcome; led to a restoration to power of the economic and political elite of prewar days; and established a foundation for the region's politics and party system that lasted well into the twentieth century. Race would remain on the nation's radar, dividing the country and polarizing its politics and parties (Woodward 2006; Perman 2012; Franklin 1994; Wilentz 2005; Cash 1991; Foner 1988, 1990, 1998, 2005; Frederickson 2002).

The struggle for African American enfranchisement has gone through a series of cycles: generations of economic servitude, political voicelessness, and citizenship in name only; the Great Migrations of World Wars I and II to the cities of the industrial North; and during the 1960s the mobilization of forces committed to changing the nation's thinking on racial matters, its politics, and its parties. The latter resulted in a window (1954–1965) of extraordinary racial achievements.

One consequence of the painstaking effort to achieve political viability and a responsiveness to its interests was a transformation of the party system—a 180-degree realignment from the party of Abraham Lincoln to that of Franklin Roosevelt and Lyndon Johnson. A practical and symbolic indication of these changes would come with the election of an African American, Barack Obama, to the presidency. Yet racism, at times more virulent than at any point since the 1960s, continued to manifest itself. Obama was attacked in personal terms, and racial attitudes showed little if any improvement over the course of his presidency. Polarization along racial lines as a consequence may have become more severe than it had been in the past, reinforcing the political patterns already in effect.

In short, race has proven to be the longest-running and most severely divisive issue in America's experience. It has constituted a severe test of the country's willingness to accept, and then apply, the principles it claimed to be founded on.

Reconstruction

Two competing forces clashed in the immediate aftermath of the Civil War. The white South refused to recognize the Northern victory as determining its future, in particular dictating the role freedmen would assume in the politics and economics of the Southern states. Instead, it was their intention to reinstitute the economic elite who had ruled prior to the war and to revitalize the devastated plantation economy, the source of the region's wealth and the basis of its rich traditions and of its mythology.

The Southern states quickly began to assert their control in reinstating the social conditions that had preceded the conflict. They acted forcefully in creating the Black Codes and laying the foundations for decades of Jim Crow laws designed to segregate the races and repress blacks. The laws were accompanied by state-sponsored violence intended to maintain the operations of the old system as well as to permit or overlook individual attacks on blacks and their churches and homes by whites, with no one held responsible (Franklin 1967, 1994; Du Bois 1962; McPherson and Hogue 1982). This was also the era of the founding of the Klan, allegedly to protect the Southern way of life and the sanctity of the white female. The Klan would come to lynch and intimidate blacks at will (Rable 2007; Wood 2011; Baker 2011).

These actions, and in particular the economic deprivations and blunted political status forced on blacks, were rationalized by Southern oppressors as necessary paternal efforts to provide for a people unable to fend for themselves. Blacks were depicted as lazy, indigent, violent, unskilled, uneducated, and generally incapable of assuming the burdens and responsibilities of citizenship. This misapprehension of the black character was one that Northerners would come to share. The necessity of having a plantation economy to make available a clear, easily mobilized, and politically neutered manpower pool in order to maximize profits for landowners was not debated. Nor was the price to be paid by those victimized a concern of those in power.

The impact of these measures was felt immediately. The end result was a society segregated by race and a politics marked by the exclusion of an African American citizenry and a one-party politics that disenfranchised blacks, and effectively poorer whites as well, and protected the class economic interests of a plantation society (and to the limited extent they existed, mining and manufacturing interests). By the 1890s, the full effect of the measures had played out. The extent of the disadvantages, hardships, and destitution, and the level of repression, voided any pretense as to the existence of a democratic society. Welcomed by Southerners who believed that the economic structure served their interests, this should have been a cause of concern for the rest of the nation. While this may have been true for a small minority, the country as a whole accepted the characterization presented of African Americans and the necessity of a paternal approach to their care. Further, rather than being mobilized by the appalling conditions to which few paid attention, most came to accept a romanticized view of the South, of the Ante-Bellum period, and of plantation life. It came to be part of the popular culture. D. W. Griffith's 1915 film *The Birth of a Nation* and Margaret Mitchell's 1936 book *Gone with the Wind* and its 1939 movie adaptation, as well as a series of other films in the early to middle twentieth century on the Ku Klux Klan, all fed these beliefs.

The consequences for blacks were devastating. The states attempted to outdo each other in establishing segregation barriers—that is, "to institutionalize white-supremacist beliefs" (Sitkoff 1993: 4; see also Fireside 2004; Perman 2012) in working conditions and through chain gangs, convict-leasing (by sheriff's offices to plantation overseers or mine owners), and fully segregating public and private facilities and activities (Blackmon 2008). Any form of interracial contact was to be prevented. Segregation of hospitals, public accommodations, parks, transportation, recreation, schools, swimming pools, residential areas, sports teams and sporting events, barber shops, funeral homes, cemeteries, courtrooms with separate Jim Crow Bibles, zoos, the playing of checkers and other board games, telephone booths, books and textbooks, taxis, houses of prostitution, and everything else conceivable was the enforced condition of society. It was "serfdom on the lower ring of the economic ladder" (Sitkoff 1993: 4). It all went unchallenged. Harvard Sitkoff, in recounting these Jim Crow laws and social practices, wrote that blacks were politically powerless to bring about change. They lived under total white dominance. "Daily facing grinding poverty, physical helplessness, and all the banal crudities of existence under an open, professed, and boasting racism, many blacks grew fatalistic. Segregation and discrimination came to seem permanent, immutable, an inevitable condition of life, and the majority of African-Americans succumbed to the new racial order" (1993: 6).

A segregated society was defended as just, humane, and necessitated by the deficiencies inherent in the newly freed race (racial eugenics were in vogue). It would be a white man's world, the care of blacks his burden. Ministers, educators, writers, and journalists provided the intellectual rationalization for a white racist society. Social Darwinism, scripture, "scientific" studies, and the implicit superiority of an Anglo-Saxon race were all employed in defense of the racial caste system. Over time, the federal government and the Supreme Court would both reinforce this fixed order in a legal and political context. In the North as well as the South the firm belief was that "for the good of all, the naturally superior whites should rule over the baser races. . . . The Southern Way had become the American Way" (Sitkoff 1993: 4).

Such ingrained racial thinking would prove exceedingly hard to change, as subsequent events would show. The tumult and violence almost a century later in the wake of the Supreme Court's decision in *Brown v. Board of Education* (1954), the reaction to *Brown,* and the open rebellion of Southern public officials and the general public that surfaced indicated that such views were held with an intensity that had not mellowed over the decades since the Civil War. They would prove to continue to be a problem, if in more subtle, less obvious ways, into the twenty-first century.

There was another, quite different vision as to the post–Civil War future of the South. "The Victorian North . . . sought to determine the meaning of freedom and the course of the transition from slavery to freedom" (Foner 2005: 96). The federal government would determine the role in the society and its politics to be assumed by African Americans. This conception of a new South, free from the old ways and freed of the heavy hand of racism, one in line more with national criteria of democratic conduct, was championed by the Radical Republicans in Congress in the immediate aftermath of the Civil War. The approach was at least as ambitious as that of the Southerners. It was one that could call on no previous record of success and had never been attempted prior to this. It went against everything that a white Southern society held to be dear.

The Radicals believed themselves to be the true heirs of the Lincoln legacy. It was their mission to ensure to the extent possible the full representation of blacks in the electorate, in public office, and in the economy of the Southern states. Through the Freedmen's Bureau they intended to make available the support programs and technical assistance needed to incorporate the newly freed blacks into the lifeblood of the Southern states. There was no questioning the sincerity or intensity of their commitment, as exemplified by the sending of federal troops into ten (of eleven) Southern states that demonstrated the greatest resistance to a new social order.

In retrospect, although of no practical importance at the time, the principal achievement of the Radical Republicans' postwar legacy was the adoption of three amendments to the Constitution. These were effectively rendered irrelevant through a form of de facto nullification during Reconstruction. Their promise would not be fulfilled for a century. The first of these Reconstruction Amendments, as they came to be called, was the Thirteenth Amendment (1865), which declared that "neither slavery nor involuntary servitude . . . shall exist within the United States."

The Fourteenth Amendment (1868) was considerably more complicated and far more ambitious. It was intended to undo the Black Codes; to repeal the *Dred Scott* decision of 1857, which declared slaves to be the property of their "masters" and denied them citizenship; and to create a new and equitable political order of universal applicability to the nation as a whole. The amendment declared that "no State shall make or enforce any law which shall abridge the privileges or immunities of citizens of the United States, nor shall any State deprive any person of life, liberty or property without due process of law, nor deny to any person within its jurisdiction the equal protection of the laws." The "due process," "privileges and immunities," and "equal protection of the law" clauses were to enjoy a robust judicial life in the twentieth century. They would eventually be used as a legal gateway by the courts to apply Bill of Rights protections uniformly throughout the country.

The Fourteenth Amendment had more overtly political goals also. It proposed to proportionally reduce the vote for electors in a state in relation to the number of black citizens denied the franchise; kept those who had engaged in rebellion from holding elective office; and rejected responsibility for the debts of the Confederacy or to offer compensation to slaveholders for the loss of their labor force. The substance of the amendment provides insight into the thinking of the Radical Republicans, specifically their objective of empowering blacks and also of penalizing the South for the insurrection. The intent of the amendment was one thing; operationalization of its provisions proved quite another.

Finally, the Fifteenth Amendment (1870) mandated that the rights of citizens to vote "shall not be denied or abridged by the United States or by any State on account of race, color or previous condition of servitude."

The objectives of the North as framed by the Radical Republicans were clear. Seemingly they would be implemented, given the victory of the North in the war and the adoption of amendments to the Constitution clearly spelling out the rights of citizenship for those newly freed. The reality during Reconstruction was that such an outcome was illusory. It would be effectively fought by the Southern states, with their views eventually to be accepted by the public in the North and by the very federal government that had attempted to establish standards for a postwar South.

A major problem for the Radicals was that not everyone in the North or in government accepted their objectives. What initially might have appeared to be close to a consensus was not. The Radical Republicans faced opposition from the beginning not only from what then existed as a Southern white presence in national politics but also from within their own ranks, from the more moderate and accommodationist party members. President Andrew Johnson, Lincoln's vice president, who had assumed office with Lincoln's assassination, was a border-state Democrat, sympathetic to the South, and a committed segregationist in his own right. The Johnson plan, announced and enacted in 1865, was to allow the Southern states to effectively do as they chose. He approved of the Black Codes, refused to sign civil rights acts or endorse the constitutional amendments, and did what he could to obstruct congressional action in general. His beliefs were unadorned: "This is a country for white men, and by God, as long as I am president, it shall be a government of white men" (quoted in Rothstein 2012: C5).

In the South, the tide ran unequivocally against the Radicals' conception of Reconstruction. Two events were to provide, first, political acceptance and legitimacy, and second, constitutional validation of the Southern creation of the repressive state. The initial and most significant political action involved the disputed presidential election of 1876. In this the Southern states supplied a solid bloc of nineteen votes in the Electoral College for the Republican candidate, Rutherford B. Hayes. His Democratic opponent, Samuel J. Tilden, the progressive governor of New York, had won the popular vote by a half-million vote margin, in the highest turnout in the nation's electoral experience (81.8 percent). The Southern total gave Hayes a one-vote victory in the Electoral College and thus the presidency. The action also brought to an end one of the longest, most intensely contested, and bitter presidential fights in history (Holt 2008).

The quid pro quo was that the federal troops would be withdrawn and the Southern states would be free of further federal interference to manage their affairs as they saw fit. A weariness in the North with decades of strife and violence, a desire to reunite the Union, the accepted belief in blacks' inability to excise the responsibilities of citizenship, and the view that it was time to move on all contributed to a Northern acceptance of what had been negotiated politically.

The second marking point in the Northern recognition of Southern racial supremacy took place in 1896 with the Supreme Court decision in *Plessy v. Ferguson*. Speaking for the majority, Justice Henry Billings Brown wrote, "Legislation is powerless to eradicate racial instincts or to abolish distinctions based on physical differences. . . . If the civil and political rights of both races be equal, one cannot be inferior to the other civically or political. If one race be inferior to the other socially, the Constitution of the United States cannot put them on the same plane." The reasoning of the chief justice says all that is needed about race relations and the thinking and views of the time. The case helped to cement the legal framework for "separate but equal" as the law of the land, extending protection for the practice in the South. It would come to apply to all aspects of the institutionalized relationships of daily life in the South. The decision would not be reversed until *Brown v. Board of Education* in 1954, in which the Court declared separate facilities to be inherently unequal (Cottrol, Diamond, and Ware 2003; see also Maltz 2007).

To implement a segregated society and insulate it from national political pressures, the region produced a "one-party" dominant face to the rest of the country. It proved to be highly effective in protecting the Southern way of life and it led to the disenfranchisement of African Americans, not to be fully reversed until the 1960s.

Should the purpose of Reconstruction have been to guarantee a full African American presence in political life, then it can be considered a failure. Blacks for a brief early period did enjoy an impressive level of participation and did elect representatives to Congress and to state and local office. But this did not last long. A Southern economic elite was able to reassert its control over the society, its economy, and its politics.

The period was repressive and racist. It operated well beyond the bounds of a representative democratic governing system. Nonetheless, much that would shape the nation's future direction and the operation of its party system was to come out of that period in time. Manufacturing and financial interests established their control over the national Republican Party, an association that despite periods of accelerated change and intermittent progressive and populist challenges has remained to this day. The nation's economy began its turn from an agricultural base to embrace industrialism, leading to the population movement to big cities. A tolerance emerged for an ethnic influx from Europe, stemming from the needs of an expanding economy for a greatly enlarged work force. This in-migration would become the electoral base of the urban machines of the era of the political boss and in time of the Democratic Party nationally. The foundation of the nation's emergence as an industrial state and an international power was put into place during the Reconstruction years, with both aspects tied to Republican Party initiatives.

A new, more expansive, more powerful nation-state had taken shape. From the creation of a national currency and a land-grant college system, to the settling of the West and the building of a transcontinental railroad, a new nation was born (Foner 1990: 9).

These developments took place in the North coming out of the Reconstruction period. The segregationist, one-party South, also a product of the era, would last for a century. Yet there were consequences that over time would prove positive. "The transformation of slaves into free laborers and equal citizens was the most dramatic example of the social and political changes unleashed by the Civil War and emancipation. . . . A new Southern class structure and several new systems of organizing labor were well on their way to being considered" (Foner 1990: xv).

A Democratic, one-party, segregationist South would continue well into the mid-twentieth century (and later). When it did finally breathe its last, the shock waves were severe enough to realign the political parties and reconstitute the nation's politics.

Disenfranchisement

The drive to deny the franchise to blacks took many forms: a poll tax (the poll tax, or any tax, as a precondition for voting, was made unconstitutional by the Twenty-Fourth Amendment to the Constitution in 1964), interpretive readings of the state and federal laws and constitutions to the satisfaction of local registrars, literacy tests, property requirements, onerous residence requirements, incarceration, and the like. All were in defiance of the postwar amendments; all were applied to prospective black voters. These, in addition to community social pressure, economic threats directed at blacks by employers, and violence were used to ensure that only whites would qualify to vote. The violence could come from state and local authorities, individual citizens acting on their own initiative and free from legal sanctions, the Klan, local sheriffs, and in effect any group or individual who chose to engage in it. It all would take its toll. The unavoidable issue was that a white majoritarian society and its government refused blacks the right to participate in its politics and did whatever it took to keep blacks economically and politically subservient.

The intimidation proved to be highly effective and affected blacks and poor whites alike. The leaders in denying blacks the vote were the five states of the Deep South: Alabama, Georgia, Louisiana, Mississippi, and South Carolina. The measures taken were unusually effective. For all practical purposes, African Americans were left, as intended, disenfranchised, politically (as well as economically) vulnerable, and unrepresented in Southern politics. In these states in presidential elections between 1892 and 1908, the average turnout, never high (except in Alabama, where two out of three voted), declined from 43 to 19 percent. In congressional elections, seen as far more important for protecting the Southern way of life, turnout was already anemic even in nonpresidential election years, but still managed to decline by half, from 14 to 7 percent. The vote itself was heavily Democratic, as to be expected in a one-party era. The Republican Party, for all practical purposes, verged on extinction (Walton, Deskins, and Puckett 2012; and Burnham 2010b).

Turnout in state, county, and local races is difficult to determine. More often than not, no voting returns were reported. This could also be the case in gubernatorial contests, the most important of elections in the Southern states, and it is particularly the case for Republican participation figures. Two of the principal weapons of the disenfranchisement effort, the grandfather clause and the literacy test (often interpretive readings of state or federal constitutions to the satisfaction of white registrars), had the designated consequences. Black voting was severely depressed, even when compared with that of a white population where lower income groups were also effectively excluded.

The extent of the exclusion of blacks and poor whites can be seen in the election returns that are available. Whatever else the politics of disenfranchisement of African Americans and the one-party system that accompanied it did, they proved to be highly effective vehicles for restricting the franchise, expressing the will of the upper economic classes to choose the representatives of their interests and maintain in place the society's power structure.

The impact of these conditions on blacks is depicted by Harvard Sitkoff. More than a thousand were lynched during the years 1900 to 1915 alone. "No records exist to tally the number beaten or tortured. Nor can one describe adequately the terror of living with a constant fear of barbarity and violence, of having your security subject to the whim of those who despise you, of having no recourse to police or courts" (1993: 5).

It was a state of affairs the actual consequences of which few, in South or North, would acknowledge. Potential remedial efforts were not to be part of the nation's political agenda.

A One-Party Politics

The South has been the land of one-party politics, in itself a basic anomaly in a nationally competitive two-party system. For the first hundred years in the post–Civil War Reconstruction phase, it was the Democratic Party that dominated. In reality, it was a no-party/factional politics that served the interests of the region, or more accurately its white population and their economic power structure. The Southern Democratic Party created a shield for the "Solid South" externally as an ambassador of the area's interests in its representation to the North. It served to protect the Solid South as seen from the North (i.e., united on racial issues and in its conservative ideological and policy outlook).

The Solid South, operating as a national stage through the Democratic Party, placed a brake on the nation's more expansionist government ambitions. It formed an uneasy, often highly tense relationship with the party's Northern electorate and its congressional representation. However severely the two wings of the party were out of sync with each other, the Northern Democrats acted as enabler for the protection of Southern interests. The explanation was that the South and its electoral vote were vital to any chance the Democrats might have of winning the presidency, and this was recognized and rewarded as such. The placement of Southerners in key party chairmanships through the application of the seniority system (in effect at the time) and their prominence in positions of legislative leadership in the Congress gave the South effective control over policymaking as it impacted its interests. The South, through the strategic placement of its congressional representatives, the loose voting discipline exercised by the party caucuses, and such institutionally accepted practices as the filibuster, was more than able as a region to exercise a veto over executive and congressional actions it disagreed with. Unfortunately for the Democrats, this impacted core interests of its Northern and particularly urban and industrial states, giving the party a schizoid presence on the national scene.

V. O. Key Jr.'s *Southern Politics* (1949) provides a guide to the region's one-party politics. The list can be long but is worth extended attention as a lesson in what democracy is not about and the objectives political parties are not intended to serve. Key saw one-partyism as characterized by the following:

- A factionalism at the state level, some of it permanent, other parts of it quasi-structured, and yet other parts more indicative of a no-party politics.
- Major variation by state in its party operations and political culture, if not in its racial views and conservatism.
- Party politics becomes more repressive in proportion to numbers of blacks in a locality. This was true by county and by state, ensuring that those counties and states of the Deep South with the largest concentrations of African Americans, and therefore more of a threat to white society, would permit the least participation in their politics.
- The inability of a factional politics to organize and operate much as a party did in a competitive environment and therefore to adequately represent the interests of the state's population.
- Low levels of voter participation in primaries (from which blacks were excluded), as well as in national and state elections.
- An ability, or more an unwillingness, to organize voters and mobilize constituency groups.
- A politics of policy confusion, uncertainty, and erratic issue positioning, as compared with the more traditional two-party approach.
- No accountability for behavior and actions in office; no consistent "ins" versus "outs" election debate; no collective party responsibility for what was done or not done.
- Uncontested terms of service, leading to a lower quality of political leadership, a receptivity to organized groups and financial interests, and a political class significantly divorced from the electoral base it purported to represent.
- A politics motivated by personal ambition and personal reward.
- Nonexistent recruiting structures for candidate selection for elective office.

- A disorganized and chaotic political culture that encourages dema-goguery, erratic behavior, and the acceptance of and reward for racial targeting.
- Government subservient to the interests of individuals, groups, and cor-porate pressures and predisposed to favoritism in its decisionmaking.
- An inability to pursue a reasoned consideration and the implementa-tion of long-run policy programs.
- State agencies and boards insulated from the shifting political winds, conducting their business as they choose and exercising no accountability, however indirect, to a party constituency or to a broader public.
- A "haves" versus "have-nots" division in the society that largely ignored the poorer classes, black or white, which were essentially excluded from politics: "the have-nots lose in a disorganized politics" (Key 1949: 307).
- One-partyism as an effective mechanism for instituting and maintain-ing an elite-driven, rigidly class-based political system.
- Redistributive programs, equitable tax structures, schools, health care, housing, and public service and social welfare expenditures as the principal policy losers in such a system.
- A one-party politics of short-term perspectives, however approached (party factionalism and discord, program enactment, leadership objec-tives, government actions).
- Political campaigns devolving into personal rivalries "uncomplicated by substantial social and economic" issues (Key 1949: 308).
- An issueless politics ensuring that upper-class economic and status interests exist in a state of uncertainty. Unanticipated changes in direction can emerge in a personalized, unpredictable politics and, on rare occasion, populist grassroots movements surface to challenge the status quo. The interests of an economic elite, and ironically those of lower classes, are more effectively represented and considerably more secure in a structured two-party system divided on a class basis. "A modicum of political conflict probably aids in the maintenance of the health of a capitalistic role" (Key 1949: 210). This is a point not often made.
- To the extent politics is organized at all, it is centered around state government issues; the isolation of the states from national politics as found in a one-party politics, makes attention to a national policy agenda exceedingly difficult.

V. O. Key, of course, was aware that the Southern states differed inter-nally and in their political operations, that all of the distinctive features of a one-party system did not apply to all states or all at any one point in time.

He also foresaw the coming of a Republican Party and with it an alignment of interests reflective of the national party's orientation and electoral group alignment. He was more optimistic than might have been justified in believing that a two-party competitive politics would evolve and that it would adequately concern itself with the social welfare and racial concerns of the South and its residents.

Finally, he, as have others, saw in the operations of a one-party/no-party system a reaffirmation of value and critical importance to a democratic state of a vital, functioning two-party competitive politics. For those who did not get the message, a one-party politics is authoritarian, status-based, unrepresentative (in the Southern case to the extreme), nonparticipation-oriented, and designed to further the interests of its economic elite. What stands out in the experience of the South is its longevity, success (whatever its internal failings) in achieving its objectives, and the degree of difficulty in bringing about meaningful change.

A More Competitive Party Politics?

The beginnings of the South's emergence from its noncompetitive one-party cocoon can be traced to a number of developments. Its discomfort with the candidacy of Democrat Al Smith in the 1928 presidential election provided a break with previous practice. Smith was a Catholic with little appeal to fundamentalist Protestants in the South, a product of Tammany Hall, a liberal governor of New York who looked and sounded like the Northeastern representative of a foreign party that he was. A dry, rural South found little of appeal in such a candidacy. Two decades later, the Dixiecrat rebellion of 1948 began when Strom Thurmond led a walkout from the Democratic National Convention that nominated Harry Truman. Southerners were angered by Truman's record on civil rights in general and by the planks on civil rights in the platform. The result was Thurmond's independent third-party candidacy, meant to deny Truman the prospect of election. Thurmond carried four Deep Southern states: South Carolina, Alabama, Louisiana, and Mississippi. Nonetheless, Truman won in an upset victory over Republican candidate Thomas E. Dewey of New York.

The popular Dwight D. Eisenhower, the commander of troops in Europe and of the Normandy invasion in World War II, running as a Republican, carried the states of Florida, Texas, Tennessee, and Virginia in the 1952 election. While he did reasonably well for a Republican in other states of the South, they remained in the Democratic Party's column. In the 1956 presidential race, Eisenhower carried Louisiana for the first time since Rutherford B. Hayes, as well as Tennessee, Kentucky, Florida, and Texas.

In more recent decades, and beginning with Barry Goldwater's embrace of a conservative states' rights agenda in the 1964 race against Lyndon Johnson, the Republican Party began to feature its "law and order" and "Southern strategy" campaign themes, code words for a racial appeal to whites in the South (and outside). It proved highly effective electorally. A permanent movement began with Richard Nixon's campaign in 1968 and 1972. Southern white support for the Republican Party was consolidated in the 1980 and 1984 Reagan elections. After 1968 and prior to Barack Obama, only two Democrats were elected president: Jimmy Carter, a conservative Democrat from Georgia, and Bill Clinton, a centrist/moderate from the border state of Arkansas.

The South has proven as effective in exercising its influence within the Republican Party coalition as it did in the Democratic Party's. It has emerged as the major faction in its congressional party, increasingly dictating its ideological tone in policymaking, setting litmus tests for its prospective presidential nominees, and establishing the policy agenda for House Republicans and by extension and to a considerable degree for the Congress as a whole (Lublin 2004; Black and Black 1992, 2002; Scher 1997; Clark and Prysby 2004; Steed, Moreland, and Baker 1997; McKee 2010).

The contemporary Republican one-party dominance of Southern politics has little in common with its Democratic predecessor in most respects. It is clearly more tolerant on racial matters; operates within a competitive, democratic context; adapts as necessary to electoral defeats; is organized and has the same policy commitments as its national party representatives; and accepts and operates within the bounds of nationwide norms of political and electoral correctness. The region's discredited Democratic one-party system did not honor such concerns. Still, in some respects, in its failure to incorporate African Americans into its coalition or to represent rather than oppose their concerns, social advancement, and policy interests, it may not be that different in this regard than its Democratic forebears. Then again, this is little different than the Republican Party nationally in its lack of commitment to such issues.

From the perspective of a mass democratic, representative, accountable, and inclusive polity offering competitive policy choices with continuity and a responsibility to act in concert with a nation's long-term interests, the one-party politics of the Democratic South offered a contradiction and a denial of the basic tenets of a democratic system. It embodied a different set of priorities and was built on a contrasting value structure, designed to serve quite different interests.

The one-party Democratic South is gone. In its place is a one-party Republican politics, equally conservative in economic terms compared to its predecessor. The Democratic Party in the South that emerged from the post-1960s realignment is based on a coalition of blacks and a small cadre of white liberals. In policy appeals and assumptions, unlike its predecessor, it is also in harmony with its non-Southern wing of the party. Unlike its predecessor within the region, it is a minority party with limited electoral success or policy impact regionally or nationally.

A Changing Racial Politics

The Great Migrations of blacks from the South to war manufacturing plants and industrial cities of the North began initially during World War I, then followed more decisively during World War II (Berlin 2010; Katznelson 1976). It was to change the nation's electoral geography and its politics. Further, the black veterans returning from a war against totalitarianism and racism were not inclined to accept a racially segregated country. Such forces would lead to restructured party alliances, especially for the Democrats. This was also to effect a decrease in the multiracial representation of minorities in the Republican Party and, within two decades, an increasingly self-conscious Republican appeal to a white electorate (Roland 1976).

Blacks had begun to mobilize in the process, moving from the Republican Party to the Democratic Party. Big city Democratic politics were the first to experience the infusion from a more politically assertive, and expanded, black urban population, soon to be followed at the national level (Weiss 1983). In time the black vote would become the largest and most loyal voting bloc in the Democratic coalition and of course culminated in the election of Barack Obama in 2008.

Whatever the demographic trends and the growing appeal of the Democratic issue agenda, the change was not to come easily. African American concerns were not a priority of the New Deal and at best came to be addressed indirectly in Franklin D. Roosevelt's class-oriented policy commitments and symbolically in Eleanor Roosevelt's strong public advocacy of black equality. The Solid South continued as a key component of the Roosevelt New Deal coalition. A Southerner served initially as FDR's vice president, and the support of Southern representatives in Congress was critical to the passage of New Deal legislation. The Republican Party had made inroads on the Democrats' coalition in 1928 (Republicans won forty states, Democrats eight), when the party ran the aforementioned Al Smith, a Catholic and a product of Tammany Hall, and the personification in speech, religion, and personal style of big city Northern politics. Smith was anathema to a Southern, rural, and fundamentalist white constituency. The later Dixiecrat walkout from the 1948 Democratic National Convention indicated what was to come.

Eisenhower's successes in the elections of the 1950s were viewed as rare exceptions brought on by the popularity of the Republican candidate and the specific circumstances of the presidential race in question. In 1964, with the nomination of conservative Barry Goldwater, matters would begin to change in fundamental ways. Goldwater lost overwhelmingly to Lyndon Johnson, paving the way for Johnson's Great Society and War on Poverty, civil rights agenda, and national health care programs, all attractive to a black constituency (Mackenzie and Weisbrot 2008; Milkis and Mileur 2005; Watson 2011). However, Goldwater's *Conscience of a Conservative* (2009 [1964]), his statement of its views in his campaign, and then its inclusion as the basis for the party's platform, would signal a massive political shift. It would lead to a rejection of the New Deal legacy that had been dominant in politics for over a generation, and to the beginning of the establishment of a Republican ascendancy that would continue into the twenty-first century. The election of Richard Nixon in 1968 began the process, and that of Ronald Reagan, a believer in Goldwaterism, would solidify the realignment and establish it as the nation's dominant political framework. Reagan was strongly conservative, a believer in eliminating New Deal social legislation, and a disciple of a limited-government agenda. The conservative movement in the Republican Party had little appeal for blacks, a view reinforced by Reagan and the Republicans' explicitly white-oriented appeals (Tate 1993; Dawson 1994).

On the other hand, and roughly parallel to these events, a moral-political awakening had begun to gain traction in US politics more generally. In 1944, Swedish social scientist Gunnar Myrdal published *An American Dilemma,* a comprehensive analysis of black conditions that would prove highly influential with the public, the political class, and the country's intellectual elite. It would give emphasis to a rethinking of racial attitudes that would come to influence the nation's politics.

Myrdal's study did not immediately transform America's approach to its racial problem, but it did significantly accelerate it and provide a solid research basis as to the striking discrepancy between values and reality in the treatment of black Americans. In this context, it could be seen as a call to conscience that proved unusually effective.

The introduction to Myrdal's study left no doubt as to how he saw social problems and what he believed was an anomaly in an otherwise democratic society. "It is embarrassing. It makes for moral uneasiness. . . . This takes on the proportion of a menace—biological, economic, social, cultural, and, at times, political. This anxiety may be mingled with a feeling of individual and collective guilt. . . . To all it is a trouble" (1944: xiv).

As for the South, "The White South *wanted the Negroes to fail as freedmen* and saw in their failure a confirmation of their own wisdom and the Northerners' folly" (emphasis in original). As for the political parties, Myrdal emphasized, "The party which works for change has the established law on its side . . . [and] wants to enforce it, but has not the political power; the party which stands for the status quo has the power but not the law" (1944: 445).

The message was clear. Myrdal's study and his advocacy of what he referred to as the American Creed have come to be seen, while concerned with race, as a standard in the assessment of American democracy and its strengths and shortcomings.

As this critical assessment was appearing, other forces were in motion. The Supreme Court, in *Smith v. Allwright* (1944), building on its *United States v. Classic* (1941) decision, ruled the "white only" Southern Democratic primary unconstitutional. The decision effectively signaled the beginning of the end for the institution that had made disenfranchisement and a one-party politics possible.

Roosevelt had issued an executive order in 1941 intended to end discrimination in the defense industry and in the government. He created the President's Committee on Fair Employment Practices (later the Fair Employment Practice Commission) to end discrimination in employment, although it lacked enforcement powers and so the committee's creation was largely a symbolic action.

The Congress of Industrial Organizations (CIO), in sharp contrast to the more established American Federation of Labor (AFL), actively recruited blacks to its union, a first for the country and an initial effort to move African Americans into the economic mainstream: "the C.I.O.'s contribution to changing patterns of race relations has been incalculable" (Meier and Rudwick, as quoted in Schuman et al. 1977: 13). Joining with the Roosevelt administration, the CIO began a decade-long campaign to increase black political participation in the South.

Harry Truman was particularly aggressive for his time in pushing civil rights issues. He appointed the Commission on Civil Rights in 1947. Its conclusions echoed those of Myrdal: "The pervasive gaps between our aims [as a nation] and what we actually do is a kind of moral dry rot which eats away at the emotional and rational basis of democratic beliefs" (quoted in Schuman et al. 1997: 8). The commission endorsed efforts to protect blacks from violence, ensure their political rights in the South, and improve their economic conditions, objectives that would take years to realize. Significantly for the era and the Democratic Party's immediate electoral fortunes, the commission called for an end to segregation.

Truman also desegregated the military, and the Democratic National Convention that nominated him in 1948 adopted civil rights amendments to its platform, resulting, as earlier mentioned, in a Southern third-party movement intended to ensure his defeat in the election.

These events were followed, of course, by what was considered the most important Supreme Court ruling of the twentieth century, the *Brown* (1954) decision, which ended segregation in schools and upheld desegregation as a principle to be applied to all of the society. This ruling of the Warren Court declaring segregation implicitly unequal and therefore unconstitutional reversed precedent, in particular the ruling in the *Plessy* (1896) case. The decision set in motion a wave of state-sanctioned mass violence, often led by elected officials and including mob and individual acts of intimidation against blacks in defiance of the Court order.

In response, the Supreme Court a year later issued a compliance standard calling for enactment with "all deliberate speed," a criterion vague enough not to satisfy any side. The decision did contribute to a mobilization of blacks, supportive whites, and eventually the federal government to force enfranchisement and desegregation.

The Civil Rights Era, 1954–1965

The movement would begin in the wake of the *Brown* decision with the national attention directed to the determined, often violence-prone attempts to thwart the realization of school desegregation. The use of state police powers to block implementation, rather than enforce it; both the official and the random terrorism targeting blacks, including children attempting to attend the white schools; the lawlessness of the period; and the disrespect and rejection of democratic procedural processes all served to educate a Northern public and its elected officials as to the intensity of racial prejudices broadly characteristic of Southern society. The actual social and living conditions encountered by Southern blacks would become a point of the nation's contention. And as a consequence, the national mood would change. Aggressive enforcement of existing laws, a mobilization of the black community along with its white supporters, and the introduction of new and more targeted federal legislation, accompanied a determined national intervention in the politics and voting practices of the South.

The renewed efforts to achieve integration, the most comprehensive since the early days of Reconstruction, began in the last half of the 1950s and reached their greatest success in the 1960s. The Eisenhower administration passed the Civil Rights Act of 1957. Sit-ins at the ice cream counter in the Woolworth store in Greensboro, North Carolina, in 1960 would lead in time to "freedom riders" and the "freedom summers" of the 1960s. With these aggressive, Northern-initiated efforts to end segregation and ensure the enfranchisement of blacks, a predictable series of violent confrontations would occur. Civil rights workers, black churches, ministers who were at the heart of the voting drives, "schools" where the activists sought to introduce local blacks to the complexities of registration and voting mechanisms, and even the buses carrying civil rights workers into the South were all to be attacked. People were beaten, homes were burned, police dogs were loosed. Eventually this violence and repression would lead to killings, as it did with the murders of Viola Liuzzo, James Cheney, Michael Schwerner, Andrew Goodman, Emmett Till, and Medgar Evers, and eventually with the assassination of Martin Luther King Jr. in 1968. King had attempted to lead a scripture-based, Ghandian movement of nonviolence against segregation.

A number of groups would come into existence to engage in the Southern civil rights struggle. These included most notably the Student Nonviolent Coordinating Committee (SNCC), to emerge as among the more aggressive of organizations. In addition to Reverend King's Southern Leadership Council, other more established groups such as the Congress for Racial Equality (CORE) and the venerable National Association for the Advancement of Colored People (NAACP, founded in 1911) became directly involved in the protests. Such groups not only functioned as on-the-ground advocates of the black vote but would come to play a more direct role in national party politics as the representatives of black aspirations. They would help push a reluctant Kennedy administration into an embrace of the movement and later would consult with Lyndon Johnson on tactical and legislative matters (Garrow 1986; Branch 1989; Williams 1987; Matthews and Prothro 1966; Woodward 2006).

The most ambitious efforts to promote black enfranchisement and a civil rights agenda more broadly would take place during Johnson's presidency. Johnson was a Southerner who had built his power and reputation as the most effective party leader in history on his support from the established core of Southerners in the Senate. In office, LBJ proved to be the most ardent advocate of the black cause and lower-class economic welfare interests more generally since the days of FDR's New Deal. Arguably, as seen in this company, Johnson would gain a place as one of the most successful presidents in history in seeing his domestic programs through to enactment. This period of intense activity during LBJ's term has been referred to by G. Calvin Mackenzie and Robert Weisbrot (2008) as the "liberal hour." It proved to be that and more, and was not to be repeated in subsequent administrations.

The Civil Rights Act of 1957 had made substantial improvements in a number of areas. It created a civil rights division in the Department of Justice; authorized the new division to prosecute election officials who denied the vote to blacks; and created a federal civil rights commission. The fatal weakness of the act was its failure to provide enforcement powers, an omission necessitated for the Southern bloc in Congress to allow its passage. The federal commission initially began a comprehensive effort to investigate racial discrimination, making its findings available to the public and doing what it could to promote a racially integrated Southern electorate. It would come increasingly under attack by Republicans with the eventual resurgence of a conservative movement that led to Republican appointees on its board of directors and staff. These included opponents to the very conception of such a commission as well as to its objectives. What followed was the progressive limitation of its activities to the point that its mission underwent a redefinition and its relevance as a force of importance in the fight against segregation faded into memory.

The 1957 Civil Rights Act would be the last such effort the Republicans would initiate. The subsequent 1964 Civil Rights Act was formulated in the Kennedy administration and passed by the Johnson administration. At least in part it was a response to the civil rights march on Washington, D.C., in the spring of 1963, the largest mass demonstration ever up to that time. It was the setting for Martin Luther King Jr.'s "I Have a Dream" speech, a powerful appeal for racial justice. The march called for new civil rights legislation, increased economic opportunity for African Americans, and the desegregation of Southern schools, which was still a point of intense resistance almost a decade after *Brown*.

Johnson pushed hard for the Civil Rights Act of 1964 and refused to compromise on its substantive provisions with either his former Southern colleagues in Congress or the Republicans. The legislation declared discrimination in public facilities and public employment illegal; mandated the US attorney general to initiate suits in the federal courts to force the desegregation of schools; and authorized the withholding of federal funds from segregated schools. What the act did not do, out of fear of a Southern and Republican backlash sufficient to bar passage of what was a controversial piece of legislation, was to address the question of black voting. This would come a year later with the Voting Rights Act of 1965.

The 1965 act was the most important legislation since Reconstruction as well as the most effective in the nation's history in ending segregated voting practices. It would increase black registration, at times through the appointment of federal registrars to enroll blacks in geographic areas of clear discrimination. It would lead not only to increased black participation in elections, but also to a basic realignment of the parties. As predicted by Johnson, the realignment would be at the expense of a Democratic majority in the electorate. The Republican control of the nation's political agenda would begin with the election of Richard Nixon in 1969. The act itself would become an object of Republican attacks whenever it came up for renewal. A series of court cases would challenge its constitutionality, or that of its most effective enforcement mechanisms, and the Supreme Court would indicate that it was receptive to hearing such challenges to the constitutionality of the legislation (Bullock and Gaddie 2009; Davidson and Grofman 1994; Parker 1990).

On a related note, and one important for black political mobilization, a rump group of blacks along with a few white liberals organized to oppose the white-dominated, segregationist official Mississippi Democratic Party, the accepted representative of the national party in the state. The Mississippi Freedom Democratic Party (MFDP), which began similar movements in other Southern states, took its case to the 1964 Democratic National Convention. The convention was designed to celebrate the Johnson administration's accomplishment, unanimously nominate LBJ, and launch his presidential general election campaign. Instead, and ironically, in a convention designed to avoid confrontation, the MFDP movement drew national attention. Johnson was not sympathetic and had the black party representatives ejected from the convention hall. Eventually, in a compromise that was rejected by the Mississippi Freedom delegation, it was proposed to allow several representatives of the group to be seated as honorary guests of the convention.

Despite its lack of short-term impact, the challenge had the desired effect. The national Democratic Party established a commission to review the issue. It recommended that any state party that excluded minorities would have its convention membership reduced proportionate to those not represented. In a major departure in the history and operation of either political party, the Democrats mandated compliance with the national party standards and authorized sanctions for noncompliance.

The action was well received within the party at the time. No one anticipated that it would come to be the basis for enforcing the post-1968 reforms of the nominating process, created after the chaos and violence of the Chicago convention. These reforms were to change the entire structure of the nominating process and to open the party and its decisionmaking on presidential candidates to the participation of grassroots supporters. For the times, and given the fundamental nature of the changes proposed, the reforms and their anticipated effect on the party (eventually on both political parties) were highly controversial and bitterly resisted. Prior to the 1972 election and their enactment, and likely since the inception of the party system, nominating processes had been at the discretion and under the control of state and local party leaders. They were most often arbitrary and closed to broad involvement. They functioned primarily as an incumbent protection and renomination plan. The reforms, in addition to the inclusion of blacks and other less represented groups, would lead to the adoption of a dominant, closely regulated primary system, open to all party members. The power to choose who would run for office on the party label was now in the hands of activists (i.e., those who chose to involve themselves) (Crotty 1978, 1983).

Whatever the immediate opposition for the changes experienced, the two party coalitions would be set and continue indefinitely into the future. The Democrats represented the North, urban areas, blue-collar workers (although the Republicans under Reagan would make serious inroads into this subgroup), blacks and most other minorities, professional women, and liberals. The Nixon and Reagan strategic appeals would lead to a predominantly white, overwhelmingly conservative, anti-statist, and, with the South added to the party's base, electorally successful coalition. The two parties would become increasingly ideological and divided, creating the polarity of political extremes that characterizes contemporary politics.

The Political World of Black and White America

A picture of the contrasting views on race can be found in survey data from the American National Election Studies (ANES) Cumulative File and its comparison across time of attitudes of blacks and whites relating to politics, government, and ideology. The lineage of the issues examined can be traced back to the beginnings of the University of Michigan national election surveys in the late 1940s and early 1950s. This is especially true for the most basic of attitudes that define the parties and establish their fundamental differences in appeal, which have proven reliable predictors of political behavior. The data also serve to establish the distinctive boundaries of the black political universe and develop its evolution over the generations.

In other areas of more recent concern, the timeline can be short; these become included in the national surveys when they emerged on the national stage. In areas other than those indicated, the level of broad agreement between the races can be considerable, approaching, within limits (relative differences in evaluations remain), a national consensus within the American culture or something reasonably close to it.

One party has proven to be historically friendly to black concerns (the Democrats), while the other has not (the Republicans). The parties' positions on social, economic, monetary, and reform matters in general have nothing in common with each other. The Republican Party, though seldom if ever characterized in this manner, comes close to being a white-only party. This can raise questions as to its role in and contribution to a pluralistic democratic society that values commitment to toleration, fairness, inclusiveness, and representativeness. The explanation, or rationalization, usually put forward is that race is not the dividing line; political opportunity and the potential for electoral success are the motivating factors. This may well be the case, but given the role and divisiveness of race in US history and the extreme difficulty in attempting to address the divide, a more accommodating, less strident view might prove more productive of the nation's welfare. Such an approach can be found on occasion in earlier generations of Republicanism, but is not part of its concern in the present age.

Seen from a campaign perspective, the white-oriented "law and order" and "Southern strategy" campaign begun by Richard Nixon in the immediate aftermath of the adoption of the Voting Rights Act (and taken from the third-party presidential campaign of segregationist governor George C. Wallace of Alabama) has proven unusually effective. The approach and its appeal were solidified in the election and presidency of Ronald Reagan. Reagan made a point of announcing his candidacy in the first of his successful campaigns in Philadelphia, Mississippi, the site of the murder of three civil rights activists: James Earl Chaney, Andrew Goodman, and Michael Henry Schwerner. The three workers were arrested by a deputy sheriff in June 1964 and then released into the hands of Klansmen. They were shot and their bodies were buried in an earthen dam. The case received national and international attention and was a mobilizing force in the adoption of the Voting Rights Act a year later.

Reagan chose to announce his candidacy within the context of this background. It was to be indicative of his thinking and can also be seen in relation to the political values of the Republican Party more broadly. Reagan began with some pointed political jokes, wished that the "Duke" could be there (the late actor John Wayne, a prominent staunch Republican and anticommunist), laid out his position on the national issues of the election, stated his belief that liberal federal social welfare programs should be returned to state control (which would serve to undermine them), and verbally attacked the Soviet Union. These all proved to be standard approaches of Reagan, to be heard repeatedly in the campaign to come. He then got to the more controversial aspect of his speech, the one that had brought him to Mississippi in the first place: "I believe in states' rights. . . . I believe we have distorted the balance of our government today by giving powers that were never intended to be given in the Constitution to that federal establishment. . . . If I do get the job I'm looking for, I'm going to devote myself to reorder those priorities and to restore to the states and local communities those functions which properly belong there" (Reagan 1980). This was a promise vague enough to be open to different interpretations. The wording used the location at which Reagan chose to announce his presidential run, and the talk of "states' rights" emphasized symbols familiar to Southerners. This was seen as a coded signal to George Wallace voters, a promise to reject extant civil rights laws, and an endorsement of support for, and even a return to, a white-dominated Southern society.

Washington Post columnist William Raspberry (2004) would later write, "Reagan took the Republican Party from virtual irrelevance to . . . ascendancy. . . . The essence of that transformation . . . is the party's successful wooing of the race-exploiting Southern Democrats. . . . Reagan's Philadelphia [Mississippi] appearance was an important bouquet in that courtship."

It may be that as African Americans move up the social and economic ladder, they might find the Republican Party's issue agenda more attractive and the party in turn might see them as a receptive group to organize. If done in large numbers (which at present is unlikely), such a development would effectively begin to transform the class-relevant nature of the political system and could help refute race-based partisan claims. Still, the Republican Party has done little to improve the standing of blacks or their position historically. The party's opposition beyond economic concerns in consistently opposing legislation seen as favorable to blacks, repeatedly attempting to repeal or render impotent the Voting Rights Act, and attempting to limit black political participation all reintroduce the racial issue. Not to be dismissed, the effectiveness of the appeal to a majority-white electorate in achieving election successes may prove too attractive to resist.

Better-defined issue domains clearly differentiate blacks and whites and fit nicely within the perceived political wisdom. With overwhelming consistency, blacks identify as Democrats and whites, though not as uniformly but still impressively, identify as Republicans. There was a closer correspondence in party associations during the Eisenhower years. Following the election of John F. Kennedy, this began to change. With the realignment of the South during the Johnson years and whites moving more decisively into Republican ranks, the party system assumed its present shape.

Liberalism is not a popular position in contemporary times. It is an identification that claims only about 20 percent of the voting population. The self-classification of liberal is down for blacks by one-third from earlier decades (the measure has been included in surveys since 1972). The realignment consolidated during Reagan's presidency depressed the liberal identification to where it has stabilized at present levels. One further difference in ideological positioning stands out: the proportion of African Americans reporting "don't know" in response to questions on ideology ran between 40 and 50 percent, at least twice as high as for whites.

There is a clear, sustained polarization in racial perceptions as to the role of government in American society, as has been indicated. Blacks believe in an activist government, involved in ameliorating social conditions and intervening in the economy and elsewhere as needed to more equitably transform the nation's social, educational, and economic opportunity structure. This belief applies in the area of domestic policy and reinforces the partisan divide over such issues as aid to minorities, unemployment insurance, tax equity, and national health care. African Americans as well as white liberals support such programs as a matter of social justice (Kinder and Sanders 1996; Schuman et al. 1997; Sears, Sidanius, and Bobo 2000; Hacker 2003).

Whites in turn favor minimal government regulation of the economy, industry, trade, the environment, the financial community, and taxes, and favor regressive taxation rates for the wealthiest. They oppose a social welfare state and the redistributive programs it would favor. On the other hand, and less discussed, they support federal and state stimulus plans for industry, enterprise zones, business start-up incentives, tax subsidies, and minimal regulation enforcement. The emphasis within this context is on a laissez-faire, free-market economic framework for distributing the resources of the society. This is accompanied by a belief that self-advancement is a matter of individual, not government, responsibility.

The races and the parties are polarized along these lines. Given the significance of their positions in meeting and advancing their own levels of needs, no obvious areas of mutual agreement receptive to consensus building are evident.

There is one perception of government the races do agree on. There is a strong tendency among both blacks and whites to fear arbitrary use of state powers, as well as a strong tendency to believe, for example, that politicians are crooks, that favoritism exists in awarding contracts, that special interests have a major impact on policy decisions, that government wastes money and is unable to efficiently administer programs, that politics is too complicated to understand, that people have little say in what government does, and so on. There has been a virtually linear growth in such attitudes, spiking in the 1970s in the age of Watergate, and continuing after that at much the same levels in the following decades and providing a contrast with more benign perceptions of the 1960s. While, as with everything else, the degree of intensity can vary by race, such beliefs have persisted, and reached new highs in the 1990s and the early twenty-first century.[1] There are occasional differences, however; for example, whites are twice as likely as blacks to think that government is too powerful. Nonetheless, the consistency of feelings of distrust, powerlessness, and governmental incompetence constitute something approaching a shared bond among blacks and whites. In more starkly political terms, Ronald Reagan's "government is the enemy" slogan undoubtedly contributed to legitimating such feelings. Overall, such a view, reinforced by what can seem like endless political abuses of the public trust, is unlikely to reinforce confidence in an activist, redistributive state.

The policy positions taken correspond closely to each party's ideological beliefs (see Chapter 2). The intra-racial levels of strength of support, as well as their consistency in distinguishing the parties, go far in determining, on a racial and party basis, where each party stands. Once the focus is moved from economic, social welfare, and redistributive politics, however, the picture changes. A good deal of cross-racial, cross-party agreement can be found in attitudes on international affairs, defense and defense-spending policy, the immediacy of a conventional war, the US role in the world community, and social agenda and lifestyle issues, such as women's equity in the workplace, approval of equal pay, and the like. This is not to say that there is relative agreement on all nondefining economic and social welfare policy areas. This is not the case, nor are the levels of intensity in approving selected positions the same. The direction such perceptions move in is related, and the gap in patterns of support is less severe.

A final point gets to the heart of the racial polarization over social welfare and aid programming. Whites believe that the condition of blacks is substantially better and its improvement more advanced than do the blacks themselves. African Americans in turn believe they live in a quite different world than do whites.

A Post-Racial Politics?

The election of an African American, Barack Obama, to the presidency led some to believe that the age of a post-racial politics, or color-blind politics, in the words of dissenting justice John Marshall Harlan in the *Plessy* (1896) case, was at hand. The foregoing does not suggest such a development. In 2008, 55 percent of whites voted against Obama and for his opponent; 95 percent of blacks voted for Obama. In the 2012 election, the results were similar, as 40 percent of whites voted against Obama and over 90 percent of blacks voted for him. While Obama's overall job approval ratings as president have sunk to below-majority lows, often into the vicinity of 40 percent or below among the electorate in general, African Americans have continued to support him, with approval ratings hovering around 90 percent or better.

Many observers had looked for, and it is fair to say hoped for, a positive improvement of consequence in racial attitudes following Obama's election, possibly even leading to the death throes of a racial prejudice in politics. It was too much to expect. In time, it may come to pass. At the present, race continues as a political force of consequence, dividing the parties in their appeal and issue advocacy and, arguably, exerting a more subtle influence among the population. It would have been far too optimistic to expect attitudes ingrained in the nation's collective consciousness for centuries to undergo such a fundamental orientation in such a short period of time, however historic the outcome of the election proved to be. During a speech in March 2008 (in reaction to Reverend Jeremiah Wright, Obama's pastor in Chicago who had made a fiery speech on race), President Obama made much the same point: "I have never been so naïve as to believe that we can get beyond our racial divisions in a single election cycle, or with a single candidacy—particularly a candidacy as imperfect as my own." Rather than speculating on a post-racial politics, a more realistic way to frame the issue, as put by Lawrence Bobo, is "whether Obama's success will permanently broaden who is seen as truly American or whether he will come to be seen as a quite special exception, with little bearing on the deeper cultural and social roots of racial division in America" (2011: 93). Bobo adds that he favors a "guarded optimism." A closer look at race in the 2008 elections may bring into question even this modest projection (Dasgupta and Yogeeswaran 2011).

Obama and the Black Community

Prior to running for president, Obama had a distant relationship to black America. He was by any standard a different type of black candidate. He had not grown up in an African American culture. His mother was white and he had little contact with his black father, a native of Kenya. He was brought up in Indonesia and later sent to a multicultural Hawaii to live with white grandparents and attend private schools. He was a graduate of an elite university and Harvard Law School. It has been said that he had returned to Chicago as a south-side community organizer to establish himself in a black environment, develop roots in the community, familiarize himself with its thinking, and begin to develop a political base. This he used to run for the US House in 2000, unsuccessfully, but then later, with better results, for the US Senate in 2004 (after serving in the Illinois legislature since 1997). He had no association with the civil rights movement, had not been an advocate for black causes, and had no identifiable support among African Americans nationally.

Obama's candidate profile was that of an articulate, prepared, knowledgeable, and highly educated candidate, projected as fulfilling the promise that was America. He could arguably be considered more a part of the mainstream white political culture than a representative of a minority, urban-based, and poor constituency. In campaigns, he made a conscious effort to appear calm, deliberate, and reasoned in speech and less combative than he might reasonably have been in public appearances. In the debates, even when under attack, he went to lengths to avoid being caricatured as an angry black man. It was both an intentional scripting as part of the campaign strategy and the measure of the man. The objective was to appeal to, or at a minimum not to alarm, the electorate's white majority. In his background and approach to campaigning, what was less clear was his appeal to and relationship with the black minority. At the start of the nomination campaign, these had yet to be established. What then to do? How was he to establish a connection and mobilize a national constituency of blacks, a critical need for a successful African American presidential campaign?

The strategy adopted was ingenious. It evolved early in the presidential election cycle and while Obama was still a minor candidate, little more than a blip on the nation's political radar. His early efforts were largely ignored by the mass media, although not by the black press. While unconventional, they would prove unusually effective.

Two events in particular define Obama's identification as a black man. The first took place in Selma, Alabama, several weeks after the announcement of his candidacy. Selma had been the site of repeated acts of violence during the 1960s directed against civil rights workers and led by the county sheriff, Jim Clark. The relevant historical background is that Reverend Martin Luther King Jr. had attempted to organize a march to the state capital to protest the situation. The marchers advanced as far as the town's Edmund Pettis bridge, where they were attacked by police dogs, state and local authorities, and bystanders. The carnage was captured on television and seen by the nation. It had immediate and significant results. President Lyndon Johnson appeared before a joint session of the Congress to push, successfully, for the Voting Rights Act. The Johnson appearance was memorable. He challenged the essence of the confrontations, warning Southerners, "It is wrong—deadly wrong—to deny any of your fellow Americans the right to vote in this country." In one of the more lasting moments of the nation's recognition of the severity of the problem, Johnson adopted the battle cry of the civil rights demonstrators: "We Shall Overcome!" It was hoped that the end of the disenfranchisement of African Americans, along with the realization of the intent of the Civil War amendments, was at hand, and that a fully inclusive political society was on the horizon.

Obama began his own Selma speech, delivered on the anniversary of the adoption of the Voting Rights Act, by acknowledging the presumptiveness of his decision to run for president. Implicitly recognizing his identification as a member of a minority, he used biblical references to place his candidacy within a religious context familiar to his listeners. In reference to others at the meeting, including Representative John Lewis (D-GA), a major organizer and participant in the Selma marches as a young man, Obama went on to say, "We're in the presence today of giants whose shoulders we stand on, people who battled, not just on behalf of African Americans but on behalf of all America . . . [who] battled for America's soul, shed blood, that endured taunts and ferment and in some cases gave the full measure of their devotion" (phrasing borrowed from Lincoln's Gettysburg Address).

He described the repressive conditions encountered by blacks and how he, through his grandfather and father, and by implication how blacks universally, were to profit from the promise that was America's. Selma, Birmingham, and the other crisis points in the civil rights struggle "sent a shout across oceans so that my grandfather began to imagine something different for his son [Obama's father]. His son who grew up herding goats in Africa could suddenly set his sights a little higher and believed that maybe a black man in this world had a chance." Obama went on: "What happened in Selma, Alabama, and Birmingham . . . stirred the conscience of the nation." And should the association have been missed, "don't tell me I don't have a claim on Selma, Alabama. Don't tell me I'm not coming home to Selma, Alabama."

> I'm here because somebody marched. I'm here because you all sacrificed for me. I stand on the shoulders of giants. I thank the Moses generation. . . .
> There are still battles that need to be fought; some rivers that need to be crossed. . . . The task was passed on to those who might not have been as deserving, might not have been as courageous, find themselves in front of the risks that their parents and grandparents had taken. . . . The previous generation . . . pointed the way. They took us 90% of the way there. We still got that 10%. . . . So the question . . . that I have today is what's called of us in this Joshua generation? What do we do in order to fulfill that legacy; to fulfill the obligations and the debt that we owe to those who allowed us to be here today?

Obama listed the problem that his campaign, and assumedly his presidency, would address, and encouraged blacks to get out and work to make it all a reality. In colloquial terms, "If Cousin Pookie would vote, get off the couch and register some folks and go to the polls, we might have a different kind of politics." It was a kind of imagery not to be heard again from candidate Obama.

Overall it was a compelling speech and one with an argument tying his campaign for office to the successes of the civil rights moment and projecting it as the realization of what in an earlier age had been little more than a dream.

This then would be the themes of Obama's appeal to blacks. He was a second-generation extension of the civil rights movement and its leaders who through their actions made his presidential candidacy possible. He framed it within a context soon to become familiar to those who followed his campaign; he was a representative not only of blacks but of all Americans in reclaiming a nation's soul, or in Myrdal's terms, in bringing to life the values contained in the American Creed. These are themes Obama would repeat both in the campaign and when in office.

The second test of Obama's candidacy in a racial context came in March 2008 in response to reports of incendiary remarks by Obama's pastor, the aforementioned Reverend Jeremiah Wright. This time the message was directed at white America. It was a call for unity in moving on to reach the realization of a better America. Obama, speaking in Philadelphia at the site of the Constitutional Convention, referred to "a Constitution that had at its very core the ideal of equal citizenship under the law; a Constitution that promised its people liberty, and justice, and a Union that could be and should be perfected over time." He continued:

> What would be needed were Americans in successive generations who were willing to do their part—through protests and struggle, on the streets and in the courts, through a civil war and civil disobedience and always at great risk—to narrow that gap between the promise of our ideals and the reality of their time.
>
> This was one of the tasks we set forth at the beginning of this campaign—to continue the long march of those who came before us, a march for a more just, more equal, more free, more caring and more prosperous America. I chose to run for the presidency at this moment in history because I believe deeply that we cannot solve the challenges of our time unless we solve them together—unless we perfect our Union by understanding that we may have different stories, but we hold common hopes; that we may not look the same and we may not have come from the same place, but we all want to move in the same direction—towards a better future for our children and our grandchildren. This belief comes from my unyielding faith in the decency and generosity of the American people. But it also comes from my own American story.

This was to be the basic theme of his presidential campaign: a call to a racially united America to realize the best of itself and its tradition of opportunity, fairness, and tolerance.

As for Reverend Wright, Obama left no doubt as to where he stood:

> The remarks that have caused this recent firestorm . . . expressed a profoundly distorted view of this country—a view that sees white racism as endemic, and that elevates what is wrong with America above all that we know is right with America. . . .
>
> Reverend Wright's comments were not only wrong but divisive, divisive . . . at a time when we need unity; racially charged at a time when we need to come together to solve a set of monumental problems—two wars, a terrorist threat, a failing economy, a chronic health care crisis and potentially devastating climate change; problems that are neither black or white or Latino or Asian, but rather problems that confront us all.

Then came reconciliation, an olive branch to Wright and by extension to the community he served:

> As imperfect as he may be. . . . He strengthened my faith, officiated my wedding and baptized my children. Not once in my conversations with him have I heard him talk about any ethnic group in derogatory terms, or treat whites with whom he interacted with anything but courtesy and respect. He contains within him the contradictions—the good and the bad—of the community that he has served diligently for so many years.

All in all it was a delicate balancing of racial perspectives couched in a rejection of what the reverend had preached and, most significantly, what it said about the United States. It was a virtuoso performance at a critical juncture in his presidential campaign. Obama took advantage of a nation's attention at a moment of racial questioning to reach out to the voting public at large.

Again the appeal was relevant to the campaign and it was effective. It tied Obama to the hopes of all Americans and positioned his campaign as a crusade to achieve the values the nation had been built on. And although Obama did not face another fundamental challenge to the legitimacy of his candidacy, he did encounter individual racial attacks, questions as to his citizenship (the "birthers"), and slurs such as those mocking his name (Sugrue 2010).

The effort to bridge the racial gap, build support as an outsider from a black constituent base, and allay the fears of whites as to the candidacy of a black man were all part of the campaign's approach. The hurdles were significant; what it took to surmount them adequately enough to be elected was at least as demanding.

What then was the impact of race on the campaign? The most comprehensive and intensive study of race in the 2008 election has been published by Michael Tesler and David Sears. They do not equivocate in stating their conclusion: "the election of our first black president was not a post-racial moment. . . . Racial attitudes were heavily implicated in every aspect of Barack Obama's quest for the White House. . . . Behind such success in the primaries and general election . . . *lay perhaps the most racialized presidential voting patterns in American history*" (2012: 159, emphasis added; on the 2012 campaign, see also Crotty 2013).

The basic point then is that race continues to be an elemental part of the country's political psyche, one that polarizes its parties and, as it has throughout the nation's history, challenges the inclusiveness and representativeness of its democratic institutions (Nunnally 2012).

A Note on Black Leadership

During the most robust period of black political mobilization and achievement in the movement of the 1960s, African American leadership, especially the mainline and more media-effective (in reaching a broader public), was led by ministers. The most notable of course was Reverend Martin Luther King Jr., who in his person and his rhetoric came to symbolize the aspirations of black America. This more conventional, nonviolent element was combined with a more aggressive Black Power strain that organized freedom riders and the volunteer efforts of civil rights workers to go to the South to educate and enroll black voters.

The ministers mobilizing and heading such drives in cities and rural areas throughout the South considered themselves to be speaking from the soul that manifested their Christian calling. They couched their rhetoric in biblical symbolism, as Obama was later to do in appealing for black support. They were the carriers of the Christian ideal to a region in need of its message as they saw it.

In the more than half century since, the political leadership of the black community has shifted to elected officials. The change is significant. Officeholders favor a more cautionary, less combative tone in dealing with the concerns of blacks. Their objective is more multidimensional; representing their constituents and getting elected requires a broader, less exclusionary civil rights rhetoric. They are also concerned with their potential for legislative effectiveness once in office. For a permanent congressional minority, this necessitates a conciliatory and more compromise-driven political approach. It involves a less angry, less outside-the-box, more mainstream political persona, one that embraces working with white representatives and one that may necessitate developing new political alliances—that is, moving beyond the

Democratic Party to develop working associations of mutual benefit with receptive conservatives and Republicans.

In this vein, Carol Swain writes, "Not only must blacks in Congress make alliances with like-minded representatives from other races and ethnic backgrounds, but they must also rethink their own priorities and the relationship of those priorities to African-American needs" (1995: 225; see also Tate 2003).

The basic problems facing the black community have not changed (Nunnally 2012; Robinson 2010). Legislative strategizing, despite the presence of a black man in the presidency, the nation's most powerful office, as to the best way to most effectively achieve some form of both conflict resolution and the improvement of social conditions, may need rethinking, and in turn a less polarizing agenda. How this would be achieved is another matter.

Conclusion

The story of African Americans' efforts to achieve representation within the political parties and more fully in the nation's political decisionmaking has been one of constant struggle. If one were seeking the extremes of polarization in the United States, race is it. The advancement of their interests is confined at present to one party; the other primarily opposes this. Blacks have had a president of their race, one they supported fully in elections and continued to identify with while in office.

The battle for political rights, however, is far from over, and predictably it continues to divide along party lines. The Republican Party has a consistent record of voting against the programs put forward to alleviate the class and political suffering of blacks, and yet has focused on minimizing the political participation of blacks (and other minorities) (Hasen 2012; Wang 2012). The party has successfully challenged the Voting Rights Act, the single most effective instrument for achieving black political participation, as seen in the Supreme Court decision in *Shelby County, AL v. Holder* (2013), which voided the process for applying the act's enforcement powers. This, as much as anything, is continuing evidence of a racial divide between the parties and in the country.

At the same time, attention has turned to class issues that profoundly affect the black community. Reverend King had indicated just such an increased concern as the focus of civil rights attention just prior to his assassination. The list of concerns is substantial, as befitting the segregated nature of the society and the history of race relations: poverty, AIDS, unemployment, education, health, income disparity, employment inequity, recession, teenage pregnancy, crime, home foreclosure, substandard housing, and residential segregation, among others. Also, and whatever the causes or potential for resolution, the high rate of incarceration of young black males has drawn critical attention. There is a negative white perception, mostly subconscious, of blacks that will continue to be troublesome. It does have political relevance. As Andrew Hacker notes, "There is scant evidence that the majority of white Americans are ready to invest in redistributive programs, let alone give of themselves in more exacting ways" (2003: xiii). The struggle of African Americans for political and economic equality continues.

As indicated earlier, Gunnar Myrdal catalogued the racial conditions and social problems of the country as he saw them in the 1940s. They were of course substantial for a minority world divorced, and largely unnoticed, by the majority of the white population. Much has improved since then, but Andrew Hacker's assessment in his 2003 book *Two Nations: Black and White, Separate, Hostile, Unequal*—his well-received evaluation of the nation's racial condition—indicates that there is much to be done. The challenge of segregated America remains. As it has in the past, it will come down to the political parties, their will to effect a broader national commitment to issues of social justice, and their level of success in achieving such objectives.

Racial issues, embedded in a politics and party system driven by class differences, have provided a particular dynamic to political polarization and have proven resistant to fundamental change. Conditions, political and economic, have clearly improved, as have racial attitudes incrementally over recent decades. More positive change can be expected. Yet there is little to indicate in the discussion in this chapter and the related research cited that despite the presidency being held by a black man, race will not continue to be a divisive force in US politics and party representation. It is one not amenable to easy or imminent resolution.

Note

1. These findings are based on an analysis of ANES data. See also Nunnally 2012.

10

Latinos, Partisanship, and Electoral Engagement

John A. Garcia

Recently there has been serious attention directed toward the Latino[1] community by political parties, campaign activities, and the mass media in the United States. At the same time, Latinos are exercising their dramatically expanding population base into greater political capital and increasing their impact on the political system. In addition, political parties have been more deliberate in their approach and appeals, while the mass media outlets are calibrating the real impact and voices for these communities. In this chapter, I explore two dimensions of the political world of Latinos. What is the extent of Latinos' electoral engagement (i.e., registration, voting, turnout, coethnic candidate support, and campaign activities)? And what are the partisan affiliations, preferences, and party interactions among this large and diverse community? Integrated into this discussion is a developmental perspective in terms of trends and changes.

It is difficult to introduce the subject of Latinos in the United States without acknowledging the "demographic imperative"—the dramatic and sustained growth rate that has increased the size of this community from one in eight Americans in 2000 to one in six Americans in 2014. This growth has driven much of the overall population growth in the United States over the same period. But my purpose in this chapter lies more with analyzing the impact of this community on the US political system, specifically political parties and elections.

In the midst of a contracted 2012 presidential election cycle, both the Democratic Party and the Republican Party made concentrated appeals to Latino voters to support their candidates. A long history of political science research has established the role of party affiliation and identification on voters' electoral choices, their ideology, and interest in elections (Campbell et al. 1960; Markus and Converse 1979; Miller 1991). Voters are also affected by their socioeconomic status, participatory orientation, and social-group identification, as well as by electoral rules. In the case of socioeconomic status, individuals with greater and more useful resources are more likely to register to vote, and to vote regularly. Higher levels of educational attainment, higher levels of income, and higher occupational status enable greater participation in political processes, greater targeting by political parties for mobilization, and more investment in the policy outcomes of government (Verba, Schlozman, and Brady 1995).

"Participatory orientation" usually refers to such cognitive categories as political efficacy, trust, and interest. Greater sense of empowerment serves as a basis and motivation for an individual to participate in the more fundamental expression of civic and political engagement, whereas political alienation and cynicism have a depressing effect on electoral participation by accentuating social distance and decreasing attachment to the political system and its processes. The act of voting is viewed as one of the foundations of a representative democracy, and the electoral "rules of the game" establish who can vote and how. Historically, electoral mechanisms such as the poll tax, literacy tests, "white primaries," and, more recently, voter identification laws have had negative and differential effects on minority communities (Fraga et al. 2012). In a broader sense, poll locations, registration periods, and redistricting schemes have also affected voter registration and turnout, especially for minorities (Davidson 1994).

The final cognitive categories are group consciousness and identification. These emphasize group affinity, attachment, and frame of reference for motivation to engage in collective action and pursue group policy and candidate preferences (Garcia 2010a). Whether described as "linked fate," the "Black utility heuristic," or "ethnic group consciousness," this sense of group unity or commonality serves as a prism through which to view and assess one's political importance (Dawson 1994; Garcia 2010b). While I focus here on the registration and turnout aspects of electoral participation (Fraga and Ramirez 2003, 2004), it should be noted that electoral participation extends beyond the acts of registration and voting. Working on campaigns, donating money to candidates and political parties, and partisan activism are also included in electoral participation.

Latinos and the US Electoral System

Even though the act of voting has been central for US democratic citizenship, this has not been an easy activity for Latinos to exercise. Voter suppression maneuvers, low levels of political knowledge about elections, low socioeconomic status, and limited English-language proficiency have reduced Latinos' electoral participation. Legislation like the Voting Rights Act of 1965 and its subsequent extensions has enabled more Latinos to be more politically engaged (Garcia 2010a). Provisions for bilingual ballots and other voting materials, pre-clearance of election-related changes, and redistricting challenges and biases in election systems have created opportunities for Latinos and civil rights organizations like the Mexican American Legal Defense and Education Fund (MALDEF) and the National Council of La Raza (NCLR) to pursue voting rights implementations. For example, the creation of majority/minority districts, or districts of influence,[2] along with judicial interventions, helped to increase the representation of Latino elected officials at every level of government during the 1980s and 1990s. These legal actions had the net results of enhancing gains in Latino voter registration and turnout.

However, the substantial growth of the Latino population has not resulted in a corresponding change in the trajectory of Latino representation among the US electorate (see Table 10.1 and Figure 10.1). As of 2000, almost 40 percent of Latino adults in the United States were foreign-born, and Latino immigrants to the United States had lower rates of naturalization than persons from other parts of the world. This reached a record low of 38 percent in 1990 and in 2011 has improved to 56 percent. If an estimated 11 million undocumented Latino immigrants are added to the population base, then the growing Latino tide could entirely redraw the landscape and politics of the United States (Patten 2010). At the same time, issues of political incorporation, effective political socialization, and movement toward citizenship come into play, affecting increased electoral participation (Fraga and Ramirez 2003). Even though undocumented Latino immigrants are not directly engaged in voting, their recent political activism has generated

Table 10.1 Voting-Eligible Population, Actual and Projected, 2012 and 2030 (millions)

	2012	2030	Share of Growth (%)
Hispanic	24	40	41
White	154	163	23
Black	27	35	21
Asian	9	16	15
All	215	256	100

Sources: Pew Hispanic Center tabulations of the August 2012 Current Population Survey, and Pew Research Center projections for 2012.

Notes: Eligibility based on age and citizenship. "White," "Black," and "Asian" include only the non-Hispanic components of those populations. American Indian/Alaska Native not shown. "Share" calculated before rounding.

Figure 10.1 The Latino Presidential Vote, 1980–2012

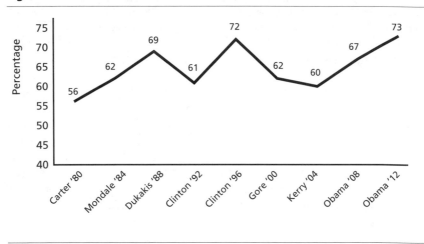

Source: Pew Hispanic Center 2012.

greater interest and involvement by the Latino electorate. This serves as a good example of the contextual factors that affect electoral participation. This air of anti-immigrant and anti-foreigner sentiment has resulted in higher rates of Latino naturalization since 2000 (Pantoja, Ramirez, and Segura 2001; DeSipio 1996) and higher than expected levels of voter registration and turnout among this group.

The primary detriment to Latino voter registration and turnout is socioeconomic status, which emphasizes the accumulation of social capital, skills, and attention attained through more education, higher income, and greater occupational status. Individuals with these attributes tend to incorporate participatory orientations and have greater political knowledge and interest, and are more likely to be contacted for voter mobilization. These attributes enable persons to devote the time, attention, and cognitive resources necessary to decipher what is at stake in an election, what candidates believe, and other matters of political importance (Garcia and Sanchez 2004; Garcia 2010a, 2010b). In the case of Latinos, education is a strong contributor to voter registration and regular turnout. Income and occupational status tend to be less salient predictors of electoral participation.

Another dominant demographic characteristic of Latinos is their youthfulness; they have a median age of 27.2 (US Census Bureau 2004), which is almost ten years younger than the median age of the US population overall. There are at least two implications of this age distribution. The first is that younger adults participate much less than their older counterparts, as the peak age grouping for active voters has historically been 35–50. Second, almost 750,000 Latinos turn 18 annually, and most of these are native-born citizens. So this addition to the Latino electorate presents a challenge of "bucking" the pattern of lower levels of electoral participation among the young, and thus development of a more participatory orientation and the exercise of political expression become the targets of outreach and mobilization efforts such as focused voter registration drives, engaging Latino youth, and generating Latino identity and group pride.

Recent research (Michelson 2005; Garcia-Bedolla and Michelson 2012) has produced evidence that directing attention to Latinos can improve voter interest and turnout. For the most part, the campaign efforts of both Democratic and Republican candidates have placed lower priority on trying to mobilize Latinos, who have been characterized as having "low propensity" and being hard to mobilize. Efforts by primarily Latino-based organizations have targeted this community for voter registration and turnout. Their approach has concentrated on one-on-one interpersonal contact and use of coethnic canvassers to connect with prospective Latino voters (Barreto, Segura, and Woods 2004). Historically, organizations like the Southwest Voter Registration and Education Project have targeted concentrated Latino areas and engaged in conversations about important concerns and issues, and the extent of responsiveness under current political regimes. Over time, one lesson learned is that the timing of voter registration matters, such that voter registration campaigns must occur close to election periods. In this manner, efforts prior to an upcoming election would encourage Latinos to vote and seek public office. Paul Frymer (2010) has suggested that outreach to Latino and other minority voters may demobilize white voters if race is a salient factor in a community, legislative district, or state. Another perspective among the major parties is that the relatively lower registration and turnout rates among Latinos may cost the party or candidate more votes than it gains.

I have identified socioeconomic status, participatory orientations, structural factors, and mobilization as key determinants of voter registration and turnout. These determinants apply to Latinos, but in somewhat differing degrees. For example, education is a strong predictor for Latino voter registration and turnout, but income and occupational status are weaker predictors. At the same time, a fuller understanding of these electoral dynamics needs to incorporate Latino-specific measures. That is, nativity versus foreign-born status, language use and proficiency, national origin, generational distance from immigration, naturalized citizen or not, and group identity and consciousness represent salient dimensions of being Latino in the United States (Fraga and Ramirez 2004). The significant percentage of Latino adults born outside the United States raises a number of issues regarding electoral participation (Cho 1999; Leal 2002). Obviously, a prerequisite for voter registration is citizenship status, such that fulfilling naturalization requirements and securing naturalized status can diminish or augment the electoral base for the Latino community. Since 1960, lower rates of naturalization among Latino immigrants, especially those of Mexican origin, have been a long-standing pattern; yet a hostile anti-immigrant climate and restrictive immigration policies have served as a catalyst for Latino immigrants to attain citizenship status (Jones-Correa 1998; DeSipio 1996).

There have been a few studies that have analyzed the naturalization rates of Latino immigrants by their country of origin and contributing factors (see Table 10.2). For the most part, Mexican-origin Latinos have had low rates of naturalization (a similar pattern holds for US immigrants of Canadian origin), but such low rates of naturalization exist for nearly all Latino immigrants, regardless of origin. Factors such as length of time in the United States, age at which immigration occurs, greater levels of acculturation, higher English-language proficiency, higher educational attainment, and stronger attachment to the United States and sense of belonging all result in increased rates of naturalization (Pantoja and Gershon 2006). In addition, a restrictive or anti-immigrant climate has served to motivate Latino immigrants to naturalize (largely to elevate their status legally) (Segura and Pan-

Table 10.2 Latino Naturalizations by Nation of Birth, 2007–2008

Nation of Birth	Number of Latino Naturalizations		Percentage Increase	Rank as Naturalization Source, 2008[a]
	Fiscal Year 2007	Fiscal Year 2008		
Mexico	122,258	231,815	90	1st
Cuba	15,394	39,871	160	5th
El Salvador	17,157	35,796	109	7th
Dominican Republic	20,645	35,251	71	8th
Colombia	12,089	22,926	90	9th
Nicaragua	8,164	17,954	120	13th
Guatemala	8,181	17,087	109	14th
Peru	7,965	15,016	89	15th
Ecuador	7,229	11,908	65	19th
Honduras	4,669	8,794	88	25th

Source: Department of Homeland Security, Office of Immigration Statistics.
Notes: a. For fiscal year 2008. This table identifies naturalizations from countries of birth of Latino ancestry. (The countries ranked 2nd to 4th are India, China, and Vietnam. The other top twenty-five countries of birth are primarily from Asia, Africa, and Caribbean regions.)

toja 2003). The latter factor has been associated with closing the gap in voter turnout rates between native-born and naturalized Latino voters.

These factors that affect Latino voter registration—especially education, and to a lesser extent income—also affect Latino voter turnout. There is also a slight gender effect, as Latinas vote at slightly higher percentages compared to their male counterparts. In terms of national origin, Cubans self-report the highest level of voting, while Salvadorans self-report the lowest levels. Again, turnout is also affected by voter contact with the political parties and their candidates. According to the results of the 2006 Latino National Survey, only 30 percent of Latino voters reported any mobilization contact (Fraga et al. 2012). If one distinguishes between native-born and naturalized Latino citizens, the latter group is largely ignored. If contacted, they are Latinos who have attained higher educational and occupational status. Socioeconomic status is a salient force, as it is expected that those with higher socioeconomic status have the skills, knowledge, and motivation to vote and are more likely to do so. In terms of voter contact by national origin, Cubans, followed by Mexicans and Puerto Ricans, are the most contacted Latino groups in the United States.

Electoral Participation and Partisanship

A discussion of Latinos' electoral participation would be incomplete without discussion of the patterns of partisanship among this group. Early work on Mexican American electoral politics (Kramer and Levy 1972) extolled three major truths: that Mexican Americans are Catholic, Democratic, and politically apathetic. It is the ascribed long-standing connection of Mexican Americans to the Democratic Party that guides the discussion of Latino electoral participation here. As already indicated, it is well accepted that Latinos in the United States, with the exception of Cuban Americans, favor the Democratic Party (DeSipio 1996; Garcia and Sanchez 2004). But the stability of Democratic Party identification among Latinos requires further inquiry. Recent evidence from the Pew Hispanic Center (Lopez and Taylor 2012) and Latino Decisions (Barreto and Segura 2012) has shown that the ratio of Latino Democrats to Latino Republicans has grown beyond a margin of 2.5 to 1.

I now turn to a discussion of partisan identification among Latinos (see Figure 10.2) and of the associated predictive characteristics, such as salience of partisan identification, ties with political ideology, and support for coethnic candidates. The political science literature on partisan identification among the nonminority population is well established (Campbell et al. 1960; Markus and Converse 1979; Fiorina 1981; McKuen, Erikson, and Stimson 1989; Miller 1991). Examination of partisan identification among minority groups is more recent, with direct application of prevailing nonminority models showing some areas of "lesser fit" with minority groups. Part of the

Figure 10.2 Party Affiliation Among Latino Registered Voters, 1999–2011

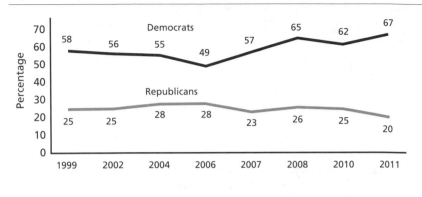

Sources: Pew Hispanic Center, 2002–2011 National Surveys of Latinos; *Washington Post,* Kaiser Family Foundation, and Harvard University, 1999 National Survey on Latinos in America.
Notes: For 2011, *N* = 557. For all years, includes respondents who say they consider themselves Democrat or Republican or lean toward the Democratic Party or the Republican Party. Responses of "don't know" and "refused" are not shown.

explanation why prevailing models of partisanship have less predictive "power" for Latinos lies with the paucity of minority respondents in many national surveys. For example, the American National Election Studies (ANES) would, from time to time, oversample the African American population, until the 2008 ANES incorporated a sampling strategy to ensure adequate numbers of Latino and African American respondents. In addition to increasing the number of Latino respondents, examination of partisanship among Latinos requires factoring in how any distinct experiences of being Latino (i.e., the immigration experience, language, cultural and social identity) may influence how Latinos relate to the major political parties.

Latino partisanship includes dimensions such as the difference between native-born and foreign-born Latinos, and the difference between naturalized and native-born Latinos, in addition to political socialization experiences as well as the more conventional factors of social class, gender, ideology, and education. The extant research literature finds a preponderance of Democratic Party affiliation among most Latinos. Bruce Cain, D. Roderick Kiewit, and Carole Uhlaner (1991) found that Latinos have become strongly more likely to identify with the Democratic Party since the rise of anti-immigrant public sentiment. Greater familiarity with and exposure to US politics have also increased Democratic identification among Latinos, and this trend continues across generations. Carole Uhlaner and F. Chris Garcia (2005) found that among national samples of Latinos of Mexican, Cuban, and Puerto

Rican origin, their identification with the Democratic Party increased the longer they lived in the United States. In the case of Cuban-origin Latinos, though, they identify more strongly with the Republican Party, due to a strong overlap of anticommunist and anti-Castro sentiment.

In addition, R. Michael Alvarez and Lisa Garcia-Bedolla (2003) reported that 56.6 percent of their Latino survey respondents identified as Democrats, 24.5 percent as Republicans, and 13.0 percent as independents. Salience of party identification was greater for Latinos of Puerto Rican and Mexican origin, while salience among Cuban Americans was significant for the Republican Party. The alignment of issue positions between Latino voters and the respective parties was a major determinant of party identification. As witnessed in the 2012 elections, the Republican Party's policy positions conflicted with Latino public opinion, to the benefit of increased Latino support for the Democratic Party. Zoltan Hajnal and Takeu Lee (2003), in their examination of Latino independents, demonstrated that levels of acculturation (both cultural and political) serve as a key factor in partisan attachment for this group. These researchers suggest that partisan attachment is more complex for Latinos than for other groups in the United States. In addition to the experience of being Latino in the United States, basic research approaches to sampling design and question wording also have a significant impact on the understanding of partisanship as well as on the clustering of established independent variables (Barreto 2010).

An interesting aspect of the generational transmission of party identification across Latinos is that of naturalized citizens. In 2006, only 12 percent of first-generation noncitizen Latinos identified as "strong Democrats," compared to almost 28 percent of first-generation naturalized Latino citizens (Fraga et al. 2012). The Democratic advantage holds generally for all Latino national subgroups by substantial margins, ranging from a low of 2.5 to 1 among Central Americans to 7.6 to 1 among Dominicans. Mexican-origin Dominicans and Puerto Ricans are the three most Democratic groups (Fraga et al. 2012). For the Cuban community, 48 percent identify themselves as Republicans and almost 27 percent identified themselves as "strong Republicans." However, a recent study of partisanship in this community shows some shift to the Democratic Party among second-generation Cuban Americans (Jensen 2008).

Consistent with the extant literature on partisanship, education and income play a role in the self-reporting of party affiliation. That is, Latinos with more education and higher levels of income are more likely to indicate a party identification. This research supports the relationship between education and income, and higher levels of political knowledge and greater access to political resources. Latinos at the lower end of this spectrum are much more likely to report that they "do not know" their party affiliation compared to Latinos at the higher end of the spectrum. Among naturalized Latino voters, those who identify as Democratic are twice as likely to register to vote as those who identify as Republican (Fraga et al. 2012). Whereas income is a good predictor of party affiliation for the general population, it is much less salient for Latinos, as the prevalence of Democratic affiliation is consistent across higher education and income levels (Fraga et al. 2012).

While the results of the 2012 elections indicated a growing and more active Latino electorate, an important concern was the extent of Latinos' enthusiasm and closeness to the Democratic Party in relation to turnout levels. Luis Ricardo Fraga and colleagues (2012) examined the extent of Latinos' attitudes toward the Republican and Democratic parties, controlling for generational status (i.e., distance from the immigration experience), citizenship, education, and income. Their results demonstrated stable and consistent attitudes among Latinos toward both parties. As their overall partisan affiliation suggests, Latinos hold much more positive attitudes toward the Democratic Party than toward the Republican Party. This pattern holds across the various national-origin subgroups of Latinos, except for Cuban-origin Latinos, whose closeness to the two parties remains more equally divided. Even across income and educational groupings, partisan attitudes among Latinos as a whole remain unchanged since the 1980s and noticeably more positive toward the Democratic Party than toward the Republican Party. At the same time, almost one-third of Latinos indicate that neither party has sufficiently advocated for their interests.

For the general population, conservative-leaning individuals tend to identify as Republican and liberal-leaning persons as Democratic (Leighley and Velditz 1999). For Latinos, just fewer than 50 percent who identify as Democrats place themselves ideologically as conservative (whether weakly or strongly) (Fraga et al. 2012). For second-generation Latino Americans, there is more of a bifurcated pattern, with 39 percent indicating a liberal leaning and 36 percent classifying themselves as conservative-leaning. This pattern holds across national-origin subgroups, and is also evident in income levels, with about 25 percent of Latinos who earn less than $15,000 annually identifying as strongly conservative, and about 20 percent of Latinos who earn more than $54,000 annually identifying as strongly liberal. The same distribution holds for education levels, with Latinos who have less than a high school education tending to be more conservative (slightly) than their college-educated counterparts.

For Latinos, how well ideological stance predicts partisan identification has not been examined to the extent as for other voter groups. Other research on Latino partisanship (Ramirez 2002; Bowler, Nicholson, and Segura 2006) indicates that Latinos are more supportive of governmental "intervention" on economic, social, and civil rights issues, but more fiscally conservative, compared to the general population. Abrajano, Alvarez, and Nagler (2008) show the importance of social and moral issues and their role in affecting Republican gains among Latinos in the 2004 presidential election. At the same time, Latinos' ideological orientation (liberal or conservative) has not ensured any greater movement of Latinos to political party, especially in terms of identifying as Republicans (Segura and Bowler 2011). In addition, ideology is a multidimensional concept, such that variations across substantive policy areas (i.e., policy preferences, priorities, and positions) can make it difficult for political parties to assume a singular unifying ideological strand to affect partisan identification and support by Latinos.

A final factor in this examination of partisanship among Latinos is the presence of coethnic candidates in elections. The long-standing literature on political parties demonstrates the strong influence of partisan affiliation on voter choice. At the same time, the role of race/ethnicity in influencing voters' self-identification and candidate choice indicates significant levels of voter polarization. At times, the race/ethnicity of voters prompts them to cross their own party lines to vote for coethnics of the "other party" (Barreto, Villarreal, and Woods 2005; Hill, Moreno, and Cue 2001; Manzano and Sanchez 2009). This has been demonstrated with African American voters, but in most cases African American candidates run as Democrats. For Latinos, how important is it to support a Latino candidate regardless of partisan affiliation? Again, Fraga and colleagues (2012) show that a clear majority of Latinos indicate that it is important to them that a candidate be Latino. This initial support declines somewhat when education and income are controlled for. An added dimension is the candidate's ability to speak Spanish. Again, a majority of Latino respondents indicate that it is important that a candidate know how to speak Spanish. This sentiment is significant across all income groups except for Latinos who earn more than $54,000 annually. A similar pattern exists across education levels, as almost three-quarters of Latinos with less than a high school degree, three-fifths of Latino high school graduates, and one-half of Latinos with college education think it important that a candidate speak Spanish. Regarding support for coethnic candidates, over three-quarters of Latinos think it is important or very important to support a candidate whose policy positions are consistent with their own. As a result, the presence of a coethnic is a favorable starting point for gaining Latino attention, but this may not lead to support for that candidate if the coethnic takes policy positions in opposition to the preferences of the Latino community (Barreto 2010).

Latinos and Partisanship in the 2012 Elections

Since 1988, while Latinos have trailed other racial/ethnic groups (i.e., whites and African Americans) in terms of voter registration and turnout levels in elections, their participation has been increasing (Taylor et al. 2012) (see Figure 10.3). This pattern, combined with continuous high population growth of

Figure 10.3 Latino Participation in Presidential Elections, 1988–2012

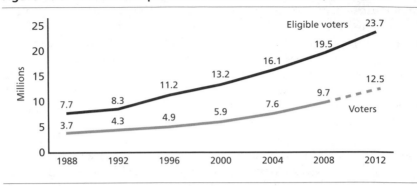

Source: For 1988 through 2008, Pew Hispanic Center tabulations of the Current Population Survey November Supplements; for 2012 number of "eligible voters" (23.7 million), Pew Hispanic Center tabulations of the August Current Population Survey; for 2012 number of "voters" (12.5 million), Pew Hispanic Center estimate based on the National Election Pool national exit poll and number of votes tallied as reported by media outlets and election turnout experts.

Note: "Eligible voters" are US citizens ages eighteen and older.

Latinos, increasing numbers of naturalized citizens, and more Latinos reaching the age of majority, has added to the size of their electoral base. Besides socioeconomic factors that affect voter registration and turnout, heightened group identification (both national-origin and pan-ethnic) and mobilization among Latinos have resulted in substantial gains for Latinos as a major electoral community. The 2012 elections served as a confirmation of the arrival of the Latino electorate, as the national media, political parties, and polling firms took their presence into greater account in campaign strategies and campaign coverage, anticipating the significant impact of Latinos on the outcome of the elections (see Figure 10.4).

Both the Pew Hispanic Center (Lopez and Taylor 2012) and Latino Decisions (Barreto and Segura 2012) exit polls reported substantial Latino voter support for the reelection of President Barack Obama: 71–75 percent for Obama and 23–27 percent for Mitt Romney. Latino Decisions reported that the Latino net effect on President Obama's vote margin was 5.4 percent, and that Latinos provided critical margins in the battleground states of Colorado, Florida, Ohio, Virginia, and Nevada. For states like Virginia and Ohio, despite smaller-percentage Latino populations, their significant levels of support for Obama (e.g., 66 percent of Latinos in Virginia, and 82 percent in Ohio) made a difference. The margin of Obama's victory in Colorado was fueled by an 87 percent Latino vote. In the Florida contest, one of the closest, 57 percent of Latinos voted for President Obama. The population gains of non-Cuban Latino Americans (i.e., Puerto Ricans and Mexicans), as well

Figure 10.4 Election Capsule, 2012

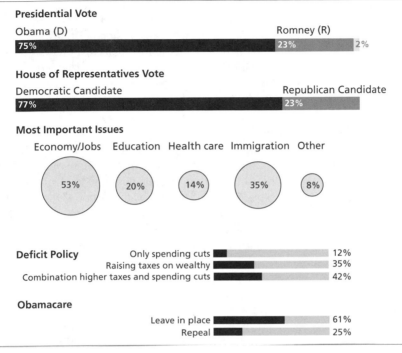

Presidential Vote

Obama (D)   Romney (R)

| 75% | 23% | 2% |

House of Representatives Vote

Democratic Candidate   Republican Candidate

| 77% | 23% |

Most Important Issues

Economy/Jobs   Education   Health care   Immigration   Other

53%   20%   14%   35%   8%

Deficit Policy
Only spending cuts — 12%
Raising taxes on wealthy — 35%
Combination higher taxes and spending cuts — 42%

Obamacare
Leave in place — 61%
Repeal — 25%

Source: Barreto and Segura 2012.

as the decline of Cuban Republican presidential support, may have helped Obama carry that state.

Latino Decisions also reported similar levels of support for Democratic candidates among Latinos in the congressional races of 2012. The Latino vote for Democratic candidates for the Senate ranged from 57 percent (Florida) to 89 percent (Massachusetts). A similar level of Latino support was demonstrated for Democratic candidates for the House, representing some partisan consistency among Latinos in voting for national offices. Both polling organizations reported that the economy was the top policy issue among Latino voters (53–60 percent), followed by immigration (30–35 percent) and then education and health. On immigration policy, an overwhelming 71 percent of Latinos supported a path toward legalization as central for immigration reform. Demographically, larger percentages of Latino college graduates, Latinos earning less than $50,000 annually, and Latino youths supported President Obama compared to Latinos' overall support for the president. Finally, Latino Decisions calculated that the magnitude of Latino voter support and turnout made the difference of President Obama winning the national popular vote.

All of this indicates a clear trajectory of increased Latino electoral participation and greater attention directed by the major political parties at ensuring Latino support. While the general media have begun focusing intently on America's changing demographics only recently, I would contend that this pattern has been evident for over a decade. The difference lies more with the realization that the behaviors of the country's "growth" segments (Latino Americans primarily, but also Asian Americans) are affecting political processes and outcomes.

So what lies ahead for Latinos' electoral participation and partisanship? The growth curve will continue well into this century. Latinos will account for 40 percent of the growth of the voting-age population in the United States between 2010 and 2040. This continued growth is the result of more Latino youth reaching the age of majority and more Latino permanent resident aliens becoming naturalized citizens. The conversion of this growth into voter gains will lie with continued mobilization of the Latino community (Fraga et al. 2010).

Political parties factor into this growth equation. For the Republicans, who have distanced themselves from a more diverse constituency and adopted a less Latino-friendly policy agenda and platform, will they see a need to reevaluate and change their strategy? Some state and local units of the Republican Party have indeed tried to soften their policy agenda (less restrictive positions on immigration, less emphasis on moral issues, etc.) to minimize negative rhetoric toward immigrants and avoid questioning who the "real Americans" are. The key test will be the development of some consensus among the Republican Party's elites and activists (including conservative media icons) toward more constructive and open dialogues with the Latino community. The latter is equally applicable for the Democrats. While they enjoy a long-standing and clear partisan edge among Latinos compared to the Republicans, there is evidence of Latino dissatisfaction with the Democratic Party over its inclusiveness, participation, and policy congruence with Latino sentiments.

The demonstrated Latino effect in the 2012 elections will raise expectations and pressures from this community to seek greater Democratic Party responsiveness. The inclusiveness and direction of its policy agenda will be critical in determining future patterns of Latino electoral participation and partisanship. The Democratic Party's current advantage can be maintained with a mutually beneficial exchange with the Latino community (i.e., incorporating and implementing priorities within the Latino policy agenda as well as supporting more Latino candidates), while the Republican Party, if it is to make significant inroads, needs to redirect its policy emphasis such that negativity about immigrants, the poor, the un-acculturated is not synonymous with Latinos and other national origin communities. In addition, greater inclusion of Latinos and their interests must become more evident in its party leadership and its representatives. Clearly, the partisan challenges for both of the major political parties lie with Democrats demonstrating concrete benefits for Latinos' continued support and Republicans' openness to greater diversity of views and priorities that are more consistent with Latino interests. To a significant extent, the 2012 elections and contemporary partisan politics crystallized Latinos' commitment to a responsive party system; they will not be satisfied with rhetoric alone.

Notes

1. Use of the term *Latino* in this chapter refers to persons of Latin American or Iberian Peninsula ancestry or origin who reside in the United States.

2. "Districts of influence" refers to legislative districts in which a "critical mass" of Latinos (i.e., composing 25–40 percent of the population) resided.

11

Gay Rights
and the Party Divide

Paul R. Brewer and Shawn C. Fettig

In late 2010, opponents and supporters of "Don't Ask, Don't Tell," a policy that barred openly gay people from serving in the US military, fought a dramatic political battle over its fate. A previous effort by President Barack Obama and his Democratic allies in Congress to overturn the policy had failed in the US Senate in September 2010, when Senator John McCain, the Republican nominee whom Obama had defeated in the 2008 presidential election, led a filibuster against a broader defense bill that would have repealed it. After the midterm elections in November 2010 gave the Republicans a new majority in the US House of Representatives, opponents of "Don't Ask, Don't Tell" knew that their only chance in the foreseeable future to overturn the policy would be the lame duck session of the outgoing Congress, in which Democrats would still hold majorities in both chambers.

The final battle over the fate of "Don't Ask, Don't Tell" began on November 30, 2010, when the US Department of Defense released a study concluding that a repeal of the policy would have little impact on military effectiveness. On December 2, Secretary of Defense Robert Gates and Admiral Mike Mullen, who chaired the Joint Chiefs of Staff, testified in favor of repeal to the Senate. The following day, however, the chiefs of the army and the marines defended the policy in their testimony to the Senate. McCain, still leading the opposition to repeal, seized on their comments to bolster his stance. On December 9, a new vote to lift his filibuster against the defense bill failed by three votes, with one Democratic senator and all of the Republican senators except for Susan Collins voting against cloture.

Immediately after the vote, Collins and Joe Lieberman (an independent senator who caucused with the Democrats) announced that they would introduce a separate bill to repeal "Don't Ask, Don't Tell." Six days later, the House of Representatives passed this standalone bill. After considerable political maneuvering, five other Republican senators joined Collins and the Democratic majority in voting on December 18 to bring the repeal bill to the floor of the Senate. That same day, the bill itself passed on a 65–31 vote, with two additional Republicans joining the winning side. On December 22, Obama signed the bill. For gay rights activists, the outcome represented a decisive victory in their seventeen-year battle to overturn the policy.

Whereas the battle over gay men and women serving in the military now seems to be settled, legal recognition of gay marriage remains an open—and highly charged—political issue. Less than two months after signing the repeal of "Don't Ask, Don't Tell," the Obama administration also weighed in on the latter subject. On February 3, 2011, Attorney General Eric Holder announced that the White House would no longer defend the Defense of Marriage Act against legal challenges. This law, passed by Congress in 1996, defines marriage under federal law as a union between a man and a woman; it also allows states to refuse recognition of gay marriages sanctioned by other states. The Obama administration's decision angered many Republican supporters of the act, and Speaker of the House John Boehner subsequently announced the formation of a "Bipartisan House Legal Advisory Group" to defend the law in the place of the Department of Justice.

In this chapter, we explore how gay rights issues such as lifting the ban on military service and legal recognition of gay marriage have emerged and evolved as partisan and ideological battlegrounds. We pay particular attention to the extent to which polarization has characterized the politics of gay rights at both the elite and mass levels. In recent years, a number of political scientists and other observers have raised concerns that US politics has become increasingly divided along partisan and ideological lines. According to this narrative, a growing chasm separates the "Red America" of Republicans and conservatives, on the one side, and the "Blue America" of Democrats and liberals, on the other. A sizable body of research supports the claim that political leaders have become increasingly polarized, particularly in terms of congressional roll call votes (see, e.g., McCarty, Poole, and Rosenthal 2006; Poole and Rosenthal 2007). There is ongoing debate, however, regarding the extent to which public opinion in the United States has grown more polarized over time (see, e.g., Abramowitz 2010; Fiorina, Abrams, and Pope 2011; Hetherington 2009; Jacobson 2007).

We begin by briefly chronicling the political history of gay rights, from the 1969 Stonewall riots to the 2010 repeal of "Don't Ask, Don't Tell" and the ongoing battle surrounding gay marriage. Next, we examine the degree to which political elites have demonstrated partisan or ideological polarization on gay rights issues in the contexts of congressional votes, presidential campaigns, and US Supreme Court decisions. We then analyze trends over time in public opinion about gay rights, with a focus on patterns of partisan or ideological polarization among citizens on the topics of military service and gay marriage. We also examine the preferences of lesbian, gay, and bisexual voters and the broader role that gay rights issues have (or have not) played in shaping voting behavior. We conclude by considering the implications of our findings for the future political trajectory of gay rights issues in general and gay marriage in particular.

The Politics of Gay Rights: A Brief History

During the first half of the twentieth century, the subject of homosexuality was politically invisible in the United States. In the 1950s, the Mattachine Society and the Daughters of Bilitis (the first gay rights and lesbian rights organizations, respectively) launched efforts to place their concerns on the public agenda, but gay rights issues garnered little attention from politicians or the mainstream media until the Stonewall riots of 1969.

From Stonewall to State Initiative Battles

On June 28, 1969, police raided the Stonewall Inn in New York City, reputed to be a popular gathering place for gay men, and began arresting patrons. Those not arrested were asked to leave; once outside, they began spreading word of the raid. Soon, a large crowd had gathered outside the inn. The police barricaded themselves inside as the crowd began throwing bottles and bricks. Thus began the Stonewall riots, which continued for many nights and drew thousands of protestors demanding that the police stop harassing the gay community. For many gay men and lesbians, Stonewall was a turning point in their awareness of and involvement in gay activism.

As young gay activists came of age, they began to demand freedom from discrimination in employment, housing, and other facets of daily life. One such activist was Harvey Milk, who became the first openly gay person to win public office in California when he was elected to the San Francisco Board of Supervisors in 1978. Prior to his assassination on November 27, 1978, his tenure was defined by his work to enact gay rights measures in San Francisco and his opposition to California's Proposition 6, a ballot initiative that would have allowed gay teachers in the state to be fired on the basis of their sexual orientation.

As the gay rights movement began to achieve political victories, it met resistance from an anti–gay rights movement that drew much of its support from socially conservative Christians. One key figure in this countermovement was Anita Bryant, a popular singer who founded the Save Our Children Foundation in response to a gay rights measure in her home state of Florida. In 1977, she led a successful campaign to repeal the ordinance and then began touring the country in support of other efforts to stop or repeal gay rights measures. In California, however, her efforts on behalf of Proposition 6 met defeat. Interestingly, one opponent of the initiative was a former Republican governor of California, Ronald Reagan.

By the beginning of the 1980s, the political battle lines between pro–gay rights and anti–gay rights groups had been drawn. In contrast, the two major political parties had yet to present clear divisions on gay rights. Instead, the subject remained largely invisible on the national political stage. Reagan, who had been elected president in 1980, said little about the spread of AIDS during the early years of his tenure (though his silence drew criticism from gay activists who mobilized to focus attention on the disease). In 1986, the battle over gay rights briefly entered the national political arena when the US Supreme Court upheld a state law banning sodomy in *Bowers v. Hardwick,* thereby turning back a legal challenge by gay rights advocates.

Not long after the decision, opponents of gay rights began another major push to achieve their policy goals through direct democracy at the state level (for a more detailed account, see Gallagher and Bull 1996). In 1988, the Oregon Citizens Alliance secured a place on the ballot for a referendum to repeal an executive order issued by the state's Democratic governor that prohibited discrimination on the basis of sexual orientation within the executive branch. The referendum, Measure 8, passed with 53 percent of the vote. In the wake of its victory, the Oregon Citizens Alliance introduced a new initiative to ban state protection or promotion of a range of sexual behaviors, including homosexuality. Its authors relied on the arguments that had worked for the Measure 8 campaign: first, that homosexuality was a threat to traditional morality; and second, that gay rights laws created "special rights." In 1992, however, the Oregon Citizens Alliance faced a well-prepared and well-funded countercampaign that emphasized the theme of equal rights for gay men and lesbians. Ultimately, Oregon voters rejected Measure 8 by a vote of 57 percent to 43 percent.

That same year, Colorado for Family Values launched its campaign for Amendment 2, a ballot initiative to bar "protected status based on homosexual, lesbian, or bisexual orientation" and, in the process, void existing gay rights laws in the cities of Denver, Boulder, and Aspen. As in Oregon, a pro–gay rights organization—here, Equal Protection Colorado—launched its own anti-initiative public relations campaign. The result in Colorado, however, was different than the result in Oregon: Amendment 2 passed with 53 percent of the vote. Opponents of the initiative immediately began a legal challenge, setting into motion a process that would eventually result in a key US Supreme Court decision.

The Emergence of a National Partisan Battle over Gay Rights

In 1992, two very different presidential candidates, Pat Buchanan and Bill Clinton, made gay rights a theme of their campaigns. In the Republican nomination campaign, Buchanan incorporated the subject into his broader message of unapologetic social conservatism. The incumbent in the race, President George H. W. Bush, had alienated many of the moral traditionalists in his party during his tenure; his reluctance to take a strong anti–gay rights stand during the nomination campaign angered them further. Buchanan took advantage of this schism by wooing religious conservatives within the Republican Party. Although he eventually lost to Bush, he successfully negotiated for a highly visible speaking slot at the Republican National Convention. In his speech, he linked the Democratic Party to the gay community, arguing that "Bill Clinton and Al Gore represent the most pro-lesbian and pro-gay ticket in history." He went on to proclaim that he stood with President Bush "against the amoral idea that gay and lesbian couples should have the same standing in law as married men and women."

On the other side of the partisan fence, Clinton made a campaign pledge to lift the ban on gay men and lesbians serving in the US military. Shortly after his inauguration, he attempted to make good on this promise and, in doing so, sparked a political firestorm. His proposal to issue an executive order ending the ban drew protests from not only Christian conservatives but also the military establishment, personified by General Colin Powell and Senator Sam Nunn. In response, gay rights supporters marched on Washington, D.C., to demand equal rights. Faced with an outcry from both sides, Clinton agreed to a compromise: the "Don't Ask, Don't Tell" policy, which barred the military from asking recruits about their sexual orientation and military personnel from openly identifying themselves as gay or lesbian. This outcome angered leaders of the gay rights movement, some of whom called Clinton's retreat a betrayal.

From there, the central front in the gay rights controversy shifted again, this time to the courts. In December 1993, a Colorado judge struck down Amendment 2 as unconstitutional. The state then appealed the decision to the Colorado State Supreme Court, which rejected the state's argument by a vote of 6 to 1. In 1996 the case reached the US Supreme Court, which ruled in *Romer v. Evans* that Amendment 2 denied gays and lesbians equal protection under the law. Although the Court stopped short of overturning *Bowers v. Hardwick,* its majority opinion (written by Justice Anthony Kennedy) rejected the notion that antidiscrimination laws create "special rights" for gays and lesbians. A minority opinion (written by Justice Antonin Scalia) criticized the majority for taking sides in a "culture war."

That same year, in 1996, Congress debated two bills dealing with gay rights: the Defense of Marriage Act and the Employment Non-Discrimination Act. The former dealt with a growing controversy over the legality of gay marriage. In 1993, the Hawaii Supreme Court had ruled in *Baehr v. Levin* that the state's ban on gay marriage violated the state constitution's equal protection clause. In response, a number of other states acted to exclude gay marriages from the "full faith and credit" provisions of their own state constitutions. The Defense of Marriage Act, which established marriage in federal law as a union between a man and a woman in addition to permitting states to refuse recognition of same-sex marriages that had been performed in other states, was passed by both chambers of Congress and signed into law by President Clinton. On the other hand, the Employment Non-Discrimination Act—which would have banned job discrimination on the basis of sexual orientation—failed in the Senate by a single vote.

Following this flurry of activity, the prominence of gay rights issues in the national political arena faded for a time. The topic of gay rights played only a minor role in the 1996 presidential campaign given that Republican nominee Bob Dole made little effort to emphasize it and that Clinton had signed the "Don't Ask, Don't Tell" policy and the Defense of Marriage Act. Two years later, the murder of Matthew Shepard, a gay student at the University of Wyoming, provoked a new discussion of hate crime legislation. Shortly afterward, President Clinton called on Congress to pass a federal hate crime bill that covered crimes based on sexual orientation; ultimately, however, no such bill made it to his desk.

In 1999, gay rights activists won a victory when the Vermont Supreme Court ruled that same-sex couples in the state should be afforded the same rights as opposite-sex couples. The state legislature subsequently passed legislation allowing same-sex couples to form civil unions that offered the same legal benefits as marriages. The advent of civil unions in Vermont brought new attention to the debate over legal recognition for same-sex relationships; nevertheless, the topic of gay rights played a relatively minor role in the 2000 presidential contest, which pitted Democratic nominee Al Gore against Republican nominee (and eventual winner) George W. Bush.

The Debate over Gay Marriage Takes Center Stage

For the next few years, the battle over gay rights continued to lie mostly dormant on the national political scene. In 2003, however, the US Supreme Court overturned *Bowers v. Hardwick* by ruling in *Lawrence v. Texas* that consensual homosexual sex is protected by the Fourteenth Amendment of the US Constitution. Later that same year, the ruling of the Massachusetts Supreme Court in *Goodridge v. Dept. of Public Health* mandated that the state legally recognize same-sex marriages. The latter decision brought an unprecedented degree of national attention to the issue of gay marriage. Not long afterward, President George W. Bush entered the fray by advocating an amendment to the US Constitution that would define marriage as a union between a man and a woman. In his 2004 State of the Union address, he said, "If judges insist on forcing their arbitrary will upon the people, the only alternative left to the people would be the constitutional process. Our nation must defend the sanctity of marriage." Shortly thereafter, the proposed amendment was introduced in both chambers of Congress, only to fail in each.

The issue of gay marriage also played a prominent role in the 2004 presidential campaign. In particular, it provided the topic for a controversy surrounding the third presidential debate between Bush and his Democratic challenger, John Kerry, which took place on October 13. In response to a question from moderator Bob Schieffer, Bush said that he did not know whether homosexuality was a choice; he then went on to advocate tolerance for gay people while reiterating his opposition to gay marriage. For his part, Kerry invoked the lesbian daughter of Vice President Dick Cheney in arguing that homosexuality was not a choice and advocating for "partnership rights" (at the same time, he also said, "I believe that marriage is between a man and a woman"). After the debate, a number of Republicans—including both Bush and Cheney—criticized Kerry for mentioning the vice president's daughter. In the end, Bush won reelection. Furthermore, voters in thirteen states passed ballot initiatives amending their constitutions to define marriage as between a man and a woman. Voters approved similar initiatives in two more states in 2005 and eight more states in 2006. Arizona voters provided the lone exception to the trend when they rejected such an initiative in 2006.

The election results on November 4, 2008, brought new victories for opponents of gay marriage. Not only did Arizona voters pass a less restrictive version of the amendment that they had rejected two years earlier, but voters in Florida and California also approved amendments to their state constitutions defining marriage as between a man and a woman. The outcome for the California measure, Proposition 8, was a particularly bitter one for gay marriage supporters given that it overturned a May 15, 2008, ruling by the California Supreme Court that mandated legal recognition for gay marriages (the Connecticut Supreme Court issued a similar ruling that year, but its decision was not overturned at the ballot box). At the same time, the election of Barack Obama as president brought new hope for opponents of "Don't Ask, Don't Tell"; during his campaign, the Democrat had pledged to repeal the policy.

The following year, 2009, saw three states (Maine, New Hampshire, and Vermont) and the District of Columbia pass laws that recognized gay marriages, though voters in one of these states (Maine) subsequently overturned such recognition through a ballot measure. Meanwhile, an Iowa Supreme Court ruling brought gay marriage to the Midwest. In 2010, a challenge to California's Proposition 8 was upheld by a federal judge; the ruling was subsequently appealed to the US Supreme Court. Later that year, Congress passed and Obama signed a bill mandating the repeal of "Don't Ask, Don't Tell." Not long afterward, the Obama administration signaled that it would no longer defend the Defense of Marriage Act against legal challenges. On

June 24, 2011, New York passed a law recognizing gay marriage, making it the most populous state thus far to do so.

Polarization on Gay Rights Among Political Elites

Since the early 1990s, national political elites have had numerous occasions to take positions on gay rights issues and thereby signal their stances to the public. Here, we examine position-taking on gay rights in all three branches of the federal government from 1992 through 2010. Specifically, we examine partisan divisions among members of Congress and presidential candidates as well as ideological divisions among justices on the US Supreme Court.[1] As we will show, all three sorts of leaders have demonstrated clear patterns of polarization on gay rights policies.

Partisan Polarization in Congressional Votes

Congress has voted on gay rights issues a number of times since the early 1990s. For example, there were congressional votes on military service in 1993 and 2010, employment nondiscrimination in 1996 and 2007, and gay marriage in 1996 and 2004. Table 11.1 reports the results of these votes by subject, chamber, and party.

To begin with, consider the three congressional votes regarding the creation of the "Don't Ask, Don't Tell" policy, which had been inserted into the National Defense Authorization Act of fiscal year 1994. As previously mentioned, this compromise involved allowing gay men and lesbians to serve in the military only so long as they kept their sexual orientation a secret, while also forbidding military officials from actively seeking to identify and remove gay service members from the military. Members of the US House of Representatives introduced two amendments that addressed "Don't Ask, Don't Tell" in different ways. Both amendments failed, but the votes on them revealed strong party divisions. Representative Duncan Hunter, a Republican, introduced an amendment that would have required military officials to ask service members about their sexual orientation, effectively nullifying the "Don't Ask, Don't Tell" compromise. Whereas 65.5 percent of the Republicans in the House supported this amendment, only 11.5 percent of the Democrats voted for it. On the Democratic side, Representative Marty Meehan introduced an amendment that would have stripped the "Don't Ask, Don't Tell" compromise from the defense bill altogether. Here, the pattern of support was reversed: 69.9 percent of House Democrats voted for his amendment, whereas only 6.3 percent of House Republicans did so. The final defense bill, which included the "Don't Ask, Don't Tell" provision, ultimately passed Congress with the support of almost all of the Democrats in the House (93.7 percent) and the Senate (92.7 percent) as well as a majority of the Republicans in the Senate (59.1 percent); on the other hand, only 29.4 percent of House Republicans voted for it.

Table 11.1 Congressional Votes on Gay Rights Issues, by Chamber and Party, 1993–2010

	House				Senate				Outcome
	Republicans		Democrats		Republicans		Democrats		
	For	Against	For	Against	For	Against	For	Against	
"Don't Ask, Don't Tell": Hunter amendment (1993)	114 (65.5%)	60 (34.5%)	30 (11.5%)	230 (88.5%)	—	—	—	—	Failed in House
"Don't Ask, Don't Tell": Meehan amendment (1993)	11 (6.3%)	163 (93.7%)	157 (60.9%)	101 (39.1%)	—	—	—	—	Failed in House
National Defense Authorization Act (1994)	50 (29.4%)	120 (70.6%)	223 (93.7%)	15 (6.3%)	26 (59.1%)	18 (40.1%)	51 (92.7%)	4 (7.3%)	Passed by both House and Senate; signed by Clinton
Employment Non-Discrimination Act (1996)	—	—	—	—	8 (15.1%)	45 (84.9%)	41 (89.1%)	41 (10.9%)	Failed in Senate
Defense of Marriage Act (1996)	224 (99.6%)	1 (0.4%)	118 (64.5%)	65 (35.5%)	53 (100%)	0 (0%)	32 (69.6%)	14 (30.4%)	Passed by both House and Senate; signed by Clinton
Federal Marriage Amendment (2004)[a]	191 (87.6%)	27 (12.4%)	36 (18.6%)	158 (81.4%)	45 (88.2%)	6 (11.8%)	3 (6.4%)	44 (93.6%)	Failed in both House and Senate
Employment Non-Discrimination Act (2007)	35 (18.0%)	159 (82.0%)	200 (88.9%)	25 (11.1%)	—	—	—	—	Passed by House
"Don't Ask, Don't Tell" repeal (2010)	15 (8.6%)	160 (91.4%)	235 (94.0%)	15 (6.0%)	8 (20.5%)	31 (79.5%)	57 (100%)	0 (0%)	Passed by both House and Senate; signed by Obama

Source: Congressional Record, 1993–2010.
Note: a. Senate vote was on cloture.

In 1996, Congress took up two bills that addressed gay rights issues. The Employment Non-Discrimination Act, a version of which has been introduced in every Congress since 1994 except for the 109th, would bar workplace discrimination on the basis of sexual orientation. In 1994 and 1995, this act did not make it out of committee and, thus, did not receive a vote on the floor of either chamber. In 1996, however, the act reached the Senate floor. It received the support of 89.1 percent of the Democrats but only 15.1 percent of the Republicans and, thus, failed on a vote of 49 to 50. The Employment Non-Discrimination Act did not again receive a full floor vote in either chamber until 2007, when the House considered a version of the bill. Once again, the vote split largely along party lines: 88.9 percent of the Democrats voted for it, compared to only 18.0 percent of the Republicans. This time, the bill passed in the House, but only to die in the Senate without a vote.

The Defense of Marriage Act, a bill to define marriage at the federal level as being between a man and a woman and allow states to deny recognition of same-sex marriages performed in other states, passed both houses of Congress in 1996 and was signed by President Clinton. Republicans supported this act overwhelmingly, with 99.6 percent of House Republicans and every Senate Republican voting for it. A majority of Democrats in each chamber also voted in favor of the act; the margin was closer here, however, with 64.5 percent of House Democrats and 69.6 percent of Senate Democrats voting in favor of the bill.

The Federal Marriage Amendment, which was introduced into both chambers in 2004, would have restricted marriage in the United States to a union between one man and one woman. Given that it was a proposed amendment to the US Constitution, it needed at least two-thirds of the votes in each chamber (290 in the House and 67 in the Senate) to proceed. Although the amendment received the support of 87.6 percent of House Republicans and 88.2 percent of Senate Republicans, only 18.6 percent of Democrats in the House and 6.4 percent of those in the Senate voted for it. Consequently, it failed to reach the two-thirds threshold in either chamber. Indeed, it did not even reach the 60 votes needed to invoke cloture in the Senate.

At the prompting of President Obama, Congress revisited "Don't Ask, Don't Tell" in 2010 by voting on a bill to repeal the provision and thereby allow gay men and lesbians to serve openly in the military. The repeal bill passed the House with the support of 94.0 percent of the Democrats but only 8.6 percent of the Republicans. The Senate then passed the bill with the support of every voting Democrat as well as 20.5 percent of the Republicans.

In sum, the votes reported in Table 11.1 reveal sharp partisan differences on gay rights. Compared to their Republican counterparts, congressional Democrats have tended to be more favorable to pro–gay rights legislation (as in the cases of the Employment Non-Discrimination Act and the "Don't Ask, Don't Tell" repeal) and less favorable to anti–gay rights legislation (as in the cases of the Defense of Marriage Act and the Federal Marriage Amendment). The partisan gaps on several votes reached or exceeded 80 percentage points (the Federal Marriage Amendment in the House; the "Don't Ask, Don't Tell" repeal in both chambers). The smallest partisan gaps were for the Defense of Marriage Act, but even here the parties differed by 30 percentage points or more.

Partisan Polarization in Presidential Campaigns

Next, we turn to the positions on gay rights taken by the Republican and Democratic nominees in every general election presidential campaign from 1992 to 2008. Table 11.2 outlines the stances of the Democratic nominees (Bill Clinton in 1992 and 1996, Al Gore in 2000, John Kerry in 2004, and Barack Obama in 2008) and of the Republican nominees (George H. W. Bush in 1992, Bob Dole in 1996, George W. Bush in 2000 and 2004, and John McCain in 2008) in four domains of gay rights: military service, employment nondiscrimination, gay marriage, and civil unions. Given that presidential candidates sometimes have the luxury of taking an ambiguous position—or no position at all—on a given issue, we are not able to identify a position for every candidate on every issue (in addition, Table 11.2 sometimes reports simplified versions of more complex stances). However, the evidence available reveals a number of distinctions between the parties in the context of presidential campaigns.

One set of differences has revolved around the issue of military service. During his 1992 campaign, Clinton pledged to overturn the ban on gay men and lesbians serving. In contrast, his opponent favored retaining the ban. Of course, Clinton ultimately signed "Don't Ask, Don't Tell" as a compromise. Since then, each of the Republican nominees (Dole, George W. Bush, and McCain) has opposed the repeal of "Don't Ask, Don't Tell." Meanwhile, each of the Democratic nominees after Clinton (Gore, Kerry, and Obama) has supported repeal.

The presidential nominees have also diverged along party lines on the topic of employment nondiscrimination. All of the Democratic presidential nominees from 1992 onward have supported the Employment Non-Discrimination Act. In contrast, at least two of the Republican nominees (George W. Bush and McCain) opposed it (George H. W. Bush did not offer an opinion in 1992, and Dole's position was unclear in 1996 given that he did not participate in the Senate vote on the bill that year).

As of 2008, no major party nominee had openly supported gay marriage while campaigning for presidential office (though Gore openly advocated for gay marriage in the years following his campaign). By 2004, however, distinctions between the parties' nominees had emerged regarding their degree

Table 11.2 Presidential Nominees' Positions on Gay Rights Issues, 1992–2008

	Military Service	Employment Nondiscrimination	Gay Marriage	Civil Unions
Democrats				
Bill Clinton (1992, 1996)	Supported overturning ban in 1992; signed "Don't Ask, Don't Tell" (DADT)	Supported Employment Non-Discrimination Act (ENDA)	Opposed gay marriage; signed Defense of Marriage Act (DOMA)	—
Al Gore (2000)	Supported DADT repeal	Supported ENDA	Opposed gay marriage	—
John Kerry (2004)	Supported DADT repeal	Supported ENDA	Opposed gay marriage; opposed DOMA and Federal Marriage Amendment (FMA)	Supported civil unions
Barack Obama (2008)	Supported DADT repeal	Supported ENDA	Opposed gay marriage[a]; opposed DOMA and FMA	Supported civil unions
Republicans				
George H. W. Bush (1992)	Opposed overturning ban	—	—	—
Bob Dole (1996)	Opposed DADT repeal	Unclear	Opposed gay marriage; supported DOMA	—
George W. Bush (2000, 2004)	Opposed DADT repeal	Opposed ENDA	Opposed gay marriage; supported DOMA and FMA	Supported civil unions in 2004
John McCain (2008)	Opposed DADT repeal	Opposed ENDA	Opposed gay marriage; supported DOMA; opposed FMA	Unclear

Source: Compiled by the authors.
Note: a. In 2012, Obama announced that he supported gay marriage.

of support for anti–gay marriage measures. For example, Kerry opposed both the Defense of Marriage Act and the Federal Marriage Amendment in 2004, whereas Bush supported both. Similarly, Obama opposed the Defense of Marriage Act in 2008, whereas McCain supported it (though the latter had voted against the Federal Marriage Amendment in 2004).

The distinctions between the two parties' nominees on civil unions have been murkier. Kerry expressed support for civil unions during his presidential campaigns, but Bush also appeared to endorse civil unions (on December 16, 2003, he said that the "position of this administration is that whatever legal arrangements people want to make, they're allowed to make, so long as it's embraced by the state or at the state level"). Obama also expressed support for civil unions, whereas McCain issued a series of ambiguous or even contradictory statements on the subject.

All in all, however, the positions summarized in Table 11.2 suggest that the presidential nominees have often split along party lines on gay rights issues. This is especially clear in the cases of military service, employment nondiscrimination, and the Defense of Marriage Act. When the Democratic nominee and the Republican nominee have differed on gay rights, the former has always taken the more pro–gay rights position.

Ideological Polarization in US Supreme Court Votes

As of 2010, three landmark US Supreme Court decisions had dealt with gay rights. In *Bowers v. Hardwick* (1986), the Court held that gay individuals do not enjoy a right of privacy related to sexual conduct. In *Romer v. Evans* (1996), the Court ruled that Colorado's Amendment 2 was unconstitutional because it denied gays and lesbians equal protection under the law. Finally, in *Lawrence v. Texas* (2003), the Court overturned *Bowers v. Hardwick* by ruling that sodomy laws deny gay individuals the right to due process and invade privacy rights. Table 11.3 reports the positions of the individual justices serving on the Court in each of these three decisions, as well as the justices' ideological positions for the term in question as captured by Martin-Quinn scores (Epstein et al. 2007; Martin and Quinn 2007). In calculating such scores, individual justices are assigned a score for each term based on their decisions for that respective term. This score can range from –6 (extremely liberal) to +6 (extremely conservative), where 0 is located at the center of the ideological spectrum. Martin-Quinn scores allow for comparisons across time and, thus, can be used to track the evolution of justices' ideologies during their tenures.

It is immediately apparent from Table 11.3 that in each of the three cases, there was a sharp ideological divide between the justices who supported gay rights and those who did not. In none of the three cases did a justice who scored below 0 vote against the pro–gay rights side of the case. Thus, no justice on the liberal side of the ideological spectrum supported the

Table 11.3   US Supreme Court Votes in Gay Rights Decisions, with Ideology Scores for Justices

	Bowers v. Hardwick (1986)	*Romer v. Evans* (1996)	*Lawrence v. Texas* (2003)
Pro–gay rights votes	Marshall (–4.07) Brennan (–3.23) Blackmun (–0.79) Stevens (–0.49)	Stevens (–3.09) Breyer (–0.74) Ginsburg (–0.66) Souter (–0.57) Kennedy (0.58) O'Connor (0.70)	Stevens (–2.46) Souter (–1.52) Ginsburg (–1.70) Breyer (–1.34) O'Connor (0.23) Kennedy (0.87)
Anti–gay rights votes	Powell (0.79) White (1.17) O'Connor (1.23) Burger (2.00) Rehnquist (3.47)	Rehnquist (1.69) Scalia (2.99) Thomas (3.62)	Rehnquist (1.23) Scalia (3.18) Thomas (4.05)
Total vote (pro–gay rights vs. anti–gay rights)	4–5	6–3	6–3

Source: Findlaw.com and Martin Quinn Scores for select years.

Note: Ideology scores are Martin-Quinn scores that range from –6 (extremely liberal) to +6 (extremely conservative).

anti–gay rights position in any of the three cases. A closer examination, however, reveals some interesting nuances in the justices' behavior. In 1996 and 2003, two justices (Kennedy and O'Connor) who fell on the conservative side of the ideological spectrum voted in favor of gay rights—and, in doing so, pushed the decision in favor of the pro–gay rights side. Furthermore, Kennedy's score in 2003 (.87), when he voted in favor of the pro–gay rights side, was more conservative than Powell's score in 1986 (.79), when he voted against the pro–gay rights side. This pattern suggests that the center position on gay rights issues may have shifted to the pro–gay rights side at the judicial level. The pattern of overall votes also suggests a pro–gay rights shift. In 1986, the Court split 4–5 in favor of the anti–gay rights position. In both 1996 and 2003, the Court split 6–3 in the other direction.

Summary
Taken together, the results show elite polarization on gay rights in all three branches of government across a range of policy domains. Such polarization has been neither universal nor entirely consistent; given the data, however, we can safely say that Republican and conservative elites have tended to

oppose gay rights policies, whereas Democratic and liberal elites have tended to offer greater support for such policies. Thus, the battle over gay rights that US political leaders have waged among themselves reflects the broader polarization that has increasingly come to characterize US politics at the elite level (McCarty, Poole, and Rosenthal 2006; Poole and Rosenthal 2007).

Polarization on Gay Rights Among the Public

As the political battle over gay rights has played out at the elite level, support for a range of gay rights policies has increased dramatically among the public as a whole (Brewer 2008; Brewer and Wilcox 2005). Figure 11.1 illustrates this shift for four policy domains: military service, employment nondiscrimination, civil unions, and gay marriage. The level of support for gay rights has varied substantially across these domains, with members of the public expressing the highest levels of support for military service and employment nondiscrimination and the lowest levels of support for gay marriage. Nevertheless, opinion has followed the same upward trajectory in all four domains (apart from a temporary decline in support for military service, civil unions, and gay marriage in 2003–2004, a pattern that presumably reflects a backlash in public opinion following the *Lawrence v. Texas* and *Goodridge v. Dept. of Public Health* decisions in 2003). Among the respondents to the 1992 American National Election Study (ANES), exactly half said that they favored allowing gays to serve in the military; by 2008, the percentage doing so had increased to 76 percent.[2] Likewise, the percentage of ANES respondents who favored laws to protect gay men and lesbians from job discrimination increased from 52 percent in 1992 to 69 percent in 2008.[3] Surveys from the Pew Research Center capture similar upward trends in support for legal recognition of gay relationships: support for civil unions grew from 45 percent in 2003 to 57 percent in 2009, and support for gay marriage grew from only 27 percent in 1996 to 45 percent in 2011.[4]

Beneath these trends, however, lies a pattern of political polarization in public support for gay rights policies. Consider public opinion about allowing gays to serve in the military. The 1992 ANES found that 57 percent of Democrats favored this policy, whereas only 38 percent of Republicans did so—a difference of 19 percentage points (see Figure 11.2a). Four years later, the gap had widened to 25 percentage points (70 percent for Democrats versus 45 percent for Republicans), presumably in response to the politicized battle over "Don't Ask, Don't Tell" in 1993. Interestingly, this partisan gap had diminished to around a third of that size (8 points) by 2008, when 78 percent of Democrats and 70 percent of Republicans favored allowing gays to serve in the military. A similar "depolarization" over time took place along ideological lines (see Figure 11.2b). In 1992, 70 percent of liberals but only 38 percent of conservatives favored allowing gays to serve in the military,

Figure 11.1 Public Support for Gay Rights, 1992–2011

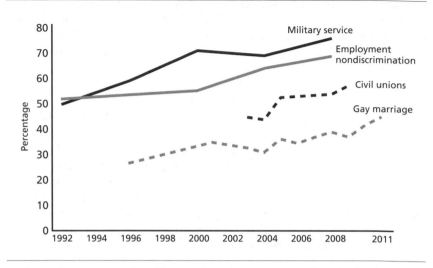

Source: Data on support for military service and employment nondiscrimination from the American National Election Studies (ANES); data on support for civil unions and gay marriage from Pew.

for a gap of 32 percentage points. As with the partisan gap, the ideological gap on the subject had widened by 1996 (to 38 points, with 89 percent of liberals in favor versus 51 percent of conservatives). Over the next twelve years the gap narrowed to 17 points, with 87 percent of liberals and 70 percent of conservatives expressing support in 2008.

In contrast to the narrowing partisan gap on military service, there was a widening partisan gap in public support for gay marriage. A 1996 Pew survey found that 33 percent of Democrats and 15 percent of Republicans supported gay marriage, for a difference of 18 percentage points (see Figure 11.3a). By the time of a 2011 Pew survey, this gap had grown to 34 percentage points, with fully 57 percent of Democrats but only 23 percent of Republicans supporting gay marriage. Pew surveys also reveal a widening ideological gap on the subject over the last half of the 1990s and the first half of the next decade (see Figure 11.3b). In 1996, 52 percent of liberals supported gay marriage, compared to 15 percent of conservatives—a gap of 37 points. By 2005, the percentage for liberals had increased to 69 percent, whereas the percentage for conservatives had remained virtually unchanged at 14 percent, pushing the gap to 55 points. That year marks the widest recorded ideological gap on the subject; as of 2011, 66 percent of liberals favored gay mar-

Figure 11.2a Public Support for Allowing Gays to Serve in the Military, by Party, 1992–2008

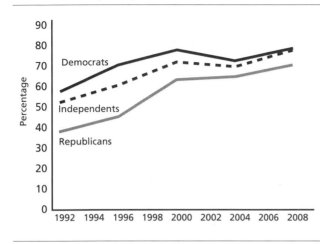

Source: American National Election Studies (ANES).

Figure 11.2b Public Support for Allowing Gays to Serve in the Military, by Ideology, 1992–2008

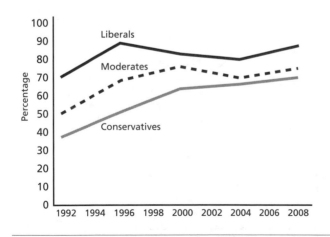

Source: American National Election Studies (ANES).

Figure 11.3a Public Support for Gay Marriage, by Party, 1996–2011

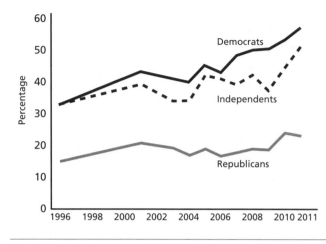

Source: Pew Research Center.

Figure 11.3b Public Support for Gay Marriage, by Ideology, 1996–2011

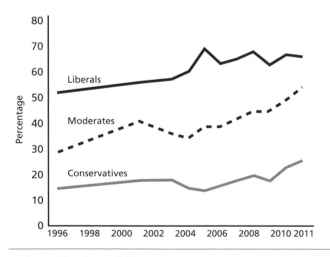

Source: Pew Research Center.

riage compared to 20 percent of conservatives, for a narrower but still wide gap of 46 points.

The most likely explanation for the polarization observed in public opinion about gay rights revolves around the tendency of citizens to follow cues sent by elites who share their political views (Zaller 1992). In the context at hand, such an account implies that Republicans and conservative citizens should tend to adopt the anti–gay rights positions taken by Republican and conservative elites. Similarly, Democrats and liberals among the public should tend to follow the more favorable signals that Democratic and liberal political elites have sent regarding gay rights.

One piece of evidence for this explanation comes from an analysis of public opinion in the aftermath of President Clinton's 1993 push to overturn the ban on military service by gays and lesbians. In August 1993, 81 percent of the respondents in a Pew Research Center survey said that they were following this issue "very" or "fairly" closely. Thus, news of the president's stance regarding the issue undoubtedly reached many citizens. To test the impact of this signal, Michael Bailey, Lee Sigelman, and Clyde Wilcox (2003) used data from an ANES panel survey in which respondents were interviewed during the 1992 presidential campaign and then reinterviewed in 1993. They found that Clinton's stand shifted public opinion toward greater support, particularly among those who strongly supported the president (they also found, however, that his popularity declined among those who opposed allowing gays and lesbians to serve in the military).

Additional support for the argument that elite signals have fostered polarization in public opinion about gay rights comes from an analysis that Paul Brewer (2008) conducted using a series of Pew Research Center surveys from 2003 and 2004. During this period, the decision of the Massachusetts Supreme Court in *Goodridge v. Dept. of Public Health* had pushed the public controversy surrounding gay marriage to a previously unseen level of prominence. Building on John Zaller's (1992) notion of "polarization effects," Brewer hypothesized that education would magnify the impact of political elites' signals on public opinion, given that highly educated citizens should be more likely than less educated ones to receive and accept signals from leaders on their end of the political spectrum. Consistent with this argument, Brewer found that the effects of ideology and presidential approval on opinion about gay marriage were strongest among the most educated respondents. Furthermore, he found that the impact of ideology on public opinion about civil unions was particularly strong among the most educated respondents. On the other hand, education did not magnify the impact of presidential approval on opinion about civil unions—a finding that makes sense given that President Bush clearly opposed gay marriage but signaled greater willingness to accept civil unions.

To provide a closer look at patterns in the underlying structure of recent public opinion regarding gays serving in the military and gay marriage, we build on another set of analyses that Brewer (2008; see also Brewer 2003) conducted using ANES data from 1992, 1996, 2000, and 2004. The theoretical framework for these analyses starts with the premise that Americans can base their opinions about gay rights issues on a variety of predispositions, including not only party identification and ideology but also feelings toward gays and lesbians as a group, beliefs about whether the Bible should be interpreted literally, and support for the values of equality and traditional morality (see also Craig et al. 2005; Haeberle 1999; Lewis and Rogers 1999; Olson, Cadge, and Harrison 2006; Stoutenborough, Haider-Markel, and Allen 2006; Strand 1998; Wilcox et al. 2007; Wilcox and Norrander 2002; Wilcox and Wolpert 1996, 2000).[5] At the same time, Brewer's model allows the impact of each predisposition to change over time. Thus, aggregate shifts in public opinion can reflect shifts in the underlying predispositions themselves, shifts in the extent to which citizens use particular predispositions to form their opinions, or both. In addition, the model incorporates the potential effects of attendance at religious services as well as a host of demographic factors (gender, self-identification as African American, age, education, and income), the effects of which may also shift over time. Here, we update Brewer's model to incorporate data from the 2008 ANES.

The Structure of Public Opinion
About Allowing Gays to Serve in the Military

Our analysis of public opinion on the issue of military service incorporates ANES data from 1992, 1996, 2000, 2004, and 2008. Respondents in each survey were asked whether they thought that gays "should be allowed to serve in the United States Armed Forces." A follow-up question captured whether respondents felt so "strongly" or "not strongly," thereby allowing for the creation of a four-category opinion measure ranging from strong opposition to strong support. In modeling the effects of the key predispositions on this variable, we treat the 1992 effects as the baselines and use *year* × predisposition terms (year multiplied by predisposition) to capture shifts from these baselines. As reported in Table 11.4, the results indicate a number of changes over time in the underlying structure of public opinion. One such shift involves the profound decline in the degree to which feelings toward gays and lesbians predicted support for allowing gays to serve in the military. From 1992 to 2008, the magnitude of this relationship declined by more than a third. Another shift involves the weakening of the negative association between moral traditionalism and support for the policy. The impact of this value was cut in half over the sixteen-year period under study. Yet another change over time in the structure of opinion involves the fading of the nega-

Table 11.4 Determinants of Public Support for Allowing Gays to Serve in the Military (ANES), 1996–2008 (1992 baseline)

Variable	Coefficient (standard error)	
Positive feelings toward gays and lesbians	.63	(.03)**
× 1996	−.10	(.05)†
× 2000	−.10	(.06)†
× 2004	−.19	(.06)**
× 2008	−.23	(.05)**
Republican party identification	−.11	(.03)**
× 1996	−.03	(.04)
× 2000	−.02	(.05)
× 2004	.05	(.05)
× 2008	.11	(.04)*
Conservative ideology	−.04	(.05)
× 1996	−.12	(.07)
× 2000	.02	(.07)
× 2004	.08	(.08)
× 2008	−.07	(.06)
Bible should be taken literally	−.11	(.03)**
× 1996	.05	(.04)
× 2000	−.02	(.05)
× 2004	.03	(.05)
× 2008	.08	(.04)*
Egalitarianism	.11	(.05)*
× 1996	−.04	(.07)
× 2000	−.12	(.08)
× 2004	−.03	(.08)
× 2008	−.04	(.07)
Moral traditionalism	−.24	(.05)**
× 1996	.04	(.07)
× 2000	.17	(.07)*
× 2004	.09	(.08)
× 2008	.12	(.07)†

$N = 6,021$

Source: American National Election Studies (ANES).

Notes: Coefficients are ordinary least squares regression coefficients. The model also included a series of year dummy variables (1996, 2000, 2004, and 2008, with 1992 as the excluded baseline) and a series of controls (attendance at religious services, gender, self-identification as African American, age, education, and income), as well as the full set of year × control terms.

†$p \leq .10$; *$p \leq .05$; **$p \leq .01$.

tive association between belief in a literal interpretation of the Bible and support for allowing gays to serve. By 2008, this once clear relationship had all but vanished.

Most important for the purpose at hand, the results shed light on the roles of partisanship and ideology across time. In 1992, there was a significant negative relationship between Republican partisanship and support for allowing gays to serve. By 2008, however, a significant decline in the impact of partisanship had essentially erased its association with opinion about the policy. Thus, the multivariate analysis confirms the pattern illustrated in Figure 11.2a: the gap between Democrats and Republicans on the issue of military service narrowed over the time period under study. As for ideology, it was not significantly related to opinion in 1992; nor did its impact change significantly over time. As of 2008, then, neither partisan nor ideological polarization characterized public opinion about allowing gays to serve in the military.

The Structure of Public Opinion About Gay Marriage

Given that the ANES only began asking about support for gay marriage in 2004, our analysis of public opinion regarding this issue is restricted to two years: 2004 and 2008. Moreover, we are unable to draw direct comparisons across these years, because the options provided to respondents varied from one survey to the other. Both asked whether "same-sex couples should be allowed to marry" or "should not be allowed to marry." In 2008, however, respondents were also presented with a third option: "should not be allowed to marry but should be allowed to legally form a civil union."[6] Thus, we treat opinion in 2004 as a dichotomous measure (opposition to or support for gay marriage), but treat opinion in 2008 as a three-category ordinal measure (opposition to gay marriage and civil unions, support for civil unions but not gay marriage, and support for gay marriage).

The results from 2004 indicate that positive feelings toward gays and lesbians were associated with support for gay marriage, whereas belief in a literal interpretation of the Bible and moral traditionalism were negatively related to support (see Table 11.5). Each of these relationships was strong in substantive terms, as well (as captured by comparing the predicted probabilities of supporting gay marriage for respondents at the minimum and maximum values for each variable). Meanwhile, egalitarianism was not significantly related to opinion. The negative relationship between Republican partisanship and support for gay marriage was relatively weak (though still significant), but the negative relationship between conservative ideology and support was both statistically significant and substantively large. All else being equal, strong conservatives had only a 16 percent probability of supporting gay marriage, whereas the figure for strong liberals was 49 percent.

Most of the predispositions that predicted opinion in 2004 also predicted opinion in 2008, despite the change in measurement strategy from one sur-

Table 11.5 Determinants of Public Support for Gay Marriage (ANES), 2004–2008

	2004			2008		
	Coefficient (standard error)	Probability of Support		Coefficient (standard error)	Probability of Support	
		at Minimum (%)	at Maximum (%)		at Minimum (%)	at Maximum (%)
Positive feelings toward gay men and lesbians	2.39** (.29)	4	75	1.48** (.15)	12	62
Republican party identification	−.41† (.23)	36	22	−.06 (.13)	35	33
Conservative ideology	−1.02** (.40)	49	16	−.46** (.18)	43	27
Bible should be taken literally	−1.25** (.22)	57	14	−.80** (.12)	53	24
Egalitarianism	.01 (.38)	29	29	.47* (.21)	24	41
Moral traditionalism	−2.62** (.39)	81	5	−1.27** (.21)	62	17
N	790			1,248		

Source: American National Election Studies (ANES).

Notes: Coefficients are probit (2004) or ordered probit (2008) coefficients. The second column for each year presents the probability of support for a respondent at the minimum observed value of the independent variable, holding all other variables at their means. The third column for each year presents the probability of support for a respondent at the maximum observed value of the independent variable, holding all other variables at their means. The models also included a series of controls (attendance at religious services, gender, self-identification as African American, age, education, and income).

†$p \leq .10$; *$p \leq .05$; **$p \leq .01$.

vey to the other. Once again, positive feelings toward gays and lesbians were associated with greater support, whereas biblical literalism and moral traditionalism were negatively related to support. This time, however, egalitarianism was also significantly and positively related to support. As before, strong conservatives were much less likely to support gay marriage (27 percent) than were strong liberals (43 percent). On the other hand, the relationship between partisanship and support was not statistically significant in 2008.

Summary
Our analysis indicates that public opinion about allowing gays to serve in the military has become not only more favorable over time but also less polarized. In a span of sixteen years, from 1992 to 2008, a once substantial gap between Republicans and Democrats on the issue largely faded. The story for public opinion about gay marriage is considerably different, at least at present. Here, public support is both lower (if also increasing) and more polarized. An initial look at trends in public opinion suggested a widening partisan divide, but our multivariate analysis reveals that ideology, rather than partisanship, played a stronger role in dividing the public on gay marriage as of 2008. One possible explanation here revolves around the fact that no president or major party presidential nominee had explicitly endorsed gay marriage up to that point. This may have led citizens to think about the issue more in terms of a clash between liberalism and conservatism than in terms of a clash between the two parties.

Gay Voters and Gay Rights Issues in Presidential Elections
It is one thing for citizens to hold opinions about gay rights issues; it is another thing for them to act on those opinions. Of course, the numerous anti–gay rights initiatives appearing on state ballots over the years have provided many voters with opportunities to have a direct say on public policy. Evaluating what role—if any—that voters' opinions about gay rights have played in presidential elections, however, is a more complicated endeavor.

Lesbian, Gay, and Bisexual Voters in Presidential Elections
Each general election exit poll conducted from 1992 to 2008 (by Voter News Service from 1992 to 2000, and by the National Election Pool in 2004 and 2008) captured vote choice among a sample of lesbian, gay, and bisexual (LGB) voters. The percentage of exit poll respondents identifying as LGB ranged from a low of 2.5 percent (in 1992) to a high of 5.0 percent (in 1996), with an average of 3.8 percent across the five elections. In each election, these voters overwhelmingly favored the Democrat over the Republican. In 1992, Clinton won 72 percent of the LGB vote, whereas George H. W. Bush

garnered only 14 percent (another 14 percent went to H. Ross Perot). Four years later, Clinton won 66 percent compared to Dole's 23 percent (and Perot's 7 percent). The 1996 election turned out to be the high water mark for the Republican share of the LGB vote. In 2000, Gore won 71 percent compared to George W. Bush's 21 percent (7 percent cast their votes for Ralph Nader). Bush's share of the LGB vote in the 2004 election was identical to his 2000 share and far less than Kerry's (79 percent). In 2008, McCain matched but did not exceed Bush's total of 21 percent in the previous two elections, while Obama won 74 percent of the LGB vote. The average share of the LGB vote captured by the Democratic candidates was 72 percent over the sixteen-year span; in contrast, the average share for the Republican candidates was a mere 20 percent.

Given that the Democratic Party's presidential nominees have typically expressed greater support for gay rights policies than have the Republican Party's nominees, a simple explanation for its advantage among LGB voters would be that these voters cast their ballots on the basis of gay rights issues. Other evidence, however, suggests that this is not necessarily the only—or even the best—explanation for the pattern. To begin with, the opinions that LGB citizens hold about gay rights, while generally much more favorable toward gay rights policies than those held by the general public, are not monolithic. For example, the 2004 National Election Pool exit poll found that although 51 percent of LGB respondents favored allowing gay and lesbian couples "to legally marry," 17 percent said that there "should be no legal recognition of their relationships" (another 35 percent said that gay and lesbian couples "should be allowed to form civil unions but not marry") (Egan and Sherrill 2005). Indeed, one study concluded that concerns about economic benefits—rather than civil rights—best accounted for the Democratic Party's edge in support among LGB Americans (Schaffner and Senic 2006). Further complicating matters, LGB voters also tend to hold more liberal views than the general public on a wide range of policy areas, from social welfare policy to foreign policy to environmental policy (Egan, Edelman, and Sherrill 2008).

The Broader Influence of Gay Rights Issues on Voting Behavior

A degree of controversy surrounds the role that public opinion on gay rights issues has—or has not—played in shaping the general public's voting behavior in presidential elections. One seemingly necessary (but not sufficient) condition for such influence would be for members of the public to perceive meaningful differences between the two parties (and their nominees) on gay rights issues. The clear differences taken by party leaders on a range of gay rights issues and the polarization observed in public opinion on these issues suggest that this condition is likely to be met at least some of the time. Then again, responses to two survey items included in the 2008–2009 ANES Panel Study should caution observers about overestimating the degree to which members of the public accurately perceive where the parties and their nominees stand on specific gay rights policies. The first of these items asked, "Does Barack Obama favor, oppose, or neither favor nor oppose an amendment to the U.S. Constitution banning marriage between two people who are the same sex?" The second asked the same question regarding John McCain. Of the respondents, 41 percent correctly stated that Obama opposed such an amendment, whereas 41 percent said that he neither favored nor opposed it and 18 percent said that he favored it. When it came to McCain, 42 percent correctly identified him as opposing such an amendment, but fully 34 percent perceived him to be in favor of it (another 23 percent said that he neither favored nor opposed it). One plausible explanation for this finding is that many respondents may have incorrectly inferred McCain's stance from his party's relatively anti–gay rights orientation. Another is that some voters may have projected their own opinions onto the candidates whom they favored (or contrary opinions onto candidates whom they opposed).

Even if one assumes that citizens will perceive clear differences between the parties on gay rights issues, another question remains: How much weight will they attach to these issues in choosing which candidate to support? The case of the 2004 election suggests that when it comes to making claims on this score, caution again appears to be in order. Some initial accounts of Bush's victory drew on National Election Pool exit poll results in attributing the outcome of the election to a public backlash against gay rights. In particular, these accounts pointed to the finding that a plurality of respondents (22 percent) chose "moral values," one of the seven options offered, when asked to name the issue that was most important to them. More skeptical observers, however, noted that the "moral values" option was conceptually broader than the other options and that the proportion of voters choosing this option did not differ significantly from the proportion choosing "the economy/jobs" or the proportion choosing "terrorism." In addition, a post-election Pew Research Center (2004) survey found that the term "moral values" meant many different things to respondents and that few respondents (3 percent) mentioned any social issue—let alone gay rights—in response to an open-ended question about the issue that mattered most to them. More rigorous analyses conducted afterward found that citizens' opinions about gay marriage played a modest role, if any, in shaping vote choice in the 2004 election (Hillygus and Shields 2005; Lewis 2005). However, some evidence suggests that the presence of anti–gay marriage amendments on the ballot had a mobilizing effect on white evangelical support for Bush (though at a cost of demobilizing secular support for him) (see Campbell and Monson 2008).

Epilogue: Gay Rights and the Parties

Looking at the issue of gay men and lesbians serving in the military, it is interesting to note that the polarization initially observed among both citizens and leaders faded among the former even as it persisted among the latter. By the time Congress repealed "Don't Ask, Don't Tell" on a heavily (though not entirely) partisan vote, public opinion had already approached a consensus that cut across political lines. Thus, elite polarization rather than mass polarization served as the final obstacle to the resolution of the issue. In light of this, it is perhaps not surprising that many potential contenders for the 2012 Republican nomination remained largely silent during the 2010 debate over the repeal of "Don't Ask, Don't Tell." Here, public opinion clearly favored President Obama's stance.

Meanwhile, the political landscape surrounding gay marriage remains polarized at both the elite and mass levels. Indeed, the contrast between the two parties became even sharper on May 9, 2012, when President Obama announced his support for gay marriage. His shift on the issue dovetailed with a growing trend among not only other Democratic leaders but also Democratic partisans among the public to endorse "marriage equality." At the elite level, Obama's announcement followed a similar statement by his own vice president, Joe Biden, as well as public endorsements by potential future presidential candidates such as New York governor Andrew Cuomo and Maryland governor Martin O'Malley (both of whom signed state laws recognizing gay marriages). At the mass level, an April 2012 Pew Research Center survey (2012a) found that 59 percent of Democratic respondents supported gay marriage.

Mitt Romney, the 2012 Republican presidential nominee, followed his party's previous nominees in opposing gay marriage and supporting the Defense of Marriage Act. If anything, he went further than the Republican Party's two previous nominees in his opposition. Unlike 2004 Republican nominee George W. Bush, Romney publicly opposed civil unions along with gay marriage; unlike 2008 Republican nominee John McCain, Romney also endorsed the Federal Marriage Amendment. Similar to Obama's new pro–gay marriage stance, Romney's anti–gay marriage stance reflected the majority sentiment in his party at both the elite and mass levels. His top rivals for the 2012 Republican nomination—most notably, former US senator Rick Santorum and former Speaker of the House Newt Gingrich—took the same position. Furthermore, the same April 2012 Pew survey that found a clear majority of Democrats in favor of gay marriage (59 percent) also found a clear majority of Republicans in opposition (68 percent).

Less clear is what role, if any, the issue of gay marriage will play in future presidential elections. Some initial media accounts suggested that Obama's announcement might hurt his chances, but most respondents in polls said it would not influence their votes either way.[7] The Romney campaign was not particularly eager to emphasize the issue in the general election campaign. It will be important to watch the trajectory that each party takes on the issue. Given the political tides within the Democratic Party, it seems unlikely that either its leaders or its followers will shift away from what now appears to be a growing party consensus in favor of gay marriage. It also appears unlikely that Republican leaders or partisans will shift toward majority support in the near future. In the longer term, however, one might expect a continuation of present public opinion trends to push the Republican Party to weaken its anti–gay rights stances in general and its anti–gay marriage stance in particular.

Notes

1. Given that the ideologies of Supreme Court justices often shift over time (Epstein et al. 2007), we focus on their ideological positions at the time of key decisions rather than the party affiliations of the presidents who initially appointed them.

2. Respondents were asked, "Do you think homosexuals should be allowed to serve in the United States Armed Forces or do you think they should not be allowed?"

3. Respondents were asked, "Do you favor or oppose laws to protect homosexuals against job discrimination?"

4. The wording of the question on civil unions was as follows: "Do you strongly favor, favor, oppose, or strongly oppose allowing gay and lesbian couples to enter into legal agreements with each other that would give them many of the same rights as married couples?" The wording of the question on gay marriage was as follows: "Do you strongly favor, favor, oppose, or strongly oppose allowing gays and lesbians to marry legally?"

5. For details on the construction of the measures for these variables as well as the measures for the controls described later, see Brewer 2008.

6. In 2004, 3 percent of the respondents were coded as volunteering this third response. In 2008, 28 percent were coded as volunteering the response, but all three options were presented to respondents as part of an "audio-computer aided self-interview" portion of the questionnaire.

7. Among these were polls sponsored by the Pew Research Center, by ABC News and the *Washington Post,* and by CBS News and the *New York Times.*

12

Aging Policy: A Partisan Paradox

Christine L. Day

Old-age politics has worked its way front and center in the partisan-ideological debates of the early twenty-first century. Opponents of Social Security and Medicare have tried for decades to chip away at their support, to little avail. The two programs, composing a third of the federal budget, are so popular that opposition among elected officials has been muted. Today, however, open challenges to the size and structure of both programs from the right and defensiveness on the left are turning Social Security—more formally, Old Age, Survivors, and Disability Insurance (OASDI)—and Medicare into lightning rods for partisan acrimony.

The change has been a long transition, not an overnight transformation, and it is attributable to a confluence of related developments. The proportion of the federal budget spent on benefits for older people is rising and projected to escalate. For one thing, the population is aging and the leading edge of the baby boom is just reaching the age of sixty-five; over the next two decades, as nearly the entire generation of boomers collect Social Security and Medicare benefits, the budgets of these programs will be strained. Medicaid's budget also is likely to fall short due to increasing need for nursing home care and home health care. Especially straining Medicare and Medicaid is the fact that medical inflation far outpaces that of the consumer price index, threatening the long-term sustainability of both programs if health care costs are not contained.

Not only are the older population and the cost of health care expanding, but so is the national debt, and the current economic situation is not conducive to reducing either the annual deficit or the debt anytime soon. Thus there is a great deal of pressure on the government to reduce spending even

285

as more money is required to meet current entitlement obligations. Finally, the conservative/libertarian wing of the Republican Party, in its ascendancy, is becoming increasingly strident in its demands to reduce the deficit by curbing spending without raising taxes. As a result, programs benefiting older Americans, especially the large entitlement programs that have been protected for decades, are increasingly and openly in the crosshairs of fiscal conservatives in government. Witness, for example, President George W. Bush's push for partial privatization of Social Security during both terms of his presidency. Wisconsin representative Paul Ryan's proposal to voucherize Medicare in 2011, and many Republicans' and even some Democrats' insistence on major entitlement reform during recent, ongoing budget negotiations. Although such attempts to cut Social Security and Medicare benefits have been stopped short by public outcry, they are gaining political viability in light of economic, budgetary, and demographic realities.

The trend toward greater partisan-ideological polarization among political elites complicates efforts to find common ground toward maintaining pension and health care benefits for older Americans, while keeping taxes low, reducing the deficit, and eventually paying down the national debt. Debates over reducing or privatizing aging-related benefits versus maintaining or increasing them have become more broadly ideological and less group-oriented in recent years. Pro-market elites, including interest-group leaders, have begun framing their opposition to social insurance programs less in terms of generational equity, and more in terms of shrinking the government in order to "save" popular programs. Consequently, debates over old-age programs and benefits increasingly are meshed with much broader debates over the role of government versus the private sector.

This partisan-ideological polarization over old-age benefits, however, remains somewhat tempered by three factors: (1) continued widespread support for Social Security and Medicare among the general public; (2) some intraparty conflict over the complexity of policies—Medicare in particular—and the role of government in providing public benefits directly, by subsidizing the private sector, or by privatizing them altogether; and (3) the dominance, among mass-membership aging-based interest groups, of AARP (formerly the American Association of Retired Persons), a relatively moderate organization with an enormous and ideologically diverse membership base.

I begin this chapter by outlining the evolving rhetoric characterizing public debate over aging-related policies. Next, I review public opinion studies demonstrating consistent, long-lived support for Social Security and Medicare. Disagreements over the extent of support tend to divide people along partisan, not age, lines, although recent policy debates show some potential for age-based conflict. Third, I examine the landscape of aging-based political organizations and the increasing ideological polarization among old-age mass-membership groups, with AARP maintaining a position of moderation. Finally, I examine partisan trends around aging policy in Congress since the mid-1990s, revealing an overall high level of polarization. Despite occasional interruptions of this polarization, the outlook for partisan compromise on major aging policy, Social Security and Medicare in particular, is not one that inspires a great deal of hope.

Competing Frames in Aging Policy Debates

Democrats favor a stronger governmental role in promoting social welfare than do Republicans, who favor a more autonomous private sector. These respective liberal and conservative views underlie the partisan conflict over Social Security, Medicare, and other programs benefiting older people. Conflict was restrained through most of the postwar period, as the programs remained popular with the public, budgetary pressures did not demand retrenchment, and the norm of bipartisan negotiation and compromise still reigned in Washington. By the late 1970s, a small but expanding number of aging-based political organizations had become active advocates for the elderly. Meanwhile, political observers called attention to the "graying of the federal budget" (Hudson 1978), or the increasing proportion of the budget consumed by programs and benefits for older Americans.

Conservative opponents of a strong governmental role in promoting social welfare began, in the 1980s, to demand "generational equity," charging that older Americans were consuming too much of the federal budget at the expense of younger generations. Liberals responded with calls for "generational interdependence," asserting that family and community ties across generations contradict the notion of zero-sum conflicts between them (Williamson and Watts-Roy 1999). Political organizations representing younger adults promoted the generational equity theme as old-age advocacy groups, defending government programs benefiting aging citizens, continued to expand in number and size. As the twentieth century rolled into the twenty-first, this age-group-based conflict was fading in prominence as the rhetoric associated with debates over Social Security and Medicare grew more broadly ideological, invoking themes of free-market versus government regulation, individual responsibility versus collective security, and even class conflict, themes that match the burgeoning partisan-ideological polarization of the early twenty-first century.

The period between the New Deal and the late 1970s is characterized by Robert Binstock (2010) as the era of "compassionate ageism"—compassionate because of widespread support for a social welfare system that does much to alleviate problems of poverty, illness, and loss in old age, and ageist because much of that support appears to be based on stereotypes of older people as poor and frail. Both the passage and amendment of the Social

Security Act in the 1930s and the creation of Medicare and Medicaid in 1965 occurred in the context of sweeping redistributive changes in social policy: first the New Deal in response to the Great Depression, and then the Great Society and War on Poverty thirty years later. Older people were not the sole beneficiaries of welfare-state expansion during either period, and even Social Security and Medicare pay benefits to younger survivors and disabled persons. But the elderly were the primary target of these two major social insurance programs, and of myriad other programs, services, and legislation created and enacted in the 1960s and 1970s, including Medicaid, which covers long-term care for poor older and disabled persons along with general medical expenses for the poor; the Older Americans Act, which provided a network of programs and services throughout the country; the Age Discrimination in Employment Act and the Employee Retirement Income Security Act, which provided protection for jobs and private pensions; and various bureaucratic agencies, research institutes, and special committees established in Congress to address aging-related issues. In addition, income security was enhanced in the early 1970s when Social Security benefits were increased and tied to the cost of living, and Supplemental Security Income established a minimum income level for the elderly (see Hudson 2010 on policy developments).

During this era of compassionate ageism, such advances in old-age security appealed to Americans across the ideological spectrum by combining principles of social welfare with those of individual responsibility and deservingness. The stereotype of the frail, poverty-stricken elderly person was not completely divorced from reality; most older people were indeed destitute prior to the New Deal, and their poverty rate remained disproportionately high on the eve of the Great Society and War on Poverty. Sympathy for the aged was enhanced by the notion of deservingness: people deserve security toward the end of their lives after decades of work and sacrifice. Social Security, with its redistributive aspects and contributory structure, could be framed as both a poverty program and a type of savings scheme resulting in earned benefits and self-reliance after retirement (Schulz and Binstock 2006: chap. 3; Béland 2005). Medicare and Medicaid represented a compromise between liberals wishing to expand social insurance to health care coverage and conservatives who opposed extending "socialized medicine" to the general population (Marmor 2000; Grogan and Andrews 2010).

Thus proponents were able to overcome multiple hurdles that set the United States decades behind other developed countries in adopting any type of social insurance program, from a culture of extreme individualism to a relatively weak and divided labor movement and the dual economy that stifled support for public pensions and old-age assistance particularly in the agrarian, plantation-based South well into the nineteenth century (Quadagno 1988). Support for old-age security remained so strong between World War

II and the 1970s that politicians of both parties claimed credit for maintaining and expanding old-age entitlements (Béland 2005).

The era of compassionate ageism, embedded within a broad liberal consensus, began to erode in the late 1970s, both in reaction to the growth of the welfare state and as a result of spiking oil prices, stagflation and slower economic growth, and the first projections of future deficits in the Social Security trust fund (Binstock 2010; Schulz and Binstock 2006; Quadagno 1989; Polivka and Estes 2009). A new old-age stereotype—that of the prosperous, hedonistic retiree—illustrated the message: older Americans, no longer poor, but in fact enjoying lives of luxurious leisure, were consuming far more than their share of societal resources through overly generous government benefits at the expense of younger generations. In 1988, *The New Republic* coined the widely used phrase "greedy geezer" on its cover, in a story portraying older Americans as prosperous and selfish (Fairlie 1988). The theme was repeated in numerous media accounts and commentaries throughout the 1980s and 1990s, with older people depicted as disproportionately wealthy and politically powerful (e.g., Kotlikoff 1992; Longman 1985, 1987; Peterson 1999; Preston 1984; Samuelson 1999).

Not that this was bad news for old-age advocates, who could point with pride to social insurance and old-age assistance programs that were working as intended; indeed, the poverty rate among people older than sixty-five had dropped lower than that for the general population. Public assistance programs establish a rather meager floor for the destitute of all ages, but the universality of social insurance programs—which in the United States are heavily oriented toward the elderly—are most effective in reducing poverty (Quadagno 1989). While there was a great deal of diversity among the elderly, and many remained below or near the poverty level, advocacy groups such as the rapidly growing AARP benefited by portraying older people as active, healthy, contributing members of society, boosting the economy with their purchasing power (Day 1990).

But proponents of small-government, pro-market policies, intent on reversing the expansion of social insurance and public assistance, latched on to the new stereotype in the mid-1980s to push the generational equity theme. Equity was lacking, they said, among age groups and among generations, with the elderly enjoying a windfall at the expense of young families and children. Government programs and benefits targeting older people, according to this view, had so overwhelmed the budget that few resources were available for younger people, and old-age benefits had become so generous that the working-age Americans supporting those benefits had become unfairly burdened in the present and would be unable to afford the same self-indulgent lifestyles in their own retirement. Not only would the unfairness escalate once the large baby boom cohort reached retirement age, but the strain on the federal budget, including on the Social Security trust fund, would reach crisis proportions requiring drastic change. Thus promoters of the generational equity frame, then and since, have appealed to liberals' sympathy for younger people, especially children, while scapegoating the elderly (Binstock 1983; Quadagno 1989). The change they espouse is not a shift of governmental resources from the old to the young, but rather a shift of resources from government to the private sector, through reduction of both taxing and spending by means-testing social insurance benefits, reducing them to public assistance levels, and partially or even fully privatizing pension and health care benefits. The generational equity frame, Jill Quadagno (1989) suggests, is meant to obscure the neoliberal free-market agenda by appearing to promote the interests of the nonelderly poor.

Advocates of preserving old-age benefits object to characterizing social welfare as a generational zero-sum game. Instead, they emphasize family and community ties under the rubric of generational interdependence, or generational solidarity (Estes et al. 2009; Williamson and Watts-Roy 1999). Far from draining resources from the young, public pensions, health care coverage, and other benefits enable Americans to retain their independence and self-reliance into old age, reducing their dependence on their children, who in turn retain more disposable income for themselves and their own children. Benefits thus are shared across generations rather than consumed by one at the expense of another. The generational interdependence view extends to the community as well, with an emphasis on collective security and mutual caring and concern, as well as universal rights to a decent standard of living. Further, although welfare states vary in their age orientation (Lynch 2006), empirical evidence disputes the zero-sum notion that the elderly benefit at the expense of children (Williamson and Watts-Roy 1999). Instead, countries with well-developed old-age welfare states tend to spend more on children as well (Pampel 1994).

Generational interdependence advocates object to the crisis rhetoric surrounding old-age entitlements as well. They do not dispute that changes are needed in order to keep the programs fiscally sound over the long term, but maintain that incremental changes to financing and benefit levels are sufficient without transforming the structure of the programs (Schulz and Binstock 2006; White 2001). This was the approach taken by the Greenspan Commission in 1983, for example, which restored actuarial balance to the Social Security trust fund for several decades in the future, without transforming the nature of the program, despite conservatives' charges that the system was then in a crisis requiring more drastic measures (Béland 2005). The crisis frame, they suggest, is not rooted in reality but is instead used to undermine public confidence in the future of social insurance, thereby reducing public support. Similarly, the call for means-testing social insurance benefits by generational equity proponents does not signify concern for the nonelderly poor; instead, it arises from the recognition that once converted from universal social insurance to low-income public assistance, the programs would lose much middle-class support and become politically easier to dismantle (Williamson and Watts-Roy 1999).

Both the generational interdependence frame, promoting maintenance or expansion of the current system for old-age health and security, and the generational equity frame, promoting reductions in governmental effort and a larger role for the private sector, claim to address the needs of children and younger adults, and extol the virtues of self-reliance for older people. Both perspectives suggest rhetorically that there is a legitimate role for government in providing for basic needs, and in the 1980s, public and congressional support remained high for existing social insurance and public assistance programs. Fay Lomax Cook and Edith Barrett's (1992) survey of congressional representatives revealed a partisan split among congressional representatives, but primarily over whether to increase or maintain current levels of support. Substantial majorities of representatives from both parties opposed cuts to Social Security, Medicare, Unemployment Insurance, Aid to Families with Dependent Children, Food Stamps, Medicaid, and Supplemental Security Insurance. Partisan disagreement over Social Security was virtually nonexistent.

All this began to change in the 1990s, as the age-group basis for promoting generational equity began to fade, becoming increasingly subsumed under broader ideological arguments about the role of government. Free-market advocates had used the generational equity argument to chip away at the notion that older people were particularly needy and deserving of governmental largesse (Quadagno 1989). Their message had penetrated Congress, as members expressed concern about rising poverty among children as living standards improved for the elderly (Cook and Barrett 1992). But Americans for Generational Equity, founded in 1985, and similar groups, faded from view by the early 1990s. The generational equity frame has not been dropped altogether; one need only Google "generational equity" or the pejorative "greedy geezers" to find thousands of contemporary references (Binstock 2010; see for example Samuelson 2011). But as partisan polarization increases, there appears to be less need to appeal to sympathy for children and young families in order to support deep cuts and major structural changes to Social Security and Medicare.

There are a number of interrelated reasons for this shift in rhetoric among conservatives. For one thing, Republicans gained a majority in both chambers of Congress in 1994 for the first time in forty years, and since then leaders of both parties have consolidated power as the rank and file became more unified within each party, and as ideological moderates became increasingly rare (Aldrich and Rohde 2000; Binder 2003). As a result, Republicans were emboldened to slash domestic spending, and bipartisan agreement on existing social welfare programs declined. Simultaneously, the pluralistic system of crosscutting groups has gradually been giving way to a more party-dominated system in which interest groups and parties are more clearly and closely aligned (Abramowitz 2010; Stonecash 2010). Thus group-based constructs like generational equity are more easily folded into broad-based multi-issue ideological frameworks.

More recently, economic recession and an expanding national debt have further emboldened conservatives intent on shrinking social welfare spending. Proponents of slashing or privatizing the major social insurance programs—whom James Schulz and Robert Binstock (2006) term "the merchants of doom"—have warned since the late 1970s that old-age benefits would not be sustainable once the large postwar baby boom cohort reached old age, and in 2011 the first of them reached the age of sixty-five. Doomsday seemed all the more imminent in the first decade of the twenty-first century, as massive tax cuts, two wars, and then the deepest recession since the Great Depression turned federal surpluses into deficits, followed by a seemingly insurmountable national debt after governmental action was taken to stimulate the faltering economy. Social Security and Medicare, along with tax policy, now shifted to the epicenter of ideological controversy, as Democrats focused their energies on sheltering the programs while Republicans dug in against any type of tax increase.

Thus conservative rhetoric about old-age social insurance is less about supporting the young versus the old, and more about reducing government by shifting the risk of illness and income loss in retirement to the individual (Hacker 2006). Conservative Republicans emphasize free-market competition, personal choice (for ourselves), and personal responsibility (for others); liberal Democrats emphasize the social insurance aspect of maintaining personal and collective security and lowering individual risk (Hacker 2006; Marmor 2000; Polivka and Estes 2009). Recognizing the popularity of Social Security and Medicare among the public, Democrats stress their defense of the programs. Republicans assert that they must be drastically transformed, or privatized, in order to "save" them, while also soft-pedaling proposed changes by substituting the term "personal accounts" for Social Security privatization (Baumgartner et al. 2009: 172) and "premium supports" for Medicare vouchers (Marmor 2000). But in general, partisan debate over old-age social insurance has become more grounded in broad ideological differences than it has been since the expansionist era of the 1960s and early 1970s. "One of the most striking features of Medicare's political evolution," notes Theodore Marmor, "is how the ideological cleavage that attended its birth reappeared, in a different guise, more than three decades later" (2000: 191).

Finally, another likely reason for diminishing use of the generational equity frame is the desire of public officials and political advocates to attract older people, and certainly not to alienate older people by scapegoating them;

this is especially important as the baby boom generation reaches the age of retirement and Medicare eligibility. Voter turnout already tends to increase with age (Wolfinger and Rosenstone 1980), and the baby boom generation is not only numerically large, but also has a long tradition of political activism and higher levels of education and income than previous generations of older people (Williamson 1998). But they are also highly diverse and politically divided, and therefore receptive to appeals from across the ideological spectrum. Astute politicians across the spectrum know that people tend to be especially sensitive to loss and risk; they tend to become more agitated over potential or actual loss than excited about potential gain (Kahneman and Tversky 1979; Quattrone and Tversky 1988). Thus each side strives to use language that does not suggest the loss of benefits for older people and those approaching old age.

One type of policy that theoretically enables members of both parties to claim credit for maintenance and expansion of government benefits, even in an ideologically polarized legislature, is "delegated governance" (Morgan and Campbell 2011), or private-sector delivery of publicly funded benefits. Medicare reforms passed during the Bill Clinton and George W. Bush administrations provide prime examples. The Medicare + Choice program, created in 1997 in conjunction with the Balanced Budget Act, gave Medicare recipients the option of obtaining Medicare benefits through private plans rather than traditional Medicare. In 2003 it was reconfigured into Medicare Advantage, as part of the Medicare Modernization Act, which also created the similarly private-sector provision of prescription drugs for Medicare recipients. The Medicare Modernization Act was primarily a Republican-supported program, because of the private, for-profit aspect and the lack of government-regulated cost controls. While the private options to traditional Medicare were supposed to save money for the federal government through competitive choices for recipients, in fact they have cost significantly more than traditional Medicare, because of the subsidies required to attract customers to the private plans. They also shift risks to individual beneficiaries, who must choose among plans of varying and unpredictable quality (Moon 2007; Morgan and Campbell 2011; Marmor 2000). The Medicare Modernization Act also resulted in taxpayer subsidies to the pharmaceutical industry (Iglehart 2004). Ironically, then, a deficit-increasing policy received most of its support from the same Republican Party intent on reducing the deficit through domestic budget cuts. Further, conservative Republicans mobilized many of their older constituents against the Patient Protection and Affordable Care Act ("Obamacare") in 2009 on the grounds that their Medicare Advantage benefits—that is, the subsidies to private insurers running the optional Medicare plans—would be cut in order to pay for expanding health care coverage to the nonelderly population (Surowiecki 2010). But whatever the normative implications of delegated governance, it does have the potential for promoting compromise between pro-market Republicans and pro–social welfare Democrats, especially because recent federal court decisions permit a more expansive and influential corporate role in the financing of federal election campaigns.

Public Opinion on Age-Related Policies: Intergenerational or Ideological Conflict?

Social Security, Medicare, and government spending on the elderly more generally are popular with the American public. Warnings about funding crises and "greedy geezers" seem to have had little effect on public opinion to date. The universality of social insurance programs gives everyone a stake in maintaining Social Security and Medicare; younger adults who are years away from collecting benefits directly recognize their importance to the financial security of their parents and grandparents; and older people tend to be seen in a sympathetic and deserving light (Campbell 2009). To the extent that the general public is divided on whether to increase or simply maintain current benefits levels, those divisions appear along partisan and income lines, with Democrats and low-income respondents demonstrating even higher support than Republicans and higher-income people. But support is high across the board (Campbell 2009; Cook and Barrett 1992; Day 1990; MacManus 1996; Ponza et al. 1988; Rhodebeck 1993). Even in the lead-up to the divisive 2012 election, majorities of voters in every age group expressed more support for maintaining Social Security and Medicare benefits than for reducing the federal deficit, and agreed that the federal government does too little for older people (Pew Research Center 2011).

Looking more broadly at policies that are particularly salient for different age groups, it is still difficult to find signs of age-based conflict. Some researchers have recognized the potential for generational conflict, as budget deficits and a growing national debt began forcing tradeoffs in budgeting, and spending priorities differed somewhat across age groups—with older people being somewhat less supportive of government spending on environmental concerns, education, and research on AIDS, for example (MacManus 1996). However, recent studies examining attitudes toward government spending on a variety of age-related policies, such as education for the young and Social Security and health care for the old, dismiss the "gray peril" thesis that older people's attitudes are influenced by age-based self-interest. Instead of an aging effect on attitudes, they attribute what age differences they find to cohort effects, or the effects of the political environment around the time they came of age and approached adulthood (Fullerton and Dixon 2011; Plutzer and Berkman 2005; Street and Cossman 2006; Pew Research Center 2011). Another study of older respondents found their attitudes toward the Medicare Catastrophic Care Act—passed in 1985, then repealed the following year in the face of protests by older people—to be related to trust in government and assessments of the national economy, and not related to factors of direct self-interest such as perceived effects on one's own tax and benefit levels (Day 1993; see also Himelfarb 1995).

Nor does age have much effect on partisan identification and voting behavior. Vote choices in national elections generally do not differ across age groups, and there is little evidence that older voters' choices are affected specifically by candidates' stances on aging-related issues (Binstock and Campbell 2011; Binstock 2009). Laurie Rhodebeck (1993) found older people to be more likely to vote on the basis of age-related concerns like Social Security and health care, but that their attitudes on those issues, and their votes, were divided along partisan lines. Voters are much more diverse within age groups than between them, and their votes are more likely to be affected by other group identities like race, religion, gender, and of course partisanship (Abramowitz 2010; Day 1990; Schulz and Binstock 2006). Partisanship may vary somewhat by age from one election to the next, as a result of generational differences, or cohort effects. For example, older people today who came of age during the New Deal period tend to swing somewhat more Democratic than those who came of age during the Republican Eisenhower era (Binstock 2009). Political consultants and observers who work to identify the electoral interests of older voters may recognize the potential for the elderly to vote as a bloc, a potential that old-age interest groups sometimes use to their advantage with what Robert Binstock (1972) terms the "electoral bluff." But the potential has yet to be actualized, even when such issues as Social Security and Medicare reforms are high on the political agenda.

Many scholars and journalists examining old-age politics in recent years, however, wonder whether we are starting to see generational conflicts in political attitudes and behavior that cut across partisan lines. Serious attempts to transform Social Security—President George W. Bush's push for partial privatization through personal accounts in 2005—and Medicare—US House Republicans' 2011 proposal to overhaul Medicare by replacing benefits with vouchers for private care—already show signs of dividing Americans by age. Numerous surveys during the Social Security privatization debate under the George W. Bush presidency revealed considerably higher opposition to the plan among people over sixty-five years of age than among younger adults, especially those under forty-five. The issue was much more salient among older people as well (Campbell and King 2010). Similarly, a study by the Pew Research Center in 2011 found that knowledge about, and opposition to, the Republicans' Medicare overhaul plan increased with age (Grossman 2011).

Another recent source of divisiveness was the Patient Protection and Affordable Care Act, signed into law in early 2010. The public has been highly polarized along partisan lines in their attitudes toward President

Obama's health care reform, but they also divide along age lines, with support dropping precipitously after the age of sixty-five (Gelman, Lee, and Ghitza 2010). The concern for older people appears to be loss aversion, as political opponents of health care reform evoked frightening visions of "death panels" and "pulling the plug on granny"; they also raised the specter of Medicare cuts, although the cuts were primarily to subsidies for inefficient private Medicare Advantage plans (Binstock 2010; Lynch 2011). Indeed, town hall meetings with members of Congress were filled with older people expressing anger at what they felt were potential losses and dangers resulting from health care reform.

Results of the 2010 congressional elections reflected these concerns, as Republican candidates did best among voters aged sixty-five and older, suggesting the emergence of a "'senior-issues' voting bloc" for the first time in four decades (Binstock 2012: 408). Older voters were most supportive of 2012 Republican presidential candidate Mitt Romney, as well, with polls showing those under age thirty strongly supported President Obama's reelection and middle-aged voters nearly evenly split between the two (Pew Research Center 2012d). An article in *The New Yorker* about the drop in support for Democrats among older voters attributed the drop to their opposition to the Affordable Care Act. The title of the article: "Greedy Geezers" (Surowiecki 2010). Thus the phrase was trotted out once again—but this time by liberal defenders of the health care reform package.

Andrea Campbell's book *How Policies Make Citizens* (2003) demonstrates the surges in political participation, especially in contacting public officials, among older people in reaction to proposed cuts to Social Security and Medicare. Lower-income seniors were especially likely to participate, contrary to the usual tendency for participation to increase with income, but since lower-income seniors depend more heavily on Social Security, their participation is a reasonable, and even a democratizing, development. Older people, then, can be mobilized in large numbers to defend the programs that insure them against illness and income loss. Aging-based membership organizations play a major role in their mobilization.

Perhaps as they confront continued attempts at radical reforms to old-age social insurance, as a polarized Congress battles over raising taxes versus slashing spending, older people may unite across party lines in defense of their programs. Reforms that shrink, voucherize, or privatize old-age benefits, however, are likely to exacerbate the degree of economic inequality among older persons, with the potential of dividing them even further along partisan, ideological, and class lines (Hacker 2006). As a result of their participation already, Frederick Lynch (2011) notes that aging baby boomers confront media stereotypes that are themselves ideologically polarized: the relatively affluent, irresponsible, and self-centered aging yuppies who stridently defend their government benefits, and the rabidly antigovernment, antitax teabaggers who stridently oppose health care reform. Certainly the political organizations that claim to speak for older Americans are divided along ideological lines.

Interest Groups: Who Speaks for Older Americans?
Diverse Groups for Diverse Seniors

Political organizations, for better or worse, have played a dominant role in US politics since the beginning. The US Constitution was based on Madisonian principles of decentralization and fragmentation of power, allowing a multitude of diverse interests to compete, and preventing any single faction or interest from dominating. Countless scholars and observers, from Alexis de Tocqueville (1945 [1835]) in the early days of the republic, to Robert A. Dahl (1956) in the twentieth century, have extolled the virtues of the pluralistic US political system. Many others have criticized the system for violating the pluralist ideal by favoring the interests that are most well-endowed and well-connected, or as E. E. Schattschneider famously wrote, "The flaw in the pluralist heaven is that the heavenly chorus sings with a strong upper-class accent" (1960: 35). Schattschneider chaired the American Political Science Association committee that issued a report in 1950 calling for stronger and more unified programmatic parties that would more easily mobilize voters and offer them a clear choice between different visions of the role of government (American Political Science Association 1950). In the spirit of being careful what you wish for, many political scientists today deplore the extent to which the major parties have polarized, becoming so unified within, and so far apart from each other, that the government is stymied by gridlock, making the country nearly ungovernable (e.g., Abramowitz 2010; Fiorina and Abrams 2009).

Political organizations representing older Americans in the early twenty-first century reflect both the diversity and the competing, overlapping nature of interest groups as envisioned by pluralist theory, and the partisan-ideological polarization that characterizes contemporary US government. Policy communities build structure out of complex issue areas through conflict and coalition, gradually turning multidimensional issue spaces into more clearly defined positions that represent the different sides (Baumgartner et al. 2009). In the case of aging policy and the representation of older Americans, interest groups over the past few decades have become increasingly aligned with the opposing political views represented by the Democratic and Republican parties, through both the evolution of long-existing groups and the creation of newer ones. Like the parties, old-age interest groups have become increasingly polarized along ideological lines. But there is still some complexity, with some policy disagreements among mostly like-minded groups, and with the largest and most dominant of the old-age political organizations, AARP, still largely holding down the middle.

The interest-group landscape that could be considered part of the aging policy community is vast, comprising hundreds of organizations at the national level, and thousands if state- and local-level chapters and standalone groups are counted. These include mass-membership groups, among which AARP stands out as the largest and best known; membership and service groups for subpopulations of the elderly, such as the Older Women's League and the National Caucus and Center on Black Aged; service and advocacy groups composed mostly of professionals and other organizations, such as the National Council on the Aging; trade associations and provider groups such as the National Association of Area Agencies on Aging and the American Association of Homes and Services for the Aging; research and outreach groups for persons afflicted by specific illnesses that tend to affect older people, such as the Alzheimer's Association; and academic and professional associations such as the Gerontological Society of America (Pratt 1976; Day 1990, 1998; Campbell 2003; Schulz and Binstock 2006; Estes 1979). The discussion here is restricted to mass-membership organizations with the mission of representing older people generally and with open memberships, whether members are mostly of the participatory or the "checkbook" variety. Even so, there are undoubtedly some groups left out of the discussion, primarily organizations that are nothing more than direct-mail or Internet fundraisers rather than active advocacy organizations, although the distinction is not always entirely clear (see Godwin 1988).

Prior to the passage of Social Security, the Townsend movement and a few other social movement organizations joined the battle for public pensions. But durable mass-membership advocacy groups for older people did not emerge or become politicized until after the passage of major aging-based programs and benefits in the 1960s and early 1970s, including Medicare, Medicaid, the Older Americans Act, and Social Security legislation that expanded benefits and introduced cost-of-living adjustments. These programs, along with the prior creation of Social Security, produced a politicized age-based identity by setting age as the eligibility criterion, thus giving older people a clear stake in government and politics (Walker 1983). Old-age advocacy thus illustrates the reciprocal effect between government action and interest-group organization.

AARP's origins date to 1947, with the formation of the National Retired Teachers Association (NRTA) for the purpose of providing health insurance—back then very difficult and expensive for retirees to obtain. The NRTA spawned and then merged with the American Association of Retired Persons in 1958, but it was much more a service organization than a political group in those early years. The labor union movement helped create the

National Council of Senior Citizens in 1961, from the remnants of its Senior Citizens for Kennedy campaign, as it lobbied for Medicare to help retirees; in 2001 it was reconfigured into a new organization, the Alliance for Retired Americans (ARA). Next came the Gray Panthers in 1970, a more radical organization with the slogan "age and youth in action," inspired by the civil rights, antiwar, and environmental movements of the time. The National Committee to Preserve Social Security and Medicare (NCPSSM) was founded in 1982 in reaction to the Reagan administration's attempts to cut Social Security benefits and reform the program. At this point, AARP was considered the conservative one of the bunch, composed mostly of white-collar professionals (Pratt 1976); although the much more conservative National Alliance of Senior Citizens had been founded in 1974, it was relatively small and little known. In the late 1980s and early 1990s a trio of conservative groups—the Seniors Coalition, the United Seniors Association (now USA Next), and the 60 Plus Association—began direct-mail fundraising and lobbying for limited government and free-market reforms. Thus over the past half century, as the parties have become increasingly polarized, the mass-membership aging-based political organizations have evolved into an array of established organizations ranging from one ideological extreme to the other. What differentiates them ideologically from the parties in Congress is that the center is not disappearing; it remains anchored by the 40 million–member AARP.

When President Obama turned fifty, he joked during a fundraiser that "by the time I wake up, I'll have an email from AARP asking me to call President Obama and tell him to protect Medicare" (Pace 2011). Everyone got the joke, because today, virtually everyone knows about AARP, including its fifty-and-over membership criterion. AARP is one of the nation's largest membership groups of any kind, and one of the most visible and politically influential (e.g., Lynch 2011; Schulz and Binstock 2006; Morris 1996; Day 1998).

Frederick Lynch, in his recent book about AARP, characterizes its ideology as "moderately liberal—largely a reflection of the culture and ideology of the upper-middle and professional classes," bipartisan, and "accept[ing] of globalization, mass immigration, [and] multiculturalism" (2011: 171). With its huge and diverse membership, many of whom join for the vast array of selective benefits, it is nearly impossible to take specific issue positions that do not anger at least some of its members, but its politics generally remains sufficiently moderate to avoid mass defections from either conservatives or liberals. Its endorsement of the 2003 Medicare Modernization Act, for example—the prescription drug law endorsed by President George W. Bush and more Republicans than Democrats in Congress—angered many of its liberal members, while its endorsement of President Barack Obama's health care reform package, the Patient Protection and Affordable Care Act, infuriated many of the group's conservatives (Lynch 2011; Binstock 2010; Schulz and Binstock 2006). Andrea Campbell and Julia Lynch (2000) note that AARP's moderate issue positions and willingness to work with groups that may compete with the elderly for government benefits, relative to the more extreme self-interested attitudes toward old-age benefits among older people themselves, make AARP unusual among advocacy organizations, which tend to be more extreme than their constituents. Most recently, AARP attracted a flurry of media attention when it announced it could accept some cuts to Social Security benefits in order to maintain the program's solvency (Lichtblau 2011).

With its size and clout, AARP has anchored a number of political coalitions, both horizontally with other aging-based groups—most notably the Leadership Council of Aging Organizations (LCAO)—and vertically with nonelderly groups. The sixty-member LCAO, founded in 1978, advocates actively on the liberal side of aging issues, supporting maintenance or expansion of old-age government programs and benefits. Its sixty members include the mass-membership groups AARP, ARA, the Gray Panthers, NCPSSM, and the Older Women's League—that is, all of the mass-membership groups on the left side of the spectrum, but none of the conservative ones—as well as a variety of service, research, trade, and professional associations; and also ethnic organizations, health care reform advocates, and labor unions. Most notable among the vertical coalitions—besides the Gray Panthers, which has always billed itself as a young/old coalition (Sanjek 2011)—is Generations United, which formed in 1986 in reaction to the drive for generational equity. Generations United includes such children's advocacy groups as the Children's Defense Fund, the Child Welfare League, and Big Brothers/Big Sisters, in addition to aging-based groups on the left—but again, not those on the right. When old-age membership groups in these coalitions disagree with each other on particular issues, the 2003 Medicare Modernization Act for example, it is AARP that is most willing to deviate from liberal Democratic orthodoxy toward the center (Beard and Williamson 2011).

The first political organization that was formed explicitly to advocate for generational equity was Americans for Generational Equity (AGE), founded in 1985 with funding from "Social Security and Medicare's prime private-sector competitors," including insurance and health care companies and banks (Quadagno 1989: 360). It lasted only a few years, but during that time it did much to insert the generational equity argument into aging policy debates among politicians, scholars, and journalists. It does not seem to have engaged in coalition building with children's advocacy groups like Generations United. Organizations that inherited the generational equity mantle included organizations speaking for younger generations—"Generation X," those born in the decade or two following the baby boom, in particular—and the Concord Coalition, founded in 1992 by investment banker Peter Peterson, who still is a prominent advocate of privatizing Social Security (Schulz and Binstock 2006). The Generation X organizations, Third Millennium and Lead or Leave, also faded before the end of the 1990s. The Concord Coalition, whose primary stated goal is fiscal responsibility and reduction of the national debt, often is cited as a major adversary of the aging-based organizations that defend Social Security and Medicare (Day 1998), but if measured against congressional Republicans in 2011, it is more flexible and less stridently conservative, because its proposed solutions for reducing the debt include tax increases as well as entitlement reform.

There is little left, then, of the organizations based on generational equity. But the conservative organizations representing older people, 60 Plus, the Seniors Coalition, and USA Next, remain active in Washington, D.C. In fact they are just three of several organizations presenting themselves as conservative representatives of older people's interests, but they are the most active and best known. The three groups were founded with the help of conservative direct-mail specialist Richard Viguerie, and some activists and political observers suggest that they are only sporadically active politically, and more active as fundraising organizations (Lynch 2011; Day 1998; Schulz and Binstock 2006). Others have charged that their primary funding is corporate; 60 Plus in particular was said to serve largely as a front group for the pharmaceutical industry in a report by consumer advocacy group Public Citizen, a charge that 60 Plus denies (Tilove 2009). At any rate, if political activity can be measured in terms of lobbying expenditures and campaign contributions,[1] the conservative groups are often as active as, or more than, some of their liberal counterparts in recent years. In the 2010 election cycle, for example, the NCPSSM, which has a sizable political action committee, spent just over $1.6 million on contributions and independent expenditures, 98 percent of it in support of Democrats; 60 Plus, in comparison, spent $6.6 million on independent expenditures, 85 percent of it *against* Democrats. (AARP does not endorse candidates or contribute to campaigns.) And while none of the three spends as much on lobbying as the giant AARP, the Seniors Coalition spent between $4 million and $9.5 million every year from 1998 to 2006, comparable to the NCPSSM's spending and much more than that of the ARA.

All of the conservative aging-based membership groups bill themselves as conservative or "responsible" alternatives to AARP—not because AARP is their polar opposite ideologically, but because of the AARP's sizable clout as a defender of maintaining or expanding current benefit levels for older Americans. Although AARP is relatively moderate and bipartisan, its issue positions place it much more often in agreement with the Democratic Party, while the conservative groups side consistently with Republicans on such issues as reducing taxes and privatizing Social Security and Medicare in order to "save" them. In addition to serving as a target of opposition by the conservative groups, AARP also has come under attack and investigation by Republican members of Congress, in 1995 to investigate the group's business dealings and tax-exempt status (Day 1998), and in 2011 to investigate possible conflicts of interest between its support for health care reform and its endorsement of health insurance policies (Roth 2011).

In sum, the paradox of the aging-based membership organizations is that they both enhance and mitigate partisan polarization. Over the years, they have grown in number and diversity so that they now range from far left (Gray Panthers) to far right (60 Plus, the Seniors Coalition, and USA Next). While existing groups once could work together on a variety of issues through coalition building, the addition of the most conservative groups starting in the late 1980s ensured that there would always be partisan and ideological strife among them. But the oldest, largest, and most politically powerful of the organizations, AARP, remains a moderating influence, steadfastly defending social insurance and other public programs and benefits for older people, but willing to compromise, at least at the margins, with those on the right who demand cutbacks in domestic spending in general and reductions in Social Security and Medicare in particular.

Aging Policy and Partisan Polarization in Congress

Increasing polarization in Congress over the past few decades is now a widely accepted truism, confirmed by the *National Journal*'s annual calculation of congressional vote ratings since 1982: the data show Democrats and Republicans moving steadily further apart, and reaching a "new peak of polarization" in 2010 (Brownstein 2011). Party polarization on aging policy issues has followed a somewhat erratic path in Congress, although the general trend also has been toward increasing polarization. In the mid-1980s, Cook and Barrett (1992) concluded, based on a survey of members of Congress as well as roll call voting patterns, that Social Security was a nonpartisan issue, because bipartisan support for maintaining current benefit levels was so high. Partisan conflict over Medicare entailed support for increasing versus maintaining current benefits. Despite the Reagan administration's attempts to make serious reductions in Social Security, deep and acrimonious ideological debates over the very nature and existence of the two social insurance programs were still years away.

Opportunities for pro-market reformers to wear down the bipartisan support for Social Security and Medicare began to appear in the mid-1990s. Republicans gained control of both chambers of Congress in 1995, with leadership that was (for the time) unusually assertive and ideologically conservative. Concern about the federal deficit had grown; Social Security, Medicare, and Medicaid already consumed a large portion of the federal budget, and population aging was projected to inflate their costs a great deal more

(Schulz and Binstock 2006; Béland 2005). In this context it is logical that partisan polarization over aging policy would increase after the mid-1990s.

One way to measure this trend is to examine old-age interest-group ratings of members of Congress over time, by party. The ratings used here are those of the Alliance for Retired Americans and its predecessor, the National Council of Senior Citizens (NCSC). Between them, the NCSC and ARA have been rating members of Congress annually for many years, based on roll call votes on ten issues in each chamber that the NCSC and ARA believe have a strong impact on the well-being of older Americans. With their labor union ties, their 4 million–strong membership, and their strong commitment to social insurance principles and "a progressive political and social agenda,"[2] they provide a useful representation of the more liberal end of the aging-based organizational spectrum. Further, there is good precedent for using these ratings: Cook and Barrett's (1992) excellent study of public and congressional support for the US welfare state uses NCSC ratings as well to gauge support for social welfare programs benefiting older people. The ratings range from 0 to 100, the latter score indicating greatest support for older people according to the ARA and NCSC.

Figure 12.1 shows the average ARA/NCSC ratings of Democratic and Republican members of the House of Representatives from 1996 through 2011. Figure 12.2 displays the same for the Senate.[3] The party difference (average Republican rating subtracted from average Democratic rating) in 1996 is relatively moderate in both House and Senate (rounding to 62 and 65, respectively). In 1997 the party difference dips precipitously to 46 in the House and remains at 65 in the Senate. After a hike in 1998 (party difference of 83 in both chambers) and another dip in 1999 (68 in the House, 81 in the Senate), the party differences remain consistently high, in the mid-80s to mid-90s range, from 2000 through 2006. In 2007 the party difference declines to a low of 37 in the House while remaining high at 83 in the Senate, and in 2008 the party difference is relatively low in both chambers, 58 in the House and 64 in the Senate. In 2009–2011, the party differences are high once again, rising past 80 in both chambers and, in 2011, rising higher than ever to 95 in the House.

In sum, partisan polarization on aging policy as measured by ARA/NCSC ratings is high for the most part since 1996, reflecting partisan polarization generally in Congress during the period. But it is not consistently high and growing throughout the period. The evidence suggests that Congress might be somewhat more willing to compromise and cross party lines on aging policy than on issues more generally during this time of escalating party conflict. A closer look at the votes suggests that there are some votes that attract members of Congress across party lines, as well as a few low-cost noncontroversial votes, during the years of lower bipartisanship. Those bipartisan votes do not, unfortunately, portend a willingness among

Figure 12.1 Average ARA/NCSC Ratings of Representatives, US Congress, 1996–2011

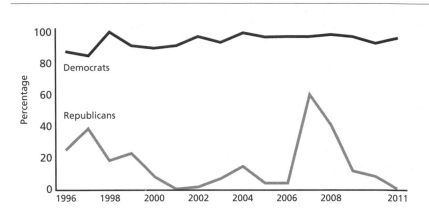

Sources: For 1996–2000, National Council of Senior Citizens, "NCSC Congressional Voting Record" annual newsletter; for 2001–2011, Alliance for Retired Americans, http://www.retired americans.org/issues/congressional-voting-record.

party members to find common ground on the major issues of keeping Social Security and Medicare solvent and reducing the deficit and the debt. After the recent rancorous budget debates, it would be surprising if they did.

The spirit of bipartisan compromise evident in the low party differences during 1997 came on the heels of the partisan rancor that characterized the first majority-Republican Congress in decades during 1995–1996, when Democrat Bill Clinton was president. The fiscal brinksmanship between the parties, led by President Clinton and Republican House Speaker Newt Gingrich, had resulted in a partial government shutdown for which the public primarily blamed Republicans; that party's demands for Medicare cuts did not endear it to the public either (Marmor 2000). In 1997 the two parties resolved to move past the previous year's disaster and pass the Balanced Budget Act, which included among many other sweeping reforms the creation of Medicare + Choice, a move toward private-sector delivery of government benefits, or "delegated governance" (Morgan and Campbell 2011; White 2001).

The 1997 spirit of compromise did not last long, of course, and what followed was several years of partisan acrimony and high polarization on aging policy, especially through most of the George W. Bush presidency. ARA ratings of congressional representatives focused on an array of broadly ideological issues affecting older people, including massive tax cuts pushed by the Bush administration that the ARA labeled "irresponsible" as the federal sur-

Figure 12.2 Average ARA/NCSC Ratings of Senators, US Congress, 1996–2011

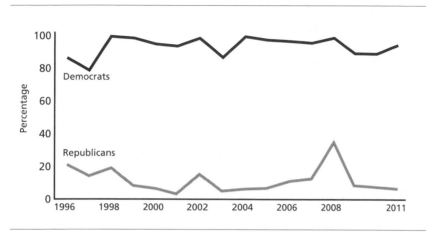

Sources: For 1996–2000, National Council of Senior Citizens, "NCSC Congressional Voting Record" annual newsletter; for 2001–2011, Alliance for Retired Americans, http://www.retired americans.org/issues/congressional-voting-record.

plus turned into a yawning deficit, proposed moves toward Social Security privatization, and the 2003 Medicare Modernization Act. The latter was another move toward delegated governance with the Part D prescription drug coverage that failed to include cost controls on the pharmaceutical industry, and enhancement of Medicare + Choice, which became known as Medicare Advantage (Morgan and Campbell 2011; Marmor 2000). The Medicare Modernization Act provided prescription drug coverage through Medicare for the first time, representing a major expansion of Medicare benefits, which led to its endorsement by AARP. But it was a partisan bill supported mostly by Republicans in Congress and by President Bush, and opposed by most Democrats as well as by the old-age membership organizations to the left of AARP—the ARA, the NCPSSM, and the Gray Panthers—because of the privatization aspect and the lack of price controls (Beard and Williamson 2011).

Why then was there a drop in partisan polarization in 2007–2008, according to the ARA congressional ratings? One likely reason is that Democrats regained control of both chambers of Congress in 2007, during the Bush presidency, creating a divided government and thereby providing incentives to make at least some agreements across party lines in order to claim credit for policy accomplishments.

Second, the votes used in calculating ARA ratings during those years included a number of issues that attracted votes, in most cases Republican votes, across party lines, or at least toward the positions preferred by the

ARA. Many of these votes related to prescription drug coverage in the wake of the Medicare Modernization Act, as members of both parties sought adjustments to the prescription drug policy that would make it more palatable to constituents. One crosscutting issue is that of drug reimportation, or permitting importation of (sometimes US-made) prescription drugs from other countries where the drugs are cheaper due to price controls. It is an issue that can meet liberal demands for cost controls and cheaper medicines as well as conservative preferences for free-market competition and choice. Other health- and drug-related bills that attracted some cross-party voting during 2007–2008 involved provision for some government negotiation of drug prices, investigation of conflicts of interest in relations between the pharmaceutical industry and the Food and Drug Administration, limited affluence testing for prescription drug coverage, and adjustments to Medicare Advantage private-plan subsidies. There were also some noncontroversial, nearly unanimous votes in 2008 to take steps to prevent elder abuse, conduct background checks on long-term care workers, continue appropriations for low-income energy assistance, and delay some Bush-supported regulations that would have cut some Medicaid nursing home benefits.

The first three years of Barack Obama's presidency, in the context of the Great Recession, saw a return to high partisan polarization on aging policy issues, debates over the highly partisan and controversial Patient Protection and Affordable Care Act, and the general partisan-ideological arguments over how to revive the economy and reduce the national debt.

In sum, as partisan polarization has increased steadily in Congress since the 1990s, it has not increased as steadily on aging policy issues. Democrats and Republicans have found ways to compromise, or at least cross party lines, on some aging-related votes apparently in resistance to the general trend toward ever-increasing polarization. However, the occasional cross-party issues and brief displays of partisan compromise generally involve low-cost noncontroversial issues or costly subsidies to the private sector. They do not necessarily suggest a future of bipartisan compromise on taxes, social insurance, the national debt, or the role of government in promoting the general welfare.

Conclusion

Paradoxically, aging policy can serve as both a catalyst for partisan polarization and a moderating force. Partisan acrimony has already broken out between Republicans who insist on balancing the budget without tax increases and Democrats who demand higher taxes in order to maintain the basic structure of old-age social insurance programs. But there are also the moderating influences of AARP's centrism, the ongoing public consensus in support of Social Security and Medicare, and policies that potentially could draw bipartisan support by both expanding and privatizing benefits.

The early years of the Obama presidency signaled a leftward shift at the federal level with the passage of the Patient Protection and Affordable Care Act (Binstock 2010). But the polarized debate since then presages a serious rightward shift toward "DIP"—decentralization, individualization, and privatization (Hudson 2007), especially with the courts empowering corporate contributors and with continuing partisan conflict over entitlement reform and the implementation of the Affordable Care Act. Further moves toward delegated governance are likely to increase the deficit, suggesting that they can only go one of two ways: they can be abandoned, the position favored by Democrats, or they can move further toward outright privatization, the position favored by Republicans. Thus the outlook for future bipartisan harmony over aging policy, despite the moderating influences discussed here, is unfortunately not very bright.

Notes

1. Data for lobbying expenditures and campaign contributions come from the website of the Center for Responsive Politics, http://www.opensecrets.org.

2. The quote is from the website of the Alliance for Retired Americans, http://www.retiredamericans.org/about, accessed in 2011.

3. I thank archivist Lynda DeLoach of the George Meany Memorial Archives at the National Labor College in Silver Spring, Maryland, for her generous help in accessing the NCSC data. Neither the collectors nor the distributors of the ARA/NCSC data are responsible for any of my interpretations.

13

The Debate
over Health Care

Thomas R. Marshall

A college student today might well believe that all American presidents will offer at least one major health care proposal early in their first term. Since 1993, that has been true: Bill Clinton, George W. Bush, and Barack Obama all made health care a major part of their first-term presidential agenda. Each of these three presidents proposed a major (and expensive) change in how health care is delivered, regulated, and paid for. Each plan aimed to fix some of the perceived flaws in the American health care system. For Clinton, this meant providing coverage for the uninsured. For Bush, this meant adding prescription drug coverage for senior citizens. For Obama, this meant covering the uninsured, restraining rising costs, and addressing other gaps in coverage. In proposing health care reform, each president fulfilled past campaign promises and sought support from powerful voter blocs. Presidents Bush and Obama passed their plans after closely divided congressional votes. President Clinton's plan died without coming up for a vote in either the House or the Senate.

American public opinion split sharply along party lines for both the Clinton and Obama plans, although far less so for Bush's plan. As each plan moved from a White House announcement to congressional debate, pollsters constantly surveyed American public opinion. By 2009 and continuing thereafter, the Obama health care plan reached a level of partisan polarization never before seen in polling over health care disputes. Large majorities of grassroots Democrats, but very few Republicans, favored the Obama plan. Health care clearly has become a hyper-partisan grassroots issue.

Congressional votes on the Obama health care proposal paralleled the polls. By overwhelming majorities, US House and Senate Democrats voted for the Obama plan on its final passage, but not a single Republican senator or House member did. Even after President Obama's health care bill became law, polls remained heavily split along partisan lines. In the ensuing 2010 midterm election, record numbers of House and Senate Democrats were defeated, in part due to heightened turnout among Republicans. Two years of lawsuits in the federal courts, resulting in a landmark June 2012 Supreme Court decision upholding most of the Obama health care bill, did not reduce the level of partisan conflict.

How did health care become such a hyper-partisan issue in US politics? Until the Clinton presidency, health care policymaking was a far less partisan issue than it is today, whether at the grassroots, in Congress, or in the federal courts. Even on far-reaching earlier health care proposals, such as those of Presidents Harry Truman, John F. Kennedy, and Lyndon Johnson, the grassroots partisan split was far smaller than it is today. For many problem-specific health care reforms, there was little evidence of partisanship at all. In this chapter, I describe the emergence of health care as a partisan issue beginning in the mid-1930s, first tracing health care as an issue on which only low levels of partisanship occurred. Next I review the growing partisanship gap over health care since the 1990s. Finally, I evaluate why and when modern health care becomes a hyper-partisan issue.

The Rise of Health Care as a Partisan Issue

Before the 1930s, health care was seldom a national policy issue, nor was it a highly partisan issue. At that time, the federal government's role in health care was still small. The federal government managed several hospitals and operated the Public Health Service. In 1906, Congress authorized the Pure Food and Drug Act, in 1917 it covered veterans' service-related injuries, and in 1921 it approved a short-lived maternal and child health program. The political support for these programs was not sharply divided along partisan lines (Carpenter 2001; Skocpol 1992). At that time, liberals and conservatives were not clearly sorted into the Democratic and Republican parties, respectively. Many and sometimes most Democrats in Congress were Southerners, and were often very conservative and oriented toward states' rights. Many congressional Republicans were progressive on health care matters. Reliable public opinion polls measuring grassroots partisan attitudes are not available for the period before the mid-1930s. However, the sponsors of and congressional votes on major health care bills show no consistent pattern of a partisan divide.

Beginning with Franklin D. Roosevelt's presidency, most US presidents offered one or more health care reforms as part of their presidential agenda (Blumenthal and Morone 2010). Many of these plans focused on specific diseases, specific groups of patients, or specific administrative reforms. Other plans were more far-reaching and comprehensive. Some presidential plans passed, some failed. Further, over time, health care grew steadily more sophisticated and expensive. No longer was medical care only a minor expense that most Americans simply paid out of pocket. Beginning in the 1940s and 1950s, many Americans, but by no means all, received health care insurance through their employer. With the origination of modern public opinion polling during the mid-1930s, it also became possible to measure grassroots partisanship on health care issues.

President Roosevelt considered several versions of a comprehensive health care plan that would cover all Americans. However, he never settled on a specific plan, and he died, shortly before World War II ended, without having enacted a comprehensive health care plan. Even so, grassroots sentiment for government involvement in health care or health research was surprisingly broad and nonpartisan. In a 1937 Gallup poll, 77 percent of Democrats and 61 percent of Republicans said yes when asked, "Should the federal government aid state and local governments in providing medical care for babies at birth?" In a 1938 Gallup poll, 83 percent of Democrats and 70 percent of Republicans said yes when asked, "Do you think the government should be responsible for providing medical care for people who are unable to pay for it?" In response to a 1939 Gallup question about efforts to find a cure for cancer—"It has been proposed that the federal government spend $3,000,000 a year to fight cancer. Do you favor this proposal?"—even larger numbers of Democrats and Republicans (85 percent and 82 percent, respectively) supported federal funding.[1] Computed as the percentage of support among Democrats minus the percentage support among Republicans, the partisanship gap on these three poll questions was surprisingly small: only 16 percent, 13 percent, and 3 percent, respectively.

Many New Deal proposals polarized Americans along party lines, but health care issues were not among them. The partisanship gaps on health care were much smaller than those on other New Deal measures of the 1930s. By comparison, Gallup put the partisanship gap at 62 percent in a 1935 poll question on whether the respondents favored the Agricultural Adjustment Act, 33 percent in a 1936 question about regulating minimum wages, 32 percent in a 1936 question on Social Security, and 68 percent in a 1937 question about Roosevelt's plan to add up to six new justices on the Supreme Court.

Although Roosevelt tabled the idea of government-run, comprehensive health care, that idea did not simply fade away. As World War II neared an end, the debate revived. In mid-1945, Gallup asked, "At present the Social Security program provides benefits for old age, death, and unemployment. Would you favor increasing the present tax rates to include payment of benefits for sickness, disability, doctor and hospital bills?" Once again, Democrats more often favored a federal role than did Republicans, but the partisan differences were much smaller than those of later years. In 1945, 58 percent

of Democrats, versus 41 percent of Republicans, favored a Social Security–
based health care plan—representing a still-small partisanship gap of 17
percent.

The debate over national health care resumed with full force when President Truman advocated a comprehensive national health care plan during his
comeback 1948 presidential election campaign. After settling for a hospital
construction program in 1946, Truman urged a nationwide "compulsory"
health care plan in his January 1948 State of the Union address. Faced with
no chance of success in a Republican-controlled Congress, Truman appointed
a special commission to design a plan; in September 1948, the commission
produced a report calling private health care a failure. Truman used that
report to call for a government-run health care insurance fund in radio
speeches and throughout his fall cross-country "whistle-stop" railroad campaign. Truman's blunt, no-holds-barred speaking style left no doubt that this
was a Democrat-versus-Republican issue (Blumenthal and Morone 2010:
82–85).

President Truman's 1948 reelection win helped to elect sizable majorities of Democrats to both houses of Congress. Nonetheless, Truman never
pushed Congress to enact a comprehensive health care plan, apparently due
to the proposal's unacceptably high costs; the Cold War and the Korean War;
the American Medical Association's vigorous opposition; and the prominence of legislation on other issues, such as civil rights, housing, and labor.
At the grassroots, the partisanship gap grew modestly larger. Gallup asked,
"Have you heard or read about the Truman Administration's plan for compulsory health insurance?" and then, if the respondent answered yes, "What
is your own opinion about it—are you for the administration's plan for compulsory health insurance or not?" For those respondents who were familiar
with the plan, three polls, in March 1949, November 1949, and November
1950, put support among Democrats at 42 percent, 37 percent, and 43 percent, respectively. Among Republicans, support was much lower: only 20
percent, 17 percent, and 13 percent. The partisanship gap (22 percent, 20 percent, and 30 percent, respectively) had grown slightly from earlier years.

That partisanship at the grassroots and within Congress is very sensitive
to the specifics of a health care plan was well illustrated by the next administration's efforts. President Dwight Eisenhower's first health care proposal
was administrative. Early in his first term as president, he asked Congress to
approve the formation of a new cabinet-level department for domestic programs, including health care. Congress quickly and overwhelmingly
approved the Department of Health, Education, and Welfare. At the grassroots, no partisan differences appeared; equally large majorities (57 percent)
of both Democrats and Republicans supported his plan. President Eisenhower's other major health care legacy was in making permanent a World
War II decision by the Internal Revenue Service allowing employer-provided

health care plans to remain tax-free. On this bill, no poll questions apparently exist, although the measure won bipartisan congressional support. During his eight years in the White House, President Eisenhower backed several targeted health care bills: health care coverage for federal employees (which passed), a reinsurance bill for high-cost patients (failed), and a proposal to provide some hospital care to low-income seniors (failed). Congressional Democrats pushed through a medical disabilities bill under Social Security. In 1960, Congress overwhelmingly passed a modest bill to subsidize states for some of the health care costs of the indigent and elderly. Throughout all these efforts, congressional support for health care plans split along both party and regional lines, with many Southern Democrats joining Republicans to oppose far-reaching plans.

President Eisenhower's track record on health care illustrates a recurring pattern. Grassroots public opinion is typically much less polarized on Republican presidents' health care plans compared to those of Democratic presidents. In part, this is because Republican presidents typically offer more narrowly targeted health care plans. However, even when Republican presidents offered major plans in terms of coverage or cost, as did Richard Nixon, Ronald Reagan, and George W. Bush, the grassroots partisanship gap remained fairly low. Further, health care did not rank near the top of Americans' "most important problems" until the early 1990s.

Presidents John Kennedy and Lyndon Johnson pressed for increased coverage for senior citizens, an effort that eventually resulted in passage of the Medicare program. During the 1960 presidential campaign, Kennedy urged a health care plan for senior citizens, but only as an occasional campaign issue. In May 1962, Kennedy ratcheted up his efforts to pass a Medicare plan, even holding a first-ever televised rally in Madison Square Garden, but his plan ran into determined opposition from the American Medical Association and from many Southern Democrats and Republicans in Congress. After suffering a narrow defeat in winning Senate approval for a Medicare program during the summer of 1962, Kennedy again raised the program as a partisan issue during the midterm elections. Despite smaller-than-usual Democratic losses in Congress in November 1962, his administration thereafter abandoned efforts to expand health care coverage (Blumenthal and Morone 2010: 157–159).

While few polls exist from the early to middle 1960s, the partisanship gaps appear to be no larger than those reported for the Truman era, and were much smaller than those reported for the Clinton and Obama plans. In March, May, and July 1962, three Gallup questions gave respondents a choice between either letting "older persons" buy a voluntary health insurance plan or covering costs through a Social Security tax. In all three polls, Democrats were more likely than Republicans to favor the Social Security option—by margins of 65 to 39 percent, 58 to 30 percent, and 54 to 30 percent, respectively. Overall poll support for the Kennedy plan steadily dropped from 55 percent to 48 percent to 44 percent over this five-month period, a pattern of falling support often found for presidential health care proposals. However, the partisanship gap itself remained quite stable, at 26 percent, 28 percent, and 24 percent, respectively.

Upon President Kennedy's death, his successor, Lyndon Johnson, wasted no time in pushing for Medicare. After his plan stalled in Congress in the fall of 1964, Johnson made Medicare a major issue during his 1964 presidential campaign, promising to make Medicare the first item on his legislative agenda if elected. The Republican presidential nominee, Arizona senator Barry Goldwater, ran as a firm opponent of Medicare and even interrupted his campaign to fly back to Washington, D.C., to vote against the Medicare bill then being debated in the Senate ("Campaign Issues: VI" 1964). Bolstered by Johnson's landslide win and by a large Democratic Party majority in the newly elected Congress, the Medicare bill soon passed, as did a low-income Medicaid plan (Blumenthal and Morone 2010: 186–195; Marmor 2000: 44–46).

As Medicare became a major campaign issue, the partisanship gap grew, as compared to years past. The polls during this period offer a preview of what would happen during the Clinton and Obama presidencies. In October 1964, Gallup asked respondents whether they approved or disapproved of a "compulsory medical insurance program covering hospital and nursing home care for the elderly" that was "financed out of increased social security taxes." More Democrats than Republicans favored this plan, by a margin of 73 to 36 percent, with a resulting partisanship gap of 37 percent.

President Richard Nixon spent little time on health care, although he did pass a major (and bipartisan) increase in funding for cancer research late in his first term. His more ambitious, albeit unsuccessful, health care proposal came during his second term, only a few months before he resigned the presidency on August 8, 1974, amid the growing Watergate scandal. His proposed Comprehensive Health Insurance Plan (CHIP) required employers to provide coverage for their employees, limited employee cost-sharing, mandated relatively generous benefits, and added a catastrophic health care program. An April 1974 Harris poll question described the bill's several provisions and reported that 30 percent of Democrats and 32 percent of Republicans favored the plan—a partisanship gap of only 2 percent, with Republicans barely more favorably inclined. The low level of public support from both parties' supporters may have been due in part to the president's low approval ratings, then at a near-record low of only 26 percent in Gallup polls.

President Jimmy Carter considered several health care plans, and eventually proposed a plan that included containment of hospital costs, a measure of catastrophic health care insurance, and additional aid for the poor and elderly. His plan went to Congress in mid-1979, but died amid the president's low approval ratings, a more sweeping plan from Democratic senator Edward Kennedy, and fierce opposition from the hospital industry. A May 1979 *Los Angeles Times* poll question asked respondents to choose from among the Kennedy plan, the Carter plan, or neither plan; 34 percent of Democrats and 38 percent of Republicans chose the Carter plan, representing a partisanship gap of only 4 percent, with Republicans slightly more favorably inclined.

President Ronald Reagan's major health care reform was enacted during his second term in office, a 1988 Medicare catastrophic health care bill for senior citizens that expanded coverage for hospital stays, doctor bills, prescription drug costs, skilled nursing care, and home health care. However, this plan was soon repealed, in November 1989, early in President George H. W. Bush's term, largely as a result of pressure from more affluent senior citizens who mobilized against the surcharges levied to pay for the program (Rice, Desmond, and Gabel 1990).

Only small partisanship gaps appeared on President Reagan's catastrophic care bill, both before it passed and before it was repealed. An August 1987 Roper poll reported that large majorities of both Democrats and Republicans (70 percent and 76 percent, respectively) favored "some form of catastrophic health insurance coverage for those on Medicare" that would provide more coverage for hospitalization, nursing care, and high medical expenses, and that would also raise premiums for the elderly. The partisanship gap of 6 percent is small, with Republicans slightly more favorably inclined. Shortly before Congress repealed the bill in November 1989, a survey by ABC News and the *Washington Post* reported that 79 percent of Democrats and 75 percent of Republicans opposed "doing away with the Medicare catastrophic health care program for senior citizens"—representing a partisanship gap of only 4 percent, with Democrats slightly more favorably inclined toward keeping the catastrophic care measure.

Health Care and the Growing Partisanship Gap

As this brief review shows, until the 1990s health care was not an intensely partisan issue. True, grassroots Democrats more often favored new federal-level health care programs, but the partisanship gaps were neither particularly large nor consistent. The partisanship gap grew considerably with the 1992 presidential election. As did Presidents Truman and Johnson, Bill Clinton made health care a major part of his first-term presidential campaign. During both the Democratic presidential primaries and the general election campaigns, Clinton backed the general idea of passing a major new health care plan. By September 1992, Clinton's plan was to include both a "pay or play" employer mandate and managed competition between insurers, although the specifics on covering the uninsured remained murky (Blumenthal and Morone 2010: 356–359). Even so, health care was clearly one of the Clinton-Gore ticket's best issues. On Labor Day 1992, a Gallup poll reported that, by a margin of 62 to 27 percent, registered voters said Clinton would better handle the health care issue than Republican president George H. W. Bush. A post-election Gallup poll reported that, by a margin of 64 to 30 percent, Americans thought the Clinton administration would improve the health care system.

Once elected, Clinton delayed for several months before sending a massive, 1,342-page health care reform bill to Congress. The proposed Health Security Act mandated that all employers cover their employees, that bare-bones plans be expanded, and that nearly all the uninsured be covered under statewide plans. The Health Security Act ran into fierce opposition from the health insurance industry, many small and medium-sized employers, and nearly all Republicans in Congress. Many congressional Democrats did not support the Clinton plan and instead favored either a single-payer plan or a more modest plan. By summer 1994, the Clinton plan had died in Congress without having come up for a vote in either the House or the Senate.

At the grassroots, the Clinton plan witnessed a sharp increase in partisan polarization. In a series of fourteen Gallup questions between September 1993 and July 1994, the partisanship gap ranged from 40 percent to 54 percent, a gap that slightly and irregularly grew over time.[2] The partisanship gap averaged 46 percent, a figure that was much larger than the gap for earlier comprehensive health care plans. As with President Kennedy's health care proposal nearly thirty years earlier, overall poll support for the Clinton plan dropped sharply (by nearly 20 percent over ten months), with Republicans showing the largest declines in support.

The average partisanship gap of 46 percent for the Clinton plan can be compared to the partisanship gaps on President Clinton's other top policy initiatives. Gallup put the partisanship gap at 49 percent on approval of the 1993 tax increase; 10 percent on approval of the 1993 "Don't Ask, Don't Tell" policy; 12 percent on approval of the 1993 North American Free Trade Agreement (NAFTA); and 26 percent on approval of Ruth Bader Ginsburg's 1993 nomination to the Supreme Court. On the 1998 House impeachment vote, Gallup put the partisanship gap at 61 percent. However, the partisanship gap was only 5 percent on Clinton's other major health care initiative— classifying nicotine as a drug and allowing the Food and Drug Administration to regulate cigarettes. In short, the partisanship gap on President Clinton's health care plan was among the largest such gaps during the Clinton presidency.

President George W. Bush's major health care legacy was in providing some prescription drug coverage to senior citizens under the 2003 Medicare Modernization Act, a measure originally priced at $400 billion over a decade. Polls point to small to medium-sized partisanship gaps, although which party's supporters more strongly backed the bill depends on the poll question's wording and timing. Five months prior to the bill's passage, Gallup reported that 81 percent of Democrats and 69 percent of Republicans favored spending "400 billion dollars over the next ten years to create a new Medicare program that would help senior citizens pay for prescription drugs"—representing a partisanship gap of only 12 percent, with Democrats more favorably inclined. Two weeks after the bill passed, despite opposition from most liberal Democrats and some conservative Republicans, another Gallup question pegged support for "the new prescription drug benefit for Medicare recipients" at 39 percent among Democrats and 63 percent among Republicans—representing a partisanship gap of 24 percent, but now with Republicans considerably more favorably inclined. By comparison, Gallup put the partisanship gaps on President Bush's other key initiatives at 40 percent on approval of the 2001 proposed tax cuts of $1.6 trillion, and 45 percent on approval of the 2003 invasion of Iraq. On approval of the Supreme Court nominations of John Roberts and Samuel Alito, the gaps were 38 percent and 46 percent. By these figures, the Bush prescription drug care plan featured neither a particularly large nor a consistent partisanship gap.

The small partisanship gaps on the Bush prescription drug care plan are typical of those on specific health or safety-related proposals. For example, obesity, smoking, and dangerous driving are now estimated to cause from several thousand to several hundred thousand deaths a year.[3] On all these issues, only small partisanship gaps exist, with Democrats typically, albeit not always, being more supportive of new regulations compared to Republicans. On obesity regulations, for example, the partisanship gap averaged only 5 percent on three separate poll questions in 2005 by the Harvard School of Public Health and International Communications Research on "convert(ing) vending machines from carrying high-sugar, high-fat foods like soda, chips, and candy to carrying healthy snacks and beverages" in grade schools, middle schools, or high schools. An average partisanship gap of only 5 percent appeared on two 1997 Gallup questions on banning cigarette vending machines and banning outdoor advertising of cigarettes, and on a 1998 Gallup question on penalizing tobacco companies if teen smoking rates were not reduced. An average partisanship gap of only 4 percent appeared on two 1984 Gallup questions on requiring seat belts to be worn when riding in a car and requiring new cars to be equipped with airbags, on a 1986 Gallup question on raising the legal drinking age to twenty-one, and on a 2010 CBS News question on banning the sending of text messages while driving.

The Obama Health Care Plan
By far the largest partisanship gaps ever found on a health care reform occurred on President Obama's health care plan, signed into law as the

Patient Protection and Affordable Care Act. Predictably, large partisanship gaps on health care reform first appeared in polls conducted during the 2008 presidential campaign, long before Congress took up the debate on the Affordable Care Act. Like the earlier campaigns of Truman in 1948, Johnson in 1964, and Clinton in 1992, the 2008 Obama campaign made reforming health care a major issue. The Obama campaign offered a far more ambitious plan than did the campaign of Republican nominee John McCain, and the Obama campaign aired a heavy schedule of attack ads criticizing McCain as favoring taxation of health care benefits (Jamieson 2009; Kenski, Hardy, and Jamieson 2010: 207–212). Although poll questions during the 2008 campaign were worded differently than those asked during the 2009–2010 congressional debate and litigation or thereafter, highly polarized attitudes along partisan lines appeared in 2008. For example, in an October 2008 poll by ABC News and the *Washington Post,* 90 percent of Democrats, but only 13 percent of Republicans, said they trusted Barack Obama more than John McCain to handle health care—representing a partisanship gap of 77 percent. That same month, on that same issue, a poll by CNN and the Opinion Research Corporation put the partisanship gap at 78 percent. In March 2009, well before Congress took up the Affordable Care Act, another poll by CNN and the Opinion Research Corporation put the partisanship gap at 68 percent on a question asking whether respondents approved of the way President Obama was handling health care policy. Thus attitudes on health care reform were already highly polarized well before the congressional debate, and even before President Obama took office. Six months of congressional debate and another two years of litigation did little to change this well-established pattern.

During the long and highly partisan congressional debate on the Affordable Care Act, the longest series of consistently worded poll questions came from Gallup, in the form, "Would you advise your member of Congress to vote for or against a health care bill this year, or do you not have an opinion?" Undecided respondents were asked whether they leaned for or against the bill. High levels of grassroots partisanship appeared throughout this polling series. Gallup's first poll during the congressional debate, conducted September 11–13, 2009, found that only 13 percent of Republicans favored the Affordable Care Act compared to 83 percent of Democrats—representing a partisanship gap of 70 percent. In January 2010, the numbers were strikingly similar: only 12 percent of Republicans, but 80 percent of Democrats, favored the Affordable Care Act—representing a partisanship gap of 68 percent. Over this entire Gallup series, the partisanship gap averaged 63 percent. The attitudes of nearly 80 percent of respondents toward the act can be correctly predicted simply by knowing a respondent's partisanship. No other attitude or experience is so strongly related to support for the act as is partisanship.

The six-month congressional debate over the Affordable Care Act did little to change this pattern. When the act reached final passage in early March 2010, the partisanship gap remained as large as ever. According to Gallup, only 9 percent of Republicans, but 80 percent of Democrats, said that they would "advise your representative in Congress to vote for a healthcare reform bill similar to the one proposed by President Barack Obama"—representing a partisanship gap of 71 percent. A year after President Obama signed the Affordable Care Act into law, a Kaiser Family Foundation poll put the post-passage partisanship gap at 52 percent, with only 12 percent of Republicans, but 64 percent of Democrats, expressing approval. In a March 2011 Gallup poll, only 18 percent of Republicans, but 79 percent of Democrats, described the act's passage a year earlier as "a good thing"—representing a partisanship gap of 61 percent.

During this period of congressional debate, the partisanship gaps on the Affordable Care Act (averaging 63 percent in Gallup's polling series) were larger than those found on any of President Obama's other major policy initiatives. For other major controversies of 2009–2010, the partisanship gaps ranged from a high of 55 percent on federal regulation of large banks and major financial institutions, to 52 percent on confirming the appointment of Sonia Sotomayor to the Supreme Court, to 47 percent on confirming the appointment of Elena Kagan to the Supreme Court, to 47 percent on transferring suspected terrorists from Guantanamo Bay, to 33 percent on an economic stimulus bill of over $800 billion. Indeed, the partisanship gap on the Affordable Care Act almost reached the magnitude of gaps found in presidential and congressional elections. According to Gallup's final pre-election polling of voters, in the 2008 presidential election, the partisanship voting gap between Republicans and Democrats was 80 percent, and in the 2010 midterm congressional elections the partisanship voting gap between Republicans and Democrats was 84 percent.

By a historical comparison, the 63 percent average partisanship gap on President Obama's Affordable Care Act is also larger than the gap for any other president's health care plan. For President Clinton's Health Security Act, the partisanship gap averaged 46 percent. For the comprehensive plans offered by Presidents Truman, Kennedy, Johnson, and Nixon, the partisanship gaps averaged 24 percent and never exceeded 37 percent. For President George W. Bush's prescription drug plan, President Reagan's catastrophic care plan, and President Carter's health care plan, the partisanship gap averaged only 12 percent. On other health-related issues, including President Clinton's nicotine regulation plan; President Eisenhower's reorganization of the Department of Health, Education, and Welfare; and President Roosevelt's maternal health and cancer plans, the partisanship gap averaged only 6 percent. Against both the contemporary and the historical record, then, health care clearly became hyper-partisan during the congressional debate over the Affordable Care Act.

Not only was this debate the most hyper-partisan health care debate in US history, but health care was also an extremely visible issue. During 2009–2010, as many as 26 percent of Americans cited health care as the country's most important problem, according to a Gallup poll. Only once before had more Americans cited health care as the nation's most important problem, when 31 percent did so during the 1993–1994 debate over Clinton's Health Security Act. No more than 9 percent of Americans cited health care as the nation's most important problem during the 2003 debate over prescription drug coverage for senior citizens. In earlier years, health care seldom reached even 3 percent in Gallup's "most important problem" category. Immediately before the 2012 Supreme Court hearings on the Affordable Care Act, only 5 percent of Americans cited health care as the nation's most important problem, and immediately after the hearings, only 9 percent of Americans did.

The Affordable Care Act was signed into law on March 23, 2010, followed by a prolonged round of legal challenges and conflicting decisions from four federal appeals courts. From March 26 to March 28, 2012, the US Supreme Court held a historic three days of oral hearings. On June 28, the Court issued a 5-to-4 decision upholding the act (except for a required expansion in state Medicaid coverage). Throughout the two-year time period between 2010 and 2012, grassroots public opinion on the Affordable Care Act remained hyper-polarized. When identically worded poll questions from 2010 and 2012 are compared, there is virtually no change apparent either in overall support for the Affordable Care Act or in the size of the partisanship gap (Pew Research Center 2012b). A Kaiser Family Foundation tracking poll asking respondents whether they had a favorable opinion of the health reform law put the partisanship gap at 65 percent in April 2010; two years later, the gap was a near identical, at 63 percent. Gallup and *USA Today* asked whether the "law that restructures the nation's health care system . . . is a good thing or a bad thing," reporting a partisanship gap of 70 percent in March 2010 and 61 percent in February 2012. By comparison, Gallup's partisanship gaps on other high-profile White House priorities of this time period were 25 percent in a May 2011 question on raising the debt ceiling, 37 percent in a June 2011 question about President Obama's schedule for withdrawing troops from Afghanistan, 53 percent in an October 2011 question about President Obama's schedule for troop withdrawals from Iraq, and 31 percent in an April 2012 question about a minimum 30 percent income tax rate on households earning $1 million a year or more. At the time of the Supreme Court's hearings on the Affordable Care Act, Gallup put the partisanship gap for an Obama-versus-Romney presidential election match-up at 74 percent. In short, between 2010 and 2012, polarization on the Affordable Care Act was higher than on any other policy initiative, and nearly as great as in the upcoming 2012 presidential contest.

The Supreme Court's 5-to-4 decision upholding the Affordable Care Act's "individual mandate" provision did not reduce partisan polarization, at least not immediately so. In a Pew Research Center survey (2012c) conducted immediately after the decision (at a time when barely half of Americans, 55 percent, could accurately describe that decision), 66 percent of Democrats approved of the Supreme Court's decision, compared to only 13 percent of Republicans—representing a partisanship gap of 53 percent. A Gallup poll, also taken immediately after the decision, asked respondents (not entirely accurately), "As you may know, the U.S. Supreme Court has upheld the entire 2010 healthcare law, declaring it constitutional. Do you agree or disagree with this decision?" to which 79 percent of Democrats agreed, compared to only 13 percent of Republicans—representing a partisanship gap of 66 percent.

The grassroots partisanship gap on the Affordable Care Act was much larger than the gap on other recent major health care controversies that reached the Supreme Court. For example, in *Pegram v. Herdich* (2000), *Rush Prudential HMO v. Moran* (2002), and *Kentucky Association of Health Care Plans v. Miller* (2003), the Supreme Court, respectively, disallowed patients' lawsuits against health maintenance organizations over claims of denial of care, upheld a Texas law allowing independent review of denials of health care claims, and upheld Kentucky's "any willing provider" law. In these three disputes, the grassroots partisanship gaps were small, averaging only 7 percent. Compared to the Health Security Act and the Affordable Care Act, the *Pegram, Rush,* and *Kentucky* cases showed very low levels of partisanship.

Further, on none of these three decisions did a clear partisan split appear among the justices themselves. In the *Pegram* and *Kentucky* decisions, all seven Republican justices joined two Democrat justices in handing down a unanimous decision. In *Rush,* three Republicans and two Democrats joined the 5-to-4 majority opinion, with four Republicans dissenting. By contrast, when the Supreme Court upheld most of the Affordable Care Act, 5-to-4, that vote came largely, albeit not entirely, along partisan lines. Chief Justice Roberts, a Republican, joined all four Democrats in upholding most of the act (except the state Medicaid provision); the remaining four Republican justices all dissented. The 7-to-2 vote to strike down the state Medicaid provision, however, was more bipartisan; all five Republican justices joined two Democrats to block the new federal coverage requirement, with two Democrats voting to uphold that provision. The Supreme Court's decision on the Affordable Care Act was therefore not a purely partisan one, but it came closer to being so than is typical. Purely partisan vote splits are not common at the Supreme Court level. Even the *Bush v. Gore* (2000) decision, allowing George W. Bush to become president, did not feature a purely partisan split on the Court, since two Republican justices (Souter and Stevens) joined two Democratic justices (Ginsburg and Breyer) in dissenting against the majority decision of five Republican justices. Among famous historical cases that greatly affected the White House, neither the 1937 "switch in time that saved nine" decisions in *West Coast Hotel Co. v. Parrish* and *National Labor Relations Board v. Jones & Laughlin Steel Corporation,* nor the executive privilege decision in *U.S. v. Nixon* (1974), featured a purely partisan vote split on the Court. Health care may be a highly partisan issue at the grassroots, but it is still somewhat less so on the Supreme Court.

The American public's hyper-partisan views on the Affordable Care Act, taken as a whole, are particularly striking, since many specific provisions in the act were not unpopular and public opinion was not particularly partisan. In a March 2011 Kaiser Family Foundation poll, large majorities of Americans favored extending tax credits to small businesses that offer health coverage to their employees (82 percent), the guaranteed issue provision (74 percent), gradually closing the Medicare "doughnut hole" (76 percent), financial help for low- and moderate-income Americans who buy their own health care coverage (72 percent), and increasing the Medicare payroll tax on the wealthy (58 percent). By comparison, the individual mandate provision (described as a provision that would "require nearly all Americans to have health insurance or else pay a fine") won support from only 27 percent of Americans. On these six specific elements of the Affordable Care Act, the partisanship gaps, respectively, were 18 percent, 23 percent, 22 percent, 42 percent, 40 percent, and 32 percent. In short, the hyper-partisan attitudes toward the Affordable Care Act as a whole did not extend to its individual provisions—a pattern one would expect given the history of health care reform efforts since the 1930s.

Conclusion

Health care is neither inevitably nor even typically a highly partisan issue. Yet depending on how presidents and the parties present the issue, it can become so. Since the 1930s, most presidents' health care plans and health-related proposals have witnessed only low to moderate levels of partisanship. Proposals that focus on specific diseases, administrative reorganizations, or specific coverage gaps never lead to highly partisan debates. Perhaps surprisingly, grassroots public opinion was not by today's standards highly polarized even on some of the more comprehensive health care plans of earlier presidents that would have created sweeping new federal regulations and mandatory coverage. During the Clinton and Obama presidencies, health care came to rank as both a highly partisan issue and a top-ranked national concern. Why does health care sometimes become hyper-partisan? Four answers may be given.

First, grassroots liberals and conservatives are now more clearly ideo-logically sorted into the Democratic and Republican parties, respectively, than they were before the 1990s. Over time, the number of liberal Republicans has dwindled, just as has the number of conservative, typically white Southern Democrats. Both parties' loyalists now take very different views of sweeping new federal spending programs and mandates, including comprehensive health care bills. For example, in a February 2011 Pew survey, Republicans, by a margin of 74 to 19 percent, favored smaller government providing fewer services rather than bigger government providing more services, but Democrats preferred the reverse, by a margin of 63 to 28 percent. This grassroots philosophical gap between Republicans and Democrats now runs surprisingly wide. In a February 2011 Pew survey, Republicans, by a margin of 70 to 27 percent, said that the Supreme Court should base its rulings on what the US Constitution meant as it was originally written, rather than on what the Constitution means in current times. Democrats said the reverse, by a margin of 65 to 29 percent. Faced with so many grassroots differences of this magnitude on the role of government, few members of Congress have either the inclination or an incentive to take a position on health care that is contrary to their party's faithful adherents (Jacobs and Skocpol 2010).

Second, grassroots Republicans and Democrats come to any debate over health care with somewhat different personal experiences and perspectives. Democrats are less likely than Republicans to rate the nation's health care system highly or to report being satisfied with the care they receive. Democrats more often worry about losing their coverage or being able to afford coverage, and Democrats more often favor universal and subsidized health care coverage (Blendon et al. 2008). Democrats are also more likely than are Republicans to favor federal spending on a wide variety of health care problems (Blendon et al. 2010). In a September 2010 Gallup poll, for example, more Democrats than Republicans (16 percent versus 10 percent, respectively) reported that they had no health care insurance at all. More Democrats than Republicans (4 percent versus 1 percent) received Medicaid. More Republicans than Democrats (46 percent versus 42 percent) received health care benefits from an employer or union. And more Republicans than Democrats received military and veterans' benefits (5 percent versus 2 percent). By comparison, the figures for Medicare are almost identical, with 30 percent of Republicans and 31 percent of Democrats receiving benefits from this program.[4] In short, nearly twice as many Democrats as Republicans are enrolled in Medicaid or have no health care plan at all, and would most obviously benefit from comprehensive federal health care reform. At the grassroots, Democrats more often focus on the problems of the uninsured and typically rank health care as a greater concern than do Republicans (McInturff and Weigel 2008; Newhouse 2010; Oakman et al. 2010).

To be sure, these partisan differences in actual health care coverage do not fully account for the large partisanship gaps described here. Differences in grassroots coverage patterns are magnified many times over when poll questions ask about a Democratic president's comprehensive plan as a whole, such as President Clinton's Health Security Act plan or President Obama's Affordable Care Act plan, rather than specific mandates within a comprehensive plan (Brodie et al. 2010). Most Americans enlarge their personal experiences with health care through the frame of a partisan heuristic, at least when comprehensive health care proposals are involved. However, this pattern does not occur when a president offers a narrowly targeted, problem-specific reform.

Third, health care spending now represents a sixth of the US economy and is steadily growing. The sheer magnitude of health care spending means that health care now has far more stakeholders than in earlier years. In any fight over federally provided and regulated medical care, a wider variety of interest groups, corporations, and labor unions will now try to defend their interests by mobilizing grassroots public opinion. Unlike earlier years, when these groups mobilize public opinion, they now often pitch their messages along partisan lines. Journalists, media celebrities, and party leaders also emphasize the tie between health care reform proposals and partisanship (Skocpol 2010; Jacobs and Skocpol 2010). The ability of interest groups to reach out to the grassroots through modern technologies, such as television and Internet ads, phone banks, and social networking, coupled with permissive laws on issue advocacy spending, virtually guarantees that a health care debate will today quickly take an intensely partisan turn.

Fourth, the two most recent hyper-partisan instances in health care policymaking both occurred under strikingly similar circumstances. A newly elected president came to the White House after making comprehensive health care a major campaign issue, while also enjoying a large majority of party members in both houses of Congress. Under these conditions, Presidents Clinton and Obama, both Democrats, had little incentive to compromise on the scope of their health care plans or to make serious concessions to Republicans. Presidents with less ambitious agendas and smaller partisan majorities in Congress have a stronger practical incentive to accept more compromises and to tone down partisan hostilities. Some observers saw equally little interest among congressional Republicans in making compromises over health care, which loomed as a promising (and eventually successful) chance to gain extra seats in the next congressional election (Blendon and Benson 2010; Jacobs and Skocpol 2010; Skocpol 1997).

This campaign context is important because evidence of early, stable, and highly polarized grassroots attitudes on health care issues clearly exists in polling data over time. Where grassroots attitudes on comprehensive health care proposals, such as the Health Security Act or the Affordable Care Act, can be tracked over time, public opinion is already strongly polarized before Congress begins to debate a health care proposal. Thereafter, grassroots polarization is little affected by congressional maneuvering and debate, or by federal court decisionmaking. In part, this pattern occurs because comprehensive health care proposals carry over from recent presidential campaigns when a newly elected president first raised the issue in a highly polarized partisan context. Not surprisingly, Americans view health care from the perspective of a partisan, campaign-related heuristic and as a part of the "permanent campaign" that now characterizes US political life. By contrast, presidential health care plans that are not initially major campaign issues never become highly partisan issues at the grassroots.

The partisan impact of health care can also be viewed as to its political repercussions. If health care becomes a highly partisan issue, not surprisingly its effects spill over into the next round of elections. Following the comprehensive health care plans of both President Clinton in 1993–1994 and President Obama in 2009–2010, Democrats suffered massive losses in the next midterm congressional election: a loss of fifty-three Democratic House seats and seven Democratic Senate seats in 1994, and a loss of sixty-five Democratic House seats and six Democratic Senate seats in 2010. These losses are among the largest midterm congressional setbacks to the president's party during the last half century.

Admittedly, not all of these losses can be attributed to the fallout from health care, since the loss of congressional seats is also tied to the strength or weakness of the current economy, how many House seats the president's party won in the prior election, and current events. Even so, this pattern of massive election losses following a president's efforts to enact a comprehensive health care plan, whether successful or not, is actually not new. For each of the seven Democratic presidents elected since 1932, from Roosevelt to Obama, the Democratic Party's losses in the House averaged forty seats in the first midterm election of that presidency if the president seriously advocated a comprehensive health care plan during his first two years, but averaged only one House seat lost if he did not. For each of the six Republican presidents elected since 1952, from Eisenhower to George W. Bush (none of whom attempted to pass a comprehensive health care bill during his first two years), the Republican Party's losses in the House in the first midterm election of that presidency averaged twelve seats. This pattern is striking and consistent. A president's early effort to pass a comprehensive health care plan is tied to larger-than-normal election losses in the first midterm congressional election of that presidency. To date, no enduring political realignments are clearly linked to health care controversies. Yet when a president pursues an ambitious, highly partisan health care plan, that effort will almost certainly have serious consequences during the next round of elections.

Will health care remain a hyper-partisan issue in the future? This seems very likely. Health care remains a major national issue. As mentioned, health care spending in the United States now consumes one-sixth of gross domestic product, and health care costs regularly grow at two to three times the rate of general inflation. Over a quarter of the federal budget is already consumed by health care spending, which is projected to increase rapidly. Health care costs and accessibility are important personal concerns to many Americans. Controversial issues such as controlling costs and expanding coverage remain politically relevant. At the grassroots, Republicans and Democrats bring different experiences, needs, and demands to the health care debate. By the evidence here, many health care reform proposals do not spark highly partisan debates. Yet when a specific combination of circumstances occurs, health care becomes hyper-partisan: when a presidential candidate proposes a comprehensive health care plan as a key campaign issue and, once elected, pursues it absent bipartisan support. These conditions seem nearly certain to recur in the foreseeable future.

Notes

1. For these three polls, a respondent's partisanship was based on reported voting behavior or voting intentions, since polls of the 1930s did not always ask for a respondent's current party preference. Later polls use self-reported party identification in computing the partisanship gap.

2. The Gallup question was, "From everything you have heard or read about the plan so far, do you favor or oppose President Bill Clinton's plan to reform health care?"

3. For 2009, the National Highway Traffic Safety Administration reported 25,488 alcohol-related fatalities and 955 fatalities due to cell phones as a distraction. For 2005, using figures from the National Center for Health Statistics, Danaei Goodarz and colleagues (2009) estimated deaths from tobacco smoking at 467,000 and deaths from obesity at 216,000.

4. These figures were recomputed from the Gallup poll of September 25–26, 2010. Unless otherwise noted, all the poll questions cited herein are based on samples of American adults nationwide and may be accessed through the searchable iPOLL database from the Roper Center for Public Opinion Research, available at http://www.ropercenter.uconn.edu/data_access/ipoll/ipoll.html.

14

Representation in a Dysfunctional Democracy

William Crotty

I hope we shall . . . crush in its birth the aristocracy of our moneyed corporations which dare already to challenge our government to a trial of strength, and bid defiance to the laws of our county.
—Thomas Jefferson in a letter to George Logan, November 12, 1816

Although the chapters in this volume have varied in their approach to the problem of polarization in the US political system, there is an overarching theme connecting the concerns expressed here: the way this polarization has made the US government democratically unaccountable and unresponsive to the public as a whole. In 1950, the American Political Science Association made a series of recommendations for making the two major political parties more democratically responsible; at that time, there were relatively few ideological or policy differences between the two parties. The events of the 1960s set in motion a partisan sorting, bringing conservatives into the Republican camp as liberals gravitated more firmly to the Democratic camp. In a way, this change has indeed provided some of what the American Political Science Association was advocating, as there are now clear distinctions between the parties and their political agendas by which voters can inform their decisions.

Unfortunately, in the current political climate, instead of these distinctions making the political parties more responsive to the public and its preferences, they have instead made them overly responsive to the interest groups—and monetary backers—who help form their political base (Gilens and Page 2014). The parties are now polarized on a wide range of issues, at a depth that precludes any room for meaningful compromise. This polarization extends to issues on which there is wide policy agreement among the public as a whole. At the core of this divide is the mass concentration of wealth in a small fraction of the population, and the corresponding influx of money into the electoral system.

Polarization frames the contemporary political as well as the economic order. In our capitalist free-market system, this has resulted in a redistribution of wealth in the population away from the middle class, believed to be the foundation for a democratic state, and upward, to the richest, at the very top of the economic pyramid. But the explanation for such a massive shift in the nation's wealth lies in politics, not economics. To repeat: the process of wealth redistribution is political. This is the key to the changes experienced. With the shift in capital accumulation, representation has undergone a transformation, servicing the interests of those with the greatest wealth. Taken together in its political and economic manifestations, it represents a revolution in the manner in which the US democratic state operates and whom it benefits, one that impacts lifestyles and opportunity structures with ramifications for the realization of social and economic objectives. The US political and socioeconomic system is now badly out of sync with the values and assumptions on which the country was founded.

A Few Basics

The restructured party alignments, as indicated, are driven by ideological values and marked by a "take-no-prisoners" partisanship. Still, factional divides of varying degrees of intensity and importance can be found in both parties. For the Democrats there has been an uncomfortable move (for liberals) to better represent the business community. The greater receptivity to corporate interests is largely traceable to the creation of the Democratic Leadership Council (DLC) following the loss of Walter Mondale ("the last of the liberals") to Ronald Reagan in the 1984 presidential election. Among its founders were Bill Clinton and Al Gore, a few short years away from the presidency and the vice presidency. The DLC was committed to moving the party closer to the center of the political spectrum, pushing it to assume a more empathetic stance toward business, and increasing its financial base. Its relationship to traditional elements of the party that emphasized the interests of the middle and working class, minorities, outgroups, and the social movements that grew out of the 1960s was strained (Chapters 7, 8, 9, 11, 12, 13). The division can be seen in the candidates recruited to run for office, the campaign appeals to party constituencies contrasted with the actions of those who win office, and the inertia and discontent that often depresses a partisan turnout (Chapter 3). The party continues to represent on a class and programmatic basis those it has always served, whatever the adjustments that must be made to what is seen as the realities of politics.

There is no sensitivity in the Republican Party to the role of money in structuring political options or in its commitment to advancing the interests of corporate America and of the most wealthy in the population. The major divide relates to the nature of the party's electoral coalition, which is white, older, better-off financially, and increasingly more conservative. As the country's social structure changes, there will be a need for a more inclusive party base to remain electorally successful. The focus by some of the more centrist and pragmatic party groups that places a greater emphasis on winning elections than ideology or maintaining the purity of the party's coalition has been centered on attracting Latinos, the newest political force to emerge (Chapter 10). Historically, efforts to make the party more representative of the electorate have not been well received, yet it would appear if "demography is destiny," an accommodation will have to be made.

Perspectives on Polarization

Polarization has shown its more virulent side over the last generation. It is a form of intense divisiveness bordering at times on a paralysis of representative processes in a socially heterogeneous if fractured society. It also happens to be a condition to which the US political system, as compared to the political systems of European democracies, is particularly susceptible. As Gerald Pomper and Marc Weiner have explored in Chapter 6, the US system, as designed by the Founders, facilitates polarization. It was meant to make policy initiatives difficult to execute. Structurally divided institutions of governance, even in the best of times, provide a test of will for even the most politically astute of officeholders, as a pluralistic society of hundreds of millions of citizens generates conflicting demands on the nation's resources. A variety of competitive social and economic needs have increasingly come into play in what often translates into a zero-sum game. The evolution of an accidental and sprawling two-party system in the United States has severely limited its capacity to represent all sectors of the voting public, as compared to the more discriminating and responsive capacities in multiparty democracies. Accumulated historical circumstances and developments, and the glorification of opposition to centralized governing, a heritage of the American Revolution, have combined to result in contentiousness, divisiveness, and even extremism (as in Barry Goldwater's much-quoted dictum "extremism in the pursuit of liberty is no vice"). Such opposition is viewed by many as a virtue, in keeping with the national character. The call to opposition is taken up by conservatives in particular, in their antagonism to collective mass action or any regulations intended to promote the public interest, which they characterize as assaults on freedom, liberty, and independence. This occurs frequently in reference to economic and fiscal policy as it relates to self-advancement. It can be seen as well in the challenge of new social ventures or, in the case of more purely political ventures intended to advance group interests, in efforts to limit the presence of minority and emerging groups in politics. The message can resonate powerfully with an electorate bred on the importance of individual responsibility and a dislike of government in the abstract.

Richard Hofstadter (1964) offers a case study of the origins of the modern polarization movement, as shaped in the 1950s and 1960s. It was a movement that broke the Democrats' welfare-state appeal, built on strains found in the American experience, and it provided a new direction, meaning, and electoral success to a politics of extremism. This was an era that included Robert Welch and the John Birch movement and its charges that President Dwight D. Eisenhower was a communist; McCarthyism and the Wisconsin senator's claim of a State Department full of communists; claims that it was the Yalta agreement that had divided Eastern and Western Europe and resulted in the Soviets gaining the atomic bomb; and the Un-American Activities Committee, with its blacklisting, thought suppression, and secrecy—all of which might not seem unfamiliar in the present era. Heading in a different direction were the Warren Court's decision in *Brown v. Board of Education* (1954), the sit-ins in the South, and the beginnings of the black rights movement that followed in the 1960s.

The comparison between the present era and the Eisenhower years, which in hindsight may be seen in a kinder light than originally deserved, is often made. But the governing ethos back then was significantly different. Policy agreements and cross-party governing coalitions were not only easier to implement but also expected and encouraged by the tenor of the times.

The presence of more factional overlapping within individual parties created the core of an effective center that could be built upon in framing legislation. Such a moderate interparty core was present and acted as a check on those who were more intensely mobilized and ideologically committed. The result was a more effective accommodation to the country's policy needs and, if this is an accurate depiction of the politics of the time, a more representative government. At a minimum, it was the argument made by those who look with nostalgia on an earlier era in which party politics, as they see it, was less divisive and more consensus-driven. Yet prior to the 1960s, social issues of a polarizing nature (such as race, feminism, and gay lifestyles) were less likely to be raised. When these issues came to the front of the political agenda in the movements of the 1960s, they served to redefine the parties and their priorities and reinforce their conflicting economic agendas.

The difference between the culture of that era and the politics of the contemporary period lies in the increasing and more inclusive embracing of a politics of distrust, and the seemingly all-encompassing divisiveness that contributes to a more severe hyper-ideological politics, of the present day. It is a party system and a politics that in its contemporary incarnation affects a broader range of issues (although economic self-interest continues to provide a base); is more difficult to overcome in policymaking; and is one that continues to feed upon itself, magnifying the disparities in wealth and life chances created. It is a condition that shows no signs of ameliorating but rather is likely to increase in intensity and impact in the years to come.

A Changing Party Politics

The dissent over the social movements of the Vietnam War era, the civil rights movement, and the social and political upheaval of the 1960s in general led to the defection of white Southern and other once-Democratic conservatives to the Republican Party. As Arthur Paulson (2000, 2007) detailed, this was to redefine both the then-dominant Democratic Party and a Republican Party on its way to decades of policy dominance. Setting the stage for the realignment was Lyndon Johnson's Great Society, whose housing, welfare, and medical programs and most explicitly the enactment of the Voting Rights Act of 1965 led to the political empowerment of Southern blacks. The effect was to break the Democratic Party's New Deal coalition. Winning presidential candidates in the neoliberal era to follow among Democrats would include the conservative Jimmy Carter and centrists Bill Clinton and Barack Obama. "Over the next forty years, the party more often than not was in the political wilderness, a congress of contending interest groups lacking a common purpose" (Wilentz 2008: xxv).

Social policy was to be redefined in the Reagan years. Redistributive programs became "entitlements" and, ignoring the massive tax cuts then and later, were targeted as the cause of budgetary imbalances and in need of severe reduction. There was nothing in Reagan's electoral victory to suggest that the public had rejected (as it clearly had the Carter presidency) the New Deal/Great Society social welfare state in favor of Reagan's "supply side" economics ("voodoo economics" according to critics). It was an economic approach that dictated a restricted role for government. The new and restrictive political framework was the interpretation to take hold in the public mind and was the basis for the party divide and policy controversies that would last into the twenty-first century.

The Democrats came to largely accept the neoliberal conservative assumptions as to the Reagan mode of governing as representative of the electorate's wishes. In effect, the Democratic Party, while it arguably did move to a more unified, moderately leftist position, was ineffective as a counter to the emergent zeal and anger of a right-wing Republican politics. It was a right-wing party politics that came to be fueled by the gross inequities in wealth establishing the foundation for an extreme adoption of a free-market partisan ideology and issue agenda. The consequence is a form of decisionmaking in governing substantial enough to threaten the essence of a broader representative democratic system.[1]

A Responsible Party System?

The greater ideological/partisan cohesion within the parties has revived talk of the evolution of a more responsible and accountable party system (on an issue basis). Such a development in a restricted two-party system as found in the nation's politics was not anticipated and was believed would be difficult to operationalize. Nonetheless, it was argued that the basics were in place in the level of antagonism and divisiveness for year-round mobilization of competing political interests and the ideological rationalization for the actions taken to a degree the country had not experienced. These all came to be identified with the potential for an emerging party system. Or it may be in truth, although unusually divisive, taken over the long run as a necessary developmental phase for the parties in need of an accommodation and potential correction of the prior system but one of more modest ambitions.

A responsible party system had been advocated by reformers and particularly academicians (Schattschneider 1942; American Political Science Association 1950) as a corrective to the existing party system, and its faults (see Arthur Paulson's discussion in Chapter 4). Not all would agree.

It is difficult to develop such a system analogous to that of the smaller European democracies within a two-party straightjacket in a country the size of the United States. We do not have that system at present, although it is more cohesively organized and policy-relevant than in former times.

The US parties have followed their own paths historically. It may be that the contemporary era is, in modest terms, a realigning period of sorts providing a correction for a party system badly in need of it. It may be that this level of transition will best serve the nation's purposes.

The Polarization of Wealth

Economic power equals political power. The point is indisputable, proven over and over in the country's history. As Thomas Ferguson has explained in-depth in Chapter 5, the consistently widening inequalities in wealth in society over recent decades have transformed US politics and led to a stalemate and polarization of political decisionmaking in governing, one serious enough to threaten the essence of a broader representative democratic system.

The political parties, and most fundamentally the Republican Party in its determined rightward movement, channel the economic power into the political arena. The Democratic Party has moved in ideological terms slightly to the left, but its efforts to be more "business friendly" in the post-Reagan years have proven to offer a weak alternative, in a dominant neoliberal economic age, to a highly motivated and ideologically extreme conservative movement.

This is the argument. It is the basis for the paralysis and bias found in policymaking and is the defining feature of contemporary politics in the United States.

A large body of research has been amassed charting the changes in income levels and the increasing disequilibrium in capital accumulation among classes. The measures of inequality employed are consistent in the picture they present of a badly divided society with its wealth concentrated at the top. The differences found are more pronounced in comparing the very richest of Americans (depending on the analysis, the top 10 percent, the top 1 percent, or even the top 0.5 percent) against the rest. The research studies diagnosing the problem are both extensive and telling. Most significant, the findings lead to the same conclusion: the very rich do exceptionally well, while the rest of the society—more specifically the middle class, which has suffered the most as the prime target of the transfer—subsidize the wealthy. The pretax earnings of the top 10 percent (or 1 percent) for the period 1917–2012 are at or above the highest level in recorded history. It is a distribution that starkly contrasts with that for the period 1936–1973, referred to as the "Golden Age" or the "Great Compression," in the levels of equality of wealth approached on a class basis. A severe maldistribution, largely a product of the 1980 presidential election and its aftermath, has grown in the intervening decades. It is a product of a conservative economic philosophy, politically engineered to redesign the social welfare–state model dominant since the 1930s.

Figure 14.1 presents the share of the nation's wealth held by the top 10 percent of income earners for the period 1917–2012. The time span analyzed allows comparisons with different political eras and their corresponding economic distributions. In the run-up to the Great Depression, a "Gilded Age" extended from the closing decades of the nineteenth century to the late 1920s. It peaked in 1929 on the eve of the depression with just under 50 percent of the total wealth for the country as a whole concentrated in the hands of the wealthiest. Franklin Roosevelt's New Deal and its redistributive, action-based government, in itself a new departure from previous conceptions, in addition to more egalitarian taxing policies, brought about a change in direction. It would lead to the greatest equalization of capital since the country's inception as the domestic programs took shape and the increased taxation began to have its impact, post-1936.

The New Deal policies were popular, as was Roosevelt's conception of the activist government that produced them. In addition to the minimization of class differences in access to wealth, an equality of interests arose

Figure 14.1 Income Share of the Top 10 Percent of Earners, 1917–2011

Source: Piketty and Saez 2003; updated to 2011 in January 2013 using IRS preliminary tax statistics.

Note: Series based on pretax cash market income, including capital gains and excluding government transfers.

unmatched both in US history or by that of any other democratic nation (and with few exceptions, if any, of any nation in the world). In response to the new economic order, the political-party system was transformed, providing electoral support for such an approach and dominating the nation's politics up through the 1960s. As testimony to the success of the New Deal's social welfare state and the belief that it had become a permanent part of the nation's landscape, there is President Dwight Eisenhower's endorsement and his accompanying contention that any opposition to such programs would be political suicide (see the opening to Chapter 5 in this volume). Such a statement from a Republican president can serve to emphasize just how monumental, and unanticipated, the Reagan economic revolution would come to be.

Jimmy Carter's conservative Democratic administration began (modestly as it was to be seen in later years) the restructuring of tax and budgetary allocations, directing funds away from social and domestic programs to fund an expanded military presence and to balance the budget and pay the costs of the Vietnam War (not concluded until 1975). The changes initiated might seem modest in hindsight, but there were indications of a new and evolving, more conservative approach to governing.

The most fundamental of changes would come with the election of Ronald Reagan, once a New Deal supporter, liberal activist, and union head, and a second-lead actor in movies with a high likeability ratio and an innate ability to sell his message. He was recruited by General Electric, a corporate leader in conservative economics and politics. Reagan would travel the country speaking to plant employees and local community groups, marketing the company's products and its message on fiscal austerity and budgetary redirections in domestic programming: the need for a strong defense (General Electric was a major beneficiary of military funding), a more combative approach to Soviet communism, limited government, and a revamped tax structure sensitive to the interests of the wealthiest. General Electric also sponsored a television program with Reagan in cowboy gear as host, thus reaching the public at large.

With the backing of similar-minded corporate executives serving as an informal cabinet and advisory board, Reagan entered politics as a reborn conservative. He was elected governor of California in a race against a popular incumbent and almost by accident burst on to the national scene in 1964. He endorsed Barry Goldwater and campaigned for him. The Goldwater consultants had half an hour of national television time the campaign was not going to use. A pretaped Reagan speech was scheduled in the slot. The talk Reagan had recorded was no different than one he had delivered hundreds of times on behalf of General Electric and in his own campaigns, but it created a sensation among conservatives. The clarity and simplicity of message and the apparent sincerity of the spokesperson would become the hallmarks of his future efforts.

Reagan went on to contest for the Republican presidential nomination, most notably in the fight with incumbent Gerald Ford in 1976. It served as a prelude to his winning of the party's presidential endorsement in 1980. He then won a close race against a highly unpopular Jimmy Carter, whose unsuccessful economic policies ("stagflation") and general indecisiveness in office, in addition to a pre-nomination challenge from liberal senator Ted Kennedy, doomed his presidency.

Whatever the pedigree, once in office Reagan would institute what amounted to an economic and political counter-revolution built on a severe if simplified application of the neoliberal economic principles he had been preaching for decades ("government is the enemy"). The effort was to eliminate social programs and services, reallocate government funds to the defense industry, take a confrontational foreign policy in opposition to Soviet communism, and install a "Star Wars" canopy at untold expense (the technology was yet to be invented) to be positioned in the skies above the United States to protect against nuclear attack. His first and most important priority, however, was to reduce taxes on the rich and, through a restructured tax system, to shift money upward in the economy to those at its heights.

Reagan did not achieve most of his objectives. What he did do, with the help of friendly Democrats, was to institute massive tax cuts that restructured the distribution of wealth within the society. The strategy paid off handsomely, along with the accompanying assumption that the ensuing budget deficits would be made up through substantial reductions in funding for social welfare programs, rewarding his supporters at levels not seen since the 1920s. Along with the accompanying assumption that the ensuing budget deficits would be made up through substantial reductions in funding for social welfare programs, the beginning of the end of the social welfare state as envisioned in the Great Depression was in sight.

The Reagan version of neoliberal economics would form the governing framework for successive administrations up to the twenty-first century, including those of Democratic centrist/conservative Bill Clinton and centrist Barack Obama. The polarization of class wealth to its extremes as experienced in the late twentieth century and the early decades of the twenty-first is a direct outcome of the Reagan fiscal policies and the accompanying economic and political restructuring.

The available data provide further support for the trend lines found for the period covered in Figure 14.1. The distribution of real income in favor of the top 10 percent of income earners following recessions (the Clinton recessions, the Great Recession) helps make the point. The wealthiest were the hardest hit by these recessions, but they recovered the most spectacularly, well out of proportion with the rest of the population (see Table 14.1). Taking the period 1993–2011 as a whole, real income growth for the richest 1 percent of Americans was 57.5 percent, compared to 5.8 percent for the bottom 99 percent. The 121 percent post–Great Recession recovery in assets particularly stands out.

Emmanuel Saez speaks in detail as to the distribution of wealth in the recovery from the Great Recession:

> From 2009 to 2011, average real income per family grew modestly by 1.7% . . . but the gains were very uneven. Top 1% incomes grew by 11.2% while bottom 99% incomes shrank by 0.4%. Hence, the top 1% captured 121% of the income gains in the first two years of the recovery. . . .
>
> This [analysis] suggests that the Great Recession has only depressed top income shares temporarily and will not undo any of the dramatic increase in top income shares that has taken place since the 1970s. Indeed, excluding realized capital gains, the top decile income share in 2011 is equal to 46.5%, the highest ever since 1917 when the series start. (Saez 2013c: 1)

In a separate account, Thomas Piketty and Emmanuel Saez show that "almost all of the income growth in the economy between 2010 and 2012— ninety-five percent of it—accrued to the one percent" (Cassidy 2014: 71). The message is clear: the nation's wealth is centered at the very top of the income pyramid and remains so regardless of circumstances.

US productivity has increased substantially, yet at the lower income levels the economic changes are not reflected in significant increases in wages,

Table 14.1　Real Income Growth, 1993–2011 (percentages)

	Average Income, Real Growth	Top 1% Incomes, Real Growth	Bottom 99% Incomes, Real Growth	Fraction of Total Real Growth (or Loss) Captured by Top 1%
Full period, 1993–2011	13.1	57.5	5.8	62
Clinton expansion, 1993–2000	31.5	98.7	20.3	45
2001 recession, 2000–2002	–11.7	–30.8	–6.5	57
Bush expansion, 2002–2007	16.1	61.8	6.8	65
Great Recession, 2007–2009	17.4	36.3	–11.6	49
Recovery, 2009–2011	1.7	11.2	–0.4	121

Sources: Piketty and Saez 2003; series updated to 2011 in January 2013 using preliminary tax statistics from the Internal Revenue Service.

Notes: Computations based on family market income including realized capital gains (before individual taxes). Incomes exclude government transfers (such as unemployment insurance and social security) and nontaxable fringe benefits. Incomes are deflated using the Consumer Price Index. The last column reports the fraction of total real growth (or loss) in family income captured by the top 1 percent of income earners; for example, from 2002 to 2007, real growth in average family income was 16.1 percent, but 65 percent of that growth accrued to the top 1 percent of income earners, while only 35 percent of that growth accrued to the bottom 99 percent of income earners.

nor do they show a tendency to level off in more equitable terms among all income groups. "From 1973 to 2011, worker productivity grew 80 percent, while median hourly compensation, after inflation, grew by just one-eighth that amount. . . . And since 2000, productivity has risen 23 percent while real hourly pay has essentially stagnated" (Lowrey 2013: 5).

The tax reductions affected all income categories but were designed to concentrate primarily on indirect sources of income, inheritances, stocks and bonds, investments, and other nonwage earnings. Wealth was reallocated from the middle class, charged with providing the balance of funds to operate the government, upward in an economic spiral that continued over successive decades. As the wealth of the richest 1 percent (to 10 percent) continued to grow, its share of the tax burden decreased virtually proportionally (see Figure 14.2). As a method for reallocating the nation's wealth, Reagan's tax policies (and those of his successors) succeeded brilliantly.

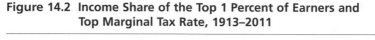

**Figure 14.2 Income Share of the Top 1 Percent of Earners and
Top Marginal Tax Rate, 1913–2011**

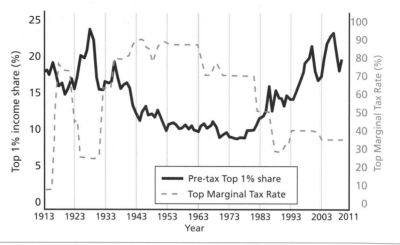

Source: Saez 2013a; Saez 2013b: 18.
Note: Income share based on pretax income.

Bad as it was for the population as a whole, the imbalance in wealth separating whites and minorities (blacks and Latinos) was magnified by the Great Recession. Post-recession, from 2008 on a white family averaged $632,000 in capital, a Hispanic family $110,000, and an African American family $98,000. Each group had less capital post-recession than pre-recession. This is one additional dimension of the economic polarization present in the society (Lowrey 2012).

There have been proposals to equalize the tax code if not bring it back more closely to the Golden Age distribution. The much-discussed Buffett Rule (proposed by billionaire Warren Buffett) would tax incomes over $1 million per year at a minimum rate of 30 percent. While receiving considerable attention, as much for its source as anything, it would in reality do little to reduce the advantages enjoyed by the richest under Republican Party proposals. For example, the proposals incorporated in Representative Paul Ryan's (R-WI) annual Tea Party budget would over time increase the benefits enjoyed by the richest, magnifying the gap already present (see, for example, Ryan's proposed "Path to Prosperity," released March 12, 2013).

There have been other reform-minded proposals, mostly as would be expected from liberal think tanks, economists, and occasionally public office-holders, that could serve to decrease the financial polarization. These can range from setting tax rates on the biggest earners anywhere from 50 to 70 or more rarely 90 percent of income. Even relatively modest increases in tax rates, such as an additional one-fifth to one-third, would add billions for government operating expenses.

Peter Diamond, an emeritus professor of economics at the Massachusetts Institute of Technology, Nobel Prize recipient, and Obama nominee to the Federal Reserve Board (blocked by Senate Republicans), in discussing these proposals in relation to research he conducted in association with Emmanuel Saez, said, "The debate in Washington is between the Bush-era and Clinton-era rates. Our finding is that the debate should be between the pre-1986 Reagan tax rate, which was 50 percent, and the rates that existed from Johnson to Reagan [which were higher]" (quoted in Lowrey 2013: 4). That would provide a beginning; others would go higher still.

There is a potential downside to such proposals beyond the impact on the biggest earners. Pretax incomes may also be affected, such as for money in prospective ventures. This impact is difficult to assess. Investment incentives and increases in economic opportunity were justifications for substantially reducing the highest rates. Tax avoidance could be projected to increase and an already-burdened Internal Revenue Service would likely be incapable of effectively policing such a development.

Unions, which can be effective as collective-bargaining instruments for the working class in shaping the distribution of income, have lost significant proportions of their memberships in recent decades. The peak union membership rate reached 35 percent in the 1950s, the consequence of a surge in unionization during the Great Depression and following World War II. It was of course a planned political outcome, the beneficiary of the pro-union administrations of Franklin Roosevelt and Harry Truman. As a consequence, unions would prove to be a primary resource for the Democratic Party, providing most of its campaign funding in elections thereafter.

With the outsourcing of manufacturing, the inability of the union movement to cross into professional occupations, and the targeting of the movement by Republicans as an essential element of their neoliberal agenda, unions faded in importance. The union membership rate at the beginning of the second decade of the twenty-first century is just over 11 percent of the work force and falling. Even then, it is disproportionately biased by the inclusion of public-sector employment (35.9 percent), which is considerably larger—by a ratio of five to one—than the rate for private-sector occupations (6.6 percent).

As the union presence weakened, the share of the nation's income going to those at the apex of the economic pyramid increased, in almost direct proportion to the loss of union membership (see Figure 14.3). American workers may well be on the verge of becoming individual entrepreneurs who sell their skills and services in the open market with little protection collectively and with considerably less bargaining power.

Figure 14.3 Unions and Shared Prosperity, 1918–2008

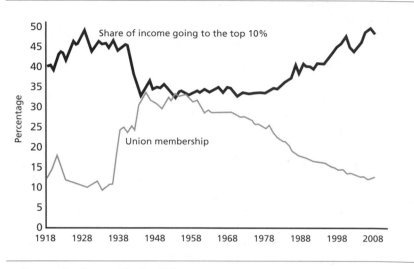

Source: Eisenbrey and Gordon 2012.

There is yet another dimension to the problem. A comparison with other advanced economies that have also been experiencing a sustained upward class movement of capital resources serves to further accentuate the disparity found in the United States. Among the advanced economies of the world, the United States ranks first in the severity of its polarization of wealth, and this for a country that likes to think of itself as a "classless society" (see Figure 14.4).

To sum up, the surge in income at the highest levels of the society can be attributed to the following factors:

- Restructuring of tax rates to increasingly reward the richest and penalize the rest. The middle class now carries the burden. In the wealthiest country in the world, the American middle class is no longer the wealthiest middle class in the world.
- Changes in the labor market and a decrease in collective efforts at worker representation.
- Indirect, nonwage income as the primary source of wealth for those at the top. Wage earners are proportionately heavily taxed. The middle class bears the cost of governing.
- Efforts to weaken, replace, privatize, or eliminate government programs that redistribute wealth, such as health care, old-age benefits,

Figure 14.4 Wealth Inequality: Europe vs. the United States, 1810–2010

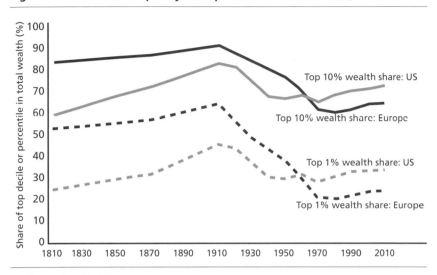

Source: Cassidy 2014.

poverty stabilization and reduction, public investments, and the funding of educational opportunity, from preschool to college.
- And most important, the political power to put in place a tax and economic structure to produce such outcomes.

The cost to the society of such an economic imbalance is high (Wilkinson and Pickett 2010, 2013; White 2014).

Follow the Money: Investing in Politics

Politics is expensive, increasingly so in a high-tech political culture. This is especially true at the national level. Congressional candidates have averaged over $1 million in campaign expenditures since the 2004 elections. Successive presidential cycles record ever higher levels of financing. The money comes from those with the funds to give and the most to gain, creating the bridge that connects and rewards the most wealthy with the political process that determines tax and budgetary priorities. It creates a political loop that feeds back into consistently higher levels of rewards for those who pay the campaign bills.

Thomas Ferguson, who addresses related issues in Chapter 5, has developed an "investment theory of politics" (1995b; see also Ferguson and

Rogers 1986). It connects the economic-political puzzle over the broad course of US history (from the eighteenth century to the mid-1990s). The argument is that, in large amounts, money invested in politics by corporations and the well-to-do largely, and often exclusively, determines candidate selection, party priorities, and election outcomes. It trumps voter impact and with it the assumed workings of a democratic electoral process. It is Ferguson's contention that the "serious discussion of money, industrial structure, and politics scarcely exists" (1995b: 9). He is correct in his belief. The economic structure of political decisionmaking—who gets what, why, and how—is a sensitive subject, one unusually complex and difficult to unravel. It brings into play questions many would choose to leave unanswered. These relate to the relationship between the real world of a corporate state and the fundamental operations of an egalitarian political order. Ferguson is one who has taken on the task.

As he has shown, such political investments have created a complex and interdependent web of influence-buying. In addition to financing campaigns, the money funds conservative think tanks, publicity ("educational") campaigns, issue ads, political action committees (PACs), interest groups, lobbying drives, public relations efforts (usually negative in character and targeted at particular legislation), ideological groups, publishing efforts, media acquisitions (Fox News and increasingly the economically vulnerable newspaper corporations), the parties themselves, and so on.

The Super PACs, which can mimic and in races of their choosing can outdo the parties in impacting candidates and voter choice, are a more recent addition for both political parties. Well-funded, the Super PACs offer all the services that a party could provide, from selecting and training the candidates to carrying their message, financing their efforts, providing expert direction and experienced consultants, and steering their choices through the demands of the pre-nomination and general election process. Their activities begin well before the election cycle gets under way. As they become more common, they may well pose a broad and more encompassing threat to the parties' traditional roles in the electoral process. Reducing the parties' importance, replacing the ties that do exist, and substituting themselves for the activists now dominant in party affairs, this would represent a further extension and one ultimately more decisive for big money and those who supply it. Ferguson is not alone in arguing that "the time has come for serious campaign finance reform" (1995b: 350).

There is a problem here that explains why so little has been attempted, much less survived, since the first effort at regulation in 1907. Members of Congress, regardless of party, are not receptive to reform initiatives. The fundraising process forms the basics of a system they were elected under and one that they feel comfortable with. Reform is not in their interests. It takes a crisis, and a substantial one that alarms the public, to bring about a consideration of campaign regulation.

Such occurred with the Watergate scandal in the Nixon administration. The break-ins and abuse of federal authority were egregious enough to raise both public and congressional concerns. The unlawful acts were attributed to the availability of excesses of unaccounted funds. True in part, it is nonetheless a benign accounting for the actions of the White House. Still, it led to the most far-reaching and fundamentally important financial campaign reforms in the nation's history. At that point, the second major barrier, and one significantly more difficult to deal with, kicked in.

The Supreme Court, historically and repeatedly in the contemporary period, has presented a virtually insuperable barrier to effective campaign reform. A succession of conservative courts has applied a series of legal stratagems to negate whatever restrictions on campaign spending, limits on donors, identification of sources, activities to be protected, ceilings on spending levels, or whatever else the Congress in one of its reform moods might propose.

The Watergate reforms came under immediate Court attack in *Buckley v. Valeo* (1976) (the 1976 presidential election was to be the first in which the reforms were to be fully enforced). The process of challenges and Court dismemberment has continued up through *Citizens United v. Federal Election Commission* (2010) and *McCutcheon v. Federal Election Commission* (2014). Both were 5-to-4 decisions, with the Court's conservative majority balanced against its centrist-to-liberal minority. This is also further evidence of politics at work; a change in administrations and an opportunistic opening could provide the potential to reverse such rulings. Still, the cumulative weight of Supreme Court decisionmaking over any period of time has been decisively anti-regulation.

The reasoning behind the Court's 2010 ruling in *Citizens United* provides insight to its commitment to a deregulation of public interest campaign restrictions. The ruling declared unconstitutional corporate and union prohibitions on independent campaign contributions. The corporations and unions (the balance heavily favors corporations and the wealthy; in the 2012 election as an illustration, the billionaire Koch brothers alone, through individual contributions, sponsoring of interest groups and PACs, information campaigns, and the like, invested $412.6 million, compared to a total of $153.4 million for the labor unions). Under Court edict, monetary interests were allowed to invest unlimited amounts in campaign advertising (mostly negative), Super PACs, and so on. All were justified as exercises in free speech analogous to those of an individual, intended to inform the voter and exercise a constitutional right. Restrictions on the use of money in campaigns, according to the Court's majority, amounted to "free speech suppression" that had a "chilling" impact on the conduct of elections.

Also according to the Court's majority, since the funds were spent independently and not coordinated with a campaign or a candidate, "they do not give rise to corruption as the appearance of corruption," an assertion to be challenged. Should funders be publicly identified through disclosure provisions, it could "chill donations to an organization by exposing donors to retaliation." The belief that donors should be identifiable was of course the intention of such legislation.

According to the justices opposed to campaign regulation, their decision was meant to further democratic ends. "The fact that a corporation or any other speaker [one morphs into the other], is willing to spend money to try to persuade voters presupposes that the people have the ultimate influence over elected officeholders." And in conclusion, to quote from the Court's decision in *McConnell v. Federal Election Commission* in 2003, "The First Amendment underwrites the freedom to experiment and to create in the realm of thought and speech. Citizens must be free to use new forms, and new forums, for the expression of ideas. The civic discourse belongs to the people and the Government may not prescribe the means used to conduct it." This ruling was followed in 2014 by that of *McCutcheon v. Federal Election Commission,* which voided any cumulative limits on total contributions to candidates, parties, or political committees.

There are several points to be made. First, campaign reform is exceptionally hard to legislate and even more difficult to sustain in light of the Supreme Court's conception of what constitutes a democracy. Second, the Court strongly supports unrestricted corporate and individual investments in politics. And third, in extension of this, the flow of money from those who have it to those who would represent the country is essentially unimpeded, and in fact is encouraged.

This conception of democratic representation forms the connection between those with the money to invest and those who would determine the tax and budgetary priorities that return to the contributors rewards well beyond the imagination of most. It is in effect a reinforcing cycle of money-politics-money that keeps on giving and one that explains the steady increases in cumulative inequality experienced.

Polarization in the Party System:
Republicans and Democrats Divided

The engine for the change in the distribution of the society's wealth is a more determined aligning of the parties, and again most decisively the Republican Party, along the economic continuum into more cohesive and disciplined political combat groups. Matthew Levendusky calls this the "partisan sort." He compares the party system of a generation or more ago with that of the present era: "In the 1950s and 1960s, Democratic and Republican elites were relatively heterogeneous, with a liberal 'Rockefeller Republican' wing and a cadre of conservative southern Democrats. But by the 1990s and 2000s, elites were more sharply polarized, with most Democrats on the left and most Republicans on the right" (2009: 2).

Polarized elites determine what it means to be a Democrat or a Republican, and the bases of the parties, and the voters, respond accordingly. The impact of these shifting ideological loyalties has resulted in a quite different party system, to an extent not only a reformulation of the partisan/ideological debate, but also a repudiation of the looser, more consensus-driven, and less rigid party coalitions found throughout the balance of US history.

The political parties translate the economic and political inequalities in the society into public policy. The parties divide along class lines. The competing views on issues, economic and social, extend from the bases of the parties up through the activist level, the most significant in clarifying and formulating issue stands, to those who represent the parties in office. There is then a clarity to each party's programmatic commitments that distinguishes and divides members at each party stratum. From this it has been contended that there is a stronger representative bond within parties that runs from grassroots identifiers to political officeholders.

One consequence of the clarification of party alignments is a bimodal party division. This largely replaces the overlapping coalitional parties familiar throughout most of US history. It also has meant, in Alan Abramowitz's (2010) terminology, "a disappearing center" in the electorate.

The clarity on issues of economic inequality—which Republicans are for, and on which Democrats seek a greater leveling across classes—among other positions (as examined in this volume), has increased decisively. The Pew Research Center (2012b), in its 2012 survey of political values, found continually widening differences over the period 1987–2012.[2] Testing partisan differences on forty-five issues, it found that the average gap between Democrats and Republicans had increased from 10 percent to 18 percent. Pew concluded that the distance between the parties in 2012 constituted the greatest magnitude of separation yet experienced. "America is more divided than ever along partisan lines. The polarization of party differences among Americans is greater than that between races, gender, ages and income. Further, the widest separation in views is to be found between Republicans and Democrats in relation to the social net."

There is, however, a difference as to the intensity of voter views in the electorate. The difference exists. This is not in question. Some do question the intensity of the differences among voters and their relevance, for example, to broader concerns of a "culture war" in politics. Morris Fiorina (1981), a leader in this regard, and others of like mind argue that voters accept class distinctions as an inherent part of the "American dream" and are best characterized as "conservative egalitarians" (Fiorina and Levendusky 2006; Fiorina, Abrams, and Pope 2008; Fiorina and Abrams 2008, 2009). Their hope is to take advantage of the opportunities offered by the system in order to move upward. Their objective is to advance to the point that the maldistributions in wealth and politics, and the tax and budgetary forces that serve those maldistributions so well, work to their advantage. According to such an approach, voters do not envy the "haves," believe they have earned whatever advantages they enjoy, and do not necessarily see themselves as the "have nots."

Others find such explanations wanting, products of a misperception of the electorate and an underestimation of the severity and compelling nature of the concerns that motivate voters. Or for some it could be the result of an ideological prism or of wishful thinking that casts things in a positive light and justifies a system in which they find little to fault. It should be acknowledged that Fiorina in particular would advocate alleviating some of the economic disparities to be found, and that he and Abramowitz (Abramowitz 2010, 2013; Abramowitz, Alexander, and Gunning 2006), an outspoken advocate of a clearly polarized party spectrum, base their interpretations on similar empirical data sources.

For some, then, the political center in the electorate has largely disappeared, leaving an ideologically sensitive, issue-driven, and significantly more partisan gulf between the parties. It results in a coherence and consistency of political views, throughout the party system, that is new to the American scene. Others believe this to be an overstatement. They find less division among party identifiers and less anger and hostility than are evident at other levels. In this regard, they argue that there is a "disconnect" between the bases of the parties and the "political classes" of the parties—those who frame party issue positions and those who represent the parties in office. The stalemate in policymaking and the intensity of the divisions found among officeholders, then, are a product of a political class who is out-of-touch with its roots in the electorate.

On one issue there is no disagreement: the critical importance of core activists in shaping the parties' message, clarifying their appeals to voters, and choosing candidates for office who share their beliefs. It is here that the policy divide is the most pronounced. Party identifiers "echo" the choices on issues presented them and support the candidates chosen to represent these.

There is agreement over the critical role of party activists in the process; these activists are considerably more ideologically driven than the average identifier, and are politically active in codifying and strengthening the parties' programmatic commitments. These are the party members who assume the decisive role in candidate selection through participation in the primaries, caucuses, and national conventions, and are the ones responsible for writing and adopting the parties' platforms.

The different party issue profiles are evident at each stage of the process, from the selection of candidates recruited and supported in general elections to the views they commit to and how they vote in the Congress. A review of the party platforms for any presidential election in the twenty-first century provides evidence of how divided and polarized each party's base and elite are.

Most activists are from the middle to upper-middle class and have the knowledge, time, and resources to devote to the work load demanded. Curiously, perhaps, an overview of the memberships of the national conventions reveals similar demographic profiles. There are differences, however. Given their class base, in terms of income levels, Republicans overrepresent the wealthiest; Democrats, in line with their electoral coalitions also, overrepresent the less affluent.

A second major difference is also apparent. The membership of the Republican convention comprises older, overwhelmingly white, and, as indicated, more affluent individuals; Democrats host a more heterogeneous mix, including among their convention membership minorities and representatives of social movements (gays, feminists, and so on).

The essential significance in values and issue beliefs motivating the core partisans as contrasted with swing voters was analyzed by Larry Bartels (2010). His focus was on the substance of the differences and the strategic tensions they create in the contemporary party system. His concern was to clarify the competing issue positions that dominate the thinking of those most instrumental in party affairs and the degree to which such opposing belief structures are moderated to appeal to a more centrist and less intense or less informed electorate. The traditional approach to explaining the campaign approaches that lead to electoral success was that a move to the center was the key to winning office.

The time frame was for six presidential elections (1988–2008). Core activists' positions on a range of issues were collected and grouped into four dimensions: social welfare conservatism, moral conservatism, racial conservatism, and antigovernment attitudes. Intense partisan differences existed in each sector, which was expected given the importance attached to such activists. Democratic core partisans scored high and cared deeply about issues in the social welfare domain, the historical calling of the party. The Republican core in turn had little interest in such areas but attached great importance to concerns relating to moral conservatism, racial conservatism, and antigovernment attitudes, none of which are priorities of the Democrats. In a reaffirmation of the distinctions between the parties and the bimodal distribution of support patterns in the electorate, neither party, and especially the Democrats, made much of an effort to moderate their views in elections to appeal to swing voters. They chose to concentrate on positions that would fortify their core support, a rejection of the centrist-oriented model believed to apply. As a consequence, this focus, in line with its appeal historically, has pushed emerging demographic groups into the big-tent Democratic Party, as John Garcia has described in Chapter 10 and Barbara Burrell in Chapter 8.

The critical focus in all of this, the culmination of all that has gone before, can be found in the political decisionmaking in Congress in particular. This is where policy is determined and the nation's issue objectives and priorities are determined. A number of factors of relevance to understanding the forces at work become clearer. First, the proportion of moderates in both parties and their influence in impacting legislative outcomes have declined significantly. The falloff is true for both parties, but in a broader policy resolution context is of more significance for Republicans. As their party's centrists exited Congress, they were replaced by extremely committed far-right conservatives.

Instead of moderating their views to reach some median voter, both parties have pushed away from the center, rejecting moderation. As Figures 14.5a and 14.5b indicate, moderates in the Republican Party have been in gradual decline for nearly fifty years, while moderate Democrats tend to lose in bunches in wave election years like 1994 and 2006 that see extreme Republicans swept into office.[3] As a result, the polarization in Congress has reached a level not seen since the era just before the Great Depression. Not coincidentally, the concentration of wealth among the few is at its highest peak since before the economic crash of 1929.

In a short span of elections, the Republican membership underwent a transformation that resulted in an increasingly ideologically committed party, one well removed from the center of the policy spectrum and of course even more distanced from the Democratic membership. The Democrats also experienced the same pressures to move left, but did so in a more moderate, centrist manner. The polarization of the parties in Congress is thus mostly a conservative Republican development.

The legislators of both parties polarized in their votes along an ideological/issue continuum (see Figures 14.6a and 14.6b). The most pronounced movement in this regard, and consequently the one of greatest importance, is the determined rightward shift of an increasingly more combative and more extreme conservative party (see Sinclair 2006; Theriault 2006).

A final point in this regard. Nolan McCarty, Keith Poole, and Howard Rosenthal (2006, 2013); Larry Bartels (1998, 2000, 2008); and Martin Gilens (2011, 2012) have all analyzed the context and motivations that explain individual congressional voting. They cite the concerns addressed in this volume and conclude that ideology tied to self-interest is a factor of consequence and potentially the most significant one. According to McCarty, Poole, and Rosenthal, "American democracy has failed the ordinary citizen. . . . Neither political party has risen to the occasion and advocated true institutional reform that would reduce the stupefying concentration of money and power in the financial sector. . . . The elites glower across an ideological divide constructed around the conflicts of the 1960s and 1970s and do little toward meaningful reform of institutions and markets that have clearly failed"

Figure 14.5a Moderates in the House, 1916–2012

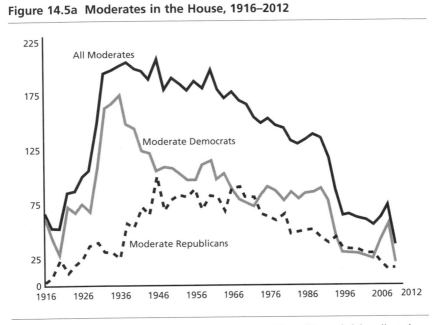

Source: Data from Jeffrey B. Lewis, Keith T. Poole, and Howard Rosenthal. http://voteview .com. Graph developed by James Dunne.

Figure 14.5b Extremists in the House, 1916–2012

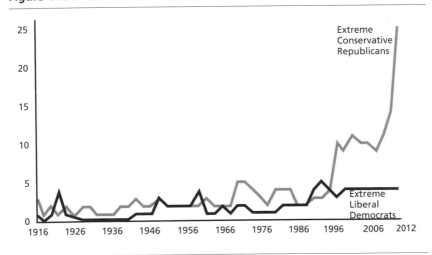

Source: Data from Jeffrey B. Lewis, Keith T. Poole, and Howard Rosenthal. http://voteview .com. Graph developed by James Dunne.

Figure 14.6a Liberal and Conservative Party Differences in the House, 1879–2011

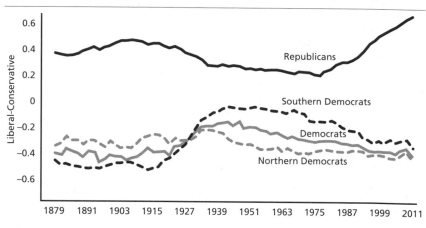

Source: http://voteview.com.

Figure 14.6b Liberal and Conservative Party Differences in the Senate, 1879–2011

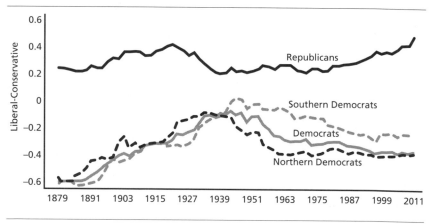

Source: http://voteview.com.

(2013: 272–273). According to Bartels, "The specific policy views of citizens, whether rich or poor, have less impact in the policy-making process than the ideological convictions of elected officials" (2008: 289). And according to Gilens, in his study of economic inequality and political power in the United States, "The preferences of the well-off groups are much more likely to be reflected in policy outcomes than those of less-affluent citizens" (2012: 241). Further, should the interests of the very wealthiest conflict with those at lesser income levels, there is no doubt as to who will prevail. The responses of those in public office to the most affluent and their concerns have steadily increased over time, illustrated most dramatically in the changed tax structure and upward shift of the society's wealth to the richest of the rich.

Conclusion

Polarization is about economic equity and social justice. One impacts the other. Polarization at varying levels has been around as far back as one can project into history. It appears to be a constant condition fostered by American society and more specifically by its institutions of political representation. Where the divide is severe, as in the contemporary period, it comes to affect all areas of policymaking, some profoundly, others with fewer consequences. The extreme economic inequality in turn feeds into and shapes the nation's politics. The carriers, or instruments, of polarization are the political parties. These accentuate the divide and provide the platforms for bringing the social and economic influences into political decisionmaking. The parties are representing their constituencies' best interests as they see them. They are reactive institutions; they do not, at least initially, create the conditions that lead to severe economic polarities. They divide along the economic fault lines in the society. They feed into the nation's decisionmaking. So aligned, they exacerbate the problem and impose it on issue concerns. The dominant of the two parties, in this case the Republican Party, has largely been able to impose its will on a weaker centrist/liberal Democratic coalition. The effect is to create a feedback loop that consistently works to increase the inequality and limit the social gains in the society. Such a division of the political universe rewards excessively those with the financial resources necessary to influence the system, and equally consistently hurts those at the middle to the bottom of the class structure. The ultimate consequence is to worsen social conditions and magnify their impact on society. The dysfunctional governance that occurs, with its failure to give "voice" to all interests and the resulting unchecked erosion of representative institutions in the culture of politics, provides no evidence of ameliorating or yielding to a better balance in distributing the country's economic resources.

The party positions are justified by ideological reasoning. For contemporary conservatives/Republicans, this means a neoliberal economic commitment that celebrates an unrestrained self-interest, one more powerful and coherent and with a clearly greater impact than any alternative approaches. The liberal/Democratic counter to such reasoning, putting forth a contrasting vision for the nation, is less well articulated, is considerably less promoted, and brings into question the effectiveness of a two-party system as representative of the basic interests of multiple hundreds of millions of citizens. The 1 percent versus 99 percent (or 10 percent versus 90 percent) division of wealth provides clear evidence of the severity of the social divisions. It also ends in a dysfunctional system and raises questions as to the relevance of eighteenth-century governing structures, and the assumptions and values they were built on, for a modern, twenty-first-century superpower.

Polarization is a political condition born of and reflective of political successes by the parties and groups with the most to benefit. It is not an immutable, uncontrollable force, the product of some "invisible hand" meant to determine policy outcomes and uncorrectable by formal functioning political forces. It is a political magnification of interest, justified by broader assumptions as to the best workings of a society and promoted in the self-interest of those with the economic resources best able to restructure political representation. Polarization is, in short, political in conception, in its operations, and in its consequences. Such a development also makes it difficult to believe polarization could sustain a serious democracy for any period of time.

The government of the contemporary period is not the one envisioned by the Founders. The issues raised in relation to the exercise of a hyper-partisan ideological politics and its impact under the conditions presently in play bring into question the country's democratic operations and their relevance for addressing equitably the needs of a mass society.

Notes

I wish to thank James Dunne for his contributions to this chapter.

1. A contemporary extension accompanying the new politics, one with echoes of the times Hofstadter reported on, has been the Tea Party movement. Theda Skocpol and Vanessa Williamson describe their research into the Tea Party movement, which was to take place largely in reaction to the election of Barack Obama. Funded and organized by billionaires and other rich donors, its focus was on economic objectives in addition to a coordinated effort to oppose President Obama's attempt to establish a national health care insurance plan. The attacks on Obama are described by Skocpol and Williamson as "paranoia." "Tea Party members [say] that Obama is a secret Muslim, a foreigner, a Socialist, a Communist, a Nazi—or maybe all of the above! Obama the un-American is the over-arching theme" (2012: 78).

The delusion of Obama as an anti-American trying to take down the country from the inside through either nefariousness or incompetence or racial bigotry or a secret commitment to socialism is no more than the reincarnation of a familiar strain in right-wing politics. The approach can be successful, as evidenced by the Tea Party's electoral victories, as for example in the 2010 off-year elections and the obstructionist force its advocates were to bring to Congress.

2. There is a rich and diverse body of research on party polarization. It includes Ansolabehere, Rodden, and Snyder 2006; Bafumi and Shapiro 2009; Baldassari and Bearman 2007; Baldassari and Gelman 2008; DiMaggio, Evans, and Bryson 1996; Evans 2003; Fiorina, Abrams, and Pope 2008; Hetherington 2009; Jacobson 2006; Mann and Ornstein 2012; and Leege et al. 2002.

3. For the purposes of the discussion and Figures 14.5a and 14.5b, extreme liberals are those with a DW-NOMINATE score between −0.7 and −1.0, and extreme conservatives are those with a score between 0.7 and 1.0. Moderates are those with a score between −0.25 and 0.25. For a full discussion of DW-NOMINATE and its methodology, visit http://voteview.com.

References

ABC News and *Washington Post*. 2011. "Economy, Gas, Partisanship, and War Gang Up on Confidence in Government." March 15. http://abcnews.go.com/Politics /abc-news-washington-post-poll-confidence-government-falls/story?id=1313 4173&page=1.

Abrajano, Marisa, R. Michael Alvarez, and Jonathan Nagler. 2008. "The Hispanic Vote in the 2004 Presidential Election: Insecurity and Moral Concerns." *Journal of Politics* 70(2): 368–382.

Abramowitz, Alan I. 2009. "Do Americans View Both Parties as Too Extreme?" July 9. http://www.centerforpolitics.org/crystalball/articles/aia2009070901/.

———. 2010. *The Disappearing Center: Engaged Citizens, Polarization, and American Democracy*. New Haven: Yale University Press.

———. 2013. *The Polarized Public? Why American Government Is So Dysfunctional*. New York: Pearson.

Abramowitz, Alan I., Brad Alexander, and Matthew Gunning. 2006. "Incumbency, Redistricting, and the Decline of Competition in U.S. House Elections." *Journal of Politics* 68(1): 75–88.

Abramowitz, Alan I., and Kyle Saunders. 2008. "Is Polarization a Myth?" *Journal of Politics* 70(2): 542–555.

Adamic, Lada A., and Natalie Glance. 2005. "The Political Blogosphere and the 2004 U.S. Election: Divided They Blog." http://www.deepdyve.com/lp/acm/the -political-blogosphere-and-the-2004-u-s-election-divided-they-blog-u0QIw X6N74.

Admati, Anat, and Martin Hellwig. 2013. *The Bankers' New Clothes*. Princeton: Princeton University Press.

Aizenman, N. C. 2011. "Legal Battle over Obama's Health-Care Law Moves to Atlanta Courtroom." June 8. http://www.washingtonpost.com/national/legal -battle-over-obamas-health-care-law-moves-to-atlanta-courtroom/2011/06/07 /AGdnZyLH_story.html.

Aldrich, John H. 1995. *Why Parties? The Origin and Transformation of Party Politics in America*. Chicago: University of Chicago Press.

Aldrich, John H., and Richard G. Niemi. 1996. "The Sixth American Party System: Electoral Change, 1952–1992." In *Broken Contract? Changing Relationships Between Americans and Their Government*, ed. Stephen C. Craig. Boulder: Westview.

Aldrich, John H., and David W. Rohde. 2000. "The Consequences of Party Organization in the House: The Role of the Majority and Minority Parties in Conditional
Party Government." In *Polarized Politics: Congress and the President in a Partisan Era,* ed. Jon R. Bond and Richard Fleisher. Washington, DC: Congressional
Quarterly.

Alexander, Herbert E. 1976. *Financing the 1972 Election.* Lexington, MA: Lexington
Books.

Alexander, Michelle. 2012. *The New Jim Crow: Mass Incarceration in the Age of
Colorblindness.* New York: New Press.

Alford, Robert R. 1962. *Party and Society: The Anglo-American Democracies.*
Chicago: Rand McNally.

Allitt, Patrick. 2009. *The Conservatives: Ideas and Personalities Throughout American History.* New Haven: Yale University Press.

Alvarez, R. Michael, and Lisa Garcia-Bedolla. 2003. "The Foundations of Latino
Voter Partisanship: Evidence from the 2000 Election." *Journal of Politics* 65(1):
31–49.

American Political Science Association. 1950. "Toward a More Responsible Two-
Party System: A Report of the Committee on Political Parties." *American Political Science Review* 44 (Supplement). https://www.apsanet.org/~pop/apsa
_report.htm.

Ammerman, Nancy. 1997. *Congregation and Community.* New Brunswick, NJ: Rutgers University Press.

Andersen, Kristi. 1976. "Generation, Partisan Shift, and Realignment: A Glance Back
at the New Deal." In *The Changing American Voter,* ed. Norman H. Nie, Sydney
Verba, and John R. Petrocik. Cambridge: Harvard University Press.

———. 1979. *The Creation of the Democratic Majority, 1928–1936.* Chicago: University of Chicago Press.

Anderson, Perry. 2013. "Homeland." *New Left Review* 81 (2nd series) (May–June):
5–34.

Ansolabehere, Stephen, John M. de Figueiredo, and James M. Snyder Jr. 2003. "Why
Is There So Little Money in U.S. Politics?" *Journal of Economic Perspectives*
17(1): 105–130.

Ansolabehere, Stephen, Jonathan Rodden, and James M. Snyder Jr. 2006. "Purple
America." *Journal of Economic Perspectives* 20(2): 97–118.

Archer, J. Clark, Fred M. Shelly, Fiona M. Davidson, and Stanley D. Brunn. 1996.
The Political Geography of the United States. New York: Guilford.

Archer, J. Clark, Fred M. Shelly, Peter J. Taylor, and Ellen R. White. 1988. "The
Geography of U.S. Presidential Elections." *Scientific American* 259: 44–51.

Aronowitz, Stanley. 1973. *False Promises: The Shaping of American Working Class
Consciousness.* New York: McGraw-Hill.

Atkeson, Lonna Rae. 2003. "Not All Cues Are Created Equal: The Conditional
Impact of Female Candidates on Political Engagement." *Journal of Politics*
65(4) (November): 1040–1061.

Atkeson, Lonna Rae, and Nancy Carrillo. 2007. "More Is Better: The Influence of
Collective Female Descriptive Representation on External Efficacy." *Politics
and Gender* 3(1) (March): 79–103.

Bafumi, Joseph, and Michael C. Herron. 2010. "Leapfrog Representation and Extremism: A Study of American Voters and Their Members in Congress." *American
Political Science Review* 104 (August): 519–542.

Bafumi, Joseph, and Robert Y. Shapiro. 2009. "A New Partisan Voter." *Journal of
Politics* 71 (January): 1–24.

Bai, Matt. 2012. "The Game Is Called Chicken." *New York Times Magazine*, April 1.

Bailey, Michael, Lee Sigelman, and Clyde Wilcox. 2003. "Presidential Persuasion on Social Issues: A Two-Way Street?" *Political Research Quarterly* 56: 49–58.

Baker, Kelly J. 2011. *Gospel According to the Klan: The KKK's Appeal to Protestant America, 1915–1930*. Lawrence: University Press of Kansas.

Baldassari, Delia, and Peter Bearman. 2007. "Dynamics of Political Polarization." *American Sociological Review* 72: 784–811.

Baldassari, Delia, and Andrew Gelman. 2008. "Partisans Without Constraint: Political Polarization and American Public Opinion." *American Journal of Sociology* 114: 408–446.

Balz, Dan. 2013. *Collision 2012: Obama vs. Romney and the Future of Elections in America*. New York: Viking.

Banaszak, Lee Ann. 2010. *The Women's Movement Inside and Outside the State*. Cambridge: Cambridge University Press.

Barker, David C. 2002. *Rushed to Judgment*. New York: Columbia University Press.

Barnard, Ellsworth. 1966. *Wendell Willkie: Fighter for Freedom*. Marquette: Northern Michigan University Press.

Barnes, Robert, and Steven Mufson. 2013. "Court Says Obama Exceeded Authority in Making Appointments." January 25. http://www.washingtonpost.com/politics /court-says-obama-exceeded-authority-in-making-appointments/2013 /01/25/b7e1b692-6713-11e2-9e1b-07db1d2ccd5b_story.html.

Barofsky, Neil. 2012. *Bailout: How Washington Abandoned Main Street While Rescuing Wall Street*. New York: Free Press.

Barone, Michael, and Chuck McCutcheon. 2013. *The Almanac of American Politics 2014*. Chicago: University of Chicago Press.

Barreto, Matt A. 2007. "*Sí Se Puede!* Latino Candidates and the Mobilization of Latino Voters." *American Political Science Review* 101(3): 425–441.

———. 2010. *Ethnic Cues: The Role of Shared Ethnicity in Latino Political Participation*. Ann Arbor: University of Michigan Press.

Barreto, Matt A., and Gary M. Segura. 2012. "ImpreMedia/Latino Decisions: 2012 Latino Election Eve Poll." Seattle: Latino Decisions.

Barreto, Matt A., Gary M. Segura, and Nathan D. Woods. 2004. "The Mobilizing Effect of Majority Minority Districts on Latino Turnout." *American Political Science Review* 98: 65–75.

Barreto, Matt A., Mario Villarreal, and Nathan D. Woods. 2005. "Metropolitan Latino Political Behavior: Voter Turnout and Candidate Preference in Los Angeles." *Journal of Urban Affairs* 27(1): 71–91.

Bartels, Larry M. 1998. "Electoral Continuity and Change, 1868–1996." *Electoral Studies* 17(3): 301–326.

———. 2000. "Partisanship and Voting Behavior, 1952–1996." *American Journal of Political Science* 44(1): 35–50.

———. 2008. *Unequal Democracy*. Princeton: Princeton University Press.

———. 2010. "Base Appeal: The Political Attitudes and Priorities of Core Partisans." Paper presented at the annual meeting of the American Political Science Association, Washington, DC.

Baumgartner, Frank R., Jeffrey M. Berry, Marie Hojnacki, David C. Kimball, and Beth L. Leech. 2009. *Lobbying and Policy Change: Who Wins, Who Loses, and Why*. Chicago: University of Chicago Press.

Beard, Renée L., and John B. Williamson. 2011. "Symbolic Politics, Social Policy, and the Senior Rights Movement." *Journal of Aging Studies* 25(1): 22–33.

Beatty, Jack. 2007. *Age of Betrayal: The Triumph of Money in America.* New York: Knopf.

Bedard, Paul. 2011. "New DNC Boss Calls GOP 'Anti-Women.'" May 26. http://www.usnews.com/news/blogs/washington-whispers/2011/05/26/new-dnc-boss-calls-gop-anti-women.

Bedlington, Anne H., and Michael J. Malbin. 2003. "The Party as an Extended Network: Members Giving to Each Other and to Their Parties." In *Life After Reform: When the Bipartisan Campaign Reform Act Meets Politics,* ed. Michael J. Malbin. Lanham: Rowman and Littlefield.

Béland, Daniel. 2005. *Social Security: History and Politics: From the New Deal to the Privatization Debate.* Lawrence: University Press of Kansas.

Bell, Daniel. 1960. *The End of Ideology: On the Exhaustion of Political Ideas in the Fifties.* New York: Free Press.

Berelson, Bernard, Paul F. Lazarsfeld, and William N. McPhee. 1954. *Voting: A Study of Opinion Formation in a Presidential Campaign.* Chicago: University of Chicago Press.

Berghahn, V. R. 1993. *Germany and the Approach of War in 1914.* 2nd ed. New York: St. Martin's.

Berlin, Ira. 2010. *The Making of African America: The Four Great Migrations.* New York: Penguin.

Binder, Sarah H. 2003. *Stalemate: Causes and Consequences of Legislative Gridlock.* Washington, DC: Congressional Quarterly.

Bingham, Amy. 2012. "'Etch A Sketch' Latest Gaffe from Romney Campaign." March 21. http://abcnews.go.com/Politics/OTUS/etch-sketch-latest-gaffe-romney-campaign/story?id=15973099.

Binstock, Robert H. 1972. "Interest-Group Liberalism and the Politics of Aging." *Gerontologist* 12(1): 265–280.

———. 1983. "The Aged as Scapegoat." *Gerontologist* 23(1): 136–143.

———. 2009. "Older Voters and the 2008 Election." *Gerontologist* 49(5): 697–701.

———. 2010. "From Compassionate Ageism to Intergenerational Conflict?" *Gerontologist* 50(5): 574–585.

———. 2012. "Older Voters and the 2010 U.S. Election: Implications for 2012 and Beyond?" *Gerontologist* 52(3): 408–417.

Binstock, Robert H., and Andrea Louise Campbell. 2011. "Politics and Aging in the United States." In *Handbook of Aging and the Social Sciences,* 7th ed., ed. Robert H. Binstock and Linda K. George. New York: Elsevier.

Black, Earl, and Merle Black. 1992. *The Vital South: How Presidents Are Elected.* Cambridge: Harvard University Press.

———. 2002. *The Rise of Southern Republicans.* Cambridge: Harvard University Press.

Blackmon, Douglas A. 2008. *Slavery by Another Name: The Re-Enslavement of Black Americans: From the Civil War to World War II.* New York: Anchor.

Blendon, Robert J., Drew E. Altman, Claudia Deane, John M. Benson, Mollyann Brodie, and Tami Buhr. 2008. "Health Care in the 2008 Presidential Primaries." *New England Journal of Medicine* 358 (January): 414–422.

Blendon, Robert J., and John M. Benson. 2010. "Public Opinion at the Time of the Vote on Health Care Reform." *New England Journal of Medicine* 362 (April): e55.

Blendon, Robert J., John M. Benson, Gillian K. Steel Fisher, and John M. Connolly. 2010. "Americans' Conflicting Views About the Public Health System, and How to Shore Up Support." *Health Affairs* 29(11): 2033–2040.

Blumenthal, David, and James A. Morone. 2010. *The Heart of Power: Health and Politics in the Oval Office.* Berkeley: University of California Press.

Bobo, Lawrence D. 2011. "Commentary: As American as Barack Obama." In *The Obamas and a (Post) Racial America,* ed. Gregory S. Parks and Matthew W. Hughey. New York: Oxford University Press.

Bolton, Alexander. 2013. "Liberals Irate as Senate Passes Watered-Down Filibuster Reform." January 24. http://thehill.com/homenews/senate/279237.

Bonk, Kathy. 1988. "The Selling of the 'Gender Gap': The Role of Organized Feminism." In *The Politics of the Gender Gap: The Social Construction of Political Influence,* ed. Carol Mueller. Newbury Park, CA: Sage.

Bowler, S., S. P. Nicholson, and G. M. Segura. 2006. "Earthquakes and After Shocks: Race, Direct Democracy, and Partisan Change." *American Journal of Political Science* 50: 146–159.

Branch, Taylor. 1989. *Parting the Waters: America in the King Years—Part I, 1954–63.* New York: Simon and Schuster.

Brewer, Paul R. 2003. "The Shifting Foundations of Public Opinion About Gay Rights." *Journal of Politics* 65: 1208–1220.

———. 2008. *Value War: Public Opinion and the Politics of Gay Rights.* Lanham: Rowman and Littlefield Publishers.

Brewer, Paul R., and Clyde Wilcox. 2005. "Trends: Same-Sex Marriage and Civil Unions." *Public Opinion Quarterly* 69: 599–616.

Brinkley, Alan. 1993. *The Unfinished Nation: A Concise History of the American People.* New York: Knopf.

Brock, David. 2004. *The Republican Noise Machine: Right-Wing Media and How It Corrupts Democracy.* New York: Crown.

Broder, David. 1978. "Introduction." In *Emerging Coalitions in American Politics,* ed. Seymour Martin Lipset. San Francisco: Institute for Contemporary Studies.

Brodie, Mollyann, Drew Altman, Claudia Deane, Sasha Buscho, and Elizabeth Hamel. 2010. "Liking the Pieces, Not the Package: Contradictions in Public Opinion During Health Reform." *Health Affairs* 29(6): 1125–1130.

Brookhiser, Richard. 2009. *Right Time, Right Place: Coming of Age with William F. Buckley and the Conservative Movement.* New York: Basic.

Brownstein, Ronald. 2007. *The Second Civil War: How Extreme Partisanship Has Paralyzed Washington and Polarized America.* New York: Penguin.

———. 2011. "Pulling Apart." *National Journal* 43(9) (February): 18–43.

Buckley, William F., Jr. 2012 (1951). *God and Man at Yale.* New York: Regnery Gateway.

Bullock, Charles S., III, and Ronald Keith Gaddie. 2009. *The Triumph of Voting Rights in the South.* Norman: University of Oklahoma Press.

Bureau of Labor Statistics, US Department of Labor. 2013. "Economic News Release: Union Members Summary." January 23. http://www.bls.gov/news .release/union2.nr0.htm.

Burke, Edmund. 2006 (1790). *Reflections on the Revolution in France.* Mineola, NY: Dover.

Burkhauser, Richard V., Jeff Larrimore, and Kosali I. Simon. 2011. "A 'Second Opinion' on the Economic Health of the American Middle Class." Working Paper no. 17164. Cambridge, MA: National Bureau of Economic Research, June.

Burner, David. 1968. *The Politics of Provincialism: The Democratic Party in Transition, 1918–1932.* New York: Knopf.

Burnham, Walter Dean. 1970. *Critical Elections and the Mainsprings of American Politics.* New York: Norton.

———. 1971. "A Political Scientist and Voting-Rights Litigation." *Washington University Law Quarterly* 2: 335–358.

————. 1972. "Political Immunization and Political Confessionalism: The United States and Weimar Germany." *Journal of Interdisciplinary History* 3: 1–30.

————. 1981. "The System of 1896: An Analysis." In *The Evolution of American Electoral Systems*, ed. Paul Kleppner et al. Westport: Greenwood.

————. 1984. "The Appearance and Disappearance of the American Voter." In *The Political Economy*, ed. Thomas Ferguson and Joel Rogers. Armonk, NY: Sharpe.

————. 1986. "Those High American 19th-Century Turnouts: Fact or Fiction?" *Journal of Interdisciplinary History* 16: 613–644.

————. 1991. "Critical Realignment: Dead or Alive?" In *The End of Realignment? Interpreting American Electoral Eras*, ed. Byron E. Shafer. Madison: University of Wisconsin Press.

————. 1996. "Realignment Lives: The 1994 Earthquake and Its Implications." In *The Clinton Presidency: First Appraisals*, ed. Colin Campbell and Bert A. Rockman. Chatham, NJ: Chatham House.

————. 2010a. "American Democracy in Peril: The American Turnout Problem and the Path to Plutocracy." New York: Roosevelt Institute.

————. 2010b. *Voting in American Elections: The Shaping of the American Political Universe Since 1788*. Palo Alto, CA: Academica.

Burns, Jennifer. 2009. *Goddess of the Market: Ayn Rand and the American Right*. New York: Oxford University Press.

Burrell, Barbara. 2010. "Political Parties and Women's Organizations: Bringing Women into the Electoral Arena." In *Gender and Elections: Shaping the Future of American Politics*, 2nd ed., ed. Susan J. Carroll and Richard L. Fox. New York: Cambridge University Press.

Burrell, Barbara, and Brian Frederick. 2007. "Political Windows of Opportunity: Recruitment Pools, Gender Politics, and Congressional Open Seats." Paper presented at the annual meeting of the Southern Political Association, New Orleans.

Bystrom, Dianne, Mary Christine Banwart, Lynda Lee Kaid, and Terry A. Robertson. 2004. *Gender and Candidate Communication: VideoStyle, WebStyle, NewsStyle*. New York: Routledge.

Cain, Bruce E., D. Roderick Kiewit, and Carole J. Uhlaner. 1991. "The Acquisition of Partisanship by Latinos and Asian Americans." *American Journal of Political Science* 35(2): 390–422.

"Campaign Issues: VI." 1964. *New York Times*, October 30.

Campbell, Andrea Louise. 2003. *How Policies Make Citizens: Senior Political Activism and the American Welfare State*. Princeton: Princeton University Press.

————. 2009. "Is the Economic Crisis Driving Wedges Between Young and Old? Rich and Poor?" *Generations* 33(3): 47–53.

Campbell, Andrea Louise, and Ryan King. 2010. "Social Security: Political Resilience in the Face of Conservative Strides." In *The New Politics of Old Age Policy*, 2nd ed., ed. Robert B. Hudson. Baltimore: Johns Hopkins University Press.

Campbell, Andrea Louise, and Julia Lynch. 2000. "Whose 'Gray Power'? Elderly Voters, Elderly Lobbies, and Welfare Reform in Italy and the United States." *Italian Politics and Society* 45 (Summer): 11–39.

Campbell, Angus, Philip E. Converse, Warren F. Miller, and Donald E. Stokes. 1960. *The American Voter*. New York: Wiley and Sons.

Campbell, Angus, Philip Converse, Warren Miller, Donald Stokes, and the National Election Studies. 1999. *American National Election Studies, 1956–1960*. Panel study. Ann Arbor: University of Michigan, Center for Political Studies.

Campbell, Angus, Gerald Gurin, and Warren E. Miller. 1954. *The Voter Decides.* Evanston, IL: Row, Peterson.

Campbell, David E., and J. Quin Monson. 2008. "The Religion Card: Gay Marriage and the 2004 Presidential Election." *Public Opinion Quarterly* 72: 399–419.

Campbell, James E. 2006. "Party Systems and Realignments in the United States." *Social Science History* 30: 359–386.

Carpenter, Daniel P. 2001. *The Forging of Bureaucratic Autonomy.* Princeton: Princeton University Press.

Carroll, Susan J., and Richard L. Fox. 2009. *Gender and Elections: Shaping the Future of American Politics.* 2nd ed. Cambridge: Cambridge University Press.

Cash, W. J. 1991 (1941). *The Mind of the South.* New York: Vintage.

Cassidy, John. 2014. "Piketty's Inequality Story in Six Charts." March 26. http://www.newyorker.com/online/blogs/johncassidy/2014/03/piketty-looks-at-inequality-in-six-charts.html.

Ceaser, James W., and Andrew E. Busch. 2001. *The Perfect Tie: The True Story of the 2000 Presidential Election.* Lanham: Rowman and Littlefield.

Centers, Richard. 1949. *The Psychology of Social Classes.* Princeton: Princeton University Press.

Chaddock, Gail Russell. 2010. "Nancy Pelosi Puts Her Stamp on the House." July 13. http://www.csmonitor.com/USA/Politics/2010/0713/Nancy-Pelosi-puts-her-stamp-on-the-House.

Cho, Wendy K. T. 1999. "Naturalization, Socialization, Participation: Immigrants and (Non-)Voting." *Journal of Politics* 61(4): 1140–1155.

Clark, John A., and Charles L. Prysby, eds. 2004. *Southern Political Party Activists: Patterns of Conflict and Change, 1991–2001.* Lexington: University Press of Kentucky.

Clark, Thomas D. 1968. *The Emerging South.* 2nd ed. London: Oxford University Press.

Clubb, Jerome M., William H. Flanigan, and Nancy H. Zingale. 1990. *Partisan Realignment: Voters, Parties, and Government in American History.* Boulder: Westview.

Clymer, Adam. 1980. "Displeasure with Carter Turned Many to Reagan." *New York Times,* November 9.

Coburn, Tom. 2011. "Why Is the Senate Stalling on the Debt Debate?" May 18. http://www.coburn.senate.gov/public/index.cfm/editorialsopinions?ContentRecord_id=e8717bcb-ffd5-4c37-827e-c3b5dbb14d97.

Cogan, Marin. 2011. "GOP Freshmen Women Go On the Offense." June 11. http://www.politico.com/news/stories/0611/57384_Page2.html.

Cole, David. 2011. "Is Health Care Unconstitutional?" *New York Review of Books,* February 24. http://www.nybooks.com/articles/archives/2011/feb/24/health-care-reform-unconstitutional.

Congressional Quarterly. 1999. "Influential Since the 1940s, the Conservative Coalition Limps into History in 1998." In *Congressional Quarterly Almanac 1998.* Washington, DC.

———. 2009. *Presidential Elections, 1789–2008.* Washington, DC.

Conlon, Richard P. 1986. "The Declining Role of Individual Contributions in Financing Congressional Campaigns." *Journal of Law and Politics* 3: 467–498.

Conradt, David P. 1983. "Political Ideologies and Belief Systems." In *Comparative Politics,* ed. Dan Jacobs, David P. Conradt, B. Guy Peters, and William Safran. Chatham, NJ: Chatham House.

Continetti, Matthew. 2006. *The K Street Gang: The Rise and Fall of the Republican Machine.* New York: Doubleday.

Converse, Philip E. 1964. "The Nature of Belief Systems in Mass Publics." In *Ideology and Discontent,* ed. David E. Apter. New York: Free Press.

Cook, Fay Lomax, and Edith J. Barrett. 1992. *Support for the American Welfare State: The Views of Congress and the Public.* New York: Columbia University Press.

Cook, Rhodes. 1996. "Dole's Job: To Convince His Own Party." In *Congressional Quarterly Guide to the 1996 Republican National Convention.* Washington, DC: Congressional Quarterly, August 3.

Cornwall, John. 1994. *Economic Breakdown and Recovery: Theory and Policy.* Armonk, NY: Sharpe.

Cottrol, Robert J., Raymond T. Diamond, and Leland B. Ware. 2003. *Brown v. Board of Education: Caste, Culture, and the Constitution.* Lawrence: University Press of Kansas.

Craig, Stephen C., Michael D. Martinez, James G. Kane, and Jason Gainous. 2005. "Core Values, Value Conflict, and Citizens' Ambivalence About Gay Rights." *Political Research Quarterly* 58: 5–17.

Crotty, William. 1978. *Decision for the Democrats.* Baltimore: Johns Hopkins University Press.

———. 1983. *Party Reform.* New York: Longman.

———, ed. 2012. *The Obama Presidency: Promise and Performance.* Lanham: Lexington Books.

———, ed. 2013. *Winning the Presidency 2012.* Boulder: Paradigm.

Currinder, Marian. 2009. *Money in the House: Campaign Funds and Congressional Party Politics.* Philadelphia: Perseus.

Dahl, Robert A. 1956. *A Preface to Democratic Theory.* Chicago: University of Chicago Press.

———, ed. 1967. *Political Oppositions in Western Democracies.* New Haven: Yale University Press.

Dasgupta, Nilanjana, and Kumar Yogeeswaran. 2011. "Obama-Nation? Implicit Beliefs About American Nationality and the Possibility of Redefining Who Counts as 'Truly' American." In *The Obamas and a (Post) Racial America,* ed. Gregory S. Parks and Matthew W. Hughey. New York: Oxford University Press.

Davidson, Chandler. 1994. "The Recent Evolution of Voting Rights Law Affecting Racial and Language Minorities." In *Quiet Revolution in the South: The Impact of the Voting Rights Act, 1965–1990,* ed. Chandler Davidson and Bernard Grofman. Princeton: Princeton University Press.

Davidson, Chandler, and Bernard Grofman, eds. 1994. *Quiet Revolution in the South: The Impact of the Voting Rights Act, 1965–1990.* Princeton: Princeton University Press.

Davis, Mike. 2013. "Last White Election?" *New Left Review* 79 (2nd series) (January–February): 55–54.

Dawson, Michael C. 1994. *Behind the Mule: Race and Class in African-American Politics.* Princeton: Princeton University Press.

Day, Christine L. 1990. *What Older Americans Think: Interest Groups and Aging Policy.* Princeton: Princeton University Press.

———. 1993. "Older Americans' Attitudes Toward the Medicare Catastrophic Coverage Act of 1988." *Journal of Politics* 55(1): 167–177.

———. 1998. "Old Age Interest Groups in the 1990s: Coalitions, Competition, and Strategy." In *New Directions in Old-Age Policies,* ed. Janie S. Steckenrider and Tonya M. Parrott. Albany: State University of New York Press.

Der Landeswahlleiter. 1995. *Election to the 13th German Bundestag in Berlin on 13 October 1994.* Final (Official) Result. Berlin: Statistisches Landesamt.

DeSipio, Louis. 1996. "Making Citizens or Good Citizens? Naturalization as a Predictor of Organizational and Electoral Behavior Among Latino Immigrants." *Hispanic Journal of Behavioral Sciences* 18(2): 194–213.

DeVries, Walter, and V. Lance Terrance. 1972. *The Ticket-Splitter: A New Force in American Politics.* Grand Rapids, MI: Eerdmans.

DiMaggio, Paul, John Evans, and Bethany Bryson. 1996. "Have Americans' Social Attitudes Become More Polarized?" *American Journal of Sociology* 102: 690–755.

Dionne, E. J. 2010. "Tuesday's Tutorial: A GOP Too Far Right." August 26. http://www.washingtonpost.com/wp-dyn/content/article/2010/08/25/AR201008 2504997.html.

Dodson, Debra. 2006. *The Impact of Women in Congress.* New York: Oxford University Press.

Downs, Anthony. 1957. *An Economic Theory of Democracy.* New York: Harper and Row.

Du Bois, W. E. B. 1962. *Black Reconstruction in America.* New York: Free Press.

Dube, Arindrajit. 2009. "The Value of (Not Having) the Public Plan." July 31. http://baselinescenario.com/2009/07/31/the-value-of-not-having-the-public-plan.

Duverger, Maurice. 1954. *Political Parties: Their Organization and Activities in the Modern State.* New York: Wiley.

Dyck, Alexander, David Moss, and Luigi Zingales. 2008. "Media vs. Special Interests." Cambridge, MA: National Bureau of Economic Research.

Egan, Patrick J., Murray S. Edelman, and Kenneth Sherrill. 2008. "Findings from the Hunter College Poll of Lesbians, Gays, and Bisexuals: New Discoveries About Identity, Political Attitudes, and Civic Engagement." New York: Hunter College. http://www.hrc.org/documents/Hunter_College_Report.pdf.

Egan, Patrick J., and Kenneth Sherrill. 2005. "Marriage and the Shifting Priorities of a New Generation of Lesbians and Gays." *PS: Political Science and Politics* 38: 229–232.

Eggers, Andrew, and Jens Hainmueller. 2011. "Political Capital: The (Mostly) Mediocre Performance of Congressional Stock Portfolios, 2004–2008." June 15. http://andy.egge.rs/papers/Eggmueller_PoliticalInvesting.pdf.

Eisenbrey, Ross, and Colin Gordon. 2012. "As Unions Decline, Inequality Rises." June 6. http://www.epi.org/publication/unions-decline-inequality-rises.

Elder, Laurel. 2008. "Whither Republican Women: The Growing Partisan Gap Among Women in Congress." *The Forum: A Journal of Applied Research in Contemporary Politics* 6(1): art. 13. http://www.bepress.com/forum/vol6/iss1/art13.

Elliot, Jonathan, ed. 1888. *Debates on the Adoption of the Federal Constitution.* 2nd ed. Research and Source Series no. 109. New York: Burt Franklin.

Entman, Robert M., and Andrew Rojecki. 2000. *The Black Image in the White Mind: Media and Race in America.* Chicago: University of Chicago Press.

Epstein, Edwin M. 1979. "The Emergence of Political Action Committees." In *Political Finance,* ed. Herbert E. Alexander. Electoral Studies Handbook no. 5. Beverly Hills: Sage.

Epstein, Lee, Andrew D. Martin, Kevin M. Quinn, and Jeffrey A. Segal. 2007. "Ideological Drift Among Supreme Court Justices: Who, When, and How Important?" *Northwestern University Law Review* 101: 1483–1542.

Epstein, Leon. 1967. *Political Parties in Western Democracies.* New York: Praeger.

Estes, Carroll L. 1979. *The Aging Enterprise.* San Francisco: Jossey-Bass.

Estes, Carroll L., Leah Rogne, Brian R. Grossman, Brooke A. Hollister, and Erica Solway. 2009. "Epilogue: From the Audacity of Hope to the Audacity of Action." In *Social Insurance and Social Justice: Social Security, Medicare, and the Campaign Against Entitlements,* ed. Leah Rogne, Carroll L. Estes, Brian R. Grossman, Brooke A. Hollister, and Erica Solway. New York: Springer.

Evans, Jocelyn Jones. 2005. *Women, Partisanship, and the Congress.* New York: Palgrave Macmillan.

Evans, John H. 2003. "Have Americans' Attitudes Become More Polarized? An Update." *Social Science Quarterly* 84: 71–90.

Evans, William McKee. 2009. *Open Wound: The Long View of Race in America.* Urbana: University of Illinois Press.

Fairlie, Henry. 1988. "Talkin' 'Bout My Generation." *The New Republic,* March 28.

Falter, Jurgen. 1991. *Hiders Wahler.* Munich: Bock.

Ferguson, Thomas. 1995a. "Deduced and Abandoned: Rational Expectations, the Investment Theory of Political Parties, and the Myth of the Median Voter." In *Golden Rule: The Investment Theory of Party Competition and the Logic of Money-Driven Political Systems,* ed. Thomas Ferguson. Chicago: University of Chicago Press.

———. 1995b. *Golden Rule: The Investment Theory of Party Competition and the Logic of Money-Driven Political Systems.* Chicago: University of Chicago Press.

———. 1995c. "Party Realignment and American Industrial Structure: The Investment Theory of Political Parties in Historical Perspective." In *Golden Rule: The Investment Theory of Party Competition and the Logic of Money-Driven Political Systems.* Chicago: University of Chicago Press.

———. 2001. "Blowing Smoke: Impeachment, the Clinton Presidency, and the Political Economy." In *The State of Democracy in America,* ed. William Crotty. Washington, DC: Georgetown University Press.

———. 2005. "Holy Owned Subsidiary: Globalization, Religion, and Politics in the 2004 Election." In *A Defining Moment: The Presidential Race of 2004,* ed. William Crotty. Armonk, NY: Sharpe. Extended version available at http://utip .gov.utexas.edu/papers/utip_32.pdf.

Ferguson, Thomas, and Jie Chen. 2005. "Investor Blocs and Party Realignments in American History." *Journal of the Historical Society* 5: 503–546.

Ferguson, Thomas, and Robert Johnson. 2009a. "Too Big to Bail: The 'Paulson Put,' Presidential Politics, and the Global Financial Meltdown." Pt. 1, "From Shadow Banking System to Shadow Bailout." *International Journal of Political Economy* 38(1): 3–34.

———. 2009b. "Too Big to Bail: The 'Paulson Put,' Presidential Politics, and the Global Financial Meltdown." Pt. 2, "Fatal Reversal: Single Payer and Back." *International Journal of Political Economy* 38(2): 5–45.

———. 2010a. "Another God That Failed: Free Market Fundamentalism and the Lehman Bankruptcy." *The Economists' Voice* 7(1): 1–7.

———. 2010b. "When Wolves Cry 'Wolf': Systemic Financial Crisis and the Myth of the Danaid Jar." Paper presented at the inaugural conference of the Institute for New Economic Thinking, King's College, Cambridge. http://ineteconomics .org/sites/inet.civicactions.net/files/INET%20C@K%20Paper%20Session %208%20-%20Ferguson%20%28Rob%20Johnson%29_0.pdf.

———. 2010c. "A World Upside Down? Deficit Fantasies in the Great Depression." New York: Roosevelt Institute. http://www.newdeal20.org/wp-content/uploads /2010/12/a-world-upside-down.

Ferguson, Thomas, Paul Jorgensen, and Jie Chen. 2013. "Party Competition and Industrial Structure in the 2012 Election." *International Journal of Political Economy* 42(2): 3–41.

Ferguson, Thomas, and Joel Rogers. 1981. "The Reagan Victory: Corporate Coalitions in the 1980 Campaign." In *The Hidden Election: Politics and Economics in the 1980 Presidential Campaign,* ed. Thomas Ferguson and Joel Rogers. New York: Pantheon.

———. 1986. *Right Turn: The Decline of the Democrats and the Future of American Politics.* New York: Hill and Wang.

Ferguson, Thomas, and Hans-Joachim Voth. 2008. "Betting on Hitler: The Value of Political Connections in Nazi Germany." *Quarterly Journal of Economics* 123(1): 101–137.

Fiorina, Morris P. 1981. *Retrospective Voting in American National Elections.* New Haven: Yale University Press.

Fiorina, Morris P., and Samuel J. Abrams. 2008. "Political Polarization in the American Public." *American Political Science Review* 11: 563–589.

———. 2009. *Disconnect: The Breakdown of Representation in American Politics.* Norman: University of Oklahoma Press.

Fiorina, Morris P., Samuel J. Abrams, and Jeremy C. Pope. 2008. "Polarization in the American Public: Misconceptions and Misreadings." *Journal of Politics* 70(2): 556–560.

———. 2011. *Culture War? The Myth of a Polarized America.* 3rd ed. New York: Pearson Longman.

Fiorina, Morris P., and Matthew Levendusky. 2006. "Disconnected: The Political Class Versus the People—Rejoinder." In *Red and Blue Nation?* vol. 1, *Characteristics and Causes of America's Polarized Politics,* ed. P. S. Nivola and D. W. Brady. Washington, DC: Brookings Institution.

Fireside, Harvey. 2004. *Separate and Unequal: Homer Plessy and the Supreme Court Decision That Legalized Racism.* New York: Carroll and Graf.

Foley, Elizabeth Price. 2012. *The Tea Party: Three Principles.* Cambridge: Cambridge University Press.

Foner, Eric. 1988. *Reconstruction: America's Unfinished Revolution, 1863–1877.* New York: HarperCollins.

———. 1990. *A Short History of Reconstruction.* New York: Harper Perennial.

———. 1998. *The Story of American Freedom.* New York: Norton.

———. 2005. *Forever Free: The Story of Emancipation and Reconstruction.* New York: Vintage.

Forcey, Charles. 1961. *The Crossroads of Liberalism: Croly, Weyl, Lippmann, and the Progressive Era, 1900–1925.* New York: Oxford University Press.

Formisano, Ronald F. 1983. *The Transformation of Political Culture: Massachusetts Parties, 1790s–1840s.* New York: Oxford University Press.

———. 2012. *The Tea Party: A Brief History.* Baltimore: Johns Hopkins University Press.

Fowler, Robert Booth, Allen D. Hertzke, and Laura R. Olson. 2010. *Religion and Politics in America: Faith, Culture, and Strategic Choices.* 4th ed. Boulder: Westview.

Fox, Richard L. 2013. "The Gender Gap and the Election of 2012." In *Winning the Presidency 2012,* ed. William Crotty. Boulder: Paradigm.

Fox, Richard L., and Jennifer L. Lawless. 2010. "If Only They'd Ask: Gender, Recruitment, and Political Ambition." *Journal of Politics* 72(2) (April): 310–326.

Fraga, Luis Ricardo, John A. Garcia, Rodney E. Hero, Michael Jones-Correa, Valerie Martinez-Ebers, and Gary M. Segura. 2010. *Latino Lives in America: Making It Home.* Philadelphia: Temple University Press.

———. 2012. *Latinos in the New Millennium: An Almanac of Opinion, Behavior, and Policy Preferences.* New York: Cambridge University Press.

Fraga, Luis Ricardo, and Ricardo Ramirez. 2003. "Latino Political Incorporation in California, 1990–2000." In *Latinos and Public Policy in California: An Agenda for Opportunity,* ed. David Lopez and Andres Jimenez. Berkeley: Berkeley Public Policy Press, Institute of Governmental Studies, University of California.

———. 2004. "Demography and Political Influence: Disentangling the Latino Vote." *Harvard Journal of Hispanic Policy* 16: 69–96.

Franklin, John Hope. 1967. *From Slavery to Freedom: A History of Negro Americans.* 3rd ed. New York: Knopf.

———. 1994. *Reconstruction After the Civil War.* 2nd ed. Chicago. University of Chicago Press.

Frankovic, Kathleen. 1982. "Sex and Politics: New Alignments, Old Issues." *PS: Political Science and Politics* 15: 439–448.

Frederick, Brian. 2009. "Are Female House Members Still More Liberal in a Polarized Era? The Conditional Nature of the Relationship Between Descriptive and Substantive Representation." *Congress and the Presidency* 36: 181–202.

———. 2011. "Gender Turnover and Roll Call Voting in the US Senate." *Journal of Women, Politics, and Policy* 32: 193–210.

Frederickson, George M. 2002. *Racism: A Short History.* Princeton: Princeton University Press.

Freeman, Jo. 1987. "Who You Know Versus Who You Represent: Feminist Influence in the Democratic and Republican Parties." In *The Women's Movements of the United States and Western Europe: Feminist Consciousness, Political Opportunity, and Public Policy,* ed. Mary Katzenstein and Carol Mueller. Philadelphia: Temple University Press.

———. 1996. "Whatever Happened to Republican Feminists?" http://www.jo freeman.com/polhistory/repubfem.htm.

Friedman, Milton. 1962. *Capitalism and Freedom.* Chicago: University of Chicago Press.

Friedman, Thomas. 2000. *The Lexus and the Olive Tree.* New York: Anchor.

Frymer, Paul. 2010. *Uneasy Alliances: Race and Party Competition in America.* Princeton: Princeton University Press.

Fukuyama, Francis. 1992. *The End of History and the Last Man.* New York: Free Press.

Fullerton, Andrew S., and Jeffrey C. Dixon. 2011. "Generational Conflict or Methodological Artifact? Reconsidering the Relationship Between Age and Policy Attitudes in the U.S., 1984–2008." *Public Opinion Quarterly* 74(4): 643–673.

Fulton, Sarah A., Cherie D. Maestas, L. Sandy Maisel, and Walter J. Stone. 2006. "The Sense of a Woman: Gender, Ambition, and the Decision to Run for Congress." *Political Research Quarterly* 59(2) (June): 235–248.

Galbraith, John Kenneth. 1954. *The Great Crash, 1929.* Boston: Houghton Mifflin.

———. 1958. *The Affluent Society.* Boston: Houghton Mifflin.

———. 1967. *The New Industrial State.* Princeton: Princeton University Press.

———. 1987. *Economics in Perspective: A Critical History.* Boston: Houghton Mifflin.

Gallagher, John, and Chris Bull. 1996. *Perfect Enemies: The Religious Right, the Gay Movement, and the Politics of the 1990s.* New York: Crown Publishers.

Ganz, Marshall Louis. 1992. "Where Have All the Voters Gone? The Decline of Voting and the Disintegration of the New Deal Alignment: A Case Study of Five Boston Wards, 1960–1988." BA diss. Cambridge, MA, Harvard University.

Garcia, John A. 2010a. *Latino Politics in America: Community of Interests and Culture.* Boulder: Rowman and Littlefield.

————. 2010b. "Latinos and Political Behavior: Defining Community to Examine Critical Complexities." In *Oxford Handbook of American Elections and Political Behavior,* ed. Jan Leighley. Oxford: Oxford University Press.

Garcia, John A., and Gabriel Sanchez. 2004. "Electoral Politics." In *Latino Americans and Participation of Latinos,* ed. S. Navarro and Armando Mejia. Santa Barbara, CA: ABC-CLIO.

Garcia-Bedolla, Lisa, and Melissa R. Michelson. 2012. *Mobilizing Inclusion: Transforming the Electorate Through Get-Out-the-Vote Campaigns.* New Haven: Yale University Press.

Garrow, David J. 1986. *Bearing the Cross: Martin Luther King Jr. and the Southern Christian Leadership Conference.* New York: HarperCollins.

Gaskins, Keesha, and Sundeep Iyer. 2012. *The Challenge of Obtaining Voter Identification.* New York: Brennan Center for Justice, New York University School of Law.

Gelman, Andrew, Daniel Lee, and Yair Ghitza. 2010. "Public Opinion on Health Care Reform." *The Forum: A Journal of Applied Research in Contemporary Politics* 8(1): art. 8. http://www.bepress.com/forum/vol8/iss1/art8.

Gelman, Andrew, David Park, Boris Shor, and Jeronimo Cortina. 2010. *Red State, Blue State, Rich State, Poor State.* Princeton: Princeton University Press.

Gentzkow, Matthew, and Jesse M. Shapiro. 2010. "What Drives Media Slant? Evidence from Daily Newspapers." *Econometrica* 78(1): 35–71.

Gienapp, William E. 1986. *The Origins of the Republican Party, 1852–1856.* New York: Oxford University Press.

Gilens, Martin. 2011. "Inequality and Democratic Responsiveness." *Public Opinion Quarterly* 69(5): 778–796.

————. 2012. *Affluence and Influence: Economic Inequality and Political Power in America.* Princeton: Princeton University Press.

Gilens, Martin, and Benjamin I. Page. 2014. "Testing Theories of American Politics: Elites, Interest Groups, and Average Citizens." March 17. http://www.polisci.northwestern.edu/people/documents/TestingTheoriesOfAmericanPoliticsFINAL forProduction6March2014.pdf.

Gladwell, Malcolm. 2010. "Small Change: Why the Revolution Will Not Be Tweeted." *The New Yorker,* October 4.

Godwin, R. Kenneth. 1988. *The Direct Marketing of Politics: One Billion Dollars of Influence.* Chatham, NJ: Chatham House.

Goldwater, Barry. 2009 (1964). *Conscience of a Conservative.* Blacksburg, VA: Wilder.

Goodarz, Danaei, Eric L. Ding, Dariush Mozaffarian, Ben Taylor, Jurgen Rehm, Christopher Murray, and Majid Ezzati. 2009. "The Preventable Causes of Death in the United States: Comparative Risk Assessment of Dietary, Lifestyle, and Metabolic Risk Factors." *PLoS Medicine* 8(1): e1000058.

Gramsci, Antonio. 1971. *Selections from the Prison Notebooks.* Ed. and trans. Quintin Hoare and Geoffrey Nowell-Smith. London: Lawrence and Wishart.

Green, John C. 2007. *The Faith Factor: How Religion Influences American Elections.* Westport: Praeger.

Green, John C., and James L. Guth. 1993. "From Lambs to Sheep: Denominational Change and Political Behavior." In *Rediscovering the Religious Factor in American Politics,* ed. David C. Leege and Lyman A. Kellstedt. Armonk, NY: Sharpe.

Green, John C., Lyman A. Kellstedt, Corwin E. Smidt, and James L. Guth. 2007. "How the Faithful Voted: Religious Communities and the Presidential Vote." In *A Matter of Faith: Religion in the 2004 Presidential Election,* ed. David Campbell. Washington, DC: Brookings Institution.

Greenhouse, Steven. 2011. "Union Membership in U.S. Fell to a 70-Year Low Last Year." January 21. http://www.nytimes.com/2011/01/22/business/22union.html.

Grogan, Colleen M., and Christina M. Andrews. 2010. "The Politics of Aging Within Medicaid." In *The New Politics of Old Age Policy,* 2nd ed., ed. Robert B. Hudson. Baltimore: Johns Hopkins University Press.

Grossman, Ron. 2011. "Aging Voters Take Issue with Ryan Overhaul Plan." *Chicago Tribune,* June 7.

Guth, James L. 2009. "Religion and American Public Opinion: Foreign Policy Issues." In *The Oxford Handbook of Religion and American Politics,* ed. Corwin E. Smidt, Lyman A. Kellstedt, and James L. Guth. New York: Oxford University Press.

————. 2010. "Religion and American Attitudes on Foreign Policy, 2008: The Case of Militant Internationalism." Paper presented at the annual meeting of the American Political Science Association, Washington, DC.

Guth, James L., John C. Green, Lyman A. Kellstedt, and Corwin E. Smidt. 1999. "Faith and the Vote: The Role of Religion in Electoral Politics." Paper presented at the annual meeting of the American Political Science Association, Atlanta.

Guth, James L., John C. Green, Corwin E. Smidt, Lyman A. Kellstedt, and Margaret M. Poloma. 1997. *The Bully Pulpit: The Politics of Protestant Clergy.* Lawrence: University Press of Kansas.

Guth, James L., Lyman A. Kellstedt, Corwin E. Smidt, and John C. Green. 2005. "Religious Mobilization in the 2004 Presidential Election." Paper presented at the annual meeting of the American Political Science Association, Washington, DC.

————. 2006. "Religious Influences in the 2004 Presidential Election." *Presidential Studies Quarterly* 36: 223–242.

Hacker, Andrew. 2003. *Two Nations: Black and White, Separate, Hostile, Unequal.* New York: Scribner.

Hacker, Jacob S. 2006. *The Great Risk Shift: The Assault on American Jobs, Families, Health Care, and Retirement—and How You Can Fight Back.* New York: Oxford University Press.

Hacker, Jacob S., and Paul Pierson. 2006. *Off Center: The Republican Revolution and the Erosion of American Democracy.* 2nd ed. New Haven: Yale University Press.

————. 2010. *Winner-Take-All Politics: How Washington Made the Rich Richer—and Turned Its Back on the Middle Class.* New York: Simon and Schuster.

Haeberle, Steven H. 1999. "Gay and Lesbian Rights: Emerging Trends in Public Opinion and Voting Behavior." In *Gays and Lesbians in the Democratic Process,* ed. Ellen D. B. Riggle and Barry L. Tadlock. New York: Columbia University Press.

Hajnal, Zoltan, and Takeu Lee. 2003. "Beyond the Middle: Latinos and the Multiple Dimensions of Political Independents." Paper prepared for presentation at the conference "A Nation of Immigrants: Ethnic Identity and Political Incorporation," Berkeley, University of California.

Hall, Kermit L., ed. 2005. *The Oxford Companion to the Supreme Court of the United States.* 2nd ed. New York: Oxford University Press.

Hamilton, Alexander, James Madison, and John Jay. 2005. *The Federalist Papers.* Ed. J. R. Pole. Indianapolis: Hackett.

Han, Lori Cox. 2010. *Women and U.S. Politics: The Spectrum of Political Leadership.* 2nd ed. Boulder: Lynne Rienner.

Hare, Christopher, Nolan McCarty, Keith T. Poole, and Howard Rosenthal. 2012. "Polarization Is Real (and Asymmetric)." May 16. http://voteview.com/blog/?p=494.

Harris, Frederick C. 2012. *The Price of the Ticket: Barack Obama and the Rise and Decline of Black Politics*. Oxford: Oxford University Press.

Hartz, Louis. 1955. *The Liberal Tradition in America*. New York: Harcourt, Brace, and World.

Hasen, Richard L. 2010. "Money Grubbers: The Supreme Court Kills Campaign Finance Reform." January 21. http://www.slate.com/articles/news_and_politics /jurisprudence/2010/01/money_grubbers.html.

———. 2012. *The Voting Wars: From Florida 2000 to the Next Election Meltdown*. New Haven: Yale University Press.

Hawkesworth, Mary. 2003. "Congressional Enactments of Race-Gender: Toward a Theory of Race-Gendered Institutions." *American Political Science Review* 97(4): 529–550.

Hayek, F. A. 1960. *The Constitution of Liberty*. Chicago: University of Chicago Press.

———. 1997. *The Collected Works of F. A. Hayek*. Vol. 10, *Socialism and War*, ed. Bruce Caldwell. Chicago: University of Chicago Press.

———. 2007 (1944). *The Road to Serfdom*. Ed. Bruce Caldwell. Chicago: University of Chicago Press.

Heberlig, Eric, Marc Hetherington, and Bruce Larson. 2006. "The Price of Leadership: Campaign Money and the Polarization of Congressional Parties." *Journal of Politics* 68: 992–1005.

Hedges, Chris. 2010. *Death of the Liberal Class*. New York: Nation.

Heller, Anne C. 2009. *Ayn Rand and the World She Made*. New York: Anchor.

Hersh, Seymour M. 1983. *The Price of Power: Kissinger in the Nixon White House*. New York: Summit.

Hetherington, Marc J. 2009. "Putting Polarization in Perspective." *British Journal of Political Science* 39: 413–448.

Hill, Kevin A., Dario V. Moreno, and Lourdes Cue. 2001. "Racial and Partisan Voting in a Tri-Ethnic City." *Journal of Urban Affairs* 23: 291–307.

Hillygus, D. Sunshine, and Todd G. Shields. 2005. "Moral Issues and Voter Decision Making in the 2004 Presidential Election." *PS: Political Science and Politics* 38: 201–209.

Himelfarb, Richard. 1995. *Catastrophic Politics: The Rise and Fall of the Medicare Catastrophic Coverage Act of 1988*. University Park: Pennsylvania State University Press.

Hoffer, Williamjames Hull. 2012. *Plessy v. Ferguson: Race and Inequality in Jim Crow America*. Lawrence: University Press of Kansas.

Hofstadter, Richard. 1948. *The American Political Tradition*. New York: Knopf.

———. 2008 (1964). *The Paranoid Style in American Politics*. New York: Vintage.

Hollihan, Thomas A. 2009. *Uncivil Wars: Political Campaigns in a Media Age*. Boston: St. Martin's.

Holt, Michael F. 2008. *By One Vote: The Disputed Presidential Election of 1876*. Lawrence: University Press of Kansas.

Hout, Michael, and Claude Fischer. 2002. "Why Americans Have No Religious Preference." *American Sociological Review* 67: 165–190.

Hudson, Robert B. 1978. "The 'Graying' of the Federal Budget and Its Consequences for Old Age Policy." *Gerontologist* 18(4): 428–440.

———. 2007. "Old Age and 'The Great Risk Shift.'" *Public Policy and Aging Report* 17(2): 2.

———, ed. 2010. *The New Politics of Old Age Policy*. 2nd ed. Baltimore: Johns Hopkins University Press.

Hunter, James. 1991. *Culture Wars*. New York: Basic.

Iglehart, John K. 2004. "The New Medicare Prescription-Drug Benefit: A Pure Power Play." *New England Journal of Medicine* 350(8): 826–833.

Jackson, Robert H. 1941. *The Struggle for Judicial Supremacy.* New York: Knopf.

Jacobs, Dan N., David P. Conradt, B. Guy Peters, and William Safran. 1983. *Comparative Politics.* Chatham, NJ: Chatham House.

Jacobs, Lawrence, and Desmond King, eds. 2009. *The Unsustainable American State.* New York: Oxford University Press.

Jacobs, Lawrence R., and Theda Skocpol. 2010. *Health Care Reform and American Politics.* New York: Oxford University Press.

Jacobson, Gary C. 1990. *The Electoral Origins of Divided Government: Competition in U.S. House Elections, 1946–1988.* Boulder: Westview.

———. 2006. "Comment: Disconnected or Joined at the Hip?" In *Red and Blue Nation?* vol. 1, ed. Pietro S. Nivola and David W. Brady. Washington, DC: Brookings Institution.

———. 2007. *A Divider, Not a Uniter: George W. Bush and the American People.* New York: Pearson Longman.

———. 2013. "How the Economy and Partisanship Shaped the 2012 Presidential and Congressional Elections." *Political Science Quarterly* 128(1) (Spring): 1–38.

Jacoby, William G. 2002. "Liberal-Conservative Thinking in the American Electorate." In *Research in Micropolitics: Political Decision Making, Participation, and Deliberation,* vol. 6, ed. Michael X. Delli Carpini, Leonie Huddy, and Robert Y. Shapiro. Greenwich, CT: JAI.

———. 2010. "Citizen Perceptions of Candidate Ideology in the 2008 Election." Paper presented at the annual meeting of the American Political Science Association, Washington, DC.

Jamieson, Kathleen Hall. 2009. *Electing the President 2008: The Insiders' View.* Philadelphia: University of Pennsylvania Press.

Jensen, Lene. 2008. "Immigrants' Cultural Identities as a Source of Civic Engagement." *Applied Development Science* 12(2): 74–83.

Jensen, Richard. 1971. *The Winning of the Midwest: Social and Political Conflict, 1888–1896.* Chicago: University of Chicago Press.

———. 1978. "Party Coalitions and the Search for Modern Values." In *Emerging Coalitions in American Politics,* ed. Seymour Martin Lipset. San Francisco: Institute for Contemporary Studies.

Jesse, Stephen. 2010. "Voter Ideology and Candidate Positioning in the 2008 Presidential Election." *American Politics Research* 38(2) (March): 195–210.

Johnson, Simon, and James Kwak. 2010. *13 Bankers: The Wall Street Takeover and the Next Financial Meltdown.* New York: Pantheon.

Jones-Correa, Michael. 1998. *Between Two Nations: The Political Predicament of Latinos in New York City.* Ithaca: Cornell University Press.

Judis, John B., and Ruy Teixeira. 2002. *The Emerging Democratic Majority.* New York: Scribner.

Kahneman, Daniel, and Amos Tversky. 1979. "Prospect Theory: An Analysis of Decision Under Risk." *Econometrica* 47(2): 263–292.

Kane, Paul. 2013. "Senate's Pragmatic Ranks Depleted by One with Chambliss's Departure." January 26. *Washington Post.* http://www.washingtonpost.com /politics/senates-pragmatic-ranks-depleted-by-one-with-chamblisss-departure /2013/01/26/932e97d0-6712-11e2-9e1b-07db1d2ccd5b_story.html.

Kaplan, Esther. 2005. *With God on Their Side: George W. Bush and the Christian Right.* New York: New Press.

Karpf, David. 2008. "Understanding Blogspace." *Journal of Information Technology and Politics* 5: 369–385.

———. 2010. "Macaca Moments Reconsidered: Electoral Panopticon or Netroots Mobilization?" *Journal of Information Technology and Politics* 7: 143–162.

Katznelson, Ira. 1976. *Black Men, White Cities: Race, Politics, and Migration in the United States, 1900–30, and Britain, 1948–1968.* Chicago: University of Chicago Press.

Kaufmann, Karen, John R. Petrocik, and Daron R. Shaw. 2008. *Unconventional Wisdom: Facts and Myths About American Voters.* New York: Oxford University Press.

Kelley, Stanley, Jr. 1960. *Political Campaigning: Problems in Creating an Informed Electorate.* Washington, DC: Brookings Institution.

Kellstedt, Lyman A., Corwin E. Smidt, John C. Green, and James L. Guth. 2007. "Faith Transformed: Religion and American Politics from FDR to G.W. Bush." In *Religion and American Politics,* 2nd ed., ed. Mark Noll and Luke Harlow. New York: Oxford University Press.

Kellstedt, Lyman A., and James L. Guth. 2011. "Religious Groups as a Force in Party Politics." Paper presented at the annual meeting of the American Political Science Association, Seattle.

Kennedy, Dan. 2008. "Political Blogs: Teaching Us Lessons About Community." http://nieman.harvard.edu/reportsitem.aspx?id=100022.

Kenski, Kate, Bruce W. Hardy, and Kathleen Hall Jamieson. 2010. *The Obama Victory: How Media, Money, and Message Shaped the 2008 Election.* New York: Oxford University Press.

Key, V. O., Jr. 1949. *Southern Politics in State and Nation.* Knoxville: University of Tennessee Press.

———. 1955. "A Theory of Critical Elections." *Journal of Politics* 17: 3–18.

———. 1956. *American State Politics: An Introduction.* New York: Knopf.

———. 1959. "Secular Realignment and the Party System." *Journal of Politics* 23: 198–210.

———. 1966. *The Responsible Electorate.* Cambridge: Harvard University Press.

Keynes, John Maynard. 1920. *The Economic Consequences of the Peace.* New York: Harcourt, Brace, and Howe.

Kinder, Donald R., and Lynn M. Sanders. 1996. *Divided by Color: Racial Politics and Democratic Ideals.* Chicago: University of Chicago Press.

King, David C., and Richard E. Matland. 2003. "Sex and the Grand Old Party: An Experimental Investigation of the Effect of Candidate Sex on Support for a Republican Candidate." *American Politics Research* 31(6): 595–612.

Kirk, Russell. 1953. *The Conservative Mind: From Burke to Eliot.* Washington, DC: Regnery.

Kirkpatrick, Evron M. 1971. "Toward a Responsible Two Party System: Political Science, Policy Science, or Pseudo Science?" *American Political Science Review* 65: 965–990.

Kirkpatrick, Jeane. 2004. "Neoconservatism as a Response to the Counter-Culture." In *The Neocon Reader,* ed. Irwin Stelzer. New York: Grove.

Kirshner, Jonathan. 2011. "Business as Usual." January–February. http://new.boston review.net/BR36.1/kirshner.php.

Klein, Ezra. 2009a. "After Health Care, We Need Senate Reform." December 28. http://www.washingtonpost.com/wp-dyn/content/discussion/2009/12/24 /DI2009122402454.html.

———. 2009b. "Winning Ugly, but Winning." December 24. http://voices.washington
post.com/ezra-klein/2009/12/winning_ugly_but_winning.html.

———. 2011. "Wonkbook: Filibuster Reform Dead." January 28. http://voices
.washingtonpost.com/ezra-klein/2011/01/wonkbook_filibuster_reform_dea.html.

Kleppner, Paul. 1970. *The Cross of Culture: A Social Analysis of Midwestern Politics, 1850–1900.* New York: Free Press.

———. 1979. *The Third Electoral System, 1853–1892.* Chapel Hill: University of North Carolina Press.

———. 1987. *Continuity and Change in Electoral Politics, 1893–1928.* Westport: Greenwood.

Kloppenberg, James T. 2011. "Liberalism." In *The Concise Princeton Encyclopedia of American Political History,* ed. Michael Kazin, Rebecca Edwards, and Adam Rothman. Princeton: Princeton University Press.

Koger, Gregory. 2010. *Filibustering: A Political History of Obstruction in the House and Senate.* Chicago: University of Chicago Press.

Kohut, Andrew, John C. Green, Scott Keeter, and Robert Toth. 2000. *The Diminishing Divide: Religion's Changing Role in American Politics.* Washington, DC: Brookings Institution.

Kopczuk, Wojciech, Emmanuel Saez, and Jae Song. 2007. "Uncovering the American Dream: Inequality and Mobility in Social Security Earnings Data Since 1937." Working Paper no. 13345. Cambridge, MA: National Bureau of Economic Research, August.

———. 2009. "Earnings Inequality and Mobility in the United States: Evidence from Social Security Data Since 1937." March 18. http://emlab.berkeley.edu/~saez/kopczuk-saez-songQJE09SSA.pdf.

Kornblut, Anne E. 2010. "O'Donnell's Primary Victory Is a Win for . . . the White House? Primaries Push More Women into General Elections, but Most Fresh Faces Now Belong to Republican Party." September 15. http://www.washington post.com/wp-dyn/content/article/2010/09/15/AR2010091503925.html.

Kotlikoff, Lawrence. 1992. *Generational Accounting: Knowing Who Pays, and When, for What We Spend.* New York: Free Press.

Kotlikoff, Lawrence J., and Scott Burns. 2005. *The Coming Generational Storm: What You Need to Know About America's Economic Future.* Cambridge: Massachusetts Institute of Technology Press.

Kousser, J. Morgan. 1974. *The Shaping of Southern Politics, 1890–1910.* New Haven: Yale University Press.

Kramer, Mark, and Michael S. Levy. 1972. *The Ethnic Factor: The Minorities Decide Elections.* New York: Simon and Schuster.

Kranish, Michael. 1994. "The House That Gingrich's PAC Rebuilt." *Seattle Times,* November 23.

Kristol, Irving. 2004. "The Neoconservative Persuasion: What It Was, and What It Is." In *The Neocon Reader,* ed. Irwin Stelzer. New York: Grove.

———. 2011. *The Neoconservative Persuasion.* New York: Basic.

Krugman, Paul. 2003. *The Great Unraveling: Losing Our Way in the New Century.* New York: Norton.

———. 2007. *The Conscience of a Liberal.* New York: Norton.

———. 2013a. "The Crazy Party." *New York Times,* September 20.

———. 2013b. *End This Depression Now.* New York: Norton.

La Raja, Raymond J. 2008. *Small Change: Money, Political Parties, and Campaign Finance Reform.* Ann Arbor: University of Michigan Press.

Ladd, Everett Carll. 1978. "Shifting Party Coalitions, 1932–1976." In *Emerging Coalitions in American Politics,* ed. Seymour Martin Lipset. San Francisco: Institute for Contemporary Studies.

———. 1981. "The Brittle Mandate: Electoral Dealignment and the Presidential Election of 1980." *Political Science Quarterly* 96: 1–25.

———. 1991. "Like Waiting for Godot: The Uselessness of 'Realignment' for Understanding Change in Contemporary American Politics." In *The End of Realignment? Interpreting American Electoral Eras,* ed. Byron E. Shafer. Madison: University of Wisconsin Press.

Ladd, Everett Carll, with Charles Hadley. 1978. *Transformations in the American Party System: Political Coalitions from the New Deal to the 1970s.* New York: Norton.

Lane, Kristin A., and John T. Jost. 2011. "Black Man in the White House: Ideology and Implicit Racial Bias in the Age of Obama." In *The Obamas and a (Post) Racial America,* ed. Gregory S. Parks and Matthew W. Hughey. New York: Oxford University Press.

Lane, Robert E. 1962. *Political Ideology: Why the American Common Man Believes What He Does.* New York: Free Press.

Lau, Richard J., and Gerald M. Pomper. 2004. *Negative Campaigning.* Lanham: Rowman and Littlefield.

Lau, Richard J., Lee Sigelman, and Ivy Brown Rover. 2007. "The Effects of Negative Political Campaigns: A Meta-Analytic Reassessment." *Journal of Politics* 69(4) (November): 1176–1209.

Lawless, Jennifer. 2004. "Politics of Presence? Congresswomen and Symbolic Representation." *Political Research Quarterly* 57(1): 81–99.

Lawrence, David G. 1997. *The Collapse of the Democratic Presidential Majority: Realignment, Dealignment, and Electoral Change from Franklin Roosevelt to Bill Clinton.* Boulder: Westview.

Lawrence, Eric, John Sides, and Henry Farrell. 2010. "Self-Segregation or Deliberation? Blog Readership, Participation, and Polarization in American Politics." *Perspectives on Politics* 8(1): 141–157.

Layman, Geoffrey. 1997. "Religion and Political Behavior in the United States: The Impact of Beliefs, Affiliation, and Commitment from 1980 to 1994." *Public Opinion Quarterly* 61: 288–316.

———. 2001. *The Great Divide: Religious and Cultural Conflict in American Party Politics.* New York: Columbia University Press.

Layman, Geoffrey, and John C. Green. 2005. "Wars and Rumors of Wars: The Contexts of Cultural Conflict in American Political Behavior." *British Journal of Political Science* 36: 61–89.

Lazarsfeld, Paul, Bernard Berelson, and Hazel Gaudet. 1944. *The People's Choice.* New York: Columbia University Press.

Leal, David. 2002. "Political Participation by Latino Non-Citizens in the United States." *British Journal of Political Science* 32(2): 353–370.

Leege, David C., Kenneth D. Wald, Brian S. Krueger, and Paul D. Mueller. 2002. *The Politics of Cultural Differences: Social Change and Voter Mobilization Strategies in the Post–New Deal Period.* Princeton: Princeton University Press.

Leighley, Jan E., and A. Velditz. 1999. "Race, Ethnicity, and Political Participation: Competing Models and Contrasting Explanations." *Journal of Politics* 61, 1092–1114.

Leip, David. 2009. *Dave Leip's Atlas of U.S. Presidential Elections.* http://www.us electionsatlas.org.

Lenhart, Amanda, and Susannah Fox. 2006. "Bloggers." July 19. http://pewinternet .org/Reports/2006/Bloggers.aspx.

Lerner, Max, ed. 1943. *The Mind and Faith of Justice Holmes.* Boston: Little, Brown.

Leuchtenberg, William E. 2005. *The White House Looks South: Franklin D. Roosevelt, Harry S. Truman, Lyndon B. Johnson.* Baton Rouge: Louisiana State University Press.

Levendusky, Matthew. 2009. *The Partisan Sort: How Liberals Became Democrats and Conservatives Became Republicans.* Chicago: University of Chicago Press.

Levendusky, Matthew, and Jeremy Pope. 2011. "Red States vs. Blue States: Going Beyond the Mean." *Public Opinion Quarterly* 75: 227–248.

Lewis, Gregory B. 2005. "Same-Sex Marriage and the 2004 Presidential Election." *PS: Political Science and Politics* 38: 195–199.

Lewis, Gregory B., and Marc A. Rogers. 1999. "Does the Public Support Equal Employment Rights for Gays and Lesbians?" In *Gays and Lesbians in the Democratic Process,* ed. Ellen D. B. Riggle and Barry L. Tadlock. New York: Columbia University Press.

Lichtblau, Eric. 2011. "AARP Is Open to Cuts for Social Security Benefits." June 17. http://www.nytimes.com/2011/06/18/us/18aarp.html.

Lightman, David. 2010. "Senate 'Holds': Where Just One Senator Makes A Majority." February 19. http://www.mcclatchydc.com/2010/02/19/86529/senate -custom-of-holds-puts-brakes.html.

Lincoln, Abraham. 1861. "First Inaugural Address." March 4. http://bartleby.com/124 /pres31.html.

Lind, Michael. 1996. *The New American Nation: The New Nationalism and the Fourth American Revolution.* New York: Free Press Paperbacks.

Liptak, Adam. 2012. "In Congress's Paralysis, a Mightier Supreme Court." *New York Times,* August 21.

Longman, Phillip. 1985. "Justice Between Generations." *Atlantic Monthly,* June.

———. 1987. *Born to Pay: The New Politics of Aging in America.* Boston: Houghton Mifflin.

Lopez, Mark Hugo, and Paul Taylor. 2012. "Latino Voters in the 2012 Election." Washington, DC: Pew Hispanic Center.

Lowrey, Annie. 2012. "French Duo See (Well) Past Tax Rise for Richest." *New York Times,* April 17.

———. 2013. "The Low Politics of Low Growth." *New York Times,* January 13.

Lubell, Samuel. 1952. *The Future of American Politics.* New York: Harper.

Lublin, David. 1997. *The Paradox of Representation: Racial Gerrymandering and Minority Interests in Congress.* Princeton: Princeton University Press.

———. 2004. *The Republican South: Democratization and Partisan Change.* Princeton: Princeton University Press.

Lucas, DeWayne L., and Iva E. Deutchman. 2010. "Electoral Challenges of Moderate Factions: Main Streeters and Blue Dogs, 1994–2008." *The Forum: A Journal of Applied Research in Contemporary Politics* 8(2).

Lynch, Frederick R. 2011. *One Nation Under AARP: The Fight over Medicare, Social Security, and America's Future.* Berkeley: University of California Press.

Lynch, Julia. 2006. *Age in the Welfare State.* Cambridge: Cambridge University Press.

MacColl, Spencer. 2011. "Citizens United Decision Profoundly Affects Political Landscape." May 5. http://www.opensecrets.org/news/2011/05/citizens-united -decision-profoundly-affects-political-landscape.html.

Macedo, Stephen, et al. 2005. *Democracy at Risk: How Political Choices Undermine Citizen Participation and What We Can Do About It*. Washington, DC: Brookings Institution.

Mackenzie, G. Calvin, and Robert Weisbrot. 2008. *The Liberal Hour: Washington and the Politics of Change in the 1960s*. New York: Penguin.

MacManus, Susan A. 1996. *Young v. Old: Generational Combat in the 21st Century*. Boulder: Westview.

Maltz, Earl M. 2007. *Dred Scott and the Politics of Slavery*. Lawrence: University Press of Kansas.

Mandle, Jay R. 1992. *Not Slave, Not Free: The African-American Economic Experience Since the Civil War*. Durham, NC: Duke University Press.

Mann, James. 2004. *Rise of the Vulcans: The History of Bush's War Cabinet*. New York: Viking.

Mann, Robert. 2007. *When Freedom Would Triumph: The Civil Rights Struggle in Congress, 1954–1968*. Baton Rouge: Louisiana State University Press.

Mann, Thomas. 2010. "The Negative Impact of Filibusters and Holds." Testimony to the US Senate Committee on Rules and Administration. June 23. http://www.brookings.edu/testimony/2010/0623 filibuster_mann.aspx.

Mann, Thomas, and Norman J. Ornstein. 2012. *It's Even Worse Than It Looks: How the American Constitutional System Collided with the New Politics of Extremism*. New York: Basic.

Mansbridge, Jane. 1999. "Should Blacks Represent Blacks and Women Represent Women? A Contingent 'Yes.'" *Journal of Politics* 61(3) (August): 628–657.

Manuel, Paul Christopher, and Anne Marie Cammisa. 1999. *Checks and Balances? How a Parliamentary System Could Change American Politics*. Boulder: Westview.

Manza, Jeff, and Clem Brooks. 1999. *Social Cleavages and Political Change: Voter Alignments and U.S. Party Coalitions*. New York: Oxford University Press.

Manzano, Sylvia, and Gabriel R. Sanchez. 2009. "Take One for the Team? Limits of Shared Ethnicity and Candidate Preferences." *Political Research Quarterly* 63(5): 568–580.

Marcus, George E., John L. Sullivan, Elizabeth Theiss-Morse, and Sandra L. Wood. *With Malice Toward Some: How People Make Civil Liberties Judgments*. Cambridge: Cambridge University Press.

Marcus, Ruth. 2010. "Fallin Plays the 'Mommy Card.'" October 28. http://www.tulsaworld.com/opinion/fallin-plays-the-mommy-card/article_c961c9fb-c716-5cd8-8c89-5d39fc79d480.html.

Markus, Gregory B., and Philip E. Converse. 1979. "A Dynamic Simultaneous Equation Model of Electoral Choice." *American Political Science Review* 73(4): 1055–1070.

Marmor, Theodore. 2000. *The Politics of Medicare*. New York: Aldine de Gruyter.

Martin, Andrew D., and Kevin M. Quinn. 2007. "Assessing Preference Change on the U.S. Supreme Court." *Journal of Law, Economics, and Organization* 23(2): 365–385.

Mason, Alpheus T., and Donald G. Stephenson Jr. 1999. *American Constitutional Law*. 12th ed. Upper Saddle River, NJ: Prentice Hall, 1999.

Matthews, Christopher. 1991. "Parenthood." *The New Republic,* May 20.

Matthews, Donald. 1959. "The Folkways of the United States Senate." *American Political Science Review* 53 (December): 1065–1073.

Matthews, Donald, and James W. Prothro. 1966. *Negroes and the New Southern Politics*. Chapel Hill: University of North Carolina Press.

Matthews, Dylan. 2010. "The Intent of Both Proposals Is to Make the Senate More Like the Senate." July 7. http://voices.washingtonpost.com/ezra-klein/2010/07/the_intent_of_both_proposals_i.html.

Mayer, William G. 1996. *The Divided Democrats: Ideological Unity, Party Reform, and Presidential Elections.* Boulder: Westview.

Mayhew, David. 1974. *Congress: The Electoral Connection.* New Haven: Yale University Press.

———. 2002. *Electoral Realignments: A Critique of an American Genre.* New Haven: Yale University Press.

———. 2010. "Legislative Obstruction." Review essay in *Perspectives on Politics* 8(4) (December): 1145–1154.

Mazzocco, Dennis. 1994. *Networks of Power.* Boston: South End.

McCarty, Nolan, Keith T. Poole, and Howard Rosenthal. 2006. *Polarized America: The Dance of Ideology and Unequal Riches.* Cambridge: Massachusetts Institute of Technology Press.

———. 2013. *Political Bubbles: Financial Crises and the Failure of American Democracy.* Princeton: Princeton University Press.

McClosky, Herbert, Paul J. Hoffman, and Rosemary O'Hara. 1960. "Issue Conflict and Consensus Among Party Leaders and Followers." *American Political Science Review* 54 (June): 406–427.

McCormick, Richard L. 1974. "Ethnocultural Explanations of Nineteenth Century American Voting Behavior." *Political Science Quarterly* 89 (June): 351–377.

McGann, James G. 1995. *The Competition for Dollars, Scholars, and Influence in the Public Policy Research Industry.* Lanham: University Press of America.

McGerr, Michael E. 1986. *The Decline of Popular Politics: The American North, 1865–1928.* New York: Oxford University Press.

McInturff, William D., and Lori Weigel. 2008. "Déjà Vu All Over Again: The Similarities Between Political Debates Regarding Health Care in the Early 1990s and Today." *Health Affairs* 27(3): 699–704.

McKee, Scott. 2010. *Republican Ascendancy in Southern U.S. House Elections.* Boulder: Westview.

McKitrick, Eric L. 1960. *Andrew Johnson and Reconstruction.* Chicago: University of Chicago Press.

McKuen, Michael B., Robert S. Erikson, and James A. Stimson. 1989. "Macropartisanship." *American Political Science Review* 73(4): 1125–1142.

McPherson, James M., and James Hogue. 1982. *Ordeal by Fire: The Civil War and Reconstruction.* New York: McGraw-Hill.

Meckler, Mark, and Jenny Beth Martin. 2012. *Tea Party Patriots: The Second American Revolution.* New York: Holt.

Michelson, Melissa. 2005. "Does Ethnicity Trump Party? Competing Voting Cues and Latino Political Behavior." *Journal of Political Marketing* 4: 1–25.

Micklethwait, John, and Adrian Wooldridge. 2004. *The Right Nation: Conservative Power in America.* New York: Penguin.

Milbank, Dana. 2010a. "Abolish the Party Committees." November 24. http://www.washingtonpost.com/wp-dyn/content/article/2010/11/23/AR2010112304217.html.

———. 2010b. "Byrd's Own Memorial Is Caught in the Senate Tangle." *Washington Post,* July 4.

Milkis, Sidney M. 1993. *The President and the Parties: The Transformation of the American Party System Since the New Deal.* New York: Oxford University Press.

Milkis, Sidney M., and Jerome M. Mileur, eds. 2005. *The Great Society and the High Tide of Liberalism.* Amherst: University of Massachusetts Press.

Miller, Marilyn. 2010. "Sutton, Supporters Turn Up Heat on GOP's 'Kitchen' Jab." *Akron Beacon Journal,* July 26.

Miller, Sean. J. 2010. "Handel Tells Deal to Put the 'Big-Boy Pants' on." August 2. http://thehill.com/blogs/ballot-box/governor-races/112111-handel-tells-deal-to -put-the-big-boy-pants-on

Miller, Warren E. 1991. "Party Identification, Realignment, and Party Voting: Back to the Basics." *American Political Science Review* 85(2): 557–568.

Miller Center. 2012. "Executive Privilege: Mapping an Extraordinary Power." Charlottesville: University of Virginia.

Montgomery, Lori. 2013. "House, Senate Negotiators Reach Budget Deal." *Washington Post,* December 10. http://www.washingtonpost.com/business/economy /house-senate-negotiators-reach-budget-deal/2013/12/10/e7ee1aaa-61eb-11e3 -94ad-004fefa61ee6_story.html.

Montgomery, Lori, and Rosalind S. Helderman. 2013. "House Votes to Suspend Debt Limit." *Washington Post,* January 23.

Moon, Marilyn. 2007. "Risky Medicare: Vouchers, Private Plans, and Defined Contributions." *Public Policy and Aging Report* 17(2): 13–15.

Morgan, Kimberly J., and Andrea Louise Campbell. 2011. *The Delegated Welfare State: Medicare, Markets, and the Governance of Social Policy.* New York: Oxford University Press.

Morone, James A. 2003. *Hellfire Nation: The Politics of Sin in American History.* New Haven: Yale University Press.

Morris, Charles R. 1996. *The AARP: America's Most Powerful Lobby and the Clash of Generations.* New York: Crown.

Mourdock, Richard. 2012. "Bipartisanship Ought to Be Democrats Siding with the GOP." May 9. http://www.huffingtonpost.com/2012/05/09/richard-mourdock -bipartisanship-indiana-senate_n_1502718.html.

Mutz, Diane C., and Byron Reeves. 2005. "The New Videomalaise: Effects of Televised Incivility on Political Trust." *American Political Science Review* 99: 1–15.

Myrdal, Gunnar. 1944. *An American Dilemma: The Negro Problem and Modern Democracy.* New York: Harper and Brothers.

National Journal. 2012. "Special Report: 2012 Vote Ratings." http://www.national journal.com/2012-vote-ratings.

National Urban League. 2013. *Redeem the Dream: 2013 State of Black America.* Washington, DC.

Newby, Idus A. 1968. *Jim Crow's Defense: Anti-Negro Thought in America, 1900–1930.* Baton Rouge: Louisiana State University Press.

Newhouse, Joseph P. 2010. "Assessing Health Reform's Impact on Four Key Groups of Americans." *Health Affairs* 29(9): 1714–1724.

Newport, Frank. 2010. "More States 'Competitive' in Terms of Party Identification." http://www.gallup.com/poll/141548/States-Competitive-Terms-Party -Identification.aspx.

Nivoli, Pietro S., and David W. Brady, eds. 2006. *Red and Blue Nation.* Vol. 1. Washington, DC: Brookings Institution.

Norrander, Barbara. 1989. "Ideological Representativeness of Presidential Primary Voters." *American Journal of Political Science* 33(3): 570–587.

———. 2008. "The History of the Gender Gaps." In *Voting the Gender Gap,* ed. Lois Duke Whitaker. Urbana: University of Illinois Press.

Nunnally, Shayla C. 2012. *Trust in Black America: Race, Discrimination, and Politics.* New York: New York University Press.

Oakman, Tara Sussman, Robert J. Blendon, Andrea L. Campbell, Alan M. Azslavsky, and John M. Benson. 2010. "A Partisan Divide on the Uninsured." *Health Affairs* 29(4): 706–711.

Ohlemacher, Stephen. 2007. "Hispanics Swing to Dems but Maybe Not for Long: Voters Also Supported Republicans in November." Associated Press, January 12.

Olson, Laura R., Wendy Cadge, and James T. Harrison. 2006. "Religion and Public Opinion about Same-Sex Marriage." *Social Science Quarterly* 87: 340–360.

Ornstein, Norman. 2010. "A Filibuster Fix." August 28. http://www.nytimes.com /2010/08/28/opinion/28ornstein.html.

———. 2011. "Worst. Congress. Ever." July 19. http://www.foreignpolicy.com /articles/2011/07/19/worst_congress_ever.

Ornstein, Norman, Thomas E. Mann, and Michael J. Malbin. 2008. *Vital Statistics on Congress 2008.* Washington, DC: Brookings Institution.

Overton, Spencer. 2006. *Stealing Democracy: The New Politics of Voter Suppression.* New York: Norton.

Pace, Julie. 2011. "Obama Celebrates 50th Birthday at White House." August 4. http://news.yahoo.com/obama-celebrates-50th-birthday-white-house -070947197.html.

Page, Benjamin I., and Robert Y. Shapiro. 1992. *The Rational Public.* Chicago: University of Chicago Press.

Palmer, Barbara, and Dennis Simon. 2008. *Breaking the Political Glass Ceiling: Women and Congressional Elections.* 2nd ed. New York: Routledge.

Pampel, Fred C. 1994. "Population Aging, Class Context, and Age Inequality in Public Spending." *American Journal of Sociology* 100: 153–195.

Pantoja, Adrian D., and S. Gershon. 2006. "Political Orientations and Naturalization Among Latino and Latina Immigrants." *Social Science Quarterly* 87(1): 1171–1187.

Pantoja, Adrian D., Ricardo Ramirez, and Gary M. Segura. 2001. "Citizens by Choice, Voters by Necessity: Patterns in Political Mobilization by Naturalized Latinos." *Political Research Quarterly* 54(4): 729–750.

Parker, Frank R. 1990. *Black Votes Count: Political Empowerment in Mississippi After 1965.* Chapel Hill: University of North Carolina Press.

Parker, Richard. 2005. *John Kenneth Galbraith: His Life, His Politics, His Economics.* Chicago: University of Chicago Press.

Parks, Gregory S., and Mattew W. Hughey, eds. 2011. *The Obamas and a (Post) Racial America?* Oxford: Oxford University Press.

Parramore, Lynn. 2010. "Money and the Midterms: Are the Parties Over?" November 12. http://www.newdeal20.org/2010/11/12/money-and-the-midterms-are-the -parties-overinterview-with-thomas-ferguson-26869.

Patten, Eileen. 2010. "Statistical Portrait of the Foreign-Born Population in the United States." Report from American Community Survey. Washington, DC: US Bureau of the Census.

Paul, Arnold M. 1960. *Conservative Crisis and the Rule of Law: Attitudes of Bar and Bench.* Ithaca: Cornell University Press.

Paulson, Arthur. 1998. "The Political Economy of Postindustrial America." In *America in the Twenty-First Century: Challenges and Opportunities in Domestic Politics,* ed. Kul B. Rai, David F. Walsh, and Paul J. Best. Upper Saddle River, NJ: Prentice Hall.

————. 2000. *Realignment and Party Revival: Understanding American Electoral Politics at the Turn of the Twenty-First Century.* Westport: Praeger.

————. 2007. *Electoral Realignment and the Outlook for American Democracy.* Boston: Northeastern University Press.

————. 2009. "The Invisible Primary Becomes Visible: The Importance of the 2008 Presidential Nominations, Start to Finish." In *Winning the Presidency 2008,* ed. William Crotty. Boulder: Paradigm.

————. 2012. "Coalitional Divisions and Realignment Dynamics in the Obama Era." In *The Obama Presidency: Promise and Performance,* ed. William Crotty. Lanham: Lexington Books.

Peikoff, Leonard. 1991. *Objectivism: The Philosophy of Ayn Rand.* New York: Meridian.

Perman, Michael. 2009. *Pursuit of Unity: A Political History of the American South.* Chapel Hill: University of North Carolina Press.

————. 2012. *The Southern Political Tradition.* Baton Rouge: Louisiana State University Press.

Peterson, Peter G. 1999. *Gray Dawn: How the Coming Age Wave Will Transform America—and the World.* New York: Times Books.

Pew Hispanic Center. 2012. "Latino Voters in the 2012 Election." November 7. http://www.pewhispanic.org/2012/11/07/latino-voters-in-the-2012-election/#fn-16829-1.

Pew Research Center for the People and the Press. 2004. "Voters Liked Campaign 2004, but Too Much 'Mud-Slinging'; Moral Values: How Important?" November 11. http://www.people-press.org/2004/11/11/voters-liked-campaign-2004-but-too-much-mud-slinging.

————. 2010. "Voters Rate the Parties' Ideologies." July 16. http://www.people-press.org/2010/07/16/voters-rate-the-parties-ideologies.

————. 2011. "The Generation Gap and the 2012 Election: Angry Silents, Disengaged Millennials." November 3. http://www.people-press.org/2011/11/03/the-generation-gap-and-the-2012-election-3.

————. 2012a. "More Support for Gun Rights, Gay Marriage Than in 2008 or 2004." April 25. http://www.people-press.org/2012/04/25/more-support-for-gun-rights-gay-marriage-than-in-2008-or-2004.

————. 2012b. "Partisan Polarization Surges in Bush, Obama Years." June 4. http://www.people-press.org/2012/06/04/partisan-polarization-surges-in-bush-obama-years.

————. 2012c. "Public Remains Split on Health Care Bill, Opposed to Mandate." March 26. http://www.people-press.org/2012/03/26/public-remains-split-on-health-care-bill-opposed-to-mandate.

————. 2012d. "Young Voters Supported Obama Less, but May Have Mattered More." November 26. http://www.people-press.org/2012/11/26/young-voters-supported-obama-less-but-may-have-mattered-more.

Pew Research Religion and Public Life Project. 2008. "U.S. Religious Landscape Survey: Religious Beliefs and Practices, Diverse and Politically Relevant." June 23. http://www.pewforum.org/2008/06/23/us-religious-landscape-survey-resources.

Phillips, Anne. 1998. "Democracy and Representation, or Why Should It Matter Who Our Representatives Are?" In *Feminism and Politics,* ed. Anne Phillips. Oxford: Oxford University Press.

Piketty, Thomas. 2014. *Capital in the Twenty-First Century.* Trans. Arthur Goldhammer. Cambridge: Belknap.

Piketty, Thomas, and Emmanuel Saez. 2003. "Income Inequality in the United States, 1913–1998." *Quarterly Journal of Economics* 118(1): 1–39.

Piven, Frances Fox, and Richard A. Cloward. 1988. *Why Americans Don't Vote*. New York: Pantheon.

Plutzer, Eric, and Michael Berkman. 2005. "The Graying of America and Support for Funding the Nation's Schools." *Public Opinion Quarterly* 69(1): 66–86.

Pole, J. R., ed. 2005. *The Federalist Papers*. Indianapolis: Hackett.

Politico.com. 2010. "The Year of GOP Women." December 15. http://www.politico .com/news/stories/1210/46374.html.

Polivka, Larry, and Carroll L. Estes. 2009. "The Economic Meltdown and Old Age Politics." *Generations* 33(3): 56–62.

Pomper, Gerald M. 1972. "From Confusion to Clarity: Issues and American Voters, 1956–1968." *American Political Science Review* 66: 415–428.

———, ed. 1993. *The Election of 1992*. Chatham, NJ: Chatham House.

———. 1996. "Alive! The Political Parties After the 1980–1992 Presidential Elections." In *American Presidential Elections: Process, Policy, and Political Change,* ed. Harvey L. Schantz. Albany: State University of New York Press.

———. 1999. "Parliamentary Government in the United States." *The State of the Parties,* ed. John C. Green and David M. Shea. Lanham, MD: Rowman and Littlefield.

———, ed. 2001. *The Election of 2000: Reports and Interpretations*. New York: Chatham.

———. 2009. "The Presidential Election." In *The Elections of 2008,* ed. Michael Nelson. Washington, DC: Congressional Quarterly.

———. 2013. "Review of *It's Even Worse Than It Looks: How the American Constitutional System Collided with the New Politics of Extremism* by Thomas E. Mann and Norman J. Ornstein." *Political Science Quarterly* 128(1): 162–164.

Pomper, Gerald M., and Susan Lederman. 1980. *Elections in America: Control and Influence in Democratic Politics*. New York: Longman.

Pomper, Gerald M., and Marc D. Weiner, eds. 2003. *The Future of American Democratic Politics: Principles and Practices*. New Brunswick, NJ: Rutgers University Press.

Ponza, Michael, Greg J. Duncan, Mary Corcoran, and Fred Groskind. 1988. "The Guns of Autumn? Age Differences in Support for Income Transfers to the Young and Old." *Public Opinion Quarterly* 52: 441–466.

Poole, Keith T., and Howard Rosenthal. 2007. *Ideology and Congress*. New Brunswick, NJ: Transaction.

Powell, E. 2010. "Where Money Matters in Congress." Paper prepared for presentation at the University of North Carolina.

Pratt, Henry J. 1976. *The Gray Lobby*. Chicago: University of Chicago Press.

Preston, Samuel H. 1984. "Children and the Elderly in the United States." *Scientific American* 251: 44–49.

Putnam, Robert D., and David E. Campbell. 2010. *American Grace*. New York: Simon and Schuster.

Quadagno, Jill. 1988. *The Transformation of Old Age Security: Class and Politics in the American Welfare State*. Chicago: University of Chicago Press.

———. 1989. "Generational Equity and the Politics of the Welfare State." *Politics and Society* 17(3): 353–376.

Quattrone, George A., and Amos Tversky. 1988. "Contrasting Rational and Psychological Analyses of Political Choice." *American Political Science Review* 82: 719–736.

Rabinowitz, George, and Stuart Elaine MacDonald. 1986. "The Power of the States in U.S. Presidential Elections." *American Political Science Review* 80: 65–87.

Rable, George C. 2007. *But There Was No Peace*. Athens: University of Georgia Press.

Rae, Nicol C. 1989. *The Decline and Fall of the Liberal Republicans*. New York: Oxford University Press.

———. 1994. *Southern Democrats*. New York: Oxford University Press.

———. 1998. "Party Factionalism, 1946–1996." In *Partisan Approaches to Postwar American Politics,* ed. Byron E. Shafer. New York: Chatham.

Ramirez, Ricardo. 2002. *Getting Out the Vote: The Impact of Non-Partisan Voter Mobilization Efforts in Low Turnout Latino Precincts*. Unpublished manuscript. San Francisco: Public Policy Institute of California.

Rand, Ayn. 1943. *The Fountainhead*. New York: Penguin.

———. 1957. *Atlas Shrugged*. New York: Signet.

———. 1990. *The Voice of Reason: Essays in Objectivist Thought*. Ed. Leonard Peikoff. New York: Meridian.

Raspberry, William. 2004. "Reagan's Race Legacy." June 14. http://www.washington post.com/wp-dyn/articles/A39345-2004Jun13.html.

Reagan, Ronald. 1980. "States' Rights Speech." August 3. http://www.onlinemadison .com/ftp/reagan/reaganneshoba.mp3.

Reardon, Sean F., and Kendra Bischoff. 2011. "Growth in the Residential Segregation of Families by Income, 1970–2009." November. http://www.s4.brown.edu /us2010/Data/Report/report111111.pdf.

Reiter, Howard L., and Jeffrey M. Stonecash. 2010. *Counter-Realignment: Political Change in the Northeast*. Cambridge: Cambridge University Press.

Republican National Committee. 1994. *Contract with America: The Best Plan by Rep. Newt Gingrich, Rep. Dick Armey, and the House Republicans to Change the Nation*. New York: Times Books.

Reynolds, John F. 1988. *Testing Democracy: Electoral Behavior and Progressive Reform in New Jersey, 1880–1920*. Chapel Hill: University of North Carolina Press.

Rhodebeck, Laurie A. 1993. "The Politics of Greed? Political Preferences Among the Elderly." *Journal of Politics* 55(2): 342–364.

Rice, Thomas, Katherine Desmond, and Jon Gabel. 1990. "The Medicare Catastrophic Coverage Act: A Post-Mortem." *Health Affairs* 9(3): 75–87.

Rich, Andrew. 2004. *Think Tanks, Public Policy, and the Politics of Expertise*. Cambridge: Cambridge University Press.

Robinson, Eugene. 2010. *Disintegration: The Splintering of Black America*. New York: Author Books.

Rokkan, Stein. 1970. *Citizens, Elections, Parties*. Oslo: Univeritetsforlaget.

Roland, Charles P. 1976. *The Improbable Era: The South Since World War II*. Lexington: University Press of Kentucky.

Rosenblatt, Gideon. 2011. "Citizens United v. United Citizens: Building a Movement to Drive Money out of Politics." January 20. http://www.huffingtonpost.com /gideon-rosenblatt/citizens-united-v-united-_b_809262.html.

Rosenof, Theodore. 2003. *Realignment: The Theory That Changed the Way We Think About American Politics*. Lanham: Rowman and Littlefield.

Rotberg, Robert I., ed. 2001. *Politics and Political Change*. Cambridge: Massachusetts Institute of Technology Press.

Roth, Bennett. 2011. "AARP Is Next on GOP Target List." March 31. http://www .rollcall.com/issues/56_103/AARP-Is-Next-on-GOP-Target-List-204487-1 .html.

Rothstein, Edward. 2012. "Lincoln Museum, Act II: The Morning After the Death." *New York Times,* February 11.

Rusk, Jerrold G. 2001. *A Statistical History of the American Electorate.* Washington, DC: Congressional Quarterly.

Ryan, Paul D. 2013. "The Path to Prosperity." March 12. http://budget.house.gov /prosperity/.

Ryden, David K., ed. 2002. *The U.S. Supreme Court and the Electoral Process.* 2nd ed. Washington, DC: Georgetown University Press.

Sabato, Larry J., and Glenn R. Simpson. 1996. *Dirty Little Secrets: The Persistence of Corruption in American Politics.* New York: Random.

Saez, Emmanual. 2013a. "Comprehensive Tax Reform: Top Incomes and Top Tax Rates." Presentation at the Stanford Institute for Economic Policy Research (SIEPR) Tax Policy Conference, Stanford, CA.

———. 2013b. "Income Inequality: Evidence and Policy Implications." Arrow Lecture, Berkeley, January. http://elsa.berkeley.edu/users/saez/lecture_saez _arrow.pdf.

———. 2013c. "Striking It Richer: The Evolution of Top Incomes in the United States." *Pathways Magazine* (Winter 2008). http://eml.berkeley.edu/~saez/saez -UStopincomes-2011.pdf.

Safire, William. 2008. *Safire's Political Dictionary.* New York: Oxford University Press.

Saloma, John S., III. 1984. *Ominous Politics: The New Conservative Labyrinth.* New York: Hill and Wang.

Samuelson, Robert J. 1999. "Off Golden Pond." *National Review,* April 12.

———. 2011. "Why Are We in This Debt Fix? It's the Elderly, Stupid." July 28. http://www.washingtonpost.com/opinions/why-are-we-in-this-debt-fix-its-the -elderly-stupid.

Sanbonmatsu, Kira. 2002. *Democrats, Republicans, and the Politics of Women's Place.* Ann Arbor: University of Michigan Press.

Sanbonmatsu, Kira, and Kathleen Dolan. 2009. "Do Gender Stereotypes Transcend Party?" *Political Research Quarterly* 62(3): 485–494.

Sanjek, Roger. 2011. *Gray Panthers.* Philadelphia: University of Pennsylvania Press.

Sapiro, Virginia, and Steven J. Rosenstone. 2004. *American National Election Studies Cumulative Data File, 1948–2002.* 12th version (ICPSR 8475). Ann Arbor: University of Michigan, Center for Political Studies, November.

Sapiro, Virginia, and Shauna Shamas. 2010. "The Gender Basis of Public Opinion." In *Understanding Public Opinion,* 3rd ed., ed. Barbara Norrander and Clyde Wilcox. Washington, DC: Congressional Quarterly.

Sargent, Greg. 2010. "In Testy Exchange, Chuck Grassley Told Obama: No Deal!" November 16. http://voices.washingtonpost.com/plum-line/2010/11/in_testy _exchange_chuck_grassl.html.

Savage, Charlie. 2009. "Obama Looks to Limit Impact of Tactic Bush Used to Side-step New Laws." March 9. http://www.nytimes.com/2009/03/10/us/politics /10signing.html?_r=0.

Scammon, Richard, and Ben Wattenberg. 1970. *The Real Majority.* New York: Howard-McCann.

Schaffner, Brian, and Nenad Senic. 2006. "Rights or Benefits? Explaining the Sexual Identity Gap in American Political Behavior." *Political Research Quarterly* 59(1): 123–132.

Schantz, Harvey L. 1996. "Sectionalism in Presidential Elections." In *American Presidential Elections: Process, Policy, and Political Change,* ed. Harvey L. Schantz. Albany: State University of New York Press.

Schattschneider, E. E. 1942. *Party Government.* New York: Rinehart.

———. 1960. *The Semisovereign People.* New York: Holt, Rinehart, and Winston.

Scher, Richard K. 1997. *Politics in the New South: Republicanism, Race, and Leadership.* Armonk, NY: Sharpe.

Schlozman, Kay Lehman, and Sydney Verba. 1979. *Injury to Insult: Unemployment, Class, and Political Response.* Cambridge: Harvard University Press.

Schneider, William. 1978. "Democrats and Republicans, Liberals and Conservatives." In *Emerging Coalitions in American Politics,* ed. Seymour Martin Lipset. San Francisco: Institute for Contemporary Studies.

Schouten, Fredreka. 2010. "Campaign Spending by Groups Gone Wild: Amount Double That of the 2006 Midterm Elections." *USA Today,* October 15.

Schulz, James H., and Robert H. Binstock. 2006. *Aging Nation: The Economics and Politics of Growing Older in America.* Baltimore: Johns Hopkins University Press.

Schuman, Howard, Charlotte Steeh, Laurence Bobo, and Maria Krysan. 1997. *Racial Attitudes in America: Trends and Interpretations.* Rev. ed. Cambridge: Harvard University Press.

Schwartz, Nelson D., and Eric Dash. 2011. "Amid Criticism on Downgrade, A&P Fires Back." August 6. http://www.nytimes.com/2011/08/07/business/a-rush-to-assess-standard-and-poors-downgrade-of-united-states-credit-rating.html?page wanted=all.

Sears, David O., Jim Sidanius, and Lawrence Bobo, eds. 2000. *Racialized Politics: The Debate About Racism in America.* Chicago: University of Chicago Press.

Segura, Gary, and Shaun Bowler. 2011. *The Future Is Ours: Minority Politics, Political Behavior and the Multi-Racial Era of American Politics.* Washington, DC: Congressional Quarterly Press.

Segura, Gary, and Adrian Pantoja. 2003. "Fear and Loathing in California: Contextual Threat and Political Sophistication Among Latino Voters." *Political Behavior* 25(3): 265–286.

Seib, Gerald F. 2010. "The Potential Pitfalls of Winning Big." *Wall Street Journal,* October 29. http://online.wsj.com/news/articles/SB10001424052702304316404575580233341173578.

Shannon, Brad. 2010. "No Clear Mandate for Health Care Bill Repeal." November 24. http://www.huffingtonpost.com/2010/11/23/no-clear-mandate-for-heal_n_787808.html.

Sifry, David. 2006. "State of the Blogosphere." October 6. http://www.sifry.com/alerts/archives/000443.html.

Silbey, Joel H. 1991. "Beyond Realignment and Realignment Theory." In *The End of Realignment? Interpreting American Electoral Eras,* ed. Byron E. Shafer. Madison: University of Wisconsin Press.

Simien, Evelyn M. 2009. "Clinton and Obama: The Impact of Race and Sex on the 2008 Democratic Presidential Primaries." In *Winning the Presidency 2008,* ed. William Crotty. Boulder: Paradigm.

Sinclair, Barbara. 1989. *The Transformation of the U.S. Senate.* Baltimore: Johns Hopkins University Press.

———. 2006. *Party Wars: Polarization and the Politics of National Policy Making.* Norman: University of Oklahoma Press.

Sitkoff, Harvard. 1993. *The Struggle for Black Equality, 1954–1992.* 2nd ed. New York: Hill and Wang.

Skocpol, Theda. 1992. *Protecting Soldiers and Mothers.* Cambridge: Harvard University Press.

———. 1997. *Boomerang: Health Care Reform and the Turn Against Government.* New York: Norton.

———. 2010. "The Political Challenges That May Undermine Health Reform." *Health Affairs* 29(7): 1288–1292.

Skocpol, Theda, and Vanessa Williamson. 2012. *The Tea Party and the Remaking of Republican Conservatism.* Oxford: Oxford University Press.

Smidt, Corwin, Lyman A. Kellstedt, and James L. Guth, eds. 2009. *The Oxford Handbook of Religion and American Politics.* New York: Oxford University Press.

Smith, Aaron. 2011. "22% of Online Americans Used Social Networking or Twitter for Politics in 2010 Campaign." January 27. http://www.pewinternet.org/2011/01/27/22-of-online-americans-used-social-networking-or-twitter-for-politics-in-2010-campaign.

Speel, Robert W. 1998. *Changing Patterns of Voting in the Northern United States: Electoral Realignment, 1952–1996.* University Park: Pennsylvania State University Press.

Stanley, Harold W., and Richard Niemi. 2010. *Vital Statistics on American Politics, 2009–2010.* Washington, DC: Congressional Quarterly Press.

Stave, Bruce M. 1970. *The New Deal and the Last Hurrah: Pittsburgh Machine Politics.* Pittsburgh: University of Pittsburgh Press.

Steed, Robert P., Lawrence W. Moreland, and Tod A. Baker, eds. 1997. *Southern Parties and Elections: Studies in Regional Political Change.* Tuscaloosa: University of Alabama Press.

Steensland, Brian, Jerry Park, Mark Regnerus, Lynn Robinson, W. Bradford Wilcox, and Robert Woodberry. 2000. "The Measure of American Religion." *Social Forces* 79(1): 291–318.

Stelzer, Irwin. 2004. "Neoconservatives and Their Critics: An Introduction." In *The Neocon Reader,* ed. Irwin Stelzer. New York: Grove.

Sternberger, D., and B. Vogel. 1969. *Die Wahl der Parlament und anderer Staatsorgane.* Berlin: De Gruyter.

Stigler, George J. 1975. *The Citizen and the State.* Chicago: University of Chicago Press.

Stiglitz, Joseph E. 2004. *The Roaring Nineties.* New York: Norton.

———. 2010a. *Freefall: America, Free Markets, and the Sinking of the World Economy.* New York: Norton.

———. 2010b. "Principles and Guidelines for Deficit Reduction." New York: Roosevelt Institute.

———. 2012. *The Price of Inequality: How Today's Divided Society Endangers Our Future.* New York: Norton.

Stonecash, Jeffrey M. 2000. *Class and Party in American Politics.* Boulder: Westview.

———. 2006. *Political Parties Matter: Realignment and the Return of Partisan Voting.* Boulder: Lynne Rienner.

———. 2010. "Changing American Political Parties." In *New Directions in American Political Parties,* ed. Jeffrey M. Stonecash. New York: Routledge.

Stoutenborough, James W., Donald P. Haider-Markel, and Mahalley D. Allen. 2006. "Reassessing the Impact of Supreme Court Decisions on Public Opinion: Gay Civil Rights Cases." *Political Research Quarterly* 59: 419–433.

Strand, Douglas Alan. 1998. "Civil Liberties, Civil Rights, and Stigma: Voter Attitudes and Behavior in the Politics of Homosexuality." In *Stigma and Sexual Orientation: Understanding Prejudice Against Lesbians, Gay Men, and Bisexuals,* ed. Gregory M. Herek. Thousand Oaks, CA: Sage.

Street, Debra, and Jeralynn Sittig Cossman. 2006. "Greatest Generation or Greedy Geezers? Social Spending Preferences and the Elderly." *Social Problems* 53(1): 75–96.

Sugrue, Thomas J. 2010. *Not Even Past: Barack Obama and the Burden of Race.* Princeton: Princeton University Press.

Sullivan, Amy. 2008. *The Party Faithful.* New York: Scribner.

Sullivan, Andrew. 2007. *The Conservative Soul: Fundamentalism, Freedom, and the Future of the Right.* New York: Harper.

Sumner, William Graham. 1919. *The Forgotten Man and Other Essays.* New Haven, CT: Yale University Press.

Sundquist, James L. 1983. *The Dynamics of the American Party System: Alignment and Realignment of Political Parties in the United States.* Washington, DC: Brookings Institution.

———. 1988. "Needed: A Political Theory for the New Era of Coalition Government in the United States." *Political Science Quarterly* 103: 613–635.

———. 1992. *Constitutional Reform and Effective Government.* Rev. ed. Washington, DC: Brookings Institution.

Surowiecki, James. 2010. "Greedy Geezers?" *The New Yorker,* November 22. http://www.newyorker.com/talk/financial/2010/11/22/101122ta_talk_surowiecki.

Suskind, Ron. 2011. *Confidence Men: Wall Street, Washington, and the Education of a President.* New York: Harper.

Swain, Carol M. 1995. *Black Faces, Black Interests: The Representation of African Americans in Congress.* Enlarged ed. Cambridge: Harvard University Press.

Swierenga, Robert. 1990. "Ethno-Religious Political Behavior in the Mid-Nineteenth Century: Voting, Values, Cultures." In *Religion and American Politics: From the Colonial Period to the 1980s,* ed. Mark Noll. New York: Oxford University Press.

———. 2009. "Religion and American Voting Behavior, 1830s to 1930s." In *The Oxford Handbook of Religion and American Politics,* ed. Corwin Smidt, Lyman A. Kellstedt, and James L. Guth. New York: Oxford University Press.

Tanenhaus, Sam. 2009. *The Death of Conservatism.* New York: Random.

Tate, Katherine. 1993. *From Protest to Politics: The New Black Voters in American Elections.* Cambridge: Harvard University Press.

———. 2003. *Black Faces in the Mirror: African Americans and Their Representatives in the U.S. Congress.* Princeton: Princeton University Press.

Taylor, Paul, Ana Gonzalez-Barrera, Jeffrey S. Passel, and Mark Hugo Lopez. 2012. "An Awakened Giant: The Hispanic Electorate Is Likely to Double by 2030." Washington, DC: Pew Hispanic Center.

Tesler, Michael, and David O. Sears. 2012. *Obama's Race: The 2008 Election and the Dream of a Post-Racial America.* Chicago: University of Chicago Press.

Theriault, Sean M. 2006. "Party Polarization in the US Congress." *Party Politics* 12: 483–503.

———. 2008. *Party Polarization in Congress.* New York: Cambridge University Press.

Tilove, Jonathan. 2009. "Seniors Group Says No to Demo Health Bills." *New Orleans Times-Picayune,* November 17.

Time. 2006. "The Rise and Fall of Ralph Reed." July 23. http://content.time.com/time/magazine/article/0,9171,1218060,00.html.

Tingsten, Herbert. 1937. *Political Behavior: Studies in Election Statistics.* London: P. S. King.

Tocqueville, Alexis de. 1945 (1835). *Democracy in America.* New York: Knopf.

———. 2000. *Democracy in America.* Ed. Harvey C. Mansfield and Delba Winthrop. Chicago: University of Chicago Press.

Tomasky, Michael. 2010. "The Specter Haunting the Senate." September 30. http://www.nybooks.com/articles/archives/2010/sep/30/specter-haunting-senate.

Tribe, Laurence. 2010. "Laurence Tribe on *Citizens United v. Federal Election Commission.*" January 25. http://www.law.harvard.edu/news/spotlight/constitutional -law/related/tribe.on.citizens.united.html.

Turner, Frederick Jackson. 1947. *The Frontier in American History.* New York: Holt.

Uhlaner, Carole J., and F. Chris Garcia. 2005. "Learning Which Party Fits." In *Diversity in Democracy,* ed. Gary Segura and Shaun Bowler. Charlottesville: University of Virginia Press.

Urofsky, Melvin I. 2005. *Money and Free Speech: Campaign Finance Reform and the Courts.* Lawrence: University Press of Kansas.

US Bureau of the Census. 1975. *Historical Statistics of the United States, Colonial Times to 1970.* Washington, DC.

Verba, Sidney, Kay Schlozman, and Henry Brady. 1995. *Voice and Equality: Civic Voluntarism in American Politics.* Cambridge: Harvard University Press.

Wald, Kenneth D. 2011. *Religion and Politics in the United States.* 6th ed. Lanham: Rowman and Littlefield.

Walker, Jack L. 1983. "The Origins and Maintenance of Interest Groups in America." *American Political Science Review* 77(2): 390–406.

Walker, Samuel. 2012. *Presidents and Civil Liberties from Wilson to Obama.* New York: Cambridge University Press.

Walton, Hanes, Jr., Donald Deskins Jr., and Sherman Puckett. 2012. *The African American Electorate: A Statistical History.* Vol. 1. Washington, DC: Congressional Quarterly.

Wang, Tova Andrea. 2012. *The Politics of Voter Suppression: Defending and Expanding America's Right to Vote.* New York: Century Foundation.

Wapshott, Nicholas. 2011. *Keynes Hayek: The Clash That Defined Modern Economics.* New York: Norton.

Ward, Robert C. 1997. "The Chaos of Convergence: A Study of Decay, Change, and Transformation Within the Telephone Policy Subsystem of the United States." PhD dissertation, Virginia Polytech Institute and State University.

Warren, Elizabeth. 2014. *A Fighting Chance.* New York: Metropolitan.

Washington Post. 2011. "(Not) Spreading the Wealth." June 18. http://www.washington post.com/wp-srv/special/business/income-inequality.

Watson, Bruce. 2011. *Freedom Summer: The Savage Season That Made Mississippi Burn and Made America a Democracy.* New York: Penguin.

Wattenberg, Martin P. 1990. *The Decline of American Political Parties.* Cambridge: Harvard University Press.

Wawro, Gregory J., and Eric Schickler. 2006. *Filibuster: Obstruction and Lawmaking in the U.S. Senate.* Princeton: Princeton University Press.

Weidenbaum, Murray L. 2009. *The Competition of Ideas: The World of Washington Think Tanks.* New Brunswick: Transaction.

Weiner, Marc D. 2005. "Fifty Years On: The American Electorate's Evolving Participation in a Responsible Two-Party System." New Brunswick, NJ: Rutgers University, Department of Political Science.

Weiss, Nancy J. 1983. *Farewell to the Party of Lincoln: Black Politics in the Age of FDR*. Princeton: Princeton University Press.

Weissert, Carol S., and William G. Weissert. 2006. *Governing Health: The Politics of Health Policy*. Baltimore: Johns Hopkins University Press.

Wesleyan Media Project. 2010. "An Uptick in Negativity." November 1. http://media project.wesleyan.edu/2010/11/01/an-uptick-in-negativity.

Whitaker, Lois Duke. 2008. *Voting the Gender Gap*. Urbana: University of Illinois Press.

White, John K. 2014. "The Unequal Divide." April 2. http://www.counterpunch.org /2014/04/02/the-unequal-divide.

White, Joseph. 2001. *False Alarm: Why the Greatest Threat to Social Security and Medicare Is the Campaign to "Save" Them*. Baltimore: Johns Hopkins University Press.

White, Theodore H. 1965. *The Making of the President, 1964*. New York: Atheneum.

———. 1975. *Breach of Faith: The Fall of Richard Nixon*. New York: Atheneum.

Wiebe, Robert. 1967. *The Search for Order, 1877–1920*. New York: Hill and Wang.

Wiecek, William M. 1998. *The Lost World of Classical Legal Thought: Law and Ideology in America, 1886–1937*. New York: Oxford University Press.

Wilcox, Clyde. 1995. *The Latest American Revolution? The 1994 Elections and Their Implications for Governance*. New York: St. Martin's.

Wilcox, Clyde, Paul R. Brewer, Shauna Shames, and Celinda Lake. 2007. "If I Bend This Far, Will I Break? Public Opinion About Same-Sex Marriage." In *The Politics of Same-Sex Marriage,* ed. Craig A. Rimmerman and Clyde Wilcox. Chicago: University of Chicago Press.

Wilcox, Clyde, and Barbara Norrander. 2002. "Of Moods and Morals: The Dynamics of Opinion on Abortion and Gay Rights." In *Understanding Public Opinion,* 2nd ed., ed. Barbara Norrander and Clyde Wilcox. Washington, DC: Congressional Quarterly.

Wilcox, Clyde, and Robin Wolpert. 1996. "President Clinton, Public Opinion, and Gays in the Military." In *Gay Rights, Military Wrongs: Political Perspectives on Lesbians and Gays in the Military,* ed. Craig A. Rimmerman. New York: Garland.

———. 2000. "Gay Rights in the Public Sphere: Public Opinion on Gay and Lesbian Equality." In *The Politics of Gay Rights,* ed. Craig A. Rimmerman, Kenneth D. Wald, and Clyde Wilcox. Chicago: University of Chicago Press.

Wilentz, Sean. 2005. *The Rise of American Democracy: Jefferson to Lincoln*. New York: Norton.

———. 2008. "Foreword." In *The Paranoid Style in American Politics,* ed. Richard Hofstadter. New York: Vintage.

Wilkinson, Richard, and Kate Pickett. 2010. *The Spirit Level: Why More Equal Societies Almost Always Do Better*. New York: Bloomsbury.

———. 2013. "Margaret Thatcher Made Britain a Less, Not More, Desirable Place to Do Business: The Ex-PM's Greatest Mistake Was Her Failure to Recognise That Social Cohesion Is Crucial to Long-Term Economic Growth." *The Guardian,* April 9. http://www.theguardian.com/commentisfree/2013/apr/10 /inequality-margaret-thatcher-britain-desirable-business.

Williams, Juan. 1987. *Eyes on the Prize: America's Civil Rights Years, 1954–1965*. New York: Viking.

Williams, Rhys, ed. 1997. *Cultural Wars in American Politics: Critical Reviews of a Popular Myth*. New York: Aldine de Gruyter.

Williamson, John B. 1998. "Political Activism and the Aging of the Baby Boom." *Generations* 22(1): 55–59.

Williamson, John B., and Diana M. Watts-Roy. 1999. "Framing the Generational Equity Debate." In *The Generational Equity Debate,* ed. John B. Williamson, Diane M. Watts-Roy, and Eric R. Kingson. New York: Columbia University Press.

Wilson, James Q. 1985. "Realignment at the Top, Dealignment at the Bottom." In *The American Elections of 1984,* ed. Austin Ranney. Durham, NC: American Enterprise Institute.

Wolbrecht, Christina. 2000. *The Politics of Women's Rights.* Princeton: Princeton University Press.

Wolbrecht, Christina, and David Campbell. 2006. "See Jane Run: Women Politicians as Role Models for Adolescents." *Journal of Politics* 68(2): 233–247.

———. 2007. "Leading by Example: Female Members of Parliament as Political Role Models." *American Journal of Political Science* 51(4): 921–939.

Wolfe, Alan. 2010. *The Future of Liberalism.* New York: Knopf.

Wolfinger, Raymond E., and Steven J. Rosenstone. 1980. *Who Votes?* New Haven: Yale University Press.

Wolfson, Adam. 2004. "Conservatives and Neoconservatives." In *The Neocon Reader,* ed. Irwin Stelzer. New York: Grove.

Wong, Janelle S. 2000. "The Effects of Age and Political Exposure on the Development of Party Identification Among Asian American and Latino Immigrants in the United States." *Political Behavior* 22(4): 341–342.

Wood, Amy Louise, ed. 2011. *Violence.* Vol. 19, *The New Encyclopedia of Southern Culture.* Chapel Hill: University of North Carolina Press.

Woodward, C. Vann. 1993. *The Burden of Southern History.* 3rd ed. Baton Rouge: Louisiana State University Press.

———. 2002 (1965). *The Strange Career of Jim Crow.* Oxford: Oxford University Press.

Woodward, J. David. 2006. *The New Southern Politics.* Boulder: Lynne Rienner.

Wright, Gerald C., Robert S. Erickson, and John P. McIver. 1985. "Measuring State Partisanship and Ideology with Survey Data." *Journal of Politics* 47: 479–489.

Wright, John R. 2000. "Interest Groups, Congressional Reform, and Party Government in the United States." *Legislative Studies Quarterly* 25: 217–235.

Wuthnow, Robert. 1988. *The Restructuring of American Religion.* Princeton: Princeton University Press.

Yeats, William Butler. 1920. "The Second Coming." In *Michael Robartes and the Dancer.* Churchtown, Dundrum, Ireland: Chuala.

Young, James P. 1996. *Reconsidering American Liberalism: The Troubled Odyssey of the Liberal Idea.* Boulder: Westview.

Zaller, John R. 1992. *The Nature and Origins of Mass Opinion.* New York: Cambridge University Press.

Ziobrowski, Alan J., James W. Boyd, Ping Cheng, and Brigitte J. Ziobrowski. 2004. "Abnormal Returns from the Common Stock Investments of the United States Senate." *Journal of Financial and Quantitative Analysis* 39: 661–676.

———. 2011. "Abnormal Returns from the Common Stock Investments of Members of the U.S. House of Representatives." *Business and Politics* 13: 1–22.

The Contributors

Paul R. Brewer is professor in the Department of Communication and the Department of Political Science and International Relations at the University of Delaware. He is author of *Value War: Public Opinion and the Politics of Gay Rights.*

Walter Dean Burnham is best known for his work on the dynamics of US electoral politics. Currently, he is professor emeritus in the Department of Government at the University of Texas at Austin.

Barbara C. Burrell is professor of political science at Northern Illinois University. She is currently working on a sequel to her 1994 book on women's campaigns for Congress, *Woman's Place Is in the House: Campaigning for Congress in the Feminist Era.*

William Crotty is Thomas P. O'Neill Chair in Public Life and professor emeritus of political science at Northeastern University. His recent publications include *Winning the Presidency 2012* and *The Obama Presidency: Promise and Performance.*

Christine L. Day is professor of political science at the University of New Orleans. She is author of *What Older Americans Think: Interest Groups and Aging Policy,* and coauthor of *Women's PACs: Abortion and Elections.*

Thomas Ferguson is professor of political science at the University of Massachusetts at Boston, and senior fellow at the Roosevelt Institute. His publications include *Right Turn: The Decline of the Democrats and the*

389

Future of American Politics and *Golden Rule: The Investment Theory of Party Competition and the Logic of Money-Driven Political Systems.*

Shawn C. Fettig has a doctorate in political science from the University of Wisconsin at Milwaukee. He is coauthor of "Be Careful with My Court: The Chief Justice and Supreme Court Legitimacy," in *The Chief Justice: Appointment and Influence,* edited by D. D. Danelski and A. Ward.

John A. Garcia is archive director of the Resource Center for Minority Data at the Inter-University Consortium for Political and Social Research (ICPSR), and visiting researcher at the Center for Political Studies at the University of Michigan. He is author of *Latino Politics in America: Community of Interests and Culture.*

James L. Guth is William R. Kenan Jr. Professor of Political Science at Furman University. He is coeditor of *The Oxford Handbook of Religion and American Politics.*

Lyman A. Kellstedt is professor emeritus of political science at Wheaton College. He is coauthor of *Rediscovering the Religious Factor in American Politics, The Bully Pulpit,* and *Religion and the Culture Wars,* and coeditor of *The Oxford Handbook of Religion and American Politics.*

Thomas R. Marshall is professor of political science at the University of Texas at Arlington. He is author of *Presidential Nominations in a Reform Age* and *Public Opinion and the Supreme Court.*

Arthur C. Paulson is professor of political science and pre-law adviser at Southern Connecticut State University. His publications include *Electoral Realignment and the Outlook for American Democracy* and *Realignment and Party Revival: Understanding Electoral Politics at the Turn of the Twentieth Century.*

Gerald M. Pomper is professor emeritus of political science at the Eagleton Institute of Politics at Rutgers University. He is author of *The Future of American Democratic Politics* and *Ordinary Heroes and American Democracy.*

Marc D. Weiner is faculty fellow and associate director of the Bloustein Center for Survey Research at Rutgers University. He is coeditor of *The Future of American Democratic Politics.*

Index

Abortion, 201
Accountability: judicial role in election law manipulation, 141; one-party politics in the Reconstructionist South, 218–219; polarization contributing to the decline of, 327; racial violence under Jim Crow, 210
Affordable Care Act: AARP endorsement, 299–300; age-related policies, 295–296; filibuster rule, 135; ideological divisions over, 322–324; partisan debate, 317–322; repeal attempts, 63, 137; Supreme Court involvement in, 142–143; threats to the aging population, 293–294
African Americans: ANES sampling strategy, 248; black leadership, 238–239; civil rights era, 225–228; demographic variables of religious partisanship, 177; disenfranchisement, 216–217; Great Migration and demographic changes, 222–225; history of racial polarization in American politics, 209–210; Obama's relationship to black America, 233–238; Obama's view of post-racial politics, 233; political realignment in the South, 80; political world of black and white America, 229–232; Reconstruction, 42–54, 210–216; religious affiliation and the Democratic Party coalition, 1940–2012, 171(table); religious affiliation and the Republican Party coalition, 1940–2012, 170(table); religious traditions and party identification, 1940–2012, 163(table),

165, 168–169; Southern Democratic electorate, 76; suffrage, 42; voting-eligible population, 2012 and 2030, 243(table). *See also* Civil rights
Age, voter turnout and, 54, 244–245
Age Discrimination in Employment Act, 288
Aging policy: congressional polarization, 302–306; era of compassionate ageism, 287–288; generational equity replacing compassionate ageism, 289–290, 292–293; generational interdependence and generational equity, 288–292; increasing costs of the older population, 285–286; interest group representation, 297–302; public opinion, 294–297
Agnew, Spiro, 78
Ailes, Roger, 101
Alford, Robert, 45
Alito, Samuel, 139
Alliance for Retired Americans (ARA), 303–306
Ambition, personal: changing the pathways of US politics, 151–153; driving politics, 131–132; one-party politics in the Reconstructionist South, 218–219
Amendment 2 (Colorado), 260–261
American Association of Retired Persons (AARP), 298–302, 304(fig.), 305, 305(fig.)
American Creed, 223–224
An American Dilemma (Myrdal), 223–224
American Federation of Labor (AFL), 224
American International Group (AIG), 103
American Medical Association (AMA), 312–313

American National Election Study (ANES), 158, 164, 166, 229, 248, 271, 275–280
American Political Science Association, 297, 327
Americans for Generational Equity (AGE), 291, 300–301
Americans for Tax Reform, 99
Anderson, John, 78
Anderson, Perry, 68–69(n29)
Anonymous holds on presidential appointments, 135–136
Anti-immigrant climate, 245–247
Apartheid, 42–54
Appointments, presidential. *See* Presidential appointments
Armey, Dick, 99, 120–121(table)
Articles of Confederation, 133
Asian population: voting-eligible population, 2012 and 2030, 243(table)
Askins, Jeri, 204
Australia: proportional representation, 31
Austrian school, 15
Authoritarianism, 12
Automobile safety, 317, 326(n2)

Baby boomers, 5, 285, 289–290, 292–293, 296–297
Bachmann, Michelle, 79
Bailout, financial, 1–4
Balanced Budget Act, 293, 304
Ballot initiative on gay rights, 260
Banfield, Edward, 108
Barbour, Haley, 98, 109
"The Battle of Blenheim," 64
Beare, Jimmy, 32–33
Bell, Daniel, 14
Bernanke, Ben, 103–104
Biden, Joe, 283
Bilingual ballots, 243
Bill of Rights, 213
Bipartisan Campaign Finance Reform, 121–122, 140–141
Bipartisan House Legal Advisory Group, 258
Bipartisanship, disdain for, 147–148
Birch, John, 330
The Birth of a Nation (Griffiths), 211
Bismarck, Otto von, 34, 65(n5)
Black Codes, 210, 213–214
Blogs, 149–150
Blue-dog Democrats, 61–62
Bobo, Lawrence, 233
Boehner, John, 137, 146, 258
Bolton, John, 139
Boston, Massachusetts: New Deal political realignment, 47–5512

Bowers v. Hardwick, 260, 262, 269, 270(table)
Boxer, Barbara, 204
Brown, Henry Billings, 56, 214
Brown v. Board of Education, 212, 214–215, 224–225, 330
Bryan, William Jennings, 37
Bryant, Anita, 259–260
Buchanan, Pat, 33, 260–261
Buckley, William F., 10, 12–13, 55
Buckley v. Valeo, 54–55, 343
Budget policy: aging policy and, 292; Bush (G. H. W.) raising taxes to close budget deficit, 97–98; divided government, 87–88; ideological nature of debate over, 71–72; increasing costs of the aging population, 285, 287; institutional gridlock over, 137; tax proposals benefiting the wealthy, 338
Buerkle, Ann, 206
Buffett, Warren, 338
Buffett Rule, 338
Burke, Edmund, 9–11, 18
Bush, George H. W.: gay rights as campaign issue, 261; LGB vote, 280–281; 1980 primary, 78; presidential nominees' positions on gay rights issues, 1992–2008, 268(table); tax hikes to close budget deficit, 97–98
Bush, George W.: *Bush v. Gore,* 33, 88–89, 140, 321–322; congressional polarization over aging policy, 304–305; dismantling the New Deal, 20; end of centrist politics, 11; expanding campaign finance, 120–121; expanding presidential power, 139; health care agenda, 309, 316–317, 319; LGB vote, 281; neoconservative movement, 14–15; neoliberal economics, 12; practice of political conservatism, 16–17; presidential nominees' positions on gay rights issues, 1992–2008, 268(table); privatization of Social Security, 286, 295; same-sex marriage, 262–263; 2000 primaries, 78
Bush v. Gore, 33, 88–89, 140, 321–322
Butterfly ballot, 33

Cain, Herman, 79
Campaign finance: committee chair assignments, 126(n28); escalation of, 68(n21); financial transformation of political operation, 109–110; Gingrich, DeLay, and Armey versus Michel, 120–121(table); Gingrich's fundraising activities, 98(table); hollowing out the

electorate, 54–55; increasing the inequality of political campaigns, 150–151; judicial role in, 56, 122, 140–143, 150–151, 343; leadership PACs, 118–119; polarization and, 114–122, 147; politics rewarding the wealthy, 341–344; religious right, 108; Republicans' campaign to defund Democrats, 99–100; Right Turn, 125(n23); spectrum of political money, 110–114, 111(fig.), 125–126(n27); spending growth through time, 1970–2008, 117(table); total campaign spending data, 126(n31); women candidates, 201–202

Campbell, Andrea, 296, 300

Canada: electoral regime, 31–32

Cannon, Joseph, 110

Capitalism: defining traditional liberalism, 19–20; Rand's objections to, 16; welfare state, 57

Capitalism and Freedom (Friedman), 12

Carter, Jimmy: gender voting, 190; health care agenda, 314–315; loss to Reagan, 335; moderate Democrats, 76; Southern electorate's voting patterns, 80; tax and budget allocation restructuring, 334

Casey, William J., 101

Castle, Michael, 63

Catholics: demographic variables of religious partisanship, 177; ideological differences and partisan polarization, 180; partisan coalitions, 169; party identification, 162, 164, 168; religion and party affiliation, 163(table), 167(table), 170(table), 171(table), 173(table), 174(table); religious divisions in parties, 157–158; restructuring perspective of partisan coalitions, 172–175

Center, political: disappearance of, 345–346; religion and partisanship, 161–162, 166–168; values and beliefs of core partisans and swing voters, 347–348

Centrists, religious, 167(table), 173(table)

Chaney, James Earl, 225, 229–230

Charitable grants, 111(fig.), 112–113

Cheney, Dick, 263

Children, aging policy and, 290, 300

China: economic recovery after 2008, 105

Chisholm v. Georgia, 154(n6)

Choate, Joseph, 38, 56

Christian Coalition, 108

Churchill, John, 64

Citizen Ambition Panel Study, 197

Citizens United v. Federal Election Commission, 56, 122, 140, 150–151, 343

Civil rights: conservative backlash, 23; Johnson's election victory, 223; liberal Democrats of 1948, 76; North-South divide, 58; origins of modern polarization, 330; religious traditions and party identification, 165; Selma, Alabama, 234; shifting party politics, 331; Southern conservative Republicans, 77; Southern political movement, 225–228; Truman's push for, 224; use of the filibuster, 133

Civil Rights Act (1957), 225–227

Civil Rights Acts (1964 and 1965), 133, 165, 227

Civil unions, 262, 267, 268(table), 269, 271, 272(fig.), 275, 278, 281, 283, 284(n4)

Civil War: American electoral regime, 31; effect of the umbrella party system, 90; ethno-religious partisanship, 159; income tax funding, 38, 56; Reconstruction, 210–216; second civil war, 64–65; voter turnout, 36–37

Class differences: demographic variables of religious partisanship, 177; Jim Crow reinforcing, 210–211; New Deal policies minimizing, 333–334; New Deal political realignment, 45–49(table), 50, 52; party divisions on class lines, 345; political activists, 347; voter turnout by socioeconomic status, 45–47

Climate change, 108–109

Clinton, Bill: campaign finance, 121; congressional polarization over aging policy, 304; Defense of Marriage Act, 262; Democratic Leadership Council, 329; divided government, 87–88; executive privilege, 139; gay rights, 260–261, 267, 275; health care agenda, 309, 315–316, 319; ideological shift in the Democratic Party, 76; impeachment prospect, 88; Krugman's criticism of contemporary conservative practice, 22–23; LGB vote, 280–281; Medicare + Choice program, 293; neoliberal economics, 336; presidential nominees' positions on gay rights issues, 1992–2008, 268(table); Republicans' refusal to accept, 64; Southern vote, 80

Clinton, Hillary Rodham, 76

Cloture rule, 133–136, 257–258

Clymer, Adam, 189

Coalition of states, partisan, 81–83, 84(fig.)

Coalitions, partisan, 169–175, 183
Coburn, Tom, 135
Coethnic candidates, 251
Cognitive categories of voters, 242
Cold War, 13
Collins, Susan, 257–258
Colorado for Family Values, 260
Colorado Republican Federal Campaign Committee v. Federal Election Commission, 55
Commission on Civil Rights, 224
Committee assignments, 99–100, 119, 123(n8), 126(n28)
Commodity Futures Trading Commission, 109
Commonweal magazine, 14
Communism: Buckley's dislike of, 13; Goldwater's view of, 17; neoconservatives' "muscular" foreign policy, 15; origins of political polarization, 330; Wilson Tariff, 38
Compassionate ageism, era of, 287–289
Comprehensive Health Insurance Plan (CHIP), 314
Compulsory health care, 312, 314
Compulsory voting, 28, 29(table)
Concord Coalition, 300–301
Conflict as polarizing issue, 91
Congress, US: aging policy, 291, 296–297, 302–306; campaign finance reform, 114–122; congressional votes on gay rights issues, by chamber and party, 1993–2010, 265(table); constitutional provisions for power, 129–131; declining political influence of moderates, 348; divided government, 72, 87–88; electoral regime, 33–34; emergence of a polarized Congress, 99–102; expanding presidential power over declaration of war, 138–139; expansion of the executive at the expense of, 152–153; gay rights debate, 257–258, 261–262; impeachment, 88; media polarization, 101–102; number of Republican and Democratic Women in Congress, 1975–2011, 196(fig.); Obama health care proposal, 309–310, 317–322; Obama's 2012 reelection, 71; partisan polarization over gay rights, 264–267; polarization of women in leadership, 202–207; progressivism as response to corruption, 143–144; Republican control after 1994 elections, 98–99; Republican "revolutionaries" attack on Democrats in the 1980s, 96–98; resisting campaign finance reform, 342–343; same-sex marriage, 263; the spectrum of political money, 110–114; TARP bailout program, 1–4; theories of political polarization, 105–108; total campaign spending data, 126–127(n31); Truman's health care plan, 312; 2010 elections, 59–60. *See also* House of Representatives; Senate
Congress for Racial Equality (CORE), 226
Congress of Industrial Organizations (CIO), 224
Congressional-district boundaries, 54
Conscience of a Conservative (Goldwater), 16–17
Conscience of a Liberal (Krugman), 22–23
Conservatism: aggrandization of judicial powers, 140–141; classical conception of, 9–10; competing ideologies of liberalism and, 24; decline of the umbrella party system, 147–148; Goldwater's political realignment vision, 73; increasing rigidity of House Republicans, 137; liberal and conservative party differences in the House and Senate, 1879–2011, 350(figs.); media polarization, 101; philosophical and political traditions, 10–16; practice of political conservatism, 16–18; Reagan's embrace of, 335; sixth-party system realignment, 85. *See also* Extremism; Ideology
Constitution, US, 154(n6); budget provisions, 138–140; competing interest groups, 297; constraining ambition, 131–132; controlling factions, 152–153; equal rights amendment, 191; judicial authority, 140–143; majoritarian principle amendments, 133–138; post-Civil War amendments, 212–213; racial equality, 236–237; real and virtual legislative provisions, 129–131; same-sex marriage, 262–263; war on terror as war on, 139–140
Constitutional system, 87–90
Consulting fees, 112
Contract with America, 16–18, 83, 87, 123(n8)
Cooper, Jim, 204
Corporate sector: Democrats' campaign finance reform, 115–117; generational equity organizations, 301; Gingrich's fundraising activities, 97, 98(table); investment in politics, 341–342; Reagan's economic restructuring, 334–335; Supreme Court undermining campaign finance restraints, 55; system

of 1896, 38–39. *See also* Campaign finance
Corruption: demobilization of the electorate, 39–41; progressivism as response to, 143–144; Republican congressmen, 99–100
Courtpacking initiative, 44
Crime: gender politics, 199
Cuban-origin voters, 247, 249–250, 253–254
Culture wars, 91, 105, 160, 180
Culture Wars (Hunter and Wuthnow), 160
Cuomo, Andrew, 283

Debt: constitutional provisions, 129–130; institutional gridlock over, 137
Defense, US Department of, 257
Defense of Marriage Act (1996), 258, 261–264, 265(table), 266, 268(table), 283
DeLay, Tom, 99, 106, 108, 120–121(table)
Delegated governance, 293
Demobilization of the electorate, 39, 40(table)
Democracy: compromise and effective politics, 2; decline of the middle class, 328; direct primary, 144–146; election law manipulation threatening, 141; electronic media trivializing democratic discourse, 150; equality and self-government, 143–144
Democratic Leadership Council, 328–329
Democratic National Convention, 75–76, 220, 227–228
Democratic Party: aging policy, 292; black America, 229; business-friendly practices, 332–333; campaign finance reform, 114–117, 126(n29); Catholic identifying with, 157–158; demographic, 347; ethno-religious identification, 162, 164; factions in, 328–329; first US republic, 36; gays in the military, 271–272, 273(fig.); gender politics, 187–191; increasing congressional polarization after 1980, 83; Latino voters, 247–251, 254–255; moderate leftward shift, 3–4; multifactional system, 73–74; neoliberal conservative approach, 331–332; number of Republican and Democratic Women in Congress, 1975–2011, 196(fig.); one-party politics in the South, 217–220; promoting social welfare, 287; realignment, 39, 75–76, 80; Reconstructionist South, 214–216; religion and partisanship, 164–169,

171(table), 174(table); Republican "revolutionaries'" attack on, 96–98; Republicans' campaign to defund, 99–100; theological factionalism, 172–175; women in state legislatures, 1983–2011, 197(fig.). *See also* Extremism
Demographic variables of religious partisanship, 175–179
Dewey, Thomas, 74, 77, 220
Diamond, Peter, 339
Direct democracy, 144, 260
Direct primary, 144–146
Disenfranchisement of voters, 67(n19), 216–217
Divided government, 72, 81–83, 87–88, 100–101, 305
Divisiveness resulting from polarization, 329–331
Dixiecrats, 74, 80, 220
Dodd-Frank financial reform legislation, 104
Dole, Robert, 262, 268(table), 281
Domestic use of executive power, 139
Dominant group relations, 1
Dominican-origin voters, 249
Donnelly, Joe, 63
"Don't Ask, Don't Tell" military policy, 257–258, 261–264, 265(table), 267, 268(table), 271–272, 283
Dred Scott decision, 213
Due process, 213
DuPont, Pete, 119
Dysfunctional politics defining polarization, 1–3

Economic conditions: decline of compassionate ageism, 289; Galbraith's liberalism, 20–22; gay voters' concerns with, 281; income share of the top 10 percent of earners, 1917–2011, 334(fig.); industrialization in the Reconstructionist South, 215; polarization of wealth, 332–341; as polarizing issue, 91–92; political conservatism, 16–17; Reagan redefining social policy, 331; real income growth, 1993–2011, 337 (table)
Economic crises (1970s), 96
Economic crisis (2008), 58, 62, 68–69(n29), 103–104, 109
Economic policy: Congress after 2008 crisis, 104; conservative and liberal ideology, 25; interest-group liberal state, 57–58; neoliberalism, 21–22, 331,

334–336, 351–352; political polarization, 148–149

Economic theory: justifying campaign spending, 103

Education level: gender politics, 199; Latino voters, 249–250; theological divisions and party identification, 166; voter turnout and, 53–54

Eisenhower, Dwight, 95(quote); anticommunist sentiment towards, 330; Buckley's dislike of, 13; Civil Rights Act, 225; conservatism, 11; electoral success, 222–223; electoral support, 220; health care, 312–313, 319–320; presidential nomination, 74, 77

Elections: age-related policies, 294–295; base strategy, 107; coalitions of states in presidential and congressional elections, 1896–2012, 84(fig.); constitutional provisions, 130; context and aftermath of, 59–65; direct primary, 144–146; gay rights referendum, 260; ideological shape shifting during campaigns, 145, 154(n10); impact of hyper-partisanship over health care, 325; insulating states from national politics, 63; Latino voters in the 2012 elections, 251–255; media participation in, 101–102; money and incumbency, 124(n10); partisan gap in women running for office, 196–200; polarization of women in leadership positions, 203–207; Social Security and Medicare issues, 294; states' rights in elections conduct, 32–33; total campaign spending data, 126–127(n31); two-party vote swings, 1892–2012, 60(table). *See also* American National Election Study; Campaign finance; Midterm elections; Presidential elections; Representation

Electoral College, 33–34, 214

Electoral reform, 39–42

Electorate: age-related policies, 294–297; characteristics of ideology, 8–9; demobilization strategies, 1890–1920, 40(table); disenfranchisement of blacks, 216–217; divided government after the New Deal, 71–72; elites hollowing out, 54–57; extremism distorting representation, 146–147; gay rights issues in presidential elections, 280–283; Imperial Germany, 65(n5); partisan coalition of states, 81; party polarization and voter intensity, 345–346; polarization over gay rights,

271–280; presidential year and off-year elections, 63; progressive reform, 39; public opinion on health care, 311–314, 316–321, 326(n1); realignment, 74–79; religious voting, 157–162; a responsible party system, 86–87; self-government, 143–144; support for Social Security and Medicare, 286; values and beliefs of core partisans and swing voters, 347–348; voter turnout among the potential US electorate, 1788–2008, 35(table); voting-eligible population, 2012 and 2030, 243(table); white vote in 2012, 62. *See also* Latinos; Public opinion; Religion and religious groups; Voter turnout and voting patterns

Eleventh Amendment rights, 154(n6)

Elites: classical conception of conservatism, 10; direct primary, 144; gaming elections, 54; Madison's vision of a virtuous elite, 131–132; party polarization, 345; potential for mass overthrow, 37–38; public opinion on gay rights, 275; theories of polarization, 107–108, 345; voter and elite realignment, 85

EMILY's List, 201

Employee Retirement Income Security Act, 288

Employer-provided health care, 311–316

Employment Non-Discrimination Act (1996), 261–262, 265(table), 266–267, 268(table)

Energy policy, 104

Enforcement Act (1870), 43

Environmental issues: climate change and energy policy, 104

Equal pay legislation, 203

Equal Protection Colorado, 260

Equal rights amendment, 191

Equality of conditions, 93

Ethno-religious perspective of party affiliation, 158–160, 162, 164–165, 168–172, 177, 181, 182(table)

Eugenics, 211–212, 214–215

Evangelical Protestants, partisanship and, 162–166, 169, 170(table), 171(table), 173(table), 174(table), 177, 180

Event analysis, 111–112

Evers, Medgar, 225

Executive power. *See* Presidential power

Executive privilege, 139, 322

Extraordinary rendition, 140

Extremism, 2–3, 146–148, 349(fig.), 353(n3)

Factionalization, 152–153, 330–331
Fairness Doctrine, 101
Fallin, Mary, 204
Federal Election Campaign Act, 55
Federal Election Commission, 117–118, 140
Federal Marriage Amendment, 265(table), 266, 283
Federal Reserve, 103–104
Federal systems, 28, 31–32
The Federalist Papers, 130–132, 135, 152
Feingold, Russ, 121–122
Ferguson, Thomas, 341–342
Fifteenth Amendment rights, 43, 213
Filibuster rule, 133–138, 152, 257
Financial market deregulation, 109
Financial reform, 104
Fiorina, Carly, 204
First Amendment rights, 140
First-past-the-post systems, 28, 32–33
Fiscal cliff, 71, 88, 137
527 campaign spending, 121–122, 127(n31)
Florida: election controversy of 2000, 88–89; presidential election of 2000, 33
Forcey, Charles, 19
Ford, Gerald, 77–78, 80, 96
Foreign policy: Goldwater's view of, 17; neoconservative movement, 14–15; policy militancy, 180–181
Fourteenth Amendment rights, 43–44, 154(n6), 213, 262
Fox News, 101, 113, 123–124(n9), 128(n39)
France: electoral regime, 31
Frankovic, Kathleen, 190
Free speech, 55, 343–344
Freedom, free-market economies as protectors of, 12
Freedom riders, 225
Freedom summers, 225
Freeman, Jo, 188
Free-market economy, 9, 11–12, 15, 18–19, 58
Friedman, Milton, 10–12
Friedman, Thomas, 105
Fundamentalists, 25, 78–79

Galbraith, John Kenneth, 20–23
Ganz, Marshall Louis, 51–52
Garfield, James, 37
Gates, Robert, 257
Gay rights: congressional votes on gay rights issues, by chamber and party, 1993–2010, 265(table); early activism, 259–260; gay marriage, 261–264;

ideological polarization in Supreme Court votes, 269–270; marriage, 261–264, 268(table), 271–275, 274(fig.), 278–280; military "Don't Ask, Don't Tell," 257–258; national partisan battle, 260–262; partisan polarization in congressional votes, 264–267; partisan polarization in presidential campaigns, 267–269; public opinion on gay marriage, 278–280; public opinion on gays in the military, 276–278; public support, 1992–2011, 272(fig.); Stonewall Inn raid, 259; voting behavior and, 281–282
Geithner, Timothy, 103
Gender gap, 189–190
Gender politics: evolution of partisan gender gaps, 187–191; normative perspectives on women's representation, 191–194; partisan gap in elective officeholding, 194–196; partisan gap in women running for office, 196–200; party organizations and women's political leadership, 200–202; polarization of women in leadership, 202–207; women as a percentage of congressional Democrats and Republicans, 1975–2011, 195(fig.)
Generation X organizations, 300–301
Generational interdependence and generational equity, 287–293, 300–301
Geographic polarization, 106
Geren Registration Act (1911), 65–66(n9)
Germany: electoral regime, 28, 31–32, 34, 57, 65(n5)
Gerrymandering, 62, 106
Gilded Age, 36
Gingrich, Newt: ascension to Speakership, 98; campaign finance, 98(table), 119–120, 125(n22), 127(n37); financial market deregulation, 109; gay rights, 283; midterm elections of 1994, 83; practice of political conservatism, 16–17; race-based politics, 23; Republican primary of 2012, 79; Republican "revolutionaries," 96–97
Glazer, Nathan, 14
God and Man at Yale (Buckley), 10–11
God gap, 158
Golden Age, 333
Goldwater, Barry: belief in the party system, 73; electoral support, 220–223; "new conservatism," 16–17; opposition to Medicare, 314; presidential nomination, 74, 77; Reagan's support,

335; Southern electorate, 80; virtues of extremism, 329–330
Gone with the Wind (Mitchell), 211
Goodman, Andrew, 225, 229–230
Goodridge v. Dept. of Public Health, 262, 271, 275
GOPAC, 119
Gore, Al, 33, 76, 80, 267, 268(table), 329
Gradualism, 18
Graham, Lindsey, 62
Gramm, Phil, 85, 98, 100–101, 108–110, 113
Gramm, Wendy, 109
Gray Panthers, 299, 302
Gray peril concept, 294
Great American Middle, 65(n8)
Great Depression, 57, 339
Great Migration, 222–225
Great Moderation (1984–2007), 58
Great Recession, 104–105, 336, 338
Great Red Scare, 65(n8)
Great Society, 20, 223, 331
Greedy geezers, 289
Greenback Party, 37
Greenspan, Alan, 16, 103
Greenspan Commission, 290–291
Griffiths, D. W., 211
Group consciousness, 242
Group interests: characteristics of ideology, 8–9
Grovey v. Townsend, 43

Hamilton, Alexander, 135, 153
Hanna, Mark, 37, 95(quote), 123(n2)
Hare system, 31
Harper v. Virginia State Board of Elections, 44
Hayek, Frederick, 10–11, 24
Hayes, Rutherford B., 214
Health care: Clinton, Bush, and Obama proposals, 309–310; growing partisanship gap, 315–317; hyper-partisanship over, 322–326; increasing costs of the older population, 285–286; interest groups of the aging policy community, 298; as a partisan issue, 310–315; Tea Party establishment as response to, 352(n1). *See also* Affordable Care Act; Medicare
Health Security Act, 316, 319–320
Hedges, Chris, 20
Heil, CeCe, 204
Holder, Eric, 258
Holmes, Oliver Wendell, Jr., 37–38, 58–59
Homestead, Pennsylvania, 45–46, 50, 53, 67(n14)

Hoover, Herbert, 44–45, 57, 62
House of Representatives: ARA/NCSC ratings, 303, 304(fig.); decline in cross-party voting, 147, 154(n11); "Don't Ask, Don't Tell" policy, 264; flight from moderation to polarization, 146–148; Latino vote, 253; liberal and conservative party differences in the House and Senate, 1879–2011, 350(figs.); moderates and extremists in the House, 1916–2012, 349(fig.); party unity votes in the House, 1953–2008, 97(fig.); pay to play system, 99–100; polarization of women, 202; Republicans increasing party divisions, 136–138; two-party vote swings, 1892–2012, 60(table); women's political gains, 194–195
House Un-American Activities Committee, 330
How Policies Make Citizens (Campbell), 296
Hunter, James, 160, 165
Hylton v. United States, 38, 56
Hyper-partisanship: defining polarization, 2–3

Identification, 242
Identity, liberal thought on, 19
Ideology: of the AARP, 299–300; aging policy, 286, 288, 297–298; arguing against a responsible party system, 86–87; budget debate, 71–72; defining partisanship, 148, 154(n14); demographic influences predicting religious-partisan affiliations, 182(table); direct primaries, 144–146; divided government after the New Deal, 71–72; era of compassionate ageism, 288; factionalization in the Republican Party, 78; gay rights, 258–259, 273(fig.), 274(fig.), 277(table), 279(table); generational interdependence and generational equity, 291–292; increasing congressional polarization after 1980, 83; interest groups and aging policy, 297–298; justifying party positions, 351–352; of Latino voters, 250–251; liberals' lack of, 20; origins and characteristics of, 7–9; partisan imbalance, 3; party differentiation, 148; party factionalization, 73–74; party polarization, 93, 345; party realignment between 1964 and 1972, 75; polarization of women in leadership,

202–207; political blogs, 149–150; post-Watergate partisanship, 52; precluding compromise, 2; Rand's objectivism, 16; religious differences and partisan polarization, 179–182; restructuring the party system, 328–329; role in party politics and policymaking, 25; Roosevelt-Willkie vision of political realignment, 73–74; roots of party divisions, 136–138; shape shifting during campaigns, 145, 154(n10); shift in party bases, 147–148; Supreme Court polarization over gay rights, 269–270; theories of political polarization, 105–106; values and beliefs of core partisans and swing voters, 347–348. *See also* Conservatism; Liberalism

Immigrants: Latinos, 243–244

Impeachment, 88

Imperial Germany, 34, 65(n5)

Income: real income growth, 1993–2011, 337(table); salaries of regulators compared with incomes of the regulated, 1949–2007, 114(fig.)

Incumbents, 59–60, 77–78, 124(n10)

Independent voters: realignment in the sixth-party system, 85

Individualism, 9, 15

Industrialization, 215

Inequality, economic and social: campaign finance structure increasing, 151; classical conception of conservatism, 10; electoral control, 113–114; Galbraith's argument for resource redistribution, 21–22; Great Recession magnifying, 338; Krugman's criticism of contemporary conservative practice, 22; mapping political polarization, 148–149; money and interest groups driving politics, 327–328; party alignment clarification increasing, 345–346; polarization of wealth, 332–341; political conservatism, 17; progressivism as response to, 143–144; wealth inequality: Europe *vs.* the United States, 1810–2010, 341(fig.)

Institutional changes: ideology, 8–9. *See also* Structural change

Intellectualism, 14–15

Interactive realignment, 80

Interest groups: age-related policies, 297–302; characteristics of ideology, 8–9; controlling policy development, 132; one-party politics in the Reconstructionist South, 219; political parties' increasing responsiveness to, 327–328

Interest-group liberal state, 57–58

Interior West states: divided government after the New Deal, 72

Internet: trivializing politics, 149–150

Interparty competition, decline of, 145–146

Interstate commerce, 142

Investment theory of politics, 341–342

Iraq, war in, 139, 180

Ireland: proportional representation, 31

Israel, 31, 180

Issue ideology, 180–181, 201–202

Jefferson, Thomas, 327(quote)

Jewish Democratic intellectuals, 14

Jews: demographic variables of religious partisanship, 177; partisan coalitions, 169; religion and party identification, 162, 163(table), 164, 168–169; religious affiliation and the Democratic Party coalition, 1940–2012, 171(table); religious affiliation and the Republican Party coalition, 1940–2012, 170(table)

Jim Crow segregation, 210–212, 214–215

Johnson, Andrew, 213–214

Johnson, Lyndon: civil rights, 226–228; election victory, 222–223; factionalization of liberal Democrats, 76; Great Society, 331; health care agenda, 310, 313–314, 319; Voting Rights Act, 234–235

Judicial powers: aggrandization of, 140–143; constitutional provision, 130; executive "recess appointments," 139; gay rights controversy in state courts, 261; judicial supremacy, 38–39, 56; presidential appointments, 135–136. *See also* Supreme Court, US

Justice argument for women's representation, 192–193

K Street Project, 99

Kagan, Elena, 319

Kennedy, Edward "Ted," 315, 335

Kennedy, John F.: Boston's political realignment, 51; Civil Rights Act, 227; health care agenda, 310, 313–314, 319; Northeast electorate, 81

Kentucky Association of Health Care Plans v. Miller, 321

Kerry, John, 263, 267, 268(table), 269

Key, V. O., 63, 86, 146, 218–220

Keynes, John Maynard, 24

King, Martin Luther, Jr., 225–226, 234

Kirkpatrick, Jeane, 14–15

Kristol, Irving, 10, 14–15
Krugman, Paul, 20–23, 64
Ku Klux Klan, 65(n8), 74, 211, 229–230

Labor force participation: women's
    electability, 199–200
Laissez-faire ideology, 53
Lane, Robert, 7–8
Latinos: defining, 255(n1); determinants of
    voter registration, 245–246; electoral
    participation and partisanship, 247–251;
    electorate, 62; expanding political
    capital, 241; ideological differences and
    partisan polarization, 180;
    naturalization rates, 245–247,
    246(table); political parties appealing
    to, 241–242; religious affiliation and
    the Democratic Party coalition,
    1940–2012, 171(table); religious
    affiliation and the Republican Party
    coalition, 1940–2012, 170(table);
    religious restructuring view of party
    coalitions, 175; religious traditions and
    party identification, 1940–2012,
    163(table), 164; 2012 elections,
    251–255; US electoral system,
    242–247; voting-eligible population,
    2012 and 2030, 243(table)
Latter-day Saints: contribution to
    conservative partisan affiliation,
    164–165; ideological differences and
    partisan polarization, 181; religious
    affiliation and the Democratic Party
    coalition, 1940–2012, 171(table);
    religious affiliation and the Republican
    Party coalition, 1940–2012, 170(table);
    religious restructuring party coalitions,
    175; religious traditions and party
    identification, 1940–2012, 163(table)
Lawrence v. Texas, 262, 269, 270(table),
    271
Leadership: classical conception of
    conservatism, 10
Leadership Council of Aging Organizations
    (LCAO), 300
Leadership PACs, 118–119, 127(n33)
Legislative elections, 29(table)
Legitimization, electoral, 57
Lewis, John, 235
Liberalism: bases for contemporary liberal
    thought and practice, 23; Buckley's
    dislike of, 13; classical conception of,
    9–10; competing ideologies of
    conservatism and, 24; decline in the
    black population, 231; decline of the

umbrella party system, 147–148;
    electability of women, 198–199; liberal
    and conservative party differences in
    the House and Senate, 1879–2011,
    350(figs.); sixth-party system
    realignment, 85; tradition and practice
    of, 18–23. *See also* Ideology
Libertarianism, 16
Libya, US intervention in, 139
Lieberman, Joseph, 85, 257–258
Lilly Ledbetter Fair Pay Act (2009), 203
Lincoln, Abraham, 27(quote), 64–65,
    213–214
Liuzzo, Viola, 225
Lobbying, 111, 111(fig.); PAC campaign
    spending, 118. *See also* Interest groups
Lodge Force Bill, 42
Lubell, Samuel, 44–45
Lugar, Richard, 63
Lynch, Frederick, 299
Lynch, Julia, 300
Lynchings, 217

Madison, James, 130–132
Main Street faction, 74
Mainline Protestants, 165–166, 167(table),
    168–169, 170(table), 171(table),
    172–175, 173(table), 174(table), 177.
    See also Protestants; Religion and
    religious groups
Majority rules, 133–138
Mama grizzlies, 204
March on Washington, 227, 234
Marriage, gay rights and, 261–264,
    268(table), 271–275, 274(fig.), 278–
    280
Marx, Karl, 27(quote)
Matthews, Christopher, 187–188
McCain, John: Bush nomination, 78;
    campaign finance reform, 121–122; gay
    rights, 257, 267, 268(table), 269; health
    care proposal, 318; presidential
    nominees' positions on gay rights
    issues, 1992–2008, 268(table);
    Republicans' campaign to defund
    Democrats, 99–100; social class of the
    electorate, 53
McCarthyism, 13, 330
*McConnell v. Federal Election
    Commission,* 344
*McCutcheon v. Federal Election
    Commission,* 343
McGovern, George, 76, 165
McMorris Rodgers, Cathy, 205
McWilliams, Wilson Carey, 143–144

Media: bigger media trivializing politics, 149–150; campaign finance, 101–102; campaign finance driving media markets, 122; campaign finance reform, 116–117; "elite" role in polarization, 107–108; following congressional polarization, 101
Medicaid, 285, 287–288
Medicare: attempts to dismantle, 285; delegated governance, 293; era of compassionate ageism, 287–288; partisan polarization in Congress, 302–303; passage of, 313–314; Reagan bill, 315; voucherization of, 286, 292, 295. *See also* Aging policy
Medicare + Choice, 304–305
Medicare Advantage, 305
Medicare Catastrophic Care Act (1985), 294–295
Medicare Modernization Act (2003), 293, 299, 305–306, 316–317
Meehan, Marty, 264
Mexican American Legal Defense and Education Fund (MALDEF), 243
Mexican-origin voters, 247, 249
Michel, Robert, 120–121(table)
Middle class: polarization and decline of, 148–149; redistribution of wealth away from, 328; tax rates penalizing, 340–341
Middle East, 180
Midterm elections: Democratic defeat in 2010, 310, 325; effects of divided government, 87–88; healthcare proposals affecting, 313, 325; partisan voting gap, 319; Republican victory in 1994, 83
Military: desegregation of, 224
Military, gay rights and, 257–258, 261–264, 267, 271, 273(fig.), 276–278, 283
Milk, Harvey, 259
Minority communities. *See* African Americans; Latinos
Mississippi Freedom Democratic Party (MFDP), 227–228
Mitchell, Margaret, 211
Moderates: bimodal party division replacing overlapping coalitions, 345–346; declining political influence of, 348; in the House, 1916–2012, 349(fig.)
Modernists, religious, 161–162, 166–168, 167(table), 173(table)
Modernization as polarizing issue, 91–92

Mondale, Walter, 328–329
Moore, Shelley, 205
Morality: Buckley's religious and political morality, 12–13; fundamentalist Christian crusade, 25
Morse, Wayne, 85
Mortgage bubble, 58, 104
Mt. Lebanon, Pennsylvania, 45–46, 50, 53, 67(n14)
Mourdock, Richard, 63, 147
Mugwumps, 41
Mullen, Mike, 257
Murdoch, Rupert, 101
Muscular foreign policy, 15
Myrdal, Gunnar, 223–224

National Alliance of Senior Citizens, 299
National Association for the Advancement of Colored People (NAACP), 226
National Committee to Preserve Social Security and Medicare (NCPSSM), 299, 301
National Council of La Raza (NCLR), 243
National Council of Senior Citizens (NCSC), 303–304, 304(fig.), 305(fig.)
National Defense Authorization Act, 265(table)
National Federation of Republican Women (NFRW), 201
National Organization for Women (NOW), 189
National security, 23
National Survey of Religion and Politics, 180–181
Naturalization, 245–246, 246(table), 249
Nature of man: characteristics of ideology, 8–9
Nazi Germany, 11–12
Neoconservatism, 14–15, 24
Neoliberalism, 21–22, 331, 334–336, 351–352
Netherlands: proportional representation, 31
New Deal: Al Smith revolution, 44–45; Buckley's religious and political morality, 13; compassionate ageism, 287–288; conservatives' opposition to, 16–17; defining traditional liberalism, 19–20; ethno-religious partisanship, 159; factional strength of liberal Democrats, 75–76; health care measures, 311–312; neoconservatives' view of, 15; party polarization and, 90; political and electoral realignment, 44–54, 80–84; redistribution

equalization capital accumulation,
333–334; religion and party
identification, 162, 164, 177–178; third
US republic, 36
New Democrats: financial transformation
of political operation, 110
New Idea men, 41
New Jersey: voter turnout, 39, 41, 41(table)
New Republic, 187–188
Nixon, Richard: disputed presidential
election, 88–89; Ford presidency,
77–78; health care agenda, 314, 319;
historical context of party polarization,
95–96; impeachment prospect, 88;
political conservatism, 11, 223;
presidential immunity, 139–140;
religion and voting patterns, 165;
Southern strategy campaign, 229–230;
Voting Rights Act, 227
Nixon v. Condon, 43
Nonvoters, 57
Normative perspectives on women's
representation, 191–194
Norquist, Grover, 99
Northeast electorate: divided government
after the New Deal, 72; post-New Deal
political realignment, 80–81
Nuclear power regulation, 116
Nunn, Sam, 261

Obama, Barack: AARP, 299; campaign
spending, 126(n31), 151; congressional
factionalism, 132; congressional
polarization over aging policy, 306;
expansion of presidential power,
139–140; Fair Pay Act, 203; gay rights,
267, 269, 282–283; gays in the military,
257–258, 263–264, 265(table), 266;
health care agenda, 309; health-care
reform in a divided government, 87;
House rigidity, 146; impact of
polarization on democracy, 89;
intractability of House Republicans,
136–137; Krugman's criticism of
contemporary conservative practice,
22–23; Latino vote, 244(fig.), 252–254;
LGB vote, 281; Libya intervention,
139; neoliberal economics, 336; older
voters' support for, 296; partisan
profile, 52–53; party ideology, 76;
presidential nominees' positions on gay
rights issues, 1992–2008, 268(table);
racists attacks on, 209–210; relationship
to black America, 233–238; Senate
control of presidential appointments,

135–136, 138; Senate factionalization,
132; social class of the electorate, 53;
Supreme Court undermining campaign
finance restraints, 55; Tea Party
establishment as response to,
352–353(n1); 2012 elections, 59–63,
71, 79; war objectives, 91. *See also*
Affordable Care Act
Obamacare. *See* Affordable Care Act
Objectivism, Rand's philosophy of, 16
O'Donnell, Christine, 63
Old Age, Survivors, and Disability
Insurance (OASDI). *See* Social Security
Old-age benefits. *See* Aging policy
O'Malley, Martin, 283
One ballot, district plurality voting
systems, 29(table)
O'Neill, Thomas "Tip," 96
One-party politics in the South, 217–220
Oregon Citizens Alliance, 260
Oregon v. Mitchell, 154(n6)
Organized labor: campaign finance reform,
115–116; campaign spending,
117(table), 127(n31); recruiting blacks,
224; shaping distribution of income,
339; unions and shared prosperity,
1918–2008, 340(fig.)

Palin, Sarah, 204
Parliamentary system, 136–138, 153
Participatory orientation, 242, 245
Parties and partisanship: Affordable Care
Act debates, 317–322; budget debate
and the fiscal cliff, 71–72; campaign
finance limits, 118; committee
assignments, 99–100, 123(n8); crossing
party lines on policy votes, 147;
declining political influence of
moderates, 348; demobilization of the
electorate, 40(table); demographic
variables of religious partisanship,
175–179; direct primary contributing to
polarization, 144–145; disputed
elections, 88–89; divided government,
72, 81–83, 87–88; economic inequality
feeding politics, 351–352; ethno-
religious perspective of party affiliation,
158–159; factionalization, 73–74;
female primary entrants by party,
1994–2010, 198(fig.); filibuster
overuse, 134–135; functional political
systems, 2; gay rights, 272–275,
273(fig.)–274(fig.), 277(table); gender
politics, 194–202; growing gap over
health care, 315–317; health care as a

partisan issue, 310–315; historical context of polarization, 95–98; ideological differentiation, 148; ideological divisions in the House, 136–138; ideological sources of religious differences, 179–182; ideology defining partisanship, 148, 154(n14); impact of polarization on democracy, 89–90; impeachment process, 88; Latino voters, 245, 247–251; media polarization, 101–102; moving economic power into the political arena, 332–341; one-party system in the South, 42–44, 215; partisan imbalance in polarization trends, 328–329; party unity votes in the House, 1953–2008, 97(fig.); party unity votes in the Senate, 1953–2008, 100(fig.); polarization in the party system, 344–351; polarizing issues, 90–93; political amateurs thesis of polarization, 108; realignment, 74–79; religious belonging, beliefs, and behavior and partisanship, 1964–2012, 167(table); religious groups and party identification, 162–169; responsible party system, 86–87, 332; rise of modern polarization, 330–331; as service organizations, 124(n11); sorting theory of polarization, 106–107; voter turnout and political partisanship after 1896, 39; women running for office, 196–200. *See also* Congress, US; Democratic Party; Extremism; Republican Party
Partisan imbalance, 3
Partisan sort, 344–345
Partnership rights, 263
Party activists, ideology driving, 346–347
Party regulars, 73–74
Party-line voting, 83, 136, 147
Paternalism, Jim Crow reinforcing, 211
Patient Protection and Affordable Care Act. *See* Affordable Care Act
Paul, Rand, 16
Paul, Ron, 16
Paulson, Henry "Hank," 103–104
Pay to play system in Congress, 99–100
Le pays légal, 56–57
Le pays reel (the real country), 34, 56–57
Pegram v. Herdich, 321
Pelosi, Nancy, 194, 196
Pension programs, 298. *See also* Social Security
Perot, Ross, 57–58, 281

Perry, Rick, 79
Peterson, Peter, 300–301
Pharmaceutical industry, 104, 112–113
Pink elephants, 204
Pittsburgh: New Deal political realignment, 47–5512
Planned economy, 11–12
Planned Parenthood, 205
Plessy v. Ferguson, 43, 214, 224–225
Pluralistic political system, 297
Polarization: defining, 1–3
Political action committees (PACs): campaign finance reform, 118, 126(n29); campaign spending data, 127(n31); campaign spending growth through time, 1970–2008, 117(table); GOPAC, 116; leadership PACs, 97, 118–119; Super PACs, 151, 342; women candidates, 201–202
Political amateurs thesis, 108
Political culture: arguing against a responsible party system, 86–87
Political Ideology (Lane), 8
Political money, the spectrum of, 110–114
Poll tax, 43–44, 216, 242
Pollock v. Farmers' Loan and Trust Co., 38, 55–56, 154(n6)
Popular vote, 214
Populist Party, 37
Post-racial politics, 233
Poverty rate among the elderly, 289
Powell, Colin, 261
Prescription drug care plan, 306, 316–317
Presidential appointments, 138; Bush's uses of executive privilege, 139; constitutional power, 139; Obama's Supreme Court nominees, 319; "recess" appointments, 139; Senate blocking, 135–136
Presidential elections: aging voters, 296; campaign spending data, 126(n31); coalitions of states in presidential and congressional elections, 1896–2012, 84(fig.); constitutional provisions, 130; disputed elections, 88–89, 214; FDR's attempt to purge conservative Democrats, 75–76; gay voters and gay rights issues, 260–262, 280–284; gender gap, 189–190; Latino participation, 244(fig.), 252(fig.); Obama's health care platform, 318; Obama's relationship to black America, 233–238; party realignment between 1964 and 1972, 75; polarization over gay rights, 267–269; presidential

nominees' positions on gay rights
issues, 1992–2008, 268(table);
Reagan's campaign, 335; realignment,
81–83, 82(fig.); Republican nomination
in 2012, 79–84; Republican
realignment since 1944, 77–79;
Roosevelt-Willkie, 45; 2012 Republican
presidential nomination, 79–85; values
and beliefs of core partisans and swing
voters, 347–348
Presidential power: constitutional
provisions, 130; expanding power over
budgets, 138–140
Primary elections, 63; constitutional
provisions, 130; direct primary,
144–146; "white only" Southern
Democratic primary, 224
Privatization of social programs, 292,
341–342
Pro-choice women, 201
Progressivism, 39, 41, 143–146
Proportional representation, 28, 29(table)
Proposition 6 (California), 259–260
Proposition 8 (California), 263
Protestants, 158–159; ideological
differences and partisan polarization,
181; religious traditions and party
identification, 1940–2012, 163(table).
See also Religion and religious groups
Pryce, Deborah, 201–202
Public opinion: gay rights, 271–280,
272(fig.), 276–280; on political
polarization, 105–106. See also
Electorate
Public relations, 111(fig.), 113
Puerto Rican–origin voters, 249, 253–254
Pure Food and Drug Act (1906), 310
Purification laws, 39, 41

Race: Buckley's conservative views,
12–13; Krugman's criticism of
contemporary conservative practice,
22–23. See also African Americans
Radical Republicans, 212–214
Rand, Ayn, 15–16, 64
Raspberry, William, 230
Reagan, Ronald: black American politics,
229–230, 232; civil rights era, 228;
dismantling the New Deal, 20;
economic restructuring, 334–336; gay
rights debate, 260; gender gap in
election behavior, 189; health care
reform, 315; historical context of party
polarization, 96; laissez-faire ideology,
53; media deregulation, 101;

neoconservative movement, 14–15;
political and economic conservatism,
11–12, 16–17; political money through
foundations and think tanks, 113;
popularization of contemporary
conservative practice, 22–23;
presidential nomination, 78; redefining
social policy, 331; Senate control of
presidential appointments, 135–136;
"signing statements," 139; solidification
of neoconservativism under, 24;
Southern vote, 80
Realignment, electoral and political,
74–79; Boston and Pittsburgh,
48–49(table); dates of US realignment,
36; divided government, 81–83;
emergence of, 75; ideological nature
and divided government, 72; New Deal,
45–54; presidential elections, 79–84;
religious groups, 164–165, 168–169;
Roosevelt and Willkie, 72–73; San
Francisco, 1948, 51(fig.); Southern
blacks, 230–232; states' voting in
presidential elections, 1896–2012,
82(fig.); voters and elites, 85
"Recess" appointments, 139
Reconstruction, 42–54, 210–216
Redistribution of wealth, 329, 331
Redistricting, 61–62, 243
Reed, Ralph, 108, 125(n20)
Reflections on the Revolution in France
(Burke), 10–11
Regulatory regime: deregulation of
financial markets, 109; liberal campaign
finance reform, 115–116; salaries of
regulators compared with incomes of
the regulated, 1949–2007, 114(fig.). See
also Campaign finance
Reichsfeinde, 34, 65(n5)
Religion and religious groups: Al Smith
revolution, 44–45; bases for continuing
conservative thought and practice, 25;
Boston's New Deal political
realignment, 50; Buckley's religious
and political morality, 13; constitutional
constraints on ambition, 131;
Democratic Party coalition, 1940–2012,
171(table); demographic variables in
party identification, 175–179; ethno-
religious perspective of partisanship,
158–159, 169–172; fiscal greed, 108;
gay rights, 259–261, 277(table),
279(table); ideological sources of
partisan polarization and religious
differences, 179–182; Mexican-

American voters, 247; partisan realignment and cleavages, 157; party identification, 162–169; political parties' ties to, 157–162; religious belonging, beliefs, and behavior and partisanship, 1964–2012, 167(table); Republican Party coalition, 1940–2012, 170(table); restructuring perspective of partisan coalitions, 159–162, 172–175. *See also specific groups*

Representation: class bases of the parties, 347; extremism distorting, 146–147; Latino electorate, 243; normative perspectives on women's representation, 191–194; partisan gap in women's elective officeholding, 194–196; polarization threatening, 1–2; voting methods worldwide, 28, 31

Republic, US, 36

Republican National Convention, 78, 261

Republican Party: aging policy, 286, 291–292; bifactional system, 74; black America politics, 229–231; budget issues after the 2008 economic crisis, 104–105; campaign to defund Democrats, 99–100; civil rights era, 226–227; congressional factionalism, 132, 136–138; demographic, 347; demographic influences predicting religious-partisan affiliations, 182(table); ethno-religious identification, 162, 164; gay rights, 271–272, 273(fig.), 283; gender politics, 187–191, 196(fig.)–197(fig.); Latino voters, 249–251, 254–255; media deregulation, 101; Medicare Modernization Act, 293–294; midterm elections of 1994, 83; number of Republican and Democratic Women in Congress, 1975–2011, 196(fig.); outspending Democrats, 151; partisan sort, 344–345; polarizing effect of direct primaries, 144–145; political realignment, 77–79; presidential nominations, 79–85; Protestants identifying with, 158; public support for gays in the military, 1992–2008, 273(fig.); racial demographics in the South, 222–224; Radical Republicans in the segregated South, 212–214; realignment towards, 80–84; religion and partisanship, 164–169, 172–175; religious affiliation and the Republican Party coalition, 1940–2012, 170(table); Republican polarization and Democratic polarization, 328–329; "revolutionaries" attack on Democrats in the 1980s, 96–98; rightward shift over time, 3, 348–349; second US republic, 36; social welfare programs, 287; Southern transformation, 220–222; tax proposals benefiting the wealthy, 338; theological factionalism, 172–175; women in state legislatures, 1983–2011, 197(fig.). *See also* Parties and partisanship

Republicanism, Madisonian, 131–132

Residential separation of income groups, 148–149

Resource distribution: defining traditional liberalism, 19–20; Galbraith's argument for, 21–22; partisan imbalance, 3

Responsible party system, 86–87, 332

Restructuring model of religious partisanship, 159–162, 165–166, 172–175, 182(table)

Reynolds, John F., 39, 41

Rights and protections, 19

Roberts, John, 142

Roby, Martha, 206

Rockefeller, Nelson, 77

Role models, female representatives as, 193

Romer v. Evans, 261, 269, 270(table)

Romney, Mitt: campaign finance, 151; gay rights, 283; ideological shape-shifting, 154(n10); Latino vote, 252; older voters' support for, 296; presidential nomination, 79–80; rightward shift, 145; swing vote in 2012, 60–61; white vote, 62

Roosevelt, Eleanor, 222

Roosevelt, Franklin D.: African Americans, 222; health care agenda, 310–311; political realignment along ideological lines, 72–73; purging conservative Democrats, 66(n11), 75–76. *See also* New Deal

Roosevelt, Theodore, 62

Rosenman, Samuel, 72–73

Rosenof, Theodore, 66(n11)

Ros-Lehtinen, Ileana, 206

Rush Prudential HMO v. Moran, 321

Ryan, Paul, 16, 60, 64, 286, 338

Ryden, David, 141, 153–154(n5)

Salvadoran-born voters, 247

Same-sex marriage. *See* Marriage, gay rights and

San Francisco: political realignment,
   51(fig.)
*Santa Clara County v. Southern Pacific
   Railroad,* 55
Santorum, Rick, 79, 283
Schattschneider, E. E., 86, 297
Schieffer, John, 263
Schultz, Debbie Wasserman, 206
Schumpeter, Joseph, 10
Schwerner, Michael, 225, 229–230
Scott v. Sandford, 154(n6)
Scranton, William, 77
Scrutin à deux tours (two ballots, two
   rounds voting system), 29(table), 31
Second civil war, 57
Segregation, 43, 133, 210–212, 214–215,
   225–228
Self-government, 143–144
Self-identified ideology, 180
Selma, Alabama, 234–235
Senate: ARA/NCSC ratings, 303; blocking
   presidential appointments, 135–136;
   constitutional provisions, 130; decline
   in cross-party voting, 147, 154(n11);
   Electoral College, 33–34; filibuster
   rule, 133–135; gays in the military,
   257–258; increasing partisanship,
   100–101, 147, 154(n12); Latino vote,
   253; liberal and conservative party
   differences in the House and Senate,
   1879–2011, 350(figs.); majoritarian
   principle amendments to the
   Constitution, 133–135; party unity
   votes in the Senate, 1953–2008,
   100(fig.); polarizing effect of direct
   primaries, 144–145; presidential
   appointments, 138; presidential
   circumvention of, 139; procedural rules
   changes, 136; women's political gains,
   194–195
Seniors Coalition, 300–302
Separation-of-powers system, 86–87
Shelby, Richard, 135–136
Shepard, Matthew, 262
"Signing statements," 139
Sixteenth Amendment rights, 67–68(n20)
Sixth-party system. *See* Realignment,
   electoral and political
60 Plus, 300–302
Slaughterhouse Cases, 42–43
Slavery, 212–213, 215
Smeal, Eleanor, 189
Smith, Al, 44–45, 62, 222
Smith, Ellison Durand "Cotton Ed,"
   66(n11)

Smith v. Allwright, 43
Social bargain, 93
Social conservatives, 180
Social Democratic Party (Germany), 34
Social issues: religious differences and
   partisan polarization, 179–182;
   theological divisions, 161
Social justice, polarization and, 351
Social media, 149–150
Social movements: contemporary liberal
   practice, 24; shifting party politics
   resulting from, 331
Social policy: conservative and liberal
   ideology, 25
Social Security: attempts to dismantle, 285;
   conservatives' push for privatization,
   286; federal control of, 311–312;
   funding health insurance, 313–314;
   Greenspan Commission, 290–291;
   partisan polarization in Congress,
   302–303; privatization of, 292. *See also*
   Aging policy
Social traditionalism, 180–181
Social welfare, 9–10, 19–20, 23, 232
Socialism, 11–12
Socioeconomic status: affecting Latino
   voters, 244; Boston's New Deal
   political realignment, 47–50;
   demographic influences predicting
   religious-partisan affiliations, 178–179,
   182(table); voter turnout, 45–47
Soft money, 117–118
Solid South, 217–218, 222–224
Sorting theory of polarization, 106–107
Sotomayor, Sonia, 319
Southern electorate: African Americans,
   76; apartheid regime, 42–54; black
   leadership, 238–239; civil rights era,
   225–228; disenfranchisement of blacks,
   216–217; high and low turnouts in the
   United States, 1866–1958, 30(table);
   one-party politics, 217–220; post-New
   Deal electoral realignment, 80;
   Reconstruction, 210–216; religious
   affiliation, 158–162; sorting theory of
   polarization, 106–107; transformation
   of the one-party system, 220–222;
   white supremacy faction of the
   Democratic Party, 73–74
Southern Politics (Key), 218–220
Southey, Robert, 64
Spain: voter turnout, 28
Specter, Arlen, 85
Split-ticket voting, 83
Spoils system, 37

Stalwarts, Republican, 78
Stassen, Harold, 77
State elections: partisan gap in women's
  representation, 195–196; poll tax, 44;
  shifting timing of, 63
States' rights: blacks' fear of arbitrary use
  of states' powers, 232; Defense of
  Marriage Act, 258; elections conduct,
  32–33; gay rights, 262–263;
  Reconstruction, 214
Status quo, 59, 92–93
Stigler, George, 111
Stock market crash, 57
Stock tips and options, 111(fig.), 112
Stonewall Inn raid, 259
Structural change: divided institutions of
  governance increasing social
  divisiveness, 329–330; expanding
  presidential power over the budget,
  138–140; extremism leading to political
  polarization, 146–148; Founders'
  barriers to personal ambition and
  injustice, 132; low economic growth,
  92–93; progressive roots of, 143–144;
  real and virtual constitutional
  permissions and constraints, 129–131
Student Nonviolent Coordinating
  Committee (SNCC), 226
Suffrage for African Americans, 42–44,
  209–210, 213
Super PACs, 151, 342
Supply side economics, 331
Suppression of voters, 62, 242–243
Supreme Court, US: aggrandization of
  judicial powers, 140–143; black
  suffrage, 43–44; *Brown v. Board of
  Education,* 212, 214–215, 224–225,
  330; *Bush v. Gore,* 33, 88–89, 140,
  321–322; campaign finance, 54–55,
  151, 343–344; *Citizens United v.
  Federal Election Commission,* 56, 122,
  140, 150–151, 343; congressional
  reversal on rulings, 154(n7); controlling
  the electoral process, 152; ending
  "white only" Southern Democratic
  primary, 224; gay rights debate,
  260–263; increasing political
  involvement, 132; Obama's health care
  bill, 142–143, 310, 319–322; opening
  the door for big campaign money, 122;
  Plessy v. Ferguson, 43, 214, 224–225;
  polarization over gay rights, 269–270;
  *Pollock v. Farmers' Loan and Trust
  Co.,* 38, 55–56, 154(n6);
  Reconstruction, 42–43; reinforcing

white supremacy, 212; system of 1896,
  56
Surge realignment, 80
Swing voters, 85, 347
Switzerland: electoral regime, 31
System of 1896, 27; judiciary supremacy,
  56; one-party system in the South,
  42–44; polarization, 65(n8); purifying
  strategies, 41

Taft, Robert, 74, 77
Tax avoidance, 339
Taxation: Carter and Reagan's economic
  restructuring, 334–335; concentrating
  wealth with the richest 1 percent,
  337–338; House Republicans' rigidity
  over, 137; *Hylton v. United States,* 56;
  penalizing the middle class, 340–341;
  proposed Buffett Rule, 338; targeting
  the wealthy, 338–339; Wilson Tariff, 38
Tea Party: increasing polarization, 79;
  opposition to bipartisanship, 147–148;
  origins and goals of, 352–353(n1); tax
  proposals benefiting the wealthy, 338;
  2010 midterm elections, 61–63
Testing Democracy (Reynolds), 39
Thatcher, Margaret, 53
Theological orientation, 160, 168. *See also*
  Religion and religious groups
Think tanks, 111(fig.), 112–113
Thirteenth Amendment rights, 212–213
Thurmond, Strom, 220
Tilden, Samuel J., 214
Till, Emmett, 225
Tobacco regulation, 116
Tocqueville, Alexis de, 93
Torture, 140
Totalitarian regimes: election law
  manipulation by, 141; Goldwater's
  claim of Democrats' adherence to, 17
Townsend movement, 298
Traditionalists, religious, 161–162, 166,
  167(table), 173(table), 177
Truman, Harry: civil rights, 224; health
  care agenda, 310, 319; national health
  care plan, 312; 1944 presidential
  nomination, 75–76; Thurmond's
  political challenge, 220; unexpected
  victory, 45
Twenty-Fourth Amendment rights, 43, 76
Twenty-Sixth Amendment rights, 154(n6)

Umbrella party system: divided party
  system, 87–88; impact of polarization
  on democracy, 89–90; liberal

Republicans and conservative Democrats, 147–148; polarizing issues, 90–93; post–New Deal political realignment, 80; responsible party system, 86–87
Undocumented immigrants, 243–244
Unions. *See* Organized labor
Unitary systems, 28
United Kingdom: voter turnout, 28, 31–32
Universal male suffrage, 42
University of Michigan national election surveys, 229
Urban areas, political realignment in, 47, 50
U.S. v. Reese, 43
USA Next, 300–302

Value in Electing Women PAC, 201–202
Values of core partisans and swing voters, 347–348
Versailles, Treaty of, 133
Veto power, 137
Vietnam War, 58, 76, 331
Viguerie, Richard, 301
Voter registration requirements, 32–33, 65–66(n9)
Voter suppression, 62, 242–243
Voter turnout and voting patterns: age and, 293; black suffrage, 42–43, 209–210, 213; coalitions of states in presidential and congressional elections, 1896–2012, 84(fig.); comparative turnouts worldwide, 29(table); disenfranchisement, 67(n19); ethno-religious perspective, 158–159; gay voters and gay rights issues, 280–283; high and low turnouts in the United States, 1866–1958, 30(table); hollowing out of the electorate, 56–57; Latino electorate, 244–245, 247–251; New Deal political realignment, 48–49(table); New Jersey, 41(table), 66(table); potential US electorate, 1788–2008, 35(table); purification laws, 39, 41; quality of the vote, 28; socioeconomic status and, 45–47, 53–54; states' voting in presidential elections, 1896–2012, 82(fig.); US political alignment, 36–37; US rates through history, 34–36; voter

realignment and elite realignment in the sixth-party system, 85
Voting Rights Act (1965), 20, 76, 165, 227, 230–231, 243, 331

Waite, Morrison R., 55
Wall Street faction, 74
Wallace, George, 76, 229–230
Wallace, Henry, 75–76
War: expanding presidential power over declaration of, 138–140; as polarizing issue, 91
War on Poverty, 223
War on terror, 139–140
War Powers Act (1973), 138
Warren, Earl, 77
Washington, George, 139
Water regulation, 116
Waterboarding, 140
Watergate scandal, 88, 139–140, 232, 343
Wayne, John, 230
Wealth: income share of the top 10 percent of earners, 1917–2011, 334(fig.); polarization of, 332–341
Weimar Germany, 57
Welch, Robert, 330
Welfare conservatism, 180–181
Welfare state, 13, 57
West Coast states: divided government after the New Deal, 72
Whigs, 90
White supremacy, 73–74, 211–212
White voters, 62, 80
Will, George, 13
Williams v. Mississippi, 43
Willkie, Wendell, 45, 72–74, 77
Wilson, James Q., 108
Wilson, Woodrow, 133
Wilson Tariff (1894), 38
WISH List, 201
Wolbrecht, Christina, 188
Wolfe, Alan, 20–21, 23
Women. *See* Gender politics
Women suffrage, 66(table)
Working class: Democratic Party factionalization, 328–329
Wright, Jeremiah, 233, 236
Wright, Jim, 96
Wuthnow, Robert, 160, 165

About the Book

What are the consequences of political polarization in the United States? Are citizens' interests adequately represented when divisive politics are the norm? What ideologies—and entrenched institutions—perpetuate these divisions, and what social groups are most affected? Answering these questions, *Polarized Politics* is a major contribution to our understanding of the causes, evolution, and impact of the politics of divisiveness in the United States.

William Crotty is Thomas P. O'Neill Chair in Public Life and professor emeritus of political science at Northeastern University. His recent books include *The Obama Presidency: Promise and Performance* and *Winning the Presidency 2012*.